CONTEMPORARY BEHAVIOR THERAPY

Conceptual and Empirical Foundations

Edited by
G. TERENCE WILSON / CYRIL M. FRANKS
Rutgers University

THE GUILFORD PRESS
New York / London

©1982 The Guilford Press
A Division of Guilford Publications, Inc.
200 Park Avenue South, New York, N.Y. 10003

Printed in the United States of America

LIBRARY OF CONGRESS CATALOGING IN PUBLICATION DATA

Main entry under title:

Contemporary behavior therapy.

Includes bibliographical references and indexes.
1. Behavior therapy.   I. Wilson, G. Terence,
1944– . II. Franks, Cyril M. [DNLM: 1. Behavior
therapy. WM 425 C761]
RC489.B4C66   616.89'142   82-949
ISBN 0-89862-614-5   AACR2

CONTRIBUTORS

DONALD M. BAER, PhD, Department of Human Development, University of Kansas, Lawrence, Kansas

ROY CAMERON, PhD, Department of Psychology, University of Saskatchewan, Saskatoon, Saskatchewan, Canada

NANCY CANTOR, PhD, Department of Psychology, Princeton University, Princeton, New Jersey

EDWARD G. CARR, PhD, Department of Psychology, State University of New York at Stony Brook, Stony Brook, New York

HANS J. EYSENCK, PhD, DSc, Department of Psychology, Institute of Psychiatry, University of London, London, England

CYRIL M. FRANKS, PhD, Department of Clinical Psychology, Graduate School of Applied and Professional Psychology, Rutgers University, Piscataway, New Jersey

FREDERICK H. KANFER, PhD, Department of Psychology, University of Illinois, Champaign, Illinois

ALAN E. KAZDIN, PhD, Department of Psychiatry, University of Pittsburgh School of Medicine, Western Psychiatric Institute and Clinic, Pittsburgh, Pennsylvania

JOHN F. KIHLSTROM, PhD, Department of Psychology, University of Wisconsin, Madison, Wisconsin

LEONARD KRASNER, PhD, Department of Psychology, State University of New York at Stony Brook, Stony Brook, New York

DONALD J. LEVIS, PhD, Department of Psychology, State University of New York at Binghamton, Binghamton, New York

PAUL F. MALLOY, PhD, Department of Psychology, State University of New York at Binghamton, Binghamton, New York

DONALD MEICHENBAUM, PhD, Department of Psychology, University of Waterloo, Waterloo, Ontario, Canada

W. ROBERT NAY, PhD, Department of Psychology, University of Illinois, Champaign, Illinois. Present address: L.I.F.E. Drug Rehabilitation and Counseling Program, Osprey, Florida

K. DANIEL O'LEARY, PhD, Department of Psychology, State University of New York at Stony Brook, Stony Brook, New York

TED L. ROSENTHAL, PhD, Department of Psychiatry, University of Tennessee College of Medicine and Mid-South Hospital, Memphis, Tennessee

GARY E. SCHWARTZ, PhD, Department of Psychology, Yale University, New Haven, Connecticut

G. TERENCE WILSON, PhD, Department of Clinical Psychology, Graduate School of Applied and Professional Psychology, Rutgers University, Piscataway, New Jersey

CONTENTS

III. MAJOR CONCEPTUAL APPROACHES

V. OUTCOME AND EVALUATION

INTRODUCTION

G. TERENCE WILSON
Department of Clinical Psychology
Rutgers University
CYRIL M. FRANKS
Department of Clinical Psychology
Rutgers University

Despite its short history, behavior therapy has exerted a variety of revolutionary influences in the field of mental health, bringing about a major reconceptualization of psychological problems and their correction. There has been a radical departure from traditional views and approaches in psychiatry, clinical psychology, and various fields related to mental health. Beginning in a relatively circumscribed area with an emphasis upon narrowly focused, specific S-R relationships pertaining primarily to specific neurotic conditions, behavior therapy has expanded to cover virtually the entire spectrum of human lives. There is virtually no discipline or subject matter to which the qualifying term "behavior" or "behavioral" cannot be meaningfully appended. Witness, for example, behavioral medicine, community behavior therapy, behavioral pediatrics, behavioral neuropsychology, behavioral economics, cognitive-behavior therapy, environmental behavior therapy, behavioral pharmacology, and behavioral genetics. The list is legion, as are the areas and points of view.

The roots of behavior therapy can be traced back to many schools of thought, to contrasting methodologies, to diverse philosophical systems, to different countries, and to various pioneers in the field. Some would lay stress on behavior therapy's origins, in classical conditioning, stemming from the Pavlovian tradition, and on its translation into practice by way of such techniques as aversion therapy, systematic desensitization, and the like. Others would place greater emphasis upon the Skinnerian legacy of operant conditioning and the experimental analysis of behavior. For still others, behavior therapy is an approach that is rooted primarily in the methodology of contemporary behavioral science, but with special reference to some form of learning theory (i.e., classical and operant conditioning) as a framework. Then there are also those for whom "behavior therapy" is cast in a much broader mold and refers to the commitment to the methods and findings of experimental psychology as a whole—including cognitive, personality, social, and developmental psychology—rather than to a more restricted reliance upon conditioning theories.

Contemporary behavior therapy has many origins and springs from the work of several pioneers in different countries. In South Africa, Wolpe completed his early research on the elimination of "neurotic" reactions in cats, and together with two of his associates, Lazarus and Rachman, laid the foundation for the modern application of behavioral methods to the treatment of adult disorders.

In the United Kingdom, dissatisfaction with traditional forms of therapeutic intervention led to a search by Eysenck and his associates for more effective alternatives stemming directly from the data and methodology of experimental psychology, rather than from impressionistic clinical folklore. This was and is in direct contrast with the bridging or dictionary-construction endeavors of such pioneers as Miller and Dollard, for whom the psychoanalytic model represented the ideal system, with learning theory appended either as a device for translating psychodynamic terminology into a language more readily understandable to behavioral scientists, or as a useful aid to the enrichment of the fundamental psychodynamic model. Primarily due to the many explicit and readily testable predictions that could be generated within a learning-theory framework in which physiological references were heavily underscored, the neobehavioral Hullian model was singled out in the first instance. This emphasis was gradually expanded to the study of a broader array of data stemming from the tradition of experimental psychology.

According to Yates, himself one of Eysenck's original enclave (now firmly ensconced in Maudsley-fabricated pockets throughout the world), the impact of Shapiro—a lifelong Maudsley citizen, but only tangentially part of Eysenck's group—is of at least equal significance in the development of behavior therapy. However, as we view it, Shapiro's contribution, with its emphasis upon intensive study of the single subject, had very little to do with the development of behavior therapy and exerts no discernible influence today.

Meanwhile, in the United States, empiricism led to the development of applied behavior analysis, deriving primarily from the work of Skinner and his students.

Evolving definitions of behavior therapy mirrored and paralleled these diverse developments. Early definitions of behavior therapy began with Eysenck's focus upon behavior therapy as the application of something called "modern learning theory." Since then, with depressing—or heartening, depending upon one's point of view—regularity, a plethora of increasingly expansive definitions has emerged. Some, such as that of Yates, with its pre-occupation with the single-case design as the *sine qua non* of behavior thera-py, are distinctly idiosyncratic. Perhaps the more generally accepted defini-tion of behavior therapy at this time is that advocated by the Association for Advancement of Behavior Therapy—originally called the Association for Advancement of the Behavioral Therapies, the change denoting a significant recognition of the commonality of principles underlying virtually all stra-tegies and techniques of behavior therapy. It goes as follows:

Behavior therapy involves primarily the application of principles derived from re-search and experimental and social psychology for the alleviation of human suffering and the enhancement of human functioning. Behavior therapy emphasizes the syste-matic and evaluation and the effectiveness of this application. Behavior therapy invol-ves environmental change in social interaction rather than the direct alteration of bodily processes by biological procedures. The aim is primarily educational. The techniques facilitate and improve self-control. In the conduct of behavior therapy, the contrac-tual agreement is usually specified in which mutually agreeable goals and procedures are specified. Responsible practitioners using behavioral approaches are guided by generally accepted ethical principles.

An advantage of this characterization of the field is its breadth. Yet there are those who will object that it is too comprehensive. Is the scope of this characterization of behavior therapy so all-encompassing that it includes any data-based, replicable procedure? Were behavior therapy to be viewed in this way, it could be argued that it ceases to be a distinctive and useful approach.

The primary advantage of a vast canvas is that many diverse positions can be accommodated and many different strategies contained under its co-ver. Within behavior therapy, there are those who accept trait theories as con-sistent with a behavioral position and those who avoid such theories as they would the plague. There are those for whom physiological and constitutional processes are believed to contribute a large amount of the total variance, and there are those for whom the environment is all-encompassing. There are those for whom self-control is a delusion and those for whom self-control is a meaningful reality. There are those for whom strict radical behaviorism is the only tenet upon which true science and behavior therapy can be predicated, and there are those for whom the only allegiance is to behavioral meth-odology and not to any form of philosophic behaviorism at all. There are those who stress external contingencies to the virtual exclusion of all else, and there are those for whom self-control and cognition are paramount. For some, the traditional model of classical and operant conditioning, perhaps with the addition of modeling, is sufficient to account for the phenomena en-compassed by behavior therapy and for the techniques generated by its prac-titioners. For others, the relationship between classical and operant conditioning is more questionable—some doubt that conditioning as a concept exists at all—and there are others who accept conditioning as a phenomenon but are distressed by the lack of evidence with respect to the existence of a general factor of conditionability or even the existence of group factors. Many would question the relationship between conditioning as conceived and studied in the laboratory, on the one hand, and conditioning in the clinic and natural environment, on the other.

Among some operant conditioners, the advent of the experimental analysis of behavior was a step forward of revolutionary importance, doing for the understanding of human behavior what Copernicus and Darwin had done for knowledge of the universe and for biology. Needless to say, this view has been challenged by both proponents and opponents of behavior therapy. Recently, it has been proposed in some circles that the introduction of cognition into the behavior-therapy model heralds a paradigm shift that is changing the entire direction of the field. We are more inclined to believe that behavior therapy, like the rest of psychology, is still in a preparadigmatic stage, rather like physics in the 16th century. There is no paradigm to shift, certainly not in behavior therapy and probably not in its parent discipline.

Within a short span of 20 years, these issues have evolved, have developed, have been discarded, and are now being taken up again. Debate, often heated and occasionally acrimonious, is characterized more by emotion than by adherence to the data-based, systematic way of thinking on which behavior therapy is supposedly based. For some behaviorists, the discussion of rival theoretical views is irrelevant at best and injurious at worst to the development of effective methods of behavioral change. They have characterized behavior modification primarily as a *methodological* approach to personal and social problems. It is doubtful, however, that methodological criteria alone can define behavior therapy or provide a basis for the choice of therapeutic strategies in clinical practice. One need only examine the theoretical differences between different approaches within the current compass of behavior therapy. Although they share common methodological priorities and prize rigorous experimental evaluation of methods, applied behavior analysis and social learning theory, for example, differ in some important respects in their conceptualizations of a model of human nature and of causal processes in psychological functioning, as well as in their implications for a technology of behavior change. The inescapable influence of theory (explicit or otherwise) on therapy is noted by Franks: "How the behavior therapist practices (including his [or her] choice of techniques, his [or her] approach to the problems of general strategy, and his [or her] specific relationships with [the] patient) thus depends both upon his [or her] explicit theoretical orientation and upon his [or her] implicit philosophical and cultural milieu."

Conversely, there are those among the behaviorally committed—and we include ourselves in this number—who stress the importance and value of theory generation and hypothesis testing. The case for the importance of being theoretical in behavior therapy has been summarized by Wilson as follows:

Confronted with the increasingly apparent multiplicity of methods and concepts encompassed by the term 'behavior therapy', a useful means of ordering the evidence, establishing priorities and filtering the good from the bad would be most useful. Whether viewed as loose metaphors or scientific guidelines, it is now widely accepted that the principles of classical and operant conditioning have been extremely successful in stimulating a wealth of experimental/clinical research and innovative therapeutic techniques over the past two decades. However, it can be argued that the heuristic value of this learning theory has reached asymptote. There is a sense of conceptual staleness in the still often useful but frequently repetitive or trivial extension of existing conditioning methods to an ever wider range of different behaviors. Replication and the empirical consolidation of advances already made are a *sine qua non* of an applied science. But a cognitive map that promises to open up new territory is needed to replace the once vibrant but now creaky guideposts of "modern learning theory." . . .

Scientific theory is also invaluable in making explicit the conceptual biases of a particular approach. Formulated so that its assumptions are testable and its procedures replicable, a theory makes it possible to refine, modify, or scrap pet therapeutic notions. Ideally, rival theoretical positions would be unnecessary if there were consensus on experimentally validated methods and outcomes. But this is a distant goal. In the meantime, unable to rely exclusively upon an empirically validated body of effective techniques, the therapist has to draw treatment strategies from some additional source. In short, the appeal is either to an organized conceptual framework or a melange of personal preference, intuition, and subjective judgment. Although the latter option will undoubtedly be helpful to some clients in certain situations, behavior therapy has always been an attempt to improve upon this state of affairs by developing an applied science of clinical behavior change.

What have been most evident over the past decade are two potent trends that, taken together, generate the potential for trouble. On the one hand, we have witnessed remarkable increases in technological know-how and methodological sophistication, leading to proliferation of techniques embracing an expanding range of psychological, educational, sociological, and medical areas. But, on the other hand, the very pace of this extremely rapid advance may well contain within it the seed of its own destruction. Little time has become available for consolidation of knowledge and the explicit testing of formalized models and generated predictions. Certain individuals mistakingly glory in the advantages of an eclecticism that gleefully abandons theory, model building, and the disciplined investigation of predictions in favor of reliance upon any technique that seems intuitively to "work." Under these circumstances, given the rapid proliferation of procedures and their accelerating application to an extraordinarily broad range of different problems, it is not surprising that the gap between theoretical developments and their application in systematically controlled fashion is widening.

It is with this problem in mind that we have planned the present volume. The marathon is not lost. Even though theoretical development lags behind the development and application of treatment techniques, it is still in the running. The overall question to which we address ourselves is as follows: Within the framework outlined above, what is the relationship between theory and practice in behavior therapy, and what does this augur for the future? The volume begins with an insightful overview by Krasner of many of the issues discussed in the earlier stages of this introduction with respect to the history and context within which contemporary behavior therapy has emerged; Krasner, in his self-generated role as a participant–observer, has been one of the more influential figures in the development of behavior therapy at the formal approach to assessment and treatment, as both a commentator on the scene and a chronicler of these developments. The next section attempts to cover in systematic fashion the conceptual foundations upon which much of behavior therapy is predicated and to which we try to be true, in concept if not always in specific detail, today. In Chapter 2, the first of these chapters, Levis and Malloy review recent evidence from the conditioning laboratory, particularly studies of fear and avoidance behavior. In view of recent criticisms of the adequacy of two-factor theory as a theoretical basis for fear-reduction methods such as systematic desensitization and *in vivo* exposure, Levis and Malloy's marshaling of the evidence and their arguments in favor of the continuing value of such a theoretical approach are of major importance. In Chapter 3, Schwartz, a pioneer and eminent leader in the rapidly burgeoning field of behavioral medicine, presents a stimulating and provocative position—namely, that behavior therapy cannot do without an informed psychobiological perspective. He insists upon a broad systems approach in which biological and behavioral variables are blended. The final chapter in this section, Chapter 4, by Cantor and Kihlstrom, provides an expert and concise summary of recent theoretical and experimental research on a novel cognitive view of personality, as well as commentary on the potential relevance of this "new look" in thinking about personality for behavior therapy.

In the third section, principles become translated into practice, and authorities in four different areas provide position statements reflecting what we feel are the four pillars of contemporary behavior therapy. First, in Chapter 5, Eysenck presents a neobehavioristic S-R approach that may be characterized as an archetype of theory, construction, and application. In Chapter 6, Baer then presents the case for applied behavior analysis, the bedrock behaviorist approach in the field. In Chapter 7, Meichenbaum and Cameron document the remarkable rise of cognitive-behavior modification and the case that can be made for cognition as the major conceptual framework for contemporary behavior therapy. Finally, in Chapter 8, Rosenthal articulates clearly what may well be the most comprehensive and sophisticated formulation of theory-based behavior therapy to date. Social learning theory, as espoused by Bandura and presented in Rosenthal's analysis, provides enough theory-based predictions to occupy skilled behavioral researchers for the next decade.

Finally, in the fourth and fifth sections, we focus upon issues of assessment, methodology, and outcome. Kanfer and Nay delineate the problems and issues of contemporary behavioral assessment in Chapter 9, and Kazdin outlines the methodological strategies available today and their strengths and weaknesses in Chapter 10. Finally, in Chapter 11, O'Leary and Carr evaluate treatment outcomes for children, and Wilson does the same for adults in Chapter 12.

Unquestionably, behavior therapy is in a stronger position now—despite many complexities and some seemingly incompatible positions—than it was 20 years ago, when all was simple and straightforward and investigators had nothing to lose but "modern learning theory." However, two decades ago, the gap between theory and application was small, because theory was rudimentary and application was limited. It is therefore perhaps not surprising that the gap is widening, since application seems to grow exponentially, whereas theoretical advances are relatively neglected and hard to come by. It is our hope that the present volume will serve, if not to close the gap, at the very least to describe the progress that has occurred, to make explicit the salient issues as the various contributors to this volume see them, and perhaps to point toward the resolution of differences.

I

BEHAVIOR THERAPY AND CLINICAL PSYCHOLOGY: A HISTORICAL PERSPECTIVE

1

BEHAVIOR THERAPY: ON ROOTS, CONTEXTS, AND GROWTH

LEONARD KRASNER

Department of Psychology
State University of New York at Stony Brook

INTRODUCTION

Writing the opening chapter in a handbook on contemporary behavior therapy is a simple task. All it requires is the placing of the early 1980s version of behavior therapy in appropriate conceptual contexts—namely, the history, philosophy, and sociology of science; the histories of psychology, clinical psychology, and psychiatry; the broader developments in "behaviorism"; and the intellectual, social, and political developments of 20th-century American and Western society. Further, these various contexts are not independent of each other and are mutually interacting. My purpose in this chapter is to present a series of contexts in which behavior therapy (as well as the subsequent chapters in this volume) can be placed in order that it may be better appreciated, understood, and utilized.

In effect, this chapter offers an outline, a series of suggestions as to relevant topics. The field of behavior therapy has become so large—not only in terms of the quantity of publications, but in terms of the range of material that it encompasses—that an adequate review of it does indeed take a handbook (it may soon require an encyclopedia). Investigators and practitioners cannot really comprehend or handle this field without awareness of the broader scientific and social contexts within which it developed. The material in virtually every section of this chapter—actually almost every paragraph—warrants at least a lengthy paper for adequate coverage, and in most instances, published books or articles are cited.

Thus, my goal is to set the stage and to offer a framework for what is to come in the remainder of this volume by putting in perspective the current (early 1980's) multiplicity of materials and "ideas" in the field. In the process of doing this, in the kinds of contexts in which the material is placed, it is acknowledged, even "intended," that there will be an influence on future developments. There is controversy about theories, models, and applications in most sections of this field, as in every field of (behavioral) science. The particular theoretical contexts in which the material is placed, in and of itself, are part of a continuous process of influence that itself will have an effect on the future behavior of individuals involved in the ever growing behavior-therapy industry.

The usual role of the author of a chapter (or article or book) in the behavioral sciences is that of a disinterested, "objective" (hence, "scientific") reviewer of a field of human endeavor, who generally does not intrude himself or herself into the material being covered. However, my own orientation (Krasner, 1980) has evolved to the point where I do not believe it possible, or even desirable, to avoid playing the role of author as participant–observer, particularly when I am dealing with any aspect of human behavior.

Can history be written objectively by a participant–observer in some of the events? Put in terms of a model that deifies "objectivity," the answer is clearly "No." However, placing material in broad social–historical contexts is not an objective restoration of *fact*, but is affected by and is a function of the current influences on the writer of history. My view is that is it necessary for an author to identify and specify his or her theoretical views and goals, particularly in a historical paper. The aim of an evaluation of the past is to provide an understanding of the present so that people may be guided in their decisions affecting future behavior. The examination of a scientific movement, such as behavior therapy, itself is subject to a process of influence and to the biases of the investigator (Mitroff, 1974). I have previously approached behavior therapy as a "case study" in the history of science, illustrating Kuhn's concept (1970) of the development of alternative "revolutionary" paradigms in science (Krasner, 1971, 1978). I have been a participant–observer in the development of the post-World War II behavioral movement, and whatever bias that has generated must be taken into consideration in evaluating the remainder of this chapter.

I would like to influence the future direction of the behavioral movement in its research and applications and its inexorable linkages with social and ethical values. My bias is a belief in the desirability of the environmental–behavioral–social learning model of human behavior as a genuine alternative to the medical–disease–pathology model. Explicating the roots and contexts of a movement in a particular framework should affect future developments.

ON LABELS AND TERMINOLOGY

It is especially crucial to determine the scope and limitation of the field of "behavior therapy," since too comprehensive a view (e.g., equating it with all of psychology) renders it meaningless, and too narrow a view (e.g., equating it with a specific technique, such as desensitization) renders it useless. As investigators plod through the vast literature of behavior therapy, they may be reminded of the parable of the blind men who described the elephant solely on the basis of their feeling of the animal. They gave excellent accounts of tusks, legs, trunk, ears, but no version of a complete elephant. My task in this chapter is to present a picture of the whole elephant and to demonstrate how it differs from other animals; for it is clear, to me at least, that the "elephant" of *behavior therapy* does indeed exist, and that it can be discriminated from other creatures of the psychological jungle.

There are a series of labels or terms that abound in this field, each of which has somewhat different origins and meanings attached to it: "behavior therapy"; "behavior modification"; "behavioral engineering"; "behavior influence"; "behavior analysis"; "behaviorism"; "cognitive-behavior modification"; "conditioning"; "operant conditioning"; "S-R approach"; "social learning"; "vicarious learning"; "reinforcement"; "contingency management"; "stimulus control"; "multimodal therapy." In this section, I describe the origins of the usage of the two most widely used labels: "behavior therapy" and "behavior modification."

I am using the label "behavior therapy" as the generic term for the entire field, that I am covering in this chapter. I do so as a matter of convenience, because that is the term used in the title of the overall volume; I emphasize, however, that it is an arbitrary choice, since several of the other terms above (e.g., "behavior modification," "applied behavior analysis") could also have been used as the generic term. It is a reasonable usage, but it is important to clarify the origin and rationale of the term. I repeatedly emphasize the fact that origins of terms are frequently lost sight of, and the terms take on a life of their own and quickly become reified. Even what should be simple historical "facts" as to the circumstances of the origin of certain terms are frequently shrouded in controversy.

A starting point in approaching the various convolutions in the usage of terminology is a straightforward dictionary definition of the ubiquitous word "behavior" (or "behaviour," the British spelling). Senn (1966) traced the change in the usage of the term:

According to the *Oxford English Dictionary*, "behaviour" has meant "manner of conducting oneself in the external relations of life" from at least 1490. From the early

16th century, it has also meant "conduct, general practice, course of life, course of action towards or to others," so that its meaning could be adequately stated in Webster's First (1909) Edition as "act of behaving either absolutely or in relation to others. . . ." But during the two hundred years following the middle of the 17th century, again according to the *Oxford English Dictionary,* another usage and meaning became more common: "The manner in which a thing acts under specified conditions or circumstances or in relation to other things. . . ." Common usage, however, kept the stress on behavior as a characteristic of a person. . . . Webster's Third Edition (1961) gives the first meaning as "the manner in which a person behaves in reacting to social stimuli or to inner need on to a combination thereof," while the earlier meaning became less commonly employed. (pp. 108–109)

The point Senn makes is that the definitions of even such a basic word as "behavior" change, and in the 20th century, even the dictionary definitions of the term "seem to have stemmed from developments in the fields of psychology, social psychology and sociology" (1966, p. 109). Thus the apparently simple definitions of "behavior" used by the *American Heritage Dictionary* (1969), "the manner in which one behaves; the actions or reactions of persons or things under specific circumstances" (p. 120), may well be the reflections of the influence of the history of behaviorism rather than of an immutable basic fact.

Senn (1966) goes into the early origins and usage of another key related term, "behavioral science." He traces the origins and multiple uses of the term and points out, as I am emphasizing herein, that "The history of science must be concerned to a large extent with the invention, development, and interrelationships of terms, concepts and things. This is especially true for the early history of behavioral science when words are important data" (p. 107). Senn attributes to Clark Hull in his *Principles of Behavior* (1943) one of the first usages of the term "behavioral science" in the manner in which it was to be utilized most generally in the decades after World War II.

The first use of the term "behavior therapy" itself in the literature was in a 1953 status report on their NIMH grant by Lindsley, Skinner, and Solomon, referring to their application of "operant conditioning" (of a plunger-pulling response) in research with psychotic patients. Lindsley (1974) suggested the term to Skinner, based on its simplicity ("behavior") and linkage (via "therapy") to other treatment procedures. Independently of this early usage, and of each other, Lazarus (1958) used the term to refer to Wolpe's application of his "reciprocal inhibition" technique to neurotic patients, and Eysenck (1959) used the term to refer to the application of what he termed "modern learning theory" to the behavior of neurotic patients (an application based in large part on the procedures of a group of investigators then working at the Maudsley Hospital in London). This influential group of early investigators consistently defined "behavior therapy" in terms of learning theory. For example, Wolpe (1973) stated that "behavior therapy, or conditioning therapy, is the use of experimentally established principles of learning for the purpose of changing unadaptive behavior. Unadaptive habits are weakened and eliminated; adaptive habits are initiated and strengthened" (p. xi).

The term "behavior modification" has also been used—interchangeably with "behavior therapy"; as a more generic term than "behavior therapy"; or as a term that solely refers to the application of operant conditioning, to distinguish it from the "behavior therapy" derived from the work of Wolpe. It initially was used to describe research studies of those investigators who were approaching the modification of behavior via the systematic application of social learning principles derived from sociopsychological research (Bandura, 1969; Kanfer & Phillips, 1970; Krasner & Ullmann, 1965, 1973). The two 1965 volumes of collected papers on research and case studies in "behavior modification" (Krasner & Ullmann, 1965; Ullmann & Krasner, 1965) represented the first use of that term in a book title. The introduction to the "research" collection (Krasner & Ullmann, 1965) placed the work of the investigators involved (e.g., Ferster, Staats, Bijou, Salzinger, Goldiamond, Patterson, Krasner, Sarason, Kanfer, Hastorf, Saslow, Colby, Bandura, and Sarbin) within the context of the broader field of "behavior influence" (Krasner, 1962; Krasner & Ullmann, 1973), which included

investigations of the ways in which human behavior is modified, changed or influenced. It includes research on operant conditioning, psychotherapy, placebo, attitude change, hypnosis, sensory deprivation, brainwashing, drugs, modeling, and education. We conceive of a broad psychology of behavior influence that concerns itself with the basic variables determining the alteration of human behavior in both laboratory and "real life" situations. On the other hand, the term "behavior modification" refers to a very specific type of *behavior influence*. (Krasner & Ullmann, 1965, pp. 1–2)

We then adopted the description of "behavior modification" offered by R. I. Watson, a historian of psychology (1962). In presenting a historical introduction to Bachrach's collection (1962) of research on the "experimental foundations of clinical psychology," Watson used the term "behavior modification" to cover a multitude of approaches:

It includes behavior modification as shown in the structured interview, in verbal conditioning, in the production of experimental neuroses, and in patient–doctor relationships. In a broader sense, the topic of behavior modification is related to the whole field of learning. Studies of behavior modification are studies of learning with a particular intent—the clinical goal of treatment. (R.I. Watson, 1962, p. 19)

Watson included among the historical forebears of "behavior modification" those investigators who were doing systematic research into the process of psychotherapy: "It was a psychologist, Carl Rogers, who in 1942, through a book. . . . and an article. . . . launched the research approach in behavioral modification through psychotherapy" (1962, pp. 20–21).

The presentation of behavior modification was placed within the context of "the clinical goal of treatment," which aimed

to demonstrate the uniformities involved in the application of social reinforcement concepts to increasingly complex behavior. This area is germane and useful to the practicing clinical psychologist. If a single label had to be given to this subject, it would be *behavior modification.* (Krasner & Ullmann, 1965, p. 1)

Ullmann and Krasner (1965) described behavior therapy as "treatment deductible from the sociopsychological model that aims to alter a person's behavior directly through application of general psychological principles." This was contrasted with "evocative psychotherapy," which was described as "treatment deductible from a medical or psychoanalytic model that aims to alter a person's behavior indirectly by first altering intrapsychic organizations" (p. 244).

Kanfer and Phillips (1970) defined four categories of behavior therapy that are still in current use: "interactive therapy" (methods requiring extended series of personal interviews using the therapist's verbal behavior to catalyze changes in the patient); "instigation therapy" (the use of suggestions and tasks to teach the patient to become his or her own therapist); "replication therapy" (the changing of behavior by replicating a critical segment of the patient's life within the therapy setting); and "intervention therapy" (disruption by the therapist of narrow response classes as they appear in the patient's interactions with his or her natural environment). Kanfer and Phillips called for establishing a well-integrated framework from which practitioners can derive new techniques with clearly stated rationales, with predictable effects, and with well-defined criteria and methods for examining their efficacy. They argued that a consistent behavioristic view requires an understanding of the entire range of psychological principles that can be brought to bear on the problems of an individual client, from presentation to discharge.

Bandura (1969), in a most influential and widely cited book, placed "the principles of behavior modification" within the "conceptual framework of social learning." "By requiring clear specification of treatment conditions and objective assessment of outcomes, the social learning approach . . . contains a self-corrective feature that distinguishes it from change enterprises in which interventions remain ill-defined and their psychological effects are seldom objectively evaluated" (p. v). Bandura integrated the by then greatly expanded investigations derived from the influence of Skinner, Wolpe, and a British group (e.g., Eysenck), and placed particular emphasis on the research on *vicarious, symbolic, and self-regulatory processes.*

Krasner (1971) conceptualized behavior therapy as comprising a series of specific techniques derived from the experimental laboratory, usually based on learning theory and applied in a situation of social influence. Behavior therapy thus involves a technology built upon a base of behavior influence. What Lazarus (1971) labeled the "nonspecific" factors, and what others call "placebo effects," include very specific social psychological variables such as expectancy, prestige, demand characteristics, set, experiment bias, and so on. The technology of behavior therapy becomes effective in modifying behavior only within the context of maximum social influence. It is important to emphasize that behavior therapy involves both the technology and its base of social influence. Some of the behavior-therapy investigators are clearly cognizant of this fact, but many ignore it. The behavior therapist is a compound of socially reinforcing and discriminative stimuli. He or she is the source of meaningful stimuli that alter, direct, and maintain another individual's behavior.

Wilson (1978) offers a useful analysis of the historical development of the term "behavior therapy" and its complicated relationship to the term "behavior modification". He observes that "despite (or possibly because of?) its elusiveness, behavior therapy might still be helpful, keeping the field broad enough to be representative of new developments but narrow enough to be useful" (Wilson, 1978, p. 94).

It is doubtful, however, whether there is any currently satisfactory definition of the model of human behavior called "behavior modification." Unfortunately, many of the developments of the past have been on the assumption that "behavior modification" does indeed "exist" (*as if* there were a reality to it separate from the behavior of the individuals endorsing it or condemning it). Numerous investigators have focused on the reification process whereby a metaphoric label takes on a life and reality of its own instead of being viewed as a set of explanatory hypotheses about human behavior.

For a considerable period of time, both the proponents and opponents of "behavior modification" and "behavior therapy" really believed in the myth of the existence of "behavior modification." There were some difficulties in defining it, but that did not prevent people from trying. Thus investigators get sidetracked on such controversies as whether "aversive" procedures are or are not really part of behavior modification. I would argue that there is indeed a field of "behavior modification" (behavior therapy), which is defined by *the behavior of those professionals who identify with it and by the historical context within which these people work.*

HISTORIOGRAPHICAL CONTEXT

In this section, I touch upon some of the issues in the writing of the history of science and of psychology that may well affect an interpretation of behavior therapy. I am not offering some highly abstract theoretical issues that should be of interest only to scholars, but issues with implications for the behavior therapist that are of relevance for current day-to-day professional activity.

A major concern about the present status of behavior therapy is that it has been not only reified as an entity but divorced from its philosophical and psychological roots. It is of major importance that those individuals who identify themselves as practitioners of behavior therapy understand and appreciate that they are dealing with a broad philosophy of human behavior, and thus that they are not merely technicians. The broadest and most pertinent context for the historical development of behavior therapy is that of "science." Virtually all researchers and practitioners of behavior therapy, from the Watsonian brand of the 1920s to the multimodel brands of the 1970s, identify with the concept of "science." "Science," socially, economically, politically, and intellectually, has grown to the point where the term is one of the highest prestige in Western society.

There are at least four historiographical contexts in which behavior therapy can and should be placed: Kuhnian paradigmatic revolutions; the Mertonian sociology of science; the "historicism–presentism" controversy; and the "externalist–internalist" dichotomy.

One of the current reigning controversies is how the growth of behaviorism or behavior therapy as a scientific movement fits with Kuhn's view (1970) of revolutions in science through paradigmatic shifts. Questions abound as to whether and how psychology itself arrived at a paradigmatic stage, or whether experimental psychology is at a preparadigmatic state (Lipsey, 1974; Mackenzie, 1972; Palermo, 1971; Warren, 1971; Weimer & Palermo, 1974). Palermo (1971) takes the position that mainstream experimental psychology has passed through the three major paradigms of structuralism, behaviorism, and cognitivism. Buss (1978) raises the number of paradigms to five, adding psychoanalysis and humanism to the other three paradigms.

Historians of psychology sometimes utilize the Kuhnian paradigm in their analysis of psychology, yet reject the view that psychology is ready for such analysis (R.I. Watson, 1971). This view is most clearly stated by R. I. Watson in his argument that "psychology is still in the preparadigmatic state. Contextually defined and internationally accepted paradigms do not yet exist in psychology" (1965, p. 133). Whether or not this concept can be applied to behavior therapy itself is currently an issue.

It can be argued that the history of the behavioral movement over the past three decades illustrates Kuhn's description (1970) of the development of alternative paradigms in science. Further, in order to understand behavior therapy and to increase the possibilities of predicting subsequent developments, the history of the behavioral movement must be presented not only as a scientific paradigm clash but also as a professional movement, as a social movement, and as an example of a continuous process of behavior influence.

The issues in the evaluation of psychology and/or behavior therapy as a paradigmatic shift are complex and involve basic questions as to definitions of "science," "behaviorism," "paradigm," and "scientific revolution." My point here is that these questions in the history and philosophy of science, which can barely be touched upon, are an integral part of understanding the nature of current behavior therapy and its future.

The line of investigation of the sociology of science initiated by Merton (1973) and his students offers an approach to conceptualizing the process of influence in the history of a behavioral science such as psychology. Ben-David (1971) has pointed out the importance of a concept of "scientific community" in the evaluation of norms and policies; this concept is based in part upon the ideas of Polanyi (1958) and Shils (1972).

Stocking (1965), in arguing for the position of "historicism" (understanding the past for the sake of the past), cites the dangers of "presenticism" (studying the past for the sake of the present); these include anachronism, distortion, misinterpretation, misleading analogy, neglect of context, and oversimplification of process. Despite these dangers, it is a basic hypothesis of my approach in this chapter that historical approaches in the behavioral sciences are, and should be, "presentistic" (Kantor, 1969; Krasner, 1965).

My current bias is also toward viewing the development of behavior therapy as a social phenomenon. In this sense, I lean to an "externalist" approach to scientific development as opposed to an "internalist" one, which focuses on developments within the particular science being investigated. Therefore, a more comprehensive understanding of behavior therapy necessitates investigating the interrelationship and mutual influence of this scientific "paradigm" with the social, political, and economic influences at work in the broader society in which it developed. Historians of the behavioral sciences are increasingly placing developments in their fields in cultural and intellectual contexts. The externalist historiography focuses on the interaction between society and particular scientific ideas and on the practice of science as a social phenomenon; it also attempts to clarify the factors that caused the developments of a particular set of scientific ideas, which in turn were affected by the science itself.

Thus, it is clear to me that the investigation of a movement in behavioral science, such as behavior therapy, is itself subject to the process of behavior influence. Approaches to the history of science in terms of broad paradigmatic models generally do not sufficiently take the process of behavior influence into consideration in the history and evaluation of behavioral sciences.

An important element in developing the historical context of behavior therapy is a belief held by many psychologists and some historians as expressed by the philosopher Popper (1966):

All scientific descriptions of fact are highly selective in that they always depend upon theories. . . . A scientific description will depend, largely, upon our point of view, our interests, which are as a rule connected with the theory or hypothesis we wish to test; although it would also depend upon the facts described. . . . In history no less than in science, we cannot avoid a point of view; and the belief that we can must lead to self-deception and to lack of critical care. . . . *History has no meaning.* . . . *Although history has no meaning,* we can give it a meaning. (pp. 444–461)

This point of view, as it involves the history of psychology, has been expressed by Marx (1977) and Braginsky and Braginsky (1974). Marx, in his review of history of psychology of the last decade, offers a set of convictions about approaches to the writing of history with which I am in close agreement:

I view history as a creative projective enterprise . . . . I view history as an interaction between the historian and the past. . . . There are no permanent solutions, only tentative constructs. . . . There are lasting ethical values . . . . I think that in history, as in psychology. . . . we need to reintroduce the doer to the doing. In order to discuss history of psychology, we have to ask about historians of psychology. . . . The historian of psychology is not a passive observer or collector, but a very active participant in the creation of the history of his [or her] discipline . . . . I believe that historians of psychology will have to come to grips with their aims, purpose and ideology. The myth of disinterested science or of objective social science is no longer tenable. (pp. 41–47)

In terms of putting material into perspective, Halle (1977) offers a useful concept. His argument is that in relatively short periods of history, it may be that chance, accident, and Heisenberg's uncertainty principle apply, but that in longer perspectives, the broader principles of evolutionary selectivity apply. In the period of the development of behavior therapy, which is so recent and, in cosmic terms, so brief, it is likely that chance may well have been a factor. However, the task of imposing an orderliness upon the history of behavior therapy will continue unabated.

Repucci and Saunders (1977) offer a view of the role of history itself as systematically mediated by a "historian" in the change process; this offers an exciting new approach to the intervention process.

By clothing himself [or herself] in the mantle of the historian, the change-oriented psychologist working in human service organizations gains a better appreciation of the universe of alternatives for action. For, while it is true that historical parallels cannot provide a blueprint for future action, they can provide an acultural foundation for asking critically important questions which have implications for action in the present. When viewed this way, the question of how much history is enough answers itself. The change-oriented psychologist needs an education in history sufficient to take him [or her] beyond total preoccupation with those issues which are defined as important solely from the perspective of the present. (p. 400)

Thus, the behavior of the historian, even the historian of behavior therapy, is mediated by his or her goals and ideology and becomes an important ingredient in a continuous process of influence.

SOCIETAL CONTEXT

The scientific and social roots of the current (early 1980s) version of the behavior-therapy movement can be traced to the half-decade immediately following World War II. We must focus on aspects of the postwar period such as the social and political Zeitgeist, developments in experimental and clinical psychology, the activities of investigators who were to become major influencers in the behavioral movement, and events in several key university settings.

The flow of events in human behavior represents a continuous process. There are antecedent influences in the history of behaviorism, as a philosophy, that are traceable back to ancient Greece, and, as a methodology, that go back at least to the 19th century. However, I am focusing in this section on the post-World War II period, because of developments that were very specifically to influence the ideology, philosophy and direction of the behavior-therapy movement.

Those who were to become influential behaviorists from the 1950s to the 1970s, in large part, products of the postwar American society, just as Skinner was to demonstrate in his autobiography (1976) that he was a product of an earlier America.

POSTWAR AMERICA

Lukacs (1978), a historian, refers to 1945 as "year zero" in the beginning of a new age. As such, it symbolized a shift from focusing on the necessities of winning a war to concern with the development of American society, economy, and "way of life." There was a strong sense of idealism on the part of returning GIs. Harold Russell (a double amputee who became symbol and spokesman for the veterans) is quoted as saying, "The guys who came out of World War II were idealistic; they sincerely believed that they were coming

home to build a new world'' (Goulden, 1976). The theme of a "better world''
was also a part of the belief system of diverse groups of professionals attracted by concepts of "utopias'' and the development of a new and optimistic model of human behavior. This view characterized not only the behaviorist perspective, but most other orientations in psychology. The theme
of optimism ran through American society: "We can do anything, having
won this war.''

The postwar period witnessed an outburst of growth in income and employment. In psychology there was unprecedented growth in the sheer numbers enteriﾗg the field, actuated by the idealistic goal of helping others in
society. With its strong scientific underpinning, it became a highly attractive
field for bright and ambitious students. Federal support for research in this
period was an outgrowth of an ever-expanding governmental paternalism.
The GI Bill was the major support for veteran students in college and
graduate school.

In contrast to the prevalent optimism of the period, there were also many
elements of pessimism in the Zeitgeist of the 1940s, including the fear of the
"bomb'' and the belief that (as expressed by Norman Cousins), "man is ob-
solete.'' The late 1940s were the beginning of the cold war in America's world
role, and, on the domestic front, the repressive movement called "McCar-
thyism'' was under way.

An important stream of ideas becoming increasingly evident was that of
the *social responsibility* deriving from science or the pursuit of knowledge.
Gregg (1948) expressed this concern eloquently in an invitational speech on
"The Profession of Psychology as Seen by a Doctor of Medicine'' to the
American Psychological Association:

Lastly, Psychology as well as Medicine must realize this inescapable sequence: Study
discovers knowledge, knowledge brings power, power entrains responsibility, and
responsibility must be prepared to survive praise or blame, dependence or passionate
resentment. One can see this sequence in the history of physics, from Archimedes to
the atomic bomb: study, knowledge, power, responsibility. If this is the sequence of
our knowledge of the physical world, can we expect the history of Psychology to
follow a different course? I think not. It may be a tragic history or it may be magnifi-
cent. Whatever its future may be, psychology will sooner or later have to face the responsibility that comes from power. (p. 401)

This theme of social responsibility was to become a dominant concern in
subsequent papers and books by many behaviorists in the following three decades (e.g., Bandura, 1969; Goldiamond, 1965; Kanfer, 1965; Krapfl &
Vargas, 1977; Krasner, 1962; Skinner, 1971).

The streams of development of behavior therapy derive from research
and applications in several diverse societies; but in its current form, to be ela-

borated on throughout this volume, it is the interaction with American society that has had the most important influence in shaping the goals and direction of the movement. Bakan (1977) aptly describes a few more of the elements in American society that affected behavioral research in the postwar period.

American psychology again rode in on the support of so-called basic research after World War II, much as it had come in on the support of science in the late nineteenth and early twentieth centuries. Between World War I and World War II psychology had established a strong experimental laboratory tradition. The recruits to psychology prior to World War II had come largely from rural areas, heavily conditioned by the successes of the mechanization of American agriculture. They were people who were heavily cathected on apparatus, and thus the laboratory was very congenial. The *Popular Mechanics* mentality of metal- and wood-working, work with electricity, motors and gears, was congruent with the experimental, behavioristic ideology. And these psychologists from their rural backgrounds were comfortable with animals. The possibility of vertical social mobility into the ever-widening vocation of scientist attracted increasing numbers of young men to the sciences, laboratory experimental psychology among them. . . . Hardly insignificant was the fact that the experimental psychological enterprise, combined with its behavioristic ideology, served the egalitarian spirit, not only with respect to personal rise, but also because of the seeming "fairness" associated with attending only to current behavior for subjects and investigators alike. The observation of behavior was a game anyone could play. It was not dependent on any richness of cultural background, social class, or special education. In the experimental laboratory the psychologists found that they could do a great deal with even the very limited capital equipment which they could scrounge, made out of common hardware, or buy with small sums of money that they could extract from their respective university administrations, and using volunteer subjects from among their students or animals which they could raise in the attic or basement of some old university building. With the kind of support they received in the decades after World War II, it became possible to acquire equipment of sophistication and complexity that had never before been possible, (p. 226)

THE CONTEXT OF BEHAVIORISM

By the end of World War II, there was already in existence a historically long-established "behaviorism" stream, solidly based on a "scientific" psychology and influenced by the laboratory studies of Pavlov (1928); the Mowrers' conditioning approach to enuresis (1938); John B. Watson's research and theoretical formulations (1924); and a stream of research and theory produced by, among others, Thorndike, Kantor, Bain, J. S. Mill, Bentham, and Locke.

The behaviorism of the postwar period which was to spawn behavior therapy is usually and appropriately linked with the influence of John B. Watson, often referred to as *the* behaviorist. There is irony in this focus on

one individual's impact, in that, more than in most psychological–philosophical movements, behaviorism can be understood as a cultural expression.

At this time as is the case in every aspect of psychology, controversy
abounds even as to the origins and prehistory of behaviorism (J. C. Burnham, 1968). At least there can be agreement in crediting John B. Watson
with "catalyzing a movement toward objectivism that was already well in
progress" (Kazdin, 1978, p. 64)

The behaviorism of John B. Watson in itself represents a wide range of
current controversy. As in any other development in the history of
psychology, historians are dealing with current views of past events; in Watson's case, some of the issues relate to Watson's originality; to the influences
on him of earlier movements such as functionalism, and of earlier investigators such as William James; and even to the specifics of his theoretical and applied contributions to psychology (Cohen, 1979; Herrnstein, 1969). J. C.
Burnham (1968) captures this aspect of Watson's career in the following:

Critics of behaviorism missed the point that Watson's originality did not consist of
simply his conception of verbal mediating responses, his interest in social control, and
his application of methods and concepts of animal psychology to humans. Watson
combined these elements into a synthesis, the whole of which was greater than its parts.
(p. 148)

Bakan (1977) further links the growth and development of behaviorism
with the change from a largely rural to an urban–industrial society in early
20th-century America, and the subsequent need for individuals to learn how
to "master" (control and predict) their environment. J. C. Burnham emphasizes this link by noting that

as in the case of other scientific developments in America during the Progressive Era,
the origins of behaviorism lie no doubt not only in the science and in the profession but
in society at large, where the idea of control, for example, so central in Watsonian
behaviorism, was already having momentous effects in other reform endeavors. (J. C.
Burnham, 1968, p. 151)

HISTORICAL PERSPECTIVES ON BEHAVIOR THERAPY

ON ORIGINS

To understand the process of the development of behavior therapy, it is
necessary to go into a detailed functional analysis of the professional
behavior of those identified with the behavioral model and to describe the
broader process of social influence as the beliefs and the research of the
"behaviorists" interacted with American society in the 1960s and 1970s.

forty years after the first enunciation of the law of effect as a formal doctrine of learning, the problem of reinforcement is still the subject of heated controversy among the proponents of rival theories of learning. (p. 489)

Postman then went on to what may well represent the first usage of the term "behavior modification" in print: "Mowrer's interpretation of effect or a satisfying state of affairs is frankly and emphatically hedonistic. Ultimately all behavior modification is mediated by pleasure (tension reduction)" (p. 500).

In experimental psychology, the studies of investigators such as Skinner, Hull, Spence, and Guthrie were beginning not only to have influence within the research field but to extend it toward applied areas as well. Training of graduate students, encouraged by the GI Bill after World War II, burst forth. But initially, few psychology programs were concerned with the linkage of behavioral theory to applications to the process of change in human behavior.

It is useful to attempt to see the commonalities and general principles that characterized the work of those early post-World War II investigators identified with "behavior therapy." Perhaps the most important of these commonalities was the role identification of the investigators themselves. Those interested in basic research saw socially important applications for their work. Those involved in applications viewed their work as derived from more basic laboratory research. They conceived of themselves as behavioral scientists investigating and applying the basic processes of change in human behavior. Thus, clinical phenomena were investigated through operationally defined and experimentally tested research studies.

The approach to "maladaptive" behavior, as to all behavior, was through a psychological rather than a "medical" model. Hence, the behavior therapist dealt *directly* with behavior, rather than indirectly with underlying or "disease" factors that "cause" symptoms. The psychological model may have been labeled as "social learning" or as "social reinforcement"—terms used to emphasize the observation that other human beings are a source of meaningful stimuli that alter, direct, or maintain an individual's behavior. The major commonality in these investigations was "the insistence that the basis of treatment stems from learning theory, which deals with the effect of experience on behavior. . . . The basis of behavior modification is a body of experimental work dealing with the relationship between changes in the environment and changes in the subject's responses" (Ullmann & Krasner, 1965, p. 1).

In effect, the term "behavior therapy" was used "to denote the modification of clinical or maladaptive behavior." Since the focus was on behavior that was *observable* and *definable*, the concern of the therapist started with the question, "What do we wish to accomplish through our application of learning theory?"

The first report of the application of the concept of "operant condition-ing" to changing a "maladaptive" human behavior was presented by Paul Fuller (1949) in a paper entitled, "Operant Conditioning of a Vegetative Human Organism." Fuller later (1974) described the influences on his think-ing at this time:

I regularly read the *Bulletin of Atomic Scientists* and a variety of nonpsychology. I had come to the psychology from geology and physics, through political theory. I kept up in some of these fields. A reaction to World War II experiences led me to the applica-tions of the principles and methods of experimental psychology to current problems.

The themes that Fuller touches upon recur again and again in this period—namely, the influence of ideas from physical sciences, particularly physics, and the impact of World War II in generating a strong desire to create a better world by the application of whatever "scientific" principles might be available.

Skinner's description (1970) of the circumstances involved in his writing of *Walden Two* further illustrates this postwar Zeitgeist:

In the spring of 1945 at a dinner party in Minneapolis, I sat next to a friend who had a son and a son-in-law in the South Pacific. I expressed regret that when the war was over they would come back and take up their old way of life. I said that some of the com-munities of the nineteenth century represented a healthy attitude. She pressed me for details and later insisted that I publish them. I was unaware that I was taking her ser-iously. A paper on "The Operational Analysis of Psychological Terms" (1945) was due on June 1, and I met that deadline. Then, to my surprise, I began to write *Walden Two* (1948). It began simply as a description of a feasible design for community living. (p. 16)

In detailing the origins of behavior therapy, particularly in the postwar period, both the *roots* and the *routes* of a group of behavioral scientists are worthy of description. The roots of what was to become the "behavior-modi-fication" and "behavior-therapy" movement in the next decade lay in the routes of several key influencers through the world of psychology and mental health. In the 1950s and 1960s the routes of the "travelling troubadors," chanting paeans to "behavior modification" and backing them up with im-pressive graphic data, led to every university and "mental health" installa-tion that had a whistle stop.

UNIVERSITY ROOTS

During the postwar period, several university settings served as focal points for developing and mediating the basic research and the training of the "com-munitites of scholars" that were to become the major source of the in-vestigators in the behavioral movement.

One of the first graduate programs to be specifically influenced by Skinnerian behaviorism was that of Columbia University, which at the same time also initiated a program in clinical psychology, approved by the Veterans Administration. The new laboratory-based experimental psychology course, with its "behavioral" orientation, was also required of the clinical students, hence fostering the training of the clinician as "scientist—practitioner." (I myself received my doctorate from this program, and I look back to those halcyon days with nostalgia.) In 1946, Keller and Schoenfeld introduced a psychology curriculum based upon operant conditioning in the undergraduate introductory course at Columbia College. The two teachers completed a text for this course, *Principles of Psychology* (1950), which was to become the first introductory textbook to give a systematic presentation of Skinner's approach to behavior change. The course was successful in terms of student interest, enrollment, and influence on curriculum in other psychology departments. Very quickly, the undergraduate and the graduate programs became integrated around principles of operant conditioning.

Indiana University was also clearly a prime influencing environment during this period. The subtleties and excitement of being in on the beginning of a social movement are nicely expressed in the following comment of Lloyd Homme (1974):

The graduate school environment at Indiana should not be overlooked. Under the influences of people like Bill Estes and Doug Ellson, there was an air of intense excitement. All the graduate students (and several undergraduates, too) were sure that behaviorism would make it big. Science Hall came to life at 7:30 each night as students returned to continue work on their experiments and to pursue their private love affairs.

A succinct description of what was to be a major event in the routes of the influence process of the behaviorist is represented by the following item in the Psychological News and Notes section of the *American Psychologist* of February 1947:

B.F. Skinner of Indiana University has been appointed the William James Lecturer in Psychology at Harvard University during the Fall term of 1947. Former William James Lecturers in Psychology were John Dewey, Wolfgang Kohler, Kurt Goldstein, and E.L. Thorndike. The subject of Professer Skinner's ten weekly lectures will be the psychological analysis of verbal behavior. He will also offer a graduate seminar on the principles of behavior. (p. 78)

Thus Skinner was linked with major figures of earlier behaviorism and psychology; the concept of "verbal behavior," which was to have major influence in later applications of "behavior therapy" was being introduced; and this was about to take place at no less an institution than Harvard University.

There were, of course, other university settings that were involved in training and influencing the behavior modifiers and therapists of later decades, particularly the Universities of Iowa and Minnesota.

It is of interest to note the origin of the term "behavior therapy" in England. A group of investigators attended semisocial evenings with H. J. Eysenck, who held regular "at-homes" for his staff and visiting colleagues. H. Gwynne Jones (1974) was at that time (circa 1958) preparing a chapter on "Applied Abnormal Psychology: The Experimental Approach" for the forthcoming textbook edited by Eysenck, *Handbook of Abnormal Psychology* (eventually published in 1960). A section of Jones's chapter was on "psychological treatment." The discussion of the group (including Payne, Inglis, Franks, and others) revolved about the term to be used in this chapter. Eysenck desired a snappy title around which a brand image might be built. Terms like "learning therapy" and "reeducational therapy" were discussed, and finally "behavior therapy" was chosen, although it is not clear which member of the group actually suggested it.

Jones used the term in his chapter of the handbook, and Eysenck (1959) used it in an earlier publication stressing the application of "modern learning theory." The unifying factor in this approach, according to Jones, was that "the emphasis is placed on observable behaviour rather than on underlying forces of a psychic nature, and the treatment suggested may be better described as 'behaviour therapy' than 'psychotherapy' " (1960, p. 775).

Although Jones was not aware of the operant work in the United States, he did recognize the importance of Peters and Jenkins's research (1954):

No specific mention has been made of the treatment of psychotic patients because neither the writer nor any of his colleagues has direct experience of such treatment. Though the aetiology of these conditions may not involve learning processes, many forms of treatment will involve such principles of learning as the gradation and spacing of practice. These principles are clearly operative in the work described in recent reports on the rehabilitation of chronic psychotic patients by vocational and other training programmes within hospitals. There is also evidence that practice with tasks of graduated difficulty has a generalized therapeutic effect on psychotic patients, as shown by the work of Peters and Jenkins (1954). (1960, p. 779)

Jones's comment as to the influences on his thinking and practice is pertinent to an understanding of the nature of the origins of behavior therapy.

I was influenced into the "scientific" clinical approach (i.e., nomothetic not idiographic) by both Eysenck and M. B. Shapiro. Eysenck, though, never saw a patient (as he would freely admit) and has no clinical "arts". Shapiro was a great teacher because one quarreled so much with many of his views. What did emerge in the 1950s was a group of people who argued a great deal, and a style of clinical work emerged which I now think was too narrow in several ways but was very influential in Britian. In relation to behavior therapy, I have been much influenced by American writers . . . but mostly by my patients who forced me to extend the range of my techniques and to take account of social and conceptual aspects of their disorders. (1974)

It is generally acknowledged by members of the Maudsley group that the first publication of a case representing the view of behavior therapy as practiced at Maudsley was the application of conditioning and learning techniques to the treatment of a psychiatric patient by H. G. Jones (1956); this publication was based on a paper presented to the British Psychological Society in April 1955.

THE CLINICAL PSYCHOLOGY CONTEXT

Since its inception, the behavior-therapy movement has been linked with the field of clinical psychology on theoretical and applied levels. Many of the postwar behavior therapists also identified (and identify) themselves as clinical psychologists.

One of the major hallmarks of the behavior-therapy movement has been the integration of experimental research with clinical procedures (Bachrach, 1962). In the postwar period, the basis for what were to be the future developments in integrating an experimental approach with clinical psychology was manifest in reports by Anastasi (1947), Sears (1946) and an APA committee on graduate training (see Shakow, 1965). The Anastasi report of a survey of graduate schools emphasized the argument that the clinician should receive intensive training in experimental psychology, with emphasis on design and methodology. Sears, in listing the approved clinical training programs for 1947, cites courses in experimental methodology as a basic requirement for the PhD in clinical psychology. (A note of historical interest is that the program at Indiana University with B. F. Skinner listed as Administrative Head was among only 18 programs then fully meeting APA criteria in clinical psychology.)

J. G. Miller (1946) accurately foresaw a new role emerging for the clinical psychologist: "From the long-range point of view it may well be that clinical psychologists, trained as they are in test construction, experimental design and the independent conducting of research, and scientific methods, will make the most significant contributions to the program in the field of research" (p. 184). Thorne (1947) emphasized certain key elements of the origins of clinical psychology in America: "In contrast with clinical psychiatry and psychoanalysis, which are direct descendants of medical psychology dating back from the ancients, clinical psychology in America has its roots in experimentally oriented academic psychology, which is more closely related to philosophy, physics, and mathematics than to medicine" (p. 159).

These observations are quite relevant to the background influences on the interests of several of the behavioral investigators of the period who helped link clinical psychology with the developing behavioral movement. For example, there were two important developments during the postwar period in the career of O. H. Mowrer, one of the major influencers of the behavioral stream: "In 1947 I came to the conclusion that there are two distinct kinds of learning and reviewed the evidence for this conclusion in a paper entitled, 'On the Dual Nature of Learning: A Reinterpretation of Conditioning and Problem Solving' " (Mowrer, 1976). The impact of this paper and the continual controversy about the "laws of learning" have, of course, continued in the behavioral movement to current times.

A second event in Mowrer's career helps put in focus the important and complex set of relationships among clinical psychology, psychoanalysis, and behavior therapy. In the mid-1940s, Mowrer, describing himself as a "discouraged and disenchanted psychoanalyst," discovered Harry Stack Sullivan. Mowrer attended a seminar of Sullivan's in the spring of 1945 at the Washington School of Psychiatry. What impressed Mowrer was Sullivan's shift from emphases on intrapersonal dynamics to the view of a disturbance in *interpersonal relations* not as a *symptom* of internal neuroses but as a *cause* of neuroses. The influence of Sullivan's views, including his concept of the therapist as a "participant–observer" in the psychotherapy situation, was beginning to be felt among psychologists and psychiatrists in the latter part of the 1940s—particularly as mediated through the William Alison White Institute in New York, which encouraged professionals to take courses and degrees in its branch of neopsychoanalysis.

One of the most important and prescient of papers in the postwar period was Shaw's paper, "A Stimulus–Response Analysis of Repression and Insight in Psychotherapy" (1946), which was one of the first to apply principles of learning based on animal work (primarily that of Mowrer) to the clinical process of psychotherapy in a systematic fashion. In the following analysis, Shaw virtually describes the approach that behavior therapists were to follow for the next three decades:

Clinical psychology has gone through a period of trial and error, and psychologists have gradually gained more and more precise knowledge of effective counseling procedures. Theoretical psychology has developed more or less independently, and many have deplored what has appeared to them to be the theoretical psychologist's preoccupation with isolated laboratory phenomena. The analysis of repression and insight in psychotherapy presented in this paper takes its departure from animal learning experiments. While it may be a far cry from these experiments to such complex phenomena as repression and insight in psychotherapy, the principles of learning discovered in animal experiments may afford the basis for a theoretical frame of reference for clinical psychology. The practical task then would become applying principles inferred from theory, which, it seems likely, would lead more rapidly to discoveries of effective techniques in counseling than a purely trial and error procedure. (1946, pp. 41–42)

Another important early linkage of psychotherapy with "learning theory" was Shaffer's article (1947) emphasizing the effects of theories of behavior on the therapist. Shaffer contended that "psychotherapy's great need for a substantial scientific basis is not fulfilled with entire adequacy by any of the existing systematic approaches" (p. 461). He focused on the one attempt to define psychotherapy in researchable terms, that of Mowrer (1939), who "applied stimulus–response concepts to the study of adjustment mechanisms" (p. 462). Shaffer conceptualized psychotherapy in terms very similar to that used by current behavior therapists, as in this statement: "Psychotherapy can be approached as a learning process through which a person aquires an ability to speak to himself [or herself] in an appropriate way so as to control his [or her] own conduct" (p. 463). (Over a period of 30 years, the cycle has gone from self-control to self-control.) A similar major influence was the 1949 paper by Shoben (then of the University of Iowa), which also attempted an integration of the "learning-therapy" approach of Mowrer with the field of psychotherapy.

On the other hand, the kind of research studies that were to become the hallmark of early behavior therapy, the operant baseline ($n = 1$) studies that combine laboratory procedures with subjects outside the laboratory and the concept of "research as therapy," had not yet appeared on the postwar scene. They would begin to develop later in the 1950s.

The lack of a reasonable methodology in clinical psychology in the postwar period was noted in Ellis's critical analysis (1949) of virtually every research paper written by members of the APA:

Contemporary researchers have a distinct tendency to follow the line of least resistance in their studies. . . . They tend to set up their researches so that they can employ experimental techniques and tests that are relatively easy to obtain and to use; . . . they tend to select their subjects from typical groups which happen to be the most readily available. (p. 494)

Interviews, special observations techniques, case studies, and other involved and time-consuming methods of gathering data were relatively unpopular with contemporary research psychologists. Influences on the psychiatrist Joseph Wolpe in this period reflect some of the experimental–clinical linkages I am describing:

1946 was the tail end of the period (1943–1946) when I was learning from conversations with professionals and from personal experiences with narcoanalysis that psychoanalytic principles were of very little use in the treatment of neuroses . . . Leo Reyna arrived as a gift from heaven at the end of 1946 . . . he spent three years in South Africa and we met on countless occasions . . . One thing he did was to encourage me to rework for publication, my MD thesis based on the cat experiments. On the basis of his personal acquaintance with Hull, I subsequently sent a revised manuscript to Hull to try to secure his endorsement, but he was too busy and too ill to even read it. Nevertheless, he sent it on to Appleton-Century [-Crofts], whose readers rejected it. The same was its fate with at least two other publishers. I made use of a good deal of material in *Psychotherapy by Reciprocal Inhibition*. The letter from Hull, though remote in tone, is a treasured possession. (Wolpe, 1974)

Another important influence in the 1940s on the clinical–experimental linkage was the work of a group of investigators at Yale (Sears, N. E. Miller, Mowrer, and Doob) who attempted to develop a "learning-theory" basis for psychoanalytic formulations. E. Lakin Phillips is prototypical of a small group of investigators who were influenced by psychoanalysis in the late 1940s as well as by learning theorists of the period (e.g., Hull, Guthrie, Spence, the Yale group). Phillips attempted to integrate the two approaches (much as the Yale group did) and eventually shifted away from the psychoanalytic into an application of behavioral learning in psychotherapy. His 1956 book, *Psychotherapy: A Modern Theory and Practice*, illustrated a learning-theory approach independent of the Skinnerian or Wolpean streams. Salter's book (1949) also offered a behavioral theory of maladaptive behavior and specific therapeutic procedures.

Eysenck (1949) published an important article, "Training in Clinical Psychology: An English Point of View." He criticized an APA Committee on Training because of their recommendation of including "psychotherapy" as a part of the training of clinical psychologists, in addition to diagnoses and research. The reason for his concern was that psychotherapy as then practiced was totally Freudian, and thus, according to Eysenck, "unscientific." Here was a clearly self-identified behavioral scientist arguing for clinical psychology as a "science." Eysenck, of course, was to have a major role in the development of the behavioral movement.

ON CURRENT TERMINOLOGY

Having placed behavior therapy in various historical perspectives, we return to issues of terminology. A useful and more current categorization of behavior therapy comes from Kazdin and Wilson (1978). They describe the different approaches in "contemporary" behavior therapy as "applied behavior analysis," a "neobehavioristic mediational S-R model," "social learning theory," "cognitive-behavior modification," and "multimodal behavior therapy."

"Applied behavior analysis" is currently used to describe those investigators whose application of operant principles derives from the Skinnerian influence in a wide range of clinical and social institutions. These are the "radical behaviorists" whose basic assumption is that behavior is a function of its consequence. Intervention procedures are evaluated in terms of single-case experimental design, in which the subject serves as his or her own control.

Applied behavior analysts utilize environmental variables to effect behavioral changes. A wide range of intervention techniques have been developed on the basis of principles generally derived from laboratory research, such as reinforcement, stimulus control, punishment, and extinction (Kazdin, 1975). Many, if not most, of the techniques used in community applications illustrate applied behavior analysis.

A second approach labeled by Kazdin and Wilson as the "neobehavioristic mediational S-R model" involves the application of the principles of classical conditioning derived from the earlier works of Pavlov, Hull, Guthrie, Mowrer, and N. E. Miller. Wolpe (1958, 1973) has been most responsible for integrating this material into a systematic treatment approach. Concepts of intervening variables and hypothetical constructs, particularly those of Hull, (1951) and Mowrer (1939, 1960a) warrant the usage of a mediational terminology. This is further exemplified by the usage of unobservable processes, such as the use of the imagined representation of anxiety-eliciting stimuli in systematic desensitization. Although the applied behavior analyst would not accept the purity of this approach, those influenced by Wolpe still consider themselves as good behaviorists, since the mediational processes are placed within a stimulus–response context. The Wolpeans, despite the use of symbolic processes such a imagery, still vehemently eschew (as of course do the Skinnerians) the utilization of cognitive formulations.

It is the newest group of behavior therapists who proudly utilize the term and concept of "cognition" to denote their approach to intervention procedures (Mahoney, 1974; Meichenbaum, 1974, 1977). These investigators emphasize the importance of, and focus on, cognitive processes and private events as mediators of behavior change. Key concepts of this group include assumptive models of reality, attributions of one's own behavior and that of others, thoughts, images, self-statements, self-instruction, sets, response strategies, and other constructs to account for "cognitive processes."

The "social learning" approach to behavior therapy has been most clearly and comprehensively conceptualized by Bandura (1969, 1977a, 1977b). Behavioral response patterns are influenced by external stimulus events (primarily through classical conditioning), by external reinforcement, and, most importantly, by cognitive mediational processes. Behavior change is effected primarily through a symbolic modeling process in which learning occurs through the observation and coding of representational processes based upon these observations or even upon imagined material.

Social learning theory emphasizes the reciprocal interaction between the individual's behavior and the environment. The individual is considered to be capable of self-directed behavior change. Bandura (1977a) has integrated the social learning approach in the concept of "self-efficacy," which emphasizes individuals' expectations about their own behavior as they are influenced by performance-based feedback, vicarious information, and psychological changes.

Lazarus's concept (1971) of multimodal behavior therapy remains highly controversial; investigators are uncertain whether it really belongs within the fold of behavior therapy or goes "beyond."

Krasner (1980) and his collaborators utilize the concept of "environmental design" in an approach to behavior change that links applied behavior analysis and social learning concepts with elements of environmental psychology, "open education," architecture, and social planning.

In the early 1970s, the self-identified behaviorists emerged from the laboratory, the clinic, and the mental hospital into the "natural" social environment. They were guided by earlier applications of behavioral principles in schoolrooms and hospitals, and they were also influenced by the national concerns about and debates on the social issues of the 1960s. A new generation of behaviorists began to take on the *total* natural and manmade environment as the focus for investigation and social change, with a purpose-namely, a "better environment" for members of society.

For example, Nietzel, Winett, McDonald, and Davidson (1977), in a chapter on "environmental problems" in a book appropriately entitled, *Behavioral Approaches to Community Psychology,* cover the topics of "litter control, recycling, energy conservation, transportation, architectural design and population change" (p. 310). Nietzel and his group place their material in the context of a quote from Fairweather (1972), who, in part, states that

population growth . . . environmental degradation . . . and human relations crises . . . face [human beings] today. [They] must solve these problems if [they are] to survive in a liveable environment. [They] must also find ways of aiding society to adopt the solutions found. Such problem-solving action requires basic social change. (p. 1)

Nietzel *et al.* use the Fairweather comments to emphasize "the urgency of finding solutions to these problems" and to accentuate the view that "the amelioration of conditions which degrade the environment may have more to do with maintaining and improving the quality of our life and 'mental health' than much of the current work conducted under the rubric of mental health" (1977, p. 310).

Thus, the behaviorists are stressing a new-old theme—namely, the *urgency* of finding solution of environmental problems of our society and the belief that the behaviorists may have the skill to contribute to the solution. The postwar theme of a "better society" as the goal of the behaviorists thus returns although, actually, it has been part of the behavioral stream throughout its history.

The attempt to influence littering behavior has been the first systematic research of the behaviorists in the environmental area, and these have become prototypical of later extensions to other environmental problems. Such studies have generally emphasized either prevention of littering by investigating antecedent events or have focused more generally on reinforcing litter removal. Nietzel *et al.* (1977) offer an excellent review of the basic studies in this area (e.g., those of Burgess, Clark, & Hendee, 1971; Geller, 1973; Kohlenberg & Phillips, 1973; Marler, 1971; and many others). The related area of recycling (a specific and important aspect of the proper disposal of litter) has also been systematically investigated by the behavior analysts.

ON PROBLEM BEHAVIORS, POPULATIONS, AND TECHNIQUES

There is virtually no human behavior that has not been studied or systematically influenced by one or more behavioral intervention procedures. This section will focus on a broad overview of the problems, populations, and techniques that have been investigated, with emphasis on the early studies which have served as the basis for the more recent studies covered in detail throughout the remainder of this volume.

In order to categorize the target problem behaviors approached by behavior therapists, the historian can utilize the official labeling system in use during the particular time period in which the investigation or application is taking place. Thus, most of the terminology in the behavioral literature comes from the second edition of the *Diagnostic and Statistical Manual of Mental Disorders* of the American Psychiatric Association (DSM-II) (1968). Thus, labels such as "neurotic disorders," "anxiety reactions," and "depressive reactions" abound.

It was in the area of the most seriously disturbed and deviant of human behaviors that the behavior therapists of the school of "applied behavior analysis" first initiated their work. The previously cited Fuller study (1949) illustrates the initial approach to those considered (in the 1940s) least approachable, the retardates. The first usage of the behavior-therapy terminology by Lindsley, Skinner, and Solomon (1953) was in a description of work with institutionalized "psychotics." Later studies focused on the development of adaptive behavior in the hospital environment, such as initiating self-care; performing jobs on and off the ward; taking medication; participating in various activities; cleaning one's room; decreasing reports of delusions and hallucinations; and altering a large variety of bizarre and antisocial behaviors, such as aggression, screaming, crying, not eating, hoarding, compulsive hand washing, and so on. The focus has been on increasing skills in severely deficit areas, such as speech, social interaction, and communication. There has been a whole series of programs to develop community-relevant behaviors, such as seeking jobs, attending social functions, and living in halfway houses and other community facilities.

Thus implicit in the behavior-therapy approach has been a reconceptualization of the group of behaviors generally labeled as "schizophrenia"; it is seen not as a product of disease, but as a product of *social learning*. Three facets of the research in this area have been (1) to demonstrate the modifiability of specific schizophrenic behaviors such as abstract thinking; (2) to analyze the behavior of schizophrenic patients in terms of their success in "impression management" and manipulative tactics; and (3) to demonstrate the reproductibility of schizophrenic behavior in normals.

In the "neurotic" category, "anxiety" and "depression" were among the first behaviors with which behavioral investigators reported success. It was Ferster (1965) who first noted that the loss of a close friend or relative constitutes a sudden shift or reduction in the schedule of reinforcements maintaining many of an individual's behaviors, and that a reduction in the rate of a person's behavior would be a logical consequence of the death of a close relative or the loss of a source of social reinforcers. Lazarus (1968) conceptualized depression as a response to "inadaquate or insufficient reinforcers." The studies of these investigators were the forerunners of the later behavioral approach to depression.

An early trend in the application of behavior therapy, insofar as the populations served were concerned, was in the opposite direction from traditional psychotherapy. In contrast with the initial focus of evocative therapy on the YAVIS (young, attractive, verbal, intelligent, successful), the behavior therapist started with the unattractive, the mute, the retardate—the one on whom everyone else had given up. For example, it is in the field of working with mental retardates that behavior therapy first had a major impact and has advanced to the point where it is "the treatment of choice." In contrast, it has only been relatively late in the history of behavior therapy that the YAVIS are getting their just due—as behavior therapy moves into the counseling area, as desensitization becomes appropriate to the full range of "neurotic" disorders, as token economies move into the home, and as to the problem behaviors of everyday life. The field of physical rehabilitation has also been strongly influenced by behavioral techniques. Behavioral medicine has extended behavioral concepts to virtually the entire population.

There are many techniques that derive from behavior modification, and they are constantly being expanded and revised. There is now a plethora of excellent textbooks to describe these current techniques and rationale (e.g.,

Gambrill, 1977; Kanfer & Phillips, 1970; Leitenberg, 1976; O'Leary & Wilson, 1976; Rimm & Masters, 1974).

Among the early techniques were positive reinforcement, modeling, and the application of reinforcement and training principles in the form of token economies. This latter procedure, "token economy," as eventually applied in classrooms; hospitals, and industry, derived from the behavior-modification streams of operant conditioning and Utopian planning.

The techniques that involve the systematic presentation of positive consequences to influence behavior derive primarily from the early operant-conditioning studies. Reynolds (1968) offers a useful introduction to operant methodology:

Operant conditioning is an experimental science of behavior. Strictly speaking, the term operant conditioning refers to a process in which the frequency of occurrence of a bit of behavior is modified by the consequences of behavior. Over the years, however, operant conditioning has come to refer to an entire approach to psychological science. This approach is characterized in general by a deterministic and experimental analysis of behavior. (p. 1)

Fuller (1949), as previously noted, was the first investigator to present a report of the deliberate application of operant conditioning in a clinical setting by "shaping" arm movements with a warm sugar–milk solution in an 18-year-old "vegetative idiot." Subsequent research was strongly influenced by the previously mentioned study by Lindsley, Skinner, and Solomon (1953) at Metropolitan State Hospital in Waltham, Massachusetts.

The research procedures with adults and children have followed the same principles and utilized the same specific techniques, such as token economies (developed originally for adults and then extended to work with children) or the training of key environmental figures (originally developed for the treatment of children and then extended to work with adults). The studies reported within this framework were increasingly characterized by greater ingenuity (artistry) in techniques, a greater range of problem behaviors tackled, and greater sophistication of design. Those studies that demonstrated experimentally that the stimulus manipulations were responsible for the behavioral changes produced were distinguished from the studies using operant techniques in a nonexperimental manner. The latter did not demonstrate that the reinforcement techniques were functional in causing the behavioral change.

The research studies based on operant conditioning placed major emphasis on the use of contingent reinforcement to strengthen specific behavior. Generally, the studies failed to emphasize the base of social influence to which the specific operant-training procedures are added. One exception were the studies of Agras, Leitenberg, Barlow, and Thompson (1969), which indicated that reinforcement is necessary for and adds to the socially influencing effects of instructions, thus linking their operant work to the process of social influence.

Baer, Wolf, and Risley (1968) made the astute and highly relevant comment that "generalization should be programmed rather than expected or lamented." This view represented an alternative to the usually futile approach, even among some behavior therapists, of changing a behavior in the laboratory or clinic and hoping that it will "carry over" to another situation, such as the home. Bijou, Peterson, Harris, Allen, and Johnston (1969) offered one of the first views of the methodology of experimental studies of young children in various *school* settings. Ferster and Simmons (1966) stressed the use of natural reinforcers available in the environment (determined by careful observation) in shaping new behavior of young children, in contrast with the more rigid dependence upon food derived from animal experimentation. Lovaas (1968) presented an overview of the rationale and procedures of his highly influential series of research studies with childhood schizophrenics. Risley and Hart (1968) reported that nonverbal behavior in preschool children can be altered by reinforcing related verbal behavior.

Patterson (1970) presented an overview of behavioral intervention procedures in the home and in the classroom. He offered a key element in behavior therapy by viewing intervention as "attempting to modify the dispensers which provide" reinforcement contingencies in the social environment. Most of the studies that used positive reinforcement also involved training individuals in the techniques of reinforcement, including ways to observe and ways to reinforce behavior. Such training was done individually and in groups, with the aid of such training devices as films, closed circuit TV, and "bug-in-the-ear," in the laboratory, in the home, and in the schoolroom. The training itself was done by the psychologists, by technicians, by parents, and by teachers.

VERBAL CONDITIONING

Research in the area of verbal conditioning has been one of the major linkages between the experimental laboratory and clinical applications (Krasner, 1958). The importance of this aspect of behavior therapy lies in the nature of the behavior involved, namely, human verbalization. The first verbal-conditioning study to attract widespread attention was that of Greenspoon (first undertaken for a doctoral dissertation in 1949 and published in 1955), in which he used a simple verbal response to influence the frequency of emission of the verbal-response class of plural nouns. From such humble beginnings have grown reams of research, numerous doctoral dissertations, much controversy, and an approach to key issues of social influence. In fact, Dollard and Miller (1950) seized upon the early reports of Greenspoon's findings to demonstrate their belief that changes in verbalization in psychotherapy were "automatic and unconscious." Whether this assessment was accurate or not (still a major controversy), Dollard and Miller anticipated the theoretical importance of verbal conditioning for clinical psychology.

In an early review of this field, Kanfer (1968) argued that research on verbal conditioning has undergone four stages: (1) demonstration; (2) reevaluation; (3) application; (4) expansion. This was a useful way of summarizing these studies, particularly as they are related to behavior-therapy research. The four stages were prototypical of the development of most of the behavioral techniques. The studies in the first stage demonstrated that verbal behavior could be brought under control of environmental stimuli; verbal behavior followed the same principles as human motor behavior and animal behavior. The early verbal-conditioning studies were similar to other early operant-conditioning studies; they demonstrated that reinforcement under certain conditions can systematically influence verbal behavior. The second stage, that of reevaluation, demonstrated that what was being dealt with was a far more complex phenomenon that at first was evidenced by a simple operant explanation. Responsivity to verbal conditioning was affected by factors such as social settings, previous experience with the examiner, expectancy, variations in the meaning of reinforcing stimuli, and other interpersonal variables. In the third stage, that of application, operant conditioning was used specifically to change verbal behavior with a therapeutic intent (e.g., Williams & Blanton, 1968, reported a study in which verbal conditioning was used as a deliberate "therapeutic" technique and found to be as effective as traditional psychotherapeutic procedures). The fourth stage of development, that of expansion, involves those studies investigating theoretical issues related to the capability of human beings for self-regulation. These included processes such as vicarious learning, the role of awareness in learning, self-reinforcement and self-control, and the associative relationship of words.

Behavior therapy involves focusing on the environmental cues that may serve as reinforcers (i.e., food, cigarettes, smiles, toys, tokens, head nods, "very good," etc.) as well as the kinds of verbal behavior that may serve as response classes. Salzinger (1967) reviewed the many studies on defining the response class in verbal conditioning and offered several ways of describing the "complexities" involved in determining what a response class is.

Goldiamond and Dyrud (1968) explicitly extended the operant investigation of verbal behavior into the area of behavior analysis of psychotherapy. They made the same observation that many of the early verbal conditioning experimenters had—namely, that there is a similarity between the operant-

conditioning strategy in research and that of the practitioner of psychotherapy.

In perspective, verbal-conditioning studies were a research technique
that developed as a combination of the operant-conditioning approach and
clinical interest in verbal behavior—hence, within the behavior-therapy
framework. Many of the early investigators were interested in the process of
psychotherapy, which during the early 1950s was primarily of the evocative
model. Here, at last, it seemed as if operant conditioning offered a technique
for setting up an analogue of psychotherapy in a rigorously objective manner. It is clear now that verbal conditioning and psychotherapy are not the
same identical process, nor is one an analogue of the other. However, some
verbal conditioning does take place in evocative psychotherapy, and some of
the relationship variables of the latter cannot and should not be eliminated
from the former.

Almost every conceivable variable in the situation has been investigated
in hundreds of studies, often with contradictory findings. The major uncontrolled variable has been that of the examiner; examiners' expectancies, their
biases, and the interactions of their reinforcing characteristics with other
variables at the same time have demonstrated complex interactional effects.
It has been this very sensitivity of verbal conditioning to the many variables
of human interaction that has given it its usefulness as a research device.

TOKEN ECONOMIES

One of the techniques emerging from the early operant studies has been the
use of tokens in place of primary reinforcers. Staats, Staats, Schutz, and
Wolf (1962) were the first to utilize a backup reinforcement system in a
reading-discrimination program. They used tokens exchangeable for a variety of edibles and toys. This meant that the therapist or experimenter was no
longer dependent upon the momentary desirability of an object (e.g., M &
Ms). Tokens opened up an almost limitless world of reinforcers.

The first reports of a token program in a psychiatric hospital were that of
Ayllon and Azrin (1965, 1968). This program evolved from previous techniques of Ayllon and his associates, which applied the earlier Skinner–Lindsley
principles of contingent reinforcement to shape desirable behavior. The early
work of Ayllon and Michael (1959) in training the psychiatric nurse as a behavioral engineer, and the use of satiation as an aversive procedure, opened
the way for the introduction of the more encompassing token program. The
Ayllon and Azrin token program functioned on a ward in a Midwestern state
hospital with a population of long-term female patients. Atthowe and
Krasner (1968) reported the successful use of a token economy program in a

VA hospital in California with patients hospitalized for up to 24 years. Schaefer and Martin (1969) reported the effectiveness of a token program in modifying a specific behavior, that of "apathy." The significance of this program lies in its reconceptualization of traditional patient withdrawal as "apathy," in the operational specification of the particular behaviors that are included in this more general category, and in the shaping of alternative, mutually exclusive behaviors that are prosocial. Since these early token programs, similar techniques have been extended to other hospital wards, to institutions for retardates and delinquents, to the schoolroom, and to the community.

Winkler (1971) reported a series of researches on token-economy programs that extend this technique into an important new dimension, that of testing predictions from economic theory and thus of studying the core of token programs. He investigated the complex relationships between the variables of prices, wages, and savings, and the ways in which these influence individual behavior. Token economies were found to operate according to principles similar to those that economists have identified in national, money-based economies. Token economies not only look like "real" economies, they function like them, and research in this field has linked behavior therapy with social and "Utopian" planning.

The use of reward itself in the classroom is of course not new, but the systematic use of contingent reinforcement by a teacher trained in the procedure does represent a basic change. The principle behind the use of tokens in the classroom—contingency reinforcement of desirable alternative behaviors— is the same as in mental hospitals, but there are problems unique to the nature of the classroom.

O'Leary and Becker (1967) introduced the first use of a token-reinforcement program to control a large class ($n = 17$) of emotionally disturbed children. The utilization of a token program resulted in a decrease of average disruptive behavior (talking, noise, pushing, and eating) from 76% in the baseline period to 10% during the 2-month token period.

A major development was the extension of the token programs beyond the hospital and the schoolroom directly into the community. L. K. Miller and O. L. Miller (1970) introduced the notion of freedom money, a token-economy approach to organizing self-help activities among low-income families. Henderson and his group at Spruce House (1968) reported a token program that bridged the gap between residential institution and the community itself with adults who had serious disturbed behaviors.

An example of a token program extended into the home with relatively intact individuals was reported by Stuart (1969), who worked with four separate couples who had sought help for marital problems. Labeling his approach "operant–interpersonal," Stuart stressed the importance of constructing situations that could increase the intensity of interpersonal reinforcement. He trained his clients in the game-like procedure, called "prostitution," of setting up a token program in the home to facilitating such forms of communication as relevant talk and sexual intimacy.

DESENSITIZATION

In terms of sheer output of research, the branch of behavior therapy making use of desensitization ranks close to that specializing in positive reinforcement. As a technique involving the gradual substitution of a favorable (i.e., relaxation) response that is incompatible with an unfavorable (i. e., anxiety) response to a stimulus, desensitization has had diverse clinical forebears. These include techniques labeled as "deconditioning," "reconditioning," "associative inhibition," and "autogenic training." However, it was Wolpe's version, "reciprocal inhibition" (1958), that eventually stimulated the outburst of research and clinical application that has characterized the next several decades.

The term "systematic desensitization" has become widely used to designate the technique used to achieve the goal of response substitution. Wolpe conceived of systematic desensitization as follows: "The breaking down of neurotic anxiety is induced in the patient, who is then exposed to a weak anxiety-arousing stimulus. The exposure is repeated until the stimulus loses completely its ability to evoke anxiety" (1958, p. 91). Based on the "conditioned inhibition" notions of Hull, Wolpe devised a series of animal experiments that resulted in the development of a technique of replacing an anxiety response by a relaxation response. Jacobson's technique of progressive relaxation (1938) offered the possibility of a response that could be influenced by the therapist and that, when developed, would be incompatible with anxiety. Wolpe paired muscular relaxation with visualized scenes and objects to which inappropriate anxiety responses had been made. Paul (1966) described a relaxation procedure that can be taught in half an hour. The potentially threatening situations to which relaxation techniques are directed are ranged in a series or "hierarchy," moving from the least to the most threatening. There have been a number of "explanations" of systematic desensitization that attribute change to "habituation" (Lader & Mathews, 1968), to operant conditioning (Leitenberg, Agras, Thompson, & Wright, 1968), to attribution theory (Valins & Ray, 1967), to interpersonal strategies, and to a Jungian analysis (Weitzman, 1967). As with each of the other techniques, the phenomenon seems far more complex than its originators had imagined. A variation is the "implosive therapy," based on extinction theory, of Stampfl and Levis (1968).

MODELING PROCEDURES

Modeling and the use of vicarious processes in the acquisition and modification of patterns of behavior have become important techniques of behavior therapy. Bandura (1969) summarized a large range of research that, through the efforts of investigators such as Bandura, Kanfer, Lovaas, Baer, and their collaborators, has become an integral part of behavior therapy:

Research conducted within the framework of social-learning theory demonstrates that virtually all learning phenomena resulting from direct experiences can occur on vicarious basis through observation of other persons' behavior and its consequences for them. Thus, for example, one can acquire intricate response patterns merely by observing the performances of appropriate models; emotional responses can be conditioned observationally by witnessing the affective reactions of others undergoing painful or pleasurable experiences; fearful and avoidant behavior can be extinguished vicariously through observation of modeled approach behavior toward feared objects without any adverse consequences accuring to the performer; inhibition can be induced by witnessing the behavior of others punished; and, finally, the expression of well-learned responses can be enhanced and socially regulated through the actions of influential models. Modeling procedures are, therefore, ideally suited for effecting diverse outcomes, including elimination of behavioral deficits, reduction of excessive fears and inhibitions, transmission of self-regulating systems, and social facilitation of behavioral patterns on a group-wide scale. (p. 118)

Research investigators in this area have used a variety of labels to classify their work, such as "modeling," "limitation," "vicarious learning," "vicarious reinforcement," "identification," and "contagion."

The application of modeling procedures to the modification of specific kinds of behavior has occured within two different but not mutually exclusive conceptual frameworks. Those working within the operant framework have tended to view the introduction of modeling procedures as an additional training technique to elicit behaviors. Baer (1968) summarized this approach to the use of imitation, particularly in its used in eliciting verbal behavior in children. Baer described the initiation of his research "not from a basis of clinical ambition to improve behavior, but rather out of a curiosity about the fundamental nature of imitation. Is imitation a type of learning qualitatively different from operant conditioning, or only a more complex organization of the results of operant conditioning than is the simple discriminated operant?" (p. 12).

On the other hand, a study of Bandura, Blanchard, and Ritter (1969) derived in part from the avoidance-learning research, particularly that of Solomon and his collaborates. The authors placed thier study within the "dual-process theory of avoidance behavior." According to this view, "threatening stimuli evoke emotional arousal, which has both autonomic and central components. It is further assumed that these arousal processes, operating primarily at the central level, excercise some degree of control over instrumental avoidance responding" (p. 173). Bandura's research and general theories of identification have forged a major link between the experimental laboratory and real-life modification of behavior (Bandura, 1977b).

The deliberate use of the behavior of the therapist (or an individual trained by the therapist) as an example, illustration, or model to influence the behavior of another person has occurred in the one-to-one interview; has been combined with reinforcement in training a retarded child; has been used as an "observational learning opportunity" with juvenile delinquents; has been used by means of a film depicting social interaction between children to enhance social behavior in preschool isolates; has helped alleviate fear of dogs in preschool children by filmed models; and has been used in treating snake phobias (Kazdin, 1978).

OTHER PROCEDURES

Control of Autonomic Functions

One of the most important recent developments, both theoretically and practically, has been the demonstration that unelicited autonomic responses can be strengthened by reinforcement after their emission. Techniques have been developed for the direct training of autonomic systems through exteroceptive feedback and operant-shaping techniques. Lang (1970), in the first comprehensive review of the research of autonomic control, credited Shearn (1962) with first demonstrating the operant conditioning of heart rate acceleration. Shapiro, Tursky, Gershon, and Stern (1969) suggested that blood pressure may be brought under control via feedback and reinforcement. Lang, Stroufe, and Hastings (1967) have also reported that heart rate may be stabilized within narrow limits when feedback is provided.

States of psychophysiological relaxation can be produced by the use of electromyograph feedback from striate muscles (Stoyva, 1968). Kamiya (1968) demonstrated that people can be taught to control some of their own brain wave patterns through hearing a feedback buzzer whenever the desired pattern is occurring. They learn to associate their sujective mental state with the buzzing, so that by reproducing that mental state they can reproduce the brain wave patterns, whether or not the buzzer is on.

The animal experiments of N. E. Miller and his associates (N. E. Miller, 1969; N. E. Miller & DiCara, 1967) on curarized rats provided the first sophisticated and convincing demonstrations of operant control of autonomic functions. Miller argued that psychosomatic conditions may develop through contingent attention and other reinforcing consequences. It should then be possible to modify the visceral responses that occur in psychosomatic disorders by extinction and differential reinforcement.

The work of this group of investigators was to provide some of the basic experimental underpinning of the current field of behavioral medicine.

Self-Control

The term "self-control" has come into increasing use among behavior therapists. One way in which the term has been used has been in the sense of "internal mediating events." However, in a broad sense, all of the behavior-therapy procedures may be viewed as training in self-control, if they are conceived of as ways of teaching individuals to regulate their own behaviors by arranging appropriate contingencies. Kanfer (1970) reviewed the considerable early contribution to research in self-regulation.

Aversive Procedures

Aversion therapy is the most controversial of the major techniques of behavior therapy in terms of theory and ethical implications. Human beings have always used noxious stimuli to influence the behavior of other humans—sometimes to coerce them; sometimes to treat them; sometimes to do one under the guise of doing the other. Within the context of behavior therapy, there are two broad types of aversive methods; those derived from operant and those derived from classical learning theory.

Bandura (1969) distinguised among types of "aversive control": the use of negative reinforcers, the use of aversive contingency systems, and the removal of positive reinforcers. Kanfer and Phillips (1970) distinguished between punishment (an aversive stimulus contingent on a response expected to decrease its frequency) and escape and avoidance (the reinforcement of an organism under noxious stimulation in any act that terminates the stimulus).

The Self-Help Movement

In its review of developments in science in the decade of the 1970s, *The New York Times* (1980) noted under "Behavior" that "more than anything else in the 1970s people helped themselves." The concept of "self-help encompassed an enormous number of books and courses promoting enlightenment or self-improvement, as well as the formation of thousands of new mutual-aid organizations in which people could discuss their problems with others who were similarly in trouble.'' This development was based on the studies that "showed that individual well-being depends more on behavior than on miracle cures, giving people renewed reason to diet, exercise and quit smoking.'' Although the influence of the behavioral movement was not the sole effect on this development, it certainly was a major one.

Glasgow and Rosen (1978, 1979) offer reviews of "self-help behavior-therapy manuals" and note the great proliferation of materials in this area. They categorize the materials in terms of the behavior problems on which the various manuals are designed to focus: phobias, smoking, obesity, sexual dysfunctions, assertiveness, child behavior problems, study skills, physical fitness, academic performance, depression, and marital and interpersonal problem-solving skills. The reviewers covered approximately 150 "commercially published or empirically evaluated behaviorally oriented books.'' They point out that there are of course many more self-help articles in newspapers and magazines, and a growing number of audiotapes and videotapes training you on doing it "yourself.''

Environmental Change

As noted earlier in this chapter, developing from the Utopian stream of behaviorism has been an extension of the scope of behavior therapy to an increasing usage to bring about an amelioration of social and ecological problems in the natural environment. In *Walden Two* (1948) the prototypical behaviorist Utopia, Skinner tackled the design of a total society. Subsequent investigators, influenced primarily by the school of applied behavior analysis, focus directly on specific problems of life in a highly complex American industrial society. Just to mention the areas in which these applications have occurred is tantamount to offering a catalogue of social and environmental problems in American society in the second half of the 20th century: pollution control; energy conservation; littering; recycling waste material; mass transportation; noise; job performance; obtaining employment; community self-government; racial integration; and military training.

The quantity and quality of studies in these areas have grown at an accelerating pace, particularly in the decade of the 1970s (e.g., Boren & Coleman, 1970; Burgess, Clark, & Hendee, 1971; Geller 1973; Geller, Chaffee, & Ingram 1975; Hayes & Cone, 1977; R. J. Jones & Azrin, 1973; Kazdin, 1975; L. K. Miller & O. L. Miller, 1970; Pierce & Risley, 1974; Winett & Nietzel, 1975). In effect, a new field of behavioral community psychology has emerged (Glenwick & Jason, 1980; Martin & Osborne, 1980; Nietzel *et al.*, 1977).

Assessment

The process of assessment is an integral part of behavior therapy. However, the goals and purposes of assessment are quite different from those of traditional psychotherapy—a difference consistent with the differences in theoretical models. The implications of these differences were summarized by Mischel (1968) as follows:

A focus on behavior change rather than on stable dispositions . . . leads to quite different emphasis in assessment and in research. In behavioral analysis the emphasis is on what a person does in situations rather than on inferences about what attributes he [or she] has more globally. . . . Social behavior assessments seek behavioral referents for the client's complaints; thereafter they identify the precise conditions that seem to be maintaining and influencing these problems so that appropriate rearrangements can be designed to achieve more advantageous outcomes. . . . Behavior assessments therefore often have to begin by establishing clear referents for highly subjective problems and goals. (p. 280)

Behavior therapists are gatherers of data that they and their clients can use as the basis of behavior decisions. Instead of asking the usual "why" or "how" questions, the focus is on "what" questions (e.g., "What are the conditions under which a particular behavior is emitted?" "What alternative behaviors should be taught?"). In addition to the contribution of a new way of approaching the assessment process, there has been a growing variety of specific assessment techniques related to specific modification procedures.

ON LEGAL-ETHICAL ISSUES

The intent of this section is to present an overview of the materials, ideas, and investigations that have to be considered in the development of a system of ethics and values for those professionally identified with the process of behavior therapy. As I have been emphasizing throughout this chapter, the model of human behavior subsumed under the label of "behavior therapy" is intricately interwoven within a social–economic–historical context, and hence within a very complex social system of ethics and values. My aim is to delineate some of the *issues* in the various controversies that touch upon ethics and behavior therapy. To do even this much is not easy, since complexities, paradoxes, and myths abound. The issues involved in this field involve concepts of freedom, justice, the nature of man and science, human and legal rights, and other abstract but "real" ideas and ideals. Thus, behavior therapists should seek resources from many astute observers of man such as novelists, poets, utopiasts, social reformers, lawyers, and social, biological, and physical scientists. Having duly pointed out the scope of the topic, I can proceed to narrow my focus to those observers identifying their work (research and theoretical) within the scope of "behavior therapy"; this work in itself represents a voluminous literature (e.g., Barrish, 1974; Begelman, 1975).

The following dictionary definition (*American Heritage Dictionary,* 1969), seems to offer a useful groundwork for the term "ethics":

The study of the general nature of morals and of the specific moral choices to be made by the individual in his relationship with others. . . . The rules or standards governing the conduct of the members of the professionals. . . . Any set of moral principles or values. . . . The moral quality of a course of action; fitness; propriety. (p. 450)

For the term "moral," the dictionary specifies,

Of our concern with the judgment of the goodness or badness of human action and character; pertaining to the discernment of good and evil. . . . Designed to teach goodness or correctness of character and behavior; instructive of what is good or bad. (p. 852)

"Ethics," then, involves decisions on the part of the behaivor therapist as to what is "good" or "bad" behavior for a specific individual. Ideally, an open-minded behavior modifier views the goal of therapy as helping individuals make these decisions for themselves. Some behavior therapists would argue that their major contribution is to reinterpret or operationalize this decision-making process as involving the assessment of the consequences of a given behavior: a behavior that leads to positive reinforcement for an individual is good; a behavior that leads to aversive consequences is bad.

I have previously argued that many investigators are inclined to hide behind a concept of "science" as a justification for avoiding the full consequences of their research (Krasner, 1965). A small segment of those involved in behavior therapy continues to separate their scientific activity and their value decisions.

Until fairly recently, it was almost an unquestioned axiom among scientists that "science" is value-free and that the pursuit of knowledge in the name of "science" was its own justification. The view within the area of behavior modification was that this scientific field, like any other within science, literally stood by itself removed from value considerations. This position was eloquently expressed by Madsen (1973): "Who decides what value/behaviors should be taught to whom has nothing to do with behavior modification." Most investigators now involved with behavior therapy would probably disagree. The question of who decides the values to be taught is at the very heart of the behavior-therapy approach.

Science is not a sacred cow, nor does it have an independent existence. Behavior therapy as a scientific discipline represents a social product in a time and place, and therapists have a social responsibility to place their own contributions in the social context of the times. The behavior therapist is an influencer and is continually being influenced.

Virtually all the early investigators in this field felt that there was a very close linkage between their research and the social and ethical applications and implications of this research. This view was most clearly influenced and led by Skinner's writings, particularly *Walden Two* (1948). This novel, written by a scientist whose basic research itself had not yet had very much impact on the field of psychology, raised issues pertaining to social systems and to ethics and morality; it anticipated the social and ethical issues arising from behavior modification that have become concerns in the 1970s and 1980s. Other investigators have also pointed out the relationship between their research and its social applications (Kanfer, 1965; Krasner, 1969; Ulrich, 1967).

Krasner and Ullmann (1965), for example, linked behavior therapy with concerns of social value:

The very effectiveness of behavior modification, the use of terms such as "manipulation," "influence," and "control of the environment," and the concept that the therapist has the responsibility to determine the treatment program, all lead to concern with social values. Behavior modification as an area of social influence, shares this problem with advertising, public relations, and education. These areas have in common individuals who have the interest and the ability to alter the behavior of other people—that is, one person determining what is desirable behavior for another. (p. 362)

As noted, these values issues were also addressed by Kanfer (1965), who argued that the ethical dilemma of the then-emerging behavior-modification procedures consisted in "justifying use of subtle influencing techniques in clinical procedures in the face of the popular assumption of the integrity, dignity, and rights to freedom of the patient. The first step in the resolution of this dilemma is the recognition that a therapeutic effort *by necessity* influences the patient's value systems as well as his [or her] specific symptoms" (p. 188).

Bandura (1969), in a most influential book, placed "the principles of behavior modification" within the "conceptual framework of social learning." He devoted an entire chapter to the discussion of value issues in the modification of behavior. He argued for the *specification of goals* as the major value feature of behavior modification:

The selection of goals involves value choices. To the extent that people assume major responsibility for deciding the direction in which their behavior ought to be modified, the frequently voiced concerns about human manipulation become essentially pseudoissues. The change agent's role in the decision process should be primarily to explore alternative courses of action available, and their probable consequences, on the basis of which clients can make informed choices. However, a change agent's value commitments will inevitably intrude to some degree on the goal-selection process. (p. 112)

These statements clearly link the behavior of those identifying their professional efforts as lying within the realm of behavior modification with a deep concern for the ethical and value implications of their work. This linkage has continued to the present day, growing ever more complex as the behavioral movement itself grows and diversifies (Graham, 1978; Krapfl & Vargas, 1978; Lickona, 1976; Skinner, 1972; Stolz, 1978).

Goldiamond (1974) offered one of the most thoughtful and provocative of suggestions for developing a basis for a system of ethics or values in behavior therapy. He argued that the Constitution of the United States should serve as a

guide for a discussion of ethical and legal issues raised by applied behavior analysis. The arguments that will be developed are that its safeguards provide an excellent guide for program development of an effective application of behavior analysis to problems of social concern, and that the violation of these rights can be counterproductive to the patient, to the aims of institutional agents whose incentives are therapeutic, and to the therapeutic aims of the society which sponsors the patient–therapist (programmer, teacher, etc.) relation. (p. 4)

On the basis of a strong civil-libertarian and legalistic position , Goldiamond offered an orientation to the changing of behavior that he termed "constructional":

This is defined as an orientation whose solution to problems is the construction of repertoires (or their reinstatment or transfer to new situations) rather than the elimination of repertoires. Help is often sought because of the distress or suffering that certain repertoires, or their absence, entail. The prevalent approach at present focuses on the alleviation or the *elimination* of the distress through a variety of means, which can include chemotherapy, psychotherapy, or behavior therapy. I shall designate these approaches as *pathologically* oriented. Such approaches often consider the problems in terms of a pathology which—regardless of how it was established, or developed, or is maintained—is to be eliminated. Presented with the same problem of distress and suffering, one can orient in a different direction. The focus here is on the production of desirables through means which *directly* increase available options or extend social repertoires, rather than *indirectly* doing so as a by-product of an eliminitive procedure. Such approaches are *constructionally* oriented; they build repertoires. (1974, p. 14)

Goldiamond thus expressed clearly and succinctly the major implication of the differences between the "disease" and the "behavioral" model—namely, the consequences of the model for the change process, and hence for the ethical–value implications. It follows from this model that, in Goldiamond's terms, "we can view the therapist not as a reinforcement machine, but as a program consultant, namely, a teacher or guide who tries to be explicit" (1974, p. 24). The intent of the "social reinforcement machine" metaphor (Krasner, 1962), indeed, was to convey the role of the "teacher," and thus I am in agreement with this formulation.

The concept of the "social contract" as the basis of value decisions can be combined with the concept of "learning environments" (e.g., Ferster & Culbertson, 1974) to provide a structure and procedures within which individuals learn to formulate their own goals as related to their interests and to contract accordingly. Individuals, options are increased by self-control and self-help procedures, as are their spheres of responsibility. Much of this ethical philosophy is consistent with the rationale behind the movement of behavior modification/therapy into the broader concept of "environmental design" (Krasner, 1980).

Concern for the ethical implications of a scientific endeavor is, of course, not unique to behavior therapy, but it is one of the outgrowths of the role of science in the atomic age. But behavior therapy, because of its promise and the possible social threat implicit in its effectiveness, has forced both society and the helping professions to face the issue of behavior control and ethics directly. Numerous papers and books have explored the implications of behavior control, and many recent books offering an overview of behavior therapy devote at least a chapter to the discussion of ethics and values.

Within the ethical overview must also be included the interest in and concern with the design of social environments to influence individual behavior. In his fictional presentation of Utopia, Skinner (1948) foresaw at a very early stage where the formulations of behavior therapy inevitably would lead. The implications of these viewpoints have been extended to the general problems of the design of cultures and "freedom."

Researchers and therapists also must take cognizance of another subtle value implication of the theoretical model that the behaviorists have been espousing. Under a "medical" or "disease" model, the role of the professional person is justified by the goal of the model, *the restoration of health*. The ethical rationale of the therapist is to restore the individual to a hypothesized state of previous health, or "normality," which implies an absence of abnormality. Thus, the therapist works in a clearly sanctioned societal role.

The behavior therapist, on the other hand, is faced with the question of which social institutions sanction the role of a behavior changer. Who determines the goals and purposes of change? The behavior therapist should not continue to hide behind the facade of health restoration, but must ask, "What social institutions sanction behavior change?"

The issues of ethics and values in behavior therapy not only are *not new* (or even unique to the behavioral field) but are ones that the investigators in the early days of behavior therapy were aware of and considered to be focal.

Throughout, the growing concern on the part of both the professionals and the public has been "Behavior therapy for what?" What is desirable behavior on the part of a human being in a given set of circumstances, and who is to decide?

This issue involves philosophical, social, political, and religious values as to the meaning and purpose of scientific inquiry, of professional application, and of life itself. Throughout recorded history and into the present day, human beings have been debating, arguing, discussing, fighting, and even killing each other in regard to such issues. A new element, reappearing periodically, is that of groups of individuals (sometimes self-identified as behaviorists) who contend that they have developed techniques of changing, controlling, influencing, and manipulating human behavior. Society responds with fear, panic, concern, indignation, and hope. What if they are right and, indeed, human behavior can be systematically changed? Humanity must then face the next, more awesome, and thus far never-resolved issue of "What is good?" and "Who decides?"

REFERENCES

Agras, W. S., Leitenberg, H., Barlow, D. H. & Thompson, L. E. Instructions and reinforcement in the modification of neurotic behavior. *American Journal of Psychiatry,* 1969, *125,* 1435–1439.

American Heritage Dictionary (W. Morris, Ed.). Boston: Houghton Mifflin, 1969.

American Psychiatric Association. *Diagnostic and statistical manual of mental disorders* (2nd ed.). Washington, D.C.: Author, 1968.

American Psychologist. Psychological News and Notes. 1947, *2,* 78.

Anastasi, A. The place of experimental psychology in the undergraduate curriculum. *American Psychologist,* 1947, *2,* 57–62.

Atthowe, J. M., & Krasner, L. Preliminary report on the application of contingent reinforcement procedures (token economy) on a "chronic" psychiatric ward. *Journal of Abnormal Psychology,* 1968, *73,* 37–43.

Ayllon, T., & Azrin, N. H. The measurement and reinforcement of behavior of psychotics. *Journal of Experimental Analysis of Behavior,* 1965, *8,* 357–387.

Ayllon, T., & Azrin, N. H. *The token economy: A motivational system for therapy and rehabilitation.* New York: Appleton-Century-Crofts, 1968.

Ayllon, T., & Michael, J. The psychiatric nurse as a behavioral engineer. *Journal of Experimental Analysis of Behavior,* 1959, *2,* 323–334.

Bachrach, A. J. (Ed.). *Experimental foundations of clinical psychology.* New York: Basic Books, 1962.

Baer, D. M. Some remedial uses of the reinforcement contingency. In J. M. Shlien (Ed.), *Research in psychotherapy* (Vol. 3). Washington, D.C.: American Psychological Association, 1968.

Baer, D. M., Wolf, M. M., & Risley, T. R. Some current dimensions of applied behavior analysis. *Journal of Applied Behavior Analysis,* 1968, *1,* 91–97.

Bakan, D. Behaviorism and American urbanization. *Journal of the History of the Behaviorial Sciences,* 1966, *2,* 5–28.

Bakan, D. Political factors in the development of American psychology. In R. W. Rieber & K. Salzinger (Eds.), *The roots of American psychology: Historical influences and implications for the future* (Annals of the New York Academy of Sciences, Vol. 291). New York: New York Academy of Sciences, 1977.

Bandura, A. *Principles of behavior modification.* New York: Holt, Rinehart & Winston, 1969.

Bandura, A. Self-reinforcement: Theoretical and methodological considerations. *Behaviorism,* 1976, *4,* 135–155.

Bandura, A. Self-efficacy: Toward a unifying theory of behavioral change. *Psychological Review,* 1977, *84,* 191–215. (a)

Bandura, A. *Social learning theory.* Englewood Cliffs, N.J.: Prentice-Hall, 1977. (b)

Bandura, A., Blanchard, E. B., & Ritter, B. Relative efficacy of desensitization and modeling approaches for inducing behavioral, affective, and attitudinal changes. *Journal of Personality and Social Psychology,* 1969, *13,* 173–199.

Barrish, I. J. Ethical issues and answers to behavior modification. *Corrective and Social Psychiatry and Journal of Applied Behavior Therapy,* 1974, *20,* 30–37.

Begelman, D. A. Ethical issues to behavior control. *Journal of Nervous and Mental Disease,* 1973, *156,* 412–419.

Begelman, D. A. Ethical and legal issues of behavior modification. *Progress in Behavior Modification,* 1975, *1,* 159–189.

Ben-David, J. *The scientist's role in society: A comparative study.* Englewood Cliffs, N.J.: Prentice-Hall, 1971.

Bijou, S. W., & Baer, D. M. *Child development* (Vol. 1). New York: Appleton-Century-Crofts, 1961.

Bijou, S. W., & Baer, D. M. *Child development* (Vol. 2). New York: Appleton-Century-Crofts, 1965.

Bijou, S. W., Peterson, R. F., Harris, F. R., Allen, K. E., & Johnston, M. Methodology for experimental studies of young children in natural settings. *Psychological Record,* 1969, *19,* 177–210.

Boren, J. J., & Coleman, A. D. Some experiments on reinforcement principles within a psychiatric ward for delinquent soldiers. *Journal of Applied Behavior Analysis,* 1970, *3,* 29–37.

Braginsky, B. M., & Braginsky, D. D. *Mainstream psychology: A critique.* New York: Holt, Rinehart & Winston, 1974.

Burgess, R. L., Clark, R. N., & Hendee, J. C. An experimental analysis of anti-litter procedures. *Journal of Applied Behavior Analysis,* 1971, *4,* 71–75.

Burnham, J. C. On the origins of behaviorism. *Journal of the History of the Behavioral Sciences,* 1968, *4,* 143–151.

Burnham, W. H. *The normal mind.* New York: Appleton, 1924.

Buss, A. The structure of psychological revolutions. *Journal of the History of the Behaviorial Sciences,* 1978, *14,* 57–64.

Cohen, D. *J. B. Watson, the founder of behaviorism: A biography.* London: Routledge & Kegan Paul, 1979.

Dollard, J., & Miller, N. E. *Personality and psychotherapy.* New York: McGraw-Hill, 1950.

Dunlap, K. *Habits, their making and unmaking.* New York: Liveright, 1932.

Ellis, A. What kinds of research are American psychologists doing? *American Psychologist,* 1949, *4,* 490–494.

Eysenck, H. J. Training in clinical psychology: An English point of view. *American Psychologist,* 1949, *4,* 173–176.

Eysenck, H. J. The effects of psychotherapy, *Journal of Consulting Psychology,* 1952, *16,* 319–324.

Eysenck, H. J. Learning theory and behaviour therapy. *Journal of Mental Science,* 1959, *195,* 61–75.

Eysenck, H. J. *Behavior therapy and the neuroses.* Oxford: Pergamon, 1960. (a)

Eysenck, H. J. (Ed.). *Handbook of abnormal psychology: An experimental approach.* London: Pitman, 1960. (b)

Eysenck, H. J. (Ed.). *Experiments in behavior therapy: Readings in modern methods of mental disorders derived from learning theory.* Oxford: Pergamon, 1964.

Fairweather, G. W. *Social change: The challenge to survival.* Morristown, N.J.: General Learning Press, 1972.

Ferster, C. B. Classification of behavioral pathology. In L. Krasner & L. P. Ullmann (Eds.), *Research in behavior modification: New developments and implications.* New York: Holt, Rinehart & Winston, 1965.

Ferster, C. B., & Culbertson, S. A psychology learning center. *Psychological Record,* 1974, *24,* 33–46.

Ferster, C. B., & Simmons, J. Behavior therapy with children. *Psychological Record,* 1966, *16,* 65–71.

Frank, J. D. *Persuasion and healing: A comparative study of psychotherapy.* Baltimore: Johns Hopkins University Press, 1961. (Rev. ed., 1973.)

Franks, C. M. Conditioning and abnormal behavior. In H. J. Eysenck (Ed.), *Handbook of abnormal psychology: An experimental approach.* London: Pitman, 1960.

Fuller, P. R. Operant conditioning of a vegetative human organism. *American Journal of Psychology,* 1949, *62,* 587–590.

Fuller, P. R. Personal communication, 1974.

Gambrill, E. D. *Behavior modification: Handbook of assessment, intervention, and evaluation.* San Francisco; Jossey-Bass, 1977.

Geller, E. S. Prompting anti-litter behaviors. *Proceedings of the 81st Annual Convention of the American Psychological Association,* 1973, *8,* 901–902.

Geller, E. S., Chaffee, J. L., & Ingram, R. E. Promoting paper recycling on a university campus. *Journal of Environmental Systems,* 1975, *5,* 39–57.

Gewirtz, J. L. The roles of overt responding and extrinsic reinforcement in "self" and "vicarious-reinforcement" phenomena and in "observational learning" and imitation. In R. Glaser (Ed.), *The nature of reinforcement: A symposium of the Learning Research and Development Center, University of Pittsburgh.* New York: Academic Press, 1971.

Glasgow, R. E., & Rosen, G. M. Behavioral bibliotherapy: A review of self-help behavior therapy manuals. *Psychological Bulletin,* 1978, *85,* 1–23.

Glasgow, R. E., & Rosen, G. M. Self-help behavior therapy manuals: Recent developments and clinical usage. *Clinical Behavior Therapy Review,* 1979, *1,* 1–20.

Glenwick, D., & Jason, L. *Behavioral community psychology: Progress and prospects.* New York: Praeger, 1980.

Goldiamond, I. Self-control procedures in personal behavior problems. *Psychological Reports,* 1965, *17,* 851–868.

Goldiamond, I. Toward a constructional approach to social problems: Ethical and constitutional issues raised by applied behavior analysis. *Behaviorism,* 1974, *2,* 1–84.

Goldiamond, I., & Dyrud, J. E. Some applications and implications of behavior analysis for psychotherapy. In J. M. Shlien (Ed.), *Research in psychotherapy* (Vol. 3). Washington,

D.C.: American Psychological Association, 1968.

Goulden, C. *The best years 1945-1950.* New York: Antheneum, 1976.

Greenspoon, J. The reinforcing effect of two spoken sounds on the frequency of two responses. *American Journal of Psychology,* 1955, *68,* 409–416.

Gregg, A. The profession of psychology as seen by a doctor of medicine. *American Psychologist,* 1948, *3,* 397–401.

Guthrie, E. R. *The psychology of learning.* New York: Harper, 1935.

Guthrie, E. R. Association by contiguity. In S. Koch (Ed.), *Psychology: A study of a science.* Study 1: *Conceptual and systematic;* Vol. 2: *General systematic formulations, learning and special processes.* New York: McGraw-Hill, 1959.

Halle, L. J. *Out of chaos.* Boston: Houghton Mifflin, 1977.

Hayes, S. C., & Cone, J. D. Reducing residential electricity energy use: Payments, information, and feedback. *Journal of Applied Behavior Analysis,* 1977, *10,* 425–435.

Henderson, J. D. The use of dual reinforcement in an intense treatment system. In R. D. Rubin & C. M. Franks (Eds.), *Advances in behavior therapy.* New York: Academic Press, 1968.

Herrnstein, R. J. Method and theory in the study of avoidance. *Psychological Review,* 1969, *79,* 49–69.

Hersen, M., & Barlow, D. H. *Single-case experimental design: Strategies for studying behavior change.* Elmsford, N.Y.: Pergamon, 1976.

Hollingworth, H. L. *Abnormal psychology.* New York: Ronald, 1930.

Homans, G. C. *Social behavior: Its elementary forms.* New York: Harcourt, Brace & World, 1961.

Homme, L. Personal communication, 1974.

Hull, C. L. *Principles of behavior: An introduction to behavior theory.* New York: Appleton-Century-Crofts, 1943.

Hull, C. L. *Essentials of behavior.* New Haven: Yale University Press, 1951.

Jacobson, E. *Progressive relaxation.* Chicago: University of Chicago Press, 1938.

Jones, H. G. The application of conditioning and learning techniques to the treatment of a psychiatric patient. *Journal of Abnormal and Social Psychology.* 1956, *52,* 414–420.

Jones, H. G. Applied abnormal psychology: The experimental approach. In H. J. Eysenck (Ed.), *Handbook of abnormal psychology: An experimental approach.* London: Pitman, 1960.

Jones, H. G. Personal communication, 1974.

Jones, M. C. A laboratory study of fear: The case of Peter. *Pedagogical Seminary,* 1924, *31,* 308–315.

Jones, R. J., & Azrin, N. H. An experimental application of a social reinforcement approach to the problem of job-finding. *Journal of Applied Behavior Analysis,* 1973, *6,* 345–353.

Kalish, H. I. *From behavioral science to behavior modification.* New York: McGraw-Hill, 1980.

Kamiya, J. Conscious control of brain waves. *Psychology Today,* April 1968, pp. 57–60.

Kanfer, F. H. Incentive value of generalized reinforcers. *Psychological Reports,* 1960, *7,* 531–538.

Kanfer, F. H. Issues and ethics in behavior manipulation. *Psychological Reports,* 1965, *16,* 187–196.

Kanfer, F. H. Verbal conditioning: A review of its current status. In T. R. Dixon & D. L. Horton (Eds.), *Verbal behavior and general behavior theory.* Englewood Cliffs, N.J.: Prentice-Hall, 1968.

Kanfer, F. H. Self-regulation: Research, issues and speculations. In C. Neuringer & J. L. Michael (Eds.), *Behavior modification in clinical psychology.* New York: Appleton-Century-Crofts, 1970.

Kanfer, F. H., & Phillips, J. S. *Learning foundations of behavior therapy.* New York: Wiley, 1970.

Kantor, J. R. Behaviorism in the history of psychology. *Psychological Record,* 1968, *18,* 151–165.

Kantor, J. R. *The scientific evolution of psychology* (Vol. 11). Granville, Ohio: Principia Press, 1969.

Kazdin, A. E. Characteristics and trends in applied behavior analysis. *Journal of Applied Behavior Analysis,* 1975, *8,* 332.

Kazdin, A. E. *History of behavior modification: Experimental foundations of contemporary research.* Baltimore: University Park Press, 1978.

Kazdin, A. E., & Wilson, G. T. *Evaluation of behavior therapy: Issues, evidence, and research strategies.* Cambridge, Mass.: Ballinger, 1978.

Keller, F. S. *Summers and sabbaticals.* Champaign, Ill.: Research Press, 1977.

Keller, F. S., & Schoenfeld, W. N. The psychology curriculum at Columbia College. *American Psychologist,* 1949, *4,* 165–172.

Keller, F. S., & Schoenfeld, W. N. *Principles of psychology: A systematic text in the science of behavior.* New York: Appleton-Century-Crofts, 1950.

Kohlenberg, R., & Phillips, T. Reinforcement and rate of litter depositing. *Journal of Applied Behavior Analysis,* 1973, *6,* 391–396.

Krantz, D. L. The separate worlds of operant and non-operant psychology. *Journal of Applied Behavior Analysis,* 1971, *4,* 61–70.

Krapfl, J. E., & Vargas, E. A. (Eds.). *Behaviorism and ethics.* Kalamazoo, Mich.: Behaviordelia, 1977.

Krasner, L. Studies of the conditioning of verbal behavior. *Psychological Bulletin,* 1958, *55,* 148–170.

Krasner, L. The therapist as a social reinforcement machine. In H. H. Strupp & L. Luborsky (Eds.), *Research in psychotherapy* (Vol. 2). Washington, D.C.: American Psychological Association, 1962.

Krasner, L. The behavioral scientist and social responsibility: No place to hide. *Journal of Social Issues,* 1965, *21,* 9–30.

Krasner, L. Behavior modification—values and training: The perspective of a psychologist. In C. M. Franks (Ed.), *Behavior therapy: Appraisal and status.* New York: McGraw-Hill, 1969.

Krasner, L. Behavior therapy. In P. H. Mussen (Ed.), *Annual review of psychology* (Vol. 22). Palo Alto, Calif.: Annual Reviews, 1971.

Krasner, L. The future and the past in the behaviorism–humanism dialogue. *American Psychologist,* 1978, *33,* 799–804.

Krasner, L. (Ed.). *Environmental design and human behavior: A psychology of the individual in society.* Elmsford, N.Y.: Pergamon, 1980.

Krasner, L., & Ullmann, L. P. (Eds.). *Research in behavior modification: New developments and implications.* New York: Holt, Rinehart & Winston, 1965.

Krasner, L., & Ullmann, L. P. *Behavior influence and personality: The social matrix of human action.* New York: Holt, Rinehart & Winston, 1973.

Kuhn, T. S. *The structure of scientific revolutions* (2nd ed.). Chicago: University of Chicago Press, 1970.

Lader, M. H., & Mathews, A. M. A physiological model of phobic anxiety and desensitization. *Behaviour Research and Therapy,* 1968, *6,* 411–421.

Lang, P. J. The application of psychophysiological methods to the study of psychotherapy and behavior modification. In A. E. Bergin & S. L. Garfield (Eds.), *Handbook of psychotherapy and behavior change.* New York: Wiley, 1970.

Lang, P. J., Stroufe, L. A., & Hastings, J. E. Effects of feedback and instructional set on the control of cardiac-rate variability. *Journal of Experimental Psychology,* 1967, *75,* 425–431.

Lazarus, A. A. New methods in psychotherapy: A case study. *South African Medical Journal,* 1958, *33,* 660–664.

Lazarus, A. A. In support of technical eclecticism. *Psychological Reports,* 1967, *21,* 415–416.

Lazarus, A. A. Learning theory and the treatment of depression. *Behaviour Research and Therapy,* 1968, *6,* 83–89.

Lazarus, A. A. *Behavior therapy and beyond.* New York: McGraw-Hill, 1971.

Leitenberg, H. (Ed.). *Handbook of behavior modification and behavior therapy.* Englewood Cliffs, N.J.: Prentice-Hall, 1976.

Leitenberg, H., Agras, W. S., Thompson, L. E., & Wright, D. E. Feedback in behavior modification: An experimental analysis in two phobic cases. *Journal of Applied Behavior Analysis,* 1968, *1,* 131–137.

Lindsley, O. R. Personal communication, 1974.

Lindsley, O. R., Skinner, B. F., & Solomon, H. C. *Studies in behavior therapy* (Status Report 1). Waltham, Mass.: Metropolitan State Hospital, 1953.

Lickona, T. (Ed.). *Moral development and behavior.* New York: Holt, Rinehart & Winston, 1976.

Lipsey, M. W. Psychology: Preparadigmatic, postparadigmatic, or misparadigmatic? *Science Studies,* 1974, *4,* 406–410.

Lovaas, O. I. Some studies on the treatment of childhood schizophrenia. In J. M. Shlien (Ed.), *Research in psychotherapy* (Vol. 3). Washington, D. C.: American Psychological Association, 1968.

Lukacs, J. *1945: Year zero.* Garden City, N.Y.: Doubleday, 1978.

Mackenzie, B. D. Behaviorism and positivism. *Journal of the History of the Behavioral Sciences,* 1972, *8,* 222–231.

Madsen, C. Values versus techniques: An analysis of behavior modification. *Phi Delta Kappan,* 1973, *54,* 598.

Mahoney, M. J. *Cognition and behavior modification.* Cambridge, Mass.: Ballinger, 1974.

Marler, L. A study of anti-litter messages. *Journal of Environmental Education,* 1971, *3,* 51–53.

Martin, G. L., & Osborne, J. G. (eds.). *Helping in the community: Behavioral applications.* New York: Plenum, 1980.

Marx, O. M. History of psychology: A review of the last decade. *Journal of the History of the Behavioral Sciences,* 1977, *13,* 41–47.

Mash, E. J. Has behaviour modification lost its identity? *The Canadian Psychologist,* 1974, *15,* 217–280.

Mead, G. H. *Mind, self, and society: From the standpoint of a social behaviorist.* Chicago: University of Chicago Press, 1934.

Meichenbaum, D. H. Cognitive modification of test-anxious college students. *Journal of Consulting and Clinical Psychology,* 1972, *39,* 370–380.

Meichenbaum, D. H. *Cognitive behavior modification.* Morristown, N.J.: General Learning Press, 1974.

Meichenbaum, D. H. *Cognitive behavior modification.* New York: Plenum, 1977.

Merton, R. K. *The sociology of science.* Chicago: University of Chicago Press, 1973.

Miller, J. G. Clinical psychology in the Veterans Administration. *American Psychologist,* 1946, *1,* 181–189.

Miller, L. K., & Miller, O. L. Reinforcing self-help group activities of welfare recipients.

Journal of Applied Behavior Analysis, 1970, *3,* 57–64.

Miller, N. E. Learning of visceral and glandular responses. *Science,* 1969, *163,* 434–445.

Miller, N. E., & DiCara, L. Y. Instrumental learning of heart-rate changes in curarized rats: Shaping and specificity to discriminate stimulus. *Journal of Comparative Physiological Psychology,* 1967, *63,* 12–19.

Miller, N. E., & Dollard, J. *Social learning and imitation.* New Haven: Yale University Press, 1941.

Mischel, W. *Personality and assessment.* New York: Wiley, 1968.

Mitroff, I. I. *The subjective side of science.* Amsterdam: Elsevier, 1974.

Mowrer, O. H. Apparatus for the study and treatment of enuresis. *American Journal of Psychology,* 1938, *51,* 163–166.

Mowrer, O. H. A stimulus–response analysis of anxiety and its role as a reinforcing agent. *Psychological Review,* 1939, *46,* 553–564.

Mowrer, O. H. *Learning theory and behavior.* New York: Wiley, 1960. (a)

Mowrer, O. H. *Learning theory and the symbolic processes.* New York: Wiley, 1960. (b)

Mowrer, O. H. The present state of behaviorism. *Education,* 1976, *97,* 4–23.

Mowrer, O. H., & Mowrer, W. M. Enuresis: A method for its study and treatment. *American Journal of Orthopsychiatry,* 1938, *8,* 436–459.

Nietzel, M. T., Winett, R. A., McDonald, M. L., & Davidson, W. S. *Behavioral approaches to community psychology.* Elmsford, N.Y.: Pergamon, 1977.

O'Leary, K. D., & Becker, W. C. Behavior modification of an adjustment class: A token reinforcement program. *Exceptional Child,* 1967, *33,* 637–642.

O'Leary, K. D., & Wilson, G. T. *Behavior therapy.* Englewood Cliffs, N.J.: Prentice-Hall, 1976.

Palermo, D. S. Is a scientific revolution taking place in psychology? *Science Studies,* 1971, *1,* 135–155.

Parsons, T. The principle structure of community. In C. Friedrich (Ed.), *Community.* New York: Liberal Arts Press, 1959.

Pascal, G. R. *Behavioral change in the clinic: A systematic approach.* New York: Grune & Stratton, 1959.

Patterson, G. R. Behavioral intervention procedures in the classroom and the home. In A. E. Bergin & S. L. Garfield (Eds.), *Handbook of psychotherapy and behavior change.* New York: Wiley, 1970.

Pavlov, I. P. [*Lectures on conditioned reflexes*] (W. H. Grantt, trans.). New York: International Publishers, 1928.

Paul, G. L. *Insight versus desensitization in psychotherapy: An experiment in anxiety reduction.* Stanford, Calif.: Stanford University Press, 1966.

Peters, H. N., & Jenkins, R. L. Improvement of chronic schizophrenic patients with guided problem-solving, motivated by hunger. *Psychiatric Quarterly Supplement,* 1954, *28,* 84–101.

Phillips, E. L. *Psychotherapy: A modern theory and practice,* Englewood Cliffs, N.J.: Prentice-Hall, 1956.

Pierce, C. H., & Risley, T. R. Improving job performance of Neighborhood Youth Corps aides in an urban recreation program. *Journal of Applied Behavior Analysis,* 1974, *7,* 207–215.

Polanyi, M. *Personal knowledge.* New York: Harper & Row, 1958.

Popper, K. R. *The logic of scientific discovery.* New York: Harper & Row, 1959.

Popper, K. R. *The open society and its enemies.* London: Routledge & Kegan Paul, 1966.

Popper, K. R. *Conjectures and refutations.* New York: Basic Books, 1967.

Postman, L. The history and present status of the law of effect. *Psychological Bulletin,* 1947, *44,* 489–563.

Rachlin, H. *Behaviorism in everyday life.* Englewood Cliffs, N.J.: Prentice-Hall, 1980.

Repucci, N. D., & Saunders, J. T. History, action and change. *American Journal of Community Psychology,* 1977, *5,* 399–412.

Reynolds, G. S. *A primer of operant conditioning.* Glenview, Ill.: Scott, Foresman, 1968.

Rimm, D. C., & Masters, J. C. *Behavior therapy: Techniques and empirical findings.* New York: Academic Press, 1974.

Risley, T. R., & Hart, B. Developing correspondence between the non-verbal and verbal behavior of preschool children. *Journal of Applied Behavior Analysis,* 1968, *1,* 267–281.

Rosenthal, R. *Experimenter effects in behavioral research.* New York: Appleton-Century-Crofts, 1966.

Salter, A. *Conditioned reflex therapy.* New York: Farrar Straus, 1949.

Salzinger, K. The problem of response class in verbal behavior. In K. Salzinger & S. Salzinger (Eds.), *Research in verbal behavior and some neurophysiological implications.* New York: Academic Press, 1967.

Sarbin, T. R. Role theory. In G. Lindzey (Ed.), *Handbook of social psychology.* Cambridge, Mass.: Addison-Wesley, 1954.

Schaefer, H. H., & Martin, P. L. *Behavioral therapy.* New York: McGraw-Hill, 1969.

Sears, R. R. Graduate training facilities: I. General information; II. Clinical psychology. *American Psychologist,* 1946, *1,* 135–150.

Senn, P. B. What is "behavioral science?": Notes toward a history. *Journal of the History of the Behavioral Sciences,* 1966, *2,* 107–122.

Shaffer, L. F. The problem of psychotherapy. *American Psychologist,* 1947, *2,* 459–467.

Shakow, D. Seventeen years later: Clinical psychology in the light of the 1947 Committee on Training in Clinical Psychology report. *American Psychologist,* 1965, *20,* 353–362.

Shapiro, D., Tursky, B., Gershon, E., & Stern, M. Effects of feedback and reinforcement on the control of human systolic blood pressure. *Science,* 1969, *163,* 588–590.

Shaw, F. J. A stimulus–response analysis of repression and insight in psychotherapy. *Psychological Review,* 1946, *53,* 36–42.

Shaw, F. J. The role of reversal in psychotherapy. *American Psychologist,* 1947, *4,* 177–179.

Shaw, F. J. Some postulates concerning psychotherapy. *Journal of Consulting Psychology,* 1948, *12,* 426–431.

Shearn, D. W. Operant conditioning of heart rate. *Science,* 1962, *137,* 530–531.

Shoben, E. J., Jr. Psychotherapy as a problem in learning theory. *Psychological Bulletin,* 1949, *46,* 366–392.

Shils, E. A. *The intellectuals and the powers and other essays.* Chicago: University of Chicago Press, 1972.

Skinner, B. F. *The behavior of organisms.* New York: Appleton-Century-Crofts, 1938.

Skinner, B. F. *Walden two.* New York: Macmillan, 1948.

Skinner, B. F. *Science and human behavior.* New York: Macmillan, 1953.

Skinner, B. F. *Verbal behavior,* New York: Appleton-Century-Crofts, 1957.

Skinner, B. F. An autobiography. In P. B. Dews (Ed.), *Festschrift for B. F. Skinner.* New York: Appleton-Century-Crofts, 1970.

Skinner, B. F. *Beyond freedom and dignity.* New York: Knopf, 1971.

Skinner, B. F. *Cumulative record: A selection of papers.* New York: Appleton-Century-Crofts, 1972.

Skinner, B. F. *About behaviorism.* New York: Knopf, 1974.

Skinner, B. F. *Particulars of my life.* New York: Knopf, 1976.

Skinner, B. F. *The shaping of a behaviorist: Part two of an autobiography.* New York: Knopf, 1979.

Staats, A. W., Staats, C. K., Schutz, R. E., & Wolf, M. M. The conditioning of textual responses using "extrinsic" reinforcers. *Journal of Experimental Analysis of Behavior,* 1962, *5,*

33–40.

Stampfl, T. G., & Levis, D. J. Implosive therapy: A behavioral therapy? *Behaviour Research and Therapy,* 1968, *6,* 31–36.

Stocking, G. W., Jr. On the limits of "presentism" and "historicism" in the historiography of the behavioral sciences. *Journal of the History of the Behavioral Sciences,* 1965, *1,* 211–217.

Stolz, S. B. *Ethical issues in behavior modification.* San Francisco, Calif.: Jossey-Bass, 1978.

Stoyva, J. *Skinnerian Zen, or control of physiological responses through information feedback.* Paper presented at Denver University Symposium on Behavior Modification, 1968.

Stuart, R. B. Operant–interpersonal treatment for marital discord. *Journal of Consulting and Clinical Psychology,* 1969, *33,* 675–682.

The New York Times. Behavior. January 1, 1980, p. 14.

Thorndike, E. L. *Human learning.* New York: Century, 1931.

Ullmann, L. P. Behavior therapy as a social movement. In C. M. Franks (Ed.), *Behavior therapy: Appraisal and status.* New York: McGraw-Hill, 1969.

Ullmann, L. P., & Krasner, L. (Eds.). *Case studies in behavior modification.* New York: Holt, Rinehart & Winston, 1965.

Ulrich, R. Behavior control and public concern. *Psychological Record,* 1967, *17,* 229–234.

Valins, S., & Ray, A. A. Effects of cognitive desensitization on avoidance behavior. *Journal of Personality and Social Psychology,* 1967, *7,* 345–350.

Warren, N. Is a scientific revolution taking place in psychology?: Doubts and reservations. *Science Studies,* 1971, *1,* 407–413.

Watson, J. B. *Behaviorism.* Chicago: The People's Institute, 1924.

Watson, J. B., & Rayner, R. Conditioned emotional reactions. *Journal of Experimental Psychology,* 1920, *3,* 1–14.

Watson, R. I. The experimental tradition and clinical psychology. In A. J. Bachrach (Ed.), *Experimental foundations of clinical psychology.* New York: Basic Books, 1962.

Watson, R. I. Prescriptions as operative in the history of psychology. *Journal of the History of the Behavioral Sciences,* 1971, *7,* 311–322.

Weimer, W. B., & Palermo, D. S. Paradigms and normal science in psychology. *Science Studies,* 1973, *3,* 211–244.

Weimer, W. B., & Palermo, D. S. (Eds.). *Cognition and the symbolic processes.* Hillsdale, N.J.: Erlbaum, 1974.

Weitzman, B. Behavior therapy and psychotherapy. *Psychological Review,* 1967, *74,* 300–317.

Williams, R. I., & Blanton, R. L. Verbal conditioning in a psychotherapeutic situation *Behaviour Research and Therapy,* 1968, *6,* 97–104.

Wilson, G. T. On the much discussed nature of the term "behavior therapy." *Behavior Therapy,* 1978, *9,* 89–98.

Winett, R. A., & Nietzel, M. T. Behavioral ecology: Contingency management of consumer energy use. *American Journal of Community Psychology,* 1975, *3,* 123–133.

Winkler, R. C. Reinforcement schedules for individual patients in a token economy. *Behavior Therapy,* 1971, *2,* 534–537.

Wolpe, J. *Psychotherapy by reciprocal inhibition.* Stanford, Calif.: Stanford University Press, 1958.

Wolpe, J. *The practice of behavior therapy* (2nd ed.). Elmsford, N.Y.: Pergamon, 1973.

Wolpe, J. Personal communication, 1974.

II

EXPERIMENTAL FOUNDATIONS
OF BEHAVIOR THERAPY

2

RESEARCH IN INFRAHUMAN AND HUMAN CONDITIONING

DONALD J. LEVIS
Department of Psychology
State University of New York at Binghamton

PAUL F. MALLOY
Department of Psychology
State University of New York at Binghamton

INTRODUCTION

The scholarly search to establish integrative lawful statements about human psychopathology has been made more difficult by the wide range of diversified and seemingly mystifying behaviors under study. For example, consider the behavior of a male who abandoned his professional career because he was afraid to leave his home out of fear that dog feces might exist in his yard. For this individual, the thought of becoming contaminated became so frightening that he repeatedly engaged in washing his clothes, hands, and body to obtain partial relief from his obsessive anxiety-eliciting thoughts. Or consider a woman who became so panic-stricken by a similar fear of dirt and disease that she required her husband to change clothes and shower immediately after entering the house. To an untrained observer, it is difficult to understand how a woman could become so frightened of bath water that she had to wear a life preserver, or how the sound of a locomotive whistle in the distance could wake such terror in an individual that he ran in a circle screaming at the top of his voice. Some individuals break out in a cold sweat at the sight of a car, airplane, or tall building, while others experience similar panic when they leave their own homes or are exposed to a crowd. Still others become so afraid of their own sexual feelings that they avoid the opposite sex, become convinced they will die and be sent to hell, become obsessed with the fear that their food contains captive people and worms, or are plagued with thoughts that they may hurt their own children or a loved one. Fears of failing, losing control, taking responsibility, expressing anger, or giving love and affection have also resulted in the behavioral and emotional inhibition of many individuals.

Not only is the mental health practitioner confronted with a wide range of symptoms to understand and treat, but the number of individuals requesting help also has dramatically increased. Lemkow and Crocetti (1958) estimated that between 14 and 20 of every 1000 children born will be hospitalized in a mental institution within their lifetime. Srole and his coworkers (Srole, Langner, Michael, Opler, & Rennie, 1962) reported that fewer than one out of four persons were judged to be psychologically healthy, and nearly one out of five persons were considered to be "incapacitated" by psychological disturbance. Recent attention has also been devoted to the possibility that between two-thirds to three-quarters of presenting physical problems may be affected by and related to psychological factors.

Response by the mental health field to these growing crises in conceptual and service needs has been characterized as slow, inefficient, and ineffectual. Existing psychotherapy movements, such as the psychoanalytic, Gestalt, existential, and humanistic approaches, have produced theoretical structures that lack operational specificity and ease of testability. Treatment techniques from these positions are costly, lengthy, and of dubious effect. Claims of therapuetic efficacy frequently are not accompanied by sufficient research support, and the support that is available generally falls short of incorporating even a minimum degree of methodological sophistication. Eysenck (1960, 1966), perhaps more than others, has cogently and at times tendentiously championed this viewpoint. Nonpsychotherapy approaches, such as chemotherapy, also have not lived up to earlier expectations. Many now view the psychopharmacology approach at best as simply providing a "holding" period, and at worst as actually delaying or preventing an individual from dealing directly with the issues that prevent corrective behavior change.

THE BEHAVIOR-THERAPY APPROACH

In a field that already has an abundance of unproven theoretical and treatment approaches, the advent of yet another therapeutic movement like behavior therapy should be viewed with a healthy skepticism. Yet it must be recognized that if the existing chaos within the mental health field is to be resolved, a new approach is needed that can provide a solid experimental and theoretical foundation upon which treatment techniques can be developed, assessed, and improved. This is precisely the strength and objective of the behavior-therapy approach and the reason why it has been labeled the "Fourth Psychotherapeutic Revolution." (The first was morale therapy; the second, psychoanalysis; and the third, community mental health. See Levis, 1970.) As Greenspoon (1965) noted, the uniqueness of this approach is reflected in its emphasis on behavior and its measurement variables, in its attempt to develop precise definitions and specifiable operations, and in its stress on experimental control.

But perhaps the greatest asset of the behavior-therapy movement is its attempt to establish an experimental foundation by highlighting, utilizing, and extending knowledge developed from the basic research areas of psychology. Such a strategy already has paid vast dividends in the establishment of new and promising treatment procedures. Furthermore, by adopting the scientific language of the laboratory, the behavior-therapy movement has greatly enhanced communication and interest between the basic and the applied researcher.

Of the basic research areas in psychology, the field of learning and conditioning clearly has had the greatest impact on the development of the applied behavioral approach. This chapter describes the rationale behind extrapolating from infrahuman and human data, as well as outlining the important conditioning models that have resulted in the development of new treatment procedures. Attention also will be paid to critical issues within the area that have important theoretical and applied implications.

THE RATIONALE FOR CONDITIONING
MODELS OF PSYCHOPATHOLOGY

Prior to the advent of the behavior-therapy movement, few systematic attempts were made to draw upon the established principles of conditioning and learning developed in the laboratory. This failure to utilize the wealth of scientific data and theory is all the more puzzling, since few clinicans would disagree with the statement that learning plays an important role in the development of psychopathological behavior. Practically all the nonbehavioral explanations of psychopathology acknowledge the role of conditioning and learning in early childhood, the effects of punishment and withdrawal of positive contact by the parents, and the importance of anxiety and fear in motivating human symptomatology. Yet there has been a reluctance to incorporate the tools and procedures of the basic researcher.

Perhaps the reluctance to utilize laboratory data is based on the premise that humans are unique and complex and that laws largely based on infrahuman research and sterile paradigms of human learning are not generalizable. Although such a thesis has merit, the history of more established sciences such as genetics and biology attests to the value of generalizing from laws established from infrahuman data. As Levis (1970) has suggested, it may turn out in the last analysis that data collected from infrahuman species will prove more useful for generalizing than work conducted with college students will. If maladaptive behavior is tied in part to conditioning of emotional or autonomic responses, and if mediated internal cues such as words, thoughts, images, and memories in the human turn out to follow essentially the same conditioning laws as exteroceptive stimuli do, the argument for infrahuman research becomes much stronger. Not only does the rat provide a less complex organism that may be more advantageous for deciphering basic laws; it also is equipped with an emotional system not too unlike that of a human. Furthermore, animals are expendable and subject to experimentation that for ethical reasons cannot be carried out on humans. Even if infrahuman and human laboratory experimentation only provides a vehicle for illustration and confirmation of suspected hypotheses about human psychopathology, the effort is more than worthwhile.

It should be noted that despite the various arguments pro and con, and the obvious need for confirmation at the clinical level, research in infrahuman and human conditioning already has had a considerable heuristic influence on the development of behavioral therapy. Wolpe's systematic desensitization, Stampfl's "flooding" or "implosive" therapy, and Skinner's operant-conditioning approach were all stimulated by such laboratory data and by their own infrahuman research. Whether justified or not, such data gave impetus to the development of promising treatment techniques that were previously undeveloped or not considered.

CRITERIA FOR EVALUATING CONDITIONING MODELS

As alluded to above, behavioral models of psychopathology that are based on the laboratory laws of conditioning have several advantages over nonbehavioral models. First, conditioning models begin with delimited, data-based behavioral laws and build systematically upon them. What may be lost in comprehensiveness is gained in precision. In contrast, nonbehavioral models often begin as "all-encompassing theories designed to analyze the whole and complete human organism" (Levis, 1970, p. 9). Such models are often impossible to put to an empirical test, since in the quest to explain and describe all, they predict nothing. Second, conditioning models are closely allied to the basic research area of learning from which they have sprung. This alliance encourages a constant interchange of ideas from which both sides benefit. The clinician is provided with potentially useful therapeutic tools, while the basic researcher is presented with diverse and challenging behaviors to reproduce and explain. Third, the commitment of conditioning models to empirical validation insures the constant revision of theory and technique that is so necessary to the advancement of present knowledge of psychopathology. Dogmatism is minimized by this system of checks and balances.

Unfortunately, impeccable pedigree and careful upbringing do not guarantee success to any child of science, and behavior therapy is no exception. Therapies based on conditioning models have been criticized by a number of writers. Breger and McGaugh (1965) noted that most behavior therapists have failed to establish a direct relationship between their treatment techniques and theoretical underpinnings. Behavior therapists also have made extravagent claims of therapeutic efficacy (e.g., Eysenck, 1960) that have not been supported by subsequent comparative studies (Bergin & Lambert, 1978; Bergin & Suinn, 1975; Rachman, 1971). Clearly, if conditioning models are truly to enhance our knowledge of psychopathology and produce useful treatments, they must meet certain theoretical and practical criteria.

For conditioning models to provide an adequate account of psychopathology, they must first provide an explanation for how human maladaptive behaviors develop. That is, what specific contingencies reliably lead to the development of phobias, obsessions, or psychoses? Second, conditioning models must account for the remarkable persistence of human psychopathology. Why does the acrophobic, for example, continue to fear and avoid high places, despite numerous nontraumatic encounters with the phobic situation throughout his life? Many conditioning models fail this criterion. Third, conditioning models should be based on data gathered not only at the infrahuman level, but also in human analogue and clinical populations. The similarities and lawfulness of the behavior in question must be demonstrated convincingly at each level (Abramson & Seligman, 1977). Finally, a useful conditioning model should suggest specific techniques whereby maladaptive behavior can be prevented, reduced, or eliminated. These techniques must then be validated in clinical populations.

CURRENT RESEARCH STRATEGIES

A careful review of existing conditioning models of psychopathology suggests two separate but not mutually exclusive research strategies. The first approach represents an attempt to reproduce within the laboratory symptomatic behavior modeled from human psychopathology. The emphasis here is on developing *response topographies* that are similar, although not necessarily identical, to those observed with human pathological behavior. For example, the study of audiogenic seizures in infrahumans has been noted to resemble hysterical convulsions in humans (Finger, 1944); the development of tonic immobility and displacements in animals has been noted respectively to resemble catatonia (Gallup & Maser, 1977) and human psychosomatic disorders (Barnett, 1955); and schedule-induced drinking phenomena in the laboratory (Staddon, 1977) have been suggested as a model for alcoholism (Gilbert, 1976). Of course, it is recognized that laboratory models are rarely exact replicas of human psychopathology and that certain symptoms, such as the disordered language of the schizophrenic, probably will not be reproduced in the laboratory because of ethical considerations. Nevertheless, such laboratory models already have enhanced researchers' and therapists' knowledge by suggesting operative principles behind the development of human symptoms and strategies for their removal. As long as such models continue to add to this knowledge and to suggest further research, the approach is more than worthwhile.

The second approach adopted in providing functional conditioning models of psychopathology represents an attempt to study within the laboratory critical learning principles that may be operative in the development, maintenance, and unlearning of symptomatic behavior. Here the emphasis is not on mimicking symptom formation, but rather on providing empirical support for *process* or *stimulus* variables believed to be involved in the learning and unlearning of psychopathology. For example, such an approach may concentrate on understanding how emotional states are learned or unlearned or on determining how such principles as experimental extinction, counterconditioning, generalization, punishment, and positive reinforcement, believed to be operative in human psychopathology or posited as critical change agents in behavioral-treatment techniques, function. It is these basic principles of learning and conditioning that behavior therapists have relied upon in developing new treatment techniques and that form the bulk of the experimental foundation of the field.

In the following sections, the major conditioning theories and principles postulated to account for symptom formation, symptom maintenance, and symptom removal are discussed. No attempt is made to be comprehensive or to summarize the vast body of conditioning literature relevant to behavior therapy. Rather, the few paradigms selected for discussion have been chosen because they have current relevance in the literature and because, as behavior models of psychopathology, they meet most of the criteria previously outlined. Particular emphasis has also been given to conditioning research that has relevance to existing behavior therapies currently in widespread use.

DEVELOPMENT OF PSYCHOPATHOLOGY

Because of problems associated with lack of experimental control and ethics, theories of symptom etiology have relied largely on clinical case material and speculation. Stimulated by a desire to establish an experimental foundation, the behavior-therapy movement has attempted to find support for its hypotheses by turning mainly to laboratory research. Documented models of symptom formation are believed to be critical not only for the establishment of a comprehensive theoretical structure, but also as an aid in enhancing the effectiveness of existing techniques and in developing new approaches. The vast amount of available conditioning literature has provided the behavior therapist with an initial data base for achieving this objective. Although the operant approach to behavior analysis is correct in its assertion that issues of etiology need not necessarily be considered in the development of effective behavioral techniques at a clinical level, the search for laws governing the establishment of psychopathology is an objective worthy of scientific undertaking.

Prior to a discussion of existing models of symptom formation, it may be helpful to provide some basic distinctions made in the learning literature. A common element of many contemporary behavior or conditioning theories is the discrimination made between a conditioned stimulus (CS) and an unconditioned stimulus (UCS). The basic distinction resides in the functional analysis of the properties of a given stimulus to those of a given response prior to any exposure to a conditioning sequence. The CS only acquires the ability to elicit a given response by being paired with a UCS. The UCS, on the other hand, is a stimulus known to evoke a regular and measurable response (UCR); for example, electric shock produces pain and escape. Repetition of the UCS will result in the continual elicitation of the UCR (excluding temporary effects of habituation or adaptation), while repetition of a CS in the abscence of the UCS will lead to a weakening or unlearning of the conditioned response (CR). Both the CS and the UCS have reinforcing properties and are capable of conditioning the organism to other stimuli.

Contemporary behavior theories also frequently make a distinction between independent variables that seem to have motivational effects upon behavior and those that direct or guide behavior. Intermediary constructs that correspond with these two groups of variables have been introduced by several theorists. For example, drives, motivations, emotions, conations, and libidos are constructs considered to function as activating agents; whereas habits, cognitive maps, and associative tendencies serve (in conjunction with external and internal stimuli) to determine the directions of behavior (Brown, 1961). The term "drive" is used in this chapter to refer to the motivational or activating aspects of behavior, and "habit strength" is used to indicate directive functions.

Traditionally, drives have been classified into primary and secondary sources of motivation. In general, primary or innate drive states, such as hunger, thirst, sex, and pain, are those that produce their effects through the action of inherited bodily mechanisms and are not dependent upon learning (elicited by a UCS). Secondary drives differ from primary drives in that their ability to serve as motivators is dependent upon learning (elicited by a CS). Such drives play an important role in the development of human behavior and include stimuli involved in the striving for prestige, social mobility, money, power, love, and status. In terms of developing maladaptive behavior, many theorists believe learned fear or anxiety to be the most relevant drive source. As Dollard and Miller (1950, p. 190) noted, fear is important to symptom formation because it can be a very strong source of motivation, because it can be attached to new cues so easily through learning, and because it is the source of motivation that produces the inhibiting responses in most conflicts. As is made clear below, conflict or drives or response tendencies is the major ingredient of most behavioral models of experimental neurosis.

CONFLICT MODELS OF EXPERIMENTAL NEUROSIS

The disruptive effects of confronting an organism with two opposing drives so as to produce a conflict in response tendencies was first noted from the results of two experiments conducted independently in Pavlov's laboratory in 1912 and 1913 by Mariya Nikolayevna Yerofeyeva and Nataliya Rudolfovna Shenger-Krestovnikova (Kazdin, 1978). In the first experiment, a salivary reflex in a dog was conditioned to a shock stimulus by pairing it with food. When the strength of shock was increased markedly, the dog continued to make the salivary response, but when the site of shock was altered, the animal became greatly agitated and the conditioned reflex broke down even when shock was returned to the original location. In the second example, a breakdown of the CR was obtained by exposing the dog to an insoluble discrimination task. In the first part of the experiment, two stimuli were presented, a circle and an ellipse. The circle presentation was followed by food leading to the conditioning of salivation to the circle. The ellipse was presented but not followed by food (UCS). After the CR was well established, the axes of the ellipse were altered progressively so that it increasingly resembled a circle. Not only did the dog's CR deteriorate, but the dog now struggled, became agitated, barked violently, and attacked the apparatus.

Stimulated by these initial findings, Pavlov (1927) further investigated the conditions underlying the behavior that he termed "experimental neurosis." Pavlov concluded that experimental neurosis could be created by manipulating other variables besides imposition of difficult discrimination, such as prolongation of CSs beyond the previous CS-UCS interval; presentation of excessively strong stimulations; rapidly changes of paradigms from excitatory to inhibitory patterns; and breakups in stereotyped response sequences. His research led him to conclude that such "neurotic" behavior was due to pathological conditions of the nervous system involving excessive excitation and/or escessive inhibition. Since the experimental neurosis paradigms did not produce pathological behavior in all animals, Pavlov postulated that constitutional predispositions contributed to neurosis; some dogs were more likely to develop behavior characterized by chronic excitation, while others tended to manifest signs of chronic inhibition.

Pavlov (1928, p. 361) considered the critical factor inherent in each of the experimental neurosis paradigms to be a *conflict* between response tendencies (excitation and inhibition). Neurotic and psychotic symptoms were seen as behavioral manifestations of the organism's attempt to reduce the conflict. Gantt (1942, 1943, 1944, 1971) replicated and extended Pavlov's work with dogs, while others found similar effects with cats (Masserman, 1943, 1946, 1950, 1971), sheep (Liddell, 1944, 1956, 1965), rats (Maier & Ellen, 1952), and human children (Krasnogorski, 1925).

Realizing the experimental and clinical importance of the approach–avoidance paradigm, N. E. Miller (1951) conducted a classic series of studies on the topic that established the experimental foundation for the learning and maintenance of such conflicts. Masserman (1943), Dollard and Miller (1950), and more recently Levis and Hare (1977) have extended this learning literature to explain symptom formation involved in the development of human psychopathology. Examples are provided to illustrate how the primary drive of pain and the secondary drive of fear can interact in a conflict situation with primary drives of hunger, sex, anger, and affection to produce psychopathology. Although the logic of these reported analyses is compelling, more experimental work is needed with the conflict paradigm, especially involving drive stimuli associated with sex, anger, and affection.

LEARNED-HELPLESSNESS MODELS

In a series of studies, Masserman (1946, 1950, 1971) demonstrated that when previously learned discrimination or avoidance tasks were made more difficult by varying the sequencing of timing requirements, by introducing disruptive auditory feedback, or by programming unpredictable shocks, the experimental animals displayed a variety of bizarre behaviors similar to those observed in Pavlov's laboratory. He departed from his earlier interpretation (Masserman, 1943) that the "neurotic" effect was a result in conflict between drive states, by proposing what he considered to be a more general etiological mechanism—the inability to control or predict important events. Masserman believed that "uncertainty" about, or loss of control over, outcomes caused dramatic increases in anxiety and pathological inhibition of adaptive behaviors.

This shift in emphasis from conflict to unpredictability finds its contemporary counterpart in the work of Seligman (1975) and his colleagues (Abramson, Seligman, & Teasdale, 1978; Maier & Seligman, 1976). Seligman improved upon Masserman's position by specifying the precise relationship between response and outcome that leads to maladaptive behavior. Three stages are postulated in the development of learned helplessness. The first stage consists of the organism's receiving information that the probability of the outcome is independent of performing a given response class. The distinction between controllable and uncontrollable reinforcement is central to the theory. The concept of controllability is defined operationally within a response-reinforced contingency space. If the conditional probability of that outcome (i. e., reinforcement), given a specific response, does not differ from the conditional probability of that outcome in the absence of that response, then the outcome is independent of responding and, by definition, uncontrollable. On the other hand, if the conditional probability of the outcome, given a specific response, is not equal to the conditional probability of the outcome in the absence of that response, then the outcome is controllable. A person or infrahuman is "helpless" with respect to some outcome when the outcome occurs independently of all voluntary responses.

The second and critical stage of the theory involves the organisms registering and processing cognitively the information obtained from the contingency exposure in which responding was independent of outcome. This event can be subdivided into two processes: (1) learning that a contingency exists concerning the independence of responding and outcome; and (2) developing the expectation that responding and outcome will remain independent on future trials. Coinciding with the second stage is a reduction in the motivation (activity) to control the outcome. Because of this factor and the emphasis on expectancy, Seligman's theory has been designated a nonmotivational, cognitive theory (Levis, 1980a). The final stage includes the generalization and transference of the developed expectation that responding and outcome are independent of new learning situations. The behavioral outcome of this generalization is referred to as the "learned-helplessness effect." The above model recently has been extended to include attribution theory (Abramson, Seligman, & Teasdale, 1978). The response class of self-esteem, which is considered orthogonal to controllability, has been added.

Uncontrollability is achieved in a laboratory setting by programming an aversive event unsystematically or randomly, while controllability is achieved by preceeding the aversive event with a signal as occurs in the standard conditioning paradigm.

The learned-helplessness model, however, is more limited than the S-R conflict model previously described in that it only purports to explain infrahuman and human depressive behavior, rather than neurotic behavior in general. Among the similarities between human depression and laboratory-induced helplessness are lowered activity levels, negative or pessimistic cognitive sets, lack of aggression, feelings of hopelessness, loss of appetite and libido, and lower norepinephrine levels.

The learned-helplessness effect has generated considerable research interest and has been observed in a wide variety of species, including dogs (Overmeir & Seligman, 1967), cats (Seward & Humphrey, 1967), rats

(Seligman & Beagley, 1975), fish (Behrend & Bitterman, 1963), chickens (Maser & Gallup, 1974), mice (Braud, Wepmann, & Russo, 1969), and humans (Hiroto & Seligman, 1975). Considerable controversy also has developed over Seligman's theoretical account, with alternative S-R models being offered to explain both the infrahuman data (Levis, 1976) and human findings (Levis, 1980a; McReynolds, 1980). Despite the existing controversy and the concern that the findings may have little to do with explaining human depression, the learned-helplessness effect that originates at the infrahuman level represents a classical example of how laboratory models can function as a heuristic stimulus. This model, perhaps more than any other factor, has generated a renewed interest in the experimental study of human depression.

AVOIDANCE MODELS

In the preceding discussion of conflict models, including those produced by the learned-helplessness paradigm, investigators (see Levis, 1976; Levis & Hare, 1977) have argued that a critical component within the paradigm involves the conditioning of aversive stimuli that are subsequently avoided. Freud (1936) was the first to advance the position that symptoms are learned because they help the individual avoid signals that elicit fear or anxiety. Behavioral therapists such as Eysenck (1968), Stampfl and Levis (1967), and Wolpe (1958) have championed this position, making it an integral part of their theoretical models. Unlike Freud, these behaviorists have extended theoretical concepts developed from laboratory data involving paradigms of infrahuman and human conditioning. Central to each of these positions is the assumption that maladaptive behavior that is labeled symptomatic is motivated by a strong, primary drive state labeled "fear."

Although a variety of theoretical accounts explain avoidance acquisition (Bolles, 1971; Herrnstein, 1969; Schofield, 1950; Seligman & Johnston, 1973), both Eysenck (1979) and Stampfl and Levis (1969, 1976) have adopted Mowrer's two-factor theory of avoidance behavior (1947). This decision was based largely on the strong research support for the model and on the ease by which it can be extended to explain human psychopathology. Wolpe (1958) selected a Hullian position (1943), which currently is rarely adopted by avoidance conditioners because of lack of support for certain basic propositions. The differences between the Hull and Mowrer models are largely academic, since both emphasize basically the same principles in the development of fear and avoidance behavior. Therefore, the emphasis will be placed on describing Mowrer's two-factor theory.

According to Mowrer's two-factor theory (1947), at least two response classes are believed inherent to the development of psychopathology. The first consists of the organism's learning to respond in a fearful manner to previously nonfearful stimuli. The sequence of events required for fear acquisition is well established in the experimental literature. Its development simply results from the pairing of initially nonfearful stimuli with an inherent aversive event producing pain. The primary drive or UCR of pain can be elicited by a variety of UCSs, such as those involved in physical punishment or generated by severe states of primary deprivation such as hunger. Following sufficient repetition of a neutral stimulus with a UCS, the nonfearful stimulus will acquire the capability of eliciting a fear response. At this point in time, the nonfearful stimulus is appropriately labeled a CS and is capable of eliciting fear even when not followed by the inherent aversive event (UCS). The aversive emotional reaction elicited by the presentation of fearful CSs is referred to as the fear CR. Although some theorists believed that the fear response solely reflected conditioning of the autonomic nervous system (Mowrer, 1947; Wolpe, 1958), recent data have questioned this assumption (Rescorla & Solomon, 1967). Nevertheless, in most cases of fear conditioning, the autonomic nervous system is affected. It is also safe to say that the fear response does not involve a unitary, well-defined set of response topographies. Many theorists believe that fear learning is governed by the laws of classical conditioning and is based solely on the principle of contiguity, the pairing of the CS and UCS (Hilgard & Bower, 1966).

The fear CR is also viewed as a secondary source of drive, possessing motivational or energizing effects (Amsel & Maltzman, 1950; Brown, Kalish, & Farber, 1951; Meryman, 1952, 1953) as well as reinforcing effects (Brown & Jacobs, 1949; Kalish, 1954; N. E. Miller, 1948). The drive properties of the fear response set the stage for learning of the second class of responses, referred to as avoidance behavior. Avoidance behavior is governed by the laws of instrumental learning, which are believed to include both a contiguity and a drive-reduction notion of reinforcement (Mowrer, 1947, 1960). Avoidance behavior is learned because of the effect of this response class on terminating or reducing the presence of the conditioned aversive state. The resulting reduction of fear (drive reduction) serves as the reinforcing mechanism for the learning of the avoidance behavior. Symptoms and defensive maneuvers developed by humans are viewed as being equivalent to avoidance behavior (Freud, 1936; Stampfl & Levis, 1967; Wolpe, 1958). They are assumed to result from attempts on the individual's part to escape previously aversive CSs that function as "danger" signals. Symptoms, like the fear response, produce varied response topographies. Although two-factor theory has not been free of criticism (Herrnstein, 1969), the theory is still considered a viable explanatory model for avoidance data for infrahumans and humans. The experimental evidence previously mentioned lends support to the basic assumptions of the position.

It should be noted, however, that the learning of the above two response classes is not in and of itself a sign of psychopathology. On the contrary, human survival is in large part dependent upon emotional learning and subsequent avoidance responding, which protect the individual from a potential source of physical pain and tissue damage. Psychopathology is assumed to occur when very low or no correlation exists between the occurrence of the above response classes and the potential presence of physical danger to the organism. Thus, for some individuals, being on the 10th floor of a building leads to a strong emotional reaction and subsequent avoidance of the building. Yet the nonoccurrence of such behavior would not physically endanger, the individuals. Or, in the case of compulsive behavior, individuals' failure to wash their hands over and over again after turning on a light switch or touching money would not significantly increase the probability of danger to the individuals. Such behaviors are labeled maladaptive because their occurrence is not biologically protective; is usually not under the individuals' control; and frequently interferes with the functioning of desired, socially adaptive responses (Levis & Hare, 1977).

Like laboratory avoidance behaviors, human symptoms are considered to be functional in that the behavior involved results in a reduction of stress immediately upon its execution. However, human symptoms are usually far more complex than are the behaviors reported in the typical laboratory experiment. Perhaps the closest analogy between the two situations is the response topography associated with the typical human phobic behavior. In the case of both the human and the infrahuman, the organism simply avoids the aversive stimulus situation, whether the feared stimulus is a car, a tall building, or a black box with grid floors. (For classical laboratory studies on the conditioning of phobia in humans, see Jones, 1924; Watson & Rayner, 1920.)

The issues of the diversity and complexity of human symptomology become less problematic for an avoidance model if the nature of the conditioned aversive stimulation being avoided is taken into consideration. Consider the two examples of obsessive–compulsive behavior described in our introduction. Both cases reported symptoms of excessive washing of hands, body, and clothes. These symptoms make sense if an individual is trying to reduce the fear of becoming contaminated by germs. Or, in the case of the woman who had to wear a lifepreserver while taking a bath, the behavior again makes sense from an avoidance model if what she feared was drowning. In a like vein, if an individual is afraid of thinking sexual thoughts, such thoughts can be prevented by the obsessive counting of heartbeats.

The above point of symptom utility is perhaps more obvious with reactions of hysterical conversion. Consider the case of a combat aviator who develops disturbances in depth perception or a soldier who develops a paralyzed arm. Not only do these symptoms have the immediate effect of preventing the individual form from reentering the feared combat situation, but an additional source of anxiety generated by feelings of guilt also is reduced by the individual's inability to conceptualize the relationship between the conversion reaction and the feared situation. Similar avoidance analyses of such symptoms as depression (Boyd & Levis, 1980; Levis, 1980a), pervasive anxiety (Hare & Levis, 1980), and psychotic symptoms (Levis, 1980b) have been made.

THE CONCEPT OF PREPAREDNESS

Recently, Eysenck (1979) has criticized the two-factor theory's account of fear acquistion on the grounds that the concept of CS equipotentiality inherent in the model needs to be modified. "CS equipotentiality" refers to the notion that one CS is as good as another. According to the two-factor theory (and most other behavioral accounts of fear acquisition), any stimulus that precedes the aversive event can be conditioned, whether the stimulus is exteroceptive (environmental) or interoceptive (thoughts, images, memories). According to Eysenck, the notion of equipotentiality is weakened by the "taste-aversion" studies (Garcia, McGowan, & Green, 1971) and by the clinical observation that phobias concern a limited set of objects such as fear of specific animals and insects, heights, and dark. In Seligman's words (1971): "And only rarely, if ever, do we have pajama phobias, grass phobias, electric-outlet phobias, hammer phobias, even though these things are likely to be associated with trauma in our world" (p. 312).

To correct this problem theoretically, Eysenck suggests the incorporation into the two-factor theory of Seligman's hypothesis of "preparedness" (1970, 1971). According to this position, the most frequently experienced phobic fears are attached to situations that threatened the survival of ancestors, and that there is a genetic predisposition or "preparedness" for acquiring these fears. Thus, "prepared" stimuli (fear of dark, snakes, etc.) are believed to be acquired more readily and to be more resistant to extinction than "unprepared" stimuli (e.g., tones, shoes, clothes, etc.).

In rebuttal to the above position, Levis (1979a) has pointed out that the interpretation of the taste-aversion studies are very controversial (Bitterman, 1975, 1976; Delprato, 1980) and that Seligman's hypothesis is not unlike Jung's concept of archetypes (1925), which was scientifically disregarded because it was deemed untestable. Furthermore, it has been argued that the concept of equipotentiality only applies when everything else is held equal. For example, contemporary conditioning theory has established that nonreinforced preexposure to a CS significantly interferes with subsequent conditioning to that stimulus (Mackintosh, 1974, p. 37). This finding is frequently referred to as "latent inhibition," and, according to Levis, may well explain why certain phobic stimuli are conditioned more easily than others.

Consider Eysenck's and Seligman's observation that phobias of electric outlets and hammers are rare, despite the possibility that such objects may well have been a source of aversive conditioning. For one thing, such stimuli are frequently exposed throughout life in nonaversive settings, and therefore past conditioning effects to these stimuli have a chance to undergo extinction and latent inhibition. For another, early discrimination training is given in how to use these objects properly to avoid danger, while such training is rarely given to differentiate a harmful from a harmless snake. In addition, the sensory consequences of common phobias characterized as "prepared" (stimuli involved in the fear of snakes, insects, and heights) are avoided more readily, reducing CS exposure and subsequent extinction effects.

Two factors must be considered when evaluating studies comparing the conditionability of prepared and nonprepared stimuli: (1) the preconditioning aversive level of each stimulus; and (2) the degree of latent inhibition from nonreinforced preexposure. When such factors are considered, little experimental support for preparedness can be found. Even Seligman's own studies (DeSilva, Rachman, & Seligman, 1977; Rachman & Seligman, 1976) provide damaging negative evidence. In the DeSilva, Rachman, and Seligman study (1977), a retrospective study was conducted on a large number of phobic and obsessive cases. The authors failed to find a systematic relationship between evolutionary criteria of preparedness and either acquisition rate or therapeutic outcome. Acceptance of the preparedness hypothesis would appear to be premature at this time until more research on the subject is completed.

MODELS OF SOCIAL AND SENSORY ISOLATION

Traditional clinical theory has long maintained that psychotic behavior is a result of social isolation and rejection occurring within the first 2 years of life. Although controlled experimental studies cannot be carried out on humans for eithical reasons, infrahuman investigators have been well aware for some time that social isolation and sensory deprivation can produce negative effects manifested through strong emotional and strange behavioral responding. For example, Tinklepaugh (1928) described a case of agitated depression and self-mutilation in a captive male rhesus monkey when his mate was replaced by other females, and Stout and Snyder (1969) reported ulcerative colitis among Siamang gibbons distressed by social disruption of care and maintenance routines.

Behavioral abnormalities have been observed by veterinarians and zoo keepers as well as by laboratory experimenters. Reports by veterinarians have included hysterical reactions in goats and cows; collective epilepsy among dogs; nymphomania in cats; emotional trauma in dogs, horses, and cats; dyspepsia, anorexia, and paroxysmal hypothenia in dogs and cats; and impotency in bulls (Chertok & Fontaine, 1963; Croft, 1951; Schmidt, 1968). Behavioral abnormalitites in zoo animals have included nonadaptive escape reactions, food refusal, excessive aggression, stereotyped motor reactions, displacement scratching, self-mutilation, homosexuality, sexual perversions, appetite irregularities, apathy, and defective mother–infant interactions (Meyer-Holzapfel, 1968). Laboratory isolation has produced insensitivity to pain and whirling behavior in dogs (Melzack & Scott, 1957; Thompson, Melzack, & Scott, 1956), convulsions in young baboons (Startsev, 1976), and apparent dissociation and hallucinations in an adult rhesus monkey (Mitchell, 1970). (See also Keehn, 1979, for additional descriptions.)

Although considerable experimental work has been performed in this area, the best known and most influential set of studies on social isolation has been carried out by Harlow and his associates (Harlow, 1958, 1964). Using monkeys as subjects, Harlow found that the most extreme form of social isolation, which involved no contact at all, led to severe disruption in social behavior. The longer the monkeys experienced social isolation, the greater the incidence of stereotyped, bizarre, and self-destructive behavior. After 12 months of life, the animals raised in isolation showed a severe lack of social and sexual behavior that could not be completely remedied by later social experience. Animals that were isolated for 24 months were totally deficient in social skill and were unable to defend themselves.

Harlow also performed a series of classic studies on maternal deprivation The results generally indicated that permanent psychological effects can ensue unless adequate substitutes for the mother are provided. Monkeys raised on surrogate mothers made of inanimate materials did not show normal sexual behavior at maturity, and if they did breed, they failed to exhibit normal maternal behavior themselves. Since both heat and food were provided by the surrogate mothers, these basic needs do not appear to be sufficient to counteract the abnormalities. Apparently the monkey's affectional system is dependent upon the contact stimulation normally provided by the mother.

OVERVIEW

It can be seen in the foregoing that symptomatic behavior similar to that observed in human neurotic and psychotic patients can be reproduced in infrahumans in a laboratory setting. There are obviously many ways in which psychopathic disorders can be achieved in an experimental setting, including fear conditioning, excessive punishment, conflict between primary drive states, uncontrollability, social isolation, and affectional separation. Such a finding is consistent with major human psychopathic states, which rarely result from the operation of a single variable. The material reviewed provides an excellent start for developing functional models of psychopathology that not only will enhance our knowledge concerning issues of etiology but will pave the way for more effective treatment techniques.

As noted earlier, the paradigms reviewed are not comprehensive. Extensive work also has been carried out on the etiology of frustration, persistence, and regression (Amsel, 1967, 1971); on dominance and aggression (Logan, 1971); and on the psychophysiology of emotions (J. V. Brady, 1970; J. V. Brady, Findley, & Harris, 1971). Furthermore, other experimental models have been offered to explain the etiology of obesity (Rodin, 1977), addiction (Siegel, 1979; Solomon, 1977), depression (Suomi & Harlow, 1977), phobias and obsessions (Marks, 1977), psychosomatic disorders (Weiss, 1977), epilepsy and minimal brain dysfunction (Gaito, 1979; Sechzer, 1977), catatonia (Gallup & Maser, 1977), and schizophrenia (Paul, 1977). This renewed interest in models of psychopathology should pave the way for significant clinical dividends.

MAINTENANCE OF PSYCHOPATHOLOGY

Behavioral theories of symptom etiology and treatment have suggested important working principles that are supported by considerable laboratory data. Such therories, however, have difficulty when addressing issues of symptom maintenance. Clinical patients emit symptoms for years in the absence of any physical danger (UCS), yet the weight of laboratory evidence suggests that conditioned fear and avoidance is short-lived when the CS is presented in the absence of the UCS (Mackintosh, 1974; Seligman & Johnston, 1973). Clinical evidence also suggests that when patients fight their symptoms by not engaging in avoidance behavior, the result is an unbearable anxiety reaction that frequently progresses to a panic-like intensity. However, laboratory data indicate that blocking of avoidance behavior results in extinction of both fear and avoidance behavior (Shipley, Mock, & Levis, 1971). Until these discrepancies are resolved, reliance on a conditioning interpretation of psychopathology remains problematic.

Unfortunately, behavior therapists have been slow to address the issue of symptom maintenance; many theorists simply ignore the problem. However, some serious attempts have been made in this critical area, and they include appeals to "traumatic" conditioning stimuli, self-punitive behavior, incubation of fears, the principle of conversation of anxiety, and cognitive expectation. Each of these suggested models is reviewed below.

THE SOLOMON–WYNNE PARTIAL-IRREVERSIBILITY HYPOTHESIS

Some behavior therapists (Eysenck, 1968, 1979; Wolpe, 1958), as well as traditional clinicians, have tended to account for the issue of symptom maintenance by appealing to the effects during conditioning of intense UCS presentations. Solomon, Kamin, and Wynne (1953) provide one of the few experiments available demonstrating that extreme resistance to extinction of avoidance responding can be obtained following UCS removal. They used a very intense shock as a UCS to establish acquisition of a shuttlebox-avoidance response with dogs. These investigations reported that after shock was discontinued, one subject mad 490 hurdle-jumping responses without showing any signs of extinction, and many responded for 200 trials without extinguishing.

To interpret the finding that CS exposure led to little extinction of the avoidance response, Solomon and Wynne (1954) suggested the principle of partial irreversibility. According to this viewpoint, a very intense or "traumatic" pain–fear reaction to a given CS pattern will result in a *permanent* increase in the probability of occurrence of a fear reaction in the presence of the CS pattern.

The partial-irreversibilty hypothesis, if correct, has profound implications at both the theoretical and applied levels. For one thing, it suggests that with the use of an intense UCS, both fear and avoidance behavior are incapable of complete extinction. For another, it suggests that treatment of such induced symptomatology cannot be effectively treated by learning principles.

Fortunately, there is little experimental support for the partial-irreversibility hypothesis. Brush (1957) tested the implication of this theory directly by manipulating the level of UCS intensity. Using the Solomon, Kamin, and Wynne avoidance situation, he found that shock intensity was not a critical variable in sustaining avoidance behavior. Rather, the critical factor was whether a drop-gate that prevents intertrial responding was used. With the use of the drop-gate, even such presumably subtraumatic shock levels such as .7 ma appeared to be significant to produce sustained avoidance responding. Furthermore, other investigators (Levis, 1966a, 1966b, 1979b; Maatsch, 1959) also have produced prolonged avoidance behavior in extinction following the use of moderate shock levels. Although it is possible that at a human level of analysis, traumatic UCSs do produce permanent fear reactions not subject to the laws of extinction, infrahuman attempts to document this have not been successful.

THE BROWN–MOWRER VICIOUS CIRCLE OR
SELF-PUNITIVE MODEL

Clinical symptomatic behavior has been described in this chapter as functional behavior in that symptoms serve as avoidance behavior to aid the individual in escaping previously conditioned aversive stimulation. However, it also should be noted that clinical symptoms are viewed as neurotic not only because the behavior persists in the absence of a real danger (UCS), but because the behavior frequently interfers with adaptive functions and results in unnecessary self-administered stress. This self-perpetuating, self-punitive, compulsive behavior of the neurotic has long been recognized in the clinical literature and was labeled by Horney in 1937 as "vicious-circle behavior."

J. S. Brown (as reported by Mowrer, 1947) developed a possible infrahuman analogue of this self-punitive component. Basically, the paradigm consists of training a rat to escape shock by placing a subject in an electrified startbox and runway, at the end of which is a safe, nonshock compartment. Animals will quickly learn to run down the alley to the safe area. Once the runway response is established, shock is turned off in the startbox but left on in other parts of the runway. Thus, the animal can completely avoid shock by staying in the startbox. Furthermore, if the animal leaves the startbox, it is punished by being exposed to shock. Such a punishment procedure might be expected to produce suppression quickly, resulting in the animal not leaving the startbox. What Brown found was the opposite result. Rats not only left the now "safe" startbox, but the effects of the shock appeared to enhance the continuation of running rather than to facilitate extinction. Thus, a vicious-circle behavior that the animal appeared unable to break was established.

Mowrer (1947, 1950) noticed the similarity of the rat's self-punitive behavior to the "neurotic paradox" phenomenon, wherein punishment of anxiety-motivated behavioral symptoms leads to their reoccurrence. Mowrer theorized that the rat leaves the "safe" startbox in extinction because of the establishment of conditioned fear to this area; fear is then maintained by the onset of punishment, while fear reduction reinforces running behavior. The punishment induced fear then generalizes through the runway, which is a stimulus homogeneous with the startbox, facilitating behavior maintenance.

Considerable research has been performed using this paradigm, with the finding that shock intensity and shock placement function as critical variables. Fear also appears to be a central factor in maintaining the behavior, which can be modified by providing discrimination training (see

Brown, 1969; Melvin, 1971). The theoretical and experimental work evolving from this area not only may provide insights in understanding human symptom maintenance, but also may prove to be an important model for understanding self-injurious behavior noted in children. Behavior therapists should pay more attention to developments in this area.

THE EYSENCK THEORY OF INCUBATION

Eysenck (1968, 1979) has advanced a conditioning model of neurosis suggesting that symptom maintenance can be accounted for by the concept of "fear incubation." Traditionally, laboratory experimenters have used the term "incubation" to refer to a growth of fear over a time interval following a conditioning sequence. This increase in fear is believed to occur in the absence of further exposure to the CS or UCS. A number of studies that suggest this phenomenon exists have been reported, but McAllister and McAllister (1967), after conducting an extensive critical review of this field, concluded that "although the incubation-of-fear hypothesis has been tested in a wide variety of situations, the phenomenon has yet to be convincingly demonstrated" (p. 189).

Eysenck (1968), however, outlined a theory of incubation in which the term is used in quite a different sense than that defined in the preceding paragraph. By the term "incubation," Eysenck referred to an increment in the fear response over a period of time that results from additional exposure or exposures to the CS. More specifically, Eysenck suggested that the CRs of fear and pain (which he called "nocive responses," or NRs) *themselves* have reinforcing properties. When paired with CSs on extinction trials, the habit strength associating CSs and NRs may increase, especially when NRs are particularly strong:

It is not the CR itself which acts as reinforcer, but rather the response-produced stimuli; not the autonomic, hormonal, and muscular reactions themselves, but rather the experience of fear/anxiety based upon them. Insofar as these CR-produced are identical with the UCR-produced stimuli, it seems automatic that they will be reinforcing in exactly the same manner; insofar as they are different, they will also act as reinforcers to the extent that they are nocive and aversive. (Eysenck, 1968, p. 313)

In his most recent presentation, Eysenck (1979) specified several conditions that favor the development of incubation: (1) Pavlovian conditioning, in which the CR is a drive; (2) a strong UCS; (3) short exposure of the CS only; and (4) individual differences in neuroticism and introversion.

To support the effect, Eysenck cites animal experiments by Napalkov (1963), Lichtenstein (1950), and Dykman, Mack, and Ackerman (1965) reporting autonomic CRs that persisted or even increased in strength over trials following CS exposure. He also refers to the "paradoxical enhancement" of fear (Rohrbaugh & Riccio, 1970; Rohrbaugh, Riccio, & Arthur, 1972; Silvestri, Rohrbaugh, & Riccio, 1970) reported in the infrahuman avoidance literature. Human studies that could be used in support of the effect are Campbell, Sanderson, and Laverty (1964); B. V. Miller and Levis (1971); and Stone and Borkovec (1975).

Eysenck's theory, however, has not been free of serious criticism, with 25 leading experts in the area expressing their concern following the publication of his 1979 paper. Levis (1979a, 1981) has been a persistent critic, arguing that enhanced fear responding following short CS exposure is expected and predicted from classical two-factor theory and does not require the concept of incubation. He also has been critical of the cited support for the incubation model, most notably the Napalkov (1963) study that greatly influenced Eysenck and that he refers to as the "Napalkov phenomenon." Napalkov reported that, following a single conditioning trial, repeated administration of the CS brought about increases in blood pressure of dogs from 30–40 mm Hg to 190–230 mm Hg. He reported that in some cases this hypertensive state lasted over a year. Levis (1979a, in press) has argued that, given our current state of knowledge in this area, such an effect is incredible to say the least as well as very difficult to reconcile with the existing literature. Furthermore, Napalkov only provided a one-paragraph summary of his work without citing a primary source of reference, making it impossible to determine exactly what experimental procedures were used. Levis noted that over 10 years have passed without a replication, making it understandable why researchers in the area have ignored or are unfamiliar with his work.

Despite criticisms of the model, we view Eysenck's contribution as important, comprehensive, and worthy of further experimentation.

THE STAMPFL–LEVIS EXTENSION OF THE
CONSERVATION-OF-ANXIETY HYPOTHESIS

The reported findings of Solomon and his colleagues, as previously noted, were that dogs could be conditioned to resist extinction to a CS for over 200 extinction trials. In reviewing these data, Solomon and Wynne (1954) made three important observations. First, the avoidance latencies of the dogs shorten considerably, with latencies between 1 and 4 seconds being common following acquisition (a 10-second CS-UCS interval was used). Second, overt signs of anxiety seemed to disappear rapidly with training and seemed nonexistent in extinction following the frequently occurring short-latency responses. Third, if a dog happened to produce a long-latency response on a particular extinction trial, signs of fear behaviorally became apparent immediately following the avoidance response, with short-latency responses returning for the next few trials.

To explain the above observations and the extremely persistent avoidance responding noted in extinction, Solomon and Wynne (1954) advanced their now classic "conservation-of-anxiety hypothesis" within the context of a fear interpretation. According to this position, extinction of the avoidance response is directly related to the repeated exposure of the CS and fear response. However, short exposures to the CS resulting from quick avoidance responding do not permit the time required for the elicitation of the classically conditioned fear reaction. Thus, this model suggests that short-latency avoidance responses at least prevent the part of this reaction centered in the peripheral autonomic nervous system from occurring, as well as conserving fear to the CS by preventing longer CS exposures. Since the short-latency instrumental act does not elicit fear, it will not be followed by fear reduction, thereby weakening the habit strength of the avoidance response. This weakened habit strength is manifested through progressively increasing response latencies, which, in turn, account for enough CS exposure to elicit the anxiety reaction. The instrumental response is again followed by anxiety reduction with a resultant increment in avoidance habit. This increased habit strength is reflected by progressively shorter response latencies, as the anxiety reaction associated with the longer CS segments secondarily conditions anxiety to the shorter CS segments.

The conservation-of-anxiety notion appears to explain the data described so far—namely, the overt signs of anxiety rapidly disappeared; that the dogs appeared to become "upset" following long-latency avoidance responses; and, finally, that with short-latency avoidance responding the laws of fear extinction are not operative. As for the theoretical merits of this position, serious difficculties present themselves upon closer inspection. If a short CS exposure does not provide sufficient time for the fear response to occur, how then can the avoidance response be elicited? The two-factor theory requires that fear be present to elicit avoidance behavior, and, if it is present, it should obey the laws of fear extinction.

Aware of these difficulties with Solomon and Wynne's interpretation, Stampfl, in an unpublished manuscript written in 1960, reinterpreted and extended the conservation principle (see Levis, 1966a, 1966b). Stampfl, in his writings with Levis (Stampfl & Levis, 1967, 1969, 1976), reasoned that if Solomon and Wynne's interpretation that short-latency avoidance responses conserved the fear to longer-latency CS exposure were correct, then the process of conservation should be maximized by dividing the CS-UCS interval into distinctive components and ordering them sequentially (e.g., tone followed by flashing lights). This conclusion was reached mainly by observing the behavior of patients (Stampfl & Levis, 1969, 1973). Such observations would suggest that instead of presenting the rat with a tone for a given time period before shock is introduced, a better procedure would be to divide the CS-UCS interval into distinctive CS segments. Thus the animals could be presented CSs sequentially in which, for example, tone (S^1) is introduced in the first 6 seconds, followed by flashing lights (S^2) for 6 seconds, followed by a buzzer (S^3) for 6 seconds, and then followed by shock.

According to the model, after the attainment of short-latency responses to the first stimulus component in the chain, S^1, subsequent extinction effects to this component should result in less generalization of extinction effects to the second component in the sequence, S^2, if the S^2 segment is highly dissimilar to the S^1 segment. The greater the reduction in generalization of extinction effects from the early part of the CS-UCS interval to the later portions, the greater the amount of anxiety that will be conserved to the components closer to UCS onset. As fear of the S^1 component extinguishes, the response latencies will become longer, eventually resulting in the exposure of the S^2 stimulus. At this point, a stimulus change from a low-fear to a high-fear state will occur. The S^2 component is viewed as being capable of functioning upon exposure as a second-order conditioning stimulus recharging the S^1 component, which in turn will again be capable of producing short-latency responses. Theoretically, as long as sufficient fear remains to the S^2 component, the process should continue to repeat itself. By adding further distinctive components (S^3) to the original conditioning sequence, the process of requiring shorter avoidance-response latencies should be increased via the principles of anxiety conservation and intermittent secondary reinforcement.

However, unlike the Solomon and Wynne interpretation, the model maintains that the fear response is elicited by the CS when short-latency avoidance-response topographies occur, such as jumping over a hurdle or running from one side of the box to the other. Asymptotic avoidance responding is quickly obtained once the response is learned. At an asymptotic state, little reinforcement (fear reduction) is needed to maintain avoidance responding, and little fear is needed to elicit responding. Short CS exposure is then viewed as eliciting a fractional anticipatory fear response, which at an asymptotic response level is capable of motivating avoidance responding for some time. Each exposure of the fractional anticipatory fear response should weaken the avoidance response, and eventually latencies will increase, exposing the subject to a greater level of fear. At the same point, this increased fear level will reinforce short-latency responses.

This extension of the conservation-of-anxiety hypothesis clearly explains why, after learning, the organism behaviorally does not show signs of fear when short-latency responses occur. The notion of the fractional anticipatory fear response also explains how avoidance responses are elicited by short-latency CS exposures. A recent study by Levis and Boyd (1979) supports both of these hypotheses. The prediction that serial CS presentations will enhance resistance to extinction in comparison with nonserial CS procedure has also been supported, with some serial CS subjects responding for hundreds of consecutive trials (Kostanek & Sawrey, 1965; Levis, 1966a, 1966b; Levis, Bouska, Eron, & McIlhon, 1970; Levis & Boyd, 1979; Levis & Stampfl, 1972). Like the Solomon and Wynne model, this position proposes that the level of fear associated with a particular segment of the CS-UCS interval is hypothesized to decrease as the segment's temporal distance from the UCS onset increases. Evidence does exist for such a relationship in the classical-conditioning literature, with both single CS (Bitterman, 1965; Ellison, 1964; Pavlov, 1927; Siegel, 1967) and serial CS presentations (Frey, Englander, & Roman, 1971; Williams, 1965). Recent findings in the avoidance literature also suggest that such a relationship may exist during shuttlebox acquisition training (Dubin & Levis, 1973; Levis & Dubin, 1973; Levis & Stampfl, 1972) and during one-way avoidance extinction (Boyd & Levis, 1976).

In summary, the argument is being made that human psychopathology resists extinction because the patient's symptoms (avoidance responses) terminate the conditioned fear cues before sufficient exposure to these cues can occur to produce a substantial extinction effect. The cues the patient is avoiding are believed to be multiple and ordered sequentially in memory storage and accessibility. Clearly, additional work is needed at both the infrahuman and human levels before the model strength can be fully assessed. Yet, considerable initial supporting data already exist, and the model has the advantage of being couched in traditional S-R theory.

THE SELIGMAN MODEL OF COGNITIVE "EXPECTANCY"

Most cognitive models of symptom or nonadaptive behavior maintenance would argue that such behavior continues because the cognition or expectation initially responsible for the behavior pattern in question has not changed or been modified. Thus, in the case of the learned-helplessness theory, Seligman (1975) would argue that helplessness will continue until the "expectation" is changed from learning that behavior does not effect outcome to learning that it does. Seligman and Johnston (1973) have extended the notion of expectancy in their formulation of a comprehensive theory of avoidance. Animals continue to avoid because they have a cognition that failure to respond will result in the occurrence of a physical harmful event, the UCS.

Seligman and Johnston (1973) were motivated to develop their position in large part because of their belief that fear interpretation cannot handle substained avoidance behavior such as that noted in the Solomon and Wynne paper (1954). Their main point has been that overt indications of fearful behavior appear to diminish shortly following acquisition. Furthermore, they argue that the available evidence from the classical-conditioning literature suggests that fear-related behavior extinguishes rapidly. They cite in their support a study by Annan and Kamin (1961) that rats extinguised within 40 trials following conditioning with a strong UCS. They also report concern over the fact that one of Solomon's dogs responded for 490 trials without extinguishing and that many others showed no signs of extinction following 200 trials. Thus, if an S-R, fear variable is not controlling behavior, an S-S, cognitive variable such as "expectancy" must be.

Historically, cognitive interpretations of avoidance behavior have not been popular, in large part because they lack theoretical precision and experimental testability. For example, Levis (1976), in criticizing learned-helplessness theory, raised the following unanswered questions: How does one determine, independent of measuring the outcome variable, when or whether a given procedural manipulation has been registered cognitively? Once registered, what are the rules and measurement criteria for determining whether or not an "expectation" will or has developed, and whether or not it will generalize to future trials? What are the parameters responsible for facilitating this generalization process, and what are the rules which determine its boundary conditions? What exactly are expectations; how are they identified; how do they link up to behavior; and how do they change? Or, more precisely, how are these constructs linked operationally to antecedent conditions?

Despite the theoretical problems encountered in developing a "predictive" cognitive theory, a cognitive position may be needed out of necessity if an alternative fear position can not handle the questions raised by Seligman and Johnston. However, in the preceding section, the Stampfl and Levis model addresses each of the issues raised by Seligman and Johnston. More specifically, Levis (Levis, 1981; Levis & Boyd, 1979) argued that Seligman and Johnston (1973) failed to equate total CS exposure when comparing 490 avoidance trials (Solomon, Kamin, & Wynne, 1953) with 40 classical-conditioning trials (Annan & Kamin, 1961). Assuming for the animal that performed 490 avoidance trials on extinction that the average pretrial response latency was about 2 seconds, total CS exposure then would be about 1000 seconds. In the Annan and Kamin study (1961), a conditioned suppression procedure was used in extinction, with pretrial CS exposure being 60 seconds. Extinction of fear followed 40 trials, but what Seligman and Johnston failed to consider was that this occurred after the animal received 2400 seconds of CS exposure. Thus, if researchers can extrapolate between studies as Seligman and Johnston do, then it is apparent that the animal which was stopped after 1000 seconds of CS may not have extinguished because of insufficient CS exposure. The critical point that Levis was making is that *CS exposure, not trials to extinction, should be considered when addressing the issue of fear extinction and fear maintenance.* Furthermore, in a recent experimental test comparing the fear and expectancy models, Levis and Boyd (1979) found support for the fear interpretation. Nevertheless, the differences between cognitive and fear interpretation have yet to be resolved fully and are in need of further experimentation.

OVERVIEW

In this section, a cursory review of the major models of symptom maintenance has been presented. We believe that the development of data-based models in the area is central for maintaining the viability of a conditioning interpretation and for addressing issues of treatment. We have also taken a more critical stance on some of the proposed models than we have in the previous section, in the hope of stimulating more interest and ultimately better functional models.

TREATMENT IMPLICATIONS OF CONDITIONING MODELS OF PSYCHOPATHOLOGY

We have noted that conditioning research has provided diverse models to explain the etiology and maintenance of psychopathology. An equally broad group of treatment approaches has been developed on the basis of these learning models of maladaptive behavior. The behavior-therapy armamentarium has thus come to include such varied techniques as systematic desensitization; social skills training; implosive (flooding) therapy; modeling; contingency management; operant methods of self-control; aversion therapy; and a variety of cognitive methods, including thought stopping and rational restructuring. Although all these treatments depend on learning theory (broadly defined) for their theoretical rationale, several are related more clearly to the conditioning models reviewed above. The emphasis of this section is on these widely used techniques (including systematic desensitization, implosive therapy, covert therapies, and operant techniques) derived most directly from the conditioning and learning literature just reviewed. In addition to describing the genesis of these behavior therapies, we also highlight controversies concerning the crucial therapeutic variables and possible disadvantages of each of these techniques. Our aim is to clarify these controversies by reference to laboratory and clinical studies of process and outcome, as well as to specify future directions for such research.

TREATMENTS BASED ON CONFLICT MODELS

In the Soviet Union, Pavlovian concepts have been central to theories of psychopathology, and the influence of Pavlov can be clearly seen in the well-known writings of Luria and other contemporary Soviet psychologists (e. g., Teplov & Nebylitsyn, 1966). For example, symptoms as diverse as depression and hysterical mutism have been attributed to "protective inhibition" resulting from pathological cortical excitation (Luria, 1966, 1970). Soviet psychotherapies developed from a Pavlovian framework have included sleep treatments designed to reduce excessive excitation, as well as the use of stimulant drugs to overcome pathological inhibition.

Pavlovian approaches to treatment have not been widely applied in the West for a number of reasons. First, Pavlov's concept of "spreading" cortical excitation and inhibition has not been supported by neurophysiological research on neural transmission and localization of function. Second, the ascendency of motivational and operant theories of learning have led to alternative formulations that have come to dominate behavioral treatment approaches. We discuss in detail below how Hullian notions led to the development of counterconditioning therapy, how two-factor theory led to extinction approaches such as implosion, and how operant conceptualizations resulted in self-control and contingency-management techniques.

As Franks (1970) has noted, however, the lack of widespread application of Pavlovian concepts to therapy seems due less to informed dismissal than to simple indifference. The provocative findings of several Pavlovian researchers concerning treatment of neurotic behavior thus have not received the attention they warrant. For example, Masserman (1971) discovered a number of procedures that would ameliorate the neurosis developed in his "uncertainty" paradigms. *Temporary* reduction in the strength of neurotic behaviors resulted from satiation of the motivating drive and from rest away from the situation in which the behavior developed. Interestingly, more *permanent* therapeutic effects were found with treatments that were later "rediscovered" in the learned-helplessness paradigm. Masserman found that animals receiving pretraining in controlling the apparatus were likely to recover normal responding when later exposed to predictable contingencies. Animals without the previous experience remained "neurotic," refusing to explore the apparatus and continuing to display bizarre behaviors. Similarly, Seligman and his associates (Hannum, Rosellini, & Seligman, 1976; Seligman, Rosellini, & Kozak, 1975) have found that infrahumans given previous experience with escapable shock could be "immunized" against the learned-helplessness effect of later inescapable shock.

Masserman also discovered that coaxing the infrahuman to respond and explore led to reassertion of normal behavior, even following conditioning of severe experimental neuroses. Similar therapeutic results were obtained if a normal monkey or mechanical monkey modeled appropriate responding in view of the neurotic animal. Seligman, Maier, and Geer (1968) and Seligman, Rosellini, and Kozak (1975) found that forcibly demonstrating to the animal that responses can produce reinforcement was also an effective method of eliminating helplessness. The learned maladaptive behavior was quite persistent, however, and most infrahumans required a large number of forced exposures before beginning to respond on their own.

Discovery of a possible neurophysiological mechanism underlying helplessness (and, by implication, depression) has led to attempts to alleviate symptoms by physiological treatment. Thomas and Dewald (1977) have found that the neurotic behavior produced by conflictual contingencies could be mitigated by blocking septal activity with drugs and by stimulating "reward centers" in the median forebrain bundle. Similar therapeutic effects have been demonstrated using electroconvulsive shock (Dorworth, 1971) and pargyline injection (Weiss, Glazer, & Poherecky, 1976).

These findings have clear implications for the prevention and treatment of depression. Susceptibility to depressive symptoms might be reduced by ensuring that children receive early experience in controlling a variety of contingencies and are exposed to a variety of environments in which their actions are clearly controlling. Once depressive symptoms have developed, they might be reduced or eliminated by encouraging clients to expose themselves to situations in which reinforcement is likely (i.e., to sample contingencies). Klein and Seligman (1976) have in fact found that experience in controlling reinforcers alleviated the behavioral deficits of both learned helplessness and depression. Further parallels between treatments for helplessness and depression have been noted in the clinical literature. Seligman, Klein, and Miller (1976) reviewed a variety of therapies for depression and concluded that successful treatments induced depressed patients to discover that their responses produce desirable outcomes; the implication is that this is the common therapeutic variable in such treatments. The implications for treatment of the neuropsychological model of helplessness (Thomas & Dewald, 1977) are somewhat less clear and must await the demonstration of similar brain mechanisms in human depressives. Additional interventions without the potential negative side effects of electroshock and neurosurgery would also be desirable from an ethical standpoint. Investigations of drug and behavioral interventions effecting the activity of the septal region, the median forebrain bundle, and other limbic structures may provide these alternatives.

Another interesting parallel between early Pavlovian notions and contemporary behavior therapy occurs in the resurrection of Gantt's "autokinesis" in the guise of Eysenck's (1968, 1979) incubation model. Both of these processes involve the tendency for maladaptive behaviors to become self-perpetuating and relatively independent of feedback from the environment

(Dykman, 1979, p. 169). Eysenck's formulation is probably theoretically superior in that it more clearly specifies the internal mechanism responsible for the process—the reinforcing properties of nocive responses. Incubation theory is examined in greater detail below in relation to implosive therapy.

Pavlovian researchers have thus laid the groundwork for several contemporary treatment approaches. Although these techniques remain in the preliminary stages of development, they appear promising for the treatment of disorders arising from conflicting drives, particualarly clinical depression.

TREATMENTS BASED ON
COUNTERCONDITIONING MODELS

It will be recalled that Wolpe (1958) believed that anxiety responses were crucial to the development and maintenance of neurotic behavior. He hypothesized that anxiety responses were persistent because they generated so little reactive inhibition, which constituted the extinction mechanism in Hullian theory. His model implied that merely exposing the client to the anxiety-provoking situation and allowing the neurotic behavior to occur would not be an effective treatment. Such exposures occur in the course of daily life, without marked therapeutic effects on neurotic behavior.

In an effort to discover a mechanism that would be effective in eliminating persistent neurotic behavior, Wolpe (1958) adopted the concept of "reciprocal inhibition" from the neurophysiological research of Sherrington (1947). Previously, the term had been used to describe the inhibition of one spinal reflex by another. Wolpe expanded this definition to encompass all instances in which "elicitation of one response appears to bring about a decrement in the strength of evocation of a simultaneous response" (1958, p. 29). He added that a decrement in anxiety responding would only be expected to occur if the opposing response were *stronger;* otherwise anxiety would become the dominant response in the situation. Since anxiety responses were considered to be mediated primarily by the sympathetic branch of the autonomic nervous system, Wolpe believed that responses maximizing parasympathetic discharge would be most effective in inhibiting anxiety.

In his initial studies, Wolpe (1958) sought to illustrate the reciprocal inhibition (or "counterconditioning") of anxiety by pairing the cues that normally evoked neurotic behavior with a variety of incompatible responses. Cats were first exposed to painful electric shocks in an experimental cage and subsequently displayed indications of conditioned anxiety, including refusal to eat, resistance to being placed in a cage, and urination and defecation. Anxiety-provoking cues were then *gradually* introduced in the presence of strong opposing responses (e.g., eating). For example, feeding was paired with gradually increasing anxiety cues by having subjects first feed from the experimenter's hand, then from the floor of a cage in which it had been previously conditioned, and finally from the food box at which shock had been delivered. Reduction in anxiety also resulted from exposure to rooms made progressively more similar to the conditioning room, and to tones previously paired with shock, which were made gradually more intense.

Clinically, Wolpe found the most effective counterconditioners to be sexual, relaxational, and assertive responses. The most commonly utilized clinical counterconditioning response has been relaxation, and this form of the technique has come to be known as "systematic desensitization" (SD). The SD procedure typically consists of specifying the stimulus situations which provoke anxiety; arranging these situations in a hierarchy from least to most anxiety-provoking; and pairing imaginal presentations of the situations with relaxation responses. It should be noted that Wolpe warned against pairing high levels of anxiety responses with relatively low levels of relaxation, because of the danger of having anxiety countercondition or overwhelm the weaker adaptive response. The therapist therefore begins SD presentations with scenes low on the hierarchy, proceeding to higher scenes only when the lower hierarchy items no longer provoke anxiety. For the same reason, individual stimulus presentations are terminated when the subject feels even a slight degree of anxiety. This mode of progression may have the additional advantage of facilitating generalization of relaxation responses to stimuli higher on the hierarchy before they are presented, making subsequent counterconditioning to high-anxiety material easier.

As Wachtel (1977) and Locke (1971) have noted, the clinical practice of SD differs in many important respects from the experimental procedures that Wolpe employed to reduce neurotic fear in his cats. The response of eating, which was used to inhibit anxiety reciprocally, was replaced with relaxation, and *in vivo* presentation of feared stimuli was replaced with imaginal presentation. On the one hand, these changes represented reasonable and practical responses to the difficulties in manipulating other counterconditioning responses and in presenting graded stimulus situations in the clinic setting. It should nevertheless be recognized that SD represents a considerable extrapolation from Wolpe's infrahuman experiments.

A more serious concern is that of whether the therapeutic mechanism in SD consists only of exposure to anxiety-provoking cues and whether the remaining complicated aspects of the procedure are superfluous. Wilson and Davison (1971) adopted essentially this position in their review of the literature on infrahuman desensitization. They noted that when the counterconditioner was manipulated independently, it led to fear reduction *only* when associated with increased CS exposure. Wilson and Davison concluded that counterconditioning responses and graduated exposure might be useful in encouraging the subject to remain in the feared situation, but that these procedures had no therapeutic effect in themselves. Rather, it was the underlying variable of total CS exposure that accounted for fear reduction.

With human subjects at the analogue and clinical level, several studies have found that relaxation is not necessary for anxiety reduction (H. R. Miller & Nawas, 1970; Nawas, Welsch, & Fishman, 1970). Other researchers have found that presenting SD scenes in an ascending order is also not critical to therapy success (Cohen, 1969; Krapfl, 1967; Krapfl & Nawas, 1970; H. R. Miller & Nawas, 1970; Nawas, Fishman, & Pucel, 1970; Wolpin & Pearsall, 1965). It also seems clear that SD can be successful when it includes only *in vivo* exposure without relaxation and when relaxation training is minimal (Rachman, 1968). Adding to the persuasiveness of the CS-exposure hypothesis is the fact that such diverse therapies as participant modeling (Bandura, 1969), reinforced practice (Leitenberg & Callahan, 1973), and flooding (Marks, 1969) share the common factor of encouraging exposure to the complex of feared stimuli (see Leitenberg, 1976, for a detailed comparison of these approaches). Wachtel (1977) has even argued convincingly that extinction by means of CS exposure is the therapeutic mechanism underlying psychodynamic therapies.

On the other hand, the evidence is not *entirely* consistent with the CS exposure hypothesis. Davison (1968) found that snake phobics who received standard SD procedure showed greater approach to the phobic object than did groups of phobics receiving imaginal exposure without relaxation, irrelevant exposure, or no treatment. Lang, Lazovik, and Reynolds (1965) found that desensitization was more effective than no treatment only when administered in the Wolpian manner, including a counterconditioning response.

At the present, it is probably most accurate to say that the inclusion of relaxation, coping, or graduated procedures in SD may be useful in ensuring that certain elements clients cooperate with CS exposure. This may be particularly true for highly anxious subjects (Schubot, 1966) or those who have difficulty producing clear imagery when aroused. The evidence that either relaxation or graduated exposure is an essential aspect of the SD procedure is mixed, with a substantial body of the literature suggesting that these procedural requirements are not necessary. With respect to relaxation training, part of the problem is that most investigators manipulate relaxation response by means of instructional procedures only. A more definitive approach would be to measure the relaxation response directly in order to determine whether the instructional set took hold. With the operational specificity of both the relaxation and the anxiety responses, the issue of their importance can be determined more readily.

TREATMENTS BASED ON EXTINCTION MODELS

It has been noted in the section on etiology that models of psychopathology based on avoidance theory consider conditioned fear to be the central motivation that maintains symptomatic (avoidance) behavior. So long as conditioned fear continues at a high level, symptoms are likely to persist. But if fear can be reduced or eliminated, there will no longer be any motivation for avoidance, and symptomatic behavior should disappear.

It has been found in the laboratory that repeatedly presenting the CS in the absence of the UCS will lead to the unlearning of the fear CR, and that reduction in fear is generally associated with reduction in avoidance. This principle of "experimental extinction" has been validated in a number of paradigms, with measures of fear ranging from behavioral-avoidance latency through suppression of consummatory responses to psychophysiological changes (Mackintosh, 1974).

Solomon, Kamin, and Wynne (1953) were among the first to suggest that the best way to *maximize* the extinction of emotional responses such as fear would be "to arrange the situation in such a way that an extremely intense emotional reaction takes place in the presence of the CS. This would be tantamount to a reinstatement of the original acquisition situation, and since the US is not presented a big decremental effect should occur" (p. 299). This statement is clearly at odds with the positions of Masserman and Wolpe (see above), who warned against the possible harmful effects of eliciting strong anxiety responses. But Solomon *et al.* (1953) recognized that interoceptive cues resulting from reexperiencing of anxiety may be important parts of the CS complex maintaining symptomatic behavior. To the extent that anxiety cues are a prominent part of the original CS complex, it is reasonable to assume that their extinction will also be necessary to eliminate symptomatic behavior. For example, it is common for agoraphobic clients to report that the *feeling* of anxiety and panic itself is what they find most disturbing (and what they seek to avoid by means of symptomatic behavior), not the external situations that elicit these feelings.

"Implosive" (or "flooding") therapy (Stampfl, 1970; Stampfl & Levis, 1967, 1969, 1973, 1976) respresents an attempt to apply this extinction principle therapeutically. As in SD, the implosive therapist first assesses the situations, thoughts, and behaviors that elicit anxiety in the client, and arranges them in a hierarchy for imaginal presentation. But rather than moving slowly through the hierarchy, carefully pairing stimuli with a counterconditioning response, the implosive therapist incorporates in initial scenes many stimuli likely to produce a strong anxiety reponse in the client. In fact, far from avoiding anxiety elicitation as in SD, the implosive therapist seeks to elicit the maximum possible anxiety reponse in the client, believing that this will hasten extinction of learned fear.

The terms "implosion" and "flooding" are often used interchangeably, and the techniques are actually similar in most important respects. But certain distinctions between the two can be discerned. "Flooding" therapists make use of both imaginal and *in vivo* exposure to feared situations, and they tend to confine themselves to "symptom-contingent" cues or cues reported by the patient; "implosive" therapists also rely on the above procedures, but they incorporate "hypothesized" cues when these are warranted. For example, when treating a client having a fear of flying, the flooding therapist would be likely to arrange for the person actually to board an airplane and to remain there until anxiety had been reduced. That is, he or she would give real exposure to most situations immediately related to anxiety evocation in the subjects daily life. An implosive therapist, on the other hand, would hypothesize that it is not airplaes or even flying per se that the client fears, but rather the possible *consequences* of flying — crashing, bodily injury, and death. Representation of these consequences would constiue one type of hypothesized cue that is believed to be stored in memory. Since these feared consequences cannot be presented *in vivo*, they are included in the latter stages of an imaginal implosive scene.

The use of hypothesized cues in implosion follows directly from the model of psychopathology on which the technique is based. The way in which serially ordered cues have been demonstrated to enhance resistance to extinction of animal and human avoidance has been described above. Unless "higher-order" cues evoking the greatest anxiety are extinguished, avoidance is likely to continue. In implosive therapy, it is therfore considered essential to present not only the anxiety-producing situation itself, but also aversive material *related* to the presenting problem, including both realistic and irrational feared consequences.

The necessity for hypothesized cues remains controversial, and few studies have examined this variable explicitly. Many investigators have made the mistake of including fear-producing material not related to the target problem (Fazio, 1970; Mathews & Shaw, 1973; Mealiea & Nawas, 1971). In one study in which appropriate, theoretically related material was employed, hypothesized cues were found to be useful (Prochaska, 1971). However, Marshall, Gauthier, Christie, Currie, and Gordon (1977) found better results when aversive cues were omitted from flooding scenes. Many behavior therapists therefore remain reluctant to utilize hypothesized cues, because of their reservations concerning the importance of dynamic cues and their fear of sensitizing subjects. These are complex issues for whose final resolution further evidence is needed, but several points can be made here. First, empirical support does exist for the usefulness of higher-order aversive cues (see Levis & Hare, 1977, for a complete review of cue categories in implosion). Second, a cue category should be rejected on the basis of empirical evidence, not of dogmatic prejudice against a theoretical orientation such as the psychodynamic. Third, the dangers of sensitization of *clinical* populations is probably overrated, as we make clear later in the discussion of incubation. Fourth, the validity of the usage of any cues is determined operationally by the implosive procedure. If the cues introduced elicit either anxiety and/or defensive behavior, the assumption is made that the affective response is a result of conditioning and therefore can be extinguished. If the behavior also changes following extinction to these cues the cues are considered relevant.

There is considerable experimental support for these extinction treatments, ranging from infrahuman laboratory work to analogue and clinical-treatment studies with humans. For example, the laboratory paradigm that closely resembles implosion is response prevention (RP). The RP paradigm is a procedure in which the subject is exposed to a fear-provoking stimulus complex and is prevented from making an avoidance response. Blocking of the response is accomplished by the imposition of barriers, by mechanical restraint, or by administration of drugs. RP is thus analogous to implosion in that feared cues are presented at a level that elicits considerable anxiety, with the expectation that such exposure will lead to significant reductions in both conditioned fear and avoidance. Consistent with the implosive-treatment model, fear reduction in RP has been found to be a direct function of total exposure to the CS complex, with the number and duration of individual trials being relatively unimportant (Bankart & Elliott, 1974; Nelson, 1966; Schiff, Smith, & Prochaska, 1972; Shearman, 1970; Shipley, 1974; Shipley, Mock, & Levis, 1971).

The conditioning literature has not been entirely supportive of the implosive approach, however. The two most prominent criticisms to arise from laboratory studies have been the possible roles of *residual fear* and *incubation* in limiting the effectiveness of implosion. Page, Riccio, and their colleagues found in animal studies that even after behavioral avoidance had been extinguished by RP, a residual level of fear to the CS complex could be measured by reluctance of the animals to reenter the shock compartment and by suppression of consummatory behavior (Coulter, Riccio, & Page, 1969; Linton, Riccio, Rohrbaugh, & Page, 1970; Monti & Smith, 1976; Page, 1955). These researchers concluded that RP was probably effective in extinguishing avoidance *not* through the extinction of fear, but rather through the conditioning of *competing responses* incompatible with avoidance (e.g., freezing, which is incompatible with running). Fear might still remain at a level sufficient to motivate later avoidance learning.

It has been questioned whether residual fear was actually being measured in these studies. It is possible that competing responses interfere with reentry or licking just as they do with running (Shipley, Mock, & Levis, 1971; Testa, 1976). Resolution of this issue awaits the unambiguous demonstration of fear independent of competing response tendencies. Nevertheless, the possibility that residual fear might remain following extinction of avoidance is certain to be a matter of concern for therapists. If a significant amount of fear remains following implosive therapy, it is possible that symptoms will be reacquired when the anxiety-provoking situation is again encountered after-therapy.

It must be noted, however, that no studies have demonstrated the reacquisition of symptoms as a function of residual fear, and it is far from clear how much residual fear would be "enough" to motivate new symptomative behavior in humans. It should be some further comfort to clinicians that even if fear is not *eliminated* by RP or implosive procedures, it is clearly significantly reduced, and prolonged flooding may well eliminate anxiety.

Until the role of residual fear is more clearly determined, cautious implosive therapists would be well advised to continue exposure of anxiety-provoking cues until all overt indices of anxiety have extinguished. In addition, since behavioral, self-report, and physiological channels may change at different rates, multiple measures of fear would help to ensure complete extinction of all aspects of the fear response (Lang, 1968; Riccio & Silvestri, 1973).

Incubation theory has been described previously, and we have noted that it has serious implications for behavior therapies based on an extinction model. If short exposures to anxiety-provoking images or situations in fact lead to increases in fear, symptomatic behavior could be *exacerbated* by flooding or implosive therapy under certian circumstances. Suppose, for example, that an agoraphobic client undergoing *in vivo* exposure to a feared crowded place were to become panic-stricken and flee the scene. Incubation of fear might occur as a result of the brief exposure, increasing the client's motivation to avoid crowded places on future encounters. Exposure could also be terminated prematurely if a client simply refused to continue to *imagine* an implosive scene before anxiety reduction had occurred; or an improperly trained therapist might become frightened at the expression of anxiety on the part of the client (crying, screaming, etc.) and end exposure too soon.

Particular risk would be predicted for neurotic introverts, who are believed to condition more easily, extinguish more slowly, and be more subject to incubation of fear than stable, extraverted clients. Incubation theory would imply that neurotic introverted subjects should be identified and provided with an alternative to flooding therapy. Neuroticism and introversion can be assessed, according to Eysenck (1979), through the administration of personality inventories (e.g., Eysenck & Eysenck, 1968) and through physiological measurements. For example, Hugdahl and his associates (Hugdahl, Frederikson, & Öhman, 1977) have shown that neurotic introverts show a higher frequency of spontaneous galvanic skin responses (GSRs) than other subjects do. Spontaneous GSRs could be assessed prior to CS exposure and used to predict response to therapy.

Alternatively, the flooding procedure could be arranged so as to minimize the possibility of incubation. Marshall, Gauthier, and Gordon (1979) recommend that exposure be continued until the subject emits a response or set of responses that are indicative of the absence of distress, and that cognitive rehearsal of coping responses be included during the latter stages of exposure. Marshall *et al.* (1979) agree with Eysenck that brief exposure may enhance fear by confirming the subject's expectation that the stimulus is to be feared and by providing insufficient time for coping rehearsal.

Implosive therapists have in fact long maintained that continuing exposure until *all* overt indices of anxiety have been eliminated is a critical element of the procedure (cf. Stampfl & Levis, 1969). It should be noted, however, that implosive therpists do *not* make this recommendation on the basis of concern with an incubation effect. Rather, implosive theory acknowledges that the *habit strength* of an avoidance response (symptom) may be strengthened by premature termination of exposure, despite the fact that the underlying *fear* may have been reduced by brief exposure.

Most theorists, then, are agreed that long exposures are preferred to brief exposures in ensuring the effectiveness of extinction therapies. There is controversy, however, as to whether incubation constitutes a real danger for clients undergoing flooding. A number of pieces of evidence would suggest that incubation seldom if ever occurs in treatment. First, in a review of the clinical literature in implosion, Levis and Hare (1977) did not find a single controlled-group study in which flooding led to a worsening of symptoms, even when it was used with low "ego-strength" subjects (Boudewyns & Levis, 1975). Rather, they found considerable support for the technique, especially with studies using patients as subjects. The oft-cited paper by Rachman (1968) purporting to demonstrate harmful effects of exposure was an uncontrolled case study in which a *single* subject displayed increased fear of snakes, and only on a self-report measure at that. Second, Shipley and Boudewyns (1980) surveyed 70 psychotherapists who had employed flooding or implosive therapy with over 3400 clients. Transient psychotic or panic episodes occurred in less than 1% of the cases, and 87% of the therapists stated that the procedures produced the same or fewer side effects than did other forms of therapy they had used. Third, implosive therapy contains a number of procedures that make premature termination of exposure unlikely. The rationale for anxiety evocation is easily understood by the client, and a single implosive session of 60 to 100 minutes is usually sufficient to produce significant symptom relief (Levis & Hare, 1977; McCutcheon & Adams, 1975). The temporary discomfort of the scene is generally viewed as minor in comparison to that produced by the symptoms for which treatment is sought (Shipley & Boudewyns, 1980). And it is often forgotten that although implosion and flooding do eventually result in high levels of anxiety in comparison to, say, SD, the treatment nevertheless proceeds in a hierarchial manner. Exposure begins with relatively low-level images, and more aversive matierial is incoporated in the scene quite gradually as a function of client reponse. Clients usually become easily involved in the task at hand, and refusal to continue imagery is rare.

TREATMENTS BASED ON OPERANT MODELS

Behaviorists of an operant orientation have long eschewed what they consider "unwarranted" theorizing in both the laboratory and the clinic. Skinner (1950), for example, has argued that it is premature to develop theories of learning, since researchers lack much essential data on critical variables. Similarly, operant clinicians have generally viewed complex models of etiology as unnecessary, preferring instead to concentrate on the conditions presently maintaining the observed maladaptive behavior. While this approach has disadvantages (such as the loss of the organizing and guiding power of theory), it has the advantage of emphasizing many of the strengths of the behaviorist approach—the strong ties with the experimental learning literature, the reliance on observable factors, and the avoidance of ill-defined constructs. In addition, operant techniques have avoided the criticisms often directed at other behavior therapies of loosely extrapolating from laboratory models. Most operant methods clearly have their genesis in the direct application to humans of infrahuman findings. In fact, many advances in treatment have resulted from the efforts of researchers with little interest in clinical issues per se.

This direct extrapolation is illustrated in the early efforts of Skinner and his colleagues, in which they applied operant principles derived from infrahuman work to various human populations. In a simple extension of Skinner's class demonstrations of cooperative behavior in pigeons, Azrin and Lindsley (1956) developed increased cooperative play in children through the use of candy reinforcement. Similarly, Ferster and DeMyer (1961, 1962) found that a key-press apparatus that recorded responses and delivered reinforcement was as useful in studying learning, discrimination, and matching abilities in psychotic children as it had been with animal subjects. Lindsley (1956, 1960, 1963) extended these techniques to psychotic adult inpatients. Subjects were placed in a room containing a lever, reinforcement magazine, and stimulus display, resembling the famous "Skinner Box" previously used with pigeons and rats. Food, cigarettes, money, music, and pictures were all used as reinforcement contingent on lever pressing. It was found that psychotics responded at rates lower than those of normal adults, and that periods of nonresponding coincided with such psychotic symptoms as pacing, incoherent vocalizations, staring, and so forth. These techniques were later expanded to study the effects of chemotherapy, psychotherapy, and other environmental manipulations on psychotic behavior.

Among the other target behaviors of early operant clinicians were elimination of hysterical blindness (J. P. Brady & Lind, 1961), increasing verbalizations and problem-solving behaviors of psychiatric patients (Isaacs, Thomas, & Goldiamond, 1960; Peters & Jenkins, 1954), and amelioration of learning disabilities (Staats, 1964, 1968). A detailed review of these early efforts at what came to be known as "applied behavior analysis"—the clinical and practical application of operant methodology—can be found in Kazdin (1978, pp. 233–275).

Much of this intial work took place at a time when the behavior-therapy movement was defining itself and reacting to prevailing psychodynamic schools of psychotherapy. Indeed, it was partly in reaction to the lack of demonstrated success of traditional therapies that many were drawn to the behavior-therapy movement. Whether by intent or necessity, operant behaviorists found themselves dealing with maladaptive behaviors and populations that had proved particularly difficult to treat. Among the most impressive successes of operant therapists working with difficult populations have been the development of token economies for chronic psychiatric inpatients, programs for eliminating self-injury and increasing language in autistic children, and techniques for improving self-help skills and classroom performance of retardates. These efforts are here described briefly.

The advent of psychotropic drugs in the early 1950s led to significant decreases in the inpatient institution population across the country. However, many chronic psychiatric patients who had been hospitalized much of their lives had lost many of the skills necessary for successful community living. Others made marginal adjustments to the community, returning frequently to the hospital in a "revolving-door" pattern. Still others were so psychotic on initial admission that involvement in treatment seemed impossible, and hospital stays were therefore extended. For all these groups, the establishment of token economies on inpatient units represented a dramatic step forward. The assumption of such programs as those directed by Ayllon and Azrin (1968) was that any patient, no matter how "regressed" his or her present behavior, could respond to a properly designed, highly structured schedule of contingencies. The hospital environment was therefore redesigned to maximize the number of reinforcers available to patients. In a departure from earlier efforts, tokens replaced primary reinforcers such as food in order to aid generalization, increase delay of reinforcement, and simplify the keeping of records. In return for performance of clearly defined self-help skills and on-the-ward jobs, patients could earn a predetermined number of tokens, which could later be redeemed for selected reinforcers such as leave from the ward, recreational opportunities, and commissary items. An interesting aspect of the system was that many of the rewards could be considered adaptive behaviors in themselves. For example, patients who consistently kept themselves well-groomed could earn tokens that they might turn in for extra social interactions with the ward psychologist. Token-economy systems were subsequently put into widespread use not only in psychiatric institutions, but also in classrooms and rehabilitation settings (Kazdin, 1977).

In the early 1960s, Lovaas and his colleagues (Lovaas, 1977; Lovaas & Newsom, 1976) embarked on a series of studies in the treatment of psychotic children. Previous attempts at treatment of severely disturbed children, such as the application of "unconditional love" (Bettelheim, 1967), had met with little demonstrable success. Among the maladaptive behaviors commonly displayed by such children were failure to respond to other humans; lack of functional language; and self-injurious behaviors, including scratching, hitting, biting, and head banging. These deficits were so severe (including, for example, biting through shoulders to the bone) that many psychotic children were confined to institutions and often restrained in bed for life.

Lovaas began the application of operant principles with the elimination of self-injurious behaviors, reasoning that these responses were the most life-threatening and did the most to prevent more adaptive interactions with the environment. When extinction proved unfeasible (since many children would emit thousands of self-injurious responses without extinguishing), it was found that a few very unpleasant electric shocks applied as contingent punishment were sufficient to eliminate self-injurious behaviors in most children. Next, attending to adults in the environment was painstakingly *shaped* through the use of contingent food rewards. The children were at first oriented toward the therapist with a physical prompt and rewarded. The prompt was gradually faded and the children rewarded for progressively longer periods of attending to the therapist. Similar shaping methods were used to establish movements of the vocal apparatus, then phonemes and words, and finally sentences. Many children thus progressed from being mute, unresponsive, and self-destructive to being verbal and cooperative. Currently, Lovaas and his group are applying operant methodology to the study of basic discriminative and attentional deficits that may underlie childhood psychosis (Koegel & Wilhelm, 1973; Lovaas, Schreibman, Koegel, & Rehm, 1971; Schreibman & Lovaas, 1973).

Perhaps the greatest frustration in these efforts has been the lack of generalization to other environments of these remarkable gains. Once the children were returned to their institutions and reinforcement for adaptive behavior was not maintained, virtually all reverted to previous maladaptive patterns (Lovaas, Koegel, Simmons, & Long, 1973). Problems in generalization of treatment gains are of course not limited to operant programs or to psychotic children, and much work in operant circles is currently directed at specifying those variables that enhance generalization (e.g., fading of reinforcement and experience in varied stimulus settings).

Bijou, Wolf, and their associates were responsible for one of the first efforts to apply operant methods to retarded children. Individually programmed lessons were coupled with food, social, and token reinforcement, with resultant improvement in academic performance. Inappropriate behaviors, such as disruption of classroom activity, were eliminated by time out from reinforcement (Bijou, Birnbrauer, Kidder, & Tague, 1966; Birnbrauer, Wolf, Kidder, & Tague, 1965). More recently, efforts have focused on increasing the self-care behavior of retardates, including dressing, bathing, and toileting (Foxx & Azrin, 1973). Other behaviors essential for community living have also been fostered by programs of reinforcement. Performance in sheltered workshops, language skills, and cooperative social behaviors have all been targets for these interventions (Kazdin, 1978). With the nationwide trend toward deinstitutionalizing large numbers of retarded and psychiatric patients, these programs are likely to become increasingly valuable.

From a few tentative efforts to extend the operant techniques discovered in the laboratory, operant models of behavior therapy have grown to encompass hundreds of programs with psychiatric patients, retardates, drug addicts and alcoholics, geriatrics, and others (Kazdin & Craighead, 1973; P. M. Miller & Eisler, 1976; Nietzel, Winett, MacDonald, & Davidson, 1977; Stahl & Leitenberg, 1976). As a result of these myriad efforts, operant techniques for increasing adaptive behavior have come to include the contingent application of positive reinforcers, termination of aversive stimuli (negative reinforcement), eliciting approximations of target behaviors through prompts, and shaping of progressively more adaptive responses. Among the techniques by which maladaptive behaviors have been reduced are contingent punishment, time out from positive reinforcement, and increases in the frequency of competing responses. Hundreds of variations and combinations of these basic strategies have been developed and applied successfully to clinical problems.

TREATMENTS BASED ON COVERT MODELS

Closely allied to the operant treatments just reviewed are a set of procedures for "covert conditioning," developed by Cautela (1966, 1967, 1970, 1971). These covert techniques are based on the assumption that stimuli presented imaginally have effects on overt and covert behaviors similar to those of stimuli presented externally. Homme (1965) was the first to suggest that covert operants (or "coverants," as he called them) followed the same laws of learning as overt behaviors. He suggested that the frequency of covert responses (such as thoughts about a term paper) could be increased by making reinforcement (such as a cup of coffee) contingent on their occurrence. He reasoned that, conversely, overt behaviors (such as smoking or overeating) could be influenced by covert events (such as thinking about the health consequences of such actions).

The treatments that were developed on these assumptions are called "covert positive reinforcement," "covert negative reinforcement," "covert sensitization," and "covert extinction." The covert procedures are essentially identical to their overt counterparts as described in previous sections of this chapter, except that the CSs, UCSs, and responses are *all* presented imaginally. Thus, in covert positive reinforcement of heterosexual interactions, a client might imagine the behavior (talking to a member of the opposite sex) to be increased, and then imagine that a reinforcing event occurs (the person responds in a friendly, interested manner). In covert negative reinforcement, a client imagines an aversive event, then shifts to imagining performance of the adaptive behavior. It is assumed that escape from the aversive imagery will reinforce (increase the probability of) the target behavior. Covert sensitization of alcoholism might consist of a client imagining raising a glass to his or her lips, but being overwhelmed by a wave of nausea as he or she is about to drink. The punishment image is believed to decrease the probability of overt drinking. Covert extinction of stuttering might involve having a client imagine engaging in the maladaptive behavior, but in the absence of consequences that are maintaining the behavior (everyone ignores the symptom).

There are several investigations suggesting that covert therapies might be successful (Ascher, 1973; Blanchard & Draper, 1973; Cautela & Baron, 1973; Flannery, 1972; Manno & Marston, 1972; Marshall, Boutilier, & Minnes, 1974; Wisocki, 1970, 1973), although they consist mostly of case reports and analogue studies. A number of other studies have tested certain theoretical assumptions of the covert position, with mixed results (Krop, Messinger, & Reiner, 1973; Ladouceur, 1974; Steffen, 1974; Zemore, Ramsay & Zemore, 1978).

Among the questions raised concerning the therapeutic effects of covert procedures have been these: Can covert processes in fact be modified in the same way as overt behavior (Rachlin, 1977)? And are the effects of covert procedures accounted for by subject expectancies, teaching, or logical analysis, rather than by conditioning processes (Heppner, 1978)? Since covert negative reinforcement more closely resembles "backward conditioning" than it does true escape conditioning, are its effects due to extinction of fear rather than to reinforcement (Zemore, Ramsay, & Zemore, 1978)?

From the perspective of conditioning and learning, perhaps the most important and interesting question is this: Can imaginal events function as effective UCSs? A basic assumption of the covert therapies is that imagined consequences can reinforce or punish behavior in much the same way as overt reinforcers can. But since they cause no pain or tissue damage, reduce no primary drive, and change no bodily state, it is difficult to see how imagined events could be considered UCSs in the usual sense. It would be more accurate to characterize them as *secondary reinforcers,* not primary ones. As such, they are likely to have real but limited power to reinforce and punish. Additionally, they are likely to lose their reinforcing properties with repetition. The techniques are therefore likely to have limited effect on maladaptive behaviors motivated by strong drives (e. g., alcoholism and sexual deviations).

It is interesting to note that covert sensitization is procedurally similar to implosion; the image of approach behavior is paired with the image of aversive consequences. And yet the expected effects are virtually opposite. In implosion, clients are expected to lose their fear and to increase their approach behavior. In covert sensitization, clients are expected to increase their aversion and to avoid the previously approached situation. The different predictions are based not just on the different target behaviors involved (one to be increased, the other decreased). It stems as well from the basically different conceptions of the effects of imagined aversive stimuli.

Parametric studies with clinical populations, in which approach or avoidance is repeatedly assessed following various numbers of imagery trials, are needed to resolve this issue. It can then be determined whether, for example, the secondary punishers used in covert sensitization can be effective with strongly motivated clinical problems, and whether such effects persist over many exposures.

OVERVIEW

In this section, the conditioning processes underlying various behavior-therapy approaches have been discussed. It has been argued that exposure to fear-evoking CSs might be the most important agent of change in a number of behavior therapies, including SD, modeling, and reinforced practice. We have presented evidence suggesting that other aspects of these techniques (such as relaxation, hierarchies, etc.) might be useful with certain clients, but not therapeutically essential. Evidence for the effectiveness of the extinction approaches of flooding and implosion has also been reviewed, and we have argued that concerns about residual fear and incubation are probably exaggerated. Some of the more prominent successes of operant clinicians have been noted, and some advantages of the operant perspective have been highlighted. Finally, we have reviewed the therapies involved in covert conditioning and discussed possible limitations in the behavioral effects of imaginal UCS presentations.

Further work is needed to resolve the many treatment issues raised in this section. Although replete with difficulties in execution, studies with clinical populations in which critical variables are parametrically manipulated hold great promise for clarifying the roles of imaginal and overt CSs and UCSs in modifying maladaptive behavior. It is to be hoped that such studies become more common than they have been in the past. Furthermore, we have suggested that considerable research advances could be made if investigators would provide an operational definition for constructs like "anxiety" and "relaxation" to insure that their procedural manipulation has an effect on each subject tested.

The laws of conditioning and learning developed in the laboratory have given rise to a wide variety of behavior-therapy techniques. In some cases, extrapolation from learning experiments has been quite direct and obvious; in others, the therapies in their final form have only vaguely resembled the laboratory paradigms from which they were derived. Without question, however, the basic research area of conditioning and learning has proven an invaluable source of inspiration to behavioral clinicians. It is likely to remain so for years to come, provided behavior therapists do not forget the "roots" from which they came.

REFERENCES

Abramson, L. Y., & Seligman, M. E. P. Modeling psychopathology in the laboratory: History and rationale. In J. D. Maser & M. E. P. Seligman (Eds.), *Psychopathology: Experimental models,* San Francisco: W. H. Freeman, 1977.

Abramson, L. Y., Seligman, M. E. P., & Teasdale, J. D. Learned helplessness in humans: Critique and reformulations. *Journal of Abnormal Psychology,* 1978, *87,* 49–74.

Amsel, A. Partial reinforcement effects on vigor and persistence: Advances in frustration theory derived from a variety of written subject experiments. In K. W. Spence & J. T. Spence (Eds.), *The psychology of learning and motivation* (Vol. 1). New York: Academic Press, 1967.

Amsel, A. Frustration, persistence and regression. In H. D. Kimmel (Ed.), *Experimental psychopathology.* New York: Academic Press, 1971.

Amsel, A., & Maltzman, I. The effect upon generalized drive strength of emotionality as inferred from the level of consummatory response. *Journal of Experimental Psychology,* 1950, *40,* 563–569.

Annan, Z., & Kamin, L. J. The conditioned emotional response as a function of intensity of the

U. S. *Journal of Comparative and Physiological Psychology,* 1961, *54,* 428–430.

Ascher, M. L. An analogue study of covert reinforcement. In R. D. Rubin, J. P. Brady, & J. D. Henderson (Eds.), *Advances in behavior therapy.* New York: Academic Press, 1973.

Ayllon, T., & Azrin, N. H. *The token economy: A motivational system for therapy and rehabilitation.* New York: Appleton-Century-Crofts, 1968.

Azrin, N. H., & Lindsley, O. R. The reinforcement of cooperation between children. *Journal of Abnormal and Social Psychology,* 1956, *52,* 100–102.

Bandura, A. *Principles of behavior modification.* New York: Holt, Rinehart & Winston, 1969.

Bankart, B., & Elliott, R. Extinction of avoidance in rats: Response availability and stimulus presentation effects. *Behaviour Research and Therapy,* 1974, *12,* 53–56.

Barnett, S. A. "Displacement behavior" and "psychosomatic" disorder. *Lancet,* 1955, *2,* 1203–1208.

Behrend, E. R., & Bitterman, M. E. Sidman avoidance in the fish. *Journal of the Experimental Analysis of Behavior,* 1963, *13,* 229–242.

Bergin, A. E., & Lambert, M. J. The evaluation of therapeutic outcome. In S. L. Garfield & A. E. Bergin (Eds.), *Handbook of psychotherapy and behavior change: An empirical analysis* (2nd ed.). New York: Wiley, 1978.

Bergin, A. E., & Suinn, R. M. Individual psychotherapy and behavior therapy. *Annual Review of Psychology,* 1975, *26,* 509–556.

Bettelheim, B. *The empty fortress.* New York: Free Press, 1967.

Bijou, S. W., Birnbrauer, J. S., Kidder, J. D., & Tague, C. Programmed instruction as an approach to the teaching of reading, writing, and arithmetic to retarded children. *Psychological Record,* 1966, *16,* 505–522.

Birnbrauer, J. S., Wolf, M. M., Kidder, J. D., & Tague, C. E. Classroom behavior of retarded pupils with token reinforcement. *Journal of Experimental Child Psychology,* 1965, *2,* 219–235.

Bitterman, M. E. The CS–UCS interval in classical and avoidance conditioning. In W. F. Prokasy (Ed.), *Classical conditioning: A symposium.* New York: Appleton-Century-Crofts, 1965.

Bitterman, M. E. The comparative analysis of learning. *Science,* 1975, *188,* 699–709.

Bitterman, M. E. Flavor aversion studies. *Science,* 1976, 192, 266–267.

Blanchard, E. B., & Draper, P. O. Treatment of a rodent phobia by covert reinforcement: A single subject experiment. *Behavior Therapy,* 1973, *4,* 559–564.

Bolles, R. Species-specific defense reactions. In F. R. Brush (Ed.), *Aversive conditioning and learning.* New York: Academic Press, 1971.

Boudewyns, P. A., & Levis, P. A. Autonomic reactivity of high and low ego-strength subjects to represented anxiety-eliciting scenes. *Journal of Abnormal Psychology,* 1975, *84,* 682–692.

Boyd, T. L., & Levis, D. J. The effects of single-component extinctions of a three-component serial CS on resistance to extinction of the conditioned avoidance response. *Learning and Motivation,* 1976, *7,* 517–531.

Boyd, T. L., & Levis, D. J. Depression. In R. J. Daitzman (Ed.), *Clinical behavior therapy and behavior modifications* (Vol. 1). New York: Garland STPM Press, 1980.

Brady, J. P., & Lind, D. L. Experimental analysis of hysterical blindness. *Archives of General Psychiatry,* 1961, *4,* 331–339.

Brady, J. V. Endocrine and autonomic correlates of emotional behavior. In P. Black (Ed.), *Physiological correlates of emotion.* New York: Academic Press, 1970.

Brady, J. V., Findley, J. D., & Harris, A. Experimental psychopathology and the psychophysiology of emotion. In H. O. Kimmel (Ed.), *Experimental psychopathology.* New York: Academic Press, 1971.

Braud, W., Wepmann, B., & Russo, D. Task and species generality of the "helplessness" phenomenom. *Psychonomic Science*, 1969, *16*, 154–155.

Breger, L., & McGaugh, J. L. Critique and reformulation of "learning-theory" approaches to psychotherapy and neurosis. *Psychological Bulletin*, 1965, *63*, 338–358.

Brown, J. S. *The motivation of behavior*. New York: McGraw-Hill, 1961.

Brown, J. S. Factors influencing self-primitive locomotive behavior. In B. A. Cambell & R. M. Church (Eds.), *Punishment and aversive behavior*. New York: Appleton-Century-Crofts, 1969.

Brown, J. S., Kalish, H. I., & Farber, I. E. Conditioned fear as revealed by magnitude of startle response to an auditory stimulus. *Journal of Experimental Psychology*, 1951, *41*, 317–328.

Brown, J. S., & Jacobs, A. The role of fear in the motivation and acquisition of responses. *Journal of Experimental Psychology*, 1949, *39*, 747–759.

Brush, F. R. The effect of shock intensity on the acquisition and extinction of an avoidance response in dogs. *Journal of Comparative and Physiological Psychology*, 1957, *50*, 547–552.

Campbell, D., Sanderson, R., & Laverty, S. G. Characteristics of a conditioned response in human subjects during extinction trials following a simple traumatic conditioning trial. *Journal of Abnormal and Social Psychology*, 1964, *68*, 627–639.

Cautela, J. R. Treatment of compulsing behavior by covert sensitization. *Psychological Record*, 1966, *16*, 33–41.

Cautela, J. R. Covert sensitization. *Psychological Record*, 1967, *20*, 459–468.

Cautela, J. R. Covert reinforcement. *Behavior Therapy*, 1970, *1*, 33–50.

Cautela, J. R. Covert extinction. *Behavior Therapy*, 1971, *2*, 192–200.

Cautela, J. R., & Baron, M. G. Multi-faceted behavior therapy of self-injurious behavior. *Journal of Behavior Therapy and Experimental Psychiatry*, 1973, *4*, 125–131.

Chertok, L., & Fontaine, M. Psychosomatics in veterinary medicine. *Journal of Psychosomatic Research*, 1963, *7*, 229–235.

Cohen, R. The effects of group interaction and progressive hierarchy presentation on desensitization of test anxiety. *Behaviour Research and Therapy*, 1969, *7*, 15–26.

Coulter, X., Riccio, D. C., & Page, H. A. Effects of blocking an instrumental avoidance response: Facilitated extinction but persistence of "fear." *Journal of Comparative and Physiological Psychology*, 1969, *68*, 377–381.

Croft, P. G. Some observations on neurosis in farm animals. *Journal of Mental Science*, 1951, *97*, 584–588.

Davison, G. C. Systematic desensitization as a counter-conditioning process. *Journal of Abnormal Psychology*, 1968, *73*, 91–99.

Delprato, D. J. Hereditary determinants of fears and phobias: A critical review. *Behavior Therapy*, 1980, *2*, 79–103.

DeSilva, P., Rachman, S., & Seligman, M. E. P. Prepared phobias and obsessions: Therapeutic outcome. *Behaviour Research and Therapy*, 1977, *15*, 65–77.

Dollard, J., & Miller, N. E. *Personality and psychotherapy*. New York: McGraw-Hill, 1950.

Dorworth, T. R. *The effect of electroconvulsive shock on "helplessness" in dogs*. Unpublished doctoral dissertation, University of Minnesota, 1971.

Dubin, W. J., & Levis, D. J. Influence of similarity of components of a serial CS on conditioned fear in the rat. *Journal of Comparative and Physiological Psychology*, 1973, *85*, 304–312.

Dykman, R. A. The Gantt and Eysenck conditioning models of neurosis. *The Behavioral and Brain Sciences*, 1979, *2*, 168–169.

Dykman, R. A., Mack, R. L., & Ackerman, P. T. The evaluation of autonomic and motor components of the conditioned avoidance response in the dog. *Psychophysiology,* 1965, *1,* 209–230.

Ellison, G. Differential salivary conditoning to traces. *Journal of Comparative and Pysiological Psychology,* 1964, *57,* 373–380.

Eysenck, H. J. (Ed.). *Behaviour therapy and the neuroses.* New York: Pergamon, 1960.

Eysenck, H. J. *The effects of psychotherapy.* New York: International Science Press, 1966.

Eysenck, H. J. A theory of the incubation of anxiety fear responses. *Behaviour Research and Therapy,* 1968, *6,* 309–322.

Eysenck, H. J. The conditioning model of neurosis. *The Behavioral and Brain Sciences,* 1979, *2,* 155–166.

Eysenck, H. J., & Eysenck, S. B. G. *Eysenck Personality Inventory Manual.* San Diego: Educational and Industrial Testing Service, 1968.

Fazio, A. F. Treatment components in implosive therapy. *Journal of Abnormal Psychology,* 1970, *76,* 211–219.

Ferster, C. B., & DeMyer, M. K. The development of performances in autistic children in an automatically controlled environment. *Journal of Chronic Diseases,* 1961, *13,* 312–345.

Ferster, C. B., & DeMyer, M. K. A method for the experimental analysis of the behavior of autistic children. *American Journal of Orthopsychiatry,* 1962, *32,* 89–98.

Finger, F. W. Experimental behavior disorders in the rat. In J. M. Hunt (Ed.), *Personality and the behavior disorders* (Vol. 2). New York: Ronald, 1944.

Flannery, R. B. A laboratory analogue of two covert reinforcement procedures. *Journal of Behavior Therapy and Experimental Psychiatry,* 1972, *3,* 171–177.

Foxx, R. M., & Azrin, N. H. *Toilet training the retarded: A rapid program for day and nighttime independent toileting.* Champaign, Ill.: Research Press, 1973.

Franks, C. M. Pavlovian conditioning approaches. In D. J. Levis (Ed.), *Learning approaches to therapeutic behavior change.* Chicago: Aldine, 1970.

Freud, S. [*The problem of anxiety*] (H. A. Bunker, trans.). New York: Psychoanalytic Quarterly Press and Norton, 1936.

Frey, P. W., Englander, S., & Roman, A. Interstimulus interval analysis of sequential CS compounds in rabbit eyelid conditioning. *Journal of Comparative and Phsiological Psychology,* 1971, *77,* 439–446.

Gaito, J. The kindling effects: An experimental model of epilepsy. In J. D. Keehn (Ed.), *Psychopathology in animals: Research and clinical implications.* New York: Academic Press, 1979.

Gallup, G. G., & Maser, J. Tonic immobility: Evolutionary underpinnings of human catalepsy and catatonia. In J. D. Maser & M. E. P. Seligman (Eds.), *Psychopathology: Experimental models.* San Francisco: W. H. Freeman, 1977.

Gantt, W. H. Origin and development of nervous disturbances experimentally produced. *American Journal of Psychiatry,* 1942, *98,* 475–481.

Gantt, W. H. Measures of susceptibility to nervous breakdown. *American Journal of Psychiatry,* 1943, *99,* 839–849.

Gantt, W. H. *Experimental basis for neurotic behavior.* New York: Harper, 1944.

Gantt, W. H. Experimental basis for neurotic behavior. In H. D. Kimmel (Ed.), *Experimental psychopathology: Recent research and theory.* New York: Academic Press, 1971.

Garcia, J., McGowan, B., & Green, K. Sensory quality and integration: Constraints on conditioning. In A. H. Block & W. F. Prokasy (Eds.), *Classical conditioning.* New York: Appleton-Century-Crofts, 1971.

Gilbert, R. M. Drug abuse as excessive behavior. *Canadian Psychological Review,* 1976, *17,* 231–240.

Greenspoon, J. Learning theory contributions to psychotherapy. *Psychotherapy: Theory, Research and Practice,* 1965, *2,* 145–146.

Hannum, R. D., Rosellini, R. A., & Seligman, M. E. P. Retention of learned helplessness and immunization in the rat from weaning to adulthood. *Developmental Psychology,* 1976, *12,* 449–454.

Hare, N., & Levis, D. J. Pervasive ("free-floating") anxiety: A search for a cause and treatment approach. In S. Turner, K. Calhoun, & H. Adams (Eds.), *Handbook of clinical behavior therapy.* New York: Wiley, 1980.

Harlow, H. F. The nature of love. *American Psychologist,* 1958, *13,* 673–685.

Harlow, H. F. Early social deprivation and later behavior in the monkey. In H. H. Garner & J. E. P. Toman (Eds.), *Unfinished tasks in the behavioral sciences.* Baltimore: Williams & Wilkins, 1964.

Heppner, P. P. The clinical alteration of covert thoughts: A critical review. *Behavior Therapy* 1978, *9,* 717–734.

Herrnstein, R. Method and theory in the study of avoidance. *Psychological Review,* 1969, *76,* 49–69.

Hilgard, E. R., & Bower, G. H. *Theories of learning.* New York: Appleton-Century-Crofts, 1966.

Hiroto, D. S., & Seligman, M. E. P. Generality of learned helplessness in man. *Journal of Personality and Social Psychology,* 1975, *31,* 311–327.

Homme, L. E. Perspectives in psychology: Control of coverants, the operants of the mind. Psychological Record, 1965, *15,* 501–511.

Horney, K. *The neurotic personality of our time.* New York: Norton, 1937.

Hugdahl, K., Frederikson, M., & Ohman, A. "Preparedness" and "arousability" as determinants of electrodermal conditioning. *Behaviour Research and Therapy,* 1977, *15,* 345–353.

Hull, C. L. *Principles of behavior.* New York: Appleton-Century-Crofts, 1943.

Isaacs, W., Thomas, J., & Goldiamond, I. Application of operant conditioning to reinstate verbal behavior in psychotics. *Journal of Speech and Hearing Disorders,* 1960, *25,* 8–12.

Jones, M. C. A laboratory study of fear: The case of Peter. *Pedagogical Seminary,* 1924, *31,* 308–315.

Jung, C. G. *Psychology of the unconscious.* New York: Dodd, 1925.

Kalish, H. I. Strength of fear as a function of the number of acquisition and extinction trials. *Journal of Experimental Psychology,* 1954, *47,* 1–9.

Kazdin, A. E. Extensions of reinforcement techniques to socially and environmentally relevant behaviors. In M. Hersen, R. M. Eisler, & P. M. Miller (Eds.), *Progress in behavior modification* (Vol. 4). New York: Academic Press, 1977.

Kazdin, A. E. *History of behavior modification: Experimental foundations of contemporary research.* Baltimore: University Park Press, 1978.

Kazdin, A. E. & Craighead, W. E. Behavior modification in special education. In L. Mann & D. A. Sabatino (Eds.), *The first review of special education* (Vol. 2). Philadelphia: Buttonwood Farms, 1973.

Keehn, J. D. Psychopathology in animal and man. In J. D. Keehn (Ed.), *Psychopathology in animals: Research and clinical implications.* New York: Academic Press, 1979.

Klein, D. C, & Seligman, M.E.P. Reversal of performance deficits and perceptive deficits in learned helplessness and depression. *Journal of Abnormal Psychology,* 1976, *85,* 11–26.

Koegel, R. L., & Wilhelm, M. H. Selective responding to the components of multiple visual cues by autistic children. *Journal of Experimental Child Psychology,* 1973, *15,* 442–453.

Kostanek, D. J., & Sawrey, J. M. Acquisition and extinction of shuttlebox avoidance with complex stimuli. *Psychonomic Science,* 1965, *3,* 369–370.

Krapfl, J. E. *Differential ordering of stimulus presentation and semi-automated versus live treatment in the systematic desensitization of snake phobia.* Unpublished doctoral dissertation, University of Missouri, 1967.

Krapfl, J., & Nawas, M. Differential ordering of stimulus presentation in systematic desensitization. *Journal of Abnormal Psychology,* 1970, *75,* 333–337.

Krasnogorski, N. I. The conditioned reflexes and children's neurosis. *American Journal of Diseases of Children,* 1925, *30,* 753–768.

Krop, H., Messinger, J., & Reiner, L. Increasing eye contact by covert reinforcement. *Interpersonal Development,* 1973, *4,* 51–57.

Ladouceur, R. An experimental test of the learning paradigm of covert positive reinforcement in deconditioning anxiety. *Journal of Behavior Therapy and Experimental Psychiatry,* 1974, *5,* 3–6.

Lang, P. J. Fear reduction and fear behavior: Problem in treating a construct. In J. M. Shlien (Ed.), *Research in psychotherapy.* Washington, D. C.: American Psychological Association, 1968.

Lang, P. J., Lazovik, A. D., & Reynolds, D. Desensitization, suggestibility, and pseudotherapy. *Journal of Abnormal Psychology,* 1965, *70,* 395–402.

Leitenberg, H. Behavioral approaches to treatment of neuroses. In H. Leitenberg (Ed.), *Handbook of behavior modification and behavior therapy.* Englewood Cliffs, N. J.: Prentice-Hall, 1976.

Leitenberg, H., & Callahan, E. J. Reinforced practice and reduction of different kinds of fears in adults and children. *Behaviour Research and Therapy,* 1973, *11,* 19–30.

Lemkow, P. V., & Crocetti, G. M. Vital statistics of schizophrenia. In L. Bellak (Ed.), *Schizophrenia: A review of the syndrome.* New York: Grune & Stratton, 1958.

Levis, D. J. Implosive therapy: II: The subhuman analogue, the strategy, and the technique. In S. G. Armitage (Ed.), *Behavioral modification techniques in the treatment of emotional disorders.* Battle Creek, Mich.: Veterans Administration Publication, 1966. (a)

Levis, D. J. Effects of serial CS presentation and other characteristics of the CS on the conditional avoidance response. *Psychological Reports,* 1966, *18,* 755–766. (b)

Levis, D. J. Behavioral therapy: The fourth therapeutic revolution? In D. J. Levis (Ed.), *Learning approaches to therapeutic behavior change.* Chicago: Aldine, 1970.

Levis, D. J. Learned helplessness: A reply and an alternative S-R interpretation. *Journal of Experimental Psychology: General,* 1976, *105,* 47–65.

Levis, D. J. A reconsideration of Eysenck's conditioning model of neurosis. *The Behavioral and Brain Sciences,* 1979, *2,* 172–174. (a)

Levis, D. J. The infrahuman avoidance model of symptom maintenance and implosive therapy. In J. D. Keehn (Ed.), *Psychopathology in animals: Research and clinical implications.* New York: Academic Press, 1979. (b)

Levis, D. J. The learned helplessness effect: An expectancy, discrimination deficit, or motivational induced persistence? *Journal of Research in Personality,* 1980, *14,* 158–169. (a)

Levis, D. J. Implementing the technique of implosive therapy. In A. Goldstein & E. B. Foa (Eds.), *Handbook of behavioral interventions: A clinical guide.* New York: Wiley, 1980. (b)

Levis, D. J. Extrapolation of two-factor learning theory of infrahuman avoidance behavior to psychopathology. *Neuroscience and Behavioral Review,* 1981, *5,* 355–370.

Levis, D. J., Bouska, S., Eron, J., & McIlhon, M. Serial CS presentation and one-way avoidance conditioning: A noticeable lack of delayed responding. *Psychonomic Science,* 1970, *20,* 147–149.

Levis, D. J., & Boyd, T. L. Symptom maintenance: An infrahuman analysis and extension of the conservation of anxiety principle. *Journal of Abnormal Psychology,* 1979, *88,* 107–120.

Levis, D. J., & Dubin, W. J. Some parameters affecting shuttlebox avoidance responding with rats receiving serially presented conditioned stimuli. *Journal of Comparative and Physiological Psychology,* 1973, *82,* 328–344.

Levis, D. J., & Hare, N. A review of the theroretical and rational and empirical support for the extinction approach of implosive (flooding) therapy. In M. Hersen, R. M. Eisler, & P. M. Miller (Eds.), *Progress in behavior modification* (Vol. 4). New York: Academic Press, 1977.

Levis, D. J., & Stampfl, T. G. Effects of serial CS presentation on shuttlebox avoidance responding. *Learning and Motivation,* 1972, *3,* 73–90.

Lichtenstein, P. E. Studies of anxiety: The production of a feeding inhibition in dogs. *Journal of Comparative and Physiological Psychology,* 1950, *43,* 16–29.

Liddell, H. S. Conditioned reflex method and experimental neurosis. In J. M. Hunt (Ed.), *Personality and the behavior disorders* (Vol. 1). New York: Ronald, 1944.

Liddell, H. S. *Emotional hazards in animals and man.* Springfield, Ill.: Charles C. Thomas, 1956.

Liddell, H. S. The challenge of Pavlovian conditioning and experimental neurosis in animals. In J. Wolpe, A. Salter, & L. J. Reyna (Eds.), *The conditioning therapies.* New York: Holt, Rinehart & Winston, 1965.

Lindsley, O. R. Operant conditioning methods applied to research in chronic schizophrenia. *Psychiatric Research Reports,* 1956, *5,* 118–139.

Lindsley, O. R. Characteristics of the behavior of chronic psychotics as revealed by free-operant conditioning methods. *Diseases of the Nervous System Monograph,* 1960, *21,* 66–78.

Lindsley, O. R. Free-operant conditioning and psychotherapy. *Current Psychiatric Therapies,* 1963, *3,* 47–56.

Linton, J., Riccio, D. C., Rohrbaugh, M., & Page, H. A. The effects of blocking an instrumental avoidance response: Fear reduction or enhancement. *Behaviour Research and Therapy,* 1970, *8,* 267–272.

Locke, E. A. Is behavior therapy behavioristic? (An analysis of Wolpe's psychotherapeutic methods). *Psychological Bulletin,* 1971, *76,* 318–327.

Logan, F. A. Dominance and aggression. In H. D. Kimmel (Ed.), *Experimental psychopathology.* New York: Academic Press, 1971.

Lovaas, O. I. *The autistic child: Language development through behavior modification.* New York: Wiley, 1977.

Lovaas, O. I., Koegel, R. L., Simmons, J. Q., & Long, J. S. Some generalization and follow-up measures on autistic children in behavior therapy. *Journal of Applied Behavior Analysis,* 1973, *6,* 131–165.

Lovaas, O. I., & Newsom, C. D. Behavior modification with psychotic children. In H. Leitenberg (Ed.), *Handbook of behavior modification and behavior therapy.* Englewood Cliffs, N. J.: Prentice-Hall, 1976.

Lovaas, O. I., Schreibman, L., Koegel, A. L., & Rehm, R. Selective responding by autistic children to multiple sensory input. *Journal of Abnormal Psychology,* 1971, *77,* 211–222.

Luria, A. R. *Higher cortical functions in man.* New York: Basic Books, 1966.

Luria, A. R. *Traumatic aphasia: Its syndromes, psychology, and treatment.* Paris: Mouton, 1970

Maatsch, J. L. Learning and fixation after a single shock trial. *Journal of Comparative and Physiological Psychology,* 1959, *52.* 408–410.

Mackintosh, N. J. *The psychology of animal learning.* New York: Academic Press, 1974.

Maier, N. R. F., & Ellen, P. Studies of abnormal behavior in the rat: XXIII. The prophylactic effects of guidance in reducing rigid behavior. *Journal of Abnormal and Social Psychol ogy*, 1952, *47,* 109–116.

Maier, S. F., and Seligman, M. E. P. Learned helplessness: Theory and evidence. *Journal of Experimental Psychology: General,* 1976, *105,* 3–46.

Manno, B., & Marston, A. R. Weight reduction as a function of negative covert reinforcement (sensitization) versus positive covert reinforcement. *Behaviour Research and Therapy,* 1972, *10,* 201–207.

Marks, I. M. *Fears and phobias.* London: Academic Press, 1969.

Marks, I. M. Phobias and obsessions: Clinical phenomena in search of a laboratory model. In J. D. Maser & M. E. P. Seligman (Eds.), *Psychopathology: Experimental models.* San Francisco: W. H. Freeman, 1977.

Marshall, W. L., Boutilier, J., & Minnes, J. The modification of phobic behavior on covert reinforcement. *Behavior Therapy,* 1974, *5,* 469–480.

Marshall, W. L., Gauthier, J., Christie, M. M., Currie, D. W., & Gordon, A. Flooding therapy: Effectiveness, stimulus characteristics, and the value of brief *in vivo* exposure. *Behaviour Research and Therapy,* 1977, *15,* 79–87.

Marshall, W. L., Gauthier, J., & Gordon, A. The current status of flooding therapy. In M. Hersen, R. M. Eisler, & P. M. Miller (Eds.), *Progress in behaviour modification* (Vol. 7). New York: Academic Press, 1979.

Maser, J., & Gallup, G. G., Jr. Tonic immobility in the chicken: Catalepsy potentiation by uncontrollable shock and alleviation by imipramine. *Psychosomatic Medicine,* 1974, *36,* 199–205.

Masserman, J. H. *Behavior and neurosis.* Chicago: University of Chicago Press, 1943.

Masserman, J. H. *Principles of dynamic psychiatry.* Philadelphia: W. B. Saunders, 1946.

Masserman, J. H. A biodynamic psychoanalytic approach to the problems of feeling and emotion. In M. E. Reymert (Ed.), *Feeling and emotions.* New York: McGraw Hill, 1950.

Masserman, J. H. *Principles of dynamic psychiatry.* Philadelphia: W. B. Saunders, 1971.

Mathews, A., & Shaw, P. Emotional arousal and persuasion effects in flooding. *Behaviour Research and Therapy,* 1973, *11,* 587–598.

McAllister, D. E., & McAllister, W. R. Incubation of fear: An examination of the concept. *Journal of Experimental Research in Personality,* 1967, *2,* 180–190.

McCutcheon, B. A., & Adams, H. E. The physiological basis of implosive therapy. *Behaviour Research and Therapy,* 1975, *13,* 93–100.

McReynolds, W. T. Learned helplessness as a schedule-shift effect. *Journal of Research in Personality,* 1980, *14,* 139–157.

Mealiea, W. L. Jr., & Nawas, M. M. The comparative effectiveness of systematic desensitization and implosive therapy in the treatment of snake phobia. *Journal of Behavior Therapy and Experimental Psychiatry,* 1971, *2,* 85–94.

Melvin, K. B. Vicious circle behavior. In H. D. Kimmel (Ed.), *Experimental psychopathology.* New York: Academic Press, 1971.

Melzack, R., & Scott, T. H. The effects of early experience on the response to pain. *Journal of Comparative and Physiological Psychology,* 1957, *50,* 155–161.

Meryman, J. J. *Magnitude of startle response as a function of hunger and fear.* Unpublished master's thesis, State University of Iowa, 1952.

Meryman, J. J. *The magnitude of an unconditioned GSR as a function of fear conditioned at a long CS-UCS interval.* Unpublished doctoral dissertation, State University of Iowa, 1953.

Meyer-Holzapfel, M. Abnormal behavior in zoo animals. In M. W. Fox (Ed.), *Abnormal behavior in animals.* Philadelphia: W. B. Saunders, 1968.

Miller, B. V., & Levis, D. J. The effects of varying short visual exposure time to a phobic test stimulus on subsequent avoidance behavior. *Behaviour Research and Therapy,* 1971, *9,* 17–21.

Miller, H. R., & Nawas, M. M. Control of aversive stimulus termination in systematic desensitization. *Behaviour Research and Therapy,* 1970, *9,* 57–61.

Miller, N. E. Studies of fear as an acquirable drive: I. Fear as motivation and fear-reduction as reinforcement in the learning of a new response. *Journal of Experimental Psychology,* 1948, *38,* 89–101.

Miller, N. E. Learnable drives and rewards. In S. S. Stevens (Ed.), *Handbook of experimental psychology.* New York: Wiley, 1951.

Miller, P. M., & Eisler, R. M. Alcohol and drug abuse. In W. E. Craighead, A. E. Kazdin, & M. J. Mahoney (Eds.), *Behavior modification: Principles, issues, and applications.* Boston: Houghton Mifflin, 1976.

Mitchell, G. Abnormal behavior in primates. In L. Rosenbaum (Ed.), *Primate behavior: Developments in field and laboratory research.* New York: Academic Press, 1970.

Monti, P. M., & Smith, N. F. Residual fear of the conditioned stimulus as a function of response prevention after avoidance or classical defensive conditioning in the rat. *Journal of Experimental Psychology: General,* 1976, *105,* 148–162.

Mowrer, O. H. On the dual nature of learning: A reinterpretation of "conditioning" and "problem-solving." *Harvard Educational Review,* 1947, *17,* 102–148.

Mowrer, O. H. Pain, punishment, guilt, and anxiety. In *Anxiety.* New York: Grune & Stratton, 1950.

Mowrer, O. H. *Learning theory and behavior.* New York: Wiley, 1960.

Napalkov, A. V. Information process of the brain. In N. Wiener & J. P. Schade (Eds.), *Progress in brain research* (Vol. 2). Amsterdam: Elsevier, 1963.

Nawas, M. M., Fishman, S. T. & Pucel, J. C. A standardized desensitization program applicable to group and individual treatment. *Behaviour Research and Therapy, 1970, 8,* 49–56.

Nawas, M. M., Welsch, W. V., & Fishman, S. T. The comparative effectiveness of pairing aversive imagery with relaxation, neurtral tasks, and muscular tension in reducing snake phobia. *Behaviour Research and Therapy,* 1970, *6,* 63–68.

Nelson, F. Effects of two counter-conditioning procedures on the extinction of fear. *Journal of Comparative and Physiological Psychology,* 1966, *2,* 208–213.

Nietzel, M. T., Winett, R. A., MacDonald, M. L., & Davidson, W. S. *Behavioral approaches to community psychology.* New York: Pergamon, 1977.

Overmier, J. B., & Seligman, M. E. P. Effects of inescapable shock upon subsequent escape and avoidance responding. *Journal of Comparative and Physiological Psychology,* 1967, *63,* 28–33.

Page, H. A. The facilitation of experimental extinction by response preverntion as a function of the acquisition of a new response. *Journal of Comparative and Physiological Psychology,* 1955, *48,* 14–16.

Paul, S. M. Movement, mood and madness: A biological model of schizophrenia. In J. D. Maser & M. E. P. Seligman (Eds.), *Psychopathology: Experimental models.* San Francisco: W. H. Freeman, 1977.

Pavlov, I. P. *Conditioned reflexes.* London: Oxford University Press, 1927.

Pavlov, I. P. *Lectures on conditioned reflexes.* New York: International Publishers, 1928.

Peters, H. N., & Jenkins, R. L. Improvement of chronic schizophrenic patients with guided problem-solving, motivated by hunger. *Psychiatric Quarterly Supplement,* 1954, *28,* 84–101.

Prochaska, J. O. Symptom and dynamic cues in the implosive treatment of test anxiety. *Journal of Abnormal Psychology,* 1971, *77,* 133–142.

Rachlin, H. Reinforcing and punishing thoughts. *Behavior Therapy,* 1977, *8,* 659–665.

Rachman, S. The role of muscular relaxation in desensitization therapy. *Behaviour Research and Therapy*, 1968,6, 159–166.

Rachman, S. *The effects of psychotherapy.* New York: Pergamon, 1971.

Rachman, S., & Seligman, M. E. P. Unprepared phobias: "Be prepared." *Behaviour Research and Therapy*, 1976, *14*, 333–338.

Rescorla, R. A., & Solomon, R. L. Two-process learning theory: Relationships between Pavlovian conditioning and instrumental learning. *Psychological Review*, 1967, *74*, 151–182.

Riccio, D., & Silvestri, R. Extinction of avoidance behavior and the problem of residual fear. *Behaviour Research and Therapy*, 1973, *11*, 1–9.

Rodin, J. Bidirectional influences of emotionality, stimulus responsivity, and metabolic events in obesity. In J. D. Maser & M. E. P. Seligman (Eds.), *Psychopathology: Experimental models.* San Francisco: W. H. Freeman, 1977.

Rohrbaugh, M., & Riccio, D. Paradoxical enhancement of learned fear. *Journal of Abnormal Psychology*, 1970, *75*, 210–216.

Rohrbaugh, M., Riccio, D., & Arthur, A. Paradoxical enhancement of conditioned suppression. *Behaviour Research and Therapy*, 1972, *10*, 33–34.

Schiff, R., Smith, N., & Prochaska, J. Extinction of avoidance in rats as a function of duration and number of blocked trials. *Journal of Comparative and Physiological Psychology*, 1972, *81*, 356–359.

Schmidt, J. P. Psychosomatics in veterinary medicine. In M. W. Fox (Ed.), *Abnormal behavior in animals.* Philadelphia: W. B. Saunders, 1968.

Schofield, W. Changes in response to the MMPI following certain therapies. *Psychological Monographs*, 1950, *64* (5, Whole No. 311).

Schreibman, L., & Lovaas, O. I. Overselective response to social stimuli by autistic children. *Journal of Abnormal Child Psychology*, 1973, *1*, 152–168.

Schubot, E. D. *The influence of hypnotic and muscular relaxation in systematic desensitization of phobic behavior.* Unpublished doctoral dissertation, Stanford University, 1966.

Sechzer, J. A. The neonatal split-brain kitten: A laboratory analogue of minimal brain dysfunction. In J. D. Maser & M. E. P. Seligman (Eds.), *Psychopathology: Experimental models.* San Francisco: W. H. Freeman, 1977.

Seligman, M. E. P. On the generality of the laws of learning. *Psychological Review*, 1970, *37*, 406–418.

Seligman, M. E. P. Phobias and preparedness. *Behavior Therapy*, 1971, *2*, 307–320.

Seligman, M. E. P. *Helplessness on depression, development, and death.* San Francisco: W. H. Freeman, 1975.

Seligman, M. E. P., & Beagley, G. Learned helplessness in the rat. *Journal of Comparative and Physiological Psychology*, 1975, *88*, 534–541.

Seligman, M. E. P., & Johnston, J. C. A cognitive theory of avoidance learning. In F. J. McGuigan & D. B. Lumsden (Eds.), *Contemporary prospectives in learning and conditioning.* Washington, D. C.: Scripta Press, 1973.

Seligman, M. E. P., Klein, D. C., & Miller, W. R. Depression. In H. Leitenberg (Ed.), *Handbook of behavior modification and behavior therapy.* Englewood Cliffs, N. J.: Prentice-Hall, 1976.

Seligman, M. E. P., Maier, S. F., & Geer, J. The alleviation of learned helplessness in the dog. *Journal of Abnormal Psychology*, 1968, *73*, 256–262.

Seligman, M. E. P., Rosellini, R. A., & Kozak, M. J. Learned helplessness in the rat: Time course, immunization, and reversibility. *Journal of Comparative and Physiological Psychology*, 1975, *88*, 542–547.

Seward, J. C., & Humphrey, G. L. Avoidance learning as a function of pretraining in the cat.

Journal of Comparative and Physiological Psychology, 1967, *63*, 338–341.

Shearman, R. W. Response-contingent CS termination in the extinction of avoidance learning. *Behaviour Research and Therapy*, 1970, *8*, 227–239.

Sherrington, C. S. *The integrative action of the central nervous system*. Cambridge, England: Cambridge University Press, 1947.

Shipley, R. H. Extinction of conditioned fear in rats as a function of several parameters of CS exposure. *Journal of Comparative and Physiological Psychology*, 1974, *87*, 699–707.

Shipley, R. H., & Boudewyns, P. A. *Flooding and implosive therapy: Are they harmful?* Unpublished manuscript, 1980.

Shipley, R. H., Mock, L. A., & Levis, D. J. Effects of several response prevention procedures on activity, avoidance responding, and conditioned fear in rats. *Journal of Comparative and Physiological Psychology*, 1971, *77*, 256–270.

Siegel, A. Stimulus generalization of a classically conditioned response along a temporal dimension. *Journal of Comparative and Physiological Psychology*, 1967, *64*, 461–466.

Siegel, S. The role of conditioning in drug tolerance and addiction. In J. D. Keehn (Ed.), *Psychopathology in animals: Research and clinical implications*. New York: Academic Press, 1979.

Silvestri, R., Rohrbaugh, M., & Riccio, D. Conditions influencing the retention of learned fear in young rats. *Developmental Psychology*, 1970, *2*, 389–395.

Skinner, B. F. Are theories of learning necessary? *Psychological Review*, 1950, *57*, 193–216.

Solomon, R. L. An opponent process theory of motivation: The affective dynamics of drug addiction. In J. D. Maser & M. E. P. Seligman (Eds.), *Psychopathology: Experimental models*. San Francisco: W. H. Freeman, 1977.

Solomon, R. L., Kamin, L. J., & Wynne, L. C. Traumatic avoidance learning: The outcomes of several extinction procedures with dogs. *Journal of Abnormal and Social Psychology*, 1953, *48*, 291–302.

Solomon, R. L., & Wynne, L. C. Traumatic avoidance learning: The principle of anxiety conservation and partial irreversibility. *Psychological Review*, 1954, *61*, 353–385.

Srole, L., Langner, T. S., Michael, S. T., Opler, M. K., & Rennie, T. A. C. *The midtown Manhattan study: Mental health in the metropolis* (Vol. 1). New York: McGraw-Hill, 1962.

Staats, A. W. (Ed.). *Human learning: Studies extending conditioning principles to complex behavior*. New York: Holt, Rinehart and Winston, 1964.

Staats, A. W. A general apparatus for the investigation of complex learning in children. *Behaviour Research and Therapy*, 1968, *6*, 45–50.

Staddon, J. E. R. Schedule-induced behavior. In W. K. Honig & J. E. R. Staddon (Eds.), *Operant behavior*. Englewood Cliffs, N. J.: Prentice-Hall, 1977.

Stahl, J. R., & Leitenberg, H. Behavioral treatment of the chronic mental hospital patient. In H. Leitenberg (Ed.), *Handbook of behavior modification and behavior therapy*. Englewood Cliffs, N. J.: Prentice-Hall, 1976.

Stampfl, T. G. Implosive therapy: An emphasis on covert stimulation. In D. J. Levis (Ed.), *Learning approaches to therapeutic behavior change*. Chicago: Aldine, 1970.

Stampfl, T. G., & Levis, D. J. The essentials of implosive therapy: A learning theory based on psychodynamic behavioral therapy. *Journal of Abnormal Psychology*, 1967, *72*, 496–503.

Stampfl, T. G., & Levis, D. J. Learning theory: An aid to dynamic therapeutic practice. In L. D. Eron & R. Callahan (Eds.), *Relationship of theory to practice in psychotherapy*. Chicago: Aldine, 1969.

Stampfl, T. G., & Levis, D. J. Implosive therapy. In R. M. Jurjevick (Ed.), *Handbook of direct and behavior psychotherapies*. Coral Gables, Fla.: University of Miami Press, 1973.

Stampfl, T. G., & Levis, D. J. Implosive therapy: A behavioral therapy. In J. T. Spence, R. C. Carson, & J. W. Thibaut (Eds.), *Behavioral approaches to therapy*. Morristown, N. J.:

General Learning Press, 1976.

Startsev, V. G. *Primate models of human neurogenic disorders*. Hillsdale, N.J.: Erlbaum, 1976.

Steffen, J. J. *Covert reinforcement: Some facts and fantasies*. Paper presented at the Annual Meeting of the Association for the Advancement of Behavior therapy, 1974.

Stone, N. M., & Borkovec, T. The paradoxical effect of brief CS exposure on analogue phobic subjects. *Behaviour Research and Therapy*, 1975, *13*, 51–54.

Stout, C., & Snyder, R. L. Ulcerative colitis-like lesion in Siamang gibbons. *Gastroenterology*, 1969, *57*, 256–261.

Suomi, S. J., & Harlow, H. F. Production and alleviation of depressive behaviors in monkeys. In J. D. Maser & M. E. P. Seligman (Eds.), *Psychopathology: Experimental models*. San Francisco: W. H. Freeman, 1977.

Teplov, B. M., & Nebylitsyn, V. D. The study of the basic properties of the nervous system and their significance for the psychology of individual differences. *Soviet Psychology and Psychiatry*, 1966, *4*, 80–85.

Testa, T. J. Comments on "Residual fear of the conditioned stimulus as a function of response prevention after avoidance or classical defensive conditioning in the rat." *Journal of Experimental Psychology: General*, 1976, *105*, 163–168.

Thomas, E., & Dewald, L. Experimental neurosis: Neuropsychological analysis. In J. D. Maser & M. E. P. Seligman (Eds.), *Psychopathology: Experimental models*. San Francisco: W. H. Freeman, 1977.

Thompson, W. R., Melzack, R., & Scott, T. H. "Whirling behavior" in dogs are related to early experience. *Science*, 1956, *123*, 939.

Tinklepaugh, O. L. The self-mutilation of a male macocus rhesus monkey. *Journal of Mammalogy*, 1928, *9*, 293–300.

Wachtel, P. L. *Psychoanalysis and behavior therapy: Toward an integration*. New York: Basic Books, 1977.

Watson, J. B., & Rayner, R. Conditioned emotional reaction. *Journal of Experimental Psychology*, 1920, *3*, 1–4.

Weiss, J. Ulcers. In J. D. Maser & M. E. P. Seligman (Eds.), *Psychopathology: Experimental models*. San Francisco: W. H. Freeman, 1977.

Weiss, J. M., Glazer, H. I., & Poherecky, L. A. Coping behavior and neurochemical changes: An alternative explanation for the original "learned helplessness" experiments. In G. Serban & A. Kling (Eds.), *Animal models of human psychobiology*. New York: Plenum, 1976.

Williams, D. R. Classical conditioning and incentive motivation. In W. F. Prokasy (Ed.), *Classical conditioning: A symposium*. New York: Appleton-Century-Crofts, 1965.

Wilson, G. T., & Davison, G. C. Process of fear reduction in systematic desensitization: Animal studies. *Psychological Bulletin*, 1971, *76*, 1–14.

Wisocki, P. Treatment of obsessive–compulsive behavior by covert sensitization and covert reinforcement: A case report. *Journal of Behavior Therapy and Experimental Psychiatry*, 1970, *1*, 233–239.

Wisocki, P. A covert reinforcement program for the treatment of test anxiety: Brief report. *Behavior Therapy*, 1973, *4*, 264–266.

Wolpe, J. *Psychotherapy by reciprocal inhibition*. Stanford, Calif.: Stanford University Press, 1958.

Wolpin, M., & Pearsall, L. Rapid deconditioning of a fear of snakes. *Behaviour Research and Therapy*, 1965, *3*, 107.

Zemore, R., Ramsay, B., & Zemore, J. Success of covert negative reinforcement is not the result of operant conditioning. *Psychological Reports*, 1978, *43*, 955–961.

3

INTEGRATING PSYCHOBIOLOGY
AND BEHAVIOR THERAPY:
A SYSTEMS PERSPECTIVE

GARY E. SCHWARTZ

Department of Psychology
Yale University

INTRODUCTION

The purpose of this chapter is to examine some of the ways that systems theory (DeRosnay, 1979) can help researchers and clinicians pursue the difficult task of integrating psychobiology and behavior therapy. My thesis is that systems theory (both general and living systems theory) can improve our understanding of the psychobiological foundations of behavior therapy, and, in the process, can improve theory, research, and applications of learning principles (broadly defined) to the prevention and treatment of psychophysiological disorders (Schwartz, 1978).

At this particular time in history, when behavior therapy is being broadened to become more cognitive, affective, and psychophysiological in orientation (e.g., Lang, 1979), the field of psychology as a whole is becoming more synthetic and "biopsychosocial." The behavior of an organism (its "psychology") is now viewed as emerging out of a complex and dynamic interaction between its biological structure (and potentials) on the one hand, and its social environment on the other.

The recent development of behavioral medicine, with its emphasis on the integration of behavioral and biomedical approaches to health and illness (Schwartz & Weiss, 1978a, 1978b), is symptomatic of this growing movement (Schwartz, 1980). For example, a major question in behavioral medicine involves the potential interaction of behavioral and drug therapies in the treatment of hypertension (Schwartz, Shapiro, Redmond, Ferguson, Ragland, & Weiss, 1979). Under what conditions can behavioral therapies such as relaxation and/or assertiveness training augment a hypertensive's response to hypertension medication? Under what conditions, in what subtypes of hypertensives, and with what kinds of drugs can additive or synergistic as opposed to antagonistic interactions occur? It is no longer appropriate to view behavioral therapies as if they were completely independent of a person's psychobiological history, in the same way that it is no longer appropriate to view biomedical therapies as if they were completely independent of a person's psychosocial history. Systems theory provides a framework for raising and addressing fundamental biohavioral issues that are critical to comprehensive and responsible health care.

This chapter highlights specific examples of theory, research, and application that move toward an integration of psychobiology and behavior therapy. The chapter is designed to be general and representative rather than specific and comprehensive.

For the purpose of this chapter, the particular examples chosen are less important than the general principles that they illustrate, since these principles can be applied to any treatment or disorder. As I propose below, the roots of behavioral psychology and systems theory were nourished in the same soil. The time may be ripe to bring them back together again.

WHAT IS SYSTEMS THEORY? BEHAVIOR AS A SUBSET OF "BEHAVIOR"

General systems theory was originally derived from the physical and biological sciences (von Bertalanffy, 1968), and it has been applied to virtually all scientific disciplines (Miller, 1978). Because general systems theory developed in part out of the engineering sciences, and because it was designed to be precise as well as general, it has tended to emphasize mathematical and/or abstract principles wherever possible (e.g., Powers, 1973). General systems theory should really be viewed as a "meta"-theory. It is more aptly described as a general scientific structure and scientific paradigm (Kuhn, 1962) than as a specific theoretical orientation (see DeRosnay, 1979, for an outstanding introduction to systems theory).

There is a curious, important, and sometimes confused link between the development of behavioral psychology in the 1920s and 1930s and the development of systems theory at this same point in history. Behavioral psychology attempted to distinguish rigidly between inference and observation by requiring that psychology deal only with observable "behavior." According to Skinner (1954), psychologists were ideally to model themselves after biologists and to measure the behavior of organisms in the same way that biologists measured the behavior of cells and tissues. Therefore, concepts of emotion and cognition were disallowed unless they could be shown to be directly measurable as "behavior."

To work within this framework, some behaviorists attempted to redefine mental events as being "covert" events that could be directly measured as "behaviors" through the use of physiological instrumentation to record muscle tension. Note that the "physiological" recording of muscular tension was viewed by psychologists like Skinner as being behavioral "psychology." The distinction between physiology and psychology was, therefore, blurred when behavioral psychology attempted to model itself after biology and to measure biology as if it were, so to speak, "invisible" behavior.

Systems theorists carried this synthesis to its logical extreme by proposing that responsible science, working at any level, was really the study of the *behavior of systems.* Therefore, in systems terms, scientists who studied the behavior of atoms were physicists; scientists who studied the behavior of chemicals were chemists; scientists who studied the behavior of cells and tissues were biologists; scientists who studied the behavior of organisms were psychologists; scientists who studied the behavior of groups and organizations were sociologists; and so forth. In fact, the journal *Behavioral Science,* which is the official publication of the Society for General Systems Research, publishes relevant articles in *all* disciplines, from subatomic physics to astronomy, to the extent that the articles adopt a general "behavioral" perspective and search for general principles that transcend their particular discipline.

General systems theory, then, is the study of the behavior of systems in general (von Bertalanffy, 1968). Living systems theory is the study of the behavior of a subset of systems that have properties of life (Miller, 1978). Behavioral psychology, were it to adopt a living systems perspective, would be defined specifically as the study of the behavior of organisms. It turns out that a systems-oriented behavioral psychology is philosophically very similar to the classic behavioral psychology that was derived from a perspective of learning theory. The major difference between these two "behavioral" psychologies is that systems-theory psychology is substantially broader than learning-theory psychology per se. Also, systems-theory psychology provides a framework for readily crossing levels of structure and analysis (e.g., from biology to psychology to social behavior).

As illustrated in Table 3-1, there are actually four different uses of the term "behavior" in science. Unfortunately, the uses are often confused. Traditional behaviorists in psychology employ the narrowest meaning to the term (derived from operant and classical conditioning learning theory). On the other hand, "behavioral science" as defined by the Society for General Systems Research employs the most inclusive meaning of the term. Note that the four definitions vary as to the level of complexity of the system that they describe (see Table 3-2) and that the last definition (i. e., the systems definition of behavior) includes the other three (and, thus, reflects the deep significance of what the original behaviorists in psychology were trying to achieve).

It is necessary, therefore, for investigators to define carefully what they

TABLE 3-1. Four Definitions of Behavior, Using Behavioral Medicine as an Example, Moving Up Levels of Complexity (in Systems Terms)

1. "Behavior" from the perspective of behaviorists and behavior therapists: "Behavior" here refers to one subarea in the discipline of psychology, emphasizing learning and the strict measurement of observable events. "Behavioral medicine" here refers to the application of behavior therapy per se (learning theory) to medicine.

2. "Behavior" from the perspective of general psychology: "Behavior" here refers to the study of behavior of organisms, broadly defined, and encompasses the entire discipline of psychology. Here psychology is "the" behavioral science. "Behavioral medicine" here refers to the application of all subareas of the discipline of psychology to medicine.

3. "Behavior" from the perspective of the arts and sciences: "Behavior" here refers to the study of behavior of organisms, very broadly defined, and encompasses not only the discipline of psychology, but the disciplines of anthropology, sociology, political science, and so forth. "Behavioral medicine" here refers to the application of all behavioral sciences (psychology being only one such science) to medicine. This is the definition of "behavioral science" used at the Yale Conference on Behavioral Medicine (Schwartz & Weiss, 1978a).

4. "Behavior" from the perspective of systems theory: "Behavior" here refers to the study of behavior of systems, not just organisms. All scientific disciplines, including physics, chemistry, and biology, in addition to the "behavioral sciences" mentioned in Definition 3, would be reclassified here as "behavioral sciences." "Behavioral medicine" here refers to the application of systems theory to, and the integration of all scientific disciplines with, medicine (Schwartz, 1979, 1980).

TABLE 3-2. Levels of Complexity in Systems and Associated Academic Disciplines

According to systems theory, in order to understand the behavior of an open system at any one level, it is essential to have some training in the academic disciplines below that level and to have training at least in the relevant discipline at the next highest level as well.

LEVEL AND COMPLEXITY OF THE SYSTEM	ACADEMIC FIELD ASSOCIATED WITH THE LEVEL OF THE SYSTEM
Beyond earth	Astronomy
Beyond nations	Ecology
Nations	Government, political science, economics
Organizations	Organizational science
Groups	Sociology
Organisms	Psychology, ethology, zoology
Organs	Organ physiology (e.g., neurology, cardiology)
Cells	Cellular biology
Biochemicals	Biochemistry
Chemicals	Chemistry, physical chemistry
Atoms	Physics
Subatomic particles	Subatomic physics
Abstract systems	Mathematics, philosophy

mean by "behavior" when they use the term in a given context. Having to define the term "behavior" continually can be frustrating if not tongue-tying at times, but it can serve the important function of replacing confusion with clarity. For clarity of presentation in this chapter, the term "behavior" will be printed in lower case letters to refer specifically to overt (or covert behavior) in a psychological sense (Definition 2), and the term "BEHAVIOR" will be printed in capital letters to refer to the *general* concept of a BEHAVING system at any level (Definition 4).

General systems theory is concerned with general principles that can be applied to any system at any level of complexity (DeRosnay, 1979). Concepts such as "information processing," "feedback," "stress and strain," "emergent property," and so forth, turn out to be general systems concepts that do not belong to any one discipline. Interestingly, learning turns out to be a general systems concept too, though until quite recently (with the development of artificial intelligence and computers that can be programmed to learn through experience) learning as a phenomenon was limited to living systems. A major goal of general systems theory is to uncover the basic principles that govern the BEHAVIOR of any system, and at the same time to uncover the rules that allow for unique BEHAVIORS to emerge in systems that vary in their biological structure and developmental history.

I will turn shortly to a discussion of specific systems principles and their application to the relationship between psychobiology/and behavior therapy. However, before leaving the "what is behavior" question, it is worth briefly discussing how this issue colors the way in which we routinely perceive "behaviors," and, therefore, the way in which they classify events as "behavioral" versus "biological" in a typical therapy situation. For example, consider a therapy situation in which the therapist asks the client, "How are you feeling?" and observes that the client looks away and moves his or her eyes to the left (adapted from Schwartz, 1978). This process of observing (from a distance) an eye movement in response to an interview question is usually defined as a psychological process involving a change in a client's "behavior." Research findings based on such eye movements would typically be published in a psychology journal.

However, if the therapist had attached electrodes to the outer corners of each eye, had displayed the eye movements as voltage shifts on a polygraph, and had computer-scored the electroculogram as indicating an eye movement to the left, this would usually be defined as a psychophysiological process involving a change in the client's "physiology," rather than as a psychological process involving a change in the client's "behavior." Research findings based on these eye movements would typically be published in a more physiologically oriented journal, such as *Psychophysiology*.

Note that the shift in discipline from psychology to physiology would continue to occur if the therapist went one step further and inferred from the eye movement to the left that the client had engaged his or her right hemisphere when he or she answered the question, "How do you feel?" In fact, part of the regular practice of clinical neurology requires that the neurologist ask the patient questions. From the nature of the overt bodily movements ("behavior") elicited by the questions, the clinical neurologist *infers* the functioning (or malfunctioning) of various parts of the nervous system. The process of making an inference about the neural mechanisms underlying bodily movements of behavior shifts the discipline from psychophysiology to "psychoneurology." Research findings based on these eye movements would typically be published in a more neurologically oriented journal, such as *Neuropsychologia.*

In what sense is the psychologist's perception any more correct than the psychophysiologist's and/or the psychoneurologist's? According to systems theory, they are all "correct." An eye movement reflects the behavior of an organism. This behavior involves the BEHAVIOR of the eye muscles as they are interfaced with the BEHAVIOR of the organism's nervous system. In more technical terms, "behavior" at the level of an organism is an emergent property of the interacting BEHAVIORS of the biological subsystems comprising the organism (as the organism interacts, of course, with its environment). This implies that behavior therapy (at the level of an organism) *always* involves the modification of various biological processes. A change in a client's behavior (at a psychological level) always involves a change in the client's biology. One change is not a "correlate" of the other; rather, *one is an emergent of the other* (see below).

For this reason, I have proposed that it is counterproductive to define psychophysiology primarily in terms of recording methods (e.g., the attaching of electrodes), since investigators can, for example, indirectly measure eye muscle BEHAVIOR simply by looking at the eye movement *in vivo* (or scoring it from a video tape record) without resorting to direct physiological monitoring. (The latter, of course, provides a more continuous and accurate, albeit intrusive, means of detecting and scoring the eye's BEHAVIOR over time.) Also, it is now possible to quantify certain physiological parameters directly without actually attaching electrodes to the body; for example, it is possible to measure skin temperature at a distance, using modern thermography equipment. From a systems perspective, it makes more sense to define psychophysiology as a *perspective*, a state of mind regarding the way in which data are to be classified and interpreted by the observer (see Schwartz, 1978), than it does to define it simply as a method of collecting data per se.

An event can be conceptualized as being behavioral (at a psychological level) or physiological, or neurological, or even biochemical for that matter, depending upon the *level of analysis* involved (see Table 3-2). For example, if a person's blood pressure drops, and the decrease is due to a decrease in peripheral resistance that is mediated by a decrease in sympathetic tone to the arterioles, *this requires* that there will be a decrease in the hormone norepinephrine secreted at the periphery. Implicit in the term "psychophysiology" is the belief that psychological and biological levels are intimately connected. Of course, taking a psychophysiological perspective should not give researchers license to forget the distinction between inference and direct measurement; for example, although a decrease in norepinephrine can be *inferred* when a decrease in peripheral resistance is measured, the peripheral resistance is not a direct measure of the hormone norepinephrine, which would be obtained using appropriate biochemical procedures.

As implied by the behaviorist movement in psychology (and expanded upon by the systems movement in science more broadly), behavior therapy is ultimately "biobehavioral" therapy having biobehavioral consequences, whether the therapist and/or the client is aware of this fact or not. Behavioral self-monitoring is, therefore, biological self-monitoring, and, as I propose below, should have biological consequences complimentary with the changes observed at the behavioral level. To modify assertive behavior is, therefore, to modify the biology of assertion—physiological concomitants of assertiveness training are, therefore, an essential component of the behavioral treatment.

This leads to a radically different view of behavior therapy (and of psychotherapy in general). Rather than promoting the mind–body split, the systems perspective leads investigators to a more unified mind–body integration. On the one hand, it facilitates the view of a fusion of biology and behavior (at a psychological level), yet, on the other hand, it simultaneously illustrates how the "mind" (behavior) emerges out of the "body" (biology). This implies that a "split" between mind and body exists in *level* rather than in function or locale. It is for this reason that I have proposed that the systems perspective as applied to psychotherapy (Schwartz, 1978) may involve a major shift in paradigm (Kuhn, 1962). Like a small point of ice seen in the sea that turns out to be the tip of a gigantic iceberg, it is possible that investigators are just beginning to see a small new point of view that may ultimately turn out to be the tip of a gigantic conceptual system for understanding and integrating behavioral and biological therapies (see DeRosnay, 1979).

WHAT IS A SYSTEM? THE BREATHING EXAMPLE

Inherent in the concept of a system is the concept of emergence and interaction. A set of parts (subsystems) becomes a system when the parts interact in unique ways, leading to certain BEHAVIORS that characterize the system as a whole. According to Miller, a system is a set of interacting units with relationships among them. The word "set" implies that the units have some common properties. These common properties are essential if the units are to interact or have relationships. The state of each unit is constrained by, conditioned by, or dependent upon the state of the other units. The units are coupled. Moreover, there is at least one measure of the sum of its units which is larger than the sum of that measure of its units. (1978, p. 16)

In other words, the properties (or BEHAVIOR) of a system as a whole emerge out of the interaction of the components comprising the system. Consequently, no one component "equals" the whole system. All properties of complex systems have multiple causes rather than single causes.

Note that the BEHAVIOR of a system, as a whole, emerges out of the BEHAVIORS (interactions) of the subsystems comprising the system. A living system is conceptualized as being an "open" system in the sense that the system continually interacts with its environment, *of which it is a part.* In other words, an organism is both a system unto itself and, simultaneously, a subsystem of various larger systems of which it is a part (e.g., an organism is a part of an ecological system). To understand the BEHAVIOR of an open system requires that an investigator understand the BEHAVIORS of the component parts of the system (in interaction) and the ways in which the system interacts with its environment (of which it is a part). This is why investigators must be familiar with disciplines of levels of complexity above as well as below that of the specific scientific discipline in which they specialize (see Table 3-2).

There are numerous implications of the concept of a system for the psychobiological foundations of behavior therapy. First, the concept of emergence allows an understanding of how biological processes can interact with each other and create functional systems of behavior. For example, as Luria (1973) explains, the function of respiration and its behavior at the level of an organism (breathing) involves a complex interaction of various biological parts , including the lungs, the diaphragm, the stretch receptors and chemoreceptors, portions of the nervous system (e.g., the "respiratory" centers in the base of the brain), and so forth. Breathing is not determined solely by the lungs, the blood, the chemoreceptors, or the lower brain nuclei involved in automatic, homeostatic breathing. Rather, breathing emerges out of the interaction of these various components. If any component of this functional system is disrupted, by any means, the system will fail to behave properly. The system will become "disregulated" (Schwartz, 1977, 1978, 1979); its behavior will appear "disordered," and the disorder may be labeled medically as a "disease."

Breathing is an excellent model system for illustrating basic tenets of systems theory. In fact, breathing turns out to be an excellent model system for teaching clients about the relationship between behavior and physiology from the systems point of view. Every bit of behavior (at the level of an organism) involves the use of energy, which directly or indirectly affects the respiratory system. Exercise and emotion can place heavy demands on an organism's need for energy (e.g., oxygen), and therefore on its breathing.

Breathing is the major bodily system that is under both "involuntary" and "voluntary" control. By "involuntary" I mean that the system regulates itself without requiring conscious, intentional control. On the other hand, a person can consciously alter breathing in various ways—for example, by deliberately holding his or her breath, or changing its rate or depth. Having clients attend to their breathing, monitor their breathing, and deliberately change their breathing in order to change their psychophysiological state is a common ingredient of most relaxation therapies. The phenomenon of breathing becomes inherently more interesting and important when viewed from the perspective of systems theory.

Of obvious relevance to behavior therapy are the following questions: How does a person learn to control breathing? Is all of breathing "automatic," or are aspects of breathing altered by learning? Accomplished musicians, athletes, actors, and so forth, typically learn to attend closely to their breathing. They learn to control their breathing and to coordinate their breathing with other aspects of their behavior in order to maximize the likelihood of reaching certain goals. Often, clients do not recognize that their breathing is out of synchrony with other aspects of their behavior. They do not recognize that this dyssynchrony not only is a symptom of "strain," but places additional "stresses" on the body and affects their thinking, emotions, and overt behavior accordingly.

Breathing also illustrates the inherent blurring that exists between something being a system in one sense and a subsystem in another sense. Breathing is not only a "discrete" behavior that can be measured and manipulated, but also a component of many higher-order behaviors (e.g., speaking). It is exquisitely sensitive to stimuli arising inside and outside the body (e. g., the oxygen concentration in a room). Breathing is neither an independent nor dependent system—it is an interdependent system (as are all open systems).

What, then, are the boundaries of the respiratory system? To include the lungs as a part of the respiratory system is obvious. But what about the throat? The nose? How are the minimum components necessary for a functioning respiratory system determined? Should the cortex be included? The cortex clearly affects breathing. But is it necessary to breathing? Removing the cortex does not eliminate involuntary breathing. However, removing the cortex does affect the stability of breathing under certain conditions. There are no easy answers to these questions, and, according to systems theory, this is as it should be. Components are more or less essential to two or more different systems simultaneously. Certain components may be shared by many different systems. For this reason, damage to one component may have a *set* of direct effects on the functioning of many different systems that all share this one component in common.

It follows that controlling certain *components* of the respiratory system must have a specific impact on breathing behavior. For example, slowing the rate of contraction of the diaphragmatic muscles has an obvious impact on the behavior of the whole respiratory system. In turn, all the systems that either include respiration as a subcomponent and/or are dependent upon breathing for their functioning (BEHAVIOR) will also be affected. It follows, therefore, that it is psychobiologically contraindicated to behave in a "Type A" fashion and also to breathe slowly and evenly. These two BEHAVIORS are incompatible. If a person is taught to breathe slowly, he or she will have to talk and walk more slowly in order to maintain this new respiratory pattern.

The BEHAVIOR of breathing, therefore, is a very complex phenomenon. Breathing marches to the beat of many different drummers, and, in turn, has an impact on the BEHAVIOR of many different drummers. I use the metaphor of the drummer also to illustrate that breathing has rhythmic qualities. It turns out that all BEHAVIOR, in all systems, can be viewed as having rhythmic components that occur repeatedly over time. Modern time-series statistics have been used to assess the dynamic relationship underlying interactions between husbands and wives (Gottman, 1979). These same statistics can be applied to any set of BEHAVIORS that occur interactively over time. In fact, a prerequisite for defining a set of parts as comprising a system is that the parts constrain each other, interact with each other, and therefore show orderly sets of relationships over time in a time-series sense.

One implication of this analysis for both psychobiology and behavior therapy is that breathing, as a behavior, should not be viewed as a simple "measure" of some related process. Breathing should not be viewed or be used as a "measure" of exercise, anxiety, speech, atmospheric oxygen saturation, or any other factor. Changes in breathing reflect complex interactions of these processes, and, for many of these processes, breathing is itself a component of the process. This implies that "a breath change is not a breath change is not a breath change," since many different variables can influence the BEHAVIOR of breathing. It follows that this same principle applies to eye movements, assertive behavior, phobic behavior, specific thought patterns, and so forth. From a systems perspective, the concept of a single cause having a single effect is a myth—causes only produce discrete effects *under certain conditions* (i.e., holding other variables constant, or letting them vary randomly, thus averaging out all the complex interactions that are actually occurring in real life). This is not to say that certain variables are not primary to some systems and secondary to others. Rather, the general conclusion is that even so-called primary variables do not have simple one-to-one impacts on the BEHAVIOR of complex living systems.

This level of abstract analysis may seem self-evident, if not trite; yet the deep significance of the analysis is quite profound. The trite conclusion, that everything is more complicated than people think, is certainly a tenet of systems thinking. However, the deep significance of the concept of a system is that the measurement of the effects of a given variable on a system ideally requires that *all* the relevant components in a system be assessed to determine the complete impact of the interaction. Measuring the behavior of only one component of the system gives us *a false picture* of (1) the nature of the intervention; (2) the complete impact of the intervention on the organism; and (3) the complex set of mechanisms that underlie the changes in behavior observed.

COMPLEXITY AND MULTIPLE EFFECTS: THE MEDITATION EXAMPLE

Consider a seemingly "simple" treatment such as meditation. As described in Schwartz *et al.* (1979) using hypertension as a model system, meditation actually involves a complex set of component processes that have an interactive impact on a complex set of psychobiological processes. This interpretation of meditation is an extension of Benson's analysis (1975) of the conditions that elicit the relaxation response.

First, people typically meditate in quiet places. Hence, the environment has been altered. Sources of environmental stress, and therefore the need for people to process stimuli in the environment, have been removed; this removal relaxes numerous psychobiological systems. Second, people typically meditate in a sitting position, with their muscles substantially relaxed. This reduces the need for people to generate overt behavior, and this reduction in turn affects all the psychobiological processes involved in skeletal muscle BEHAVING; for example, energy consumption is markedly reduced while sitting quietly, as compared to standing, walking, "behaving," and so on. Third, people typically meditate on a "mantra"—a pleasant-sounding word—and often the mantra is coupled to the rhythm of breathing. The use of a mantra reduces the spontaneous generation of cognitions and also links people's thinking to their breathing. Finally, people typically meditate by adopting a "passive" attitude. They are instructed not to become engaged with their own spontaneous thoughts (i.e., not to allow their thoughts to trigger related cognitive–affective–overt patterns of behavioral response, with all the inherent psychobiological components involved). Rather, people are told simply to let their thoughts go by, so to speak, and to return their attention both to their mantra and to their breathing. Hence, "meditation" is not a simple technique, and meditation techniques can vary greatly from one another in regard to these and other components.

It follows that the consequences of mediation can involve multiple psychobiological processes. What, then, are the "primary" effects of meditation? Becoming relaxed cognitively? Becoming relaxed somatically? Becoming more responsive to external stimuli upon the stopping of mediation? Regulating one's 24-hour biological rhythms, including sleep–wake cycles? (Typically, people are instructed to meditate twice a day every day, and to do so at similar times—this requires that people better regulate their lives in order to comply with the instructions, and this regulation process may result in people's sleeping better, eating better, etc.) In systems terms, what one defines as primary or secondary effects, main effects or side effects, depend more upon the interests of the *observer* than upon the system being observed.

For the clinician interested in using meditation to lower high blood pressure, for example, the decrease in blood pressure may be viewed as the "main" effect of meditation, whereas changes in cognitive relaxation and in the subjective experience of anxiety may be viewed as "secondary" or "side" effects. Improvement in a person's sleeping (which typically is not assessed in hypertension studies) would at best be considered an unintended "side" effect of meditation. However, for the clinician interested in using meditation to treat insomnia, the improved sleep would be considered the "main" effect of meditation. Waking anxiety levels might be considered a "secondary" effect of the meditation, whereas decreases in a person's blood pressure (which typically is not assessed in insomnia studies) would at best be considered a "side" effect of meditation. The conclusion, therefore, that "one clinician's main effect is another clinician's side effect" turns out to be well recognized in pharmacology (see Schwartz et al., 1979).

To a systems theorist, *all treatments have multiple effects.* Therefore, a true "cost–benefit" analysis of treatment from a systems perspective should require that the functioning (BEHAVIOR) of all the relevant subsystems and their interactions be assessed. Consider the example of hypertension again. It could be argued that a decrease in blood pressure of 10 mm Hg occurring with meditation is not "clinically" significant. However, this conclusion views the decrease in blood pressure as if it occurred in a vacuum (by itself). It is possible, however, that achieving a 10 mm Hg decrease in blood pressure with meditation would make it possible for the physician to reduce the dosage of certain hypertension drugs needed to control the high blood pressure. Reducing the drug dosage might also reduce some of the unpleasant "side" effects of the drugs, thereby increasing compliance. Drug–behavior interactions become a central issue for the systems theorist.

Equally important to a systems theorist is that meditation has an impact on many other processes than just the control of blood pressure. Unlike diuretic drugs (which selectively reduce blood pressure by reducing blood volume), meditation training can have an impact on other psychophysiological processes (symptoms) and thereby increase the general health of a person. The regular practice of meditation may help prevent the development of other stress-related diseases in the future, whereas highly selective drugs (such as diuretics) will have a smaller, more limited spread of effect. The practice of meditation may have a much better cost–benefit ratio when health is examined from a systems view.

From a systems perspective, before conducting basic research or clinical evaluations of presumed treatment effects, it is critical first to consider as broadly and completely as possible the nature of a given treatment and the various component processes it may alter. Investigators would ideally consider various component processes *within* a given level (between subsystems within a given level, such as between various physiological subsystems), as well as *across* different levels (e.g., from behavior to physiology to biochemistry, with one level being an emergent property of the others). This requires that researchers and clinicians become more "wholistic" and view their clients in a biobehavioral framework. Such a perspective encourages researchers and clinicians to look for interactions continually, either between specific treatments (within and/or across levels), and/or between specific treatments and specific clients. As I have mentioned in the introduction, interactions between treatments can be complementary or antagonistic, and their interactions may vary as a function of specific personal variables (e.g., the type of psychological and/or physical disorder; the specific personality; the person's styles of health behavior, such as diet; etc.).

SYSTEMS THEORY AND DIFFERENTIAL DIAGNOSIS: THE FACIAL PAIN–INSOMNIA–HYPERTENSION EXAMPLE

The systems perspective has far-reaching implications for differential diagnosis. Ideally, differential diagnosis should be the hallmark of responsible clinical care. Consider the following example. One person goes to his or her dentist complaining of serious pain in the jaw region (possibly indicative of a temporomandibular joint dysfunction). It turns out that the person is also not sleeping well and has high blood pressure, but these "symptoms" are viewed as secondary both by the person and the dentist, and a mouth appliance is prescribed by the dentist. Another person goes to a psychologist complaining that he or she is not sleeping well. It turns out that this person also has facial pain and has high blood pressure, but these "symptoms" are viewed as secondary by both the person and the psychologist, and relaxation training plus stimulus control is initiated by the psychologist. Finally, yet another person goes to an internist complaining that he or she has high blood pressure (as measured by a nurse in his or her factory). It turns out that this person also has facial pain and is not sleeping well, but these "symptoms" are viewed as secondary by both the person and the physician, and antihypertensive medication plus exercise is prescribed by the physician.

Clearly, these three people could just as well have been one person with multiple "symptoms." Unfortunately, strict adherence to a specialty perspective (rather than a systems perspective) by the people and/or the professionals leads each person to be dissected as if he or she consisted of totally independent parts, each diagnosable and treatable as if they were completely separate entities. Systems theory leads to a view of the whole person as a set of interacting subsystems operating within and across different levels. Systems-oriented therapists, be they specialists in dentistry, behavioral psychology, or medicine, would ideally adopt a common, *biopsychosocial* perspective for diagnosing, and thereby for conceptualizing the best course of treatment (Leigh & Reiser, 1980).

The specific implications of this perspective for behavior therapy should be self-evident. For instance, in the above example, relaxation training could have multiple effects on the person for whom it has been prescribed, reducing his or her jaw tension, improving his or her sleep, and lowering his or her blood pressure, all relatively simultaneously. Thus, a "single" treatment could have multiple effects and therefore multiple ramifications for health. On the other hand, even "muscle relaxation is not muscle relaxation is not muscle relaxation." Jaw pain will be better aided by relaxing the muscles specifically in the jaws, while the lowering of blood pressure may be better aided by relaxing the muscles in the arms and legs. Muscle relaxation for insomnia may be useful primarily for those persons suffering chronic muscle tension prior to going to sleep.

Note that, from a systems perspective, relaxation training is often a symptomatic treatment. For example, if a person is chronically tensing his or her jaw because he or she handles conflict situations poorly, then the direct training of jaw relaxation (if it is effective) will remove one of the "side" effects (jaw pain) involved in not handling conflict situations effectively, rather than directly correcting the problem of conflict resolution per se.

Note, too, that another person could have all of the symptoms listed above and yet could find that relaxation training was of little use in reducing any of the symptoms. The jaw pain might be primarily mediated by faulty jaw position due to misaligned teeth. The insomia might be due primarily to excessive coffee consumption, while the high blood pressure might be due to an interaction of high salt levels and genetic predisposition to sodium-sensitive hypertension. Even for this person, however, all the problems could still relate to a *common* factor—in this case, to faulty *health behavior* involving the general use of the mouth (failure to brush teeth, get braces, or alter dietary habits). These problems with health behavior might be corrected by education and behavior therapy in combination with some physical intervention (e.g., restorative dentistry). To round out this already complex picture, the person's poor health behavior involving his or her mouth region might have stemmed from early anxiety that led the person to become skeletally tense *and* have poor health behavior (including diet). For such a person, a combination of relaxation training, education in health behavior, behavior therapy, and restorative dentistry might be indicated.

A systems-oriented, consultation–liaison psychiatrist might add another dimension to the above example. This professional might notice that the person was actually depressed but was avoiding recognizing (e.g., was denying) that he or she was depressed. The depression could have various causes, including poor self-concept and/or specific life stresses, coupled with a genetic predisposition to respond to life crises with depression. Adding depression to the picture might suggest the possibility that the jaw pain, insomnia, and high blood pressure were all different manifestations of a general depression syndrome, rather than of a general syndrome of somatic anxiety and/or a general syndrome of health behavior. The psychiatrist might therefore prescribe antidepressant medication plus psychotherapy. The lifting of the depression might be accompanied by the simultaneous decrease in other "secondary" symptoms, such as jaw pain, insomnia, and hypertension!

Of course, the diagnosis of depression can be viewed from a behavior-therapy perspective (Beck, Rush, Shaw, & Emery, 1979), and various cognitive–behavioral approaches to therapy can be considered, with or without the combination of antidepressant medication, diet modification, and other factors. The important point here is not to imply that the perspective of one specialty is in general more important than another. Rather, the significant point here is that professionals in different specialties tend to focus their attention at different levels (see Table 3-2), whereas responsible health care requires that all their skills somehow be integrated by a common perspective.

Leigh and Reiser (1980) have proposed that all health professionals should utilize a general Patient Evaluation Grid (PEG) to help promote a biopsychosocial framework for diagnosis. As shown in Table 3-3, the biological, psychological, and social levels are considered by PEG in terms of present status, immediate past, and long-term biopsychosocial developmental history. Leigh and Reiser imply that to arrive at a *complete* diagnosis, a professional must extend behavioral assessment from a behavior-therapy perspective to the biological and social levels and perform a more comprehensive BEHAVIORAL assessment (using the systems language adopted in this chapter). Since behavior therapists typically have little training in biology and have relatively little training in social psychology and sociology, adop-

TABLE 3-3. Patient Evaluation Grid (PEG): Organization of Relevant Information

DIMENSIONS	CONTEXTS		
	CURRENT (CURRENT STATES)	RECENT (RECENT EVENTS AND CHANGES)	BACKGROUND (CULTURE, TRAITS, CONSTITUTION)
Biological	Symptoms Physical examination Vital signs Status of related organs Medications Disease	Age Recent bodily changes Injuries, operations Disease Drugs	Heredity Early nutrition Constitution Predisposition Early disease
Personal	Chief complaint Mental status Expectations about illness and treatment	Recent illness, occurrence of symptoms Personality change Mood, thinking, behavior Adaptation, defenses	Developmental factors Early experience Personality type Attitude to illness
Environmental	Immediate physical and interpersonal environment Supportive figure, next of kin Effect of seeking help	Recent physical and interpersonal environment Life changes Family, work, others Contact with ill persons Contact with doctor or hospital	Early physical environment Cultural and family environment Early relations Cultural sick-role expectation

Note. "Biological dimension" refers to the components of the patient, such as the organ systems, tissue, and chemical composition. "Personal dimension" refers to attributes of the whole person, including the psychological and behavioral aspects. This includes personal habits such as smoking and drinking. "Environmental dimension" refers to the psychosocial and physical environments surrounding the patient. (From Leigh & Reiser, 1980.)

ting a systems perspective requires not only that therapists use more caution in arriving at a diagnosis, but also that they develop collaborative arrangements with professionals trained in the other levels to help make comprehensive differential diagnosis. Of course, physicians typically have little training in behavioral psychology and relatively little training in social psychology and sociology, so they too need to be more cautious in making differential diagnosis and should seek appropriate collaboration with professionals trained in those levels. I believe that clients who fail to respond to relatively effective behavioral therapies often do so because of incomplete (and, therefore, faulty) diagnosis of their total status and problems.

EMERGENCE RECONSIDERED:
THE DEPRESSION EXAMPLE

Systems theory does more than illustrate the need to consider the biological, psychological, and social levels in order to make appropriate diagnoses and provide appropriate treatment. As mentioned previously, systems theory shows how subcomponents combine and interact to produce new and more complex systems that have unique properties (BEHAVIORS). This brings me back to the primary concern of this chapter—the relationship between biological processes and behavioral processes in behavior therapy. The concept of "emergent property" is profound precisely because it proposes that all behavioral treatments involve modulations and/or modifications in underlying psychobiological processes. By definition, behavioral therapies operate at a higher level (in emergent terms) than biological treatments do. However, behavioral therapies are only effective to the extent that they modulate and/or modify a person's underlying psychobiological state. Most physicians and psychologists alike tend to think about biological and psychological therapies as if each operated by different laws and represented essentially independent interventions. Systems theory changes this perspective in a radical way.

For example, if a person reports being depressed as a result of the death of a loved one, it is appropriate to conclude that the person is probably (1) having depressed thoughts; (2) having an imbalance of neurotransmitters in his or her brain; and (3) showing alterations in the chemistry of his or her immune system. It follows that a professional could conceivably correct the immune imbalance by chemical intervention acting at the periphery, or could possibly correct both the neurotransmitter imbalance in the brain and the immune balance at the periphery by various antidepressant drugs. However, according to systems theory, the professional could conceivably correct both the neurotransmitters and the immune system by helping the person to mourn the death and to redirect his or her thoughts from less negative to more positive images. In fact, one way to relieve all of these psychological and biological problems would be to help the person find someone else with whom to be in love!

From a systems perspective, the more researchers and clinicians learn about the underlying *biological* processes involved in learning, thinking, and emotion, the better justification they have for employing *psychological* interventions to alter psychobiological processes. In other words, biology is providing a foundation for the use of psychological and social interventions in specific situations. The classic reductionistic logic that "if a problem can be described biologically, then the treatment should be given directly at the biological level" is modified by systems theory in a novel and far-reaching manner.

As the connection between biology and behavior is made more strongly (from a level–emergent perspective), the distinction between medical versus nonmedical therapies begins to blur in terms of its ultimate effects. If psychological treatments can have psychobiological consequences that impinge on biological health, then psychological treatments are of medical importance and potentially become "medical" treatments. The legal and ethical implications of this paradigm shift have yet to be grasped by the various professions involved. We are just beginning to see the tip of the iceberg on this issue, and the ramifications should be great indeed for the training and licensing of future health professionals. A major challenge for the evolving interdisciplinary field of behavioral medicine is to provide a framework and structure for teaching future clinicans to have, in Neal Miller's terms, "two skills in one skull" (see Schwartz & Weiss, 1978a). These future clinicians should be better able to work effectively and responsibly at the biological, psychological, and social levels of health and illness.

SELF-REGULATION AND DISREGULATION: THE REPRESSION–CEREBRAL DISCONNECTION EXAMPLE

The concept of self-regulation is fundamental to behavior therapy; not surprisingly, it is also fundamental to living systems theory. J. G. Miller (1978) describes the various feedback mechanisms by which a system can regulate itself to support its autonomy as a system, and therefore to maintain its health. At the level of organs, it becomes possible and meaningful to view the brain as a "health care system" (Schwartz, 1979). The brain is designed biologically to detect strain (e. g., injury) in peripheral organs and to regulate itself (i.e., its BEHAVIOR) to maintain the health of the organ and the organism as a whole. For minor degrees of strain, intraorganism self-regulation may be all that is needed; for more serious degrees of strain, however, appropriate self-regulation requires crossing levels so as to seek the assistance of groups (and higher levels) to reduce the strain (e.g., going to a hospital to have the damaged organ repaired).

If the brain fails to detect strain in the peripheral organs, and/or fails to adjust itself accordingly, it will fail to act as a health care system for the body. I have called the failure to receive and appropriately respond to negative feedback "disregulation" (Schwartz, 1977, 1979). It follows that disregulation can promote disorder and disease. There are many reasons why the brain may fail to register peripheral feedback appropriately. For example, a person may find it necessary to remain in a highly stressful situation, despite negative feedback from his or her body; for example, consider the student who must fight against fatigue and anxiety in order to study for three final exams given in a single day. In other cases, psychological defense mechanisms, such as repression, may be employed to block awareness of peripheral feedback. Repressors can learn to block symptoms of anxiety and even pain from awareness. As a result of not attending to these important feedback cues, a repressor may remain in the stressful situation, placing continued strain on his or her body instead of engaging in more adaptive, health-promoting behavior.

My colleagues' and my recent research on the psychophysiology of repression is consistent with this hypothesis. Subjects who reported low anxiety on a paper-and-pencil scale tapping anxiety, but also scored high on a second scale tapping defensiveness (these high scorers were defined as "repressors"), showed autonomic and behavioral responses to a moderately stressful laboratory situation that were equal to if not greater in magnitude than responses of subjects reporting high anxiety! Only subjects who reported low anxiety and also scored low on the scale tapping defensiveness (these subjects were defined as "true low-anxious") showed appropriate moderate levels of autonomic and behavioral responding to the laboratory stressor (Weinberger, Schwartz, & Davidson, 1979).

My colleagues and I are currently examining the hypothesis that people who "think that things are positive, when the converse is actually the case" may be engaged (at a neuropsychological level) in disconnecting the left hemisphere (which appears in right-handed subjects to be associated with verbal processes and positive emotions) functionally from the right hemisphere (which appears in right-handed subjects to be associated with spatial processes and negative emotions—e.g., Ahern & Schwartz, 1979). The psychological defense mechanism of disattention may involve (1) a relative neuropsychological disconnection between the left and right hemispheres, promoting (2) disregulation in all the psychobiological processes normally kept in balance by the interaction of the two hemispheres, resulting in (3) disordered BEHAVIOR (at subjective, behavioral, and physiological levels), which (4) would be labeled medically as disease. Schwartz and Schwaab (1982) have found evidence linking repression, cerebral disconnection, and heart rate disregulation (the latter assessed as increased beat-to-beat heart rate variability in response to stress, which is an indirect measure of a breakdown in the normal, rhythmic heart rate pattern).

It is possible that correcting this sort of psychobiological disregulation will have consequences at various social, psychological, and biological levels. We have hypothesized that self-attention, when the feedback is interpreted appropriately, can reestablish essential neuropsychological connections, thereby promoting self-regulatory (including homeostatic) BEHAVIOR. This will be observed as increased "order" in the BEHAVIOR, which we may label as health or "ease." Self-attention can be increased by means of self-monitoring, with appropriate instructions as to how to process the enhanced feedback. Concepts like "self-awareness," "insight," and so forth, may be translated into enhanced psychobiological self-regulation (e.g., see Schwartz, 1979).

SOCIAL DISREGUALTION: A NEGATIVE SIDE EFFECT OF SUCCESSFUL SYMPTOMATIC TREATMENT?

Combining the concept of "disregulation" with the concept of "levels" improves our ability to evaluate some of the unintended negative side effects of various biological and behavioral interventions. We can consider the effects that direct treatment of symptoms expressed in a subpart of a system has on the stability of the larger system as a whole. Disregulation theory predicts that if stress from a higher level is causing strain at a lower level, then treating the lower-level strain directly without regard for the higher-level causes of strain can have potential disregulatory effects on the larger system (Schwartz, 1977, 1979).

A disturbing implication of this theory is the hypothesis that modern society, in its quest to develop behavioral and biomedical procedures for directly repairing the body and/or reducing the symptoms of distress, is inadvertently disconnecting human beings from the larger living system of which they are a part, and therefore disregulating the larger system. To the extent that certain physical symptoms represent lower-level strain (feedback) caused by higher-level psychological and social stress, then treating the symptoms at the level of organs (rather than treating the causes at the levels of groups, organizations, nations, or "beyond nations") will further lead the larger system to become disregulated and go out of control.

It is ironic that even research on biofeedback does not necessarily address this fundamental health issue. I have proposed that when biofeedback is used as a "nonpharmacologic pill"—a means of reducing symptoms at the individual level to encourage the person merely to cope with higher-level stresses, rather than to encourage the person actively to reduce these stresses—it may contribute to short-term personal health of the organism at the expense of longer-term social as well as personal health (Schwartz, 1977, 1979). It is becoming increasingly apparent that it is essential to consider the potential disregulatory "side effects" of "successful" behavioral and biomedical treatments.

For example, teaching people how to divert their attention (via meditation) and/or how to take pain killers to reduce pain is self-regulatory, at the level of the organism, whereas at higher social levels, the effects of these interventions may potentially be disregulatory. For example, consider the impact of psychological and biological pain killers on the promotion of violence and the production of physical injuries in competitive sports. Or, teaching people how to assert themselves and seek personal satisfaction is self-regulatory, at the level of the organism, whereas at higher social levels the effects of these interventions may be disregulatory. For instance, consider what the large-scale impact of certain assertiveness-training courses might be on the long-term stability of marriages, families, and friendships. In fact, it is possible to argue that the oversimplistic, wholesale recommendation that people should, for example, jog to improve their physical health and reduce their feelings of anxiety may have certain unintended, disregulatory consequences—people, so to speak, may run away from their problems of living, rather than face them head on.

This is a very controversial issue, and I cannot do justice to it here. I raise the issue of social disregulation not to suggest that pain killers or relaxation training or assertiveness training are necessarily always disregulatory, but rather to suggest that symptomatic treatments can potentially have unintended disregulatory side effects that should be considered as part of the cost–benefit analysis of deciding to employ them. Systems theory can help investigators to navigate across the various levels, from chemical to biological to psychological to social, so as to evaluate self-regulatory and disregulatory processes more comprehensively.

SUMMARY AND CONCLUSIONS: THE SHIFT
FROM BEHAVIOR TO "BEHAVIOR" THERAPY

This chapter has presented a few fundamental tenets of systems theory and has considered some of the implications of these principles for the integration of psychobiology and behavior therapy. It has been proposed that there is a curious and potentially important historical parallel between the development of behavioral psychology and therapy, and the development of BEHAVIORAL science and systems theory. I have considered the basic definition of a system, and I have also pursued some of the ramifications of this definition for conceptualizing what is behavior and what is biology (e.g., when is an eye movement a behavior vs. a physiological change vs. a manifestation of a neurochemical reaction?). The ways in which thinking about biology in BEHAVIORAL terms can lead therapist and client alike to view health in a more synthetic and interdependent manner have also been considered.

The interrelated concepts of levels and emergent property have been discussed, considered, and some of their implications for biopsychosocial diagnosis and treatment have been explored. It has been illustrated that thinking in systems terms does not reduce behavioral therapy to biological therapy (with the goal of replacing the former with the latter). Rather, from a systems perspective, it has been suggested that biology is actually providing a rationale for the importance of psychological and social interventions in the promotion of biopsychosocial health. This includes redefining what is meant by "primary" versus "secondary" effects, as well as the ways in which cost–benefit ratios for different therapies having different sets of effects in different individuals are computed. In this context, I have discussed the concept of interaction and the ways in which different treatments at different levels may interact in complementary or antagonistic ways.

The concept of self-regulation has been briefly described in systems terms and applied to the concept of the brain's BEHAVING as a health care system. The potential consequences of disregulating (by psychological or biological means) a self-regulating system, and the ways in which this disregulation can potentially promote disorder, have been considered. I have included in this discussion the controversial consideration of the potential social disregulatory side effects of successful behavioral or biomedical treatments aimed primarily at symptom removal.

This chapter has not reviewed the psychophysiological research literature on behavior therapy per se, nor has it evaluated the clinical impact of various procedures such as biofeedback, relaxation, cognitive-behavior therapy, and so forth, on psychophysiological disorders. This chapter has not reviewed the neuroendocrinology of emotion and stress. It also has not developed many other important principles in systems theory, such as stress–strain relationships and the concept of multicausation. Finally, this chapter has not developed in any detail the ways in which systems theory can be used with clients to promote a new cognitive view of themselves and their environment.

However, what this chapter has done, I hope, is to alert the reader to the potential importance of systems theory, not only for understanding future developments in psychobiology and behavior therapy, but also for understanding the emerging field of behavioral medicine more broadly. In his superb introduction to systems theory, DeRosnay (1979) has described systems theory as a "new scientific world view." If this chapter has increased the reader's awareness of the emergence of the concepts of BEHAVIOR therapy and BEHAVIORAL assessment as they relate to more traditional behavior therapy and behavioral assessment, then it has achieved its goal.

REFERENCES

Ahern, G. L., & Schwartz, G. E. Differential lateralization for positive versus negative emotion. *Neuropsychologia,* 1979, *17,* 693–697.

Beck, A. T., Rush, A. J., Shaw, B. F., & Emery, G. *Cognitive therapy of depression.* New York: Guilford, 1979.

Benson, H. *The relaxation response.* New York: William Morrow, 1975.

DeRosnay, J. *The macroscope.* New York: Harper & Row, 1979.

Gottman, J. *Marital interaction: Experimental investigations.* New York: Academic Press, 1979.

Kuhn, T. S. *The structure of scientific revolutions.* Chicago: University of Chicago Press, 1962.

Lang, P. A bio-informational theory of emotional imagery. *Psychophysiology,* 1979, *16,* 495–512.

Leigh, H., & Reiser, M. *The patient: Biological, psychological, and social dimensions of medical practice.* New York: Plenum, 1980.

Luria, A. R. *The working brain.* New York: Basic Books, 1973.

Miller, J. G. *Living systems.* New York: McGraw-Hill, 1978.

Powers, W. T. *Behavior: The control of perception.* Chicago: Aldine, 1973.

Schwartz, G. E. Psychosomatic disorders and biofeedback: A psychobiological model of disregulation. In J. D. Maser & M. E. P. Seligman (Eds.), *Psychopathology: Experimental models.* San Francisco: W. H. Freeman, 1977.

Schwartz, G. E. Psychobiological foundations of psychotherapy and behavior change. In S. L. Garfield & A. E. Bergin (Eds.), *Handbook of psychotherapy and behavior change* (2nd ed.). New York: Wiley, 1978.

Schwartz, G. E. The brain as a health care system. In G. Stone, N. Adler, & F. Cohen (Eds.), *Health psychology.* San Francisco: Jossey-Bass, 1979.

Schwartz, G. E. Behavioral medicine and systems theory: A new synthesis. *National Forum,* Winter 1980, pp. 25–30.

Schwartz, G. E., & Schwaab, M. *Lateral eye movements and cardiovascular disregulation in repressors.* Manuscript in preparation, 1982.

Schwartz, G. E., Shapiro, A. P., Redmond, D. P., Ferguson, D. C. E., Ragland, D. R., & Weiss, S. M. Behavioral medicine approaches to hypertension: An integrative analysis of theory and research. *Journal of Behavioral Medicine,* 1979, *2,* 311–363.

Schwartz, G. E., & Weiss, S. M. Yale conference on behavioral medicine: A proposed definition and statement of goals. *Journal of Behavioral Medicine,* 1978, *1,* 3–12. (a)

Schwartz, G. E., & Weiss, S. M. Behavioral medicine revisited: An amended definition. *Journal of Behavioral Medicine,* 1978, *1,* 249–251. (b)

Skinner, B. F. *Science and human behavior.* New York: Macmillan, 1954.

von Bertalanffy, L. *General systems theory.* New York: George Brazillier, 1968.

Weinberger, D. A., Schwartz, G. E., & Davidson, R. J. Low anxious, high anxious, and repressive coping styles: Psychometric patterns and behavioral and physiological responses to stress. *Journal of Abnormal Psychology,* 1979, *88,* 369–380.

4

COGNITIVE AND SOCIAL
PROCESSES IN PERSONALITY

NANCY CANTOR
Department of Psychology
Princeton University

JOHN F. KIHLSTROM
Department of Psychology
University of Wisconsin

The field of personality may be defined as that subdiscipline of psychology concerned with the distinctive patterns of thought, behavior, and experience that characterize the individual's unique adjustment to his or her life situation. This means, first and foremost, that personality theory must be general psychological theory; here knowledge of physiological, cognitive, social, and developmental processes is synthesized into a comprehensive view of individual behavior and experience, as people attempt to understand, respond to, and change the physical and social world in which they live. There was a time when the domain of personality was defined by and restricted to the study of individual differences. However, at present the field has broadened to include a number of general processes relevant to interpersonal behavior, so that it is especially difficult to draw sharp distinctions between the domain of personality and those of cognitive, social, and clinical psychology. The family resemblance is especially strong between personality and clinical psychology. Historically, the field of personality emerged from the psychiatry of 19th-century Paris and Vienna at least as much as it did from the psychometry of 19th-century London. The ranks of major personality theorists have numbered many practicing clinicians, including Freud, Murray, Carl Rogers, and Kelly; more recently, the emergence of behavioral and cognitive–behavioral approaches to treatment has gone hand in hand with the development of a new approach to personality emphasizing cognitive processes and social learning.

There is an important sense, then, in which personality and clinical psychology are related to each other as basic and applied sciences. Just as earlier forms of behavior therapy were closely linked to theory and data emerging from the laboratory study of learning, so it appears that current forms are closely linked to theory and data developed in laboratories studying cognitive and social processes. In this chapter, we seek to paint a broad picture of a cognitive–social approach to personology that seems to us to provide a reasonable scientific basis for clinical practice. After spelling out some of the features of this approach, we trace its historical evolution and compare it with other prominent theoretical views of personality. Then we illustrate some of the salient empirical work associated with this view of personality, particularly emphasizing the processes involved in social cognition and self-perception. Finally, we try to explicate some of the implications of this work for the clinical enterprises of assessment and intervention.

COGNITIVE AND SOCIAL PROCESSES IN PERSONALITY

The central idea of the cognitive–social approach to personality is that people respond flexibly to situations, as they construct them cognitively, and that they act behaviorally to transform situations so that they correspond more closely to their expectations. The proposition is important because it focuses the attention of personologists on the interaction of persons and the social contexts in which they live their lives, rather than on traits, motives, defenses, or "objective" environmental contingencies. It explicitly recognizes both the exquisite sensitivity of human behavior to even subtle features of the situational context, and the extraordinary power of the human cognitive system to give meaning to these contexts. The approach is explicitly dynamic in nature, because it focuses on the cognitive and behavioral transformations that occur as the elements of the social interaction—the person and the situation—assimilate each other and accommodate to each other over the course of time. While the approach is clearly cognitive, giving center stage to the processes by which social information is acquired, organized, and utilized, it seeks to understand the consequences of the mental processes for social interactions, as represented in the overt actions of individuals. While it encompasses the traditional interest of personologists in individual differences, it is centrally concerned with the general processes mediating social cognition and social behavior. Furthermore, by recognizing the importance of the individual's personal constructs in giving idiosyncratic meaning to persons and events, it includes a commitment to idiographic research on the manner in which these general cognitive and behavioral processes are played out in the lives of individual men and women.

For the purposes of explicating the approach further, cognitive–social personology may be divided into four subareas: structure (the elements of personality); dynamics (the ways in which structural elements interact with each other and with external factors); development (the ways in which structural features and dynamic interactions naturally arise); and change (the ways in which structural and dynamic factors can be altered by means of some intervention). These are topics to which any theory of personality must speak if it is to be comprehensive, and social–cognitive personology is no exception. Briefly stated, the structural and dynamic features of personality may be identified with the structural and dynamic features of the cognitive system that processes social information. These structures, then, may be construed as memory structures representing declarative and procedural knowledge (Winograd, 1975; for a general outline of a cognitive system particularly relevant to personality and social psychology, see Hastie & Carlston, 1980). The principles of personality development and change, accordingly, are the principles of social learning by which declarative and procedural knowledge is acquired and altered on the basis of direct and vicarious experience (Bandura, 1977b; Flavell, 1977; Mischel, 1968, 1973b).

STRUCTURE AND DYNAMICS

Following Hastie and Carlston (1980), the structural features of personality may be identified with that subset of the individual's declarative knowledge that is relevant to social interaction, including both conceptual and event memory. The conceptual aspect includes the individual's implicit theories of personality (D. J. Schneider, 1973); categorical knowledge concerning generalized types of people and situations (Cantor & Mischel, 1979a; Cantor, Mischel, & Schwartz, 1982a); descriptions of historical events; and detailed representations of particular other persons (Hastie, Ostrom, Ebbesen, Wyer, Hamilton, & Carlston, 1980), including the self (Markus & Sentis, 1980; Markus & Smith, 1981; T. B. Rogers, 1981). Another aspect, event memory, includes the individual's record of personal experiences, embedded in a context of space and time (Chew & Kihlstrom, 1981; Robinson, 1976). This is the store of knowledge representing people's understanding of themselves, significant others, and the world in which they live—in other words, the knowledge by which they plan their behavior in the social world.

Similarly, the dynamic features of personality may be identified with that subset of the individual's procedural knowledge that guides the organization and transformation of social information and the process of social behavior. These procedures include the interactional skills that individuals employ in the course of social exchange (Athay & Darley, 1981); self-presentational strategies (E. E. Jones & Pittman, 1980); scripts guiding social interaction (Schank

& Abelson, 1977); preferred strategies of focusing on different sources of social information (Cantor, 1981a); the algorithms by which people make attributions of causality and other inferences (E. E. Jones & Davis, 1965; Kelley, 1967, 1972; Nisbett & Ross, 1980) and form global impressions of themselves and others (D. J. Schneider, Hastorf, & Ellsworth, 1979); and the means by which they encode and retrieve social and personal information (Hastie & Carlston, 1980). This procedural knowledge, then, represents the rules by which individuals supply missing information, make predictions about the future, and generate and test plans for responding.

It should be understood that declarative knowledge and procedural knowledge are intimately related, and ultimately extremely difficult to separate, because a great deal of declarative knowledge is not represented in a form that permits direct, immediate access. The world knowledge employed by an individual to understand himself or herself, to understand another person, or to engage in a social interaction must be generated as needed by applying inferential and transformational procedures to available knowledge (e.g., Nisbett & Ross, 1980; D. J. Schneider *et al.,* 1979). Similarly, few personal experiences are fully represented in the memory store; rather, they appear to be reconstructed by inferential problem-solving procedures applied to fragmentary trace material and general world knowledge (e.g., Neisser, 1967, 1976).

DEVELOPMENT AND CHANGE

These structures and processes develop in the same manner as the other declarative and procedural aspects of the cognitive system—that is, they are largely learned. There are clear developmental trends in such social–cognitive tasks as impression formation (Peevers & Secord, 1973), attribution of causality (DeVitto & McArthur, 1978; Karniol, 1978), and self-regulation (Mischel, 1974). While some of these trends must reflect the course of cognitive development generally (Flavell, 1977), so that children become better able to integrate large amounts of information as they mature, the process of social learning must be crucial to mastering the specifics of declarative and procedural knowledge within a sociocultural and familial framework (Bandura, 1977b; Mischel, 1968). A major point of social learning theory underscores the importance of vicarious learning: Human knowledge about self and others, the rules of social interaction, and strategies for self-regulation may be acquired through observation, modeling, and imitation as much as they are through direct experience. In addition, the importance of language acquisition as a medium for acquiring the specific content of social categories, scripts, and causal judgments cannot be overestimated. Similarly, it is obvious that the socialization process, as well as television and other media, permits the culture to communicate normative expectations, possible (and acceptable) interaction strategies, values, and the like.

It follows from this view of personality development that personality change also occurs as a function of direct and vicarious experience. Of course, the processes involved here have been analyzed extensively for decades in the form of clinical behavior therapy. These underscore the importance of the environmental context and learning experience in shaping personal and social behavior. Whether their roots were in the systematic behavior theory of Hull (Wolpe, 1958), the functional behaviorism of Skinner (Ayllon & Azrin, 1968), or some other system, all the early approaches to behavior therapy were anchored to the environment: Maladaptive behaviors represented maladaptive learning. Accordingly, the early behavior therapists sought to teach their clients to make more adaptive, realistic responses to situations that troubled them, as well as to change the clients' environment in order to foster behavioral change. With the emergence of a cognitive viewpoint within experimental psychology, there arose in clinical psychology an almost irresistible trend toward a cognitive–behavioral hybrid whose central tenets were that maladaptive cognitions cause maladaptive behaviors and that behavioral change was mediated by cognitive change (e.g., Mahoney & Arnkoff, 1978; Wilson, 1978). Accordingly, cognitively oriented behavior therapists now seek to arrange learning experiences in which their clients can acquire new ways of perceiving themselves, others, and social situations; new scripts for social interaction; new plans for self-regulation; and other aspects of socially relevant declarative and procedural knowledge. When these change, to the extent that they do change, personality may be said to have changed as well.

COMPARISON WITH OTHER APPROACHES

Along with trait and psychoanalytic approaches, the cognitive–social viewpoint outlined here represents a third major paradigm available to guide the study of personality. The distinction between this theoretical approach and the others may be obvious, but it should be stated briefly for the record. Trait theories represent the structure of personality as a matrix of relationships among ostensible underlying behavioral dispositions; psychoanalysis focuses on the topographical division of the mind into id–ego–superego and conscious–preconscious–subconscious. By contrast, "structure" for the cognitive–social viewpoint refers to the mental structures by which social knowledge is organized. Similarly, personality dynamics are construed by trait theorists in terms of variables of individual differences, which moderate the relations between generalized traits and specific behavioral outcomes; psycho-analysis sees them in terms of the conflict among primitive sexual and aggressive drives, environmental and cultural demands, and internalized defenses. Cognitive–social personology, on the other hand, construes "dynamics" in terms of the mental processes by which social information is acquired, organized, retrieved, and translated into behavior.

Trait theorists characteristically pay little attention to development, except (among some) for an emphasis on the heritability of personality traits; psychoanalysts, for their part, emphasize an inexorable sequence of crises and stages. By contrast, cognitive–social personology construes personality as something that is learned, shaped by particular features of the sociocultural context. Finally, trait theories emphasize the relative stability of personality once it has been established; psychoanalysts are pessimistic about the possibility of doing anything more than coping more effectively with biological and cultural inevitables. Optimism and meliorism are the watchwords of cognitive–social personology, as it affirms that individuals can come to see themselves and their social worlds in new ways, change their environments, and so lead new lives.

THE EVOLUTION OF MODERN PERSONOLOGY

The cognitive–social, process-oriented view of personality outlined above has emerged as the latest step in a historical progression of personality theories, each of which arose in response to specific theoretical and empirical pressures.

FROM TYPES TO TRAITS

According to Greek medicine, as defined and practiced by Hippocrates and Galen, one of four biological substances ("humors") predominated in each individual, leaving him or her with a characteristic temperament: sanguine, melancholic, choleric, or phlegmatic. In his *Anthropology* of 1798, Kant construed these types as pigeonholes into which people could be sorted. There was no possibility of partial expression or combinations of types, and therein lies the problem. Typological approaches to personality have great intuitive appeal and are rewarding from a literary standpoint, because their character portraits seem to capture the gist of many of the people with whom the average person comes into contact on a daily basis. From a scientific point of view, however, they are intrinsically unsatisfying. Any attempt to pigeon-hole people must fail because it is too simplified; some people are more representative of a particular type than others are, and some people seem to present a combination of features from many types.[1] In order to allow for partial expression and combinations of types, investigators began to describe personality in terms of a person's location in multidimensional space, rather than his or her location in particular discrete categories.

The movement from a categorical to a dimensional conceptualization of individual differences was initiated by Wundt (1903) as an outgrowth of his concern with analyzing the elements of mental life. Wundt's contribution was to transform Kant's categorical-type system into a dimensional-trait system, in which people could be described in terms of the characteristic strength and rate of change of their emotions. This had the obvious benefit of allowing for partial and combined expression, and it gave a feeling of greater accuracy in describing an individual than was possible with the old pigeonholes. The abandonment of categorical types allowed people to be represented more accurately, but it brought with it its own special problem: namely, how many dimensions are needed to accurately describe the individual? This problem was clearly articulated by Allport and Odbert (1936) in their study of "the problem of trait names." They searched through an unabridged dictionary for any term that could be used to distinguish one person from another, turning up a total of 17,953 adjectives, representing relatively stable traits (4504), temporary states of mind or mood (4541), social judgments (5226), and miscellaneous descriptions of physical qualities, talents, and explanations of behavior. Clearly, if the type approach was in danger of being too simple, the trait approach was in danger of being too complex. What was needed was a system for organizing the chaos of descriptive terms, for reducing it to manageable size while keeping it representative. The desired psychometric techniques soon became available with the introduction of correlational methods, especially factor analysis, and these were applied by Cattell, Guilford, Eysenck, and many others.

The psychometric approach yielded a number of benefits to psychology. Most important was a sophisticated body of test theory, as represented by Cronbach and Meehl's work on construct validity (1955) and Campbell and Fiske's analysis of convergent and discriminant validity (1959). It also produced a rich body of statistical techniques for determining the relations among variables, including factor analysis, cluster analysis, and multidimensional scaling. Finally, it led to the development of complex actuarial models

---

1. Of course, other typological schemes have been prominent in 20th-century personology. For example, Kretchmer (1921/1925) construed his three temperaments as discrete categorical types, while allowing for variations in intensity of expression. On the other hand, Jung's types (1921/1971) are not exclusive: All attitudes and functions are present in the individual, with one of each dominating conscious life while the others are repressed to form the "personal unconscious."

for predicting behavior (Wiggins, 1973). However, there were also some negative consequences, principally a preoccupation with determining the exact number of dimensions making up the structure of personality (Eysenck, 1977; Guilford, 1975, 1977). In part, these discrepancies can be attributed to differences in the methods of factor analysis adopted by the investigators involved—for example, the choice of orthogonal over oblique rotation or primary over superordinate factors. But even within a single method of analysis, the number of dimensions depends on the kind of data that are being analyzed: observations of subjects in everyday life situations, self-ratings, or performance on laboratory tests. Thus, after more than 50 years of factor analyses, the structure of personality traits remains obscure and controversial.

One attempted resolution has focused on a single domain of data—the universe of trait terms in English. These attempts have all begun with the Allport–Odbert list and have applied factor analysis or similar techniques to determine the relations among the items (Cattell, 1943a, 1943b, 1945; Goldberg, 1977; Norman, 1963; Wiggins, 1979). Another proposed solution rejects the program of determining a universal structure of personality in favor of finding those traits that are important for understanding a single individual. This *idiographic* as opposed to *nomothetic* approach to traits was best articulated by Allport (1937), who rejected most of the notions of trait theorists without at the same time rejecting the notion of traits. Yet a third proposed solution focuses on narrowly defined dimensions of individual differences. This approach retains the assumptions of trait theory, but abandons interest in determining (idiographically or nomothetically) the structure of personality as a whole. This is the traditional area of personality that is familiar to all of us (Crowne, 1979). It emphasizes the questionnaire as an instrument for collecting information concerning individual differences in generalized behavioral tendencies, and it relates these test scores to nontest behavioral indices of the constructs under consideration. Validation of these individual personality constructs, then, yields formulation of narrow theories pertaining to specific domains of personality.

No matter what form the trait position takes, however—nomothetic or idiographic, multidimensional or unidimensional—it still comes up against some serious problems. First is the difficulty in predicting behavior in specific situations from questionnaire scores. This literature, portions of which have been reviewed by Mischel (1968), typically shows a correlation of approximately + .30 between test and nontest manifestations of a trait (Mischel has named this the "personality coefficient"). The second difficulty has to do with demonstrating behavioral stability across situations. Again, literature reviewed by Mischel (1968) shows that the personality coefficient also applies when correlating behavior in one situation with behavior in another situation. Furthermore, the best evidence for temporal stability comes from studies relying on highly abstract dispositional categories that obscure the flexibility of behavior in concrete situations (Block, 1971, 1977). These two problems, taken together, are generally known as the "consistency issue"; apparently behavior is not as consistent across time and contexts as the trait concept would lead us to expect. A third problem with the psychology of traits is the issue of "realism" versus "idealism." There are reasons to think that much of the structure revealed by factor-analytic studies of personality traits can be attributed to conceptual similarity, as opposed to actual co-occurrences among behaviors—that is, that the structure of personality resides at least as much in the mind of the perceiver as it does in the real world (Mischel, 1968; Passini & Norman, 1966; Schweder & D'Andrade, 1979).

The counterclaim, of course, is that the use of alternative prediction models would yield better results (e.g., Block, 1977; Epstein, 1979; Hogan, DeSoto, & Solano, 1977), or that the structure of personality remains intact when cognitive factors biasing self-reports and observer ratings are eliminated (Block, 1965; Block, Weiss, & Thorne, 1979). While there is certainly merit in these positions, from our point of view the empirical findings call for a different perspective on the person, rather than an ever-more-refined methodology based on the traditional view. This view must be dynamically sensitive and must take account of the processes by which individuals make sense of their world, plan and execute responses to it, and so respond flexibly and creatively to their life situations. Such a perspective is explicitly offered by modern interactionism in personology, and specifically by the cognitive-social brand of dynamic interactionism outlined earlier in this chapter.

INTERACTIONISM

The conceptual and empirical challenges to trait views of personality came to a head in the 1950s and 1960s. At this time a major alternative to conceptualizations of personality according to individual differences emerged in the hands of the behaviorist movement in psychology, with Skinner (1953) as its guiding spirit. The behaviorists eschewed unobservable constructs such as traits and motives in favor of overt behavior, and focused on the controlling power of environmental contingencies rather than intrapsychic tendencies. The situationist approach to personality held, first, that behavior reflects the prior learning history of the organism (a tenet that, in itself, was not incompatible with the trait position). In addition to direct experience, the social behaviorists drew attention to the possibilities of vicarious learning of event–event and response–outcome contingencies. They further held that behavior change occurred when there was a change in the supporting environmental contingencies, or—perhaps more broadly—in the situational demands.

There was little if any explicit concern with traditional variables of individual difference, and certainly no concern with documenting the larger structure of personality traits. Moreover, situationist personality theory was primarily concerned with personality change rather than with stability and consistency, and was closely tied to the behavior-therapy movement within clinical psychology.

The situationist movement clearly documented the extraordinary sensitivity of behavior to changes in the environmental context. Somewhat gradually, however, there was a reawakening of explicit interest in person variables within the situationist movement. With the cognitive revolution of the 1960s, interest in person variables took a new turn. Mental constructs were no longer hypothetical, but were clearly reflected in overt behavior. The person reemerged, not in the form of the usual traits, but rather in the form of the cognitive structures and processes that mediate the individual's perception of and response to the environment.

Interactionism was not an entirely new position within personality (Ekehammar, 1974). Its earliest anticipation was in the tradition of field theory within Gestalt psychology, especially the work of Lewin (1935), which held that behavior was a function of both the person and the environment. A little later, Murray (1938) introduced a conceptualization of personality in terms of personal needs and environmental press, and proposed to analyze the individual in terms of the "themas," or combinations of needs and press, which characterized his or her life. Kelly (1955), for his part, proposed that behavior was influenced by the person's construal of events and expectations of outcomes. His "individuality corollary" holds that individuals differ in the way they construe events, while his principle of "constructive alternativism" asserts that the same individual can construe events in different ways. Finally, within cognitive psychology, Neisser (1967) argued that perceptual activity was constructive and that memory was reconstructive. From his point of view, the individual combines fragmentary stimulus or trace information with inferences from preexisting knowledge structures ("schemata") to construct percepts and memories. These schemata are influenced by the individual's expectations and goals, explicitly creating a place for personality within the higher mental processes.

Interactionism provides a framework for thinking about personality, but does not solve the problem of how to go about the task of investigating the subject. In fact, there are a number of approaches within interactionism that, for the moment, need to be kept separate. Among the most prominent of these positions is one modeled on the multidimensional analysis of variance or multivariate correlation; for that reason, it may be labeled "statistical interactionism." One representative of this tradition within contemporary personality research makes use of the "S-R inventory" technique, which poses a number of specific situations to the subject and asks him or her to indicate the strength of various responses within that situation (e.g., Endler & Hunt, 1966). A typical finding is that the interaction terms account for more variance in test scores than the main effects do (e.g., Bowers, 1973; but see Sarason, Smith, & Diener, 1975). A second type of research is concerned with "aptitude-by-treatment" interactions (ATI), and has been chiefly promulgated by Cronbach (1957, 1975), and his associates. They have examined a number of applied situations, such as educational settings and industry, and have found that the outcome of training programs is best when there is an appropriate match between characteristics of the people and those of the situation in which they are learning or working. Yet a third type is represented by D. J. Bem's emphasis (D. J. Bem & Allen, 1974; D. J. Bem & Funder, 1978; D. J. Bem & Lord, 1979) on variables moderating cross-situational consistency. Bem and his colleagues have employed the Q-sort technique in many of their studies to provide a profile of the characteristics of individuals who behave in particular ways in laboratory and real-life situations.

It should be noted that most of these studies are essentially variants on the familiar trait psychology; agreeing that different people act differently in different situations, they seek through more fine-grained personality assessment to determine *just which* kind of person behaves in such and such a way. "Kind" is assessed, as in traditional trait psychology, in terms of relatively broad behavioral dispositions. Moreover, the interactions are construed as unidirectional: Persons and environments are considered to influence behavior jointly, but the possibility of reciprocal, feedback relations among persons, settings, and behaviors—with each influencing the others—is not addressed openly. Other statements have led to the development of a more truly *dynamic* interactionism. Bowers (1973), for example, responding to what he perceived as an extreme situationist position, pointed out that individuals cognitively construct mental representations of the situations they find themselves in, and suggested that they may actually generate or select these situations through their behavior.

Mischel (1973b) has articulated a highly developed cognitive–social learning approach to personality that remains the most explicit statement of "dynamic interactionism" available to date. Mischel begins with the observation that individual behavior varies across situations; this he attributes not to inconsistency, but, rather, to discriminative facility and adaptive flexibility in active coping behavior. According to his analysis, behavior in a given situation is a function of the individual's prior experiences with related situations, the detailed features of the particular situation at hand, and the meaning that the situation has acquired for the individual. Idiosyncratic personal histories yield idiosyncratic meanings, and these meanings are themselves modifiable by cognitive transformations—in short, what is in a person's head determines what he or she will do. Mischel goes on to describe five categories of person variables that mediate the individual's response to situations: competencies in cognitive and behavioral construction; encoding strategies and personal constructs; expectancies about outcomes; the subjective values attached to these expectancies; and plans for self-regulation. In a later essay, Mischel (1977) makes clear that these person variables—which, not coincidentally, are also situational variables—must be assessed from the point of view of the subject, not in terms of the experimenter's own categories.

Cognitive–social personology consists of more than simply a point of view and an attempted integration of concepts in personality with those in cognitive and social psychology. The cognitive–social approach to personality rests on a substantial body of empirical research bearing on the processes involved in social cognition and their reciprocal relations with social behavior. This research is of relatively recent vintage and covers a wide variety of specific topics. For this reason, no attempt is made to cover exhaustively the area, or to take a particularly evaluative stance with respect to the methods, findings, and conclusions of individual studies.

INTERPERSONAL PERCEPTION: TASKS AND PRINCIPLES OF NAIVE PSYCHOLOGY

Central to a dynamic interactionist conception of personality are the cognitive–social determinants of individual behavior: The individual's behavior is heavily influenced by the social situation and the individual's cognitive construction and interpretation of social experience. Consequently, we need to ask about the cognitive underpinnings of interpersonal perception and the perception of social events and situations. In other words, it is necessary to creep into the head of the perceiver–actor and see what the world looks like—how it is constructed, remembered, causally analyzed, and reinterpreted after the fact. In this section, we briefly review the tasks of the social perceiver and the principles that seem to characterize the perceiver's accomplishment of these tasks. The underlying theme connecting these tasks and principles is that social stimuli and social knowledge structures are both extremely rich and complex, and it may not be possible to engage in efficient social interactions without applying some shortcuts in information processing. Social cognition, then, involves achieving a tradeoff between the richness and complexity of belief systems and knowledge on the one hand, and the heuristics and processing shortcuts employed by the cognitive system on the other. Environmental information is assimilated to this cognitive structure at the same time as this structure is accommodated to the environmental input. In the course of this balancing act, the perceiver creates a stable picture of the world in the face of buzzing confusion and crossed signals.

CATEGORIZATION AND CONSTRUCTIVE ALTERNATIVISM

One of the main tasks of the social perceiver–actor is to form abstract generalizations about the social world—that is, to learn from experience about the variety of types of people, events, and situations that he or she is likely to encounter. Individuals come to know the physical world of natural objects and artifacts—birds and trees and chairs and cars—in part by sorting similar objects into categories and assigning names to objects with similar physical and functional properties (Bruner, Goodnow, & Austin, 1956; Markman & Siebert, 1976; Piaget, 1956; Rosch, 1978). So, too, do they come to know their way around the social world by sorting and labeling people, events, and situations on the basis of common features and resemblances (Cantor, 1981b; Cantor & Mischel, 1979a; Cantor, Mischel, & Schwartz, 1982b; Cohen, 1977; Hamilton, 1979). It only requires a brief foray into the dictionary or the "Personals" columns of the *New York Review of Books* for proof of the richness, breadth, and complexity of the social perceiver's implicit personality theories and categorical knowledge of persons and social situations (e.g., Cantor & Mischel, 1979a; Cantor *et al.,* 1982b; Cohen, 1977; Pervin, 1976; Schank & Abelson, 1977).

The social perceiver has an enormous load of cognitive and linguistic baggage with which to structure the social world and communicate about it. A recent content analysis of the features associated with prototypical exemplars of representative categories in the domain of persons (Cantor & Mischel, 1979a), for example, yielded the following distribution[2]: physical appearance or possessions, 7%; socioeconomic status, 2%; trait dispositions, 73%; behaviors, 18%. The social perceiver has rich categories for situations as well as for persons. A similar analysis of features associated with situation prototypes (Cantor *et al.,* 1982b) yielded the following distribution: physical appearance of people in the situation, 8%; physical appearance of the situation, 28%; feelings and traits associated with people in the situation, 19%; behaviors typically observed in the situation, 18%; atmosphere of the situa-

---

2. These percentages reflect the distribution of different kinds of attributes in freely generated consensual prototypes of persons and situations, averaged across several "basic-level" categories. See the studies referred to for details of procedure.

tion, 11%; social roles of people in the situation, 7%; events and places associated with the situation, 9%.

These content analyses indicate that many social categories, while mainly focused around either persons or situations, actually cross these traditional boundaries; person categories can convey a great deal of information about the social contexts in which exemplars are found, while situation categories contain substantial information about the people typically encountered in their exemplars. Moreover, the perceiver also seems to possess compound categorical schemes—information about the typical behavioral scripts associated with situations (Schank & Abelson, 1977) and about the prototypical person for a situation (Cantor, 1981a).

A primary principle characterizing social categorical knowledge is "constructive alternativism" (Kelly, 1955). There are multiple, alternative schemes according to which the same set of people, events, or situations can be categorized. Perhaps more than the common object world, the social world provides for numerous cognitive constructions. Any given individual person, for example, can be "interpreted" in terms of numerous personality, social, gender, and occupational categories; by contrast, there seems to be a limited set of alternative constructions for a car or a chair or a bird. Consequently, in studying social categorization, it is particularly crucial to focus on factors that seem to make certain categories salient and cognitively available for particular people under specified conditions. Recent literature in social cognition has isolated a number of factors that influence the salience of particular social categories and induce the perceiver to interpret social experience in certain ways.

1. *Goal set.* Jeffery and Mischel (1979) and Cohen and Ebbesen (1979) have shown that perceivers use dispositional categories to organize information about a person seen in various episodes when they are under instructions to form an impression of the person; however, they focus on contextual attributes when under instructions to recall the information.

2. *Exposure frequency and perceptual perspective.* Higgins and his colleagues (e.g., Higgins & King, 1981) have demonstrated the effects of exposure frequency on the salience and accessibility of category labels. Moreover, perceptual highlighting of certain people or behaviors cues perceivers to organize their interpretations of the events around those perceptually salient aspects (Taylor & Fiske, 1978).

3. *Individual differences.* Numerous personologists have suggested that people differ in the tendency to focus on external, social cues as opposed to more internal, subjective attitudes and dispositional attributes (e.g., Buss, 1980; Rotter, 1966; Snyder, 1979). For example, Snyder and Cantor (1980) found that individuals low on the Self-Monitoring Scale had richer, more

cognitively available images of themselves with regard to a variety of trait domains, while individuals high on that scale produced richer images when they
considered prototypical exemplars of these trait domains in the abstract,
without reference to themselves.

4. *Self-schemata.* Another factor that seems to influence the salience of
particular social categories is the particular pattern of domains (both traits
and situations) that are important to an individual's own self-image. For example, trait domains that people see as particularly relevant to and representative of their own personalities tend to be very salient in their interpretations
of information about others (e.g., Kuiper & Derry, 1981; Markus & Smith,
1981).

Another aspect of the variability of social categorizations concerns the
level of inclusiveness of the categories chosen to describe people or events or
situations. The same person, for example, could be characterized with a very
inclusive category such as "extravert" or a group of more specific categories
like "car salesman" or "clown." In this regard, work by Eleanor Rosch and
her colleagues (Rosch, 1978) in the domain of artifacts (e.g., tables and cars)
suggests that there are levels of categorization that are particularly salient and
"basic" in object perception—that is, levels that are used most frequently in
naming objects, learned first by children, verified fastest in category membership tasks, and so on. These basic-level categories are characterized by a
rich set of attributes common to all category members that do not overlap a
great deal with the attributes of other related categories.

The notion of a basic-level social category is very appealing as an internal control mechanism to simplify the task of social categorization. A number of researchers recently have argued for the investigation of this idea in the
social domain (e.g., Brown, 1980; Cantor & Mischel, 1979a; Goldberg, 1977;
Wiggins, 1980). For example, Cantor, Smith, French, and Mezzich (1980)
showed that psychiatrists have rich and distinctive feature sets associated
with some diagnostic categories (e.g., schizophrenia, affective disorder); but
that other standard diagnostic categories are either very impoverished (e.g.,
functional psychosis) or very redundant (e.g., chronic undifferentiated and
paranoid schizophrenia). Similarly, Cantor *et al.* (1982b) have considered
the notion of the "basic category" in the domain of everyday social situations. Under most circumstances, the label "party" conveys more information than "social situation," while more specific categories (e.g., "cocktail
party" vs. "fraternity party") may be highly redundant. It may be possible
to demonstrate that certain social categories (those with rich and distinctive
features associated with the category members) are also naturally most
salient in naming and category-verification tasks. If so, the salience of these
basic categories may again simplify the task of ordinary social perception.

Of course, people *can* categorize at either more specific or more inclusive levels as well, and some conditions may foster or require such categorizations. The goal or purpose of the categorization or the expertise of the perceiver in the domain under consideration would certainly also be expected to influence the relative salience of different categories (Brown, 1980; Wiggins, 1980). However, it is interesting to speculate that there exist natural differences in category salience that may serve a cognitive function of economy in the face of the complexity of the task of social categorization.

IMPRESSION FORMATION

In addition to abstracting generalizations about different social categories, the naive perceiver must also form specific impressions and categorizations of particular individuals, events, and situations that he or she encounters. This, of course, is a companion task to the categorization task described above; to "type" and label particular individuals, the lay perceiver uses the salient person categories in his or her cognitive repertoire. Each of these categories has its own set of features typical of members of the category; we refer to this set of features characteristic of category members as the "category prototype" (Rosch, 1978; Smith & Medin, 1979). The prototype features are only characteristic of members; any given category exemplar would not be expected to possess all features represented in the prototype, but, rather, some subset of these features. Therefore, different category members bear only a *family resemblance* to each other (Rosch & Mervis, 1975; Wittgenstein, 1953). Together, the set of features in the prototype captures the meaning of the category and represents the perceiver's general beliefs about what objects, people, or situations of that sort are like.

Earlier, we spoke of the complexity characterizing the categorization task in terms of the number of different social categories into which people, events, and situations might be placed. There is another level of complexity that also makes the impression formation task difficult: People possess very rich prototypes for all of these different social categories, consisting of a large number of attributes, none of which is necessary or sufficient to define the category. Moreover, there is a whole continuum of *prototypicality* among the exemplars of each category, depending on the number of prototypical features that they possess. To complicate matters further, individual behavior is greatly variable across different situations. The varied set of features in social prototypes, the variety of category exemplars, and the variability of human behavior over time and across situations all serve to complicate the task of impression formation. However, each of these factors forms the basis for a cognitive heuristic or processing shortcut that actually simplifies this task:

1. *Similarity matching.* Early views of categorization described it as a simple feature-checking process: to see whether the four-legged object was a chair, a person simply checked each defining feature of the category "chair" and labeled the object so if and only if it possessed all of these singly necessary and jointly sufficient features (Bruner *et al.,* 1956; Vygotsky, 1965). Given the variety of features in category prototypes and the continuum of prototypicality of category members, the notions of defining features and all-or-none categorizations do not apply well to natural categories. Instead, the "revisionist" view describes categorization as a simpler process of "similarity matching," in which the perceiver takes the features of the target item, checks for overlap with the features in the category prototype, and makes a probabilistic estimation of the degree of category membership (Rosch & Mervis, 1975; Tversky, 1977; Tversky & Kahneman, 1974). Such a prototype-matching process has been documented with respect to personality and psychiatric categorizations by Cantor and her colleagues (Cantor, 1978; Cantor *et al.,* 1980).

2. *Context cues.* Similarly, the naive perceiver can use the fact that people generally adapt to situations, follow norms for situationally appropriate behavior, and are thus variable in their behavior across situations to provide cues that facilitate the task of person categorization. For example, categorization of a person observed acting loud and cheery both at a party and in a library is greatly facilitated by the observation of cross-situational consistency in behavior, but is also enhanced by the observation of loud and cheery behavior in a situation—the library—in which such behavior is counternormative: This person is a prototypical extravert. Similarly, the categorization "extravert" is inhibited if the target person is observed acting cheery and loud in the library but quiet and shy at the party (Cantor, 1978; E. E. Jones & Davis, 1965). Contexts, and the match between behaviors and contexts, serve as powerful cues in the similarity-matching task of person categorization.[3]

3. *Order effects.* The categorization task of impression formation is also simplified by primacy and recency effects—the tendency to give differential weight to both early- and late-arriving information about a person or event. The particular conditions under which first impressions assimilate new information to existing expectancies, or under which old impressions are accommodated to newly learned facts, are not entirely understood (E. E. Jones & Goethals, 1972). Generally, it seems that primacy effects and assimilation are the more prevalent trends in the social domain. The perceiver–actor typically receives a rich and variable set of cues about a target person; giving differen-

---

3. As Goffman (1959) pointed out and as most clinicians will attest, a pattern of counternormative, situationally inappropriate behavior might well serve to facilitate the categorization of a person as "weird" if not "crazy."

tial attention and weight to a subset of the information not only reduces the strains on attentional and memory capacity, but probably also allows the perceiver to build a more consistent (though perhaps less faithful) overall picture or impression of the person.

MEMORY AND SCHEMATIC PROCESSING

The perceiver–actor strives not only to draw generalizations about the social world from social experience and categorizations of different individuals, but also to remember facts and events involving specific people and social interactions (Hastie *et al.,* 1980). Cognitive psychologists have devoted considerable effort to documenting a variety of organizational devices and methods used to facilitate the encoding and retrieval of information. Common to all of these methods is the notion that new information is remembered better if it is elaborated in terms of available knowledge or inferences (Bartlett, 1932; Bobrow & Norman, 1975; Hastie, 1980b; Norman & Bobrow, 1979). Schematic processing serves to guide encoding and retrieval, so that extra attention and emphasis is placed on schema-relevant (i.e., both congruent and incongruent) material (Hastie, 1980b). Of course, while this kind of schematic processing saves cognitive effort, it also leads to memory errors, since at retrieval time the perceiver may be prone to remember some schema-consistent features as having been possessed by the particular target that actually were not possessed by it (Cantor & Mischel, 1977, 1979b; Cohen, 1977). Similarly, all of the attention at the time of encoding that is devoted to idiosyncratic, atypical features of the particular stimulus may also result in an over-representation of these features at the time of retrieval (Hastie, 1980a; Hastie & Kumar, 1979).

Snyder and Uranowitz (1978) have dramatically illustrated this schema-based reconstructive process. After reading a story about a woman, half of the subjects were told that she was now a homosexual, while the other half were told that she was a heterosexual. Subsequent to this labeling manipulation, memory for facts presented in the story was biased in the direction of the current schema: Subjects selectively recalled information consistent with their current impression of the target and made errors by falsely claiming to have read schema-consistent items that were not in the story. Similarly, Owens, Bower, and Black (1979) showed than when subjects took the point of view of or empathized with a particular character in a story, they were much more likely to remember that character's successes and skills, as opposed to his or her failures and inabilities. Schematic processing simplifies and facilitates the work of person memory, giving organization and coherence to it, but at the cost of some loss of veridicality. The measure of this cost ultimately depends on the degree of distortion involved, the importance of the selectively ignored or forgotten material, and the sensitivity of the perceiver to new information that should elicit a reevaluation of previous schematic impressions. These factors, in turn, most likely vary tremendously both across particular perceivers and across particular stimulus situations.

ATTRIBUTIONS AND PREDICTIONS: NONNORMATIVE ERRORS

The lay perceiver–actor has frequently been viewed as an intuitive scientist, performing causal analyses of the social world and making predictions about future events and behavior on the basis of past experience (E.E. Jones, Kanouse, Kelley, Nisbett, Valins, & Weiner, 1972). Beginning with the work of Heider (1958) and E. E. Jones and Davis (1965), a number of investigators have studied the way in which people infer causal responsibility from behavior. Heider pointed out that while any behavioral outcome was a function of both personal and environmental forces, people showed an enduring tendency to attribute these outcomes to personal (dispositional) factors. Jones and Davis formalized this statement with their theory of "correspondent inference," in which people assume that actions correspond to intentions, which in turn correspond to dispositions; therefore, actions correspond to dispositions. Correspondence is especially strong, according to the theory, when the behavioral act under consideration deviates from social desirability or is in some other way nonnormative, infrequent, or unexpected. The tendency to downplay the causal role of situational factors in behavior has been thoroughly documented (E. E. Jones, 1979) and is so pervasive that it has come to be known as "the fundamental attribution error" (L. Ross, 1977).

Other theorists have provided extended formal models of the attribution process. The covariation model of Kelley (1967), for example, holds that attribution to internal (personal) or external (situational) causes is a function of three ways in which the actor relates to the target of his or her action: consistency (the degree to which the actor behaves in the same way toward the target across situational contexts); distinctiveness (the degree to which the actor treats other targets in the same manner); and consensus (the degree to which other actors behave in the same way toward the target). This model, of course, requires that the perceiver have available a great deal of information concerning those involved in the interaction. Later, Kelley (1972) proposed a causal-schemata model of attribution, which acknowledges causal inferences to be made under circumstances where the perceiver has only extremely limited information about the interaction. Finally, Weiner and his colleagues (Weiner, Frieze, Kukla, Reed, Rest, & Rosenbaum, 1972) have noted that individuals make attributions to stable or variable causes as well as to internal or external ones; within the domain of achievement motivation, they have provided a model of the ways in which the perceiver uses consistency and consensus information to attribute success and failure to ability, effort, difficulty, and chance. These and other theories, then, provide a set of rules according to which the perceiver may make plausible attributions about the causes of social outcomes.

However, once again, the actual attributions and predictions of the intuitive psychologist are characterized more by deviations from normative principles of inference and decision making than by adherence to the canons of accepted scientific method (Nisbett & Ross, 1980; L. Ross, 1977). Relying on a host of cognitive heuristics and processing shortcuts, the perceiver–actor performs his or her attributional and prediction tasks—specifying the reasons for another's behavior, making predictions about the likely success of a particular job candidate, estimating the co-occurrence of two events, and so on. These tasks are performed efficiently, easily, and with confidence because the perceiver–actor seems to rely on a variety of shortcuts or intuitive principles, a few of which are listed below.

1. *Salience and availability biases.* Causal candidates are frequently evaluated simply on the basis of perceptual salience or the ease with which they come to mind (Tversky & Kahneman, 1974; Taylor & Fiske, 1978).
2. *Fundamental attribution error and false consensus.* People overattribute the causes of another's behavior to internal dispositions, often underemphasizing situational determinants of the behavior (e.g., E. E. Jones, 1979; L. Ross, 1977; L. Ross, Amabile, & Steinmetz, 1977). Similarly, there is a tendency for perople to perceive other people as holding similar opinions to their own concerning events (L. Ross, 1977).
3. *Base-rate fallacy and representativeness.* Predictions about people and social events are often influenced too heavily by the degree of similarity or representativeness of the target person's attributes to a stereotype or prototype and too little by the prior odds of finding such a person in the given population (Nisbett & Ross, 1980).

There is no question that it would be more accurate to seek out all the relevant information, carefully and cautiously weigh all information available (including base rates and anecdotes), correct for the potential unreliability and lack of validity of some sources (e.g., first impressions, test scores), search for all possible behavioral determinants (e.g., situational pressures, less available or less salient information), and the like when making a social judgment. Nevertheless, it is also clear that the lay perceiver's heuristics facilitate social decision making and interpersonal communication. The cost of jumping to conclusions about another's dispositions on the basis of insufficient evidence or faulty judgmental processes will vary as a function of the judgmental context. In an everyday interaction, the cost of making precipitous judgments about others may be relatively small; people will frequently have the chance to correct their impressions, or they may simply leave the judgmental situation. However, again, these costs will increase both as the judgmental consequences for the other person become more severe (e.g., a clinical or legal situation), and as the opportunities for revising opinions or encountering disconfirming evidence lessen.

HYPOTHESIS TESTING AND THEORY REVISION

We have repeatedly indicated that the costs of employing schematic processing strategies and judgmental heuristics depend in part on the willingness or proclivity of the perceiver–actor to test and evaluate his or her theories fairly and to revise impressions in the face of disconfirming evidence. To the degree that constructions and impressions of people, events, and social situations are open to change, it is probably most efficient to make decisions on the basis of schematic shortcuts. The tradeoff in costs and benefits depends heavily on achieving a delicate balance between assimilation (of new information to old theories) and accommodation (of old theories to new information). Unfortunately, the evidence to date (though clearly only a partial picture) suggests that the hypothesis-testing procedures of intuitive scientists are biased toward theory confirmation (Snyder, 1980; Wason & Johnson-Laird, 1972), and that the intuitive scientists themselves have proclivities toward theory conservation (Nisbett & Ross, 1980). For example, Snyder and his colleagues (Snyder & Cantor, 1979; Snyder & Swann, 1978b) have asked subjects to test hypotheses about another person's personality either by choosing questions from a list or by retrieving information from memory. These investigations reveal a persistent preference for gathering and/or retrieving theory-consistent data as opposed to facts that might potentially disconfirm the theory. Not surprisingly, people can provide answers to theory-confirming questions—human behavior and experience is varied enough that even the most prototypical introverts will enjoy themselves at *some* parties—and the theory tester leaves the situation quite confident in the validity of the theory.

This bias in hypothesis testing toward theory confirmation is also complimented by a proclivity for theory conservation in the face of disconfirming evidence. L. Ross and his colleagues (e.g., L. Ross, Lepper, & Hubbard, 1975; L. Ross, Lepper, Strach, & Steinmetz, 1977) have demonstrated that experimentally induced impressions of self and others persist even when the original basis for the impressions has been thoroughly discredited. They explain this reluctance to abandon discredited beliefs by suggesting that, in the process of thinking about the beliefs, subjects marshal other belief-consistent pieces of data (real and imagined); as a result, the discrediting manipulation only serves to harm one weapon in the entire evidentiary stockpile. The validity of this perseverance, of course, depends on the weight of truth in the marshaled data; but ordinary perceiver–actors—not to mention professional scientists—have been known to persist in holding beliefs for which all relevant evidence has been discredited (Nisbett & Ross, 1980). It does appear that human hypothesis-testing and theory-revision procedures are skewed in the direction of assimilation and conservation though the magnitude of the kurtosis varies across contexts, people, and belief domains and has not yet been thoroughly evaluated.

SELF-PERCEPTION: THE NATURE AND FUNCTION OF THE SELF-CONCEPT

Along with the categorization of people, studies of the self-concept are central to the domain of cognitive–social personology. Historically, most speculations concerning the self-concept have argued that the self is a unified concept representing those characteristics of the person that he or she regards as central to his or her personality; on the other side are those who argue that the person has many "selves," depending on the number of social roles in which he or she is engaged and the number of social contexts in which he or she is found (for a review, see Epstein, 1973). More recently, Epstein (1973) has offered a view of the self-concept as a theory about oneself, part of a person's broader (implicit) theory concerning the entire range of his or her experiences. Mancuso and Ceely (1980), on the other hand, have joined others (e.g., Kuiper & Derry, 1981; Markus & Sentis, 1980; Markus & Smith, 1981; T. B. Rogers, 1981) in thinking of the self as a schema or cognitive structure involved in the processing of self-relevant information.

We begin by defining the self-concept in the same manner as any other concept: as a structured set of features and attributes defining a category represented in semantic memory. The problem, then, is to find out just what attributes belong in the self-concept, how that information is organized, and how the self-concept influences social–cognitive processes and social interactions. Research on the nature and function of the self-concept is in its infancy, but it is clear that the self is no longer simply a topic for speculation; its structure can be explored by means of procedures familiar in cognitive psychology, and its consequences for social interaction can be revealed by methods familiar in personality and in social psychology.

CONTENT OF THE SELF-CONCEPT

The most common techniques for assessment of the self-concept have been reactive: The subject is asked to rate himself or herself on a number of dimensions chosen by the investigator. Carl Rogers (e.g., C. R. Rogers & Dymond, 1954) introduced the Q-sort technique to the study of the self-concept, requiring the subject to sort a batch of first-person statements into categories representing levels of self-descriptiveness. Similarly, T. B. Rogers (1981) has employed an adjective list, in which a set of representative trait terms is rated on a scale of self-descriptiveness. In contrast to Carl Rogers's technique, the subject is not forced to conform to a normal distribution of ratings. It is unclear, however, that either method is appropriate for assessing the self-concept. People may be willing to describe themselves in a particular way, even though that is not ordinarily the way they think about themselves. The categories of self-perception may or may not correspond to those represented on the experimenter's protocol. Markus (1977) has introduced a variation on the self-rating technique, in which trait adjectives are rated in terms of both descriptiveness and importance to the self-concept. An adjective is categorized as part of the person's self-schema (self-concept) if it is rated as both extremely self-descriptive and extremely important to the person's self-concept; where these two conditions do not apply, the person is classified as "aschematic" on the dimension in question, meaning that the dimension is not a salient part of his or her self-concept. The addition of the importance rating is an advance in the assessment of the self-concept; in fact, it may be that the importance rating is the crucial one and that the self includes those features that are important to the person, regardless of how self-descriptive they actually are.

A more important consideration, however, is an idiographic one. Whether an investigator chooses adjectives or first-person statements, forces the subject to use a normal distribution of ratings or not, or chooses descriptiveness or importance as the rating dimension, subjects are still forced to employ the investigator's categories in describing themselves. This is a problem because the investigator's categories may not adequately sample the features of the self-concept. The favorite categories for psychologists are trait adjectives; however, we have noted that in describing other persons, people employ a much more diverse set of features, including physical appearance, socioeconomic status, and typical behaviors. So must it be with the categories representing the self-concept. And, of course, even if trait adjectives were predominant features of self-schemata, there would be no guarantee that the subject would be satisfied with the investigator's choice of trait dimensions, or that subject and investigator would impute the same meaning to a trait term.

Investigators such as McGuire (e.g., McGuire & Padawer-Singer, 1976) and R. A. Jones (R. A. Jones, Sensenig, & Haley, 1974) have recently reintroduced a free-response approach to the assessment of the self-concept, based on earlier techniques such as the Who Am I? Test and the Twenty Sentences Test. In the procedure employed by McGuire, the subject is simply asked to respond, orally or in writing, to the probes "Tell me about yourself" and "Describe what you look like"—questions intended to elicit the general and physical self-concepts, respectively. McGuire and Padawer-Singer (1976) administered these two tasks to a group of sixth-grade pupils in a culturally heterogeneous urban school. A content analysis of the resulting self-descriptions yielded the following results: habitual activities, 24%; relationships with significant others, 20%; attitudes, 17%; school status, 15%; demographic information, 12%; self-evaluation, 7%; physical descriptions, 5%; miscellaneous, 1%.

McGuire's method allows subjects to describe themselves in their own terms without being forced into the experimenter's categories, but gives no information about how the self-concept is organized in the individual. Such information, which is likely to be of great value to practicing clinicians, is provided by Pervin's adaptation (1976) of Rosenberg's technique (1976) for studying personal constructs. In a demonstration study, four subjects provided a list of specific situations encountered in their own current lives, and then described the features of the situations and the ways in which they felt and behaved in them; then every situation was rated on every feature, feeling, and behavior. Factor analysis was employed to produce clusters of situations defined by common features, feelings, and behaviors. Interindividual comparisons revealed appreciable commonalities across the subjects: home-family, friends–peers, relaxation–recreation, work, school, and being alone were commonly represented in the individual factor spaces. However, the characteristics defining these factors were quite different from one person to another. Moreover, comparison of the individual descriptor loadings across factors, within subjects, indicated idiosyncratic patterns of those feelings and behaviors that were relatively consistent across situations, as well as those that were fairly unique to particular situations.

STRUCTURE OF THE SELF-CONCEPT

Whatever they are, the contents of the self-concept are most likely represented in a manner similar to that of any other aspect of semantic memory (for reviews, see Anderson, 1976; Smith, 1978). For example, a number of investigators have construed the self in terms of currently popular network models of memory, such as HAM or ACT (Bower & Gilligan, 1979; Mancuso & Ceely,

1980; Markus & Smith, 1981). According to this view, the self is represented as a conceptual node in memory, embedded in an associative network that links it to other generic concepts and specific episodes. The self-concept, then, includes all other nodes to which the self-node is directly and strongly linked; where the associative links are indirect and/or weak, the concept or event lacks self-relevance. Self-reference involves searching the associative network for concepts linked to the self-node. Alternatively, others have argued that the self-concept consists of a hierarchically ordered collection of self-descriptive features, including traits, values, and specific episodic memories (Kuiper & Derry, 1981; T. B. Rogers, 1981). According to this view, the features vary on a dimension of perceived self-descriptiveness, with those features that are most characteristic combining to form the *prototype* of the self; other features, not perceived as self-descriptive, are not represented in the self-prototype. The self-prototype is conceived as a fuzzy set, with no feature being necessary or sufficient. Self-reference, from this point of view, involves comparing the features of a stimulus with features contained in the self-prototype.

The work of McGuire and Pervin suggests that the self-concept may be much less stable and monolithic than most previous analyses have assumed. What is salient in the self-concept may depend on the particular social context in which it is elicited. More important, perhaps, the self-concept may have some situational specificity, so that people see themselves differently depending on the situation they are in. Thus, instead of a monolithic self-concept, represented as a single node in memory or a prototypical set of features, there may be many "contextual selves." This proposal does not preclude the existence of a unified self-concept as well, consisting of features that are consistent across a wide variety of situations, or perhaps of the rules governing the relationships among different contextual selves.

Features of episodic memory are also important aspects of the self-concept, for the self must serve to organize the individual's autobiographical record of personal experience as much as it organizes the person's conceptual knowledge about his or her characteristic features. Unfortunately, autobiographical memory has not yet been intensively studied by psychologists (Neisser, 1978), so that answers to many questions about the encoding, representation, and retrieval of personal experiences must be speculatively generalized from theoretical accounts developed in the domains of verbal learning and person memory. Network models of memory, such as HAM or ACT, can represent both concepts and events as a series of interconnected nodes (Anderson, 1977; Anderson & Hastie, 1974; Hastie, 1980a; Hastie & Kumar, 1979). According to this view, encoding an episode of experience in memory involves forming associations among nodes representing the facts of the event (e.g., subject, object, and action) and the context (e.g., time, place, internal state) in which it occurred. It is the explicit representation of context information that distinguishes episodic (event-related) from semantic (conceptual) memory structures (Tulving, 1972). The episode as a whole is represented by a superordinate node, which may be linked to other conceptually or contextually related episodes. All the episodes, in turn, are linked to the conceptual node representing the self.

SELF-PERCEPTION

There is every reason to suppose that the self-concept is acquired in much the same manner as knowledge about other persons is: It is constructed from direct and vicarious observations of a person's own behavior, the behavior of others toward that person, and the context in which these behaviors occur (D. J. Bem, 1967, 1972; Locksley & Lenauer, 1981). Affirming this unified view of the person does not mean that the self-concept is not special in at least some ways. It is likely to be the richest concept that most people possess, and it may have the strongest emotional valence associated with it; and E. E. Jones and Nisbett (1972) have shown that actors are more likely to make situational attributions concerning their own behavior, while observers strongly attribute the same behavior to trait dispositions. We assume, however, that it is based on the same principles of categorization, impression formation, schematic memory processing, attributional and judgmental heuristics, and hypothesis testing just described. For this reason, it does not seem necessary to go into a great deal of detail on the processes of self-perception; what follows is a small sample of the relevant research.

Earlier, it was suggested that the principles of schematic processing operate in such a way as to favor the encoding of highly informative (unpredicted) features of a person, as well as the retrieval of those that are consistent with an overall impression (Hastie, 1980a; Hastie & Kumar, 1979). Both these processes can be observed with respect to the self-concept. In a series of studies, McGuire and his colleagues (McGuire & McGuire, 1980; McGuire, McGuire, Child, & Fujioka, 1978; McGuire, McGuire, & Winton, 1979; McGuire & Padawer-Singer, 1976) have obtained evidence and support of their "distinctiveness postulate"—namely, that a person notices aspects of himself or herself to the extent that they are infrequent in the social context. For example, schoolchildren who are atypical with respect to age, birthplace, hair and eye color, weight, sex, and handedness (compared to their classmates or family members) are more likely to mention these characteristics in their self-descriptions than their more typical counterparts are. On the other side, Markus (1977) found that individuals who possessed well-developed self-schemata for dependence had better access to memories of specific situations in which they behaved dependently, and vice versa, than did their counterparts who were aschematic on this dimension. Similarly, in a series of self-description tasks, subjects classified as self-schematic on such dimensions as independence–dependence, creativity, masculinity–femininity, and body weight made faster judgments about the self-descriptiveness of relevant trait terms than aschematics did (Markus & Sentis, 1980; Markus & Smith, 1981).

Self-attributions of causality are also made according to the same kinds of rules of thumb, and subject to the same kinds of heuristic biases, as those described for observers' attributions. There is, as clearly documented by E. E. Jones and Nisbett (1972), a tendency for actors to make situational attributions concerning their own behavior, in contrast to the dispositional attributions preferred by observers. As they note, this seems likely to be due more to differences in available data than to differences in the attributional process itself. The observer has only the behavioral event(s) at hand and normative information, which has probably been inferred from biased and unrepresentative samples of other behavior, upon which to base conclusions. Because the actor knows his or her past better than any observer, he or she may possess information about consistency and distinctiveness (Kelley, 1967) that, if known to an observer, would lead the latter to make a situational attribution as well; moreover, it is likely that the actor's attention is focussed more on contextual cues that, again, if noticed by the observer, would lead to a situational attribution. Studies of intrinsic motivation, in which interest in a task can be undermined by rewarding its performance, provide a good example of the operation of one of Kelley's causal schemata (1972) in self-attribution (Lepper & Greene, 1976). In these situations, there are at least two plausible reasons for subjects to perform a task: because they want to do it, and because it is rewarded. Under conditions where the controlling features of the reward are made salient (e.g., by being made contingent on performance level), subjects apparently discount their intrinsic interest in the task (Harackiewicz, 1979).

From time to time, individuals are given the opportunity to test and revise their hypotheses about themselves. In a recent study, Markus (1977) placed subjects classified as schematic or aschematic on the dimension of dependence–independence in a situation where this feature of their self-concept was contradicted. After administration of a putative suggestibility test, subjects for whom independence was part of their self-schema were told that they were highly susceptible to suggestions, while others who viewed themselves as dependent were told that they were highly resistant to social influence; half the aschematics were given each kind of false feedback. The schematics of either type were less likely to endorse the accuracy of the description, and more likely to express frank disagreement or disbelief , than were the aschematics. Moreover, when asked to rate their suggestibility, the schematics were significantly less influenced by the feedback than the aschematics were. Finally, the subjects were asked to rate themselves on a variety of adjectives pertaining to independence and dependence. Compared to self-ratings made at the beginning of the experiment, the schematics showed longer response latencies but more stable ratings than those of the aschematics. Thus the schematics were more likely to consider, but finally to reject, information contrary to their self-concepts. Here, then, may be observed the same sorts of assimilative and conservative tendencies that influence the testing of hypotheses and revising of theories about other persons.

AUTOBIOGRAPHICAL MEMORY

A fair amount of effort is now being devoted to understanding the processes involved in encoding and retrieving episodic memories in general and autobiographical memories in particular (Kihlstrom, 1981). Both encoding and retrieval can be described in terms of the "depth-of-processing" account offered by Craik and his associates (Craik & Lockhart, 1972; Jacoby & Craik, 1979; Lockhart, Craik, & Jacoby, 1976). According to this view, perceptual events can be more or less elaborately processed in the cognitive system at the time of their occurrence; the degree of elaboration depends in part on the task orientation of the subject and in part on the congruity between the event and the cognitive structures brought to bear on it; elaborate processing yields distinctive encodings; and distinctive traces are more memorable. Once an event has been encoded, retrieval depends on the interaction of information supplied by the retrieval cue and that contained in the target memory trace and associated knowledge structures. Early and sufficient overlap between the two kinds of information supports a problem-solving, reconstructive activity until an adequate memorial representation of the event has been formed. In the case of autobiographical memories, remembering involves reconstructing the spatiotemporal and experiential context in which the event originally took place.

From this point of view, a number of factors should combine to produce rich, distinctive, and highly accessible encodings of autobiographical memories. First, autobiographical memories by definition contain unique spatiotemporal context features that must make them distinctive—although, as Tulving (1972) argues, these features may be particularly fragile and prone to decay or interference. Also, many personal experiences are associated with some affective valence that should serve to heighten their distinctiveness; again, however, there is evidence that this valence diminishes over time, negative valence at a faster rate than positive valence (Holmes, 1970, 1974). To the extent that these contextual features are lost or obscured, the episode will be harder to retrieve as a uniquely specified event, and the memory may take on a more generic, semantic quality (Reed, 1979). Furthermore, the central tasks of the perceiver–actor—impression formation, inference, judgment, and causal attribution—must promote extensive processing of personal experiences. Merely a self-referent task orientation, which would seem to be a necessary aspect of having any personal experiences at all, appears to produce more memorable traces than does any other encoding condition studied to date (Keenan & Baillet, 1980; T. B. Rogers, 1981). When perceptual events are incongruent with prior expectations, thus calling for extra attentive effort in order to revise an impression or inference, the events involved will be especially highly memorable (Hastie, 1980a; Hastie & Kumar, 1979). The good encoding of unexpected events of high personal relevance is clearly exemplified by the "flashbulb" memories of the sort that most readers have for the assassination of John F. Kennedy (Brown & Kulik, 1977).

In the past, most research on autobiographical memory has focused on people's earliest recollections from childhood, as collected in clinical interviews (Ansbacher, 1947) or questionnaires (Dudycha & Dudycha, 1941; Kihlstrom & Harackiewicz, in press). Recently, investigators have begun to study the retrieval phase of autobiographical memory with a broader range of targets and more controlled procedures. A particular popular technique, introduced by Crovitz (Crovitz & Quina-Holland, 1976; Crovitz & Schiffman, 1974) and Robinson (1976), involves presenting words as cues for the retrieval of discrete personal experiences related to them. In research by Chew and Kihlstrom (1981), words varying on such dimensions as concreteness, meaningfulness, pleasantness, and self-relevance were employed as cues for memories of events occurring in the recent or remote personal past. Examination of response latencies and the characteristics of the memories recovered in this manner has begun to reveal the interactive process in which the individual extracts relevant semantic and contextual features from the retrieval cue, matches these with the stored contents of memory, and so begins to reconstruct the original experience. Another paradigm has been introduced by Linton's marathon study (1975, 1978) of her own autobiographical memories: Every day for 6 years she recorded a sample of the day's events, along with ratings of their uniqueness, importance, and emotionality; and every month she tested her memory for these events in terms of recognition and temporal ordering. The individual test protocols from Linton's research, like the eyewitness testimony studies of Loftus (e.g., Loftus & Loftus, 1980), clearly underscore Bartlett's (1932) point that memory for experiences in the real world is reconstructive rather than reproductive, and that the final product of the retrieval process is based as much on inference as on fragments of the original memory trace (Jenkins, 1974; Neisser, 1967, 1976; Norman & Bobrow, 1979).

COGNITIVE AND BEHAVIORAL CONSEQUENCES OF SELFHOOD

At this point, investigators are beginning to know something about the content and structure of the self-concept, but we have not discussed the cognitive and behavioral consequences of having one. As already noted, it appears that making a self-referent decision about a stimulus—deciding whether a trait adjective is self-descriptive, for example—facilitates later retrieval of that information (e.g., Kuiper & Rogers, 1979; T. B. Rogers, Kuiper, & Kirker, 1977). This is what would be expected if the self-concept is a richly differentiated aspect of the cognitive system. Moreover, a self-referent orientation during encoding can lead to false recollections of self-relevant information (T. B. Rogers, P. J. Rogers, & Kuiper, 1979)—just as in interpersonal perception, where cognitive economics and the vicissitudes of reconstructive memory can lead to a confusion between the veridical and inferred attributes of a person or event. Moreover, Markus (1977) has shown that having a clear concept of the self in a particular domain leads to shorter response times when rating schema-relevant traits for self-descriptiveness, greater accessibility of schema-relevant behaviors in memory, greater temporal stability in schema-relevant self-descriptions, and more confidence in the prediction of schema-relevant behavior. Most interesting, subjects with self-schemata for independence and dependence were more likely to consider, and finally to resist, information contrary to their self-concept.

Markus and Smith (1981) and Kuiper and Derry (1981) indicate that the contents of the self-concept influence person perception in a variety of ways. Briefly put, the same categories appear to be involved in the perception of self and of others: People ascribe to others traits that they see themselves as possessing, attribute to them more extreme attitudes on issues in which they are personally involved, and believe that the behaviors and opinions of others conform more closely to or diverge more widely from their own than actually is the case. For example, Shrauger and Patterson (1974) gathered free descriptions of acquaintances from subjects, coded them in terms of 57 representative dimensions, and also collected self-ratings on these same traits. For each subject, a subset of categories was classified as salient or nonsalient, according to a joint criterion of frequency and order of output. On the self-rating task, salient categories were rated higher on both self-relevance and self-satisfaction than were nonsalient categories. More recently, research by T. B. Rogers and Kuiper (1981) has found that when rating others, subjects made significantly faster judgments on trait dimensions that they had rated as extremely high or low in self-descriptiveness, compared to their judgments on moderately self-descriptive items. Similarly, Markus and Fong (1981) found that subjects with self-schemata for dependence–independence were more discriminating about the independence of a target person than were aschematics.

These findings are reminiscent of the psychoanalytic concept of projection. However, projective attribution is not restricted to undesirable qualities. Moreover, as Holmes (1968, 1978) has pointed out, the projective attribution of undesirable qualities is as commonly directed to desirable as to undesirable targets, and does not lead to more favorable evaluation of these qualities or any other kind of stress reduction. Apparently, the self-concept provides readily accessible categories against which the perception of social stimuli can be structured, as well as baseline information that serves as an anchor point for various sorts of quantitative judgments.

The apparent relation between the categories involved in the perception of self and perception of others exemplifies a primary feature of social–cognitive processes: their egocentrism. There appears to be an enduring tendency for people to attribute more than is warranted to themselves. Much of the relevant evidence has been summarized by Greenwald (1980), who has argued that the self may be construed as a historian who observes and records the life of the person. The self as historian has certain peculiar properties, however. For example, it appears to be extremely egocentric; self-relevant information is easier to process and dominates perception and memory, and self-generated material is easier to remember than that generated by others. It is also self-aggrandizing; under conditions of a threat to self-esteem, the "reverse Zeigarnik effect" favors the recall of successes as opposed to failures, and even where outcomes were determined entirely by chance or external manipulation, there is a tendency for the person to assert that he or she had control over them. Finally, it is revisionist; it seeks information from memory and the perceptual field that confirms its hypotheses, and it reencodes memories so that they correspond more closely to current attitudes and knowledge. In these respects, Greenwald argues that the ego as historian operates in the same manner as do the official historians of a totalitarian state, such as the ones described by Orwell in *1984*. In the totalitarian state, Orwell argues, these qualities are motivated by considerations of power. As in the case of projective attribution, however, the totalitarian appearance of the ego seems to reflect less on motives and more on the properties of schematic processing and other vicissitudes of cognitive economics. Just as people make attributions about themselves in the same way as they make attributions about others, self-perceptions are subject to the same sorts of biases as perceptions of other people.

Egotism in self-attributional judgments has been repeatedly demonstrated, especially in the domain of ability-linked attributions (Snyder, Stephan, & Rosenfield, 1976, 1978; Weiner *et al.*, 1972). For example, people show a marked tendency to ascribe a success to their own ability and a failure to task difficulty, especially if the task has been ego-involving and important to the subject (e.g., Miller, 1976). Moreover, as M. Ross and Sicoly (1979) have found, subjects are very likely to exaggerate their own contributions to joint enterprises (book chapters, household work, team sports) as compared to those of their collaborators. Similarly, Snyder and his colleagues (Snyder et al., 1976) have demonstrated an actor–observer divergence in ability attributions: Actors take more credit for their successes and less blame for their failures than observers attribute to them. Interestingly, this "glow effect" is diminished in the self-ratings of depressives; while normals present inflated self-characterizations relative to observer ratings, depressives see themselves as *less* socially adept and successful (Lewinsohn, Mischel, Chaplin, & Barton, 1980). In either case, that of the unrealistically positive self-assessments of normals or that of the unrealistically negative ones of depressives, it is important to point out that a self-theory or self-schema that leads the perceiver to overemphasize certain data or experience in a theory-confirming manner is operative. This process is conceptually similar to that underlying person perception in general; it need not necessarily be attributed to "special" motives associated with self-perception. If an actor has a relatively positive self-theory, then theory-congruent past and present behavior and experience may be overly salient and available, leading the actor to see a simple failure experience as relatively unique or rare in comparison with his or her entire history. This biased sampling of self-relevant information may induce the actor toward a pattern of egocentric attribution.

THE LINKS BETWEEN SOCIAL COGNITION AND SOCIAL BEHAVIOR

A main tenet of the cognitive–social interactionist view of personality is that individual social behavior emerges out of a process involving *reciprocal determinism* between the social world (both as a physical and a social force) and the individual's constructions and reactions to that world (as manifested in perceptions of self and others, emotional experiences, etc.). Conceptual transitions in the work of personologists in the behavioral tradition (e.g., Bandura, 1977a; Mischel, 1980) provide illustrations of developments in this direction. For example, consider Mischel's work on the determinants of delay of gratification in children (1974, 1980). This work has evolved from concern with the influence of objective stimulus factors in isolation (e.g., the presence or absence of the desired reward) to studies of cognitive strategies and plans that children spontaneously use to transform the perceived situation in order to facilitate delay (e.g., imagining a desired marshmallow as a cloud floating in the sky or some other nonconsummatory image). The child's waiting behavior is determined, then, through a reciprocal interaction between features of the situation and the child's behavioral and cognitive operation on that situation. It is easy to see that adult self-regulation processes may be similarly shaped through a process of assimilation and accommodation between the individual and his or her social environment.

GENDER DIMORPHISM

The course of psychosexual dimorphism, as recounted by Money and Ehrhardt (1972; see also Ehrhardt & Meyer-Bahlburg, 1979), is an excellent example of a full-fledged, dynamic, reciprocal interaction between the person and the environment, involving biological, behavioral, and cognitive variables. In a series of fascinating cases of hermaphrodism, sex reannouncement, sex reassignment, and sex reversal, delayed and precocious puberty, and transsexualism, these investigators have shown how the program for psychosexual dimorphism is passed from the chromosomes to the hormones to the genitals, and then exchanged continually between the person and his or her social environment. Nothing is given, in a biological sense, except the appearance of the external genitalia. One aspect of the reciprocal interaction between person and situation is represented by the manner in which the appearance of the external genitalia structure the social environment, as parents, siblings, and others respond differently to and impose different demands on children who are declared to be boys and girls. The wider social environment contributes another aspect to the interaction, as cultural stereotypes of masculinity and femininity determine how children will be treated and which of their behaviors will be positively reinforced. As a third component of the interaction, the child identifies himself or herself as a boy or a girl on the basis of the appearance of external genitalia, and thus begins to search for cues in the environment concerning sex-appropriate behavior. Social demands are no more "givens" than biological factors, however, as evidenced by those "androgynes" who seek to adopt attitudes and behaviors consistent with cultural stereotypes of both masculinity and femininity (S. L. Bem, 1979; Spence & Helmreich, 1978, 1979), as well as by those women identified with the feminist movement (and men influenced by it) who seek to transcend and abolish these stereotypes altogether.

The scope of the reciprocal interaction between person and situation as it affects gender identity and gender role is made particularly clear in cases of children who are genetically male or female, with a normal chromosome count, but whose sexual anatomy is improperly undifferentiated. Typically, this involves fetal androgenization in genetic females or a failure of androgenization in genetic males. Correct diagnosis of these conditions is difficult, so that the child's sex is often reassigned postnatally or reannounced during infancy or childhood, followed by corrective surgery and hormone treatment. When the social environment is clear about the sex of the child, the process of gender-identity establishment and gender-role identification unfolds smoothly; when the environment is more ambiguous, the child matures uncertain of his or her identity and role. When sex is reassigned neonatally, the environment is extraordinarily flexible, and the parents (with professional and social support) shift easily from one set of socialization practices to another; after the child has begun to establish his or her identity and to practice appropriate role behaviors (at about 18 months), the shift is much more difficult. In any event, initial uncertainty with respect to a child's sex may lead parents to be more sensitive to cross-sex-typed behavior, and to reinforce behavior appropriate to the reassigned or reannounced sex more strongly, than parents who have never doubted whether their child was a boy or a girl may do. Even young children have clear expectations about sexual dimorphism in body features, the timing of the changes involved, and behaviors appropriate to sex roles: if the original reassignment or reannouncement is not successful from their point of view, they may well seek another one. Here the reciprocal interaction reaches completion, as the dissatisfied child attempts to transform his or her own environment behaviorally so that it more closely matches his or her expectations.

SKEWED INTERACTIONISM

Thus far, we have pointed to links between social cognition and social behavior in cases where there is a fairly balanced or reciprocal interaction between the actor's cognitive–behavioral constructions and the actual "objective" social environment. However, the cognitive heuristics emerging in the literature on perception of self and others imply an interaction more heavily skewed toward cognitive assimilation (of the perceived event toward cognitive expectancies) and conservation (of cognitive–social theories). Assimilation and conservation at the cognitive level should be reflected at the behavioral level in an interaction skewed in the direction of the perceiver–actor's prior expectancies—an interaction in which the perceiver–actor's power to shape that social environment is demonstrated. This form of imbalanced interactionism has also been investigated, principally by social psychologists.

Social psychologists have gathered a great deal of empirical evidence suggesting that cognitive expectancies can often lead an actor to treat another person in such a way as to elicit from that other person behavior that confirms the actor's original expectations, thus creating a *self-fulfilling prophecy* (for a review, see Darley & Fazio, 1980). This phenomenon of cognitive-behavioral confirmation has frequently been demonstrated in interactions involving asymmetric natural power relationships such as teacher–student (Rosenthal, 1973; Rosenthal & Jacobson, 1968), experimenter–subject (Orne, 1962, 1973; Rosenthal, 1963; Rosenthal & Rubin, 1978), and interviewer–interviewee (Snyder & Swann, 1978b; Word, Zanna, & Cooper, 1974). Snyder and his colleagues (Snyder & Swann, 1978a; Snyder, Tanke, & Berscheid, 1977) have also demonstrated the phenomenon of behavioral confirmation among sets of randomly paired undergraduates in laboratory studies. For example, Snyder and Swann (1978a) had subjects playing an experimental game involving reaction time in which each partner could disrupt the performance of the other by means of a burst of noise. One partner, randomly selected as the perceiving labeler, began the session with an experimentally induced expectation (categorization) of the target partner as a hostile person. During the course of their interaction, the perceiving labeler treated the target with more hostility than would ordinarily be expected; the target returned this show of hostility, thus confirming the perceiving labeler's original expectancy. Moreover, under some conditions the randomly labeled "hostile" target came to perceive himself or herself as more hostile, and the experimentally induced hostile behavior generalized to another interaction with yet a third, naive perceiver. The expectancy or interpersonal categorization of the labeling perceiver with regard to his or her target so guided behavior in these laboratory interactions that the data available in the environment were shaped by and assimilated to that prior categorization.

Cognitive expectancies can also produce contrast effects in which only the slightest bit of disconfirmatory evidence from a partner in an interaction leads the actor to reverse his or her original categorization and to take an even stronger position in the opposite direction. However, such phenomena of behavioral contrast have been difficult to study under the controlled conditions of the laboratory. Nevertheless, in both confirmation and contrast phenomena, the reciprocal interaction between the perceiver–actor and others in his or her environment is skewed in the direction of the perceiver–actor's construction of the social world. In other words, the perceiver–actor takes a primary role in creating the environmental data base.

Another sphere in which actors take controlling roles in shaping the environment is in the domain of strategic *self-presentation* (Goffman, 1959; E. E. Jones & Pittman, 1980). This may be defined as the deliberate attempt on the part of an actor to shape an observer's definition of a situation, impression of the actor, attribution of causality, or some other social judgment. This is not to imply that such a judgment is necessarily false or erroneous, but only that it is deliberately fostered by the actor, usually in the service of augmented power. Jones and Pittman have reviewed a number of self-presentational strategies, including ingratiation (i.e., creating an impression of likability; E. E. Jones, 1964; E. E. Jones & Wortman, 1973); intimidation (creating an impression of dangerousness); self-promotion (creating an impression of competence); exemplification (creating an impression of integrity); and supplication (creating an impression of dependence). Jones and Pittman make it clear that this is not just another typology of persons. Rather, these are strategies that are available for use under appropriate circumstances; people are capable of shifting from one to another. Similarly, while self-presentation and management of impressions are common components of social interactions, they are not necessary ones; there are many circumstances in which strategic self-presentations will be modulated by social goals overriding those goals having to do with power relationships.

As an example of self-presentation in the area of success and failure, consider the strategy that Jones and his colleagues have called "self-handicapping." The self-handicapper strategically avoids giving others the opportunity to make an ability-linked attribution for his or her performance by setting up roadblocks to good performance or withdrawing effort before or during the task. Berglas and Jones (1978) demonstrated this self-handicapping pattern in the controlled conditions of the laboratory. Subjects were given success feedback after working on a set of insoluble problems (noncontingent success) or soluble problems (contingent success). They were then given the opportunity to take an ostensibly performance-inhibiting or performance-facilitating drug (actually a placebo) before engaging in a retest on similar problems. Males in the noncontingent success condition showed a unique preference for the performance-inhibiting drug, thus creating attributional ambiguity with regard to their likely failure on the retest problems. There is clearly an interaction of person and environment embedded in this pattern of self-handicapping. Yet, as in the sequence of behavioral confirmation described earlier, here the actor has taken a decided and disproportionate role in shaping the social environment according to his or her prior expectations. And the behavioral reflection or playing out of the social perceiver's cognitive heuristics may be seen here—schematic processing in the phenomena of behavioral confirmation, and ego-defensive attribution in self-handicapping.

SOME UNRESOLVED ISSUES

The cognitive–social approach to personality is well developed in some areas (e.g., impression formation and attribution theory), while other areas (e.g., the self-concept and links between cognition and action) remain relatively unexplored. Research proceeds apace on all of these fronts and others. As research and theory continue to progress, a number of difficult topics will have to be addressed.

COGNITION AND BEHAVIOR:
AFTER-THE-FACT RATIONALE?

A persisting thorn in the side of a cognitive–social theory of personality is the apparent variability and discriminativeness of behavior—so finely tuned to the nuances of situations—in contrast with the rather entrenched, stable, and conservative foundations of social knowledge. In constructing a view of the social world, the perceiver–actor seems to abstract a very smoothed, consistent, ego-protective picture, using a host of schematic memory processes and attributional–judgmental heuristics. Individual behavior seems to be far more discriminative and open to change and revision than individual cognition is. It is sometimes difficult to fit the pieces in this cognitive–behavioral puzzle together: Can such a conservative cognitive system mediate behavior that is fundamentally variable and situation-specific? Perhaps the cognitive descriptions of social reality given by the perceiver–actor are orthogonal to actual behavior—closer, that is, to after-the-fact rationalizations than to causal determinants. Nisbett and Wilson (1977) and Langer (1978) have recently argued this position. According to their analyses, social behavior is often "mindless"; individuals' after-the-fact introspections on their own behavior are frequently inaccurate because they rely on naive causal theories about the cognitive determinants of behavior. As an example, Nisbett and Wilson (1977) cite people's misinterpretations of their supermarket-shopping behavior: People claim to buy what they like, while their actual choices can be shown to be determined by serial position on the shelf. Despite persistent beliefs in the cognitive control of behavior, then, it may be that attributions, categorizations, and memories serve mostly to provide a stable view of social life, operating independently of behavior as a post hoc explanatory system.

It is certainly the case that some social behavior is reflexive in quality and that implicit causal theories can interfere with accurate introspections. Clearly, cognitive heuristics do help paint a consistent and secure social world at very little cost in processing energy. However, it may also be that the laboratory approach—restricted as it frequently is to short-term interactions and superficial decisions—underestimates the degree of reciprocal determinism that obtains between cognition and behavior in the natural social environment and overestimates the conservative, entrenched nature of everyday social cognition. Perhaps if investigators took larger temporal chunks of social interactions, varying as they naturally do over tasks and interaction partners, a truer picture of reciprocal determinism would emerge in which cognition and behavior are seen to be more intimately connected. Moreover, if researchers studied social cognition and behavior in more significant life domains (such as parent–child interactions) and with respect to more weighty social decisions (such as whether or not to drop out of college), again, the self-reports and cognitive constructions of social actors might turn out to have more impact and credibility. Therapists are in a unique position to chart the extended course of social cognition and social behavior in important life domains and to monitor changes in both thought and behavior.

THE PROBLEM OF CONSCIOUSNESS

For a time, the need for a more dynamic approach to personality was satisfied by psychoanalytic theory as developed by Freud and those who followed him. With the introduction of the "iceberg" metaphor, psychoanalysis initiated a tradition of "depth" psychologies that hypothesized invisible processes mediating surface behavior. Unfortunately, psychoanalysis suffered its own set of conceptual and empirical problems, which space does not permit us to review here (Kline, 1972; Mischel, 1973a). It is, in part, the intention of the cognitive–social personology proposed here to develop a dynamic theory of personality that does not rely on primitive drives, defenses against them, and a conceptualization of men and women as fundamentally irrational and motivated by fear. There is one issue in psychoanalytic theory which is not explicitly addressed by cognitive–social personology, however—the possibility of unconscious mental processes.

The concept of unconscious mental processes has a long and rich history in psychology (Ellenberger, 1970). Although there has been a tendency to identify them with the motives and defenses of psychoanalysis (e.g., Erdelyi, 1974; Erdelyi & Goldberg, 1979), an alternative conceptualization has been available at least since the time of James, Janet, and Prince, and has been revived as the "neodissociation" theory of divided consciousness by Hilgard (1977). The theory begins with the fact that attention can be divided and simultaneously directed to multiple cognitive tasks (Kahneman, 1973; Neisser, 1976). In some instances, one of these tasks appears to be performed subconsciously—that is, outside of the person's awareness. In an experiment by Spelke, Hirst, and Neisser (1977), for example, subjects were taught to read prose and take dictation simultaneously. With practice, they achieved high levels of performance, as measured by tests of comprehension and accuracy. The subjects were largely unable to recall the words that had been dictated to them, however. Similar divisions in awareness may be observed in a variety of clinical and experimental settings. In cases of cerebral commisurotomy, patients are unable to name stimuli processed in the nonverbal hemisphere

(Gazzaniga, 1970); normal subjects who are unequivocally asleep may respond to instructions given by an experimenter, yet have no recollection of these activities upon awakening (Evans, 1979). In the well-known phenomenon of state-dependent learning, both human and infrahuman subjects may show poor memory for material learned while under the influence of a drug until that drug state has been reinduced (Eich, 1977; Weingartner, 1978).

Hypnosis offers a particularly good medium for studying these processes, because some hypnotizable subjects appear to have a high capacity for dividing consciousness in such a way that percepts, memories, thoughts, and actions are processed outside of phenomenal awareness (Brenneman, Kihlstrom, & Hilgard, 1981; Hilgard, 1965). In hypnotic analgesia, subjects appear to be able to reduce or eliminate their awareness of pain, even though psychophysiological responses to the stimulus are unaffected (Hilgard & Hilgard, 1975). Subjects experiencing posthypnotic amnesia are unable to remember the events and experiences which transpired during hypnosis; nonetheless, these memories may be recovered after the administration of a prearranged cue, and while outside of awareness can still affect ongoing cognitive processes (Kihlstrom, 1981; Kihlstrom & Evans, 1979). Although the phenomenon has not yet been systematically studied in the laboratory, clinical lore has it that hypnotized subjects may be able to remember material that ordinarily is not accessible to them. There is also evidence that subjects can act posthypnotically on suggestions given during hypnosis, without knowing the reason for their actions (Bowers, 1966, 1975).

These and other phenomena, encountered in the clinic, the laboratory, and everyday life, converge on the conclusion that complex, intentional cognitive processes related to perception, memory, and action can take place subconsciously—that is, without being controlled or monitored by a central executive structure. The "unconscious" of neodissociation theory is different from that of some other conceptions of the unconscious in contemporary cognitive psychology (e.g., W. Schneider & Shiffrin, 1977), in that it is not limited to procedural knowledge and can carry out complex and controlled mental processes; it is also different from that of psychoanalysis in that it is not restricted to primitive sexual and aggressive contents and not necessarily employed for purposes of defense.

In contrast to its reigning position in psychoanalytic theory, the concept of consciousness is not central to the cognitive–social personology described here. Yet the notion of multiple systems for monitoring and controlling thought and action, as well as the possibility that divisions in consciousness may occur in such a manner that the lines of communication between two or more systems may be cut, is entirely compatible with recent theoretical developments in cognitive psychology and ought to be incorporated into any cognitive personology. The ability to divide consciousness so that some aspects of behavior and experience are not represented in phenomenal awareness is a cognitive competency that some individuals, at least, can bring into the service of personality. From a clinical point of view, the concept of divided consciousness is important in understanding a diverse set of complaints, from the dramatic symptoms of multiple personality to the more common ones of functional amnesia, anesthesia, analgesia, and paralysis.

COGNITION AND AFFECT

Another important issue concerns the relation between cognitive and affective aspects of personality and social behavior. Ours is not a view of men and women as coldly calculating processors of information. In fact, we see cognition and emotion as interacting reciprocally, just as persons and situations do. First, it appears to be the case that affective experiences are cognitively constructed. There are no unique patterns of psychophysiological response associated with any particular emotional experience (Johnson, 1970; Mandler, 1975). Following Schachter and Singer (1962) and Mandler (1975), we may assert that an emotional experience is a joint function of (relatively undifferentiated) physiological arousal and the situational context in which that arousal occurs (for limitations on this assertion, see Marshall & Zimbardo, 1979, and Maslach, 1979; for a stronger objection, see Zajonc, 1980). In effect, the individual explains his or her perceived arousal state in terms of available situational cues. The arousing situation, of course, is itself cognitively constructed according to the principles of social categorization, and the inference from arousal to emotion is subject to the kinds of heuristics and biases inherent in any judgmental process. Changes in the perception of the situation or in the processes guiding social inference may well alter the quality of the emotional experience elicited by an arousal state.

Moreover, once an emotional experience has been cognitively constructed, it in turn can influence the course of cognitive processing (Kihlstrom, 1980). Affective valence, whether positive or negative, is a common attribute of percepts and memories (Bower, 1967; Underwood, 1969; Wickens, 1972), even among young children (Kail & Siegel, 1977). Given the availability of evaluative and affective features in perception and memory, there is no reason to suppose that the selectivity that pervades the human cognitive system cannot bias the processing of emotionally colored material (Erdelyi, 1974; Erdelyi & Goldberg, 1979; Mandler, 1975). At the least, emotional–evaluative attributes increase the salience or availability of the information with which they are associated (Holmes, 1970, 1974), thus probably interacting with the availability bias in judgment discussed earlier.

There is appreciable evidence that mood can affect performance on both semantic (Weingartner, Miller, & Murphy, 1977) and episodic (Bower, Monteiro, & Gilligan, 1978; Nasby, 1980) memory tasks. While most of these studies have not employed stimulus materials relevant to perceptions of self or others, Monteiro and Bower (1979), employing a story-recall task, found better memory for information about a happy character when the story was read by an elated subject, and for information about a sad character when it was read by a depressed one. Lloyd and Lishman (1975) and Teasdale and Fogarty (1979), working respectively with clinically and experimentally depressed patients, found that retrieval times associated with pleasant and unpleasant autobiographical memories were related to the mood (normal or depressed) experienced by the subjects at the time of the test. Whether positive and negative moods exert complementary effects on positive and negative memories, and whether mood can induce "state dependency" in memory, is not yet clear (Kihlstrom, 1981; Kihlstrom & Nasby, 1981). Nevertheless, the apparent reciprocal influence of cognition and emotion leaves open the possibility for a maladaptive, vicious cycle—one that will be extremely hard for a therapist to correct (Beck, 1967).

ASSIMILATION AND ACCOMMODATION IN SCHEMA-BASED COGNITION

Another important detail that has not been satisfactorily resolved concerns the precise nature of schematic effects on perception and memory (Hastie, 1980a, 1980b; Taylor & Crocker, 1980). One of the functions of schemata is to anticipate environmental events, facilitating the pickup of relevant information from the perceptual field or its retrieval from memory. According to Neisser (1967, 1976), schemata accept information and are modified by it— the process of assimilation and accommodation referred to earlier. One of the signs of the assimilative process is the good retention of schema-consistent information as compared to schema-irrelevant information (e.g., Hastie, 1980a), coupled with inference-based false recall or recognition of other information, also schema-consistent, that was not actually represented in the stimulus material (e.g., Cantor & Mischel, 1977, 1979b; Snyder & Uranowitz, 1978). Schema theory is less clear, however, on the fate of information that is incongruent with the expectations represented by active schemata. Hastie (1980b), reviewing the large literature that has accumulated on schematic processing in visual perception, verbal learning, and person memory, has proposed that schematic principles operate to favor the encoding of schema-incongruent and the retrieval of schema-congruent information. According to his argument, information perceived as incongruent with expectations receives more attention as the individual attempts to comprehend its relation with other stimulus-based information and schema-based expectations and inferences; this results in a rich, highly memorable trace. At the point of retrieval, on the other hand, the schema supplies cues that facilitate contact with congruent information represented in trace fragments, as well as congruent inferences on which memorial reconstruction is based. These proposals are consistent with the outcomes of a large number of experiments on person memory performed by Hastie (1980a) and his collaborators.

The assimilative function of schemata sometimes seems to dominate cognition to such an extent that a person might seem able to perceive and remember events in almost any way that he or she desires (Kelly, 1955). In domains where the available stimulus is relatively rich and explicit, of course—as in the case of visual or auditory perception—the operation of schemata is greatly constrained by the stimulus information. In memory, however, where trace information is likely to be rather fragmentary, there is much more latitude for schemata to operate (e.g., Bartlett, 1932; Bower, 1976; Jenkins, 1974; Paul, 1959). In social cognition tasks, even when available information is not fragmentary, it is often extremely ambiguous, so that it can be just as easily assigned one meaning as another. Taylor and Crocker (1980) have shown that schematic processing can have powerful distorting effects on social cognition, as when the person applies the wrong schemata to the task of perception, judgment, or memory. They also document a number of other liabilities of schematic processing: Schemata may provide an illusory data base for making evaluations and decisions; they may lead the individual to accept as schema-consistent information that is widely at variance with prevailing expectations; and they may alter the perceived magnitude of empirical covariations between events or attributes.

While the assimilative aspect of schematic processing has by now been well documented, there is a much less clear understanding of accommodation —the ways in which schemata change in response to violations of expectancies, and the circumstances promoting such change. In social cognition studies —such as Hastie's (1980a), for example—the effect of presenting information incongruent with a first impression of a person on the final impression is not yet known. The results of experimental research on social cognition, which document so well the assimilative power of schemata, lead us to be pessimistic about the degree of accommodation which may reasonably be expected to occur. Given the assumptions of a cognitive–social approach to personality concerning personality change as outlined earlier, and the assumption of many behavior therapists that behavior change is mediated by cognitive change, this problem would seem to be worth vigorous pursuit.

THE ROLE OF INDIVIDUAL DIFFERENCES

Throughout this chapter, we have emphasized the central concern of cognitive-social personology with the general processes involved in social cognition and social interaction. However, at some point both personologist and clinician must confront the problem of individual differences. That problem is this: individual differences *in what?* Throughout most of its history, differential psychology has focused on traits on such dimensions as intellectual capacity, cognitive style, interests, values, or behavioral dispositions (e.g., Tyler, 1978; Willerman, 1979). However, as pointed out by Mischel (1968, 1973b) and many others, these trait dimensions, assessed objectively or projectively and largely without regard for the situational context, do not have much validity or utility in predicting actual behavior in laboratory or real-world settings. As made clear by Mischel (1973b, 1977), a cognitive–social approach to personology does not ignore individual differences; however, it does construe them quite differently—no longer in terms of cross-situational behavioral dispositions, but in terms of categorization systems, attentional foci, expectations, inferences, incentives, aversions, and strategies and plans relating to self-regulation and social interaction. Some of these categories of individual differences have been described in detail by Mischel (1973b); others are represented by such specific constructs of individual differences as self-monitoring (Snyder, 1979); self-awareness (Buss, 1980); locus of control (Rotter, 1966); and attributional style (Abramson & Metalski, 1981).

An interesting aspect of Mischel's summary (1973b) is that there is no attempt to develop a finite list of these variables, exhaustively representing all the dimensions within each domain on which people could vary. Thus the traditional concern with documenting an overarching, comprehensive matrix of social–cognitive individual differences, analogous to those developed to represent the "structure" of intellectual or personality traits, has disappeared. Moreover, cognitive–social personology gives little sense that its person variables are necessarily to be construed as stable, enduring, or resistant to change. Human beings are adaptive and flexible, capable of changing goals and expectations, modifying personal construct systems and inferences, learning new plans, and shifting from one plan to another. For cognitive–social personology, stability and consistency are more empirical questions than they are pretheoretical assumptions.

Regardless of whether the personal variables of cognitive–social personology are conceived as enduring or transient dispositions, they must be assessed if they are to play a role in experimentation, therapy, and theory development. The primary purpose of such assessments must be to develop a picture of how individuals view themselves and their social world. In the service of this goal, a cardinal feature of assessment procedures dictated by cognitive–social personology must be that they allow people to speak for themselves, in their own terms, without being forced to employ constructs named and defined by the clinical or laboratory investigator (Kelly, 1955; McClelland, 1980; Mischel, 1977). Actions speak louder than words, and for this reason personality assessment must expand its use of direct observational techniques to determine which situations people prefer to place themselves in, how they present themselves, how they act to transform these settings to more nearly fit their expectations and goals, and how they conduct themselves in situations requiring social exchange—a theme, not coincidentally, that is prominent in the functional analyses advocated by behavior therapists. Similarly, more attention should be paid to the assessment of features of environments, especially of their psychological as opposed to their physical properties (Magnusson, 1980).

As already indicated, the cognitive–social approach to personology provides its own set of person variables. In assessing such features of personality, the temptation is to introduce a new set of questionnaires and similar objective tests into the psychologist's armamentarium. The literature on the comparative validity and utility of various types of objective assessment instruments (e.g., Ashton & Goldberg, 1972; Hase & Goldberg, 1967; Mischel, 1968, 1972, 1977), however, indicates that the best technique involves asking people directly about their goals, expectations, inferences, and the like, under conditions that allow them to reflect honestly and dispassionately on themselves. If investigators want to know what people can tell them, they should ask them. But sometimes people cannot tell them—either because they do not have good introspective access to knowledge of themselves and their social environment, or because they cannot articulate that knowledge. Under these conditions, some indirect assessment methodology may be desirable. Rather than advocate a new generation of projective personality tests, it seems more appropriate to attempt to adapt existing laboratory paradigms, originally developed for research purposes, to the task of clinical assessment. Kihlstrom and Nasby (1980) have suggested a number of techniques that may permit assessment of the declarative and procedural knowledge involved in social cognition and social interaction.

Whatever assessment method is chosen, personality assessment must be functional and idiographic from a cognitive–social point of view, at least in spirit. In order to understand what people do in social situations, investigators must understand the knowledge, competencies, and expectations that they bring into the behavior setting; their goals and plans for carrying out the interaction itself; and the ways in which these factors change as the interaction unfolds. Person variables are not to be assessed in the abstract, but rather with a view toward their reciprocal relations with social behavior and the contexts in which they occur. We see little advantage to the collection of norms, in the usual sense of standards against which individual persons or situations are to be compared. In some instances, of course, it may be helpful to have knowledge concerning gross departures from normative competencies, expectations, goals, scripts, and plans. For the most part, however, we would advocate criterion-referenced rather than norm-referenced assessment (e.g.,

McClelland, 1973; Mischel, 1977), in which investigator and subject, clinician and client, collaborate to clarify the subject's or client's perceptions of the social environment in the service of adaptive social behavior.

CLINICAL IMPLICATIONS

The cognitive–social perspective on personality presented here has definite implications for clinical assessment and intervention. According to the position sketched in this chapter, behavior change is cognitively mediated by a process of assimilation (of social reality to existing cognitive structures) and accommodation (of cognitive structures to social reality). The client is, like anyone else, first and foremost an intuitive psychologist, trying to make sense of his or her life situation. The troubles that bring him or her to the attention of the clinician reflect just this sense—the way in which the person has come to categorize the world, make attributions and predictions, draw inferences, test hypotheses, and plan behavior. To facilitate behavior change, the clinician must get "inside the head" of the client and see the world as he or she does; and then must arrange the client's experience to alter persistent, dysfunctional declarative and procedural knowledge.

TAKING EVERYDAY SOCIAL COGNITION SERIOUSLY

The first clinical task—that of seeing the world as the client does—requires an understanding of the principles of categorization, schematic memory, and attribution that characterize everyday social cognition. As an initial lesson, it is clear that even the most "normal" of information processors among individuals relies on heuristics and shortcuts that may result in nonveridical and nonnormative perceptions, memories, and judgments. While the model of a hypothesis-testing scientist has facilitated research in social cognition, the naive perceiver–actor, not surprisingly, turns out to be far from the ideal or prototypic scientist (Nisbett & Ross, 1980). However, empirical research on social cognition has documented a variety of everyday cognitive tricks that do characterize social cognition and can be useful in clinical analysis. It may be useful to think of many clinical syndromes as having a basis in an overapplication or distortion of many of these standard cognitive heuristics on the part of the client. For examples of such an approach, we suggest the following analyses: attributional analyses of learned helplessness in terms of expectancies and attributions (Abramson, Seligman, & Teasdale, 1978; Seligman, 1975); analyses of delusions in terms of attributions and biased hypothesis testing (Maher, 1974; Maslach, Zimbardo, & Marshall, 1979); and analyses of depression in terms of schematic memory processes (Beck, 1967). These analyses raise a familiar theme in psychology—namely, that "abnormal" behavior may be fed by cognitive processes that share more than a family resemblance to those processes characteristic of "normal" social cognition (see also Kihlstrom & Nasby, 1981).

The second clinical task—that of arranging experiences so as to teach new, perhaps more functional cognitive rules and structures—is a central goal of contemporary behavior therapy (see Chapter 7 of this volume). Social skills training, for example, attempts to provide clients with new scripts for coping with troublesome life experiences (Lazarus, 1966), while attributional therapy (Valins & Nisbett, 1972) seeks to lead the client to make proper judgments about the nature of his or her difficulties as a first step toward coping with them. Readers of this volume do not need to be reminded of these and other cognitively oriented therapeutic approaches. It is simply our intention to stress the utility of gearing such retraining experiences so that they articulate with and build upon the known properties of everyday social cognition. Once again, this requires careful attention to the social environment as it is cognitively constructed by the client, and to individual differences in competencies and styles in cognitive construction. Moreover, it is fundamental that researchers and clinicians learn to be more sensitive to the impact of social interactions in shaping clients' self-perceptions and behavior. Social cognition has too frequently been studied in isolation from social interaction, and social behavior has too often been analyzed in a vacuum, independent of the actor's perceptions, beliefs, and rules.

PITFALLS IN CLINICAL APPLICATION

Empirical research on social cognition and social behavior clearly has a great deal to contribute to the work of the applied behavior analyst (e.g., Kihlstrom & Nasby, 1981; Mischel, 1979). Yet some of the research covered in this chapter suggests that this application may not be a straightforward enterprise. We have suggested that the clinician needs to provide the client with experiences and information that will promote cognitive change—experiences that facilitate theory revision and the development of new processing heuristics. The literature on social cognition, by contrast, paints a picture of cognitive beliefs and heuristics that are greatly resistant to change, quite entrenched, and perhaps not easily abandoned. Similarly, we have more or less explicitly worked under the assumption that cognitive change will lead to behavioral change. Yet recent evidence suggests a less than clear causal connection between cognition and behavior. Such inconsistencies cause us to wonder whether empirical personality research will, in fact, prove useful in the clinical domain. And, in the course of such cognition, we confront two of our own beliefs. First, we believe that cognition and behavior are intimately related and that cognitions do change, if perhaps slowly. Second, we do not feel that the standard laboratory paradigms are sufficiently ego-involving, dynamic, interactive, or temporally extended to capture or induce cognitive change and accompanying behavior change. Consequently, the tables are in some sense turned: It is the clinical behavior therapist who is now in the position to help provide the data for a cognitive–social theory of personality.

In considering the task of the clinician from the point of view of cognitive–social personology, we cannot help but remark on the pitfalls inherent in the clinical enterprise. The scientist–practitioner, despite training in statistics and experimental methodology, is also an intuitive psychologist and thus is prey to such foibles in data gathering, memory, and judgment as have been documented in the literature on social cognition (e.g., Chapman & Chapman, 1967; Nisbett & Ross, 1980). The clinician may be theory-driven in data gathering and interview techniques, and the clinical hour is a social interaction subject to the same problems of cognitive and behavioral confirmation as those of any other interpersonal encounter. So a psychoanalytically oriented therapist enters a clinical interview with a very different set of salient preconceptions than does a behavior therapist (Langer & Abelson, 1974; Mischel, 1976): The psychoanalyst focuses on psychosexual stages, is interested in developmental data and information about childhood experience, and elicits information from the patient concerning dreams, memories, and fantasies; in the same manner, the behavior therapist comes to the interaction with a set of beliefs about specific behavioral problems, is concerned with the current environments in which the client is operating, and asks questions about current situational stresses and goals. The course of each of these clinical interactions is shaped, at least to some degree, by the clinician's particular beliefs and expectancies and by his or her tendency to focus on, ask about, and differentially recall certain aspects of the client's current and past life. In order to get into the client's head, the clinician must strive to overcome the many biases that characterize the social information-processing system.

We have argued that the clinician will need to get beyond his or her own cognitive schemata and take the point of view of the client in analyzing the situation as it is perceived by and functions for the client. Yet taking the role of the client in analyzing social experience brings another problem for the clinician. The literature on social cognition suggests that once a person takes another's point of view, he or she easily falls prey to a host of cognitive biases that serve to construct an image of the world in an ego-enhancing and ego-protective light, from the perspective of that other person. Consequently, if the clinician does too good a job of seeing the world from the client's point of view, he or she may comfortably fall into some of the same cognitive traps as the client has done. For example, successfully adopting the perspective of a client who has a certain theory about a particular stressful interpersonal relationship may lead the clinician also to focus on the negative aspects of that relationship; to gather data confirming its problematic nature; and to recall an overrepresentation of hurtful, stressful events. This, of course, involves accepting the client's theory of his or her problem at face value, when the true source of difficulties lies elsewhere and remains untouched.

In order to create theory-disconfirming experiences for the client that will promote cognitive change and thus behavior change, the clinician must both enter the world of the client and retain a distance from it. Otherwise, he or she may achieve the first goal of therapy (to take the client's perspective), but fail to reach the second one (to provide experiences that will retune and retrain the client's cognitions and thus change maladaptive behavior). If both clinician and client get swept away by their theories, all is lost. This problem of achieving a tradeoff between empathy and distance is not a new one, and it is certainly not unique to behavior therapy. But the literature on social cognition and social behavior makes it painfully clear just how difficult a task that may be. The fundamental task for the cognitively oriented behavior therapist is to remain objective when everything about the therapeutic enterprise—the formal theories of the clinician as scientist and the implicit theories of the client as scientist—militates against objectivity.

ACKNOWLEDGMENTS

Preparation of this chapter was supported in part by Grant BNS-8022253 from the National Science Foundation and by Grants MH-35856 and MH-33737 from the National Institute of Mental Health. We would like to thank our colleagues, Beverly R. Chew, Judith M. Harackiewicz, Reid Hastie, Walter Mischel, William Nasby, and Mark Snyder, for their helpful comments during the preparation of this chapter.

REFERENCES

Abramson, L. Y., & Metalski, J. Attributional styles in adults. In P. C. Kendall & S. D. Hollon (Eds.), *Assessment strategies for cognitive–behavioral interventions.* New York: Academic Press, 1981.

Abramson, L. Y., Seligman, M. E. P., & Teasdale, J. D. Learned helplessness in humans: Critique and reformulation. *Journal of Abnormal Psychology,* 1978, *87,* 49–74.

Allport, G. W. *Personality: A psychological interpretation.* New York: Holt, 1937.

Allport, G. W., & Odbert, H. S. Trait-names: A psycho-lexical study. *Psychological Monographs,* 1936, *47*(Whole No. 211).

Anderson, J. R. *Language, memory, and thought.* Hillsdale, N.J.: Erlbaum, 1976.

Anderson, J. R. Memory for information about individuals. *Memory and Cognition,* 1977, *5,* 430–442.

Anderson, J. R., & Hastie, R. Individuation and reference in memory: Proper names and definite descriptions. *Cognitive Psychology,* 1974, *6,* 495–515.

Ansbacher, H. L. Adler's place today in the psychology of memory. *Journal of Personality,* 1947, *3,* 197–207.

Ashton, S. G., & Goldberg, L. R. In response to Jackson's challenge: The comparative validity of personality scales constructed by the external (empirical) strategy and scales developed intuitively by experts, novices, and laymen. *Journal of Research in Personality,* 1972, *7,* 1–20.

Athay, M., & Darley, J. M. Toward an interpersonal action centered theory of personality. In N. Cantor & J. F. Kihlstrom (Eds.), *Personality, cognition, and social interaction.* Hillsdale, N.J.: Erlbaum, 1981.

Ayllon, T., & Azrin, N. H. *The token economy: A motivational system for therapy and rehabilitation.* New York: Appleton-Century-Crofts, 1968.

Bandura, A. Behavior theory and the models of man. *American Psychologist,* 1974, *29,* 859–869.

Bandura, A. Self-efficacy: Toward a unifying theory of behavioral change. *Psychological Review,* 1977, *84,* 191–215. (a)

Bandura, A. *Social learning theory.* Englewood Cliffs, N.J.: Prentice-Hall, 1977. (b)

Bandura, A., & Walters, R. H. *Social learning and personality development.* New York: Holt, Rinehart & Winston, 1963.

Bartlett, F. C. *Remembering: A study in experimental and social psychology.* Cambridge, England: Cambridge University Press, 1932.

Beck, A. T. *Depression: Clinical, experimental, and theoretical aspects.* New York: Harper & Row, 1967.

Bem, D. J. Self-perception: An alternative interpretation of cognitive dissonance phenomena. *Psychological Review,* 1967, *74,* 183–200.

Bem, D. J. Self-perception theory. In L. Berkowitz (Ed.), *Advances in experimental social psychology* (Vol. 6). New York: Academic Press, 1972.

Bem, D. J., & Allen, A. On predicting some of the people some of the time: The search for cross-situational consistencies in behavior. *Psychological Review,* 1974, *81,* 506–520.

Bem, D. J., & Funder, D. C. Predicting more of the people more of the time: Assessing the personality of situations. *Psychological Review,* 1978, *85,* 485–501.

Bem, D. J., & Lord, C. G. Template matching: A proposal for probing the ecological validity of experimental settings in social psychology. *Journal of Personality and Social Psychology,* 1979, *37,* 833–846.

Bem, S. L. Theory and measurement of androgyny: A reply to the Pedhazur–Tetenbaum and Locksley–Colten critiques. *Journal of Personality and Social Psychology,* 1979, *37,* 1047–1055.

Berglas, S., & Jones, E. E. Drug choice as a self-handicapping strategy in response to noncontingent success. *Journal of Personality and Social Psychology,* 1978, *36,* 405–417.

Block, J. *The challenge of response sets.* New York: Appleton-Century-Crofts, 1965.

Block, J. *Lives through time.* Berkeley, Calif.: Bancroft, 1971.

Block, J. Advancing the psychology of personality: Paradigmatic shift or improving the quality of research? In D. Magnusson & N. S. Endler (Eds.), *Personality at the crossroads: Current issues in interactional psychology.* Hillsdale, N.J.: Erlbaum, 1977.

Block, J., Weiss, D. S., & Thorne, A. How relevant is a semantic similarity interpretation of personality ratings? *Journal of Personality and Social Psychology,* 1979, *37,* 1055–1074.

Bobrow, D. G., & Norman, D. A. Some principles of memory schemata. In D. G. Bobrow & A. Collins (Eds.), *Representation and understanding.* New York: Academic Press, 1975.

Bower, G. H. A multicomponent theory of the memory trace. In K. W. Spence & J. T. Spence (Eds.), *The psychology of learning and motivation* (Vol. 1). New York: Academic Press, 1967.

Bower, G. H. Experiments on story understanding and recall. *Quarterly Journal of Experimental Psychology,* 1976, *28,* 511–534.

Bower, G. H., & Gilligan, S. G. Remembering information related to one's self. *Journal of Research in Personality,* 1979, *13,* 420–432.

Bower, G. H., Monteiro, K. P., & Gilligan, S. G. Emotional mood as a context for learning and recall. *Journal of Verbal Learning and Verbal Behavior,* 1978, *17,* 573–585.

Bowers, K. S. Hypnotic behavior: The differentiation of trance and demand characteristic variables. *Journal of Abnormal Psychology,* 1966, *71,* 42–51.

Bowers, K. S. Situationism in psychology: An analysis and critique. *Psychological Review,* 1973, *80,* 307–336.

Bowers, K. S. The psychology of subtle control: An attributional analysis of behavioral persistence. *Canadian Journal of Behavioral Science,* 1975, *7,* 78–95.

Bransford, J. D., & Johnson, M. K. Contextual prerequisites for understanding: Some investigations of comprehension and recall. *Journal of Verbal Learning and Verbal Behavior,* 1972, *11,* 717–726.

Brenneman, H. A., Kihlstrom, J. F., & Hilgard, E. R. *Patterns of hypnotic abilities.* Manuscript in preparation, 1981.

Brown, R. *Natural categories and basic objects in the domain of persons.* Paper presented at the Katz–Newcomb Memorial Lecture, University of Michigan, Ann Arbor, May 1980.

Brown, R., & Kulik, J. Flashbulb memories. *Cognition,* 1977, *5,* 73–99.

Bruner, J. S., Goodnow, J. J., & Austin, G. A. *A study of thinking.* New York: Wiley, 1956.

Buss, A. *Self-consciousness and social anxiety.* San Francisco: W. H. Freeman, 1980.

Campbell, D. T., & Fiske, D. W. Convergent and discriminant validation by the multitrait–multimethod matrix. *Psychological Bulletin,* 1959, *56,* 81–105.

Cantor, N. *Prototypicality and personality judgments.* Unpublished doctoral dissertation, Stanford University, 1978.

Cantor, N. Perceptions of situations: Situation prototypes and person–situation prototypes. In D. Magnusson (Ed.), *The situation: An interactional perspective.* Hillsdale, N.J.: Erlbaum, 1981. (a)

Cantor, N. A cognitive–social analysis of personality. In N. Cantor & J. F. Kihlstrom (Eds.), *Personality, cognition, and social interaction.* Hillsdale, N.J.: Erlbaum, 1981. (b)

Cantor, N., & Mischel, W. Traits as prototypes: Effects on recognition memory. *Journal of Personality and Social Psychology,* 1977, *35,* 38–48.

Cantor, N., & Mischel, W. Prototypes in person perception. In L. Berkowitz (Ed.), *Advances in experimental social psychology* (Vol. 12). New York: Academic Press, 1979. (a)

Cantor, N., & Mischel, W. Prototypicality and personality: Effects on free recall and personality impressions. *Journal of Research in Personality,* 1979, *13,* 187–205. (b)

Cantor, N., Mischel, W., & Schwartz, J. Social knowledge: Structure, content, use, and abuse. In A. Hastorf & A. Isen (Eds.), *Cognitive social psychology.* New York: Elsevier North-Holland, 1982. (a)

Cantor, N., Mischel, W., & Schwartz, J. A prototype analysis of psychological situations. *Cognitive Psychology,* 1982, *14,* 45–77. (b)

Cantor, N., Smith, E. E., French, R. D., & Mezzich, J. Psychiatric diagnosis as prototype categorization. *Journal of Abnormal Psychology,* 1980, *89,* 181–193.

Cattell, R. B. The description of personality: I. Foundations of trait measurement. *Psychological Review,* 1943, *50,* 559–592. (a)

Cattell, R. B. The description of personality: II. Basic traits resolved into clusters. *Journal of Abnormal and Social Psychology,* 1943, *38,* 476–507. (b)

Cattell, R. B. The description of personality: III. Principles and findings in a factor analysis. *American Journal of Psychology,* 1945, *58,* 69–90.

Chapman, L. J., & Chapman, J. P. Genesis of popular but erroneous psychodiagnostic observation. *Journal of Abnormal Psychology,* 1967, *72,* 193–204.

Chew, B. R., & Kihlstrom, J. F. *Probing for remote and recent autobiographical memories.* Manuscript in preparation, 1981.

Cohen, C. E. Cognitive basis of stereotyping: An information-processing approach to social perception (Doctoral dissertation, University of California at San Diego, 1976). *Dissertation Abstracts International,* 1977, *38,* 421B. (University Microfilms No. 77-13681)

Cohen, C. E., & Ebbesen, E. B. Observational goals and schema activation: A theoretical framework for behavior perception. *Journal of Experimental Social Psychology,* 1979, *15,* 305–329.

Craik, F. I. M., & Lockhart, R. S. Levels of processing: A framework for memory research. *Journal of Verbal Learning and Verbal Behavior,* 1972, *11,* 671–684.

Cronbach, L. J. The two disciplines of scientific psychology. *American Psychologist,* 1957, *12,* 671–684.

Cronbach, L. J. Beyond the two disciplines of scientific psychology. *American Psychologist,* 1975, *30,* 116–127.

Cronbach, L. J., & Meehl, P. E. Construct validity in psychological tests. *Psychological Bulletin,* 1955, *52,* 281–302.

Crovitz, H. F., & Quina-Holland, K. Proportion of episodic memories from early childhood by years of age. *Bulletin of the Psychonomic Society,* 1976, *7,* 61–62.

Crovitz, H. F., & Schiffman, H. Frequency of episodic memories as a function of their age. *Bulletin of the Psychonomic Society,* 1974, *4,* 517–518.

Crowne, D. P. *The experimental study of personality.* Hillsdale, N.J.: Erlbaum, 1979.

Darley, J. M., & Fazio, R. Expectancy confirmation processes arising in the social interaction sequence. *American Psychologist,* 1980, *35,* 867–881.

DeVitto, B., & McArthur, L. Z. Developmental differences in the use of distinctiveness, consensus, and consistency information for making causal attributions. *Developmental Psychology,* 1978, *14,* 474–482.

Dudycha, G. J., & Dudycha, M. M. Childhood memories: A review of the literature. *Psychological Bulletin,* 1941, *38,* 668–682.

Ehrhardt, A. A., & Meyer-Bahlburg, A. F. L. Pre-natal sex hormones and the developing brain: Effects on psychosexual differentiation and cognitive function. *Annual Review of Medicine,* 1979, *30,* 417–430.

Ekehammar, B. Interactionism in personality from a historical perspective. *Psychological Bulletin,* 1974, *81,* 1026–1048.

Eich, J. E. State-dependent retrieval of information in human episodic memory. In I. M. Birnbaum & E. S. Parker (Eds.), *Alcohol and human memory.* Hillsdale, N.J.: Erlbaum, 1977.

Ellenberger, H. F. *The discovery of the unconscious: The history and evolution of dynamic psychiatry.* New York: Basic Books, 1970.

Endler, N. S., & Hunt, J. M. Sources of behavioral variance as measured by the S-R Inventory of Anxiousness. *Psychological Bulletin,* 1966, *65,* 336–346.

Epstein, S. The self-concept revisited, or a theory of a theory. *American Psychologist,* 1973, *28,* 404–416.

Epstein, S. The stability of behavior: I. On predicting most of the people much of the time. *Journal of Personality and Social Psychology,* 1979, *37,* 1097–1126.

Erdelyi, M. H. A new look at the New Look: Perceptual defense and vigilance. *Psychological Review,* 1974, *81,* 1–27.

Erdelyi, M. H., & Goldberg, B. Let's not sweep repression under the rug: Toward a cognitive psychology of repression. In J. F. Kihlstrom & F. J. Evans (Eds.), *Functional disorders of memory.* Hillsdale, N.J.: Erlbaum, 1979.

Evans, F. J. Hypnosis during sleep: Techniques for exploring cognitive activity during sleep. In E. Fromm & R. E. Shor (Eds.), *Hypnosis: Developments in research and new perspectives.* New York: Aldine, 1979.

Eysenck, H. J. Personality and factor analysis: A reply to Guilford. *Psychological Bulletin,* 1977, *84,* 405–411.

Flavell, J. H. *Cognitive development.* Englewood Cliffs, N.J.: Prentice-Hall, 1977.

Gazzaniga, M. S. *The bisected brain.* New York: Appleton-Century-Crofts, 1970.

Goffman, E. *The presentation of self in everyday life.* Garden City, N.Y.: Doubleday Anchor Books, 1959.

Goldberg, L. R. *Language and personality: Developing a taxonomy of trait-descriptive terms.* Paper presented at the meeting of the American Psychological Association, San Francisco, August 1977.

Greenwald, A. G. The totalitarian ego: Fabrication and revision of personal history. *American Psychologist,* 1980, *35,* 603–618.

Guilford, J. P. Factors and factors of personality. *Psychological Bulletin,* 1975, *82,* 802–814.

Guilford, J. P. Will the real factor of extraversion–introversion please stand up? A reply to Eysenck. *Psychological Bulletin,* 1977, *84,* 412–416.

Hamilton, D. A cognitive–attributional analysis of stereotyping. In L. Berkowitz (Ed.), *Advances in experimental social psychology* (Vol. 12). New York: Academic Press, 1979.

Harackiewicz, J. M. The effects of reward contingency and performance feedback on intrinsic motivation. *Journal of Personality and Social Psychology,* 1979, *37,* 1352–1363.

Hase, H. D., & Goldberg, L. R. Comparative validity of different strategies of constructing personality inventory scales. *Psychological Bulletin,* 1967, *67,* 231–248.

Hastie, R. Memory for behavioral information that confirms or contradicts a personality impression. In R. Hastie, T. F. Ostrom, E. Ebbesen, R. Wyer, D. L. Hamilton, & D. Carlston (Eds.), *Person memory: The cognitive basis of social perception.* Hillsdale, N.J.: Erlbaum, 1980. (a)

Hastie, R. Schematic principles in human memory. In E. T. Higgins, P. Herman, & M. P. Zanna (Eds.), *Social cognition: The Ontario symposium.* Hillsdale, N.J.: Erlbaum, 1980. (b)

Hastie, R., & Carlston, D. Theoretical issues in person memory. In R. Hastie, T. F. Ostrom, E. Ebbesen, R. Wyer, D. L. Hamilton, & D. Carlston (Eds.), *Person memory: The cognitive basis of social perception.* Hillsdale, N.J.: Erlbaum, 1980.

Hastie, R., & Kumar, P. A. Person memory: Personality traits as organizing principles in memory for behaviors. *Journal of Personality and Social Psychology,* 1979, *37,* 25–38.

Hastie, R., Ostrom, T. M., Ebbesen, E. B., Wyer, R. S., Hamilton, D. L., & Carlston, D. E. (Eds.). *Person memory: The cognitive basis of social perception.* Hillsdale, N.J.: Erlbaum, 1980.

Heider, F. *The psychology of interpersonal relations.* New York: Wiley, 1958.

Higgins, E. T., & King, G. Accessibility of social constructs: Information-processing consequences of individual and contextual variability. In N. Cantor & J. F. Kihlstrom (Eds.), *Personality, cognition, and social interaction.* Hillsdale, N.J.: Erlbaum, 1981.

Hilgard, E. R. *Hypnotic susceptibility.* New York: Harcourt, Brace & World, 1965.

Hilgard, E. R. *Divided consciousness: Multiple controls in human thought and action.* New York: Wiley-Interscience, 1977.

Hilgard, E. R., & Hilgard, J. R. *Hypnosis in the relief of pain.* Los Altos, Calif.: William Kaufman, 1975.

Hogan, R., DeSoto, C. B., & Solano, C. Traits, tests, and personality research. *American Psychologist,* 1977, *32,* 255–264.

Holmes, D. S. Dimensions of projection. *Psychological Bulletin,* 1968, *69,* 248–268.

Holmes, D. S. Differential change in affective intensity and the forgetting of unpleasant personal experiences. *Journal of Personality and Social Psychology,* 1970, *15,* 234-239.

Holmes, D. S. Investigations of repression: Differential recall of material experimentally or naturally associated with ego threat. *Psychological Bulletin,* 1974, *81,* 632-653.

Holmes, D. S. Projection as a defense mechanism. *Psychological Bulletin,* 1978, *85,* 677-688.

Jacoby, L. L., & Craik, F. I. M. Effects of elaboration or processing at encoding and retrieval: Trace distinctiveness and recovery of initial context. In L. S. Cermak & F. I. M. Craik (Eds.), *Levels of processing and human memory.* Hillsdale, N.J.: Erlbaum, 1979.

Jeffery, K., & Mischel, W. Effects of purpose on the organization and recall of information in person perception. *Journal of Personality,* 1979, *47,* 397-419.

Jenkins, J. J. Remember that old theory of memory? Well, forget it! *American Psychologist,* 1974, *29,* 785-795.

Johnson, L. C. A psychophysiology for all states. *Psychophysiology,* 1970, *6,* 501-516.

Jones, E. E. *Ingratiation: A social-psychological analysis.* New York: Appleton-Century-Crofts, 1964.

Jones, E. E. The rocky road from acts to dispositions. *American Psychologist,* 1979, *34,* 107-117.

Jones, E. E., & Davis, K. E. A theory of correspondent inferences: From acts to dispositions. In L. Berkowitz (Ed.), *Advances in experimental social psychology* (Vol. 2). New York: Academic Press, 1965.

Jones, E. E., & Goethals, G. R. Order effects in impression formation: Attribution context and the nature of reality. In E. E. Jones, D. E. Kanouse, H. H. Kelley, R. E. Nisbett, S. Valins, & B. Weiner (Eds.), *Attribution: Perceiving the causes of behavior.* Morristown, N.J.: General Learning Press, 1972.

Jones, E. E., Kanouse, D. E., Kelley, H. H., Nisbett, R. E., Valins, S., & Weiner, B. (Eds.). *Attribution: Perceiving the causes of behavior.* Morristown, N.J.: General Learning Press, 1972.

Jones, E. E., & Nisbett, R. E. The actor and observer: Divergent perceptions of the causes of behavior. In E. E. Jones, D. E. Kanouse, H. H. Kelley, R. E. Nisbett, S. Valins, & B. Weiner (Eds.), *Attribution: Perceiving the causes of behavior.* Morristown, N.J.: General Learning Press, 1972.

Jones, E. E., & Pittman, T. S. Toward a general theory of strategic self-presentation. In J. Suls (Ed.), *Psychological perspectives on the self.* Hillsdale, N.J.: Erlbaum, 1980.

Jones, E. E., & Wortman, C. *Ingratiation: An attributional approach.* Morristown, N.J.: General Learning Press, 1973.

Jones, R. A., Sensenig, J., & Haley, J. V. Self-descriptions: Configurations of content and order effects. *Journal of Personality and Social Psychology,* 1974, *30,* 36-45.

Jung, C. G. Psychological types. In H. Read, M. Fordham, & G. Adler (Eds.), *The collected works of C. G. Jung* (Vol. 6). Princeton: Princeton University Press, 1971. (Originally published, 1921.)

Kahneman, D. *Attention and effort.* Englewood Cliffs, N.J.: Prentice-Hall, 1973.

Kail, R. V., & Siegel, A. W. The development of mnemonic encoding in children: From perception to abstraction. In R. V. Kail & J. W. Hagen (Eds.), *Perspectives on the development of memory and cognition.* Hillsdale, N.J.: Erlbaum, 1977.

Karniol, R. Children's use of intention cues in evaluating behavior. *Psychological Bulletin,* 1978, *85,* 76-85.

Keenan, J. M., & Baillet, S. D. Memory for personally and socially significant events. In R. S. Nickerson (Ed.), *Attention and performance VIII.* Hillsdale, N.J.: Erlbaum, 1980.

Kelley, H. H. Attribution theory in social psychology. In D. Levine (Ed.), *Nebraska Symposium on Motivation* (Vol. 15). Lincoln: University of Nebraska Press, 1967.

Kelley, H. H. Causal schemata and the attribution process. In E. E. Jones, D. E. Kanouse, H. H. Kelley, R. E. Nisbett, S. Valins, & B. Weiner (Eds.), *Attribution: Perceiving the causes of behavior.* Morristown, N.J.: General Learning Press, 1972.

Kelly, G. A. *The psychology of personal constructs.* New York: Norton, 1955.

Kihlstrom, J. F. Posthypnotic amnesia for recently learned material: Interactions with "episodic" and "semantic" memory. *Cognitive Psychology,* 1980, *12,* 227–251.

Kihlstrom, J. F. On personality and memory. In N. Cantor & J. F. Kihlstrom (Eds.), *Personality, cognition, and social interaction.* Hillsdale, N.J.: Erlbaum, 1981.

Kihlstrom, J. F., & Evans, F. J. Memory retrieval processes during posthypnotic amnesia. In J. F. Kihlstrom & F. J. Evans (Eds.), *Functional disorders of memory.* Hillsdale, N.J.: Erlbaum, 1979.

Kihlstrom, J. F., & Harackiewicz, J. M. The earliest recollection of childhood: A new survey. *Journal of Personality,* in press.

Kihlstrom, J. F., & Nasby, W. Cognitive tasks in clinical assessment: An exercise in applied psychology. In P. C. Kendall & S. D. Hollon (Eds.), *Assessment strategies for cognitive–behavioral interventions.* New York: Academic Press, 1981.

Kline, P. *Fact and fantasy in Freudian theory.* London: Methuen, 1972.

Kretchmer, E. *Physique and character.* New York: Harcourt, 1925. (Originally published, 1921.)

Kuiper, N. A., & Derry, P. A. The self as a cognitive prototype: An application to person perception and depression. In N. Cantor & J. F. Kihlstrom (Eds.), *Personality, cognition, and social interaction.* Hillsdale, N.J.: Erlbaum, 1981.

Kuiper, N. A., & Rogers, T. B. Encoding of personal information: Self-other differences. *Journal of Personality and Social Psychology,* 1979, *37,* 499–514.

Langer, E. Rethinking the role of thought in social interaction. In J. H. Harvey, W. J. Ickes, & R. F. Kidd (Eds.), *New directions in attribution research* (Vol. 2). Hillsdale, N.J.: Erlbaum, 1978.

Langer, E., & Abelson, R. A. A patient by any other name . . . : Clinician group differences in labelling bias. *Journal of Consulting and Clinical Psychology,* 1974, *42,* 4–9.

Lazarus, A. A. Behaviour rehearsal vs. non-directive therapy vs. advice in effecting behavior change. *Behaviour Research and Therapy,* 1966, *4,* 209–212.

Lepper, M. R., & Greene, D. On understanding "overjustification": A reply to Reiss and Sushinsky. *Journal of Personality and Social Psychology,* 1976, *33,* 25–35.

Lewin, K. *A dynamic theory of personality.* New York: McGraw-Hill, 1935.

Lewinsohn, P. M., Mischel, W., Chaplin, W., & Barton, R. Social competence and depression: The role of illusory self-perceptions. *Journal of Abnormal Psychology,* 1980, *89,* 203–212.

Linton, M. Memory for real-world events. In D. A. Norman, D. E. Rummelhart, & the LNR Research Group (Eds.), *Explorations in cognition.* San Francisco: W. H. Freeman, 1975.

Linton, M. Real world memory after six years: An *in vivo* study of very long term memory. In M. M. Gruenberg, P. E. Morris, & R. N. Sykes (Eds.), *Practical aspects of memory.* New York: Academic Press, 1978.

Lloyd, G. G., & Lishman, W. A. Effect of depression on the speed of recall of pleasant and unpleasant experiences. *Psychological Medicine,* 1975, *5,* 173–180.

Lockhart, R. S., Craik, F. I. M., & Jacoby, L. Depth of processing, recognition and recall. In J. Brown (Ed.), *Recall and recognition.* New York: Wiley-Interscience, 1976.

Locksley, A., & Lenauer, M. Considerations for a theory of self-inference processes. In N. Cantor & J. F. Kihlstrom (Eds.), *Personality, cognition, and social interaction.* Hillsdale, N.J.: Erlbaum, 1981.

Loftus, E. F., & Loftus, G. R. On the permanence of stored information in the human brain. *American Psychologist,* 1980, *35,* 409–420.

Magnusson, D. (Ed.). *The situation: An interactional perspective.* Hillsdale, N.J.: Erlbaum, 1980.

Maher, B. A. Delusional thinking and perceptual disorder. *Journal of Individual Psychology,*

1974, *30,* 98–113.

Mahoney, M. J., & Arnkoff, D. B. Cognitive and self-control therapies. In S. L. Garfield & A. E. Bergin (Eds.), *Handbook of psychotherapy and behavior change: An empirical analysis.* New York: Wiley, 1978.

Mancuso, J. C., & Ceely, S. G. The self as memory processing. *Cognitive Therapy and Research,* 1980, *4,* 1–25.

Mandler, G. *Mind and emotion.* New York: Wiley, 1975.

Markman, E., & Seibert, J. Classes and collections: Internal organization and resulting holistic properties. *Cognitive Psychology,* 1976, *8,* 561–577.

Markus, H. Self-schemata and processing information about the self. *Journal of Personality and Social Psychology,* 1977, *35,* 63–78.

Markus, H., & Fong, G. *The role of the self in other processing.* Manuscript in preparation, 1981.

Markus, H., & Sentis, H. The self in social information processing. In J. Suls (Ed.), *Social psychological perspectives on the self.* Hillsdale, N.J.: Erlbaum, 1980.

Markus, H., & Smith, J. The influence of self-schemata on the perception of others. In N. Cantor & J. F. Kihlstrom (Eds.), *Personality, cognition, and social interaction.* Hillsdale, N.J.: Erlbaum, 1981.

Marshall, G. D., & Zimbardo, P. G. Affective consequences of inadequately explained physiological arousal. *Journal of Personality and Social Psychology,* 1979, *37,* 970–988.

Maslach, C. Negative emotional biasing of unexplained arousal. *Journal of Personality and Social Psychology,* 1979, *37,* 953–969.

Maslach, C., Zimbardo, P. G., & Marshall, G. D. Hypnosis as a means of studying cognitive and behavioral control. In E. Fromm & R. E. Shor (Eds.), *Hypnosis: Developments in research and new perspectives.* New York: Aldine, 1979.

McClelland, D. C. Testing for competence rather than "intelligence." *American Psychologist,* 1973, *28,* 1–14.

McClelland, D. C. Motive dispositions: The merits of operant and respondent measures. *Review of Personality and Social Psychology,* 1980, *1,* 10–41.

McGuire, W. J., & McGuire, C. V. Salience of handedness in the spontaneous self-concept. *Perceptual and Motor Skills,* 1980, *50,* 3–7.

McGuire, W. J., McGuire, C. V., Child, P., & Fujioka, T. A. Salience of ethnicity in the spontaneous self-concept as a function of one's ethnic distinctiveness in the social environment. *Journal of Personality and Social Psychology,* 1978, *36,* 511–520.

McGuire, W. J., McGuire, C. V., & Winton, W. Effects of household sex composition on the salience of one's gender in the spontaneous self-concept. *Journal of Experimental Social Psychology,* 1979, *15,* 77–90.

McGuire, W. J., & Padawer-Singer, A. Trait salience in the spontaneous self-concept. *Journal of Personality and Social Psychology,* 1976, *33,* 743–754.

Miller, D. T. Ego involvement and attributions for success and failure. *Journal of Personality and Social Psychology,* 1976, *34,* 901–906.

Mischel, W. *Personality and assessment.* New York: Wiley, 1968.

Mischel, W. Direct versus indirect personality assessment: Evidence and implications. *Journal of Consulting and Clinical Psychology,* 1972, *38,* 319–324.

Mischel, W. On the empirical dilemmas of psychodynamic approaches: Issues and alternatives. *Journal of Abnormal Psychology,* 1973, *82,* 335–344. (a)

Mischel, W. Toward a cognitive–social learning theory of personality. *Psychological Review,* 1973, *80,* 252–283. (b)

Mischel, W. Processes in delay of gratification. In L. Berkowitz (Ed.), *Advances in experimental social psychology.* New York: Academic Press, 1974.

Mischel, W. *Introduction to personality* (2nd ed.). New York: Holt, Rinehart & Winston, 1976.

Mischel, W. On the future of personality assessment. *American Psychologist,* 1977, *32,* 246–254.

Mischel, W. On the interface of cognition and personality: Beyond the person–situation debate. *American Psychologist,* 1979, *34,* 740–754.

Mischel, W. *Objective and subjective rules for delay of gratification.* Paper presented at the Symposium on Cognitions in Human Motivation, Louvain, Belgium, 1980.

Money, J., & Ehrhardt, A. A. *Man and woman, boy and girl: Differentiation and dimorphism of gender identity from conception to maturity.* Baltimore: Johns Hopkins University Press, 1972.

Monteiro, K. P., & Bower, G. H. *Using hypnotic mood induction to study the effect of mood on memory* (Hypnosis Research Memorandum #155). Stanford, Calif.: Laboratory of Hypnosis Research, Department of Psychology, Stanford University, 1979.

Murray, H. A. *Explorations in personality: A clinical and experimental study of fifty men of college age.* Oxford, England: Oxford University Press, 1938.

Nasby, W. *An experimental approach to the study of affect and memory in children.* Unpublished doctoral dissertation, Harvard University, 1980.

Neisser, U. *Cognitive psychology.* New York: Appleton-Century-Crofts, 1967.

Neisser, U. *Cognition and reality: Principles and implications of cognitive psychology.* San Francisco: W. H. Freeman, 1976.

Neisser, U. Memory: What are the important questions? In M. M. Gruneberg, P. E. Morris, & R. N. Sykes (Eds.), *Practical aspects of memory.* New York: Academic Press, 1978.

Nisbett, R. E., & Ross, L. *Human inference: Strategies and shortcomings of social judgment.* Englewood Cliffs, N.J.: Prentice-Hall, 1980.

Nisbett, R. E., & Wilson, T. D. Telling more than we can know: Verbal reports on mental processes. *Psychological Review,* 1977, *84,* 231–259.

Norman, D. A., & Bobrow, D. G. Descriptions: An intermediate stage in memory retrieval. *Cognitive Psychology,* 1979, *11,* 107–123.

Norman, W. T. Toward an adequate taxonomy of personality attributes: Replicated factor structures in peer nomination personality ratings. *Journal of Abnormal and Social Psychology,* 1963, *66,* 574–583.

Orne, M. T. On the social psychology of the psychological experiment: With particular reference to demand characteristics and their implications. *American Psychologist,* 1962, *17,* 776–783.

Orne, M. T. Communication by the total experimental situation: Why it is important, how it is evaluated, and its significance for the ecological validity of findings. In P. Pliner, L. Krames, & T. Alloway (Eds.), *Communication and affect: Language and thought.* New York: Academic Press, 1973.

Owens, J., Bower, G. H., & Black, J. The "soap opera" effect in story recall. *Memory and Cognition,* 1979, *7,* 185–191.

Passini, F. T., & Norman, W. T. A universal conception of personality structure? *Journal of Personality and Social Psychology,* 1966, *4,* 44–49.

Paul, I. H. Studies in remembering: The reproduction of connected and extended verbal material. *Psychological Issues,* 1959, *1*(Whole No. 2).

Peevers, B. H., & Secord, P. F. Developmental changes in attribution of descriptive concepts to persons. *Journal of Personality and Social Psychology,* 1973, *27,* 120–128.

Pervin, L. A. A free-response description approach to the analysis of person-situation interaction. *Journal of Personality and Social Psychology,* 1976, *34,* 465–474.

Pervin, L. A. The representative design of person–situation research. In D. Magnusson & N. S. Endler (Eds.), *Personality at the crossroads: Current issues in interactional psychology.* Hillsdale, N.J.: Erlbaum, 1977.

Piaget, J. *The origins of intelligence in the child.* New York: International Universities Press, 1956.

Reed, G. Everyday anomalies of recall and recognition. In J. F. Kihlstrom & F. J. Evans (Eds.),

Functional disorders of memory. Hillsdale, N.J.: Erlbaum, 1979.

Robinson, J. A. Sampling autobiographical memory. *Cognitive Psychology,* 1976, *8,* 578–595.

Rogers, C. R., & Dymond, R. F. (Eds.). *Psychotherapy and personality change: Co-ordinated studies in the client-centered approach.* Chicago: University of Chicago Press, 1954.

Rogers, T. B. A model of the self as an aspect of the human information-processing system. In N. Cantor & J. F. Kihlstrom (Eds.), *Personality, cognition, and social interaction.* Hillsdale, N.J.: Erlbaum, 1981.

Rogers, T. B., & Kuiper, N. A. *Processing personal information about others: Effects of familiarity and self-relevance.* Manuscript in preparation, 1981.

Rogers, T. B., Kuiper, N. A., & Kirker, W. S. Self-reference and the endocing of personal information. *Journal of Personality and Social Psychology,* 1977, *35,* 677–688.

Rogers, T. B., Rogers, P. J., & Kuiper, N. A. Evidence for the self as a cognitive prototype: The "false alarms effect." *Personality and Social Psychology Bulletin,* 1979, *5,* 53–56.

Rosch, E. Principles of categorization. In E. Rosch & B. B. Lloyd (Eds.), *Cognition and categorization.* Hillsdale, N.J.: Erlbaum, 1978.

Rosch, E., & Mervis, C. Family resemblances: Studies in the internal structure of categories. *Cognitive Psychology,* 1975, *8,* 382–439.

Rosenberg, S. New approaches to the analysis of personal constructs in person perception. In A. W. Landfield (Ed.), *Nebraska Symposium on Motivation* (Vol. 23). Lincoln: University of Nebraska Press, 1976.

Rosenthal, R. On the social psychology of the psychological experiment: The experimenter's hypothesis as unintended determinant of experimental results. *American Scientist,* 1963, *51,* 270–282.

Rosenthal, R. *On the social psychology of the self-fulfilling prophecy: Further evidence for Pygmalion effects and their mediating mechanisms.* New York: MSS Modular Publications, 1973.

Rosenthal, R., & Jacobson, L. *Pygmalion in the classroom.* New York: Holt, Rinehart & Winston, 1968.

Rosenthal, R., & Rubin, D. B. Interpersonal expectancy effects: The first 345 studies. *Behavioral and Brain Sciences,* 1978, *3,* 377–415.

Ross, L. The intuitive psychologist and his shortcomings. In L. Berkowitz (Ed.), *Advances in experimental social psychology* (Vol. 10). New York: Academic Press, 1977.

Ross, L., Amabile, T. M., & Steinmetz, J. L. Social roles, social control, and biases in social-perception processes. *Journal of Personality and Social Psychology,* 1977, *35,* 485–494.

Ross, L., Lepper, M. R., & Hubbard, M. Perseverance in self-perception and social perception: Biased attributional processes in the debriefing paradigm. *Journal of Personality and Social Psychology,* 1975, *32,* 880–892.

Ross, L., Lepper, M. R., Strach, F., & Steinmetz, J. L. Social explanation and social expectation: The effects of real and hypothetical explanations upon subjective likelihood. *Journal of Personality and Social Psychology,* 1977, *35,* 817–829.

Ross, M., & Sicoly, F. Egocentric biases in availability and attribution. *Journal of Personality and Social Psychology,* 1979, *37,* 322–336.

Rotter, J. B. *Social learning and clinical psychology.* Englewood Cliffs, N.J.: Prentice-Hall, 1954.

Rotter, J. B. Generalized expectancies for internal versus external control of reinforcement. *Psychological Monographs,* 1966, *80*(Whole No. 609).

Sarason, I. G., Smith, R. E., & Diener, E. Personality research: Components of variance attributable to the person and the situation. *Journal of Personality and Social Psychology,* 1975, *32,* 199–204.

Schachter, S., & Singer, J. E. Cognitive, social, and physiological determinants of emotional state. *Psychological Review,* 1962, *69,* 379–399.

Schank, R., & Abelson, R. *Scripts, plans, goals, and understanding: An inquiry into human knowledge structures.* Hillsdale, N.J.: Erlbaum, 1977.

Schneider, D. J. Implicit personality theory: A review. *Psychological Bulletin,* 1973, *79,* 294–309.

Schneider, D. J., Hastorf, A. H., & Ellsworth, P. C. *Person perception* (2nd ed.). Reading, Mass.: Addison-Wesley, 1979.

Schneider, W., & Shiffrin, R. M. Controlled and automatic human information processing: I. Detection, search, and attention. *Psychological Review,* 1977, *84,* 1–66.

Schweder, R. A., & D'Andrade, R. G. Accurate reflection or systematic distortion? A reply to Block, Weiss, and Thorne. *Journal of Personality and Social Psychology,* 1979, *37,* 1075–1084.

Seligman, M. E. P. *Helplessness: On depression, development, and death.* San Francisco: W. H. Freeman, 1975.

Shrauger, J. S., & Patterson, M. B. Self-evaluation and the selection of dimensions for evaluating others. *Journal of Personality,* 1974, *42,* 569–585.

Skinner, B. F. *Science and human behavior.* New York: Free Press, 1953.

Smith, E. E. Theories of semantic memory. In W. K. Estes (Ed.), *Handbook of learning and cognitive processes* (Vol. 6: *Linguistic functions in cognitive theory*). Hillsdale, N.J.: Erlbaum, 1978.

Smith, E. E., & Medin, D. *Representation and processing of lexical concepts.* Paper presented at the Sloan Conference on Cognitive Science, San Diego, March 1979.

Snyder, M. Self-monitoring processes. In L. Berkowitz (Ed.), *Advances in experimental social psychology* (Vol. 12). New York: Academic Press, 1979.

Snyder, M. Seek, and ye shall find: Testing hypotheses about other people. In E. T. Higgins, C. P. Herman, & M. P. Zanna (Eds.), *Social cognition: The Ontario symposium.* Hillsdale, N.J.: Erlbaum, 1980.

Snyder, M., & Cantor, N. Testing hypotheses about other people: The use of historical knowledge. *Journal of Experimental Social Psychology,* 1979, *15,* 330–342.

Snyder, M., & Cantor, N. Thinking about ourselves and others: Self-monitoring and social knowledge. *Journal of Personality and Social Psychology,* 1980, *39,* 222–234.

Snyder, M., Stephan, W. G., & Rosenfield, D. Egotism and attributions. *Journal of Personality and Social Psychology,* 1976, *33,* 435–441.

Snyder, M., Stephan, W. G., & Rosenfield, D. Attributional egotism. In J. H. Harvey, W. Ickes, & R. F. Kidd (Eds.), *New directions in attribution research* (Vol. 2). Hillsdale, N.J.: Erlbaum, 1978.

Snyder, M., & Swann, W. B. Behavioral confirmation in social interaction: From social perception to social reality. *Journal of Experimental Social Psychology,* 1978, *14,* 148–162. (a)

Snyder, M., & Swann, W. B. Hypothesis-testing processes in social interaction. *Journal of Personality and Social Psychology,* 1978, *36,* 1202–1212. (b)

Snyder, M., Tanke, E. D., & Berschied, E. Social perception and interpersonal behavior: On the self-fulfilling nature of social stereotypes. *Journal of Personality and Social Psychology,* 1977, *35,* 656–666.

Snyder, M., & Uranowitz, S. W. Reconstructing the past: Some cognitive consequences of person perception. *Journal of Personality and Social Psychology,* 1978, *36,* 941–950.

Spelke, E., Hirst, W., & Neisser, U. Skills of divided attention. *Cognition,* 1976, *4,* 215–230.

Spence, J. T., & Helmreich, R. L. *Masculinity and femininity: Their psychological dimensions, correlates, and antecedents.* Austin: University of Texas Press, 1978.

Spence, J. T., & Helmreich, R. L. The many faces of androgyny: A reply to Locksley and Colten. *Journal of Personality and Social Psychology,* 1979, *37,* 1032–1046.

Taylor, S. E., & Crocker, J. Schematic bases of social information processing. In E. T. Higgins, P. M. Herman, & M. P. Zanna (Eds.), *Social cognition: The Ontario symposium.* Hillsdale, N.J.: Erlbaum, 1980.

Taylor, S. E., & Fiske, S. T. Salience, attention, and attribution: Top of the head phenomena. In L. Berkowitz (Ed.), *Advances in experimental social psychology* (Vol. 11). New York: Academic Press, 1978.

Teasdale, J. D., & Fogarty, S. J. Differential effects of induced mood on retrieval of pleasant and unpleasant events from episodic memory. *Journal of Abnormal Psychology,* 1979, *88,* 248–257.

Tulving, E. Episodic and semantic memory. In E. Tulving & W. Donaldson (Eds.), *Organization of memory.* New York: Academic Press, 1972.

Tversky, A. Features of similarity. *Psychological Review,* 1977, *84,* 327–352.

Tversky, A., & Kahneman, D. Judgment under uncertainty: Heuristics and biases. *Science,* 1974, *185,* 1124–1131.

Tyler, L. E. *Individuality: Human possibilities and personal choice in the psychological development of men and women.* San Francisco: Jossey-Bass, 1978.

Underwood, B. J. Attributes of memory. *Psychological Review,* 1969, *76,* 559–573.

Valins, S., & Nisbett, R. E. Attribution processes in the development and treatment of emotional disorder. In E. E. Jones, D. E. Kanouse, H. H. Kelley, R. E. Nisbett, S. Valins, & B. Weiner (Eds.), *Attribution: Perceiving the causes of behavior.* Morristown, N.J.: General Learning Press, 1972.

Vygotsky, L. S. *Thought and language.* Cambridge, Mass.: MIT Press, 1965.

Wason, P. C., & Johnson-Laird, P. N. *Psychology of reasoning: Structure and content.* Cambridge, Mass.: Harvard University Press, 1972.

Weiner, B., Frieze, I., Kukla, A., Reed, L., Rest, S., & Rosenbaum, R. M. Perceiving the causes of success and failure. In E. E. Jones, D. E. Kanouse, H. H. Kelley, R. E. Nisbett, S. Valins, & B. Weiner (Eds.), *Attribution: Perceiving the causes of behavior.* Morristown, N.J.: General Learning Press, 1972.

Weingartner, H. Human state-dependent learning. In B. T. Ho, D. W. Richards, & D. L. Chute (Eds.), *Drug discrimination and state-dependent learning.* New York: Academic Press, 1978.

Weingartner, H., Miller, H., & Murphy, D. L. Mood-state-dependent retrieval of word associations. *Journal of Abnormal Psychology,* 1977, *86,* 276–284.

Wickens, D. D. Characteristics of word encoding. In A. W. Melton & E. Martin (Eds.), *Coding processes in human memory.* Washington, D.C.: V. H. Winston, 1972.

Wiggins, J. S. *Personality and prediction: Principles of personality assessment.* Reading, Mass.: Addison-Wesley, 1973.

Wiggins, J. S. A psychological taxonomy of trait-descriptive terms: The interpersonal domain. *Journal of Personality and Social Psychology,* 1979, *37,* 395–412.

Wiggins, J. S. Circumplex models of interpersonal behavior in personality and social psychology. In L. Wheeler (Ed.), *Review of personality and social psychology* (Vol. 1). Beverly Hills, Calif.: Sage, 1980.

Willerman, L. *The psychology of individual and group differences.* San Francisco: W. H. Freeman, 1979.

Wilson, G. T. Cognitive-behavior therapy: Paradigm shift or passing phase? In J. P. Foreyt & D. P. Rathjen (Eds.), *Cognitive-behavior therapy: Research and applications.* New York: Plenum, 1978.

Winograd, T. Computer memories: A metaphor for memory organization. In C. N. Cofer (Ed.), *The structure of human memory.* San Francisco: W. H. Freeman, 1975.

Wittgenstein, L. *Philosophical investigations.* New York: Macmillan, 1953.

Wolpe, J. *Psychotherapy by reciprocal inhibition.* Stanford, Calif.: Stanford University Press, 1958.

Word, C. O., Zanna, M. P., & Cooper, J. The nonverbal mediation of self-fulfilling prophecies in interracial interaction. *Journal of Experimental Social Psychology,* 1974, *10,* 109–120.

Wundt, W. *Frundzüge der physiologischen Psychologie* (5th ed.). Leipzig: Engelmann, 1903.

Zajonc, R. B. Feeling and thinking: Preferences need no inferences. *American Psychologist,* 1980, *35,* 151–175.

III

MAJOR CONCEPTUAL APPROACHES

5

NEOBEHAVIORISTIC
(S-R) THEORY

HANS J. EYSENCK
Department of Psychology
Institute of Psychiatry, London

DEFINITION OF TERMS

The terms used in the title of this chapter are in need of discussion and explanation. There is little agreement on the meaning of such a term as "neobehaviorism." "Behaviorism" in its fundamentalist aspects can easily be identified with the writings of J. B. Watson, but when "neobehaviorism" is introduced, some readers will expect to hear about B. F. Skinner; others will include the Mowrer–Miller type of theory under this heading; and others will prefer to refer to any or all of the many theories concerning conditioning and learning that have been put forward recently by experimental learning psychologists, such as Rescorla, Herrnstein, and others. I adopt the rather unorthodox course of putting forward what I consider to be the most viable theory of behavior therapy, based on learning theory and observations from the conditioning laboratory, mentioning alternative theories in passing only. Thus, readers may prefer to think of this as *a* neobehaviorist theory, rather than *the* neobehaviorist theory of neurosis and therapy.

The theory is labeled "S-R" because, in a very real sense, it is the insistence on stimuli and responses that singles it out from other social and cognitive theories; yet this symbolism, too, is somewhat inaccurate. I have always argued, more than perhaps any other behaviorist, that the organism (O) intervenes vitally between stimuli and responses; indeed, it creates "stimuli" from a welter of arbitrarily conjoined sensory impressions, and also creates "responses" from a mish-mash of muscle twitches. (For a definition of "responses," see Patterson & Moore, 1979.) In addition, the organism imposes motivations and reaction strategies that interact with stimuli, responses, and the links that learning and conditioning forms between them, in order to determine the total reaction of the organism to the situation. Much of what the organism contributes to behavior is genetically determined, and this contribution can best be recognized through the study of personality, intelligence, and individual differences generally (Eysenck, 1967, 1980a). Thus the minimum symbolic representation that might do justice to the facts is S-O-R, but of course to this should be added arrows to indicate that responses also usually act as stimuli, that stimuli may originate in the organism, and that the organism itself can be changed through learning and conditioning.

The term "behavior therapy" itself requires brief discussion, particularly in relation to the term "behavior modification," often used as a synonym. When I originally introduced the term "behavior therapy" in its present meaning (Eysenck, 1959), I contrasted it with psychotherapy on 10 crucial points; Table 5-1 sets out these differences and implicitly defines "behavior therapy." It defines "neurotic behavior" in terms of Pavlovian conditioning, and "treatment" in terms of extinction of autonomic conditioned responses (CRs). On the whole, this definition and the theory implicit in it have stood the test of time remarkably well; the changes that more recent experimental work has necessitated in the original formulation are described in later sections.

Here I wish to draw attention to certain important differences between this conception of "behavior therapy," and the notion of "behavior modification" as currently understood by most clinical psychologists (Leitenberg, 1976). "Behavior modification" is more usually used to designate the use of instrumental-conditioning techniques in connection with implementing changes in outward behavior that is in some way regarded as socially disadvantageous; this contrasts it with "behavior therapy," which is usually used to designate the use of classical-conditioning techniques in connection with implementing changes in autonomic reactions of patients who regard their own behavior as maladaptive. It is not suggested that these differences in usage are universally adopted; it is merely suggested that such a distinction is frequently made, and that researchers and clinicians may with advantage adopt it in talking about methods of treatment. The distinction seems to parallel in many ways that made by Eysenck and Rachman (1965) between neuroses of the first and the second kind. Table 5-2 indicates the nature of the division here suggested.

The brief notation in Table 5-2 hides many problems, of course, particularly that of the degree to which the distinction between classical and instrumental or operant conditioning can be called absolute (Bindra, 1971; Guthrie, 1935; Hearst & Jenkins, 1974; Hull, 1943; Kimble, 1961; Konorski & Miller, 1937; Mowrer, 1947; Rescorla & Solomon, 1967; Schlosberg, 1937; Skinner, 1935; Thorndike, 1932; Tolman, 1932). It would be idle to pretend that the last word on this controversy has been spoken: Let me merely state the obvious fact that there are considerable differences between the two

TABLE 5-1. Alternative Systems of Treatment of Neurotic Disorders

FREUDIAN PSYCHOTHERAPY	BEHAVIOR THERAPY
1. Based on inconsistent theory never properly formulated in postulate form.	1. Based on consistent, properly formulated theory leading to testable deductions.
2. Derived from clinical observations made without necessary control observation or experiments.	2. Derived from experimental studies specifically designed to test basic theory and deductions made therefrom.
3. Considers symptoms the visible upshot of unconscious causes ("complexes").	3. Considers symptoms as unadaptive conditioned responses (CRs).
4. Regards symptoms as evidence of *repression*.	4. Regards symptoms as evidence of faulty learning.
5. Believes that symptomatology is determined by defense mechanism.	5. Believes that symptomatology is determined by individual differences in conditionability and autonomic lability, as well as accidental environmental circumstances.
6. All treatment of neurotic disorders must be *historically* based.	6. All treatment of neurotic disorders is concerned with habits existing at *present*; their historical develpment is largely irrelevant.
7. Cures are achieved by handling the underlying (unconscious) dynamics, not by treating the symptom itself.	7. Cures are achieved by treating the symptom itself, that is, by extinguishing unadaptive CRs and extablishing desirable CRs.
8. Interpretation of symptoms, dreams, acts, and so on, is an important element of treatment.	8. Interpretation, even if not completely subjective and erroneous, is irrelevant.
9. Symptomatic treatment leads to the elaboration of new symptoms.	9. Symptomatic treatment leads to permanent recovery provided autonomic as well as skeletal surplus CRs are extinguished.
10. Transference relations are essential for cures of neurotic disorders.	10. Personal relations are not essential for cures of neurotic disorder, although they may be useful in certain circumstances.

Note. From Eysenck (1959).

TABLE 5-2. Differences between Behavior Therapy and Behavior Modification

AREAS OF DIFFERENCE	BEHAVIOR THERAPY	BEHAVIOR MODIFICATION
Mode of conditioning	Classical	Instrumental
Type of neurosis	Neuroses of the first kind	Neuroses of the second kind
Symptomatology	Emotional disorders	Behavior disorders
Hypothetical defect	Overconditioned	Underconditioned
Treatment	Extinction	Positive conditioning
Basic mediator	Law of contiguity	Law of effect

methods; whether these can be called "absolute" is in the last resort a semantic question (Gray, 1975; Mackintosh, 1974). The main task of researchers must surely be to define and investigate both similarities and differences, rather than make absolute judgments that are too all-embracing to carry much meaning. On these grounds, I believe that the two methods are sufficiently differentiated and can be shown to apply largely to different bodily systems, so that a clear distinction becomes desirable. It must be agreed that the terms "behavior therapy" and "behavior modification" are not always used in the manner suggested; the only answer can be that if they are not, they certainly should be, in the interests of intellectual clarity and experimental rigor. It is not suggested, of course, that in most real-life situations traces of both classical and instrumental conditioning cannot be found; but, rather, that in the usual types of emotional disturbance or behavioral misconduct, treatment along one line or the other is pretty clearly indicated, even though in each case elements of the theoretically irrelevant type of conditioning may be found and may have to be used as an adjunct to treatment.

However that may be, and whether or not the suggestions contained in the previous paragraphs are adopted, I deal in this chapter with "behavior therapy" as so defined; "behavior modification" is essentially dealt with in Chapter 6. My own approach to the problems of behavior disorders is probably somewhat different from the one adopted there (Eysenck, 1977b, 1980b, 1980c), but this is not the place to enter into discussion of such differences. This chapter deals essentially with theories of neurotic disorders of the first kind (anxieties, phobias, obsessive–compulsive states, reactive depressions) and their treatment, using theories of classical conditioning and extinction; instrumental conditioning will only be referred to insofar as it seems to interact with certain aspects of the treatment. I begin with a brief outline of the behavioristic position adopted by J. B. Watson and his followers, and I detail some of the criticisms that have necessitated the novel formulations adopted by neobehaviorists; I then set down the neobehaviorist position in the following sections.

Before taking up these topics, a brief word must be said about the general definition of behavior therapy as a neobehavioristic discipline. Originally I defined "behavior therapy" (1960) as "a large group of methods of treatment, all of which owe their existence and their theoretical justification to modern learning theory; they thus derive from Pavlov, Watson, and Hull, rather than from Freud, Jung, and Adler" (p. ix). And 4 years later (1964), I abbreviated this to read: "Behaviour therapy may be defined as the attempt to alter human behaviour and emotion in a beneficial manner according to the laws of modern learning theory" (p. 3). This statement has been much criticized, particularly by Breger and McGaugh (1965), Locke (1971), and London (1972); more recently, Wolpe (1976a, 1976b), MacKenzie (1977), and Erwin (1978) have also joined the critics. The major source of criticism would appear to be the (correct) belief that there is no single "modern learning theory" accepted by all psychologists working in this area, and that consequently "behavior therapy" cannot be defined in terms of this nonexistent theory. Eaglen (1978), Eysenck (1972, 1976), and Rachman and Eysenck (1966) have answered the various points made in some detail, and this is not the place to reopen this particular controversy; it may be useful to say a few words about the place of theory in science generally, however, as much of the criticism seems to be based on an erroneous notion of just what theory does and can do in science. Other points of criticism are taken up later in this chapter.

It is universally agreed in science (meaning by this the hard sciences that constitute the present model) that there are *no* theories that do not generate anomalies and counterinstances (Suppe, 1974). As a consequence, it is often found that in alive and thriving sciences two or more theories are found useful in aiding research, applied work, and the general advance toward a more inclusive type of theory. To say that because there is no universal agreement on a given theory, because there are anomalies defying explanation in terms of given theories, and because alternative theories are advocated by experts, therefore it is impossible to argue for the application of such theories as there may be, is to fly in the face of the history of science. If such a view had been taken seriously by pure and applied physicists and chemists, let alone astronomers, then no advance would have been made in the past 2000 years. Critics of behavior therapy who rely on the argument that no universally agreed theory of learning and conditioning exists, and that there are many anomalies that puzzle existing theories, are in error if they go on to argue that principles of behavior therapy cannot be deduced from such theories as do exist. Indeed, it can be argued that the testing of deductions from existing theories in the field of behavior therapy can be of great help in deciding between rival theories, in disproving given theories, and in providing material for further improvement in other theories.

Examples from the hard sciences may make clear some of these points. Newton's theory of universal gravitation was based on the hypothesis of "action at a distance"; this hypothesis was universally abandoned in recent times, and physicists now have two alternative theories of gravitation—namely, Einstein's field theory and the quantum theory of particle exchange ("gravitons"). The failure of Newton's original hypothesis and the existence of two alternative theories have not inhibited applied scientists from using these theories to the full and putting a man on the moon! Or consider the theory of heat, where the thermodynamic and the kinetic theories exist side by side. The kinetic theory, which derives from Bernoulli's famous treatise on hydraulics, gives a good understanding of atomic processes responsible for the observations and experiments carried out in the laboratory; many phenomena, however, are still quite intractable to kinetic interpretations even today, yet yield easily to a thermodynamic solution. A similar duality obtains with regard to the theory of light. Ever since the struggle between Huygens and Newton concerning the wave or corpuscular nature of light, there have been two alternative theories, until finally physicists have been reduced to regarding light as combining properties of both wave and corpuscular nature. In effect, they treat light as a wave phenomenon on Mondays, Wednesdays, and Fridays; as a corpuscular phenomenon on Tuesdays, Thursdays, and Saturdays; and as a combination on Sundays! Perhaps psychologists should do the same with classical and instrumental conditioning.

What often seems to happen in physics is that theories have the same experimental consequences, but a very different conceptual basis—Newtonian and Lagrangian mechanics, for instance, or the Schrödinger and Heisenberg interpretations of quantum mechanics. Although expressing the same experimental knowledge of present-day physics, such alternative views suggest different kinds of development and different intuitions about the reality of matter. From the point of view of future research, such differences are vital; from the point of view of application, they are much less important and may offer no hindrance at all to successful use in practice. This would appear to be the position in psychology also; the arguments concerning the major bases for a universal theory of learning and conditioning are important, but they need not prevent researchers and clinicians from applying such knowledge as they have in the way of theory to the problems of neurotic behavior. Sir George Thomson, Nobel Laureate in physics, once put this point very concisely when he said:

If differences of opinion, or at least of emphasis are still possible about space, time, and gravitation, this is an example of something very common in physics. Very different points of view may lead to identical or nearly identical conclusions when translated into what can be observed. It is the observations that are closest to reality. The more one abstracts from them the more exciting indeed are the conclusions one draws and the more suggestive for further advances, but the less can one be certain that some widely different viewpoint would not do as well. (1961, p. 74)

The mistake that the critics of my formulation make may be summed up by saying that if the good is the enemy of the best, the unattainable ideal may also be the enemy of the attainable and useful, if imperfect, reality. To rest content with good but suboptimal theories and methods is not recommended if better ones can be supplied but to decry what can be done with the best theories and methods available because they fall short of some Platonian ideal of science laid up in Heaven, and to refuse to take seriously the existing theories because they are not perfect, is to do a disservice to science, both "pure" and "applied." It is only by applying such theories as do exist that investigators shall learn their limitations, as well as their excellencies; to wait until some perfect, universally agreed-upon theories emerge is to postpone the time when psychology can be made practically useful, sine die. Nothing can show up the deficiencies of theories as well as efforts to apply them to practical problems can; the anomalies thus generated should then act as spurs to improve these theories, or even drastically to revise them. The benefits of close cooperation between "pure" and "applied" science are not one-sided; the applied scientist gains immeasurably from having good theories to apply, but the pure scientist gains equally in having important feedback from situations he or she could not easily create in the laboratory. Both these interactions are amply illustrated in the following sections.

WATSON'S ORIGINAL THEORY

In order to criticize J. B. Watson's original theory and to contrast it with neobehavioristic theories, it is of course essential first of all to state what Watson's theory was. This is not as easy as might be thought, because Watson did not write a detailed outline of this theory in any of his papers or books, but dropped hints, made suggestions, and outlined vague models that can hardly aspire to the appellation of "theories." Furthermore, as D. Cohen (1979) has pointed out, Watson was too sensible and too much in touch with the real world to accept the logical restrictions of his own theories, so that he often talked and wrote in ways that seemed to contradict what he had said elsewhere. This of course happens to all theorists, but it is particularly noticeable in Watson.

Watson's theory of neurosis may be said to have begun with his paper on "Behavior and the Concept of Mental Disease" (J. B. Watson, 1916); in this paper, he began by stating: "The simple truth that I think Freud has given us is that *youthful, outgrown, and partially discarded habits and instinctive systems of reaction can and possibly always do influence the functioning of our adult systems of reactions, and influence to a certain extent even the possibility of our forming the new habit systems which we must reasonably expect it to form*" (p. 590). He goes on to say that "such habit systems need never have been 'conscious' (and here all I mean by being 'conscious'— and all I believe the psychopathologists mean by it—is that *the patient cannot phrase in terms of words the habit twists which have become part of his [or her] biological equipment*). The implication is clear that in the psychoneuroses I should look for *habit disturbances*—maladjustments—and should attempt to describe my findings in terms of the inadequacy of responses, of wrong responses, and of the complete lack of responses to the objects and situations in the daily life of the patient'' (p. 591).

According to Watson,

The chief difficulty in the description in terms of the everyday language of habit formation lies in our failure to look upon *language* . . . as being only a system of motor habits. As a short cut—a system of economy—the human animal has formed a system of language habits (spoken words, inner speech, etc.). These language habits are built up from and always correspond more or less closely to the general system of bodily habits (p. 591).

Watson goes on:

If now we can take what appears to me to be a sensible point of view about language habits (''thought'') and come to look upon them as obeying the laws of all other habits, and describe our patient's symptoms wholly in terms of habit disturbance, and trace the conditions which have led to the disturbance, we shall have come a long way. . . . All such disturbances of habit—superfluous and useless conditioned reflexes—may be found to date back to some primary stimulus (possibly to sex trauma, exposure, masturbation, etc., in childhood) which is a conditioning cause. (p. 593)

Having dealt with motor habits, Watson turns to emotion:

Every motor reaction calls for a simultaneous response in the glandular system (corresponding in part at least to the *affective values* of the psychologist and psychopathologist). Now the chief symptom in many cases of mental disease is the disturbance of ''affective values'' . . . as I view the matter we have here just the situation for arousing *conditioned emotional reflexes.* Any stimulus (nonemotional) which immediately (or shortly) follows an emotionally exciting stimulus produces its motor reaction before the emotional effects of the original stimulus has died down. A transfer (conditioned reflex) takes place (after many such occurrences) so that in the end the second stimulus produces in its train now not only is proper group of motor integrations, but an emotional set which belonged originally to another stimulus. (p. 596)

Watson's theory was elaborated in the paper with Rayner (J. B. Watson & Rayner, 1920), which set forth the story of ''little Albert,'' the infant in whom Watson and Rayner conditioned a phobic response to rats; this paper is too well known to be discussed in detail, although, as Harris (1979) has pointed out, the way the experiment is described in many textbooks involves serious inaccuracies. Jones (1924a, 1924b) took up the story and employed a number of therapeutic methods that adumbrated modern methods of behavior therapy, often very successfully, in her attempts to cure children of various neurotic disorders.

In all this, the language is the language of Pavlov and conditioning, but, as a perusal of Watson's book (1919) makes clear, he deviated in many ways from the narrow behaviorism that is so often associated with his name nowadays. Thus, for instance, he would define the stimulus in human behavior as "stimulus or situation"; thus the stimulus could be a quite complex object or event in the external environment, involving different ways of identifying the total situation and its perception. Equally, Watson's concept of a response was much broader and more permissive than would be acceptable to some modern theorists. Nor would it be correct to say that Watson was in reality a pure S-R psychologist. In his list of determiners of an act, he cited as a fourth determiner the state of the organism, both emotionally and physiologically. Watson also anticipated Skinner in emphasizing the previous history of the individual (reinforcement history). These are all aspects of his work that are seldom emphasized nowadays.

If Watson's theory had to be characterized, it might be reduced to a number of simple statements. The first of these would be that behavior is largely determined by habit, and that habit is produced by Pavlovian conditioning. The second point would be that among the habits that are being conditioned are language and emotional habits, as well as motor ones. The third point would be that the habits so conditioned are often inappropriate, and that this gives rise to what are called neurotic and generally abnormal reactions. The fourth and final point would then be that the cure of such inappropriate conditioned reactions must lie in their *extinction,* using methods suggested by laboratory experiments, mostly on animals. These points might still be acceptable to most behavior therapists, but they do give rise to many difficulties, uncertainties, and criticisms; a restatement, or at least a change in meaning, is required before the theory can be accepted. Neobehaviorism provides such a change in meaning of the terms used and such an explanation of the anomalies that made Watson's original theory ultimately unacceptable. Some of the criticisms, anomalies, and difficulties to which Watson's theory gave rise must therefore be stated next. I have provided a more extensive statement of these points elsewhere (1979), so that I shall list them here very briefly.

The first objection is that the experiment with little Albert only involves a single case, and even then is not as impressive when looked upon in detail as it may seem at first sight. Harris (1979) has made this point in some detail. Furthermore, other authors, (e.g., Bregman, 1934; English, 1929) have failed to replicate Watson's results. Thus the experimental support for Watson's theory is really quite inadequate to bear the large structure that he erected upon it. Watson seems to have had some premonition that the experiment might not be easily replicable, because, remarking upon the persistence of the CRs in little Albert, he also stated that "one may possibly have to believe that such persistence of early conditioned responses would be found only in persons who are constitutionally inferior" (Watson & Rayner, 1920, p. 14). This is an interesting sentence because it goes entirely counter to Watson's well-known environmentalist philosophy; it suggests that one important set of variables that must be added to his original statement relates to personality. It is made clear in a later section of this chapter that this premonition was amply justified, and that indeed the omission of personality from the behaviorist position is one of its greatest weaknesses. Watson never returned to this hypothesis of "constitutional inferiority," and of course as it stands it has no assignable meaning, other perhaps than that children who develop neurotic responses are constitutionally predisposed to the development of neurotic responses (not a very illuminating concept). In this sentence Watson was paying lip service to genetics, just as Freud and Skinner did; none of these writers took or has taken seriously the task of specifying the precise nature of the genetic component, or of performing the necessary experiments to demonstrate the validity of the hypothesis.[1]

The second point of criticism arises from the finding that phobias, which are perhaps the most clear-cut instances of emotional CRs, are relatively restricted in the kinds of conditoned stimuli (CSs) that give rise to them. As Seligman (1971, p. 312) has pointed out, phobias "comprise a relatively nonarbitrary and limited set of objects; agoraphobia, fear of specific animals, insect phobias, fear of heights, and fear of the dark, and so forth. All these are relatively common phobias. And only rarely, if ever, do we have pyjama phobias, grass phobias, electric-outlet phobias, hammer phobias, even though these things are likely to be associated with trauma in our world." The set of potentially phobic stimuli thus seems to be nonarbitrary and to be related to the survival of the human species through the long course of evolution, rather than to recent discoveries and inventions that are potentially far more rational sources of phobic fears, such as motor cars, airplanes, and guns (Geer, 1965, Landy & Gaupp, 1971; Lawlis, 1971; Rubin, Katkin, Weiss, & Efran, 1968; Wolpe & Lang, 1964). Watson seems to have accepted the postulates of equipotentiality—that is, the notion that one CS is as good as another in producing conditioned responses. The nonarbitrary and limited choice of objects and situations that predominantly produce phobic fears in humans is difficult to explain along the lines of equipotentiality, and a new theory is obviously required.

A third difficulty that arises in connection with Watson's theory is the assumption that neurotic disorders start with a single traumatic conditioning event or with a series of relatively traumatic events of this nature. This is not

---

1. It is interesting to note that in our work on eyeblink conditioning (Eysenck & Levey, 1972), we have found a subgroup of subjects who completely failed to extinguish the CR in spite of the large number of unreinforced CSs presented to them. Perhaps little Albert belonged to this subgroup! Recent unpublished work on this subgroup suggests that the result is not due to partial reinforcement or to strength of original conditioning.

usually true, however, of peacetime neuroses; in wartime, traumatic events often occur to provide the appropriate unconditioned stimulus (UCS), but in peacetime the onset of neurotic disorders tends to be insidiuous, and frequently, if not usually, a traumatic UCS is completely lacking. It seems that here, too, certain objects or situations provide a fertile ground for an association with nontraumatic UCSs, thus contradicting the postulate of equipotentiality. From the psychiatric point of view, this difficulty with Watson's theory may be considered fatal, at least as the theory is stated in the original form.

Another problem that Watson seems to have disregarded quite deliberately is the dependence of the typical laboratory CS-UCS connection on very refined and precise experimental conditions, particularly on the time relations involved. For eyeblink conditioning, to take but one example, the CS has to precede the UCS by between 500 and 2500 msec; if the timing is outside these limits, very little conditoning will be found. But such precision is unobtainable, except by chance and occasionally, in real-life situations, and consequently the question arises: How can conditioning be made responsible for the acquisition of neurotic habits in real life, when the conditions for producing such habits are only very occasionally encountered?

The next objection to Watson's theory is one that has often been raised by experimental psychologists (e.g., Kimmel, 1975). As is well known, unreinforced CRs extinguish quickly (Kimble, 1961), and neurotic reactions should be no exceptions to this rule. Eysenck and Rachman (1965) have suggested that the well-documented prevalence of spontaneous remission in neurosis (Rachman, 1971) may be due to extinction of this type; however, extinction does not take place in many cases and it is the task of a good theory to account for these "nonfitting" cases, as well as for those that behave according to expectation. Watson himself put forward the view, based on his experiments with little Albert, that "conditioned emotional responses as well as those conditioned by transfer . . . persist in modified form throughout life" (J. B. Watson & Rayner, 1920). (By "transferred response," Watson means what would now be called "stimulus and response generalization," a term not then widely used.) Watson must have known of the experimental phenomenon of extinction; it is difficult to see why he did not mention the problems this would present to any such theory as that advocated by him. Of course, Pavlov's work had not been translated at that time, and he had to base his theories on casual reports; this might account for his failure. Nevertheless, he based his methods of treatment on principles of extinction, so he cannot have been ignorant of the principle itself.

If the previous difficulty is one that has been raised mostly by experimental psychologists, the next one is more likely to be raised by clinical psychologists. In many neuroses, investigators not only fail to observe the expected extinction of the unreinforced CS, but they find an incremental (enhancement) effect, such that the unreinforced CS actually produces more and more anxiety (CR) with each presentation of the CS. This finding is of course related to the fact, mentioned before, that in peacetime neuroses the UCS is very frequently not traumatic at all, but relatively mild; how is it possible that such mild UCS can give rise to CRs that are much stronger than the unconditioned response (UCR)? As Mackintosh (1974) points out, "CRs, even if they resemble the UCR very closely, are usually weaker and of lesser amplitude" (p. 97). Yet the very notion of "subtraumatic UCS" implies something of this sort—the final CR (neurotic breakdown) is stronger (involves more anxiety) than the UCR! This goes counter to all that is known of the fate of UCRs; these are known to habituate, rather than to increase in strength. The failure of traumatic UCSs to occur in peacetime neuroses is well documented (Gourney & O'Connor, 1971; Lautsch, 1971), as are the insidious onset of many neuroses (I. M. Marks, 1969; Rachman, 1968) and the rather more frequent occurrence of traumatic UCSs in wartime (Grinker & Spiegel, 1945).

Watson stresses the importance of pain or physical restraint as the major UCSs producing fear and anxiety. But while simple physical pain has frequently been used as the UCR in laboratory conditioning of animals, and even of humans, it is quite clear from the literature mentioned above that in the origin of neurotic disorders physical pain seldom plays any great part (except in wartime neuroses). This leaves a great question mark against Watson's theory, because once loss of support, physical constraints, and very intense physical stimuli of various kinds are removed from consideration, Watson really has little to offer in the way of UCSs appropriate for the production of neurotic disorders in adult humans. I have suggested elsewhere (1979) that instead of pain the UCR in human neuroses is more usually to be found in frustrative nonreward (Gray, 1971), different types of conflict (Yates, 1962), uncertainty (Kimmel, 1975), uncontrollability, and so on. These concepts can be defined operationally, and their use does not render our theory "cognitive."

Apart from the general failure of Watson's theory to be logically consistent, these are the major anomalies and difficulties that arise when attempts are made to apply his theory to what is known about the origins of human neurosis. An extinction theory of treatment might still be acceptable, even though the conditioning theory of the origins of neurosis might not; however, it will be argued that to have a proper theory of treatment, a proper theory of the origins of neurosis is required. Having now dealt in some detail with the original behavioristic theory, I now turn to the ways in which it has to be altered in order to provide a more acceptable neobehavioristic account.

THEORETICAL ADVANCES

PREPAREDNESS

Some of the difficulties with the original behavioristic theory of neurosis and treatment arise from the fact that Watson unnecessarily took part in a controversy that has roots going back to the differences between John Locke, the British philosopher of empiricism, and Immanuel Kant, the German philosopher of nativism. For Locke, mind was a tabula rasa, an empty tablet on which experience could write anything it chose. To him, there was nothing in the mind that had not been put there by sensation (i.e., by sensory impressions). To Kant, it seemed obvious that the mind contributed at least the categories of classification and understanding, and that these were genetically given and were not themselves the product of experience.

The battle between these originally philosophical ideas has since taken many forms, and it may be said to be the basis of the current debates between environmentalists and geneticists. In Watson's day the debate was between those who maintained the importance of instincts for human behavior and motivation (e.g., William McDougall) and those who denied the importance of instincts as far as possible and rather favored learning and conditioning (i.e., environmental factors) as explanatory concepts. It is not necessary for behaviorism to take any part in this controversy, but Watson did so, and rather disastrously adopted the wrong—namely, the environmentalist —position. As Bergmann (1956) makes clear, Watson's "third pseudomethodological tenet is an extreme environmentalism. . . . According to Watson, the child is at birth equipped with nothing but the structure of its body and a few elementary unlearned responses. All the rest is learning" (p. 274). He was thus a very active participant in the "instinct controversy," which lasted only half a dozen years but had fateful consequences for the development of psychology. Cravens (1978) has pointed out that "before 1917 it was difficult to find any psychologist who questioned the instinct theory. By 1922 it was almost impossible to identify more than a handful of psychologists who still accepted the human instinct theory as a legitimate category of scientific explanation" (p. 191). Behaviorism is not logically linked with the rejection of phylogenetic hypotheses, or even with the rejection of ontogenetic hypotheses, but through Watson the marriage was accomplished. As a result, psychology became divorced from evolution and ended up in a cul-de-sac of its own construction. It is only in recent years that this trend has been reversed.

One field in which this reversal has been particularly rapid and impressive is that of perception, where the work of Hubel and Wiesel (1959,

1963, 1965) has demonstrated beyond any doubt that certain areas in the striate cortex are set aside for specific visual sensations, so that experience is organized very much as Kant had hypothesized—in terms of genetically determined properties of the brain.

Another area that has seen a tremendous change from the purely environmentalistic mode (Skinner, 1957) is that of linguistics, where the work of Chomsky (1957, 1959, 1964, 1965, 1972, 1975) has demonstrated beyond serious doubt that as N. Smith and Wilson (1979) put it, "human beings were innately disposed to learn certain types of language. In other words, the languages that actually exist are the ones we are predisposed to learn" (p. 27). The major established facts in the field can only be "explained on the assumption that children are innately equipped to learn only certain types of language, and that the form their linguistic development takes is genetically determined" (p. 27). There is no serious doubt that Chomsky is right in emphasizing the importance of phylogenetic factors in the development of language, and again it can only be said that there is no necessary correlation between environmentalistic theories and behaviorism; Skinner could be perfectly right in his positive assertion that languages are in fact acquired, without also making a negative assertion as to the absence of phylogenetic factors in the structuring of language.

It would not be quite correct to say that Watson entirely eschewed phylogenetic factors in human motivation. He claimed that fear, love, and rage were innate reactions to certain specific situations, such as being dropped, being stroked, and being restrained physically. Fighting, too, he assumed to be largely an instinct, and he also seems to have accepted gregariousness as such. Manipulation and constructiveness are other instincts sometimes mentioned by him. His view seemed to be that "the geneticist is likely to overestimate, to emphasize the number of original tendencies; the psychoanalyst to under-estimate them" (J. B. Watson, 1919, p. 114). He himself, he thought, had hit upon the right medium. In part, Watson's reputation as a total environmentalist is therefore undeserved; he suffered, very much as Skinner was to suffer later, from the sins and follies of his followers, who vulgarized, oversimplified, and subtly changed his teaching.

The change in our way of looking at phylogenetic factors in the determination of behavior and motivation began with the work of the ethologists, which demonstrated, at least in animals, a far greater degree of instinctive predisposition than had previously been thought possible outside the insect field. Evolutionary principles, such as those adopted by E. O. Wilson (1975, 1978), may tilt too much in the opposite direction, but they do redress the balance unfairly disturbed by the extreme environmentalism of the past 50 years (Eysenck, 1980d).

An important aspect of this new emphasis on evolutionary principles and phylogenetic predispositions is Seligman's theory of "preparedness" (Seligman, 1970, 1971). According to this theory, "phobias are highly prepared to be learned by humans, and, like other highly prepared relationships, they are selective and resistant to extinction, learned even with degraded input, and probably non-cognitive" (Seligman, 1971, p. 312). Seligman gives many examples of the fact that some contingencies are learned much more readily than others—that is, with highly degraded input, such as single-trial learning, long delays of reinforcement, and so forth; the work of Garcia, McGowan, and Green (1971) has become a classical example of this.

The notion of preparedness integrates well with the hypothesis of innate fears (Breland & Breland, 1966; Hinde & Stevenson-Hinde, 1973; Seligman, 1971); presumably, it is mainly a question of *degree* of fear experienced which separates the two concepts. When the fear upon first encountering the stimulus object is strong, it is considered innate; when it is weak, but easily conditioned, the label "preparedness" would be used. The underlying physiological connections and the hypothetical evolutionary development are identical. The concept is a valuable one, and it appears necessary for a full understanding of phobic neuroses in particular. Seligman does not stress the importance of individual differences in relation to "preparedness"; however, different personality types will presumably show different degrees of "preparedness" as well as differences in the strength, or even the presence and absence, of innate fears.[2]

There are now a number of empirical studies that have subjected the concept of "preparedness" to experimental investigation, such as the recent work of Hugdahl, Frederikson, and Öhman (1977) and Öhman and his colleagues (Öhman & Dinsberg, 1978, Öhman, Eriksson, & Olofson, 1975; Öhman, Erixson, & Löfberg, 1975; Öhman, Frederikson, Hugdahl, & Rimmö, 1976). Using galvanic skin response (GSR) conditioning to picture slides, these investigators have demonstrated very clearly that "prepared" stimuli (pictures of rats and spiders) acquired CS-UCS connections much more quickly than did nonprepared CS (pictures of flowers and mushrooms, or even rifles and revolvers; Öhman & Dinsberg, 1978). It was also found that conditioning mediated by such "prepared" stimuli was more resistant to extinction; this point is important for subsequent discussion in this chapter and should be kept in mind. Rachman (1978a) has prepared a critique of the con-

---

2. The general ideas underlying the notion of preparedness are of course not new; thus Stekel (1912/1923) wrote, referring to Hall's (1897; see also 1914) article on fears: "The kernel of truth in his doctrine is the fact that fear is in part inherited. It is of course unthinkable that fear should not be inherited through the flight of ages. Millions of years of fear certainly do not remain without influence on the brain" (p. 384). Even Freud himself might be cited in evidence: "Constitution is everything," he told a much surprised Binswanger (1953, p. 21).

cept, and a paper by Rachman and Seligman (1976) indicates that even "unprepared" fears can show features in the theory associated with "preparedness."

It will be clear that accepting the notion of "preparedness" will account
for some of the difficulties with Watson's theory, and it may be suggested
that any neobehavioristic theory of neurosis would be required to incorporate "preparedness" (as well as the associated notion of innate fears within
itself. The theory can account for the fact that Bregman (1934) and English
(1929) failed to obtained fear conditioning in their replication of Watson's
experiment with little Albert; they used common household goods such as
curtains and blocks or a wooden duck, none of which would have the
"preparedness" value of furry animals. Another problem that may be explained by this concept is the choice of CS—why, in a traumatic situation (or
in a series of subtraumatic situations), does the person concerned pick one
rather than another equally prominent stimulus to become the CS? On
Seligman's evidence, the choice would be determined very much by innate
"preparedness," in addition to the usual chance factors.

The lack of equipotentiality that has been noted can also be explained in
terms of "preparedness." The most frequently experienced phobic fears are
attached to objects or situations that during the 4 million years of human evolution have possessed special dangers; these danger have made the acquisition
of the innate or "prepared" fears extremely useful to the individuals and the
species concerned. Open spaces make it difficult to hide from enemies; closed
spaces make it difficult to escape from enemies. Some small animals (such as
snakes and spiders) are poisonous, and these constituted dangers to humans.
Heights had obvious dangers before protective fencing became customary.
Altogether, the attractiveness of the hypothesis is obvious, although, as with
all evolutionary arguments, direct evidence must inevitably be difficult to
come by.

The last point that is explained by the postulation of "preparedness" is
the fact that in typical laboratory conditions CS-UCS intervals are of critical
importance, while in real-life situations no such precise timing can be
guaranteed. As Seligman points out, learning with a prepared CS can occur
with severely degraded input—that is to say, in circumstances that would lead
to complete failure under typical laboratory conditions (i. e., with nonprepared CS). Even with rats, Garcia *et al.* (1971) and Logue (1978) could
delay the UCS by as much as 1 whole hour after the presentation of the
"prepared" CS, and could nevertheless obtain significant evidence of conditioning. It can thus be seen that a neobehavioristic theory adopting "preparedness" instead of equipotentiality is enabled to deal with many of the problems presented by the genesis of neurotic fears.

Even with the addition of "preparedness," ordinary conditioning may not be the causal factor in all or even most phobias. Rachman (1977, 1978a) has indeed suggested that direct conditioning of any kind accounts for relatively few phobias, and the work of Murray and Foote (1979) would seem to support his view, suggesting that observational and instructional learning, rather than direct conditioning, appears important in the acquisition of fear of snakes. In this they differ from Rimm, Janda, Lancaster, Nahl, and Dittman (1977), who found, in the study of the acquisition of a heterogeneous group of phobic fears, that there were more reported experiences suggestive of direct conditioning than of vicarious experience or informational instruction. Clearly, the matter is very much in need of direct empirical study; as I point out later on, however, it should not be assumed that vicarious experiences or informational instruction cannot be themselves viewed or explained in terms of conditioning, particularly when the concept of the incubation of anxiety (to be developed in the next section) is employed. To this discussion one further point should be added—namely, the role played by approach contingencies in phobic behavior (Hayes, 1976; Hayes, Lattal, & Myerson, 1979). Simple questionnaire studies such as those just mentioned are probably insufficient to elucidate the nature of the acquisition of phobic responses.

In criticism of the concept of "preparedness," it should be pointed out that it is neither as original nor as clear-cut as it might seem at first sight. Historically, Thorndike's concept of "belongingness" (Thorndike, 1935) anticipated the notion that *associations* are prepared and that differential associability plays an important part in learning. What Seligman has done essentially is to add an evolutionary dimension to Thorndike's concept, but psychologically the two are very similar.

Among other criticisms of the theory, it should be noted that taste-aversion learning is about the only kind of learning mentioned in the Seligman and Hager book of studies in the literature (1972) that is not susceptible to alternative hypotheses. One criticism concerns the criteria for "preparedness," such as conditioning in spite of input degradation. As Schwartz (1974) has pointed out, indices such as number of trials, delay of reinforcement, and so forth "are sensible and useful within the context of the well-studied experimental paradigms to which they refer, like Pavlovian and instrumental conditioning paradigms" (p. 187). Given a particular paradigm, it is relatively easy to compare alleged instances of "preparedness" with contrary instances, with respect to a large number of parameters that might reflect degradation of input.

The problem is this: any assessment of degradation of input assumed that the paradigms on which the assessment is based are reliable measuring instruments. To compare taste-aversion learning to the laws of Pavlovian conditioning and conclude that taste-aversion learning is prepared is at the same to invest Pavlovian conditioning with the status of a unitary, reliable process; that is, such a comparison assumes that all instances of Pavlovian conditioning have something in common aside from the procedure that produces them. (Schwartz, 1974, p. 188)

If, however, investigators should encounter a phenomenon that appears to be "prepared," that must be because the procedure that produced it differed significantly (input is degraded) from past procedures that have produced other familiar phenomena. What, then, is the justification for comparing this new phenomenon with the familiar ones to assess its preparedness? The point can be extended to looking at taste-aversion learning as an instance of avoidance learning. A good deal of avoidance learning is characterized by rapid acquisition (Bolles, 1970) and resistance to extinction (Solomon & Wynne, 1954); this illustrates that prepared taste-aversion learning is dependent upon the paradigm it is evaluated against, and that there are no clear criteria other than the procedures themselves for labeling phenomena as one kind of learning or another.

Another example given by Schwartz (1974) is autoshaping. "Preparedness" has been demonstrated in regard to autoshaping in pigeons' pecking keys, but what decides whether the phenomenon itself is instrumental or not? (Seligman and Hager include papers on autoshaping in their section on instrumental learning.) "Whether or not key pecking is prepared, is, at present, unresolvable, not especially because of weaknesses in the notion of preparedness, but because of weaknesses in the distinctions we make among different kinds of learning" (Schwartz, 1974, p. 189). Key pecking clearly is not a simple example of either Pavlovian or instrumental conditioning alone (Gamzu & Schwartz, 1973; Gamzu & Williams, 1971; Jenkins & Moore, 1972; Schwartz & Williams, 1972). A good discussion of this issue is given by Gray (1975).

Another problem that arises in the recognition of "preparedness" is that the criteria for preparedness, such as degradation of input, do not by themselves permit a distinction between phenomena resulting from prepared *associations* and those resulting from the choice of specially salient stimuli or especially probable responses. Another problem is the difficulty of distinguishing between species-specific characteristics (phylogenetic and characteristics capitalizing on the organism's past history (ontogenetic). "A simple determination that an association is prepared does not carry with it a determination of the origin of the preparedness" (Schwartz, 1974, p. 190; see also Lehrman, 1953, 1970). These and many other problems that arise in connection with "preparedness" require an empirical answer before the concept is as firmly established as investigators might wish it to be.

THE INCUBATION OF ANXIETY

It is suggested in this section that many of the difficulties with Watson's original formulation are due to faults in the generally accepted notions about extinction, and that a drastic revision of the law of extinction is necessary before investigators can begin to cope with the experimentally observed facts. In part, as I point out, the difficulty lies in the common but unjustified belief that Pavlovian conditioning is in some sense a unitary mode of learning that cannot be broken down into different types. This belief is unfounded.

The classical theory of extinction has always been beset by experimental anomalies; the simple belief that the presentation of the unreinforced CS (to be symbolized by $\overline{CS}$) inevitably leads to extinction was shown to be erroneous as early as the 1950s by Razran (1956), who stated in his review of 40 years of American and Russian experimentation that "extinction continues to be clearly a less than 100% phenomenon. Instances of difficult and even impossible extinction are constantly reported by classical CI experimenters" (p. 39). I have suggested (1968) that the classical law of extinction only applies to certain types of conditioned responses, but that for others the $\overline{CS}$ presentation may be followed by an actual enhancement (incubation) of the CR.

It may be useful to begin a discussion of the incubation phenomenon by considering Grant's classification of conditioning paradigms (1964). He distinguishes between "Pavlovian A conditioning" and "Pavlovian B conditioning." The former is exemplified by the familiar bell–salivation experiment; Pavlovian B conditioning, however, shows essential differences from this familiar type of experiment. As Grant puts it in his description of Pavlovian B conditioning:

This subclass of classical conditioning could well be called Watsonian conditioning after the Watson and Rayner (1920) experiment conditioning fear responses in Albert, but Pavlov has priority. The reference experiment for Pavlovian B conditioning might be that in which an animal is given repeated injections of morphine. The UCR morphine involves severe nausea, profuse secretion of saliva, vomiting, and then profound sleep. After repeated daily injections Pavlov's dogs would show severe nausea and profuse secretion of saliva at the first touch of the experimenter (Pavlov, 1927, pp. 35–36). In Pavlovian B conditioning, stimulation by the UCS is not contingent on [a subject's] instrumental acts, and hence there is less dependence upon the motivational state of the organism, *and the CS appears to act as a partial substitute for the UCS.* Furthermore, *the UCS elicits a complete UCR* in Pavlovian B conditioning, whereas in Pavlovian A conditioning the organism emits the UCR of approaching and ingesting the food. A great deal of interoceptive conditioning (Bykov, 1957) and autonomic conditioning (Kimble, 1961) apparently follows the Pavlovian B paradigm. (Grant, 1964, p. 138; see also Kalat & Rozin, 1973; italics added)

The notion that "the CS appears to act as a partial substitute for the UCS" is basic to my own theory, as is the fact that "the UCS elicits a complete UCR." In Pavlovian A conditioning, motivation in the animal is already present at the beginning of the experiment; if the dog is not hungry, neither conditioning nor evocation of CRs can occur. Thus, in the nonhungry animal, the UCS does not elicit the UCR—the dog does not salivate. In Pavlovian B conditioning, the motivation is itself provided by the UCS, which elicits the UCR irrespective of whatever prior motivation may have been present in the animal. Thus it may be said that the major difference between Pavlovian A conditioning and Pavlovian B conditioning lies in the fact that in the latter *the UCS acts as a drive*.

It seems likely that the other property of Pavlovian B conditioning—namely, that the CS appears to act as a partial substitue for the UCS—is a consequence of the fact that the UCS acts as a drive; if the UCS acts as a drive, then the CS, by being associated with the UCS, can also act as a drive, and will thus produce UCRs similar to those produced by the UCS. A profound difference is thus apparent between Pavlovian A conditioning, in which presentation of the $\overline{CS}$ leads to extinction, and Pavlovian B conditioning, in which presentation of the $\overline{CS}$ may, under certain circumstances to be specified later, lead to incubation (enhancement of the CR). The reasons for this prediction are as follows.

Extinction occurs essentially because the $\overline{CS}$ is not followed by the UCR for a number of trials; the absence of the UCR weakens the CR and finally eliminates it. In the case of Pavlovian B conditioning, however, the presentation of the $\overline{CS}$ evokes a CR that is similar to or identical with the UCR. Hence an entirely different situation now exists; the $\overline{CS}$ is not followed by the absence of reinforcement, but by a CR that itself may act as a reinforcing agent by virtue of its similarity to the UCR. What is being suggested, therefore, is that conditioning sets in motion a positive feedback cycle in which the CR provides reinforcement for the $\overline{CS}$. Usually the extinction process will be stronger than this form of reinforcement, leading to overall extinction and making the action of $\overline{CS}$-CR reinforcement unobservable, but under certain circumstances (e.g., when the UCS is exceptionally strong), the extinction process may be weaker than the $\overline{CS}$-CR reinforcement process, and observable incubation will result. I suggest that UCRs that fit the Pavlovian B conditioning model particularly well are those related to fear–anxiety; it is well known that fear–anxiety can act as a drive, and, hence, that responses of this kind are likely to obey the precepts of Pavlovian B model. It seems possible that sexual responses may also fall within the purview of this model. Certainly sexual stimuli can usually elicit a complete UCR, and CSs are particularly likely here to act as partial substitutes for the UCS (many stimuli conditioned to sexual UCSs produce erection; i.e., the CR = UCR). Unfortunately too little work has been done in the field of sex, as compared with that in anxiety, to pursue this analogy further.

I have developed the theory of incubation in greater detail elsewhere (1979); I will not here go into any of the details presented there. However, before going on to the specification of the parameters of the model that enable it to be tested, a word needs to be said about the shift in emphasis in this model from the stimulus (which is all-powerful in the Watsonian behaviorist model) to the response (which I believe is a more important feature in the neobehavioristic model). Where the classical account links the CS with the UCS, I would partly ignore the UCS and concentrate largely on the UCR. The differentiation between UCS and UCR is usually somewhat artificial from the point of view of the organism being conditioned. Consider aversive conditioning, using shock. The shock is the UCS, and pain + fear the UCR; this makes sense from the point of view of experimenters, who administer the UCS, while subjects experience the pain. However, from the subjects' point of view, they do not feel shock (UCS) that produces pain (UCR); they experience a painful shock—that is, UCS and UCR are experienced simultaneously and not as separate, consecutive entities. It is this Gestalt-like NR (nocive response) that is being linked with the CS through contiguity, and to which the CR eventually adds another increment of pain–fear that is introspectively very difficult or even impossible to differentiate from the original NR.

In other words, the differentiation between UCS and UCR reflects preoccupation with control (the UCS is under the control of an experimenter, and causes the UCR in the sense that what the experimenter does produces the response in the subject); from a subject's point of view (and, after all, it is in the subject that the process of conditioning takes place), the differentiation is of doubtful relevance or value. UCS and UCR are temporally close together—so close that the subject often cannot differentiate between them—and, in consequence, it is difficult to disentangle the links that contiguity forces between CS and either. This difficulty can best be sorted out when UCS and UCR are temporally separated.

Such sorting out is possible in the case of apomorphine aversive conditioning (e.g. for alcohol addiction); the drug (UCS) is given several minutes before the nausea it causes (UCR) supervenes. Orthodox opinion would have it that conditioning takes place when the CS precedes the UCS; when the UCS comes first, backward conditioning, which is weak and often nonexistent, is said to occur. In practice, it is well known (Franks, 1963) that strong CRs are obtained also when the CS immediately precedes the UCR and follows the UCS by several minutes. This shows clearly the importance of the CS-UCR link and the relative unimportance of the CS-UCS link—a distinction that has been hidden in most research because of the temporal contiguity (or even identity) of UCS and UCR. A particularly clear example of the irrelevance of the UCS is the experiment by Campbell, Sanderson, and Laverty (1964), in which temporary interruption of respiration (UCR) was produced by intravenous injection of succinylcholine chloride dihydrate (UCS). "The [subjects] were all unaware of the process of injection, which was part of a lengthy process of injection of saline solution and sometimes of atropine (to reduce salivation); the CS was so timed as to precede the first sign of UCR—usually a sudden drop in skin resistance" (1964, p. 628). Here the patients were completely unaware of the UCS; furthermore, the UCS preceded the CS. This would mark the case as one of backward conditioning; yet, as Kimble (1961) points out, "it is apparent that backward conditioning in which the UCS precedes the CS leads to little conditioning" (p. 158; but see Eysenck, 1975). Actually, in the Campbell *et al.* (1964) experiment, the CRs produced were exceptionally strong and long-lasting, giving support to the view voiced here, which emphasizes the importance of the UCR and plays down the importance of the UCS. The point is an important one for the understanding of the process of conditioning as a whole and of incubation in particular.

My theory agrees in important points with views that have been voiced by other authors. Thus Razran (1956) has already stated that "the automatic deconditioning in the early stage of extinction is a direct result of the loss of the interoceptive and the proprioceptive conditional stimuli (feedback CSs) which in the original conditioning were an integral part of the CR situation and which when the unconditional stimulus is withheld and the evoked reaction is reduced, cease to be present" (p. 48). In the case of anxiety conditioning, these interoceptive and proprioceptive CSs remain, if in somewhat reduced forms; they are sufficient to avoid extinction and instead to produce enhancement. There is also some common ground between the concept of "incubation" in conditioning theory, and that of "sensitization" in habituation theory (Groves & Thompson, 1970), although not too much should be made of the obvious similarities, in view of the clear differences in pertinence and methodology. Nevertheless, the differentiation between extinction and habituation is easier to make in theory than to apply in practice.

What are the conditions under which incubation would be expected to occur? I have argued that when the CR acts as a drive (as in the case of anxiety), the CS can be regarded as a partial substitute for the UCS, and the CR as partly identical with the UCR. On this hypothesis, the CR acts as a reinforcement for the CS-CR connection, but will only do so provided it is strong enough to overcome the natural extinction tendency common to all $\overline{CS}$s. Hence, incubation will only be observed if the UCS is strong enough in the first place for its partial substitute ($\overline{CS}$) to overcome extinction normally following the presentation of the $\overline{CS}$. The strength of the UCS is thus a crucial matter.

Related to the question of strength of the UCS is also the question of the duration of exposure to $\overline{CS}$. In general, the longer the exposure to $\overline{CS}$ is, the weaker the CR will be (Borkovec, 1972, 1974; I. M. Marks & Huson, 1973; Mathews, Johnston, Shaw, & Gelder, 1974; Mathews & Shaw, 1973; Nunes & Marks, 1975; Stern & Marks, 1973; J. P. Watson, Gaind, & Marks, 1972).

Figure 5-1 may serve as a illustration of the general theory in question. It illustrates the hypothetical events that take place upon presentation of $\overline{CS}$. A strong CR is evoked that is felt as fear–anxiety by the patient or the experimental animal. This CR habituates or extinguishes (Curve A) as $\overline{CS}$ presentation is prolonged, just as the UCR would habituate or extinguish. When strong, the CR can act as reinforcement in much the same way as the UCR can. Below a critical point, the CR is too weak to act in this manner, and hence below this point only extinction, rather than enhancement of the CR, is obtained. Above this critical point, incubation is obtained.

FIGURE 5-1. Hypothetical fate of the CR during prolonged exposure of the unreinforced CS.

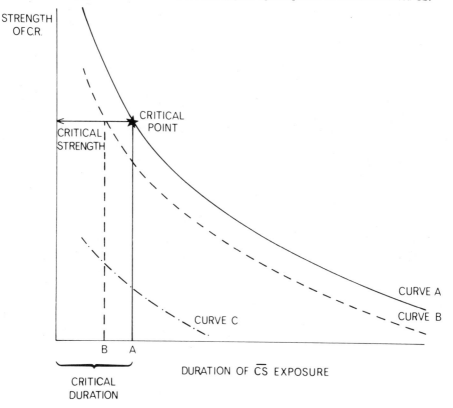

The curve shows that essentially identical stimuli ($\overline{CS}$) can produce extinction (spontaneous remission in neurosis; curative effects of different types of therapy) and enhancement of the CR (the positive feedback cycle producing neurotic behavior once emotional CRs have been established). The crucial factors in the distinction are the position of the critical point on Curve A, related to the strength of the CR (which in turn is related to the strength of the UCS) and the duration of $\overline{CS}$ exposure. It will be seen that there is a critical duration, just as there is a critical strength: If duration of $\overline{CS}$ exposure is longer than the critical duration, then extinction will take place; if it is shorter, then enhancement (incubation) will occur.

The remaining curves (Curve B and Curve C) are more relevant to the next section, in which I discuss the theory of treatment of neurosis, but essentially Curve B represents the general lowering of CR strength as a result of extinction, so that the difference between Curves A and B represents the extinction effects. Curve A may be regarded as a typical sample of "flooding" therapy; Curve C, which never rises above the critical point, may be regarded as a typical example of desensitization. I return to these points later on.

To return now to the discussion of the parameters involved in incubation, it would seem likely that individual differences in personality are important in this field; as already mentioned, Watson and Rayner (1920) suggested the importance of "constitutional inferiority" in little Albert. There is strong evidence to indicate that extraversion–introversion and neuroticism—stability are closely involved with the origins of neurosis (Eysenck, 1967, 1976, 1977b, 1977c; Eysenck & Rachman, 1965), in the sense that people who are high on neuroticism and low on extraversion are much more likely to develop neurotic disorders than persons not in that quadrant of the personality space are. I return to a discussion of personality in relation to the development and treatment of neuroses in a later section. Here, I go on to discuss the experimental and clinical evidence for incubation. Not all relevant studies are discussed here, as the number is much too large for a single section; I simply mention some of the more important historical ones and then go on to studies specifically done to test the incubation hypothesis.

Illustrative of the older type of study is the work of Napalkov (1963), who worked with dogs in a Pavlovian paradigm. He found that various nocive stimuli (NSs) produced increases in blood pressure of less than 50 mmHg, with complete adaptation occurring after some 25 applications (Figure 5-2). A single conditioning trial, however, followed by repeated administrations of the $\overline{CS}$ (never the UCS), brought about increases in blood pressure of 30–40 mm Hg at first, rising to 190–230 mm Hg; the hypertensive state produced lasted over a year in some cases. Figure 5-2 shows in diagrammatic form the fate of the UCR and the $\overline{CR}$ in this experiment. Rapid habituation of this (subtraumatic) UCS, and the tremendous increment in the CR follow-

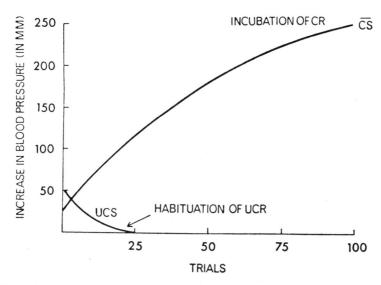

FIGURE 5-2. Incubation of CR following unreinforced CS exposure, as opposed to habituation of the UCR. (From Eysenck, 1968.)

ing presentation of the $\overline{CS}$, present an interesting contrast. Unfortunately, the account of the experiment given by Napalkov is insufficiently detailed to regard his paper as proof rather than as an illustration; replication of his work is urgently needed.

In an earlier study, Lichtenstein (1950) reported on the inhibition of feeding responses in dogs following shock administered while the eating response was occurring. He noted that "a prominent feature of the anxiety symptoms is their tendency to develop and fixate after shock reinforcement has been discontinued" (p. 29). He wrote:

A further striking feature of anxiety symptoms is that they may be formed, increased in strength, and fixated some time after shock has been discontinued. We have mentioned, for example, the fact that resistance to entering the stock increased over a period of days. Tremors and tic-like movements, not observed directly after shock application, appeared later. The conditioned respiratory gasp likewise did not appear in some dogs until after the acquisition of the feeding inhibition. (1950, p. 29)

His experiments descriptively present a good example of incubation, although his own theory goes along quite different lines from those of incubation theory and has been criticized (Eysenck, 1979).

The work of Dykman, Mack, and Ackerman (1965) was concerned with conditioning and extinguishing specific and general responses in dogs; they deliberately stress the importance of nonspecific CRs and point out the importance of recording as many of these as possible. They summarize their findings as follows: "In general, extinction was more upsetting than conditioning, and this finding is contrary to expectation. *Apparently to some dogs the threat is more traumatic than the presence of shock.* The median of 'symptoms' during all conditioning phases was 5.0, and the median number during extinction was 13.0 ($p < 0.01$ binomial test)" (p. 228). In several other studies, Dykman and Gantt (1958, 1960a, 1960b) and Galbrecht, Dykman, and Peters (1960) have suggested that "the threat of trauma continues to operate in extinction . . . sometimes preserving the CR and sometimes interfering with it as real behavioural pathology appears. . . . We suggest that spontaneous recovery could stem from a failure of the experimenter to desensitize all relevant cues, the most important being, of course, the UCS. If this conjecture is correct, we could then obtain a more stable extinction by bringing back the UCS at reduced intensity, or better, by gradually decreasing the intensity of the UCS to zero level" (Dykman, Gantt, & Whitehorn, 1956, p. 228). Dykman, Murphee, and Ackerman (1966) go on to demonstrate the longitudinal data, as well as genetic data from litter differences "support the conception that the CR is dependent upon innate patterns of reactivity" (1966, p. 430.) This seems to support the "preparedness" view of Seligman, dealt with in the preceding section.

The potency of "threat" (CSs) as compared with UCS has also been demonstrated in the human field (Bridger & Mandel, 1964); the principle appears to have wide applicability (see also Cook & Harris, 1937). Maatsch (1959), like the authors mentioned, has reported a similar continued increase in an avoidance CR—in his case, in rats subjected to a single shock trial over a fixation criterion of 100 massed extinction trials.

Studies of "partial irreversibility" or conditioned fear responses, such as those of Solomon, Kamin, and Wynne (1953) and Solomon and Wynne (1953, 1954), show an increment in CR strength, indexed by decreased latency after withdrawal of the UCS; some of their data suggest close affinity with the concept of incubation put forward here. Unfortunately, their data are complicated by the fact that these experiments employed avoidance-learning paradigms, so that simple incubation is complicated by newly acquired avoidance responses.

Somewhat similar in nature to the work of Solomon and his colleagues, but employing human subjects, in the study of Campbell *et al.* (1964) already mentioned. They found enhancement effects after a single, traumatic experience of respiratory paralysis (UCR); despite repeated extinction trials—30 administered 5 minutes after conditioning, 30 1 week later, and 40 2 weeks after that—GSR continued to gain strength over time. This is a particularly important and impressive study relevant to the concept of incubation.

Other more recent studies are those of Reynierse (1966), who found that both time and duration of $\overline{CS}$ exposure were influential in deciding on the course of extinction or enhancement (see also Baum, 1970, and Sartory & Eysenck, 1976). More recently, Rohrbaugh and Riccio (1970), Silvestri, Rohrbaugh, and Riccio (1970), and Rohrbaugh, Riccio, and Arthur (1972) have attempted to test incubation theory directly. They exposed rats to $\overline{CS}$ in the form of apparatus cues between conditioning and testing, and they succeeded in demonstrating enhancement effects. They also tested the hypothesis that duration of $\overline{CS}$ exposure was an important variable, and they succeeded in demonstrating that short $\overline{CS}$ exposures produced enhancement and long $\overline{CS}$ exposures produced extinction.

More recently still, Sartory and Eysenck (1978) studied five different strains of rats that were repeatedly subjected to extinction trials following Pavlovian fear conditioning, the duration of the extinction trials being varied for different groups of animals. Results showed that fearfulness of the animals (strain differences) and duration of extinction trials were jointly and severally causal in determining the degree of extinction of the fear CR.

In another study, Morley (1977) used two different strains of rats—namely, the emotionally reactive and nonreactive Maudsley strains (Eysenck, 1964b). He found that "the two strains differ in the nature of their responses to the present experimental conditions . . . the data confirm the hypothesis that individuals of the *emotional* type are most likely to develop neurotic avoidance behaviour . . . moreover the present experiment indicates that the avoidance behaviour may incubate and thus not be manifest until some time after the initial exposure to the CS-UCS pairing" (1977, p. 367). Morley's use of a punishment-contingency procedure makes it somewhat more difficult to assess its relevance to the theory here under discussion.

More relevant to the hypothesis is the work of Siegeltuch and Baum (1971) and Baum (1969b), in which they showed that the length of response prevention must be increased if the level of fear is enhanced, either by having a session of unavoidable shocks prior to training, or by increasing shock during training. This is exactly the prediction that follows from my hypothesis relating to the "crucial point." Also relevant are findings by Baum (1969a, 1970) relating to the relationship between intensity of shock and duration of response prevention. Ward (1976) failed to repicate these findings, but Weinberger (1965), Spring, Prochaska, and Smith (1974), and Reynierse and Wiff (1973) all report that the longer the duration of response prevention is, the quicker the extinction of the avoidance response is.

There are a number of other papers, mostly of a clinical nature or relevant to therapy, that will be discussed in the next section. Reviews of the literature by Woods (1974) and Eysenck (1979), and critiques such as that of Bersh (1980), suggest that while there is a good deal of evidence compatible with the incubation theory, many of the studies supporting it have certain weaknesses that would make it inadvisable to cite them as conclusive proof for the adequacy of the theory. It would seem highly desirable for further studies, specifically designed to investigate the parametric predictions of the model, to be carried out with both animals and humans in order to resolve this ambiguity. The problem is clearly a very important one for general psychology, where the law of extinction has been a vital part of the conditioning paradigm, and for behavior therapy in particular, where extinction may be the major variable mediating therapeutic success.

A UNIFIED THEORY OF TREATMENT

It is undeniably true that at present there is little agreement on the effects of psychotherapy, and there have been practically no attempts to create a unified theory of treatment that would account for such facts as are reasonably well established. I merely list here those effects that I believe have been firmly established, or at least that have some empirical support in the literature and are likely to be confirmed by later, better controlled studies. I simply quote the major summaries citing the references on which I have based my view; this is clearly not the place to review the whole literature again. The first point to be noted, then, is that "spontaneous remission" is extremely powerful in producing an improvement in neurotic disorders. This clearly is an important benchmark against which all psychiatric methods of treatment must be evaluated (Rachman & Wilson, 1980). The effectiveness of spontaneous remission (or, rather, of all the events happening in life once a neurotic disorder has become established, and occurring during a period of no psychiatric treatment) is the first and perhaps the most important fact that has to be explained by any theory of neurosis and its extinction. It is an interesting fact that the majority of psychiatric treatises and textbooks, including psychoanalytic works, do not even mention this vitally important variable, in spite of the fact that spontaneous remission probably contributes all or nearly all of the effectiveness that is claimed for psychotherapeutic, psychoanalytic, and other methods of treatment.

Second, psychotherapy of the traditional kind (including psychoanalysis) is effective in improving the condition of neurotic patients, but has not been shown to be superior to spontaneous remission (Rachman & Wilson, 1980). Claims have been made recently (e.g., Bergin & Lambert, 1978; M. L. Smith & Glass, 1977) that there now exists such evidence, but as the Rachman and Wilson book makes clear, these claims are essentially unfounded.

The third point to be explained is the existence of a possible biphasic effect of psychotherapy, particularly of the Freudian kind. It appears that if some patients are benefited, others may be made worse (Hadley & Strupp, 1976; Strupp, Hadley, & Gomes-Schwartz, 1977). The evidence is far from conclusive (Mays & Franks, in press), but is sufficiently suggestive to make it likely that such negative effects do occur, at least occasionally.

This suggestion is supported by evidence favoring the view that the personality and approach of the therapist may be of considerable importance in producing improvement, irrespective of theoretical position (Truax, 1963; Truax, Frank, & Imber, 1966). The work summarized in these studies suggests that empathy, genuineness, and warmth appear to be favorable qualities in therapists, whereas their absence would seem to produce negative effects in patients. Sutherland (1977) gives an interesting account of how the behavior of the therapist and the negative effects of treatment may have been linked in a particular case.

The fifth point requiring explanation is that behavior therapy is significantly better in its effects than is either spontaneous remission, psychotherapy of the orthodox kind, or psychoanalysis (Kazdin & Wilson, 1978). These authors discuss all the qualifications needed to make this generalization acceptable, and also discuss the difficulties of research in this field; there is no need here to recapitulate their warnings.

The last point summarizing existing knowledge is that disorders of the first kind (anxiety states, reactive depressions, obsessive–compulsive disorders, phobic states, and dysthymic neurosis generally) are much more easily cured than are disorders of the second kind (hysteria, personality disorders, psychopathy, alcoholism and drug addiction, and hypochondria); this distinction has been elaborated by Eysenck and Rachman (1965). This distinction is an important one, but no attempts seem to have been made in the literature to explain the particular difficulties encountered in treating disorders of the second kind, although the facts relating to this difficulty are very widely known.[3]

In this section, my concern is to demonstrate that all six of these important facts can be explained in terms of the theory briefly outlined in the last section and summarized in Figure 5-1—that is, a theory asserting that as all neurotic disorders are due to Pavlovian conditioning, so all therapeutic success is due to Pavlovian extinction.[4] It is my contention that such a theory will account for the effects given and will present a unified neobehaviorist theory of neurosis and treatment.

---

3. A possible seventh fact in this field would seem to be that psychosomatic disorders can be explained in terms of classical conditioning, and that their treatment is also subject to extinction procedures (Lachman, 1972; Martin & Levey, 1980). Because of space limitations I do not go in detail into a discussion of this, but the two references given here may serve as an introduction to this aspect of the topic.

4. Lader and Mathews (1968) have drawn an analogy between systematic desensitization and habituation. Gray (1980) prefers using the principles of habituation, rather than the principles of extinction, in accounting for the success of neurosis therapy. This is an important point to be discussed later.

In discussing the suggestion that all methods of treatment, including spontaneous remission, may be subsumed under the heading of Pavlovian extinction, there is inevitably a break between the discussion of behavior therapy and the discussion of the other types of treatment. The reason, of course, is that while behavior therapy has been explicitly based on the principles in question, this is not true of psychotherapy, psychoanalysis, cognitive approaches, or spontaneous remission. As a consequence, there is practically no empirical literature to document my assertion that psychotherapy too is subject to the same rules as behavior therapy, and that it works, insofar as it does work, through simple Pavlovian extinction. As a consequence, my discussion will have to be much more speculative and interpretative than might be desirable. My excuse can only be that this presentation may serve to encourage others to carry out empirical work in connection with the views put forward.

I begin with spontaneous remission, this being, as it were, the fundamental baseline with which everything else must be compared. The evidence suggests that it is not the elapse of time that produces the effect, but rather the events taking place in that time (Eysenck, 1963). It is well known that people suffering from neurotic disorders may not approach a psychiatrist with their troubles, but may rather seek advice and help from friends, relatives, priests, teachers, or persons in authority (Rachman & Wilson, 1980). What happens during the consequent interactions is not at all well documented, but it may reasonably be expected that the patients will discuss their problems in the presence of these friendly and usually supportive lay therapists. Thus these situations have two major elements of behavior therapy in them. In the first place, there is the reassuring, relaxing presence of a friend whose advice is being sought; this will usually serve to reduce any anxiety that may be felt in the situation. In the second place, there is a presentation of the $\overline{CS}$ that is much reduced in intensity, being not *in vivo,* but in a semantic, imaginal form, very much as in Wolpe's type of desensitization. A situation resembling that of desensitization behavior therapy thus exists, although of course the approaches involved are very much suboptimal, occurring by chance rather than by planning. Nevertheless, my theory would suggest that the method should work, and apparently this prediction is borne out by the very high remission figures published in connection with this type of "treatment."

Essentially, psychotherapy (of any type), psychoanalysis, and cognitive types of therapy follow very much the same kind of approach. The friend, relative, teacher, priest, or other person is replaced by the professional therapist, who may be a psychiatrist, a clinical psychologist, or a counselor, but who essentially seeks to provide a reassuring and relaxing atmosphere and to discuss the patient's problem with him or her, thus leading the patient to face the $\overline{CS}$ under conditions that keep the resulting anxiety below the critical point. Again, a success no less than that obtained in spontaneous remission, but not necessarily superior to it, would be expected. Again, the expectation is borne out, on the whole.

Why should psychoanalysis and psychotherapy in some cases produce a worsening rather than an improvement in the condition of the patient? The answer to this problem is probably tied up intimately with the personality of the therapist or analyst who produces this type of effect. As already pointed out, there is some evidence to suggest that therapists who are supportive, friendly, and genuine, and who generally provide a relaxing atmosphere, are more successful than are those who show the opposite characteristics. Thus a classical psychoanalyst who restricts himself or herself to interpretation, who does not show much sympathy with the patient's problems, who refuses to give the patient advice, and who is generally remote in his or her approach is likely to put the patient in a situation where the $\overline{CS}$ produces a CR that is above the critical point, so that instead of extinction there is incubation—in other words, the patient gets worse. It is unfortunate that the situation has not been looked at empirically from this point of view, so that this hypothesis cannot be supported with any quantitative or empirical data. The problem is such a serious one, however, that it must be hoped that such studies will soon be undertaken so that therapists can at least avoid harming their patients, even though they may not be able to benefit them!

When behavior therapy is considered, it may be noted immediately that for many people there is no unity to the concept at all; they prefer to talk about "behavior therapies" as if these constituted a set of unconnected methodologies. It is suggested here that, in terms of my theory, this is entirely the wrong conclusion. What seems to be the case is that there are many ways in which the patient can be confronted with the $\overline{CS}$ in such a way that his or her reaction does not exceed the critical point. The best way to begin the discussion may be by considering two rather different methods—namely, desensitization and "flooding." Apparently the procedures are not only different, but contradictory. Thus Wolpe stresses the point that if in the course of desensitization too much anxiety is aroused in the patient (i.e., if the CR rises above the critical point), the therapy is disrupted, and the patient may revert to previous levels of symptomatology. On the other hand, in "flooding," the patient is intentionally exposed to high levels of anxiety, which yet are suggested to improve his or her neurotic condition drastically (Rachman & Hodgson, 1980). Eysenck (1978) has suggested that the reason for the difference lies in the duration of the exposure of the $\overline{CS}$. In typical "flooding" therapies, the exposure tends to be relatively lengthy, thus making sure that the CR drops below the critical point; whereas in desensitization, where, following Wolpe's advice, the therapist will usually stop the presentation of the $\overline{CS}$ once a high degree of anxiety is produced, this short presentation ensures that the

CR will not drop below the critical point, thus producing incubation and enhancement rather than extinction.

The experimental evidence in favor of these deductions from my theory is quite impressive, both in the animal field and in the field of behavior therapy with human patients. Rapid extinction of responses has been found with flooding in animals (e.g., Baum, 1966; Page & Hall, 1953; Polin, 1959), and also with neurotics (e.g., Hodgson, Rachman, & Marks, 1972b; Rachman, Hodgson, & Marks, 1971; Rachman, Marks, & Hodgson, 1973; see also a review by Baum, 1970). These studies all used lengthy $\overline{CS}$ presentations; with short presentations failures of extinction to occur had been observed, and in many cases incubation effects. Woods (1974) has reviewed the literature; some of the most impressive studies are those by Rachman (1966), where one of three spider-phobic subjects, exposed for 10 sessions to $\overline{CS}$ presentations of spiders for 2-minute periods, reported that her fear of spiders *increased* during treatment. Periods of 1 hour or so seem best for producing extinction effects. Several investigators have recently studied experimentally the effects of short versus long exposures to $\overline{CS}$ in human subjects. Miller and Levis (1971) succeeded in verifying the importance of length for $\overline{CS}$ exposures on the fate of the CR. Proctor (1968) and Watts (1971) studied the influence of intraitem exposure time to aversive stimuli on systematic desensitization. Ross and Proctor (1973) found long single exposure to hierarchy items more effective in reducing avoidance behavior than short exposure was. Sue (1975) has reviewed a number of successful and unsuccessful extinction-like studies in humans ($\overline{CS}$ exposure only) and found that success depended crucially on length of exposure; his own study gave similar results. There are also studies showing that exposure to symbolic representations of feared stimuli can elicit unexpected *increases* in autonomic responses, whether the stimuli were visual displays (Borkovec & Glasgow, 1973), verbal descriptions (Boulougouris, Marks, & Marset, 1971), or self-induced thoughts (Breznitz, 1967; Rankin, Nomikos, Opton, & Lazarus, 1964). Stone and Borkovec (1975) have also found evidence of paradoxical effects of brief $\overline{CS}$ exposure on analogue phobic subjects, in a study replicating that of Miller and Levis (1971), but with certain additions which serve to test, and disprove, hypotheses regarding the phenomenon of fear incubation advanced by Staub (1968) and others.

I next look at sets of theories that have become very popular recently, and that have given rise to fairly specific methods of treatment—namely, the so-called "cognitive theories" and the varieties of "social learning" theories. Of the many presentations that might be cited, the following are probably sufficient to illustrate the variety of approaches associated with these terms: Bandura (1977); Beck (1976); Bower (1978); G. Cohen (1977); Goldfried (1977); Gutsch and Ritenour (1976); Mahoney (1974); Meichenbaum (1977); and Rosenthal and Zimmerman (1978). Ryle (1978) has argued that these "cognitive" developments may lead to a common language for the psycho-therapies, and Sarason (in press) has also argued for a possible reconciliation through such theories between behavior therapy and psychoanalysis. Wolpe (1978) has voiced criticisms of these approaches, many of which are undoubt-edly justified and may represent the typical reactions of many behavior thera-pists to these new developments. It is not my intention here to go into details concerning these criticisms; I merely wish to point out that cognitive thera-pies and social learning therapies both involve exposure of the patient to the CS, and consequently fall under the general paradigm I have outlined as a universal therapeutic medium for all methods of treatment. Thus they, too, join the list of methodologies that can be subsumed under the unified theory here outlined. However, in view of the popularity of the theories underlying these methods (considered apart from the methods of treatment themselves), a few words may be necessary to rectify the common assumption that these theories differ importantly from conditioning theories, and that they pro-duce results superior to those associated with orthodox behavior therapies. Taking the second point first, it must be noted that the number of studies comparing methods of cognitive therapy or social learning therapy with be-havior therapy and other methods is very limited (e.g., Morris, 1975; Rush, Beck, Kovacs, & Hollon, 1977; B. F. Shaw, 1977; Taylor & Marshall, 1977). These and similar studies, even if they could be accepted as free of quite serious faults, could hardly be accepted as proof of the superiority or even the equivalence of the therapies to orthodox behavior therapies. In a critical sur-vey of cognitive-behavior therapy with children, Hobbs, Moguin, Tyroler, and Lahey (1980) have evaluated such studies in terms of subject popula-tions, adequacy of outcome measures, experimental and statistical method-ology, and consistency of findings. "In general, deficiencies were found on all dimensions. Although some studies have reported promising results that merit further investigation, methodological improvements are necessary be-fore the clinical utility of cognitive behaviour therapy with children can be documented" (p. 147). It would be my view that the same judgment can be made of the work that has been done with adults, using cognitive therapies and also social learning therapies.

Turning now to the theories underlying these methods of treatment, I may perhaps begin by stating that in my view it is quite erroneous to talk about "cognitive theory" or "social learning theory"; neither theory exists as such, even in the least rigorous sense of the term "theory." There do exist ways of talking about certain phenomena that recognizably employ cognitive terms, or terms of social learning, but these do not begin to constitute a theory. For a theory to exist, there must be a consistent body of propositions from which testable deductions can be made; furthermore these deductions should be different from those made by alternative and better established theories. No such body or proposition exists, and no such firm predictions can be made.

The situation has been reviewed by Allport (1975), who concludes his examination of the "cognitive" field by stating that it is characterized by "an uncritical, or selective, or frankly cavalier attitude to experimental data; a pervasive atmosphere of special pleading,˙a curious parochialism in acknowledging even the existence of other workers, and other approaches, to the phenomena under discussion; interpretations of data relying on multiple, arbitrary choice points; and underlying all else a near vacuum of theoretical structure within which to interrelate different sets of experimental results, or direct the search for significant new phenomena" (p. 150). This evaluation may seem uncomplimentary, but it mirrors reality to an uncomfortable degree. If such theories wish to be taken seriously as psychological theories, then they will have to be framed in a much more rigorous manner than has been the case hitherto, and the investigators framing them will have to undertake the serious business of differentiating predictions made by these revamped theories from those deriving from conditioning theory.

Specific criticisms of specific theories are of course quite numerous; as an example, I quote the journal issue edited by Rachman (1978b) summarizing criticisms of Bandura's "self-efficacy" theory (1977). The set of criticisms there recorded may serve as an indication of the difficulties still attending the formulation of a proper "cognitive" or "social learning" theory encompassing the phenomena in question.

Much of the difficulty in differentiating conditioning and cognitive theories lies in the misunderstanding of behavioristic principles common among critics. Thus it would be quite untrue to say that the behaviorist position disregards cognitive factors, or leaves out considerations of language, imagery, or symbolism. Pavlov (1927) has already insisted on the importance of the "second signaling system"; he pointed out that "a word is as real a conditioned stimulus for man as all the other stimuli in common with animals, but at the same time more all-inclusive than other stimuli" (p. 284). And again: "Owing to the entire preceding life of a human adult, a word is connected with all the external and internal stimuli coming to the cerebral hemisphere, signals all of them, replaces all of them and can, therefore, evoke all the actions and reactions of the organism which these stimuli produce" (p. 285). Platanov (1959), in his monograph *The Word as a Physiological and Therapeutic Factor,* has emphasized this point, and Staats (1963, 1968) has made many important contributions to demonstrate its validity. To demonstrate the independence of cognitive factors in neurosis from simple theories of Pavlovian conditioning, it would be necessary to demonstrate experimentally that radically different predictions follow from radically different theories. To simply say that cognitive factors must be taken intò account is not to differentiate the two approaches.

What is often suggested by cognitive theorists is that humans have direct introspective access to higher-order cognitive processes, and that investigators should capitalize on this direct access. Such an approach would certainly differentiate cognitive theorists from conditioning theorists, but the evidence is strongly opposed to any such intepretation (Nisbett & Wilson, 1977). As they show, subjects are sometimes unaware of the existence of a stimulus that importantly influenced a response, unaware of the existence of the response, and unaware that the stimulus has affected the response. They propose "that when people attempt to report on their cognitive processes, that is, on the processes mediating the effects of the stimulus on the response, they do not do so on the basis of any true introspection. Instead, their reports are based on a prior, implicit causal theories, or judgments about the extent to which a particular stimulus is a plausible cause of a given response" (p. 231). Cognitive theorists have taken too little trouble to discount experimentally the findings summarized by Nisbett and Wilson, and have instead assumed that the facts are different from what they actually are. This is not a recommended procedure in science.

It may be concluded, then, that the cognitive and social learning therapies involve typical Pavlovian extinction in their application to neurotic subjects; that the theories on which they are based are not supported by proper experiments, are not internally consistent, and are not capable of making testable predictions; and that the general assumptions on which these theories are based are contrary to empirical fact. This does not mean that cognitive factors must be or should be excluded from behavior therapy; the Pavlovian system makes provision for their inclusion, and as Wolpe (1978) has pointed out, they do in fact form an important part of the behavior therapist's armamentarium. This is particularly clear in the use of imagery in desensitization; it has been objected that this is not a "behavioristic" concept or methodology, but this criticism is not justified, as I point out in a later section.

PERSONALITY AND THE DIATHESIS–STRESS MODEL

Most if not all modern theories of neurosis accept in some form or other the diathesis–stress model (Gossop, 1980); such acceptance may be implicit or explicit. According to this model, neurosis (or psychosis) occurs when a particular stress impinges upon a person whose genetic constitution (and reinforcement history) is such as to make him or her particularly susceptible to the stress in question. Figure 5-3 shows in diagrammatic form the essential features of the model (Edwards, 1969). On the abscissa is plotted the genetic predisposition (neuroticism or psychoticism; Eysenck & Eysenck, 1976); the ordinate represents the number of cases (frequency of occurrence) pertaining to each degree of predisposition. The resulting distribution is shown in the

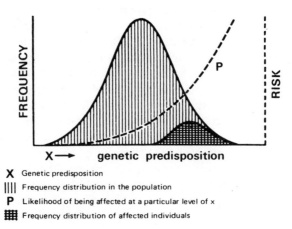

X **→** genetic predisposition

X   Genetic predisposition

|||| Frequency distribution in the population

P   Likelihood of being affected at a particular level of x

⊞ Frequency distribution of affected individuals

FIGURE 5-3. Model of the diathesis–stress theory of psychiatric disorder.

normal curve with vertical hatching. Line "P" presents the probability of persons with given genetic predispositions developing neurosis (or psychosis); this represents the risk for persons at given positions along the abscissa. The cross-hatched normal curve at the right end of the abscissa represents actual cases of neurosis (or psychosis); obviously the picture is somewhat idealized, because in reality the correlation between predisposition (diathesis) and disease would be much less clear-cut.

This "continuum" type of theory is of course opposed to the "disease model" traditionally preferred by medical writers, but the advantages of a quantitative over a qualitative view are so obvious that a detailed criticism of the latter view may be dispensed with (Eysenck, 1970a, 1970b; McGuire, 1973). The most direct proof for a quantitative view has come through the application of criterion analysis to both psychotic and neurotic disorders (Eysenck, 1950, 1952), favoring the dimensional view in both cases. Granted the validity of the dimensional approach, the next question is the number of dimensions required; in particular, do neurosis and psychosis constitute a single dimension, with the former intermediate between normality and psychosis, or are two dimensions required? Here too the evidence is very strong, suggesting that the two dimensions are largely independent of each other, and that consequently two continuua are required—one of psychoticism, the other of neuroticism (Eysenck, 1977b, pp. 17–20).

To these two dimensions must be added a third, extraversion–introversion, because both introverted and extraverted varieties of neurotic and psychotic disorders can be isolated, and they present with different symptoms related to different personality traits. Figure 5-4 shows the differences in personality and behavior between introverted and extraverted adult neurotics (Eysenck, 1947), and Figure 5-5 shows a similar picture for children (Eysenck, 1970b). For psychosis, too, such differences between extraverted and introverted symptomatology have been observed (Verma & Eysenck, 1973). There are thus three major dimensions of personality that can be shown to be intimately related to neurotic and psychotic disorders, and it would seem that any thoery of neurosis that is concerned with behavior would need to bring these factors into contact with other parts of a neobehavioristic theory of neurosis. (I am here concerned almost entirely with neurosis and disregard psychotic disorders; these have been discussed elsewhere, e.g., Eysenck & Eysenck, 1976.)

It must suffice here to state very briefly and dogmatically how the personality factors are believed to be connected with neurotic disorders of both the first and second kind (Eysenck & Rachman, 1965) and with psychosomatic disorders (Pancheri, 1979).

1. The three major personality factors (psychoticism, extraversion, and neurosis) are strongly determined by genetic factors (Fulker, 1980). They fail

FIGURE 5-4. Extraverted and introverted neurotic symptoms in adult patients. (From Eysenck, 1947.)

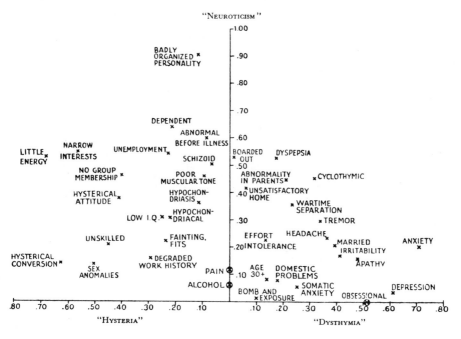

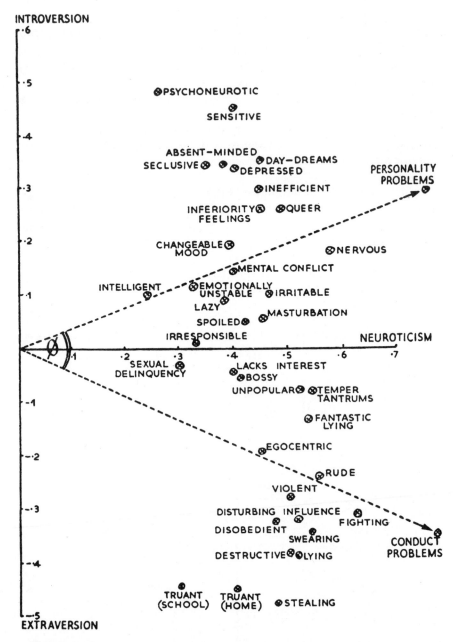

FIGURE 5-5. Extraverted and introverted symptoms in children attending a child guidance clinic. (From Eysenck, 1970b.)

to show dominance or assortative mating (both of which can be found very strongly in the inheritance of mental abilities), and environmental effects are of the "within-family," not the "between-family" variety.

2. There are biological factors underlying the manifest personality differences—for example, differences in cortical arousal in extraversion–introversion and differences in limbic system responsiveness for neuroticism (Stelmack, 1980).

3. Differences in cortical arousal, probably mediated by the reticular formation, produce differences in ease and strength of formation of conditioned responses (Levey & Martin, 1980).

4. Personality differences so caused and mediated produce observable differences in social behavior, particularly in relation to neurosis, criminality, and antisocial behavior generally (G. Wilson, 1980).

5. Disorders of the first kind (dysthymic neuroses) are produced by a combination of predispositions to the formation of strong and lasting emotional reactions (neurosis), and ease of formation of CRs (introversion); disorders of the second kind (psychopathy; hysteria) are produced by a combination of predispositions to formation of strong and lasting emotional reactions (neurosis), and the failure to produce strong CRs readily (Eysenck & Rachman, 1965). In other words, too ready conditioning of strong emotional responses is responsible for dysthymic reactions; failure to produce socially acceptable conditioned responses ("conscience") is responsible for psychopathic and other "behavior disorder" responses (Eysenck, 1977b).

6. Alternative theories to explain the observed relationships are in existence (Gray, 1980), but would not alter in any essential way the discussion in this section.

It will be clear that these facts are relevant not only to a discussion of the origins of neurotic disorders, but also to a discussion of their treatment. It has been shown, for instance, that differences in extraversion–introversion can be of crucial relevance for the appropriateness of such different therapies as Ellis's rational–emotive psychotherapy and C. Rogers's client-centered psychotherapy, with the former benefiting introverts, the latter extraverts; for the nonappropriate type of therapy, success was no better than no treatment was (DiLoreto, 1971). Wolpe's desensitization therapy worked equally well for both personality types. Clearly information of this type is of considerable importance for the practicing behavior therapist, and it raises theoretical problems that require an answer if the study of neurosis and its treatment is ever to be put on a scientific footing. Traditionally, of course, behaviorists have neglected the study of personality, although as pointed out previously, Watson himself suggested the relevance of such personality variables as "constitutional inferiority" in connection with little Albert's development of a phobic disorder. As far as neobehaviorism is concerned, it is often thought (erroneously) that Skinner has disavowed the existance of genetically determined individual differences as much as Watson did (in his programmatic writings). This is not so; as Jensen (1973) has pointed out, Skinner has often been misinterpreted in this respect by his followers. Skinner's own writings show that he does not deny the existence and importance of such factors, although he has not shown much interest in studying them himself.

Given that, roughly at least, these various hypotheses are along the right lines, what sort of predictions can be made regarding the relationships between neurosis and personality? One obvious expectation, in view of the hypothesized lower arousal level of extraverts, would be a higher rate of extinction for them (Hemming, 1979); there is known to be a negative correlation between speed of acquisition and speed of extinction of CRs (Franks, 1963). Thus extraverts, ceteris paribus, would be expected to recover more quickly from dysthymic disorders. In making this prediction, introverts and extraverts need not be defined in terms of questionnaire responses; equally useful would be other (laboratory) measures known to be correlated with extraversion, such as spontaneous fluctuations of the GSR. Quick extinction of the CR is also found to be accompanied by quick recovery (Franks, 1963); thus, if there are any relapses, they might be found more readily in extraverts.

General drive level, theoretically expected to be higher in dysthymics, would be expected to summate with anxiety (according to Hullian teaching), thus making recovery more difficult, and acquisition of CRs easier.[5] Altogether, the intensity of the fear-inducing stimulus should be able to be traded against personality, in the sense that lower stimulus levels should produce the same effects in dysthymics as higher drive levels do in stable extraverts. These and other predictions should be considered in terms of the complete personality theory in question, not in terms of the very dogmatic and abbreviated outline given above. Thus, for instance, Pavlov's principle of transmarginal in-

---

5. General drive level must of course be presumed to vary from time to time in accordance with day-to-day events and with internal events such as menstrual cycle changes (Baker, Mishara, Kostin, & Parker, 1979; Vila & Beech, 1978). This concept may have considerable explanatory function in connection with anomalies that otherwise might be difficult to explain. Thus Rachman and Hodgson (1980) have found that while cleaning and other rituals in obsessive–compulsive patients generally led to a lowering in anxiety, occasionally they produced no change or might even lead to an increase in anxiety. These occasional departures from theoretical expectations might be explained in terms of accidental rises in drive level of the kind suggested above, leading to states of anxiety above the critical point and thus not containable by the compulsive acts. Incubation effects might be expected to be found under these circumstances; unfortunately, Rachman and Hodgson do not seem to have looked for such effects. This might be an interesting research project.

hibition suggests that with particularly strong UCSs, introverts will show protective inhibition, thus giving extraverts the opportunity to condition more quickly and strongly under these conditions (Eysenck & Levey, 1972). These and other qualifications should always be borne in mind in evaluating the research literature. One possible prediction from this postulate might be, for instance, that under wartime conditions, when very strong UCSs are quite common, extraverted disorders such as hysteria might be much more common than in peacetime—a deduction that seems to be in accord with the facts.

The genetic element in personality was linked with the development of phobic disorders by Torgersen (1979), who carried out a twin study to throw light on the etiology and nosology of phobic fears. Factor analysis revealed five factors (separation fears, animal fears, mutilation fears, social fears, and nature fears). The study demonstrated that, apart from separation fears, genetic factors played a part in the strength as well as the content of the phobic fears. Young, Fenton, and Lader (1971) and Slater and Shields (1969) have come to similar conclusions. Torgersen finds correlations between personality traits of the dysthymic (though not the hysterical) kind and phobic fears. Clearly, genetic personality traits are important in the development of phobic fears.

With strength of fears genetically determined to some extent, how would such differences in drive level affect therapy? Kass and Gilner (1974) hypothesized, following some earlier work by Lang (1969), that "in the low drive group, any incentive will serve to keep the subjects attending to the feared stimuli so that extinction occurs. . . . However, in the high avoidance groups, only relaxation will enable the subjects to attend to the feared stimuli" (p. 100). This hypothesis states, in a more readily testable form, the same sort of notion that is stated in a previous section of this chapter in relation to the apparent worsening effects of psychoanalysis under certain circumstances (i.e., when the therapist is not providing relaxing stimuli for the patient). The Kass and Gilner study furnished some support for the hypothesis, although for reasons discussed by them the results could not be taken to enable a definitive conclusion.

Hugdahl et al. (1977) preferred to speak of "arousability" rather than drive level; they indexed it by means of spontaneous electrodermal responses. They compared groups that were high and low on this variable (which is highly correlated with introversion) during differential conditioning to potentially phobic or neutral stimuli. "It was found that the effects of these two factors were essentially additive, i.e., conditioning and resistance to extinction were better for phobic stimuli and for high-arousal groups" (p. 345). The high-arousal group with phobic stimuli "was the only group that failed to extinguish during 20 trials, which indicates that high arousal gives superior resistance to extinction particularly for phobic stimuli" (p. 345).

Gordon (in press) has suggested that "complex phobias, involving fear of many situations or events (agoraphobia, social phobias) occur in people with a higher level of physiological reactivity than those who develop simple monosymptomatic phobias'' (see also Cooper, Gelder, & Marks, 1965; Lader, 1967). The reason, it is suggested, may be "that heightened arousal leads to wider stimulus generalization. . . . Thus a wider range of stimuli would come to evoke fear reaction in the highly aroused agoraphobic than in less susceptible persons.'' An experiment carried out by Gordon, using three groups of subjects (complex phobias, monophobias, normals), showed results significantly in agreement with the hypothesis. In addition, the groups were differentiated in the expected direction on the neuroticism scale of the Eysenck Personality Inventory (EPI); this scale correlated very significantly with the generalization test used ($r = .47$). Stimulus generalization is undoubtedly an important element in any behavioristic theory of neurosis, and further work linking it with personality would be of considerable interest.

I turn next to treatment.[6] One of the mechanisms underlying extinction, which is certainly the most promising theoretical concept with regard to fear reduction during treatment, is habituation of autonomic responses (Stelmack, 1980). B. D. Smith and Wigglesworth (1978) tested high- and low-extraversion scorers' habituation to tones of varying intensity. No difference emerged between groups in their skin conductance responses to soft tones. However, it took introverts more trials to cease responding to tones of 100 dB than it took extraverts. The former also produced higher-amplitude responses to a novel tone of different frequency after the original series and more dishabituation (i.e., a larger response to a repetition of the original tone) than did extraverts. When a fixed number of tones was given (Wigglesworth & Smith, 1976) low-extraversion scorers did not differ from high-extraversion scorers in rate of habituation (presumably because some had not yet completely habituated by the end of the series) but high-extraversion scorers showed a greater amount of dishabituation at the return of the original stimulus after an interspersed, novel one. Orlebeke (1973) hypothesized that low-extraversion scorers have a low tolerance for strong stimulation and are likely to react with a defensive reflex rather than with an orienting reflex, the former of which is less subject to habituation. The differentiation between the two types of responses can, however, only be shown up in the bidirectional responses of the cardiovascular system. Orlebeke (1973) obtained support for his notion in peripheral vasomotor responses. Other studies using electrodermal measures only and low-intensity stimulation found less clear-cut differences between high- and low-extraversion scorers' rate of habituation (e.g., Coles, Gale, & Kline, 1971; Sadler, Mepperd, & Honcks, 1971). Deitz (in press) reports positive findings.

---

6. I am indebted to Gudrun Sartory for her assistance with the remainder of this section.

The predicted relationship between extroversion and speed of extinction derives some support from clinical studies. I. M. Marks, Boulougouris, and Marset (1971) found a positive correlation ($r = .62$) between extroversion as measured with the EPI, and change in ratings of the "main phobia" following flooding treatment. Treatment had been carried out for a set number of sessions, after which high-extraversion scorers showed greater improvement than low-extraversion scorers. The correlation between extraversion and outcome was not significant following systematic desensitization. There was, however, a significant negative correlation ($r = -.55$) between extraversion and change in spontaneous fluctuations of skin conductance, indicating that high-extraversion scorers showed less change during the treatment procedure than low-extraversion scorers did. This latter result is difficult to interpret, as pretreatment levels of spontaneous fluctuations were not reported. It is therefore impossible to conclude whether high-extraversion scorers showed less habituation during the treatment and a higher level of spontaneous fluctuation, or else whether their initial level was lower than that of low-extraversion scorers. The same criticism does not apply to the first result, since scores obtained for the "main phobia" were one of the selection criteria for admitting patients to the trial and can therefore be assumed to have been high for all subjects.

A similar result was found by Mathews *et al.* (1974). Following 15 sessions of either flooding, desensitization, or a control treatment, in phobic patients high-extraversion scorers clinically improved more than low-extraversion scorers. The stability of this result was confirmed at a follow-up assessment after 6 months. At the end of treatment, the same relationship between extraversion and treatment outcome was found, with Cattell's 16-PF scales related to extraversion—namely, "venturesome," "extraversion," "happy-go-lucky," and "outgoing." However, only the result found with the "outgoing" scale proved stable at follow-up. All results were reported in terms of comparison of extraversion scores between "more" and "less" improved subjects of the whole sample. It would have been helpful to know whether extraversion scores were the same in the three treatment groups. Since control subjects were less improved than those in the two treatment groups, presumably more control subjects were to be found in the "less improved" groups; in the event of a randomization error, the personality effect could be confounded with the treatment effect.

The possibility of this error was avoided in Hallam's study (1976) on personality factors and treatment outcome. Phobic patients had been treated to reach a criterion of "no noticeable further improvement." Eysenck Personality Questionnaire scales were completed before treatment and again after 6 months. Initial scores were correlated with outcome but not with extraversion ($r = .03$). Hallam found that high-extraversion scorers needed marginally fewer treatment sessions to reach the criterion, but that extraversion was uncorrelated with final outcome. There was, however, a positive relationship between treatment outcome and increase in the extraversion score, which may have been due to the improvement of the social phobics in the sample (14 out of 49) who were engaging in more social activities after effective treatment.

Gelder, Marks, and Wolff (1967) and Martin, Marks, and Gelder (1969) have reported direct evidence that patients with higher extraversion scores improve more readily than other patients do. The Martin *et al.* study is of particular interest in that it included a measure of speed of conditioning. Their main finding was that "patients who improve with treatment were shown on present evidence to condition faster than those who do badly" (p. 123) (see also Sarason, 1958). However, this paper also includes the warning that "if there is one clear-cut conclusion of the present study it is that the complex pattern of relationships present among variables demands an equally complex *multivariate* analysis in order that the pattern can be properly interpreted" (p. 123).

In summary, it appears that these clinical studies, if beset with methodological frailty, provide some support for the notion that extraversion predicts the speed of extinction. It is possible that, if this is true of simple extinction (flooding) treatments, patients high on introversion–conditioning may do better with counterconditioning-type treatments; this distinction deserves careful experimental checking.

Neuroticism as a personality dimension is hypothesized to be related to a high degree of reactivity of the autonomic nervous system, which predisposes high-neuroticism scorers to react strongly to emotional stimuli and show slower habituation than low-neuroticism scorers do (Coles *et al.,* 1971; Orlebeke, 1973). Although subjects who suffer from neurotic disorders show markedly higher neuroticism scores than control subjects do, differences between neuroticism scores within patient samples failed to be predictive of treatment outcome in studies using behavioral techniques (Hallam, 1976; I. M. Marks *et al.,* 1971; Mathews *et al.,* 1974). A possible reason for this failure might be the clinical practice of extending all patients' exposure to the fear-eliciting stimulus until their fear has subsided (i.e., of achieving a certain criterion of habituation within each session rather than adhering to a certain time limit). If a standard time limit is chosen for all patients, it is usually gauged to allow habituation to take place in all patients. Individual differences in autonomic reactivity are thus likely to be swamped by long-duration exposures during treatment. Lengthy exposures to fear-eliciting stimuli have been shown to induce extinction in emotionally reactive and nonreactive rats alike, whereas short exposures achieved extinction in nonreactive animals only (Sartory & Eysenck, 1976). Unfortunately, the strain differences are confounded with the strength of the CR in this study of passive avoidance conditioning; emotionally reactive animals were shown to condition faster during the predetermined number of conditioning trials. Hence it is impossible to decide whether this need for longer exposures to achieve extinction was due to their stronger CR or to strain properties. In a study of active avoidance conditioning (Sartory, 1977), no difference was obtained in the rate of extinction between emotionally reactive and nonreactive rats; the difference between levels of avoidance reactions during extinction trials is again confounded with differences between preextinction levels. In order to investigate strain differences during extinction of fear responses unambiguously, animals would have to be conditioned to reach a criterion level.

The question of whether an initally intense fear response takes longer to extinguish than a mild one does has not yet been resolved by clinical trials. Intense fear responses can be expected to take longer to extinguish than milder ones do. In the study by I. M. Marks $et\ al.$ (1971) mentioned above, a negative correlation ($r = -.51$) was found between initial ratings of "total phobia" and improvement in the main phobia after a set number of desensitization trials. Hence patients with a greater number of phobias improved less in their main phobia, presumably because some of the treatment time in their case, was devoted to dealing with minor phobias. Following flooding treatment, a positive correlation ($r = .5$) was found between scores of the phobic checklist and improvement in "main phobia"—a result that is presumably due to a ceiling effect. These results relating initial fear level to outcome were not replicated by Mathews $et\ al.$ (1974). The inherent difficulty of evaluating results of outcome studies has been mentioned before; owing to ethical considerations, treatment studies are characterised with a certain amount of "overkill" regarding therapeutic effect, so that they contribute little to the theoretical debate of therapeutic processes.

Initial level of fear intensity proved to have little or not predictive value for treatment outcome (but see Rabavilas, Boulougouris, Perissaki, & Stefans, 1979). A possible reason for this could be, as has been mentioned above, that the overall treatment effect is too powerful to show up subtle individual differences. Another reason might be that the initial variance between subjects' ratings, is, in fact, too small; most subjects who are prepared to register as psychiatric cases can be expected to suffer considerable distress, and measures are usually taken with regard to their most prominent complaint. Owing to biological constraints, the panic an agoraphobic might suffer when going out is in no way different from the panic attack of a spider phobic when confronted with a spider. There are however, other important differences between these two groups of patients that may be apparent only during treatment. Lader and Wing (1966) found differences in the rate of habituation of skin conductance responses to neutral stimuli (tones) between nonanxious controls and specific phobics on the one hand, and agoraphobic social phobics and patients suffering from chronic anxiety states on the other. The latter groups are characterized by spontaneous panic attacks that cannot be attributed to any particular stimulus but are generated by high autonomic arousal. Lader, Gelder, and Marks (1967) divided phobics into "habituators" and "nonhabituators" on the basis of their diminution in skin conductance response to a series of tones and found that "habituators" had a better clinical outcome in desensitization treatment than did "nonhabituators." The former comprised mostly specific phobics, and the latter mostly agoraphobics. Agitated depressive patients were also shown to have a high level of responding without habituating to a series of tones (Lader & Wing, 1966). More recently, Foa (1979) identified treatment failures among obsessive–compulsive patients as being those who failed to habituate (measured by subjective fear ratings) during treatment sessions, as was the case in depressed obsessionals; or else those who showed resensitization between treatment sessions, as was the case with patients who had overvalued ideas. (These patients believed in the potential danger of the stimulus they avoided.) The basic level of autonomic arousal has to be considered a powerful factor in maintaining anxiety responses and counteracting extinction processes.

As dysthymic reactions are consistently correlated with introversion and high arousal, so psychopathic and hysteric reactions are correlated with extraversion and low arousal (Eysenck, 1980c). Extraverts and introverts also differ with respect to stress-induced affect, labeling the emotion "anger" and "fear" respectively (Sipprelle, Ascough, Detrio, & Horst, 1977). These personality traits have already been shown to be related to therapy outcome (e.g. Martin *et al.,* 1969), but on the whole there has not been sufficient reserarch on these variables to produce any very definitive conclusions. Sloane, Staples, Cristol, Yorkston, and Whipple (1976) suggested as a result of their extensive study that psychotherapy was least effective with extraverted subjects (i.e., those scoring high on the MMPI hysteria and psychopathic deviate scales). On the other hand, extraverts did better than introverts did in behavior therapy. This would seem to be in contradiction to DiLoreto's results (1971) quoted earlier, but direct comparisons are not really feasible in view of the divergence of patients, therapies, and personality measures. The issue is potentially an important one, and, taken together with the suggestion that extraversion–introversion differences might be relevant to the choice between simple extinction methods of treatment and counterconditioning methods, ought to be investigated more thoroughly than has been the case hitherto. Such research ought also to follow up such findings as those of Fouts and Click (1979) indicating important differences between extraverts and introverts in reacting to observational learning contingencies.

This section has been rather inconclusive; the research reviewed tends to show that personality differences can be of crucial importance, but the volume of work done and the lack of proper hypothesis testing has precluded any definitive conclusions.[7] It would seem impossible to deny personality differences an important place in any neobehavioristic theory of neurosis and treatment, yet the bad old habits of Watsonian denigration of personality concepts seem still to inhibit investigators from looking at these variables as seriously as they ought to. Indeed, many investigators do not include personality among the variables studied. Until this course is reversed, research will constantly come up with results that are difficult to replicate, are out of line with prediction, and are difficult to reconcile with theory; patients are not a homogeneous group, and their individuality deserves recognition in research designs.

In this survey, I have omitted two areas of work that could be of considerable importance—one because there is too little evidence, the other because there is too much. The former area is that of therapist personality (e.g. Baird, 1979; Goodwin, Geller, & Quinian, 1979); the latter that of animal work (e.g., Broadhurst, 1975; Franklin & Broadhurst, 1979; Satinder, 1977; Wilcox & Fulker, 1973). The possible interaction between therapist personality and patient personality could throw much light on the development of neurotic disorders, but hitherto there has not been sufficient or sufficiently well-planned work to make this more than a promise. On the other hand, work with genetically purebred strains of animals is not only of considerable potential importance, but there has been so much work that has already given interesting results than any systematic review would go well beyond the boundaries of this chapter. Hence only passing mention has been made of some of these studies; in any neobehavioristic scheme, they will undoubtedly assume a major degree of importance.

DESYNCHRONY, IMAGERY, AND CONDITIONING

In this section, I discuss a number of issues that are closely related with the general neobehaviorist theory outlined here, that might be considered as criticisms of the theory, or that have importance regarding its application for therapeutic practices. There are of course many other areas that might have been chosen, but within the limits of a single chapter there has to be restraint.

---

7. There is much evidence that high-psychoticism scorers suffering from neurotic disorders respond very poorly to psychotherapy and behavior therapy (Eysenck & Eysenck, 1976). Possibly this tendency could be counteracted by suitable administrations of phenothiazine or other antipsychotic drugs, during the duration of treatment at least; there is some evidence for the potential value of this method.

A number of criticisms have been made and answered in connection with my paper in the peer review journal *The Behavioral and Brain Sciences* (Eysenck, 1979); these are not rehearsed again here.

DESYNCHRONY

"Desynchrony" refers to the fact that anxiety and fear do not come as "lumps" (Rachman, 1974). Lang (1970) pointed out that the major three aspects of anxiety—namely, the physiological, the behavioral, and the introspective—are far from perfectly synchronized; in fact, they may wax and wane almost independently of each other, at least as long as anxiety is not overwhelmingly strong (Hodgson & Rachman, 1974; Rachman & Hodgson, 1974). This fact seems to present difficulties to a conditioning theory of neurosis, because if the conditioned fears and anxieties are not unitary emotions but are made up of independent behavioral, autonomic, and cognitive elements, then the theory would seem to have to find a way of recognizing this differentiation.

In answer, I would say that the dissociation observed is more imaginary than real. Synchrony would only have been expected under certain rather special conditions—conditions that would rarely obtain. Consider a man who "goes over the top" in trench warfare; his behavior seems indicative of lack of fear, although his autonomic system may be strongly involved and his introspections may indicate strong fear. But his behavior is not determined only by his autonomic responses and his cognitive anxieties; it is also determined by other factors, such as the likelihood of a court-martial if he should refuse to go over the top, with the consequence that he might be shot out of hand. In other words, this is a situation in which behavior is determined by the outcome of an avoidance–avoidance conflict, and failure to act in accordance with one set of avoidance stimuli does not mean that there should be no autonomic reactions motivating an individual in that direction.

Another case might be a candidate in an examination, whose autonomic system is again strongly involved, but who denies any introspective fears; in this case, there is the possibility that other cognitions related to the examination situation have preempted thought processes.

On the autonomic side, it is of course well known that such responses are highly specific, both to the person and also to the situation. Thayer (1970) has shown that different autonomic measures do not correlate at all highly with one another, but they do correlate quite well with introspection; it is as if the mind can integrate the sum of all autonomic responses, suitably weighing each in conformity with a situation and in line with a particular pattern of individual reactivity. While there will therefore be considerable desynchrony between changes in introspection and changes in particular electrophysiolog-ical recordings, this does not mean that there is any pronounced dysynchrony between the weighted sum of all electrophysiological recordings and verbal report (introspection).

These arguments should be taken together with the fact that desyn-chrony mainly appears when relatively weak states of emotional arousal are considered (i.e., states well below the "critical point" in Figure 5-1). From all this it may be concluded that, while the discovery of desynchrony may pre-sent some problems to the theory, these are by no means insuperable. It seems desirable that further work should be done on desynchrony, but using much more comprehensive recording of psychophysiological responses than has been customary hitherto. Even then, it is of course quite likely that both the speed of conditioning and the speed of extinction of these components of the anxiety state may be correlated rather less strongly than might at first be sup-posed; again, there is no reason to expect that verbal responses should be con-ditioned at the same speed as behavioral or autonomic ones.

Rachman (1977) has suggested that there are different combinations of the three components of the anxiety state, as well as three methods of acquir-ing fears—namely, conditioning, vicarious learning, and informational learning. He maintains that "we can hazard the speculation that [for] fears acquired by a conditioning process . . . the components which will be most markedly involved are the psychophysiological and behavioural, with the subjective component playing a comparatively minor role. In the case of fears transmitted indirectly (i.e., vicariously or informationally) one might expect the subjective aspect to be predominant and the psychophysiological changes in behavioural effects to be comparatively minor" (p. 380). He also expects prepared fears to have large physiological and behavioral compon-ents, but expects nonprepared fears to have a larger cognitive element. These suggestions are worthy of being followed up by suitable experimentation. So are hypotheses about the relationship between desynchronous changes and high-demand types of *in vivo* treatment (Grey, Sartory, & Rachman, 1978). Altogether, this is an interesting and important area within the neobehavior-istic model of neurosis.

IMAGERY

The use of imagery in desensitization treatment, as suggested by Wolpe, has often been held to violate in some way the behavioristic properties of behav-ior therapy. Such a criticism does not seem very appropriate, because images can be tied into a behavioral chain by defining the stimulating conditions (in-structions) and the behavioral changes that emerge at the other end of the chain; thus, images would seem to fulfill Hull's prescription for intervening variables acceptable within a behavioristic or neobehavioristic framework.

Consider an imaginary experiment in which a male subject is instructed to imagine a certain type of explicit sexual situation. The investigator predicts (and finds, through the use of a penis plethysmograph) that after a given period of time an erection results. Thus a causal chain can be inferred from the instruction to the erection, involving an intervening variable that itself cannot be observed from the outside, but that has the same status as a drive or a habit. Furthermore, it is possible to correlate differential changes with reports on the part of the subject about the vividness of his imagery; where such correlations are significant and positive, they may be taken as further behavioral evidence for the meaningfulness of postulating the concept "imagery."

Such evidence is indeed readily available. W. A. Shaw (1940) showed that muscle tension varied systematically with the imagined performance of a perceptual task, and this relationship was closer in subjects reporting more vivid imagery. Electromyographic activity showed a monotonic increase with the imagination of weights of increasing heft. Deckert (1964) and B. B. Brown (1968) tested the relationship between a perceptual task (e.g., visually following a beating pendulum) and the performance of the same task in imagination. All three studies showed similarities in response between actual performance and performance in imagination. Responses in imagination tend to be degraded in specificity, but less so in good imagers than in poor ones. A similar correlation can be observed within subjects between the vividness of an image and the degree of concordance between actual observation and image effect.

In these studies, subjects were given an actual percept or act to perform before being called upon to produce an image; similar effects can be produced in the absence of a perceptual template. The early studies of Perky (1910) were followed by the well-known work of Jacobson (1930, 1931) and more recently that of McGuigan (1973). D. F. Marks and Barron (quoted in D. F. Marks, 1972) have studied the role of instructional information on image production, demonstrating that the presence or absence of sensory adjustment response in imagery could be controlled by instruction. These were more clearly effective for "good visualizers."

The relationship between emotional imagery and autonomic arousal is equally well documented. The early work of Rowland (1963) was followed by the better controlled studies of Grossberg and Wilson (1968), who studied the physiological responses of 46 subjects to imagined fearful and neutral scenes. A correlation of .6 was found between reported vividness of the images and heart rate change during imagery. Lang, Melamed, and Hart (1970) found high correlations between heart rate and fear ratings in imagined situations related to the phobic fears of their subjects. They, like Grossberg and Wilson

(1968), found correlations in the neighborhood of .5 between the vividness of visualization and heart rate responses. Van Egeren, Feather, and Hein (1971) and I. M. Marks and Huson (1973) report similar results. J. P. Watson *et al.* (1972) found greater heart rate and skin conductance responses with the imagination of fearful scenes as compared with neutral scenes in eight patients flooded with imagery instructions relevant to their clinical fears; they compared results with exposure to actual phobic objects.

Also of considerable importance in monitoring the effects of imagery are studies such as those of Mendoza and Wichman (1978), and Vandell, Davis, and Clugston (1943), in which physical skills executed in imagination have been shown to produce measurable effects on the actual demonstration of these skills afterwards, as compared with the results for a control group not having the practice in imagination. The positive results of these studies demonstrate again that it is possible to attach the intervening variable "imagination" to instructions at the one end and to measurable effects at the other.

Finally, in relation to treatment, the work of Foa and Chambless (1978) and Grayson and Borkovec (in press) has shown that the use of imagery can be controlled through instruction and can be shown to give specific effects in behavior therapy. There seems to be little doubt that imagination can be conceptualized within a neobehavioristic framework and does not require special "cognitive" theories for its understanding. The situation would be altered if it could be shown that such cognitive theories make predictions other than those that would be made within a neobehavioristic framework, and if it could also be shown that these predictions were in fact borne out by experimental studies, while those made by neobehavioristic theories were disproved. No such evidence exists at the moment.

CONDITIONING

The process of conditioning is clearly vital to the neobehavioristic theory of neurosis, and consequently must be discussed at least in some brief detail here. Other aspects are covered in more detail elsewhere in this volume. As a beginning, I must comment on a well-known paper by Brewer (1974), in which he alleges that "there is no convincing evidence for operant or classical conditioning in adult humans" (p. 1). His argument is too lengthy to be dealt with in full here, and in any case is being answered in considerable detail by Levey and Martin (in press). Instead, I merely list a few facts from eyeblink conditioning to illustrate the absurdity of Brewer's claim.

It is well known that the CS-UCS interval in eyeblink conditioning has to be within a very narrow range (from approximately 500 msec to 2500 msec) in order to produce CRs. If investigators wish to explain the phenomena of Pavlovian conditioning in terms of expectancies, awareness, and other cognitive variables, it is difficult to see why the adult human should be able to create such cognitive "expectancies" within such very limited time periods, but be unable to extend them beyond 2 or 3 seconds. No explanation of this oddity is available in Brewer's paper.

It is also well known that voluntary eyeblink responses have a much shorter latency than eyeblink CRs have, and indeed there is practically no overlap between the two curves. This fact has been used to eliminate "voluntary responders" from his studies. Brewer does not explain the difference, which poses a severe problem for any form of cognitive or "expectancy" theory. The differentiation is perfectly well in line with Pavlovian hypotheses.

Martin and Levey (1969) have shown that two properties of the eyeblink CR can be isolated. One is frequency; the other is effectiveness (i.e., success in shutting out the noxious stimulus from impinging on the cornea). These two effects are quite unrelated, and it is difficult to see how any cognitive theory would deal with the problem of "expectancy" producing two independent reaction patterns. Brewer gets over this problem by not even mentioning the Martin and Levey study; indeed, throughout his paper, he avoids awkward factual confrontations of this kind. Until the challenge of these and many other established facts is met, his argument can hardly be taken very seriously.

There are many other questions that Brewer fails to answer. Thus one might ask how any form of expectancy or cognitive theory would manage to deal with the Mowrer paradox of neurosis—that is, the problem of why, in spite of the failure of life experiences to be in line with the patient's "expectancies," nevertheless these "expectancies" grow stronger and stronger. Again Brewer evades the challenge. The truth would seem to be that, far from "expectancies" explaining conditioning phenomena, conditioning creates not only autonomic and motor responses but also mental responses of the kind we may label "expectancies"; in this way, these may be regarded as epiphenomena, having no causal effect. Introspectively revealed "expectancies" might then be regarded as simply an index or monitor of the strength of CRs, thus explaining the alleged correlation between verbalized insight into the conditioning paradigm and the appearance of CRs.

Brewer seems to admit the existence of classical conditioning in animals, but not in man. Logically, this implies that he must explain why what has usually been regarded as human conditioning follows much the same laws as animal conditioning; if the mechanisms are entirely different, why are the contingencies so similar? Is not the most probable explanation simply that under certain circumstances humans form CRs, just as animals do? Certainly Occam's Razor would suggest accepting alternative theories only after much scrutiny.

Of greater interest is a study by Tryon (in press) in which he attempts to give an operant explanation of Mowrer's neurotic paradox. The attempt is an ingenious one, but too complex to be discussed here in any detail. Essentially, the explanation centers on the suggestion that neurosis "involves an approach–avoidance conflict over the non-occurrence of a particular behavior whose absence is the basis for naming the phobia" (p. 209).

The attempt fails ultimately because it considers omission of the feared behavior as a reinforced stimulus, comparable to the punished occurrence of the feared behavior itself. It is doubtful whether it has much meaning to label the nonoccurrence of a behavior a "stimulus" in the orthodox sense; to use Tryon's own example, when is nondriving (in a person with a car phobia) to be considered as a stimulus? Such a person, like most people, is in a state of nondriving most of the time; yet not driving a car would only be considered a stimulus in this connection when there was a definite choice between driving or not driving in the person's mind.

Even if Tryon's theory could account for Mowrer's paradox, it is doubtful whether it could account for the phenomena of incubation of anxiety (i.e., the actual increase of anxiety when nonreinforced stimuli are presented). To say all this is not to say that it might not be possible to account for the facts in terms of operant conditioning; it is merely to say that the present effort, though ingenious, is unlikely to account for all the facts as readily as Pavlovian conditioning is.

A final comment, in virtue of the importance of conditioning for any neobehavioristic theory of neurosis, must be made concerning the meaning of Pavlovian conditioning itself. In this chapter, I have purposely ignored the detailed discussion of the nature of Pavlovian conditioning, but it should not be assumed that the old-fashioned S-S type of substitution hypothesis is adequate to account for the facts that have emerged since Watson presented his behavioristic version, or since Mowrer advocated the two-stage model of avoidance learning. Notterman, Schoenfeld, and Bersh (1952) were among the first to show the inadequacy of such a substitution theory, by demonstrating in human subjects that, while the UCR to an electric shock was an *acceleration* of heart rate, the CR to a tone paired with the shock was a *deceleration* of heart rate. (Other examples are given in Terrace, 1973.) This conclusion does not necessarily lead to regarding classical conditioning simply as an example of discriminative operant conditioning (Sheffield, 1965), but it does lead to some novel ways of looking at classical conditioning. Thus Rescorla (1967) has suggested that the CS transmits information about the occurrence of the US, thus suggesting that contiguity is not the important element in producing the CS-UCS link, but rather the fact that the CS reduces *uncertainty* about the occurrence of the UCS.

Work on "autoshaping" (P. L. Brown & Jenkins, 1968) or "sign-tracking" (Hearst & Jenkins, 1974) can also be looked upon as depending on informational processes (Gamzu & Schwartz, 1973). This and other possible changes in the precise denotation of Pavlovian conditioning would leave the neobehavioristic model unaffected; indeed, they may serve to differentiate it from the simplistic Watsonian model that preceded it. It would clearly be wrong to argue here for any of the alternatives offered, if only because there is no space to discuss their advantages and disadvantages; one of the more attractive ones, perhaps, is Bindra's (1974, 1978) perceptual–motiviational account of conditioning.[8] However that may be, clearly the precise nature of the conditioning process must remain a research objective within the general field of a neobehavioristic approach to the neuroses.

LIMITATIONS OF A THEORY

In the literature, there appear many misunderstandings concerning the nature and the limitations of a theory such as that presented here as neobehaviorism. Some of these misunderstandings are obvious; thus, some people have objected that the views of human nature underlying the theory are unacceptable because they do not account for much that is valuable in human conduct. But of course the principles involved are not meant to cover *all* of human behavior; they are strictly related to the origins of *neurotic* behavior and the extinction of the CRs involved. McLean (1963) has popularized the concept of the "triune brain" (i.e., the relative morphological and functional differentiation of the brain into the reptile brain, the paleocortex, and the neocortex); the details may not always be right, but the concept as a whole is almost certainly in line with modern neurophysiological thinking (Uttall, 1978).

It is the paleocortex that is concerned with emotional behavior, and it is Pavlovian conditioning that speaks the language of the paleocortex. To deny that Pavlovian conditioning accounts for *all* of human behavior is not to

---

8. Interesting attempts have been made, although with questionable success, to combine the laws of Pavlovian conditioning with cognitive theories; a good example is King's "image approach" to conditioning (1979). It is unfortunate that cognitive theorists insist on trying to disregard classical conditioning altogether and on building up an entirely novel set of principles. It would have been much more helpful if they had restricted themselves to the more prosaic but more important task of elaborating the principles underlying the second signaling system within a conditioning framework.

deny that it accounts for *some* of human behaviour, and my point would be that neuroses are primitive reactions appropriately linked with the paleocortex. The theory does not pretend to go outside this limited field, and objections to its doing so are therefore irrelevant.

Other objections relate to the fact that the theory does not take into account many facts that are reasonably well established and clearly relevant to neurosis. Thus it might be said that the "secondary gain" that some neurotics derive from their illness uses principles of operant conditioning and hence would seem to contradict the priority of Pavlovian conditioning accorded it in the present account. There are no doubt many ways in which an existing neurosis may be maintained, and operant conditioning undoubtedly may play a part in this; my theory is concerned with the *origin* of the neurosis, not so much with its maintenance. There are undoubtedly many factors that play a part in this, but it is not the purpose of this chapter to elucidate them all. "Secondary gain," envisaged as a function of operant conditioning, almost certainly plays an important part in individual cases. To admit this is not to deny the preeminence of Pavlovian conditioning in the production of the neurosis in the first place.

One important aspect of the theory that critics do not always recognize is the fact that it deals with the core of neurotic genesis and treatment; the activities of clinical therapists may take them well beyond these limits, and different and novel concepts may be required to take account of all the complexities issuing therefrom. An example may make clear the kinds of complexities this statement is meant to cover.

Consider aversion therapy of alcoholics, homosexuals, fetishists, and other such patients. It is usually agreed that the original treatment may work, in the sense that the positive appeal of the alcohol, homosexual stimuli, or other stimuli involved can be neutralized by aversive conditioning; what is usually found also, however, is a rapid relapse. At first sight, this might seem to contradict the statement that relapse is rare and almost unheard of in behavior therapy; however, that statement pertains to the *dysthymic* disorders (i.e., disorders the treatment for which is the extinction of existing CRs). Aversion therapy is appropriate for disorders of the second kind—namely, those in which where there has been a failure of conditioning to produce abstinence from certain types of stimuli, and in which treatment consists of producing the requisite Pavlovian conditioning in the patient. Obviously such CRs are subject to extinction, and there are many reasons to predict that such extinction should occur quite frequently.

What therapists do, almost inevitably, is to put "cured" patients back into the situations in which they found themselves before treatment, with all the old CSs (friends, social stimuli, bars, homosexual acquaintances, etc.) that were associated with the development of their original disorders. Little effort is made to alter the environment in such a way as to withdraw these stimuli, or to provide others that might usefully take their place.

Thus, treatment of homosexuals that does not go beyond extinction and neutralization of homosexual tendencies is almost certain to lead to a resumption of homosexual activities, because the patients lack the desire to form relations with the opposite sex, lack the ability to do so should they desire it, and are not commonly in a position to meet members of the opposite sex for the purpose. Instead, they are of necessity reduced to satisfy their social needs by meeting old friends (usually homosexuals), being tempted again by them into resuming their former way of life, and often being reinforced for doing so. Under these conditions (i.e., the appearance of old CSs associated with undesirable behavior), it is to be wondered at that aversion therapy has any lasting effects at all, even in a small number of cases.

This analysis does not only conform with common sense; it also derives considerable support from animal studies of drug addiction and tolerance that demonstrate the importance of situational cues in a framework of Pavlovian conditioning (Hinson & Siegel, in press; Siegel, 1976, 1978a, 1978b, 1979; Siegel, Hinson, & Krank, 1978, 1979). These studies demonstrate the tremendous influence that environmental stimuli associated with drug taking have on the various processes associated with drugs; it does not seem unreasonable to extrapolate from this work with animals to human environmental conditioning related to drug abuse, sexual habits, or other behavior patterns of an antisocial kind.

What would be required, therefore, to turn the successful extinction process into a general therapeutic success would be an intervention in the lives of patients that goes well beyond the laboratory-like treatment prescribed by behavior therapists. For example, it might be necessary to move homosexual patients into a different environment; to make them disown their former friends; and to give them special "social skills" training in meeting, attracting, and seducing members of the opposite sex, as well as training in turning their sexual energies in that direction. Efforts to do that would be well in line with the conditioning theory, but seriously hampered by lack of resources and by ethical considerations that might make such behavior on the part of therapists undesirable in the eyes of many administrators.

The situation might be compared with that of dentists. The core activity of dentists is filling teeth; however, lasting success in keeping their patients from having toothaches, having teeth pulled out, and generally suffering the various dental disorders that humans are prone to requires much more than that. They have to persuade their patients (particularly children) to brush their teeth regularly, not to eat too many sweets, to come to see them regularly, and so forth. In addition, they must be careful not to put off patients by charging too much, by causing them distress, by giving painful injections, and so on. In other words, there is a whole therapeutic set of activities irrelevant to the core treatment, but without which the core treatment itself could not be carried out, might not have lasting consequences, and would at best be somewhat irrelevant to the needs of patients. Nevertheless, no one would cavil at a textbook stating that the rules according to which teeth are filled constitute a central part of the training of dentists, and that filling teeth is what constitutes dentists' special skill. A person may be a good dentist, but may fail at the other activities outlined here, and thus may be a failure in his or her profession. The same may be said of clinical psychologists. All this does not detract from the fact that clinicians should be concerned, as I have been concerned in this chapter, with the central portion of the activity of the clinical psychologist—namely, a recognition of the causes and cures of neurosis. It is freely acknowledged that this by itself is not enough for the successful psychiatric treatment of the patient, but this realization does not lessen the importance of the central aspects of the treatment.

Once it is acknowledged that the central concept of treatment is extinction, it may also be acknowledged that there are many ways of embodying the extinction process in a set of procedures and that these ways may differ widely from each other. Thus extinction is implied in modeling as much as in desensitization; in flooding as much as in psychoanalysis; and in spontaneous remission as much as in client-centered therapy. The task of the research worker is to match the particular method best suited to bring the extinction process to bear on the disorder with both the nature of the neurotic disorder itself and the personality of the patient. Failure to recognize this need has resulted in a dearth of factual knowledge on this vital topic, and it is to be hoped that future work along the lines suggested in this chapter will remedy this unsatisfactory state. Some types of therapy may appeal more to extraverts and others to introverts, as I have noted; the fact that extinction is central to both methods does not mean that the appeal of one method over another for particular types of patients should be neglected. This is a topic of enormous complexity, but the fact of its existence does not deny the primacy of extinction for the cure of neurotic disorders.

The question of cognitive factors, expectancies, imagery, and thought processes generally has already been discussed, at least briefly. There is no doubt that these may interact with the conditioning process in many different ways, and to that extent it is certainly true to say that cognitions must be recognized as a real aspect of human behavior. To do this is not necessarily to go outside the field of neobehaviorism. It is well known on an experimental basis that stimulus generalization may proceed along cognitive lines (i.e., through synonyms, verbal associations, etc.). Once this can be shown, verbal stimuli of this type can be regarded as just that—stimuli; the fact that they are verbal does not alter their status in a theory of conditioning. As Pavlov has already pointed out, "A word is as real a conditioned stimulus for man as all the other stimuli in common with animals, but at the same time more all-inclusive than any other stimuli" (quoted by Platanov, 1959, p. 3).

For a cognitive or social learning theory of neurosis, such as Bandura's theory of "perceived self-efficacy," to be accepted as a proper alternative to a conditioning theory, it has to be shown that the concepts involved and the rules invoked can be established independently of conditioning theory in the laboratory and can lead to different predictions. As the issue of *Advances in Behavior Research and Therapy* edited by Rachman (1978b) indicates, critics are by no means convinced that Bandura's theory stands up to this test. Smedslund (1978, 1979) has put forward criticisms rather similar to those made by some of the contributors to the Rachman volume. In a sense, cognitive theorists make their task too easy for themselves; it would be valuable if they would present a proper alternative theory to that of conditioning, but hitherto they have not succeeded in doing so.

One last word concerns the recent decision on the part of the American Psychiatric Association to delete the term (and concept) of "neurosis" from their vocabulary. It is hardly necessary to stress that such committee decisions, based on political pressures and scholastic infighting, have no scientific standing; abolishing the term does not abolish the underlying reality. As Figures 5-4 and 5-5 have shown, there is strong evidence for the existence of a "positive manifold" of symptoms defining "neurosis," and this evidence has not even been considered by the individuals who defined "neurosis" out of existence. How would psychologists define "neurosis"? In principle, they should perhaps follow the practice of the "hard" scientists, which is to define concepts in terms of theories, preferably using quantitative deductions in the process. This procedure may at times look excessively arbitrary, but it has been shown to work exceptionally well. Why is mercury used in thermometers, and not linseed oil? The answer is that mercury behaves as predicted by the kinetic theory of heat, while linseed oil does not; the former, but not the latter, gives results in line with the formula for the mixing of two similar fluids of masses m_1 and m_2, and of initial temperatures t_1 and t_2, resulting in a final temperature t_f:

$$t_f = (m_1 t_1 + m_2 t_2)/(m_1 + m_2)$$

If the task of theory construction is taken seriously, "neurosis" would therefore be defined in terms of the conditioning theory outlined here; if it should be found that certain mental aberrations, behavioral oddities, or autonomic dysfunctions do not originate in the manner suggested, then they automatically fall outside the concept "neurosis." Provided that a sufficiently large number of phenomena are covered by the definition, there is nothing unusual in such drastic surgery; physicists and chemists proceed along these lines all the time. The mutual interplay suggested between fact and theory, definition and concept, seems a better method for arriving at the truth than does the arbitrary committee procedure of the American Psychiatric Association, which steps outside science altogether.

I would conclude that the neobehavioristic theory of neurosis and treatment, with all the anomalies and defects that may still exist, does account for most of the phenomena observed in the laboratory and in the clinic, and that it unifies them in a relatively satisfactory manner. Until some other theory that does the job at least equally well is advanced, and until it can make predictions of a testable and verifiable kind that are different from those made by neobehavioristic theories of conditioning, it would seem desirable to regard conditioning theory as a paradigm for all workers in this field—not as a Holy Grail to be preserved at all costs, but rather as a useful tool in research and therapy, to be improved and (if need be) discarded when something better turns up. At present there is little evidence for the emergence of a different theory capable of carrying out this function (Gossop, 1980).

REFERENCES

Allport, D. A. The state of cognitive psychology. *Quarterly Journal of Experimental Psychology,* 1975, *27,* 141–152.

Antrobus, J. S., Antrobus, D. A., & Singer, J. L. Eye movements accompanying daydreaming, visual imagery, and thought suppression. *Journal of Abnormal and Social Psychology,* 1964, *69,* 244–252.

Baird, P. Relationships between certain MMPI factors and psychotherapeutic preferences. *Psychological Reports,* 1979, *44,* 1317–1318.

Baker, A. H., Mishara, B. L., Kostin, I. W., & Parker, L. Menstrual cycle affects kinesthetic after-effect: An index of personality and perceptual style. *Journal of Personality and Social Psychology,* 1979, *37,* 234–246.

Bandura, A. Self-efficacy: Toward a unifying theory of behavioral change. *Psychological Review,* 1977, *84,* 191–215.

Baum, M. Rapid extinction of an avoidance response following a period of response prevention in the avoidance apparatus. *Psychological Reports,* 1966, *18,* 59–64.

Baum, M. Extinction of an avoidance response following response prevention: Some parametric investigations. *Canadian Journal of Psychology,* 1969, *23,* 1–10. (a)

Baum, M. Extinction of an avoidance response motivated by intense fear: Social facilitation of the action of response prevention (flooding) in rats. *Behaviour Research and Therapy,* 1969, *7,* 57–62. (b)

Baum, M. Extinction of avoidance responding through response prevention (flooding). *Psychological Bulletin,* 1970, *74,* 276–284.

Beck, A. T. *Cognitive therapy and the emotional disorders.* New York: International Universities Press, 1976.

Bergin, A. E., & Lambert, M. J. The evaluation of therapeutic outcomes. In S. L. Garfield & A. E. Bergin (Eds.), *Handbook of psychotherapy and behavior change* (2nd ed.). New York: Wiley, 1978.

Bergmann, G. The contribution of John B. Watson. *Psychological Review,* 1956, *63,* 265–276.

Bersh, P. J. Eysenck's theory of incubation: A critical analysis. *Behaviour Research and Therapy,* 1980, *18,* 11–17.

Bindra, D. A unified account of classical conditioning and operant training. In A. H. Black & W. F. Prokasy (Eds.), *Classical conditioning* (Vol. 2): *Current theory and research.* New York: Appleton-Century-Crofts, 1971.

Bindra, D. A motivational view of learning, performance, and behavior modification. *Psychological Review,* 1974, *81,* 199–213.

Bindra, D. How adaptive behavior is produced: A perceptual–motivational alternative to response–reinforcement. *The Behavioral and Brain Sciences,* 1978, *1,* 41–91.

Binswanger, L. *Sigmund Freud: Reminiscences of a friendship.* London: Grune & Stratton, 1953.

Bolles, R. Species-specific defense reactions and avoidance learning. *Psychological Review,* 1970, *77,* 32–48.

Borkovec, T. D. Effects of expectancy on the outcome of systematic desensitization in implosive treatment for analogue anxiety. *Behavior Therapy,* 1972, *3,* 29–40.

Borkovec, T. D. Heart rate process during systematic desensitization and implosive therapy for analogue anxiety. *Behavior Therapy,* 1974, *5,* 636–641.

Borkovec, T. D., & Glasgow, R. E. Boundary conditions of false heart-rate feedback effects on avoidance behavior: A resolution of discrepant results. *Behaviour Research and Therapy,* 1973, *11,* 171–177.

Boulougouris, J. C., Marks, I., & Marset, P. Superiority of flooding (implosion) to desensitization for reducing pathological fear. *Behaviour Research and Therapy,* 1971, *9,* 7–16.

Bower, G. H. Contacts of cognitive psychology with social learning theory. *Cognitive Therapy and Research,* 1978, *2,* 123–146.

Breger, L., & McGaugh, J. L. Critique and reformulation of "learning-theory" approaches to psychotherapy and neurosis. *Psychological Bulletin,* 1965, *63,* 338–358.

Bregman, E. An attempt to modify the emotional attitudes of infants by the conditioned response technique. *Journal of Genetic Psychology,* 1934, *45,* 169–198.

Breland, K., & Breland, M. *Animal behavior.* New York: Macmillan, 1966.

Brewer, W. F. There is no convincing evidence for operant or classical conditioning in adult humans. In W. B. Weiner & D. S. Palermo (Eds.), *Cognition and the symbolic processes.* Hillsdale, N. J.: Erlbaum, 1974.

Breznitz, S. Incubation of threat and duration of anticipation and false alarm as determinants of the fear reaction to an unavoidable frightening event. *Journal of Experimental Research in Personality,* 1967, *2,* 173–179.

Bridger, W., & Mandel, I. J. A comparison of GSR fear responses produced by threat and electric shock. *Journal of Psychiatric Research,* 1964, *2,* 31–40.

Broadhurst, P. L. The Maudsley reactive and non-reactive strains of rats: A survey. *Behavior Genetics,* 1975, *5,* 299–319.

Brown, B. B. Visual recall ability and eye movements. *Psychophysiology,* 1968, *4,* 300–306.

Brown, P. L., & Jenkins, H. M. Auto-shaping of the pigeon's key peck. *Journal of the Experimental Analysis of Behavior,* 1968, *11,* 1–8.

Burks, J., & Rubenstein, M. *Temperament styles in adult interaction: Application in psychotherapy.* New York: Brunner/Mazel, 1979.

Bykov, K. M. [*The cerebral cortex and the internal organs*] (W. H. Gantt, trans.). New York: Chemical Publishing, 1957.

Campbell, D., Sanderson, R., & Laverty, S. G. Characteristic of a conditioned response in human subjects during extinction trials following a simple traumatic conditioning trial. *Journal of Abnormal and Social Psychology,* 1964, *68,* 627–639.

Chomsky, N. *Syntactic structures.* New York: Mouton, 1957.

Chomsky, N. Review of Skinner's *Verbal behavior. Language,* 1959, *35,* 26–58.

Chomsky, N. *Current issues in linguistic theory.* New York: Mouton, 1964.

Chomsky, N. *Aspects of the theory of syntax.* Cambridge, Mass.: M.I.T. Press, 1965.

Chomsky, N. *Language and mind.* New York: Harcourt Brace Jovanovich, 1972.

Chomsky, N. *Reflections in language.* London: Temple Smith, 1975.

Cohen, D. *J. B. Watson.* London: Routledge & Kegan Paul, 1979.

Cohen, G. *The psychology of cognition.* London: Academic Press, 1977.

Coles, M. G., Gale, A., & Kline, D. Personality and habituation of the orienting reaction: Tonic and response measures of electrodermal activity. *Psychophysiology,* 1971, *8,* 54–63.

Cook, S. W., & Harris, R. E. The verbal conditioning of the galvanic skin reflex. *Journal of Experimental Psychology,* 1937, *21,* 202–205.

Cooper, J. E., Gelder, M. G., & Marks, I. M. Results of behaviour therapy in 77 psychiatric patients. *British Medical Journal,* 1965, *1,* 1222.

Cravens, H. *The triumph of evolution.* Philadelphia: University of Pennsylvania Press, 1978.

Deckert, G. H. Pursuit eye movements in the absence of moving visual stimulus. *Science,* 1964, *143,* 1192–1193.

Deitz, S. R. Individual differences in electrodermal response conditioning and self-report of discomfort: A phobia analogue. *Behaviour Research and Therapy,* in press.

DiLoreto, A. *Comparative psychotherapy.* New York: Aldine-Atherton, 1971.

Dykman, R. A., Gantt, W. H., & Whitehorn, J. C. Conditioning on emotional sensitization and differentiation. *Psychological Monographs,* 1956, *70,* 15.

Dykman, R. A., & Gantt, W. H. Cardiovasular conditioning in dogs and humans. In W. H. Gantt, (Ed.), *Physiological basis of psychiatry.* Springfield, Ill.: Charles C Thomas, 1958.

Dykman, R. A., & Gantt, W. H. A case of experimental neurosis and recovery in relation to the orienting response. *Journal of Psychology,* 1960, *50,* 105–110. (a)

Dykman, R. A., & Gantt, W. H. Experimental psychogenic hypertensions: Blood pressure changes conditioned to painful stimuli (schizokinesis). *Bulletin of Johns Hopkins Hospital,* 1960, *107,* 72–89. (b)

Dykman, R. A., Mack, R. L., & Ackerman, P. T. The evaluation of autonomic and motor components of the unavoidance conditioned response in the dog. *Psychophysiology,* 1965, *1,* 209–230.

Dykman, R. A., Murphee, O. D., & Ackerman, P. T. Litter patterns in the offspring of nervous and stable dogs: II. Autonomic and motor conditioning. *Journal of Nervous and Mental Disorders,* 1966, *141,* 419–431.

Eaglen, A. Learning theory versus paradigms as the basis for behavior therapy. *Journal of Behavior Therapy and Experimental Psychiatry,* 1978, *9,* 215–218.

Edwards, J. H. Familial predispositions in man. *British Medical Bulletin,* 1969, *25,* 58–64.

English, H. B. Three cases of the "conditioned fear response." *Journal of Abnormal and Social Psychology,* 1929, *34,* 221–225.

Erwin, E. *Behaviour therapy.* Cambridge, England: Cambridge University Press, 1978.

Eysenck, H. J. *Dimensions of personality.* London: Routledge & Kegan Paul, 1947.

Eysenck, H. J. Criterion analysis: An application of the hypothetico-deductive method to factor analysis. *Psychological Review,* 1950, *57,* 38–53.

Eysenck, H. J. Schizothymia–cyclothymia as a dimension of personality. *Journal of Personality,* 1952, *20,* 345–384.

Eysenck, H. J. Learning theory and behavior therapy. *The Journal of Mental Science,* 1959, *105,* 61–75.

Eysenck, H. J. *Behaviour therapy and the neuroses.* London: Pergamon, 1960.

Eysenck, H. J. Behavior therapy, spontaneous remission and transference in neurotics. *Ameri-*

can *Journal of Psychiatry,* 1963, *119,* 867–871.

Eysenck, H. J. *Experiments in behaviour therapy.* London: Pergamon, 1964. (a)

Eysenck, H. J. (Ed.). *Experiments in motivation.* London: Pergamon, 1964. (b)

Eysenck, H. J. *The biological basis of personality.* Springfield, Ill.: Charles C Thomas, 1967.

Eysenck, H. J. A theory of the incubation of anxiety/fear response. *Behaviour Research and Therapy,* 1968, *6,* 319–321.

Eysenck, H. J. A dimensional system of psychodiagnostics. In A. R. Mahrer (Ed.), *New approaches to personality classification.* New York: Columbia University Press, 1970. (a)

Eysenck, H. J. *The structure of human personality* (3rd ed.). London: Methuen, 1970. (b)

Eysenck, H. J. Behavior therapy is behavioristic. *Behavior Therapy,* 1972, *3,* 609–613.

Eysenck, H. J. A note on backward conditioning. *Behaviour Research and Therapy,* 1975, *13,* 2101–2202.

Eysenck, H. J. Behaviour therapy: Dogma or applied science? In M. P. Feldman & A. Broadhurst (Eds.), *Theoretical and experimental bases of the behaviour therapies.* London: Wiley, 1976.

Eysenck, H. J. *Crime and personality.* London: Routledge & Kegan Paul, 1977. (a)

Eysenck, H. J. *You and neurosis.* Los Angeles: Sage, 1977. (b)

Eysenck, H. J. Neurotizismusforschung: Der Neurotizimus und die Theorie de Neurose. In L. J. Pongratz (Ed.), *Handbuch der Klinischen Psychologie.* Göttingen: Göttingen Verlag für Psychologie, 1977. (c)

Eysenck, H. J. What to do when desensitization goes wrong? *Australian Behaviour Therapist,* 1978, *5,* 15–16.

Eysenck, H. J. The conditioning model of neurosis. *The Behavioral and Brain Sciences,* 1979, *2,* 155–199.

Eysenck, H. J. (Ed.). *A model for personality.* New York: Springer, 1980. (a)

Eysenck, H. J. A psychological theory of hysteria. In A. Roy (Ed.), *Hysteria.* New York: Wiley, 1980. (b)

Eysenck, H. J. Psychopathie. In U. Baumann, H. Berbalk, & G. Seidenstücker (Eds.), *Klinische Psychologie: Trends in Forschung und Praxis* (Vol. 3). Vienna: Hans Huber, 1980. (c)

Eysenck, H. J. Man as a biosocial animal: Comments on the sociobiology debate. *Political Psychology,* 1980, *2,* 43–51. (d)

Eysenck, H. J., & Eysenck, S. B. G. *Psychoticism as a dimension of personality.* London: Hodder & Stoughton, 1976.

Eysenck, H. J., & Levey, A. Conditioning, introversion–extraversion and the strength of the nervous system. In V. D. Debylitsyn & J. A. Gray (Eds.), *Biological bases of individual behavior.* London: Academic Press, 1972.

Eysenck, H. J., & Rachman, S. *The causes and cures of neurosis.* London: Routledge & Kegan Paul, 1965.

Foa, E. B. Failure in treating obsessive–compulsives. *Behaviour Research and Therapy,* 1979, *17,* 177–188.

Foa, E. B., & Chambless, D. L. Habituation of subjective anxiety during flooding in imagery. *Behaviour Research and Therapy,* 1978, *16,* 391–399.

Fouts, G. T., & Click, M. Effects of live and TV models on observational learning in introverted and extraverted children. *Perceptual and Motor Skills,* 1979, *48,* 863–867.

Franklin, R. V., & Broadhurst, P. L. Emotionality in selectively bred strains of rats mediates prior shock effects on escape–avoidance conditioning. *Behaviour Research and Therapy,* 1979, *17,* 349–354.

Franks, C. M. Ease of conditioning and spontaneous recovery from experimental extinction. *British Journal of Psychology,* 1963, *54,* 351–357.

Fulker, D. W. The genetic and environmental architecture of psychoticism, extraversion and neuroticism. In H. J. Eysenck (Ed.), *A model for personality*. New York: Springer, 1980.

Galbrecht, C. D., Dykman, R. A., & Peters, J. The effect of traumatic experiences on the growth and behavior of the rat. *Journal of Genetic Psychology,* 1960, *50,* 227–251.

Gamzu, E., & Schwartz, B. The maintenance of key pecking by stimulus-contingent and response-independent food presentations. *Journal of the Experimental Analysis of Behavior,* 1973, *19,* 65–72.

Gamzu, E., & Williams, D. R. Classical conditioning of a complex skeletal act. *Science,* 1971, *171,* 923–925.

Garcia, J., McGowan, B. K., & Green, K. F. Biological constraints on conditioning. In A. H. Black & W. F. Prokasy (Eds.), *Classical conditioning* (Vol. 2): *Current theory and research.* New York: Appleton-Century-Crofts, 1971.

Geer, J. H. The development of a scale to measure fear. *Behaviour Research and Therapy,* 1965, *3,* 45–53.

Gelder, M., Marks, I., & Wolff, H. Desensitization and psychotherapy in the treatment of phobic states. *British Journal of Psychiatry,* 1967, *113,* 53–73.

Goldfried, M. R. The use of relaxation and cognitive relabeling as coping skills. In R. B. Stuart (Ed.), *Behavioral self-management strategies, techniques and outcomes.* New York: Brunner/Mazel, 1977.

Goodwin, W. B., Geller, J. D., & Quinian, D. M. Clinical responses of A and B practising psychotherapists and neurotic patient prototypes. *British Journal of Medical Psychology,* 1979, *52,* 17–27.

Gordon, D. K. The role and stimulus generalization in the development of complex phobias. *Behaviour Research and Therapy,* in press.

Gossop, M. *Theories of neurosis.* New York: Springer, 1980.

Gourney, A. B., & O'Connor, P. J. Anxiety associated with flying. *British Journal of Psychiatry,* 1971, *119,* 159–166.

Grant, D. A. Classical and operant conditioning. In A. W. Melton (Ed.), *Categories of human learning.* New York: Academic Press, 1964.

Gray, J. A. *The psychology of fear and stress.* London: World University Library, 1971.

Gray, J. A. *Elements of a two-process theory of learning.* London: Academic Press, 1975.

Gray, J. A. Is there any need for conditioning in Eysenck's conditioning model of neurosis? *The Behavioral and Brain Sciences,* in press.

Gray, J. A. Alternative theories of personality. In H. J. Eysenck (Ed.), *A model for personality.* New York: Springer, 1980.

Grayson, J. B., & Borkovec, T. D. The effects of expectancy and imagined response to phobic stimuli on fear reduction. *Cognitive Therapy and Research,* in press.

Grey, S., Sartory, G., & Rachman, S. Synchronous and desynchronous changes during fear reduction. *Behaviour Research and Therapy,* 1978, *17,* 137–147.

Grinker, R., & Spiegel, J. *Men under stress.* London: Churchill, 1945.

Grossberg, J. M., & Wilson, H. F. Physiological changes accompanying the visualization of fearful and neutral stiuations. *Journal of Personality and Social Psychology,* 1968, *10,* 124–133.

Groves, P. M., & Thompson, R. F. Habituation: A dual-process theory . *Psychological Review,* 1970, *77,* 419–450.

Guthrie, E. R. *The psychology of learning.* New York: Harper, 1935.

Gutsch, K. V. & Ritenour, J. V. *Nexus psychotherapy.* Springfield, Ill.: Charles C Thomas, 1976.

Hadley, S. W., & Strupp, H. H. Contemporary views of negative effects of psychotherapy. *Archives of General Psychiatry,* 1976, *33,* 1291–1303.

Hall, G. S. A study of fears. *American Journal of Psychology,* 1897, *8,* 147–249.

Hall, G. S. A synthetic genetic study of fear. *American Journal of Psychology,* 1914, *25,* 149–200, 321–392.

Hallam, R. S. The Eysenck Personality Scales: Stability and change after treatment. *Behaviour Research and Therapy,* 1976, *14,* 369–372.

Harris, B. Whatever happened to little Albert? *American Psychologist,* 1979, *34,* 151–160.

Hayes, S. C. The role of approach contingencies in phobic behavior. *Behavior Therapy,* 1976, *7,* 28–36.

Hayes, S. C., Lattal, K. A., & Myerson, W. A. Strength of experimentally induced phobic behavior in rats: Avoidance versus dual-component formulations. *Psychological Reports,* 1979, *44,* 891–894.

Hearst, E., & Jenkins, H. M. *Sign-tracking: The stimulus–reinforcer relation and direct action.* Austin, Tex.: Psychonomic Society, 1974.

Hemming, J. H. Personality and extinction of a conditioned electrodermal response. *British Journal of Social and Clinical Psychology,* 1979, *18,* 105–110.

Hinde, R. A., & Stevenson-Hinde, J. *Constraints on learning.* London: Academic Press, 1973.

Hinson, R. E., & Siegel, S. The contribution of Pavlovian conditioning to ethanol tolerance and dependence. In H. Tigter & J. C. Crabbe (Eds.), *Alcohol tolerance, dependence, and addiction.* Amsterdam: Elsevier North-Holland, in press.

Hobbs, S. A., Moguin, L. E., Tyroler, M., & Lahey, B. B. Cognitive behavior therapy with children: Has clinical utility been demonstrated? *Psychological Bulletin,* 1980, *87,* 147–165.

Hodgson, R., & Rachman, S. Desynchrony in measures of fear. *Behaviour Research and Therapy,* 1974, *12,* 319–326.

Hodgson, R. J., Rachman, S., & Marks, I. M. The treatment of chronic obsessive–compulsive neurosis: Follow-up and further findings. *Behaviour Research and Therapy,* 1972, *10,* 181–189.

Hubel, D. H., & Wiesel, T. N. Receptive fields of single neurons in the cat's striate cortex. *Journal of Physiology,* 1959, *148,* 574–591.

Hubel, D. H., & Wiesel, T. N. Receptive fields of cells in striate cortex of very young, visually inexperienced kittens. *Journal of Neurophysiology,* 1963, *26,* 994–1002.

Hubel, D. H., & Wiesel, T. N. Receptive fields and functional architecture in two nonstriate visual areas (18 and 19) of the cat. *Journal of Neurophysiology,* 1965, *28,* 279–289.

Hugdahl, K., Frederikson, M. & Öhman, A. "Preparedness" and "arousability" as determinants of electrodermal conditioning. *Behaviour Research and Therapy,* 1977, *15,* 345–353.

Hull, C. L. *Principles of behavior.* New York: Appleton-Century-Crofts, 1943.

Jacobson, E. Electrical measurements of neuromuscular states during mental activities: III. Visual imagination and recollections. *American Journal of Physiology,* 1930, *95,* 694–702.

Jacobson, E. Electrical measurements of neuromuscular states during mental activities: IV. Evidence of contraction of specific muscles during imagination. V. Variations of specific muscles contracting during imagination. *American Journal of Physiology,* 1931, *96,* 115–121.

Jenkins, H. M., & Moore, B. The form of autoshaped response with food and water reinforcers. *Journal of the Experimental Analysis of Behavior,* 1972, *20,* 163–181.

Jensen, A. Skinner and human differences. In H. Wheeler (Ed.), *Beyond the punitive society.* San Francisco: W. H. Freeman, 1973.

Jones, M. C. The elimination of children's fears. *Journal of Experimental Psychology,* 1924, *7,* 383–390. (a)

Jones, M. C. A laboratory study of fear: The case of Peter. *Pedagogical Seminary,* 1924, 31, 308–315. (b)

Kalat, J. W., & Rozin, P. You can lead a rat to poison but you can't make him think. In M. P.

Seligman & J. Z. Hager (Eds.), *Biological boundaries of learning.* New York: Appleton-Century-Crofts, 1973.

Kass, W., & Gilner, F. H. Drive level, incentive conditions and systematic desensitization. *Behaviour Research and Therapy,* 1974, *12,* 99–106.

Kazdin, A. E., & Wilson, G. T. *Evaluation of behavior therapy: Issues, evidence, and research strategies.* Cambridge, Mass.: Ballinger, 1978.

Kimble, G. A. *Hilgard and Marquis' conditioning and learning.* New York: Appleton-Century-Crofts, 1961.

Kimmel, H. D. Conditioned fear and anxiety. In C. D. Spielberger & I. G. Sarason (Eds.), *Stress and anxiety* (Vol. 1). New York: Wiley, 1975.

King, D. L. *Conditioning: An image approach.* New York: Gardner, 1979.

Konorski, J., & Miller, S. On two types of conditioned reflex. *Journal of General Psychology,* 1937, *16,* 264–272.

Lachman, S. J. *Psychosomatic disorders: A behavioristic interpretation.* New York: Wiley, 1972.

Lader, M. H. Palmar skin conductance measures in anxiety and phobic states. *Journal of Psychosomatic Research,* 1967, *2,* 271–281.

Lader, M. H., Gelder, M. G., & Marks, I. M. Palmar conductance measures as predictors of responses to desensitization. *Journal of Psychosomatic Reasearch,* 1967, *11,* 283–290.

Lader, M. H., & Mathews, A. M. A physiological model of phobic anxiety and desensitization. *Behaviour Research and Therapy,* 1968, *6,* 411–421.

Lader, M. H., & Wing, L. *Physiological measures, sedative drugs, and morbid anxiety* (Maudsley Monographs). London: Oxford University Press, 1966.

Landy, F. J., & Gaupp, L. A. A factor analysis of the Fear Survey Schedule III. *Behaviour Research and Therapy,* 1971, *9,* 89–93.

Lang, P. J. The mechanisms of desensitization and the laboratory study of human fear. In C. M. Franks (Ed.), *Behavior therapy: Appraisal and status.* New York: McGraw-Hill, 1969.

Lang, P. J. Stimulus control, response control and desensitization of fear. In D. Levis (Ed.), *Learning approaches to therapeutic behavior change.* Chicago: Aldine, 1970.

Lang, P. J., Melamed, B. G., & Hart, J. A psychophysiological analysis of fear modification using an automated desensitization procedure. *Journal of Abnormal Psychology,* 1970, *76,* 229–234.

Lautsch, H. Dental phobia. *British Journal of Psychiatry,* 1971, *119,* 151–158.

Lawlis, G. F. Response styles of a patient population on the fear schedule. *Behaviour Research and Therapy,* 1971, *9,* 95–102.

Lehrman, D. S. A critique of Konrad Lorenz's theory of instinctive behavior. *Quarterly Review of Biology,* 1953, *28,* 337–363.

Lehrman, D. S. Semantic and conceptual issues in the nature–nurture problem. In I. R. Aronson, E. Toback, D. S. Lehrman, & J. S. Rosenblatt (Eds.), *Development and evolution of behavior.* San Francisco: W. H. Freeman, 1970.

Leitenberg, H. *Handbook of behavior modification and behavior therapy.* Englwood Cliffs, N. J.: Prentice-Hall, 1976.

Levey, A. B., & Martin, I. Personality and conditioning. In H. J. Eysenck (Ed.), *A model for personality.* New York: Springer, 1980.

Levey, A. B., & Martin I. Cognition, evaluation and conditioning: Rules of sequence and rules of consequence. *Behaviour Research and Therapy,* in press.

Lichtenstein, P. E. Studies of anxiety: I. The production of a feeding inhibition in dogs. *Journal of Comparative and Physiological Psychology,* 1950, *43,* 16–29.

Locke, E. A. Is "behavior therapy" behavioristic? *Psychological Bulletin,* 1971, *76,* 318–327.

Logue, A. Waiter, there is a phobia in my soup. *Psychology Today,* 1978, p. 36.

London, P. The end of ideology in behavior modification. *American Psychologist,* 1972, *27,* 913–920.

Maatsch, J. L. Learning and fixation after a single shock trial. *Journal of Comparative and Physiological Psychology,* 1959, *52,* 408–410.

MacKenzie, B. D. *Behaviorism and the limits of scientific method.* Atlantic Highlands, N. J.: Humanities Press, 1977.

Mackintosh, N. J. *The psychology of animal learning.* London: Academic Press, 1974.

Mahoney, M. J. *Cognition and behavior modification.* Cambridge, Mass.: Ballinger, 1974.

Marks, D. F. Individual differences in the vividness of visual imagery and their effect on function. In P. W. Sheehan (Ed.), *The function and nature of imagery.* New York: Academic Press, 1972.

Marks, I. M. *Fears and phobias.* London: Academic Press, 1969.

Marks, I. M., Boulougouris, J., & Marset, P. Flooding versus desensitization in the treatment of phobic patients: A crossover study. *British Journal of Psychiatry,* 1971, *119,* 353–375.

Marks, I. M., & Huson, J. Physiological aspects of neutral and phobic imagery: Further observations. *British Journal of Psychiatry,* 1973, *122,* 345–356.

Martin, I., & Levey, A. B. *The genesis of the classical conditioned response.* London: Pergamon, 1969.

Martin, I., & Levey, A. B. Classical conditioning. In M. Christie & P. Mellett (Eds.), *Psychosomatic approaches in medicine.* New York: Wiley, 1980.

Martin, I., Marks, I. M., & Gelder, M. Conditioned eyelid responses in phobic patients. *Behaviour Research and Therapy,* 1969, *7,* 115–124.

Mathews, A. M., Johnston, D. W., Shaw, P. M., & Gelder, M. G. Process variables and the prediction of outcome in behaviour therapy. *British Journal of Psychiatry,* 1974, *125,* 256–264.

Mathews, A. M., & Shaw, P. Emotional arousal and persuasion effects in flooding. *Behaviour Research and Therapy,* 1973, *11,* 587–598.

Mays, D. T., & Franks, C. M. Getting worse: Psychotherapy or no treatment. The jury should still be out. *Professional Psychology,* in press.

McGuigan, F. J. Electrical measurement of covert processes as an explication of "higher mental events." In F. J. McGuigan & R. A. Schooner (Eds.), *The psychophysiology of thinking.* New York: Academic Press, 1973.

McGuire, R. J. Classification and the problems of diagnosis. In H. J. Eysenck (Ed.), *Handbook of abnormal psychology.* London: Pitman, 1973.

McLean, P. D. *A triune concept of the brain and behavior.* Toronto: University of Toronto Press, 1963.

Meichenbaum, D. *Cognitive-behavior modification: An integrative approach.* New York: Plenum, 1977.

Mendoza, D., & Wichman, H. "Inner" darts: Effects of mental practice on performance of dart throwing. *Perceptual and Motor Skills,* 1978, *47,* 1195–1199.

Miller, B. V., & Levis, D. J. The effects of varying short visual exposure time to a phobic test stimulus on subsequent avoidance behaviour. *Behaviour Research and Therapy,* 1971, *9,* 17–21.

Morley, S. The incubation of avoidance behaviour: Strain differences in susceptibility. *Behaviour Research and Therapy,* 1977, *15,* 365–367.

Morris, N. E. *A group self-instruction method for the treatment of depressed outpatients.* Unpublished doctoral dissertation, University of Toronto, 1975.

Mowrer, O. H. On the dual nature of learning: A reinterpretation of "conditioning" and "problem-solving." *Harvard Educational Review,* 1947, *17,* 102–148.

Murray, E. J., & Foote, F. The origins of fear of snakes. *Behaviour Research and Therapy,* 1979, 489–493.

Napalkov, A. V. Information process of the brain. In N. Wiener & J. P. Schade (Eds.), *Progress in brain research* (Vol. 2: *Nerve brain and memory models*). Amsterdam: Elsevier, 1963.

Nisbett, R. E., & Wilson, T. D. Telling more than we can know: Verbal reports on mental processes. *Psychological Review*, 1977, *84*, 231–259.

Notterman, J. M., Schoenfeld, W. N., & Bersh, P. J. Conditioned heart-rate responses in human beings during experimental anxiety. *Journal of Comparative and Physiological Psychology*, 1952, *45*, 1–8.

Nunes, J. S., & Marks, I. M. Feedback of true heart-rate during exposure *in vivo*. *Archives of General Psychiatry*, 1975, *32*, 983–994.

Öhman, A., & Dinsberg, V. Facial expressions as conditioned stimuli for electrodermal responses: A case of "preparedness"? *Journal of Personality and Social Psychology*, 1978, *36*, 1251–1258.

Öhman, A., Eriksson, A., & Olofson, C. One-trial learning and superior resistance to extinction of autonomic responses conditioned to potentially phobic stimuli. *Journal of Comparative and Physiological Psychology*, 1975, *88*, 619–627.

Öhman, A., Erixon, G., & Löfberg, I. Phobias and preparedness: Phobic versus neutral pictures as conditioned stimuli for human autonomic responses. *Journal of Abnormal Psychology*, 1975, *84*, 41–45.

Öhman, A., Frederikson, M., Hugdahl, K., & Rimmö, P.-A. The promise of equipotentiality in human classical conditioning: Conditioned electrodermal responses to potentially phobic stimuli. *Journal of Experimental Psychology: General*, 1976, *105*, 313–337.

Orlebeke, J. F. Electrodermal, vasomotor and heart-rate correlates of extraversion and neuroticism. *Psychophysiology*, 1973, *10*, 211–212.

Page, H. A., & Hall, J. F. Experimental extinction as a function of the prevention of a response. *Journal of Comparative and Physiological Psychology*, 1953, *46*, 33–34.

Pancheri, P. Stress, personality and interacting variables: An interpretive model for psychoneuroendocrine disorders. In L. Carenza, P. Pancheri, & L. Zichella (Eds.), *Clinical psychoneuroendocrinology in reproduction*. London: Academic Press, 1979.

Patterson, G. R., & Moore, D. Interactive patterns as units of behavior. In M. E. Lamb, S. Suomi, & G. R. Stephenson (Eds.), *Social interaction analysis: Methodological issues*. Madison: University of Wisconsin Press, 1979.

Pavlov, I. P. *Lectures on conditioned reflexes*. New York: International Publishers, 1927.

Perky, C. W. An experimental study of imagination. *American Journal of Psychology*, 1910, *21*, 422–425.

Platanov, K. [*The word as a physiological and therapeutic factor.*] Moscow: Foreign Languages Publishing House, 1959.

Polin, J. T. The effect of flooding and physical suppression as extinction techniques on the anxiety-motivated locomotor response. *Journal of Psychology*, 1959, *47*, 253–255.

Proctor, S. Duration of exposure of items and pretreatment training factors in systematic desensitization therapy. In R. D. Rubin & C. M. Franks (Eds.), *Advances in behaviour therapy*. London: Academic Press, 1968.

Rabavilas, A. D., Boulougouris, J. C., Perissaki, C., & Stefans, S. Pre-morbid personality traits and responsiveness to flooding in obsessive–compulsive patients. *Behaviour Research and Therapy*, 1979, *17*, 575–580.

Rachman, S. Studies in desensitization: II. Flooding. *Behaviour Research and Therapy*, 1966, *4*, 1–6.

Rachman, S. *Phobias: Their nature and control*. Springfield, Ill. Charles C Thomas, 1968.

Rachman, S. *The effects of psychotherapy*. London: Pergamon Press, 1971.

Rachman, S. *The meaning of fear*. Middlesex: Penguin, 1974.

Rachman, S. The conditioning theory of fear-acquisition: A critical examination. *Behaviour Research and Therapy*, 1977, *15*, 375–387.

Rachman, S. *Fear and courage*. San Francisco: W. H. Freeman, 1978. (a)

Rachman, S. (Ed.). Perceived self-efficacy. *Advances in Behaviour Research and Therapy,* 1978, *1.* (b)

Rachman, S., & Eysenck, H. J. Reply to a "critique and reformulation" of behavior therapy. *Psychological Bulletin,* 1966, *65,* 165–169.

Rachman, S., & Hodgson, R. J. Synchrony and desynchrony in fear and avoidance. *Behaviour Research and Therapy,* 1974, *12,* 311–318.

Rachman, S., & Hodgson, R. J. *Obsessions and compulsions.* New York: Appleton-Century-Crofts, 1980.

Rachman, S., Hodgson, R. J., & Marks, I. M. Treatment of chronic obsessive–compulsive neurosis. *Behaviour Research and Therapy,* 1971, *9,* 237–247.

Rachman, S., Marks, I. M., & Hodgson, R. J. The treatment of obsessive–compulsive neurotics by modelling and flooding *in vivo. Behaviour Research and Therapy,* 1973, *11,* 463–471.

Rachman, S., & Seligman, M. E. P. Unprepared phobias: "Be prepared." *Behaviour Research and Therapy,* 1976, *14,* 333–338.

Rachman, S., & Wilson, G. T. *The effects of psychotherapy.* New York: Pergamon, 1980.

Rankin, N. O., Nomikos, M. S., Opton, E. M., & Lazarus, R. S. *The roles of surprise and suspense in a stress reaction.* Paper delivered at Western Psychological Association Meeting, 1964.

Razran, G. Extinction re-examined and re-analysed: A new theory. *Psychological Review,* 1956, *63,* 39–52.

Rescorla, R. A. Pavlovian conditioning and its proper control procedures. *Psychological Review,* 1967, *74,* 71–80.

Rescorla, R. A., & Solomon, R. L. Two-process learning theory: Relationship between Pavlovian conditioning and instrumental learning. *Psychological Review,* 1967, *74,* 151–182.

Reynierse, J. H. Effects of CS-only trials on resistance to extinction of an avoidance response. *Journal of Comparative and Physiological Psychology,* 1966, *61,* 156–158.

Reynierse, J. H., & Wiff, L. J. Effects of temporal placement of response prevention on extinction of avoidance in rats. *Behaviour Research and Therapy,* 1973, *11,* 119–124.

Rimm, D. C., Janda, L. H., Lancaster, D. W., Nahl, M., & Dittman, K. An exporatory investigation of the origin and maintenance of phobias. *Behaviour Research and Therapy,* 1977, *15,* 231–238.

Rohrbaugh, M., & Riccio, D. V. Paradoxical enhancement of learned fear. *Journal of Abnormal Psychology,* 1970, *75,* 210–216.

Rohrbaugh, M., Riccio, D. V., & Arthur, S. Paradoxical enhancement of conditioned suppression. *Behaviour Research and Therapy,* 1972, *10,* 125–130.

Rosenthal, T. L., & Zimmerman, B. J. *Social learning and cognition.* New York: Academic Press, 1978.

Ross, S. M., & Proctor, S. Frequency and duration of hierarchy item response in a systematic desensitization analogue. *Behaviour Research and Therapy,* 1973, *11,* 303–312.

Rowland, L. W. The somatic effects of stimuli graded in respect to their exciting character. *Journal of Experimental Psychology,* 1963, *19,* 547–560.

Rubin, B. M., Katkin, E. S., Weiss, B. W., & Efran, J. S. Factor analysis of a fear survey schedule. *Behaviour Research and Therapy,* 1968, *6,* 65–75.

Rush, A. J., Beck, A. T., Kovacs, M., & Hollon, S. Comparative efficacy of cognitive therapy and imipramine in the treatment of depressed outpatients. *Cognitive Therapy and Research,* 1977, *1,* 17–37.

Ryle, A. A common language for the psychotherapies. *British Journal of Psychiatry,* 1978, *132,* 585–594.

Sadler, T. G., Mepperd, R. B., & Honcks, R. L. The interaction of extraversion and neuroticism in orienting response habituation. *Psychophysiology,* 1971, *8,* 312–318.

Sarason, I. G. Interrelationships among individual difference variables, behavior in psychotherapy, and verbal conditioning. *Journal of Abnormal and Social Psychology,* 1958, *56,* 339–344.

Sarason, I. G. Three lacunae in cognitive therapy. *Cognitive Therapy and Research,* in press.

Sartory, G. The fearless avoiders: Comparison of various strains of rats in an active avoidance task. *Behaviour Research and Therapy,* 1977, *15,* 149–157.

Sartory, G., & Eysenck, H. J. Strain differences in acquisition and extinction of fear responses in rats. *Psychological Reports,* 1976, *38,* 163–187.

Sartory, G., & Eysenck, H. J. Fear conditioning and extinction in rats at different times of day. *Journal of General Psychology,* 1978, *99,* 87–92.

Satinder, K. P. Arousal explains difference in avoidance learning of genetically selected rat strains. *Journal of Comparative and Physiological Psychology,* 1977, *91,* 1326–1336.

Schlosberg, H. The relationship between success and the laws of conditioning. *Psychological Review,* 1937, *44,* 379–394.

Schwartz, B. On going back to nature: A review of Seligman and Hager's *Biological boundaries of learning. Journal of the Experimental Analysis of Behavior,* 1974, *21,* 183–198.

Schwartz, B., & Williams, D. R. Two different kinds of key pecks in the pigeon: Some properties of responses maintained by negative and positive response-reinforcer contingencies. *Journal of the Experimental Analysis of Behavior,* 1972, *18,* 201–216.

Seligman, M. E. P. On the generality of the laws of learning. *Psychological Review,* 1970, *77,* 406–418.

Seligman, M. E. P. Phobias and preparedness. *Behavior Therapy,* 1971, *2,* 307–320.

Seligman, M. E. P., & Hager, J. *Biological boundaries of learning.* New York: Appleton-Century-Crofts, 1972.

Shaw, B. F. Comparison of cognitive therapy and behavior therapy in the treatment of depression. *Journal of Consulting and Clinical Psychology,* 1977, *45,* 543–551.

Shaw, W. A. The relation of muscular action potentials to imaginal weight lifting. *Archives of Psychology,* 1940, *No. 245,* p. 50.

Sheffield, F. D. Relations between classical conditioning and instrumental learning. In W. F. Prokasy (Ed.), *Classical conditioning.* New York: Appleton-Century-Crofts, 1965.

Siegel, S. Morphine analgesic tolerance: Its situation specificity supports a Pavlovian conditioning model. *Science,* 1976, *193,* 323–325.

Siegel, S. Tolerance to the hyperthermic effect of morphine in the rat is a learned response. *Journal of Comparative and Physiological Psychology,* 1978, *92,* 1137–1149. (a)

Siegel, S. A Pavlovian conditioning analysis of morphine tolerance. *National Institute of Drug Abuse Research Monograph Series,* 1978, *18,* 27–53. (b)

Siegel, S. The role of conditioning in drug tolerance and addiction. In J. D. Keehn (Ed.), *Psychopathology in animals.* New York: Academic Press, 1979.

Siegel, S., Hinson, R. E., & Krank, M. D. The role of predrug signals in morphine analgesic tolerance: Support for a Pavlovian conditioning model of tolerance. *Journal of Experimental Psychology: Animal Behaviour Processes,* 1978, *4,* 188–196.

Siegel, S., Hinson, R. E., & Krank, M. D. Modulation of tolerance to the lethal effect of morphine by extinction. *Behavioural and Neural Biology,* 1979, *25,* 257–262.

Siegeltuch, M. B., & Baum, M. Extinction of well-established avoidance through response prevention (flooding). *Behaviour Research and Therapy,* 1971, *9,* 103–108.

Silvestri, R., Rohrbaugh, M., & Riccio, D. V. Conditions influencing the retention of learned fear in young rats. *Developmental Psychology,* 1970, *2,* 389–395.

Sipprelle, R. C., Ascough, J. C., Detrio, D. M., & Horst, P. A. Neuroticism, extraversion, and response to stress. *Behaviour Research and Therapy,* 1977, *15,* 411–418.

Skinner, B. F. Two types of conditioned reflex and a pseudotype. *Journal of General Psychol-*

ogy, 1935, *12,* 66–77.

Skinner, B. F. *Verbal behavior.* New York: Appleton-Century-Crofts, 1957.

Slater, E., & Shields, J. Genetical aspects of anxiety. In M. J. Lader (Ed.), *Studies of anxiety. British Journal of Psychiatry Special Publications,* 1969, No. 3.

Sloane, R. B., Staples, F. R., Cristol, A. H., Yorkston, N. J., & Whipple, K. Patient characteristics and outcome in psychotherapy and behavior therapy. *Journal of Consulting and Clinical Psychology,* 1976, *44,* 330–339.

Smedslund, J. Bandura's theory of self-efficacy: A set of common sense theorems. *Scandinavian Journal of Psychology,* 1978, *19,* 1–14.

Smedslund, J. Between the analytic and the arbitrary: A case study of psychological research. *Scandinavian Journal of Psychology,* 1979, *20,* 129–140.

Smith, B. D., & Wigglesworth, M. J. Extraversion and neuroticism in orienting reflex dishabituation. *Journal of Research in Personality,* 1978, *12,* 284–296.

Smith, M. L., & Glass, G. P. Meta-analysis of psychotherapy outcome studies. *American Psychologist,* 1977, *32,* 752–760.

Smith, N., & Wilson, D. *Modern linguistics.* London: Penguin, 1979.

Solomon, R. L. Kamin, L. J., & Wynne, L. C. Traumatic avoidance learning: the outcome of several extinction procedures with dogs. *Journal of Abnormal and Social Psychology,* 1953, *48,* 291–302.

Solomon, R. L., & Wynne, L. C. Traumatic avoidance learning. *Psychological Monographs,* 1953, *67*(4).

Solomon, R. L., & Wynne, L. C. Traumatic avoidance learning: The principles of anxiety conservation and partial irreversibility. *Psychological Review,* 1954, *61,* 353–385.

Spring, D., Prochaska, J., & Smith, N. Fear reduction in rats through avoidance blocking. *Behaviour Research and Therapy,* 1974, *12,* 29–34.

Staats, A. W. *Complex human behavior.* New York: Holt, Rinehart & Winston, 1963.

Staats, A. W. *Learning, language, and cognition.* New York: Holt, Rinehart & Winston, 1968.

Staub, E. Duration of stimulus-emotion as determinant of the efficacy of flooding procedures in the elimination of fear. *Behaviour Research and Therapy,* 1968, *6,* 131–132.

Stekel, W. [*Conditions of nervous anxiety and their treatment.*] London: Kegan Paul, French, Trubner, 1923. (Originally published, 1912.)

Stelmack, R. M. The psychophysiology of extraversion and neuroticism. In H. J. Eysenck (Ed.), *A model for personality.* New York: Springer, 1980.

Stern, R., & Marks, I. M. Brief and prolonged flooding. *Archives of General Psychiatry,* 1973, *28,* 270–276.

Stone, N. M., & Borkovec, T. D. The paradoxical effect of brief CS exposure on analogue phobic patients. *Behaviour Research and Therapy,* 1975, *13,* 51–54.

Strupp, H. H., Hadley, S. W., & Gomes-Schwartz, B. *Psychotherapy for better or worse.* New York: Jason Aronson, 1977.

Sue, D. The effect of duration of exposure on systematic desensitization and extinction. *Behaviour Research and Therapy,* 1975, *13,* 55–60.

Suppe, F. *The structure of scientific theories.* London: University of Illinois Press, 1974.

Sutherland, S. *Breakdown.* London: Temple Smith, 1977.

Taylor, F. G., & Marshall, W. L. Experimental analysis of a cognitive–behavioral therapy for depression. *Cognitive Therapy and Research,* 1977, *1,* 59–72.

Terrace, H. S. Classical conditioning. In J. A. Nevin (Ed.), *The study of behavior.* Glenview, Ill.: Scott, Foresman, 1973.

Thayer, R. E. Activation states as assessed by verbal report and four psychophysiological variables. *Psychophysiology,* 1970, *7,* 86–94.

Thomson, G. *The inspiration of science.* London: Oxford University Press, 1961.

Thorndike, E. L. *Fundamentals of learning.* New York: Teachers College Press, 1932.

Thorndike, E. L. *The psychology of wants, interests and attitudes.* New York: Appleton-Century-Crofts, 1935.

Tolman, E. C. *Purposive behavior in animals and man.* New York: Century, 1932.

Torgersen, S. The nature and origin of common phobic fears. *British Journal of Psychiatry,* 1979, *134,* 343–351.

Truax, C. Effective ingredients in psychotherapy. *Journal of Counseling Psychology,* 1963, *10,* 256–263.

Truax, C., Frank, I., & Imber, S. Therapist empathy, genuineness, and warmth and patient outcome. *Journal of Consulting Psychology,* 1966, *30,* 395–401.

Tryon, W. W. An operant explanation of Mowrer's neurotic paradox. *Journal of Applied Behavior Analysis,* in press.

Uttall, W. R. *The psychobiology of mind.* Hillsdale, N. J.: Erlbaum, 1978.

Vandell, R. A., Davis, R. A., & Clugston, H. A. The function of mental practice in the acquisition of motor skills. *Journal of General Psychology,* 1943, *29,* 243–250.

Van Egeren, L. F., Feather, B. W., & Hein, P. L. Desensitization of phobias: Some psychophysiological propositions. *Psychophysiology,* 1971, *8,* 213–228.

Verma, R. M., & Eysenck, H. J. Severity of type of psychotic illness as a function of personality. *British Journal of Psychiatry,* 1973, *122,* 573–585.

Vila, J., & Beech, H. R. Vulnerability and defensive reactions in relation to the human menstrual cycle. *British Journal of Social and Clinical Psychology,* 1978, *17,* 93–100.

Ward, W. D. The effects of manipulation of the CS and variations in the duration of response prevention on extinction of avoidance response. *British Journal of Social and Clinical Psychology,* 1976, *15,* 167–177.

Watson, J. B. Behavior and the concept of mental disease. *Journal of Philosophy, Psychology and Scientific Methods,* 1916, *13,* 589–597.

Watson, J. B. *Psychology from the standpoint of a behaviorist.* Philadelphia: Lippincott, 1919.

Watson, J. B., & Rayner, R. Conditioned emotional reactions. *Journal of Experimental Psychology,* 1920, *3,* 1–14.

Watson, J. P., Gaind, P., & Marks, I. M. Physiological habituation to continuous phobic stimulation. *Behaviour Research and Therapy,* 1972, *10,* 269–278.

Watts, F. Desensitization as an habituation phenomenon: I. Stimulus intensity as determinant of the effects of stimulus length. *Behaviour Research and Therapy,* 1971, *9,* 209–217.

Weinberger, N. M. Effects of detainment on extinction of avoidance responses. *Journal of Comparative and Physiological Psychology,* 1965, *60,* 135–138.

Wigglesworth, M. J., & Smith, B. D. Habituation and dishabituation of the electrodermal orienting reflex in relation to extraversion and neuroticism. *Journal of Research in Personality,* 1976, *10,* 437–445.

Wilcox, J., & Fulker, D. W. Avoidance learning in rats: Genetic evidence for two distinct behavioral processes in the shuttle box. *Journal of Comparative and Physiological Psychology,* 1973, *82,* 247–253.

Wilson, E. O. *Sociobiology: The new synthesis.* Cambridge, Mass.: Harvard University Press, 1975.

Wilson, E. O. *On human nature.* Cambridge, Mass.: Harvard University Press, 1978.

Wilson, G. Personality and social behavior. In H. J. Eysenck (Ed.), *A model for personality.* New York: Springer, 1980.

Wolpe, J. Behavior therapy and its malcontents: I. Denial of its bases and psychodynamic fusionism. *Journal of Behavior Therapy and Experimental Psychiatry,* 1976, *7,* 1–15. (a)

Wolpe, J. Behavior therapy and its malcontents: II. Multimodal eclecticism, cognitive exclusivism and exposure empiricism. *Journal of Behavior Therapy and Experimental Psychiatry,* 1976, *7,* 109–116. (b)

Wolpe, J. Cognition and causation in human behavior and its therapy. *American Psychologist,*
    1978, *33,* 437–446.
Wolpe, J., & Lang, P. J. A fear survey schedule for use in behaviour therapy. *Behaviour Re-
search and Therapy,* 1964, *2,* 27–30.
Woods, D. J. Paradoxical enhancement of learned anxiety response. *Psychological Reports,*
    1974, *35,* 295–304.
Yates, A. J. *Frustration and conflict.* London: Methuen, 1962.
Young, J. P. R., Fenton, G. W., & Lader, M. H. The inheritance of neurotic traits: A twin study
of the Middlesex Hospital Questionnaire. *British Journal of Psychiatry,* 1971, *119,* 393–
398.

6

APPLIED BEHAVIOR ANALYSIS

DONALD M. BAER
Department of Human Development
University of Kansas

FORMS OF VERBAL BEHAVIOR CONTROLLING APPLIED BEHAVIOR ANALYSIS

This argument is written explicitly as one of the four arguments that constitute Section III of this book; its three companions are Chapters 5, 7, and 8, and their existence requires that it be one of them but not the same as any of them. The structure of Section III asserts that there are at least four conceptual positions possible and real in the field of behavior therapy, that applied behavior analysis is one of them, and that Chapter 6 describes it as a conceptual approach that is not the same as some other conceptual approaches named "neobehavioristic S-R," "cognitive-behavior therapy," and "social learning theory."

In fact, Chapter 6 proceeds as if there is a conceptual approach called "applied behavior analysis" that can be described as such. However, if Chapter 6 is to be behavior-analytic, it should first proceed as if applied behavior analysis is the collective verbal behavior (as defined by Skinner, 1957) of a number of people, and is under the control of certain environmental events that also are forms of verbal behavior. Some of these environmental events are relatively easy to specify:

1. Any affirmation that a proper and valuable domain of study is the behavior of organisms, and that behavior is orderly, predictable, and controllable, has a positive stimulus function; and any rhetorical assumption that it is impossible to understand what organisms do without first understanding what organisms are has negative stimulus function.[1] (Occasionally, rhetoric is answered with rhetoric: An organism *is* very much what it does.)

---

1. "Positive stimulus function" means that the event is at least a positive reinforcer; "negative stimulus function" means that the event is at least a negative reinforcer. Behaviors producing or maximizing positive reinforcers are increased thereby, as are behaviors removing, minimizing,

2. Any description of behavior that consists of observable responses by an organism has positive stimulus function, and any description that includes unobservable responses has negative stimulus function, except under rather special circumstances. Any reference to stimuli as observable environmental events to which the analyst, the analyst's subject organism, and the analyst's audience all respond observably has positive stimulus function; and any reference to stimuli as unobservable–nonenvironmental events or as events to which the analyst, the analyst's subject organism, and the analyst's audience do not respond observably has negative stimulus function, except under rather special circumstances.[2]

---

escaping from, or avoiding negative reinforcers. If the affirmation that behavior is the direct and central topic of study has positive stimulus function, then any forms of verbal behavior displaying that property will increase. Thus, there will be experiments aimed at the analysis of behavior; subsequent descriptions of how behavior works; discoveries that behavior is extremely sensitive to environmental contingencies; explanations of behavior that will be considered complete because they related the behavior to contingencies adequate to account for it; and so forth. If affirmations that behavior is merely a by-product of some other, much more central phenomena (such as mind or physiology) have negative stimulus function, then any forms of verbal behavior that counter, minimize, escape from, or avoid that content will increase. Thus, there will be a good deal of ignoring such affirmations; arguing against them; pointing out the so far apparent self-sufficiency of the behavioral science and technology that does take behavior as its central topic; rhetoric; and so on. For this chapter, "stimulus function" also means the discriminative properties that such events easily can have: Positive events set the occasion for further analysis, both logical and empirical; negative events set the occasion for explanations of why further attempts at analysis are useless, and for studied ignoring (Krantz, 1971), which unfortunately often resembles ignoring the event's proponent.

2. Descriptions of behavior and stimuli that include unobservable elements always have negative stimulus function for the behavior of those applied behavior analysts who are also methodological behaviorists, but not always for the behavior of those who are also radical behaviorists (Skinner, 1974). Radical behaviorists do not ignore, escape from, or avoid descriptions of private behaviors observable only to their possessor; they do, however, strenuously avoid any implication that such private events are different in kind or function from observable behaviors. Thus, they assume that private events are behaviors subject to environmental control, which is what they assume about observable behaviors. In consequence of this assumption, they conclude that private events in no sense are autonomous causes of observable behaviors, even though many other approaches to the study of behavior do presume that currently autonomous attitudes, interpretations, styles, wishes, decisions, affects, self-instructions, and computations are the source of the observable (subsequent) acts of the organism. For the radical behaviorists, private events are certainly possible; probably all radical behaviorists observe those events operating in their own individual behavior, and, as an act of probability (or at least charity), will suppose that similar events operate unobservably in the behavior of others, too. The question is not whether they operate, but how they operate. The assumption of radical behaviorism is that they operate as elements in chains that begin with observable environmental events and end with observable responses by the organism; thus, their thorough analysis is environmental and empirical, as is the analysis of observable behavior. For this reason, I have ensconced this special tolerance for private events by the radical behaviorists (of whom I consider myself one, except for occasional lapses) in a footnote.

3. Any research that experimentally correlates a response with environmental stimuli—either as antecedents, as consequences, or as both—is an analysis ("an" analysis is not the same as "the" analysis) of that response and has positive stimulus function; the greater this correlation is, the more positive the stimulus function is. Analyses that show nonexperimental correlations between a response and environmental stimuli have for some analysts a very slight positive stimulus function; for some other analysts no stimulus function; and for very many analysts a negative stimulus function (apparently inhering in the extraordinary range of totally different cause-and-effect analyses implicit in virtually all nonexperimental correlations).

4. Stimulus–response, response–stimulus, and stimulus–response–stimulus correlations are essentially statements about contingencies between stimuli and responses. When many such analyses have been made, a relatively few patterns of contingencies emerge again and again, and consequently gain names such as "reinforcement," "punishment," "schedule," "discrimination," "stimulus and response classes," "deprivation," and "satiation." Thus, any new analysis has positive stimulus function if it shows that this relative handful of patterns can describe (at the level of function) the new correlation as well as it has so far described the already analyzed correlations. The less the new correlation resembles the so-far-analyzed correlations, and yet is describable in the same terms, the more positive the stimulus function of the analysis is (Sidman, 1960). When the new correlation does not seem to be easily described in the same terms, its function is to occasion new analyses aimed specifically at clarifying whether, with more information, it will be clear that the new correlation is describable in the usual terms, after all, or whether it will require additional or different terms. The latter conclusion has negative stimulus function; it occasions a great deal of reexamination of the issue and still further analysis. While such reexamination and further analysis is ongoing, the correlation at issue is made very salient in the literature of the field as a topic of central importance.

5. Any analysis that experimentally correlates a response with environmental stimuli and does so within the behavior of a single organism at a time has positive stimulus function for analysts whose current curiosity is functional, process-oriented, and analytic; and any analysis that experimentally correlates the average response of a group of organisms with environmental events has positive stimulus function for analysts whose current curiosity is actuarial (rather than functional, process-oriented, and analytic).[3]

---

3. The phrase " . . . whose current curiosity is . . . " should be recognized as a nonbehavioral shorthand for yet another statement about stimulus functions. To say that a behavior analyst is curious about process, function, or analysis means that explanations of how behavior works, what makes it occur more and less in one organism at a time (which is where it resides), have positive stimulus function. To say that a behavior analyst is curious about actuarial facts is to say

6. Any analysis that deals with a response that seems to constitute a personal problem for the organism displaying it (or lacking it), or a problem for the society in which that organism lives, has especially strong positive stimulus function. It it were not for this special positive function, there would be no distinction between the behavior of behavior analysts and applied behavior analysts. This function, furthermore, implies a number of corollary functions, as described in paragraphs 7 through 9.

7. Any research or development that tends to maximize behavioral technology has strong positive function. Technology makes what otherwise is only a conceptual approach into something that can be implemented on a wide scale by a large number of people with less training than that (apparently) required to produce the technology and its underlying analyses. Thus, effective manuals, workbooks, and recipes, organized when necessary into systems analyses, have very strong positive stimulus function.[4]

---

that statements about how a process comes out on the average have positive stimulus function. For example, applied behavior analysts could initially be curious about how to alter the critical behaviors of persons identified by their society as juvenile delinquents, and could answer that curiosity by a series of experimental analyses of those behaviors in individual delinquents. With those answers in hand, the same (or other) applied behavior analysts could well become curious about whether the treatment approach implicit in those answers would produce better results, on the average, than the society's current (probably rigidified) treatment technique does, on the average. Given an agreement about the meaning of "better results" (a chapter of its own), this curiosity naturally becomes actuarial: Will a typical group of delinquents handled in the new way show better average outcomes than those of a perfectly comparable group handled in the old way? Group averages are exactly what this actuarial curiosity seeks, for societal implementation is the underlying issue now, and a society typically (and reasonably) wants to know not how Johnny Jones will fare in one approach as opposed to another, but how most of its delinquents will fare in one approach as opposed to another. Note that neither curiosity is less applied than the other or less behavioral than the other, although it may fairly be said that actuarial curiosity is less analytic than single-subject process-oriented curiosity. Currently, applied behavior analysis as a discipline is increasingly devoted to pressing on from analytic facts about process to actuarial tests of treatments embodying those processes against alternative treatments. Persons pursuing such actuarial curiosities are no less applied behavior analysts; they are justifiably more applied and less analytic than they were (or their discipline was) a moment previous, but they are able to be so by virtue of having been very analytic in that previous moment. That is, the stimulus function of statements about process, while still strongly positive, is now less positive than the stimulus function of actuarial statements about the effectiveness of societal treatment approaches built on that knowledge of process.

4. Much of the character of applied behavior analysis is determined by the discovery that the actual production of manuals, workbooks, and recipes (organized when necessary into systems analyses) *that actually work well* is itself a problem requiring a very high level of intensive applied behavior analysis. It is not engineering as contrasted to research; it is not easy as contrasted to sophisticated; it is not routine as contrasted to creative; and it is not trivial as contrasted to ultimately valuable. It is instead a problem in knowing enough about the ultimate analysis of a behavior to be able to state *all* the procedures that can control that behavior enough to be worth-

8. Any clarification and assessment of both the costs and the benefits of achieving a given degree of effectiveness in the remediation of a given problem will have strong positive stimulus function; the more comprehensive, precise, and objectively quantitative this assessment is, the more positive its stimulus function is.

9. Any principles and techniques that show how to translate a personal or societal problem into observable behaviors that, if changed, would then constitute a solution to the problem (Baer, 1975) have positive stimulus function. Sometimes, problems are stated behaviorally (a child cannot read, or the crime rate of the society is very high) and correctly, in which case no translation is needed. Sometimes, problems are stated behaviorally but incorrectly (a child is nominated for special-track schooling by a teacher supposedly because of high rates of aggression, whereas in fact the teacher is responding to the child's low rate of compliance with classroom instructions), and these require better translation. And sometimes, problems are not stated behaviorally at all ("I don't know what to do with my life; nothing is worthwhile," or

---

while, and then it is a problem in being able to state those procedures so that readers and auditors will in fact respond to those statements with just those procedures (rather than with fewer procedures or other procedures). The behaviors called "implementation of recipe" are themselves behaviors that require behavior analysis; and they clearly are problem behaviors for any society that sets some of its people the task of solving some of its problems by "the implementation of recipes." The analysis of implementation responses is not different in principle from the analysis of bar-pressing responses or paired-associates memorizing; but it is an analysis largely undone at the level of detail, and it is an analysis hugely more important to a society than those other analyses are. So-called basic research, using bar pressing or paired-associates memorizations (or any other task suiting the research mainly because of its convenience to the researcher) may indeed on occasion produce abstract generalizations that underlie much of the behavior that perplexes society; but until those underlying generalizations can be brought to the point of application, society will continue on its course unaffected by the fact that the principle controlling the solution of some of its problems has been stated and proven. It is not at all unlikely that these principles already have been stated and proven to quite some considerable extent; the unsolved problem is the translation of those principles into actions that actually contact social life. Actual contact requires a recipe and a recipe implementer, and we are not yet good at writing such recipes, at training their reader–auditor–implementers, or (ultimately) at writing recipes so effective that any reasonable reader–auditor will implement them correctly. Nor have we done much more than recognize the next behavioral problem: Given the existence of effective recipes that can be implemented easily, what controls the behavior of implementing them? What conditions lead a society to use its recipes (Stolz, 1981)? Finally, this point is not too well served by terms such as "recipe" and "recipe implementer": They have a certain clarity (and have been used here mainly because of that), but they do not emphasize enough that any social science that does not know how social science becomes applied to society misses a crucial part of *all* social science—not how societies have changed, but how societies *can be* changed. To know how societies have changed is probably quite partial knowledge, compared to knowing how societies can be changed. Thus, pursuing the application of knowledge reflects a value based not only on pragmatism, but also on the completeness of knowledge.

"American workers no longer embody the values and responsibilities of true artisans"), in which case translation becomes the first problem of any attempt at applied behavior analysis, and its absence or failure cancels any subsequent usefulness of the approach. (When that is the case, then this corollary becomes the most crucial aspect of the entire discipline. An understanding of the current status of applied behavior analysis hinges on the recognition that this stimulus function has not yet generated enough of the behaviors that logic indicates are essential to the discipline's future utility. That point is developed later in this chapter.)

10. For certain members of this discipline, any demonstrations of its approach that are labeled "applied behavior analysis" have the stimulus function of positive models: They are imitated. As in any conceptual approach, some of its proponents are responsive not so much to the positive and negative stimulus functions that may define the approach as to the models of the approach that are publicly agreed to characterize it. Most people do not understand the logic of our culture; they simply practice it, largely in imitation of its models, past and present. Similarly, many applied behavior analysts have by now been socialized in the discipline, rather than worked it out or worked through its philosophical texts; for them, its defining stimulus functions may often operate largely unrecognized and unexamined, or may not operate at all. But the behavior of those who are responsive to the defining stimulus functions may well change as new ways of maximizing those functions are found; when that happens, their new behaviors will constitute new models for the essentially imitative, if their new behaviors are publicly labeled "applied behavior analysis."

If "applied behavior analysis" is the collective behavior of people who call themselves "applied behavior analysts," and is controlled by all or some of these stimulus functions, then the definition of the approach should be behavioral—specifically, a problem in anthropology. Is there indeed a tribe whose behavior can be described best as serving these 10 stimulus functions? (See Horowitz, 1975, for a description of life among the ABA.) Or are there two tribes, one whose behavior serves the first nine functions; and another whose behavior serves the 10th? Or is there a single core of persons whose behavior is dependably controlled by the sixth through ninth functions—those that define the applied nature of the approach—but is responsive to the other functions only selectively or sporadically?

Given that the first and sixth functions (the affirmation of behavior as the central subject matter and the analysis of personal or societal problems into behaviors) are essential to calling any form of behavior analysis "applied," there remain eight other functions that are clearly (anthropologically) not essential. The first and sixth functions can be combined with the remaining eight, according to combinatorial analysis, in 255 different ways. (One of the remaining eight can be combined with the first and sixth in any of eight ways; two in any of 28 ways; three in any of 56 ways; four in any of 70 ways; five in any of 56 ways; six in any of 28 ways; seven in any of eight ways; and all eight in just one way: $8 + 28 + 56 + 70 + 56 + 28 + 8 + 1 = 255$.) Potentially, then, there are 255 kinds of applied behavior analysts, each kind perhaps somewhat regretfully deprecating the 254 other kinds for either woefully incomplete or pitifully overrestrictive subscription to the eight optional functions. Perhaps some of those other kinds are "neobehavioristic S-R," "cognitive-behavior therapy," or "social learning theory"; if so, let it be known that there are still 251 unlabeled approaches waiting to be adopted and exploited for whatever useful (or otherwise reinforcing) insights they may provide.

Even if there are 255 possible kinds of applied behavior analysts, there is no necessity that each type exists in fact. However, the Law of Large Numbers suggests forcefully that as the ranks of applied behavior analysts increase, the probability of each of these types actually appearing also increases. What if the 252 types not preempted from calling themselves "neobehavioristic S-R," "cognitive-behavior therapy," or "social learning theory" all claim that they are the true applied behavior analysts? Is there some way that a mere chapter writer could show (other than arrogantly) that unless they embody the first nine of the functions cited here, or at least the tenth (but in imitation only of those who do embody the first nine), they are not truly applied behavior analysts?[5]

An arrogant proclamation, more or less in the manner of planting the flag on the moon just because the flag planter is there and no one else is, is indeed one potential answer to the problem of this chapter—distinguishing applied behavior analysis from its three companions of Section III. But it is not a behavior-analytic answer. A behavior-analytic answer, it now seems clear, should assert that there is no such thing as "applied behavior analysis" other than in titles. Instead, there are stimulus functions that can be found in control of the behaviors of some students of behavior; and as many ways as there are for each of those stimulus functions to be strongly operative, moderately operative, slightly operative, or inoperative in any student's behavior is as

---

5. There is always the possibility of proceeding empirically, in the manner of survey sociology. All persons remotely connected with the field are asked whether they are applied behavior analysts. Those who reply that they are then are asked about the stimulus function, for them, of each of the ten candidates at issue (a quick but not very ethical question); or they are analyzed for the actual functions, for them, of each of the candidates (a slow but more ethical process). A composite picture then would be calculated: For example, it could be said that the typical applied behavior analyst is very responsive to the first three functions, somewhat to the fourth, weakly to the fifth, overwhelmingly to the sixth, strongly to the seventh, and so on. Apart from such surveys, the problem remains arbitrary.

many ways as there are to study behavior. Why some of those ways, or one of them, should be called "applied behavior analysis" is thus a problem for behavior analysis rather than for logic or philosophy. The stimulus functions are the important realities; the best question is whether the 10 listed here are sufficient to yield an analytic picture of the study of behavior as an enterprise, or whether the list is seriously incomplete. It seems likely, in fact, that the list changes with time and experience (i.e., contingencies). Some people developing a science of behavior began to examine its effectiveness in solving personal and societal problems, and progressively added the sixth through ninth functions to the list; in doing so, they may occasionally have abandoned or depreciated some of the earlier listed functions (Birnbrauer, 1979; Dietz, 1978; Hayes, 1978; Michael, 1980; Pierce & Epling, 1980). As the adventure continues, similar sorts of changes are always possible. Indeed, any adventure consisting of verbal behavior under the control of a number of stimulus functions also consisting of verbal behavior will have no definite boundaries: More and more behavior is likely to be generated, and its content becomes part of the controlling functions to generate still newer behavior. In other words, such adventures grow like Topsy.

The remainder of this chapter argues that some of the behavior generated by the 10 functions listed above has not yet become as thoroughly a part of the controlling functions as might be possible; that it would be better if it did; and that some verbal behavior might be useful in causing some of that to happen. Specifically, the ninth function—the translation of personal or societal problems into a correct list of behaviors to be changed—has not yet attracted the intense experimental analyses that seem possible for it, the results of which might well be invaluable to the future effectiveness of applied behavior analysis.

TURNING PROBLEMS INTO BEHAVIORS

In application, analysts begin with a complaint. The complaint may be presented by someone else, or it may be their own complaint. The complaint always centers on a problem—something is wrong, painful, harmful, inappropriate; at least, something is less than optimal when it could be optimal. Such words are not behavioral, but the display of such words—"complaining"—is a very prominent behavior class in most organisms. The analytic challenges for anyone who deserves to be called an "applied behavior analyst" are (1) to restate the complained-of problem in behavioral terms; (2) to change the behaviors indicated by that restatement; and then (3) to see whether changing them has decreased the complaining response.

By way of example, consider a relatively simple case: "loneliness" in several residents of retirement homes (Goldstein & Baer, 1976). An analyst, working in such homes on other problems, was presented repeatedly with the complaint that these residents, while "comfortable," were "unhappy." Upon questioning—pointedly behavioral questioning—"unhappy" was refined to "lonely"; upon further questioning, "lonely" was specified not as receiving few callers (which was well accepted, because relatives and friends happened to live far away) but as receiving few letters from them. Thus, the complaint of loneliness was focused finally on the rate of letters received. The question then was this: What behaviors of whom were responsible for that low rate? Further pointed questioning led the analyst to suspect that before anything was done, the letters written by the lonely complainers in response to the few letters that they received should be examined. Past responses were not available, of course, as these had been mailed without retention of copies; but an examination (with the consent of the elderly complainers) of their next several responses to the few letters that they received showed a common enough content: the complainers reproached their correspondents for not having written in so long, and imputations of guilt were added through reminders that a complainer was, after all, only a correspondent's mother, father, grandmother, grandfather, aunt, uncle, best friend, and so on. The analyst immediately guessed that such letters punished the correspondents. Questioning showed that the elderly complainers never wrote except to answer a letter received, which they did immediately upon receiving it. Thus, a clear contingency seemed to operate on their correspondents' letter-writing behavior: If they wrote to their elderly friends or relatives, they were promptly punished by return mail; if they did not write, there were no consequences. That contingency, if functional, would indeed explain a low rate of letters received.

Was it functional? To find out, the analyst had only to change the letter-writing behavior of the elderly complainers, so that their letters would be neither reproachful nor accusatory. That change was a very easy one, requiring only the slightest application of any behavioral technology—a nonreproachful letter that asked at least one question meriting an answer was modeled, and the next several letters written by the elderly complainers were read and commented on, approvingly or disapprovingly according to their content, before they were mailed. A few early ones needed rewriting; the complainers always agreed readily to do so. The analyst then prompted the complainers to write to relatives or old friends who rarely or never wrote to them. Within a very few tries, the complainers were now writing totally nonreproachful, nonaccusatory letters to everyone. Perhaps to fill the space formerly occupied by that reproachful kind of content, they now wrote about their daily lives, happenings of interest, and memories of their past experiences with their correspondents, which probably made it easy for their correspondents to reply responsively and may well have reinforced rather than punished the correspondents' letter writing. Furthermore, the complainers were taught to include self-addressed, stamped envelopes in their letters, with comments explaining that they wanted to make a reply easy—their correspondents shouldn't have to "hunt up" their address.

These changes in the complainers' letter writing were made in a multiple-baseline design, across three complainers. In perfect response to the staggered timing of that design, the three complainers began to receive prompt replies to their letters, almost tripling their average rate of receiving letters. Furthermore, presumably in part because of gratified communication among their pool of potential correspondents, and in part by their prompted writing to some long-silent people, they began to receive letters from new correspondents. This led them to begin writing to yet other potential correspondents, and to receive prompt answers, accomplishing still higher rates of letters received—and letters to answer. All this activity filled time in otherwise often empty days.

That behavior change and its snowballing effects were accompanied by a thorough absence of complaints about loneliness. Unfortunately, while the changes in letter writing and in rates of letters received were carefully quantified, in the usual tradition of applied behavior analysis, the previous and subsequent rates and contents of complaining were not—unfortunately, also in the usual tradition of applied behavior analysis.[6] Yet the complaints were the source of the behavior change that was so easily made in this case. The value of this study for applied behavior analysis was not in the behavior change; while that change was invaluable to the subjects of the study, it was trivially easy to do and added nothing to behavior-change principles or their technology. The value of the study to the discipline was that it correctly translated a problem—a complaint of loneliness—into a set of behaviors to be changed, which, once changed, satisfied the complaint.

This discipline needs to know exactly that—how to translate any complaint into behaviors to be changed, which, if changed, will end the complaining behaviors to the satisfaction of the complainer. Exactly because it is a behavioral discipline, it has always moved as quickly as possible from complaints, which are not behavioral, to behaviors to be changed. Complaints, being nonbehavioral, probably have negative stimulus function for us—what can we do with them? Behaviors to be changed, on the other hand, have positive stimulus function for us—we often know exactly what to try on them; if

---

6. The complainers told the analyst that they now were much happier and no longer lonely. Furthermore, several of them still write to the analyst; their letters are always cheerful and pass on news from their correspondents, and are never reproachful or accusatory (although the analyst sometimes is slow to reply). Is that a measure of having satisfied the complaint? Why not (cf. Wolf, 1978)?

we don't know, we are eager to find out, and we do know quite a bit about how to find out.

Moving quickly from complaints to behaviors to be changed is the only tactic that makes applied behavior analysis possible and relevant when the complaints are nonbehavioral; when the complaints are behavioral, deciding quickly whether they are correct in the behaviors that they cite as the problem, or whether some other behaviors are the ones that must be changed if the complaint is to be satisfied, again is the essential tactic that enables a discipline of behavior change to become an applied discipline. The problem with moving quickly is that while it complies with the negative stimulus function of nonbehavioral complaints, it also tends to preempt the analysis of *how* the translation is done. Indeed, it tends to reinforce us for being shrewd, intuitive, and reliant on past experience to yield a probable translation, rather than for being analytical, questioning, skeptical, and experimental with the translation process. If we were questioning, skeptical, and experimental much more often with this problem, we would have a chance of becoming systematic and valid, rather than (or at least as well as) intuitive, shrewd, and experienced. The process of translating complaints into behaviors to be changed is so crucial to applied behavior analysis that if it does not become systematic and valid, the future of the entire discipline may well be at risk. Thus, this process deserves at least as much research as any other part of the discipline, yet it seems to have received the least.

Still, the problem has undergone some systematic research. An example of this quite small body of inquiry can be seen in an attempt to accomplish a behavioral analysis of conversational skill (Minkin, Braukmann, Minkin, Timbers, Timbers, Fixsen, Phillips, & Wolf, 1976), so as to be able to design a training program in that skill for predelinquent girls deficient in it and needful of it. The research proceeded on the assumption that conversational skill with conventional adults is important in both work and social settings and thus functional in delinquency-prevention programs. (That delinquency gives rise to social complaints about it needs no argument.) In contrast to the analysis of successful correspondence just discussed, in which the analyst simply guessed at the probable behavioral components of the problem, this analysis attempted to discover the important behaviors that make for successful conversation. To do so required a four-step experiment.

1. Five junior-high-school girls and five university women were asked, one at a time, to converse for 4 minutes with an unknown adult and then again for another 4 minutes with another unknown adult while being videotaped. These tapes were then examined repeatedly on the assumption that the university women probably possessed better conversational skills than the junior-high-school girls did. The question was this: What behaviors seemed to differentiate the women from the girls? The experimenters found that, on

the average, the university women asked more questions, gave more positive feedback to answers received, and talked more but avoided the extremes of talking very much or very little. Thus, it was hypothesized that these three behaviors might represent a behavioral analysis of good conversation.

2. Next, 13 rather diverse adult judges listened to these tapes and rated each conversation on a 7-point bipolar scale ranging from "poor" to "excellent." The tapes had already been measured for their rates of questioning, positive feedback, and duration of time spent in talking. The judges' ratings of the conversational quality of the tapes correlated + .70 with rate of questioning, + .56 with rate of positive feedback, and + .43 with duration of time spent in talking. Furthermore, on the average, the judges rated the university women as 5.25 in conversational quality (a score of 7 representing "excellent"), and the junior-high girls as 3.4, thereby confirming the experimenters' supposition that a comparison of these two groups ought to reveal the critical differences that make up relative conversational skill.

2a. Using the same definitions and procedures as before, the study was repeated with fresh subjects and judges to accomplish cross-validation. Strikingly similar results were produced, except that the judges' rating of conversational excellence this time correlated + .63 with rate of questioning, + .64 with rate of positive feedback, and + .65 with duration of time spent in talking (the last correlation being appreciably better than its predecessor).

3. Four predelinquent junior-high-school girls who volunteered for training were taught to increase their rates of questioning and positive feedback; their time spent in talking was not subjected to training, presumably on the assumption that increases in questioning and positive feedback necessarily would accomplish appropriate increases in time spent in talking. Training consisted of a conventional package of instructions on how to perform each skill, accompanied by rationales of why it was good to learn these skills; demonstrations of how to perform each skill; and repeated periods of practice at each skill and at both skills, with feedback and eventually with small monetary reinforcers for each instance of questioning and positive feedback. The girls learned quite rapidly, evidencing appreciable increases in their rates of these skills.

4. Pretraining and posttraining videotapes were made of each girl's conversations. These tapes were then rated by judges for their excellence in conversation, exactly as the previous tapes had been rated. Prior to training, the girls were rated, on the average, as 2.8 (on the 7-point scale in which 7 was "excellent"); subsequent to training, they were rated as 4.3, a figure that put them about midway between the ratings of normal junior-high-school girls (3.7) and university women (5.0) that the same judges had produced.

Clearly, the behavioral analysis of conversational excellence into appropriate rates of the behaviors of questioning, positive feedback, and time spent in talking has some considerable validity. On the other hand, equally clearly, it has some appreciable lack of validity; correlations between judges' ratings of conversational excellence and the rates of these behaviors were never higher than $+.70$, and were as low as $+.43$. The conventional practice of squaring these correlations to show what proportion of variance in the judges' ratings is explained by the rates of these behaviors shows that at most about 50% of that variance was accounted for, and at least, about 20%. The multiple regression of the judges' ratings against these three behaviors operating interactively was not calculated; it might have been more impressive. However, it might not; the experimenters noted that one of their four subjects learned questioning as well and positive feedback almost as well as the other three girls, yet was considered by only seven judges to have improved in conversational excellence, by five judges to have remained unchanged, and by three judges to have worsened. This might suggest that there is something more to people's ratings of conversational ability than these particular performances had captured.

However, a very significant finding of this study was a relative lack of reliability in these judges' ratings of conversational skill. Judges showed average reliabilities of only $+.68$ (in one sample) and $+.61$ (in the other sample) when their ratings of each subject's two conversations were compared; the statistical measure of their consensual agreement as a group (the Kendall coefficient of concordance) was estimated at only $+.61$ (in one sample) and $+.46$ (in the other sample). These are not very high levels of reliability or concordance. That could mean that the judges' ratings were measured imperfectly; it could also mean that there is no uniform attribute of behavior that can be called "conversational excellence," and that one person's estimate of it is as good as another's and quite likely rather different from another's. In that case, rather than suggesting that there is something more to people's ratings of conversational ability than these particular performances had captured, it might be more appropriate to ask whether there is a goal here to be captured. We will never be able to teach someone a set of behaviors that constitute what everyone considers "conversational skill," if there is no such thing as a universally appreciated excellence in conversation; in that case, one person's sparkle is another person's boredom. Thus, the behavioral analysis of complaints into behaviors to be changed may be the necessary characteristic of an applied behavior analysis that can deal only with behaviors that need changing, but it may also occasionally assign applied behavior analysts the problem of finding out first whether they are attempting to satisfy one person's complaint or many persons' complaints. If it is the latter case, then they must next discover whether those complaints function uniformly across complainers. If they do not, there can be no behavioral analysis of all those complaints, but only of one of them at a time or of some of them (the uniformly functioning ones of them) at a time. This necessitates a quite forcible return to the logic of single-subject (single-complainer) experimental design.

Note the prevalence of a systematic research logic in this example, in contrast to the "loneliness" example (Goldstein & Baer, 1976) discussed previously. Instead of proceeding intuitively, this study embodied a rationale for discovery of the necessary underlying behavioral analysis of conversational excellence. It first found examples of complaints (the conversations of the junior-high-school girls) and noncomplaints (the conversations of the university women); it then argued that the behavioral differences essential to conversational excellence must contrast in those two cases, and proceeded to examine the behavior of both cases for contrasts. Upon detecting some, it went on to change just those behaviors in cases previously considered complainable, and found that by doing so, it had rendered them less complainable. This is much more systematic than the previous example, and is certainly to be recommended for a great deal of future research. Yet it does not completely rationalize the problem: In examining the ways in which the complaint cases' behavior contrasted with the noncomplaint cases' behavior, the experimenters had no system for choosing what behaviors to examine. There must have been very many ways in which the behaviors of the junior-high-school girls contrasted with those of the university women, as the behaviors could be seen and heard in their videotapes. Why, then, did the experimenters choose only three of these differences for their hypothesis about the behavioral analysis of conversational ability? And why those three? No doubt they were prominent differences, and no doubt they made some sense in the analysis of good versus poor conversation. But would not, say, the content differences between the conversations of the two sets of talkers also have made some sense in the same quest? Perhaps there appeared to the experimenters to be no systematic content differences as they examined the videotapes; even so, is it not likely that a careful search for some with an analytic code would have yielded some? In the final analysis, then, even this very desirable method begins with some experimenter decisions that seem to be intuitive—subject to the biases and hypotheses that theoretical, pretheoretical, and metatheoretical commitments, recognized and unrecognized, compel. None of this precludes the use of this method very widely in the future; it only asks whether there is not also a possible analysis of the first question: What differences should analysts look for when contrasting complaint and noncomplaint cases?

THE THEORETICAL SIGNIFICANCE OF
IDENTIFYING TARGET BEHAVIORS

The next example of behavioral analysis indicates just how profound a problem the identification of target behaviors can be for the discipline of behavior analysis, applied or not. An understanding of reading was the germinal question for this analysis, as pursued by Sidman and his colleagues in a still ongoing research program (Sidman, 1971; Sidman & Cresson, 1973; Sidman, Cresson, & Willson-Morris, 1974). The failure to teach reading adequately to all children by currently known teaching techniques is a matter of widespread complaint in most societies. Workers in that field often say that the literature of research into what is optimistically called "remedial reading" contains more than 5000 studies, yet does not display a demonstrable solution to the entire problem. Thus, any behavioral analysis of reading is potentially a piece of exceptionally important applied behavior analysis.

The Sidman group argues that reading is, on analysis, a set of relations among four events: (1) the thing being referred to (or its icon, such as a picture of it or a toy model of it); (2) the word that a person hears spoken in reference to that thing; (3) the same word written (usually, printed); and (4) the speaking of that word by the person. The relations that comprise reading are a set of discriminative functions that make any one of these events the occasion for one or more of the other events. If the terms "thing" to denote the thing referred to, "hear word" to denote someone else saying the word that refers to that thing, "WORD" to denote the same word written, and "say word" to denote speaking the word oneself are used, then those discriminative functions can be diagrammed[7] as follows:

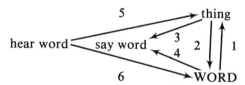

In this kind of diagram, an arrow leading from one event to another means that the event from which the arrow proceeds is discriminative for the event to which it proceeds. Thus the diagram above summarizes six relations:

1. Look at a written word and selectively indicate the thing to which it refers.
2. Look at a thing and selectively indicate the written word for that thing.
3. Look at a thing and say its word.

---

7. Sidman and his colleagues, in the studies cited here, offered a somewhat different diagram to display the same discriminative functions of these events for one another. The diagrams of this chapter obviously are derived from that original, and I am indebted to Sidman and his colleagues for the inspiration to diagram these functions so that they may be looked at and appreciated for both their complexity and their simplicity. I have placed the events "hear word" and "say word" in close juxtaposition (in contrast to the original diagram) to emphasize the importance of their mutual function (in most persons) for the analysis of generalization patterns among these functions when some of them are taught and others are not. These points are made clear in the next few pages.

4. Look at a written word and say it.
5. Hear a word spoken and selectively indicate the thing to which it refers.
6. Hear a word spoken and selectively indicate the written form of that word.

Anyone who can do these six things across a reasonable universe of things and their words may be called a reader. (And anyone who not only can indicate the written word in relations 2 and 6 above but also can write the word, as well as display the other four relations, may be called a writer.)

This analysis in itself qualifies as a very important piece of behavioral analysis. However, this is an analysis that has led to empirical research aimed exactly at its analytical potential, which has in turn moved the analysis to more fundamental (and more analytical) levels. That research has taken the form of experimentally establishing one or more of these six relations, to see if any of the others would then emerge without being established directly (e.g., Sidman, 1971; Sidman & Cresson, 1973; Sidman, Cresson, & Willson-Morris, 1974). For example (Sidman & Cresson, 1973), with some severely retarded subjects, these six relationships all were missing at the outset of training. First, training established the match-to-sample skill necessary for the experimental format that the researchers were using to display these relations. Subsequently, two particular relations were taught (5 and 6 in the diagram): Upon hearing a word, the subjects were taught to indicate a picture of the thing that word referred to, and to indicate the written form of the same word. Diagrammatically, the relations established by training were as follows:

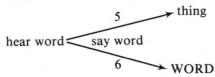

When these two relations had been taught for a small sample of things and their written words, probing showed that the remaining four relations then emerged without direct teaching, as diagrammed below (where directly taught relationships are indicated by solid-line arrows, and emergent, untaught relations are indicated by dashed-line arrows):

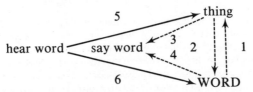

In another example (Sidman, Cresson, & Willson-Morris, 1974), with similarly deficient subjects, only relations 2 and 5 were established: Subjects were taught to indicate the correct thing upon hearing its word spoken, and to look at a thing and indicate its written word:

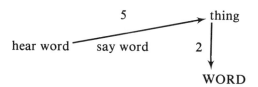

Again, after sufficient experience with the teaching of these two relations across a small sample of things and their words, heard and written, the remaining four relations emerged without direct teaching:

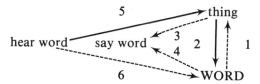

With examples like these and others as empirical facts of clear reliability and at least modest generality (cf. Dixon & Spradlin, 1976; Gast, vanBiervliet, & Spradlin, 1979; Spradlin & Dixon, 1976; vanBiervliet, 1977), the urgent questions become these: Why is it possible to train only a pair out of six relations and see the other four emerge without direct training? Why is it that various pairs will serve equally well? What is the behavioral analysis of that?

Sidman and his colleagues, in their discussion of these studies, and Sidman (1981), in a very recent summary of the logic underlying those studies, have offered a beginning analysis. That analysis seems to be predicated on five demonstrable characteristics of *typical* discriminative function.

1. Two identical yet separate events can be discriminated as such. Thus, in a match-to-sample format, if A and B are the sample events, and A and B are also used as the comparison events, a reinforcement contingency operating consistently on matching a comparison stimulus to the sample stimulus will produce a consistent identity discrimination: The comparison A will reliably be chosen rather than the comparison B when the sample is A; and the comparison B will reliably be chosen rather than the comparison A when the sample is B.If it were not for the relative ease of accomplishing this generalized form of discrimination, the questions to follow about functionally equivalent classes of events could hardly be answered in the match-to-sample format.

2. When an event, A, is made an effective sample for a comparison event, B, it will be found that B has become an effective sample for A when A serves as a comparison event. In more general terms, if A controls B, then B will control A; they are functionally equivalent events.

3. When an event, A, is made an effective sample for a comparison event, B, and if in another context, B is made an effective sample for a comparison event, C, then it will be found that A has become an effective sample

for the comparison event C. In more general terms, if A controls B and B controls C, then A will control C as well as B.

4. When two events, A and B, are made equally effective samples for the same comparison event, C, they become functionally equivalent: Now, if A is made the sample, and the comparison events are B and, say, D, B will be chosen as the match to A; when B is made the sample, and the comparison events are A and, say, E, A will be chosen as the match to B. In more general terms, when A and B both control C, A will also control B, and B will also control A. As a corollary, when two events, A and B, are made equally effective comparisons for the same sample event, C, they also become functionally equivalent. Now, when A is the sample, and the comparison events are B and, say, F, B will be chosen as the match to A; when B is the sample, and the comparison events are A and, say, G, A will be chosen as the match to B. In more general terms, when A and B are both controlled by C, A will also control B, and B will also control A.

5. The events of saying a word and hearing a word are usually functionally equivalent events, at least in any hearing subject who has been taught vocal imitation. "Vocal imitation" means that an individual can say a word that is heard; "hearing" means that when the individual says a word, he or she hears it as well.

One or another, or combinations, of these typical characteristics of discriminative function allow the derivation of all six of the functions that characterize reading from the teaching of quite a variety of pairs of those functions. To see this, consider the Sidman, Cresson, and Willson-Morris (1974) example described previously: Retarded subjects lacking any of the six functions constituting reading were taught to indicate the correct thing when they heard its word spoken, and were taught to indicate the correct written word when they were shown the thing. Diagrammatically:

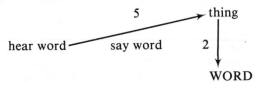

Since these subjects were hearing, vocally imitative persons, the fifth characteristic from the preceding list implies that the actual relations among events in this training were as follows:

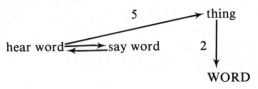

This diagram makes it clear that the event "hear word" controls the events "say word" and "thing"; the corollary of the fourth characteristic from the preceding list implies, then, that "say word" and "thing" are functionally equivalent. Alternatively, the fact that "say word" controls "hear word" and that "hear word" controls "thing" allows the third characteristic from that list to imply that "say word" will control "thing"; the second characteristic, then, implies that if "say word" controls "thing," then "thing" will control "say word." Thus, either way, the diagram becomes:

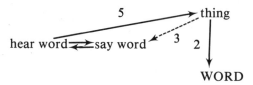

Furthermore, these diagrams show that "hear word" controls "thing" and that "thing" controls "WORD"; the third characteristic from the preceding list implies, then, that "hear word" will also control "WORD," and the diagram then is:

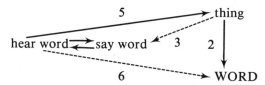

Now it is clear that "say word" controls "hear word" and that "hear word" controls "WORD"; the third characteristic from the preceding list again operates to imply that "say word" will also control "WORD," and the second characteristic then implies that "WORD" will thereby control "say word." Alternatively, the diagram now shows that "hear word" controls both "say word" and "WORD"; the corollary of the fourth characteristic from the preceding list again operates to imply that "say word" and "WORD" are functionally equivalent. Either way, the diagram becomes:

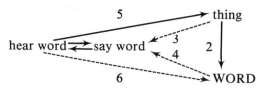

Finally, the diagram makes clear that "thing" controls "WORD"; the second characteristic from the preceding list implies, then, that "WORD" will control "thing." Alternatively, since "hear word" controls both "thing" and "WORD," the corollary of the fourth characteristic implies that "thing" and "WORD" are functionally equivalent. Interestingly, the corollary is not actually needed; the fact that "thing" and "WORD" both control "say word" allows the fourth characteristic to imply the functional equivalence of "thing" and "WORD" without its corollary. And, in addition, since the diagram shows that "WORD" controls "say word," which in turn controls "hear word," which in turn controls "thing," then the third characteristic of the preceding list can be extended to suggest that "WORD" could thereby control "thing." Thus, it is rather overdetermined that the diagram display the last of the six needed relations:

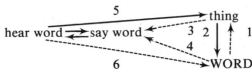

This indeed describes the data of the experiment: After relations 2 and 5 were taught across a few examples, the remaining relations emerged without direct teaching. And, in fact, these four characteristics of typical discriminative function, coupled with the fifth fact that saying a word and hearing a word usually are functionally equivalent, will analyze the patterns of generalization observed in all of the studies that so far have examined the effects of training various pairs of the six relations constituting reading. (The derivations of these analyses are left as an exercise for the reader.) Furthermore, it seems true, as Sidman has argued, that the fourth characteristic and its corollary are not needed for this analysis; in the example just given, their applications always could be ignored in favor of either the second or the third characteristic, or their joint operation. The same can be found when the data of all the other extant studies are subjected to similar analysis. (This claim, too, is left as an exercise for the reader: pursuit of it in this chapter would require too many pages.) However, reliance on the second and third characteristics requires invocation of the fifth as well—that the subjects of these studies are hearing, vocally imitative persons. In the analysis just pursued here, the fourth characteristic of typical discriminative function and its corollary were included and used mainly because they are typically characteristic of such functions; because they are descriptive of the operation of event classes (stimulus and response classes); and because they conceivably may be found to operate when some aspect of the second or third characteristic fails to operate.

Note that in logic, the fourth characteristic and its corollary are implicit in the second and third characteristics: if A controls C and B controls C, A should also control B, and B should also control A. This is so because of the second characteristic, which says that if A controls C, then C controls A, and that if B controls C, then C controls B; and because of the third characteristic, which says that since A controls C and C controls B, then A controls B, and also says that since B controls C and C controls A, then B controls A.

Thus, it follows that A controls B and that B controls A. As for the corollary, if A controls B and also controls C, then the second characteristic says that B will also control A and that C will also control A, and the third characteristic says that if B controls A and A controls C, then B controls C, and that if C controls A and A controls B, then C controls B. Thus, it follows that B controls C and C controls B. Then why have I added the fourth characteristic and its corollary to the briefer, neater analysis offered by Sidman and his colleagues? Because a characteristic may be logically implicit in two other characteristics, and yet conceivably need not exist in nature for only that reason. The fourth characteristic and its corollary may sometimes be true of discriminative functioning, not *because* the second and third characteristics are true, but conceivably even when one or the other of them is not true. True, *if* the second and third characteristics are true, then automatically the fourth and its corollary are too. But what is known about the conditions in which the first three characteristics are true? I submit that not enough is known to be sure that they always operate together, and that not enough is known to be sure that the fourth would not operate even in the absence of one of the other three.

The major underlying point is that these characteristics always have to be described as "typical," and the meaning of "typical" does not include "inevitable" or "universal." There is no necessity that all discriminative functioning displays the first, second, third, or fourth characteristics listed here, just as there is no necessity that all persons hear or be vocally imitative. Given these characteristics, or at least some of them, then the generalization patterns found when pairs of the six functions that constitute reading are taught become understandable: Those generalization patterns are analyzed by these characteristics. Now the question becomes this: What is the analysis of these characteristics? Under what conditions do they characterize discriminative functioning, and under what conditions (if any) do they not? Given these characteristics, a certain behavioral analysis of reading becomes possible—but when are we indeed *given* these characteristics? By contrast, when must we make them happen—teach them—before we can rely on them? If there are such times or conditions, then how do we teach those characteristics so that they are indeed characteristic—so that they are generalized functions? Thus, a given behavioral analysis of reading into six components rests on an underlying behavioral analysis of generalization amongst its components, which in turn rests on yet another even more deeply underlying behavioral analysis of the nature of discriminative functions and of stimulus and response classes. The act of pursuing a behavioral analysis, therefore, is not simply an act of application—of finding the behavior changes that constitute the solution to some complaint. It is also, at least sometimes, one of the most fundamental research operations possible for the discipline. Perhaps, if every behavioral analysis always is questioned about the behavioral analysis that must underly *it,* and if this questioning is pressed again and again upon its own results, the outcomes will be exceptionally valuable to establishing the most fundamental structure of knowledge about behavior.

A POSSIBLE TACTIC FOR FUTURE ANALYSIS

The final example of behavioral analysis for this chapter has been chosen to represent a *possible* tactic for the future analysis of a great many behaviors (Meichenbaum & Goodman, 1971). *Possible* must be emphasized, for reasons that soon become evident. On the face of it, the study constituting this example dealt with children about whose behavior there was systematic and important social complaint, in that they were students in a remedial second-grade public-school classroom. Students usually are assigned to those classrooms because of academic deficiencies or inappropriate classroom conduct, or both. The study attempted a behavioral analysis of some of these behaviors, in that it observed the children's classroom conduct and also had their teachers rate it, to see whether it changed after the experimental intervention; in addition, the study attempted a behavioral analysis of some psychological-test performances, chosen mainly for their presumed reflection of "impulsivity" as some children's generalized style of responding to problems of all sorts. "Impulsivity" might be thought to represent a behavioral analysis of both academic deficiencies and inappropriate classroom conduct, but this is hardly clear. Thus, the study asked whether observations and ratings of classroom conduct, together with low scores in three components of an IQ test, many errors and short latencies in a test of impulsivity, and many maze-tracing errors interpretable as a result of impulsivity, could be analyzed as an absence of appropriate forms of self-instruction in being reflective rather than impulsive. But since there is scant point in teaching children to instruct themselves literally to be reflective rather than impulsive, a prior behavioral analysis of impulsivity–reflectivity was required. That was proposed in the form of the following training program, which required four half-hour sessions.

1. The experimenter modeled for each child performances of a variety of tasks, such as copying line patterns, coloring within boundaries, and solving visual-form problems. The model displayed self-questions about the nature of each task and self-answers in the form of plans and rehearsals (especially to "go slow" and "be careful"), as well as ongoing self-instructions to continue carrying out the plan as rehearsed. Performances were accompanied by self-acknowledgments when the model was follow-

ing the plans, as well as self-acknowledgments of occasional mistakes, which were followed by self-reassurances, self-correction, and the reassertion of the plans. Self-approval was modeled when the task was going well and when it was finished correctly.

2. The subjects then performed the same task while the experimenter instructed them to do all of what the experimenter had just modeled.
3. The subjects then performed the task again and were asked to instruct themselves aloud.
4. The subjects then performed the task again and were asked only to whisper the self-instructions.
5. The subjects then performed the task again and were asked to instruct themselves silently and without lip movements.

The design of this study used three groups of five children each, matched on sex composition and prior IQ levels. One group, after measurement of all its dependent variables, encountered the training program just described. A second group, similarly measured, had an equal number of sessions with the experimenter, during which they were exposed to the same tasks for as many trials as were the first group's members; however, they received no training in self-instruction, although occasions were found to offer them as much experimenter approval as was given to the first group. The third group was measured similarly, encountered no training program or any other set of experiences with the experimenter, and was measured again when the first two groups were (i.e., promptly after their intervening experiences, and 1 month later).

In general, the mean postintervention measures showed changes in a variety of performances for the experimental group trained in self-instruction, and these changes for the most part were interpretable as decreases in test-displayed impulsivity. (The crucial role of self-instructional training was not always affirmed; some of these changes were also displayed, but always to a lesser extent, by some of the children who had been given familiarity with the training tasks and an equal amount of attention without the training in self-instruction.) However, classroom observations of the children's inappropriate conduct and teachers' ratings of it ("self-control," "activity level," "cooperativeness," "likeability," etc.) showed no changes from their mean levels prior to the intervention, in any group. Thus, training this class of self-instructional skills did not prove to be a behavioral analysis of inappropriate classroom conduct, but did constitute at least a partial behavioral analysis of several psychometric measures of IQ and impulsivity. Thus, the theory that those aspects of IQ and impulsivity are part of a behavioral analysis of inappropriate classroom conduct was now less credible than previously (although it can always be doubted that the best measures of it had been used, or that this study's training program was sufficiently comprehensive for its results to generalize that far). What can be said is that training in self-instruction improved one set of performances in situations that might be like those prevailing in academic work, but were not identical to them; yet it did not improve another set of actual classroom performances that might be thought to be related to the first set.

These patterns were still evident 1 month later. Thus, should anyone want a behavioral analysis of children's response to certain IQ-test components and certain measures of psychometric impulsivity, a durable one embodied in an impressively short, simple, and logical training program for certain self-instructional skills is in hand.

Given that some complaints (about impulsivity) can be analyzed as an absence of appropriate self-instruction, what other complaints might be shown to derive from a similar absence of their appropriate self-instructions? It is intriguing that what amounts to little more than a proposal to explore just that question (Meichenbaum, 1977) has created a methodological storm within applied behavior analysis, so that some workers are careful to identify themselves as "cognitive-behavior" modifiers in distinction to unprefixed behavior modifiers, and some others are careful to point out that their absence of prefix is in token of their systematic abstention from the invocation of anything called "cognitive," as if "cognitive" were necessarily in contradistinction to "behavioral." Two sources of this storm may be discerned: the methodological behaviorists and the radical behaviorists (see footnote 2). The methological behaviorists have made it a point of systematic procedure never to deal with anything unobservable by public means; to the extent that cognitive events are private, they will not be dealt with to that extent by methodological behaviorists. ("Dealt with" in this context almost surely means "observed and manipulated," and if that is so, then they seem to be on firm ground—most of the phenomena called "cognitive" are, most of the time, not observable by public means. But is there perhaps a way in which they are nevertheless manipulable? Wait and see.) The radical behaviorists have not made it a point of systematic procedure never to deal with anything unobservable by public means; what they have done instead is to assume that no unobservable events ever operate independently of observable antecedents to affect behavior (see Skinner, 1957, for an example of a thorough willingness to deal with a wide range of unobservable events). To the extent that cognitive events are said to operate as if they were autonomous causes of observable behavior—that is, as events that, once they exist, are thenceforth almost immune to environmental influence, while themselves exerting extreme environmental influence—they will not be dealt with in radical behaviorism. ("Dealt with" in this context probably means "related to observable antecedents and consequences." Is there a way in which cognitive events, even though postulated by their theorists to be autonomous, nevertheless can be examined for their reality and possibly related to a controlling environment, rather than postulated as the controlling environment? Wait and see.)

The context of this chapter is the possibility of systematizing the process of analyzing complaints into behaviors to be changed. The major point is that this process is crucial but not widely appreciated as such, and consequently is far from achieving the systematization that might be possible. Methodological storms over as simple a proposal as seeing to what extent training in self-instruction skills can constitute a behavioral analysis of some complaint are an irrelevant distraction from that enterprise, which in the long run may prove more important than the orthodoxies that its deeper (and optional) implications seem to threaten. Thus, my goal now is to argue in defense of trying that line of behavioral analyses, mainly to see whether it will be worth anything, while maintaining the stance of a radical behaviorist and at the same time trying to tempt methodological behaviorists to see sufficiently methodological behavior in this kind of work.

The defense of a generic class of self-instruction trainings as potential behavioral analyses of complaints might well start with a modest yet perfect example that is actually quite familiar to each reader—which is why it has been chosen. The problem is that of extracting the square root of any real number from the infinite class of real numbers; the complaint is that virtually no beginning secondary-school student can do this, and yet he or she is supposed to need the skill. (Perhaps I will be excused if I do not question this thesis too closely.) Consequently, late in secondary school, it is taught routinely. (A little later, it is forgotten routintely, which is part of its perfection as an example for this argument.) The skill desired is a generalized one: Every student should be able to extract the square root of any real number whatsoever, not just of 1, 4, 9, 16, 25, . . . 144, which were memorized earlier as parts of the multiplication tables. It is impossible to teach each member of an infinitely large response class separately; the only recourse is to teach a little of that and insure that generalization to the remainder occurs. This is accomplished by teaching a self-instruction skill, called an "algorithm" by mathematicians and computer programmers. The specific algorithm is retaught here, because most readers will have forgotten it, and because its characteristics need to be clear and complete to support some of the argument to follow. The reteaching is attempted as the working through of a single example: extracting the root of 660.49.

First, sort the number into pairs of digits to the left and right of its decimal point, thus:

$$06 \ 60 \ . \ 49$$

Starting with the leftmost pair, find a number whose square is equal to or less

than the leftmost pair. That is 2; write it above the leftmost pair and then
write its square below the pair:

$$
\begin{array}{r}
2 \\
\hline
06\ 60\ .\ 49 \\
4
\end{array}
$$

Subtract that 4 from the pair it is written under and write the remainder, 2,
appending to it the next pair of digits:

$$
\begin{array}{r}
2 \\
\hline
06\ 60\ .\ 49 \\
-4 \\
\hline
2\ 60
\end{array}
$$

Double the number extracted so far, 2, to make 4; write that 4 to the left of the
new term, 260:

$$
\begin{array}{rr}
 & 2\qquad . \\
\hline
 & 06\ 60\ .\ 49 \\
 & -4 \\
\cline{2-2}
4 & 2\ 60
\end{array}
$$

Find the largest digit, x, that can be appended to that 4 to make a number in
the 40's, such that this number multiplied by x will be equal to or less than the
current term, 260. The digit must be 5: 5×45 is 225, which is less than 260,
whereas 6×46 is 276, which is more than 260. Append this 5 to the 4 to make
45, write it above the next pair, and do the multiplication just specified:

$$
\begin{array}{rr}
 & 2\ \ 5\ . \\
\hline
 & 06\ 60\ .\ 49 \\
 & -4 \\
\cline{2-2}
45 & 2\ 60 \\
 & 2\ 25
\end{array}
$$

Subtract the 225 just produced from the 260 it is written under and write the
remainder, 35, appending to it the next pair of digits:

$$
\begin{array}{rr}
 & 2\ \ 5\ . \\
\hline
 & 06\ 60\ .\ 49 \\
 & -4 \\
\cline{2-2}
45 & 2\ 60 \\
 & -2\ 25 \\
\cline{2-2}
 & 35\ \ 49
\end{array}
$$

Double the number extracted so far, 25, to make 50; write that 50 to the left of
the new term, 3549 (and note that you are repeating the operation of three
steps ago; you are now cycling):

```
        2  5 .
     06 60 . 49
      - 4
45    2 60
    - 2 25
50     35  49
```

Find the largest digit, x, that can be appended to that 50 to make a number in the 500's, such that this number multiplied by x will be equal to or less than the current term, 3549. That digit must be 7. Append this 7 to the 50 to make 507, write it above the third pair, and do the multiplication just indicated (and compare this step to the one three steps ago):

```
         2  5 . 7
      06 60 . 49
       - 4
45     2 60
     - 2 25
507     35  49
        35  49
```

Subtract the 3549 just produced from the 3549 under which it is written and write the remainder, 0; the fact that it is 0 indicates that a perfect square root now has been written above the starting number. And indeed, 25.7^2 is exactly 660.49. Note that this algorithm is a repetitive cycle of generalizable operations that can be applied to any real number, repeatedly, until a square root is extracted (or one sufficiently close for practicality).

Teaching this algorithm to secondary-school students requires a few weeks of classwork in mathematics. Those students memorize the algorithm, practice it over some few dozen examples, fortify their memories against the final exam in which it will inevitably play some role, and are for a time able to perform an infinitely generalized response class: They can extract the square root of any real number, previously taught or not, previously encountered or not. If only there were some truly important social significance to this ability, its teaching would be displayed as a triumph of applied behavior analysis, because the training program is short and easy and the resultant generalization is breathtaking. True, maintenance is unimpressive, but, on the other hand, recovery of the skill is relatively easy. (Conceivably, as a result of these pages, every reader who learned this algorithm in secondary school and has since forgotten it now recalls it again, and will be able to use it in the future—for the next few weeks.)

Note that this infinitely generalized response class requires very few skills: The ability to add, subtract, multiply, and divide, as well as the ability to memorize a reasonably formidable sequence of doing just that, analyzes it perfectly. Note that it is a clear example of a mediating response. Thus secondary-school students have been taught a small repertoire with which they can in the future mediate any stimulus from the class of real numbers into its corresponding response, its square root. Note also that this mediating response is, during its teaching, in no sense exotic, nonbehavioral, or unobservable; it is the simple stuff of arithmetic done in a specific sequence, the teaching of which seems to upset no behaviorist, methodological or radical. But perhaps other mediating responses have acquired their somewhat suspect reputation because they are often *inferred* to account for some behavioral skill, and by inference are given characteristics that cannot be verified or denied by direct observation. This algorithm, by contrast, is thoroughly observable; well known (in secondary-school circles, at least); easily taught; and, perhaps just because of all that, uncontroversial.

Given all that, then notice that once the algorithm is taught, its practice quickly becomes unobservable. At first, students can be heard instructing themselves in its sequential steps; soon, their lips move, but what they are saying to themselves cannot be heard. Their pencils still are detailing every step on paper, however. But not too long later, even their observable pencil-on-paper responses will begin to disappear here and there, where private shortcuts are possible and easy. Eventually, all that will be seen when the students are presented with the stimulus is a skeleton of the pencil responses necessary to its solution; the guiding algorithm behind those pencil responses is now completely invisible. Have the students left the realm of methodological behaviorism by becoming efficient?

Perhaps so; quite a variety of behavior analysts and applied behavior analysts will refuse to deal with an unobservable behavior, and this algorithm is now quite unobservable. I submit that this case is different, however: This one may be unobservable now, but it was taught, and it was observable (briefly) while it was taught; and having taught it, teachers know its behavioral components, none of which was scandalous or heretical to anyone under the control of a positive stimulus function for observable events. Teachers thus do not need to *infer* what unobservable processes their secondary-school students are possessed of that enable them to extract square roots across an infinite class of stimuli; the teachers *know* what they are using because the teachers gave it to them, knowing also that it would become unobservable rather quickly.

If there are grounds for methodological disquiet, they must consist of the current unobservability of the results of this routine installation of the prosaic algorithm. How do teachers know that it hasn't changed, now that it is unobservable? It may very well have changed; the point is whether or not a student's ability to extract accurate square roots has changed too. If it has not, then the teacher still knows that the advent of square-rooting responses in this student was accomplished by the teaching of the algorithm; whatever transformations it may have undergone within the unobservable privacy of the student are not necessary to an understanding of its continuing function, or to an understanding of the student's continuing ability.[8] The teaching of the original algorithm remains the behavioral analysis of the student's enduring root extractions. On the other hand, if the student's ability to extract square roots has changed, then the teacher does not know what is now miscontrolling that behavior—only what is no longer controlling it. That is not an unusual situation when behavior escapes from experimental control; it is no more a disadvantage in this context than in any other.

Another characteristic of this response class is important to the argument: There is no way imaginable of teaching an efficient, generalized skill of extracting square roots, other than by teaching one of its mediating algorithms (or by acquiring a calculator with a square-root function—irrelevant to this argument). Endless trials of differential reinforcement for correct square roots, even with punishment for incorrect ones, will not yield the skill. The class is too large to memorize; and iterative squarings of possible roots, hunting for closer and closer ones, while actually related to the algorithm, still is so inefficient a tactic as to fail in the comparison. Here is a response class that can be acquired only through a mediator. Granted, we tend to prefer analyses of behavior that do not involve mediation over analyses that do, simply on the grounds of parsimony. This example is a good one because it makes clear that parsimony is always on the side of necessity, and in this case, mediation is a necessity.

This argument is not meant to serve as a call for a prominent role of inference in applied behavior analysis. I distrust inferences, largely because I trust the Law of Large Numbers. The Law of Large Numbers says that the larger the number of opportunities is, the more likely it becomes that even very unlikely events will occur at least once. Baer's Corollary of that law, applied to the problem of inferring what unobservable ability a behaver must have if we are to explain the behavior exhibited, says that you can never collect enough data to support only one inference to explain them: If enough inferrers can be set to inferring, the probability of at least one of them producing an alternative inference to explain the same data can be made as high as

---

8. Indeed, I have had an experience that suggests to me quite forcibly that such algorithms do change form without changing function, with time and especially with disuse. There came a moment in my life when I had not extracted a square root by hand in many years, and suddenly needed one (for other than research purposes). I found that I could not recall the verbal algorithm sufficiently: What doubled? I was completely stalled, until I simply took up a pencil and applied it to paper as if I did recall the algorithm. My experience, as best I can report it, was that my hand still knew the algorithm, although "I" did not. I recovered the algorithm by watching my hand solve the problem; I induced what doubled from what my hand wrote in extracting the root.

you wish (or higher than you wish, if the original inference is known as your inference). A science in which the firmness of an inference depends so much on the number of inferrers who are attempting inferences from the same data does not have positive stimulus function for me. I prefer sciences in which response classes are analyzed by teaching them, rather than by inferring what their possessor must have learned some time previously. If we encounter a square rooter already possessed of the infinitely generalized ability, we are helpless to analyze the origin of that ability; analysis of it can only be accomplished by installing it (through teaching, most likely) in someone who does not yet possess it. Then what we need most are teaching curricula, together with experimental designs powerful enough to show that behavior changes following the teaching of some skill are attributable to that teaching rather than to some extraneous variable.

The need for teaching curricula recalls inference for a less than prominent role in the construction of behavioral analyses. If a certain response class seems to defy establishment through simple means such as differential reinforcement, and we reluctantly consider the possibility of establishing it through mediating skills, we will then need some guess about what a successful mediator could be. We may very well try to infer what successful behavers are using in being successful. Given the inference, however, our characteristic recourse as applied behavior analysts should be not to see what other data this inference seems to agree with, or what data can be gathered for it to agree or disagree with; our tactic should be to teach the skill inferred as crucial, to see what happens as a result.

If this argument has convinced the reader that the usual invisibility of the square-root algorithm shortly after it is taught does not debar the case from inclusion in the class of successful and (formally) impressive behavioral analyses crucial to a discipline of applied behavior analysis, then perhaps the reader will consider a minor extension of some of the detail of the argument. Use of a square-rooting algorithm is simply a special case of self-instruction. The Meichenbaum and Goodman study (1971) described earlier was also a special case of self-instruction. Their self-instructions, rather than recommending sequences of arithmetic operations, recommended sequences of recalling a problem's necessities, going slowly and carefully, correcting errors without drama, acknowledging good work as it proceeded, and using self-praise when successful. That seems to be a matter of detail, rather than of principle. Then surely there is no bar to considering the Meichenbaum and Goodman study as an example of applied behavior analysis, too. Its troubles are not at the level of principle, but at the level of circumstance: It chose self-instructions considerably less precise than those of sequential arithmetic operations ("go slow" and "be careful" are a little like "be good," the classic example of an uncompliable instruction). And, perhaps most significant of all, it taught self-instructions that, unlike the arithmetic operations of the square-root algorithm, could be wrong in some real cases. The square-root algorithm always leads to a correct answer; that is the way the world of numbers works. The self-instruction to go slowly and be careful is only likely to lead its practitioner to success in the form of correct answers to problems—it is not certain to do so, especially with those problems that the practitioner of these self-instructions is unequipped to solve, no matter how slowly or carefully they are attempted. That is the way the world of behavior works. In the simple language of applied behavior analysis, use of the square-root algorithm is always reinforced with a correct answer; use of many other generalized problem-solving algorithms is only sometimes reinforced with a correct answer. This is especially true of self-instructions of the form, "If I try harder, I'll get it right." For a given student, there always are problems for which no amount of harder trying will accomplish a correct answer.

But self-instructions of the form to go slowly, be careful, and try harder are clearly very good self-instructions to practice and follow, even when they are lies: How could anyone know that the instructions will not work in a given instance unless they are tried? And when they are tried, people believe, they can sometimes convert an otherwise almost certain failure into a successful problem solution. Thus, they seem undeniably positive skills to have. Furthermore, their theoretical function most often is to mediate one of the favorite processes of applied behavior analysis—the contingencies of reinforcement, punishment, and extinction. The intent of these self-instructions usually is to compensate for absences of reinforcement and to mitigate the weakening effects of punishment and extinction. If they are applied to desirable behaviors, they should have desirable effects—if they work. If their function is to mediate the most basic behavior-change processes of a discipline, then surely they are a crucial part of that discipline—if they work. Pragmatically and theoretically, they seem undeniably central to our concerns—but only if they work.

Seeing whether they work, on the face of it, should have two major components. One is simply to examine them experimentally in a wide variety of situations, with the best measurement and experimental designs that can be applied. The other is for the experimenters to apply them as artfully, shrewdly, and technologically as they know how. If they want to see whether or not they work, should they not give them the best opportunity to work? To a considerable extent, the first of these components is in place. Studies of the effects of teaching a variety of self-instructions abound; the journals in which they are published proliferate to the point of sometimes publishing nothing else (clearly a poor tactic for seeing whether they are merely a distinctive part of a larger discipline); and books containing their descriptions, theories, and subtheories are increasingly available as undergraduate textbooks as well as professional-level arguments. The second component, however, does not yet seem strong. Self-instructions are not always being taught with the best technological expertise that the discipline can provide, and they hardly ever seem to be maintained artfully against encounters with disconfirming experiences in the real world—not with the same exquisite attention to scheduling that any laboratory-based operant conditioner can give a key peck or bar press to buttress it against a great deal more extinction than reinforcement.

If applied behavior analysts will agree that the still undeveloped art of transforming complaints into the correct behaviors to be changed, so as to satisfy those complaints, is vital to the discipline;

and if applied behavior analysts will agree that teaching the square root algorithm represents an imporant form of that art (even if not an important outcome);

and if applied behavior analysts will agree that the typically unobservable character of the square-root algorithm in practice is no bar to its inclusion in the discipline, considering that it is taught as an observable skill, that the teaching of it is a public and replicable intervention, and that the results of that teaching are clear, observable, and impressive in their correctness and generality (if not in anything else);

and if applied behavior analysts will then agree that the similar teaching of a variety of other forms of self-instruction, to see whether they too can yield clear, observable, and impressive results, not only in correctness and generality, but quite possibly in social significance as well, is an essentially similar adventure of essentially similar respectability according to the basic values of the discipline;

then surely applied behavior analysts will assist that adventure, by evaluating its accomplishments rather than reacting to its nomenclature, at least when it conforms to these characteristics, and by offering such studies the best technological support available in the discipline, to see this variant of the behavioral analysis of complaints into behaviors to be changed at its best;

for its face logic is very appealing, and its postulated role is at the heart of bedrock contingencies; thus, its potential is very great—

unless it isn't. But how could we tell without trying it out as well as we know how?

REFERENCES

Baer, D. M. In the beginning, there was the response. In E. Ramp & G. Semb (Eds.), *Behavior analysis: Areas of research and application.* Englewood Cliffs, N.J.: Prentice-Hall, 1975.
Birnbrauer, J. S. Applied behavior analysis, service, and the acquisition of knowledge. *The Behavior Analyst,* 1979, *2,* 15–21.

Dietz, S. M. Current status of applied behavior analysis: Science versus technology. *American Psychologist,* 1978, *33,* 805–814.

Dixon, M. H., & Spradlin, J. E. Establishing stimulus equivalences among retarded adolescents. *Journal of Experimental Child Psychology,* 1976, *21*(1), 144–164.

Gast, D. L., vanBiervliet, A., & Spradlin, J. E. Teaching number–word equivalences: A study of transfer. *American Journal of Mental Deficiency,* 1979, *83*(5), 524–527.

Goldstein, R. S., & Baer, D. M. R.S.V.P.: A procedure to increase the personal mail and number of correspondents for nursing home residents. *Behavior Therapy,* 1976, *7,* 348–354.

Hayes, S. C. Theory and technology in behavior analysis. *The Behavior Analyst,* 1978, *1,* 25–33.

Horowitz, F. D. Living among the ABA's: Retrospect and prospect. In E. Ramp & G. Semb (Eds.), *Behavior analysis: Areas of research and application.* Englewood Cliffs, N.J.: Prentice-Hall, 1975.

Krantz, D. L. The separate worlds of operant and nonoperant psychology. *Journal of Applied Behavior Analysis,* 1971, *4,* 61–70.

Meichenbaum, D. H. *Cognitive-behavior modification.* New York: Plenum, 1977.

Meichenbaum, D. H., & Goodman, J. Training impulsive children to talk to themselves: A means of developing self-control. *Journal of American Psychology,* 1971, *77*(2), 115–126.

Michael, J. L. Flight from behavior analysis. *The Behavior Analyst,* 1980, *3,* 1–21.

Minkin, N., Braukmann, C. J., Minkin, B. L., Timbers, G. D., Timbers, B. J., Fixsen, D. L., Phillips, E. L., & Wolf, M. M. The social validation and training of conversational skills. *Journal of Applied Behavior Analysis,* 1976, *9*(2), 127–139.

Pierce, W. D., & Epling, W. F. What happened to analysis in applied behavior analysis? *The Behavior Analyst,* 1980, *3,* 1–10.

Sidman, M. *Tactics of scientific research.* New York: Basic Books, 1960.

Sidman, M. Reading and auditory–visual equivalences. *Journal of Speech and Hearing,* 1971, *14,* 5–13.

Sidman, M. Equivalence relations. *Division 25 Recorder,* 1981, *16*(1), 3.

Sidman, M., & Cresson, O., Jr. Reading and cross-modal transfer of stimulus equivalences in severe retardation. *American Journal of Mental Deficiency,* 1973, *77*(5), 515–523.

Sidman, M., Cresson, O., Jr., & Willson-Morris, M. Acquisition of matching to sample via mediated transfer. *Journal of the Experimental Analysis of Behavior,* 1974, *22*(2), 261–273.

Skinner, B. F. *Verbal behavior.* New York: Appleton-Century-Crofts, 1957.

Skinner, B. F. *About behaviorism.* New York: Knopf, 1974.

Spradlin, J. E., & Dixon, M. H. Establishing conditional discriminations without direct training: Stimulus classes and labels. *American Journal of Mental Deficiency,* 1976, *80*(5), 555–561.

Stolz, S. B. Adoption of innovations from applied behavioral research: "Does anybody care?" *Journal of Applied Behavior Analysis,* 1981, *14*(5), 491–505.

vanBiervliet, A. Establishing words and objects as functionally equivalent through manual sign training. *American Journal of Mental Deficiency,* 1977, *82*(2), 178–186.

Wolf, M. M. Social validity: The case of subjective measurement, or how applied behavior analysis is finding its heart. *Journal of Applied Behavior Analysis,* 1978, *11,* 203–214.

7

COGNITIVE-BEHAVIOR THERAPY

DONALD MEICHENBAUM
Department of Psychology
University of Waterloo

ROY CAMERON
Department of Psychology
University of Saskatchewan

In a recent review of the behavior-therapy literature, Ledwidge (1978) has noted the proliferation of articles on cognitive-behavior modification (CBM) published in behavior-therapy journals. It is this increasing trend that has led such observers as Mahoney (1974) and Meichenbaum (1977) to announce that behavior therapy is going cognitive, as is psychology in general (see Dember, 1974). The editors of the *Annual Review of Behavior Therapy,* Cyril W. Franks and G. Terence Wilson, each year attempt to characterize the previous year's progress in behavior therapy in terms of some overriding influential or controversial development. In the 1977 *Annual Review* (Franks & Wilson, 1977), they designated 1976–1977 as the "year of cognition" for the theoretician and practitioner alike. The cognitive trend is also evident in a variety of publications, including a new journal, *Cognitive Therapy and Research;* several books on cognitive-behavior therapy (e.g., Beck, Rush, Shaw, & Emery, 1979; Foreyt & Rathjen, 1979; Kendall & Hollon, 1979; Mahoney, 1974; Meichenbaum, 1977; Turk, Meichenbaum, & Genest, in press); an annual research conference on cognitive-behavior therapy; and innumerable workshops. It is even possible to find job descriptions for cognitive-behavior modifiers (whoever they are). Cognitive–behavioral approaches are clearly riding the crest of a wave of popularity. Indeed, as we note below, we are concerned that the current enthusiasm for cognitive–behavioral techniques seems to outstrip the empirical data base in the area (see Mahoney & Arnkoff, 1978, and Meichenbaum, 1977, for critical reviews of the empirical work).

Our intention in the present chapter is to highlight, and to attempt to clarify, central conceptual issues that are emerging as the field develops. In the first section, we consider the nature and origins of CBM. We then move on to consider conceptual developments in CBM with children and adults. In the final portion of the paper, we present an embryonic cognitive–behavioral model of therapeutic change, in which we attempt to identify the central objectives and processes of therapy.

THE NATURE AND ORIGINS OF COGNITIVE-BEHAVIOR MODIFICATION

The shift to a cognitive orientation has not been without its critics. Indeed, the concern with the role of cognitive processes in behavior modification has elicited what Mahoney and Kazdin (1979) have characterized as "strong and vituperative reactions." These reactions are especially apparent among those with a behavioral orientation, who have viewed the recent interest in cognitive processes as a "mentalistic resurrection." Consider the following:

Cognitivism constitutes a counter-revolution to the behavioristic revolution that promised to promote psychology to a scientific status. . . . Students of scientific psychology cannot but deplore the regressive tendencies of cognitive psychology. ("Observer," 1978, pp. 157, 159)

In a similar vein, Wolpe (1976) has branded as "malcontents" those who espouse a cognitive orientation. Such sentiments have been echoed by a number of other critics, including Ledwidge (1978), who considers CBM a "step in the wrong direction," and Greenspoon and Lamal (1978) who ask, "Cognitive-behavior modification: Who needs it?"

Since our main purpose is to present our own overview and critique of the area, we do not want to become sidetracked by reviewing systematically all the contentious issues that are being debated. The interested reader is encouraged to refer to recent papers by some of the protagonists, including Beck and Mahoney (1979); Eysenck (1979); Greenspoon and Lamal (1978); Ledwidge (1978); Locke (1979); Mahoney and Kazdin (1979); Meichenbaum (1979); "Observer" (1978); Wilson (1979, 1980); and Wolpe (1976, 1978). In the present context, we would like to offer only a few brief comments on the debate that is under way. We recognize that critical discussion plays a vital role in the development of ideas and technologies. We welcome criticism that challenges us to clarify our thinking. When our critics (e.g., Ledwidge, 1978) argue that supporters of CBM require more empirical data to support their notions, we heartily concur; it is important to remember that CBM conceptions and approaches are quite new, and that further well-designed research studies, especially studies involving clinical populations, are required to assess adequately the possibilities and limitations of CBM (Meichenbaum,

1979). We share the concern about the dangers of uncritical acceptance of CBM. Other points of debate have touched on heady philosophical issues related to metaphysics and epistemology (e.g., Beck & Mahoney, 1979; Wolpe, 1978). We have nothing to add to this discussion; we doubt that consensus will be achieved on these points. The philosophically inclined reader may find Allport's philosophical perspective (1955) on behavioristic versus cognitive theories in psychology to be pertinent to the points presently at issue. We would endorse Mahoney and Kazdin's position that "in the final analysis, it will, or should, be the theoretically sound and empirically established techniques that are embraced by the field. What these are called, how they develop, and the purity of their philosophical heritage will be interesting but not of ultimate importance" (1979, p. 1046).

While we find ourselves agreeing with critics of CBM at some points, and intellectually challenged at others, we are also concerned that some of the criticism of CBM appears to be based upon misconceptions about the nature of CBM. Since there do appear to be misconceptions in some quarters, we feel that it would be prudent to begin by describing briefly the nature and origins of CBM as we see them (see also Mahoney & Arnkoff, 1978; Meichenbaum, 1977; and Wilson, 1979).

We turn first to the question of the nature of CBM. There are two main points we would like to emphasize. The first is that "CBM" is a rubric applied to a wide variety of therapeutic techniques that are based upon a number of different conceptual models. A recent, major review of cognitive and self-control therapies (Mahoney & Arnkoff, 1978) covers such diverse approaches as rational–emotive therapy, cognitive therapy, coping skills therapies, problem-solving therapies, self-control approaches, and covert conditioning. All these approaches tend to be characterized as "cognitive–behavioral." The essential common denominators across approaches appear to be (1) interest in the nature and modification of client cognitions and (2) some commitment to the use of behavior-therapy procedures in promoting change. However, the differences across approaches are at least as striking as the similarities. There are differences in theoretical underpinnings (ranging from theories of conditioning to those of cognitive information processing and social learning); different aspects of cognitive experience (beliefs, attributions, expectations, coping self-statements and images, problem-solving cognitions, etc.) are emphasized; different prescriptions may be offered about the best point of intervention in the cognition–affect–behavior–consequence complex; different strategies for intervention (ranging from direct frontal attacks on irrational beliefs to encouraging clients to produce adaptive behaviors before focusing on cognitions) are described; there are differences in the nature of the treatment rationales offered to clients (if indeed a rationale is provided at all); differences in style of intervention (ranging from highly directive to collaborative) appear to be striking; and differences in the emphasis placed upon the use of behavior-therapy procedures are evident. In short, the term "CBM" has as its referents a rather broad assortment of strange bedfellows.

This makes it difficult and indeed misleading to discuss CBM in general terms. To do so is to impose what Kieslar (1966) has characterized as a "myth of uniformity" on CBM. As research progresses, it would not be surprising to discover that some of the evolving CBM conceptualizations and treatment procedures are productive, while others are not. There is reason to believe that this crucial point is sometimes overlooked. For instance, in his review, Ledwidge (1978) conducts a "box score" comparison of the relative efficacy of "traditional behavior therapy" versus "cognitive-behavior modification." We regard such a dichotomous classification as a misguided oversimplification of a very complex body of literature (see Ledwidge, 1978, 1979; Mahoney & Kazdin, 1979; Meichenbaum, 1979; and Wilson, 1980, for a full discussion of Ledwidge's review). In our view, such oversimplification obscures the rich diversity that exists in behavior therapy (Wilson, 1979) as well as among CBM procedures.

The second major point we wish to emphasize in describing the nature of CBM is that CBM approaches incorporate behavior-therapy procedures. There appears to be a misconception that a clear discontinuity exists between behavior therapy and CBM. Ledwidge (1978), for example, while acknowledging that "CBM therapists include behavioral components" when conducting therapy, goes on to declare that "despite these behavioral constituents . . . the primary focus of each of these methods is on thought processes" (p. 357). By the end of his paper, he is referring to CBM as "this new verbal therapy" (p. 372). However, the researchers most closely identified with the development of most CBM approaches appear to regard behavioral procedures as *central* to the therapy process. An excerpt from Mahoney and Kazdin's response to Ledwidge offers an interesting perspective on this point:

According to Bandura—and many other persons labeled "cognitive-behavior modifiers"—the processes that govern human adjustment (and maladjustment) are cognitive in nature (i.e., they involve attentional processes, aspects of information storage and retrieval, etc.). However, in almost comic irony, it now appears that behavioral procedures may be among the most powerful methods for activating those cognitive processes. Thus, if any clear distinction can be drawn, the major difference between cognitive and less cognitive behavior modifiers does not lie in their therapeutic procedures so much as in their rationale and selection of a given procedure in an individual case. (Mahoney & Kazdin, 1979, p. 1045)

Research by Bandura and his colleagues, in particular, has suggested that behaviorally oriented intervention procedures result in greater positive change in both objective and subjective measures of psychological functioning that do verbal, imaginal, or vicarious interventions (Bandura, 1977; Bandura, Blanchard, & Ritter, 1969). However, Bandura (1977) argues that the therapeutic impact of these behavioral procedures is mediated by alterations at a cognitive level: The change *procedures* are behavioral in focus, but the *process* of change is viewed as largely cognitive. The behavioral procedures are seen as more potent than are purely cognitive procedures for eliciting change in cognitive self-regulating processes, which in turn result in constructive behavioral changes.

It is instructive to consider CBM in historical perspective to appreciate further the blurred distinction between behavior therapy and CBM approaches. It is noteworthy that learning theorists and the behavior therapists who have built on their work have not denied the role of cognition in the process of behavior change. Techniques such as desensitization, flooding, covert conditioning, and anxiety-relief conditioning have all attended explicitly to modifying or making therapeutic use of the client's imagery and self-statements. Originally, cognitions were conceptualized in terms of conditioning theories: Cognitions were seen as responses or response-produced stimuli that were thought to be subject to the same "laws of learning" as overt behavior was.

This point of view is reflected, for instance, in the writings of Dollard and Miller (1950) and Skinner (1953). Dollard and Miller set out to translate Freudian psychoanalytic procedures into terms of learning theory. In doing so, they indicated that the client's higher mental processes, such as the labels he or she uses in a situation, can be viewed as "cue-producing responses" that may facilitate or inhibit subsequent responses. The labels the client employs are viewed as learned responses that in turn may be stimuli for succeeding responses. Within such a mediational view, the explicit use of learning techniques to teach new and more adaptive labels can be effective in altering the individual's emotional reaction (e.g., in reducing anxiety). Dollard and Miller suggested that an important consequence of changing labels and reducing anxiety is an increase in the client's problem-solving capacities. The client's newly learned "cue-producing response" leads to significant behavior change.

Skinner's operant-conditioning model of self-control contends that individuals control their own behavior in precisely the same way that they would control the behavior of anyone else—namely, through manipulation of the variables of which the behavior is a function. For example, to decrease an undesirable personal behavior, an individual makes the undesirable response less probable by altering the rewards and punishments on which it depends. A behavior therapist with an operant orientation might ask this question: What is the immediate effect of a disruptive thought or image (e.g., a depresssing or anxiety-arousing idea)? Frequently, the immediate effect is that the person labels himself or herself depressed or anxious and hence feels that he or she is incapable of continuing work. Often, the act of thinking such thoughts eventually leads to escape from an unpleasant situation, and, thus reinforced by the termination and future avoidance of an aversive stimulus, the act is maintained. The operant behavior theapist suggests that the client's thinking processes can be influenced significantly by systematically manipulating the consequences of these processes.

Thus, within a framework of learning theory, there has been a tradition of viewing the client's cognitions as behaviors to be modified in their own right, subject to the same "laws of learning" as are overt nonprivate behaviors. The behavioral techniques that have been used to modify overt behaviors, such as operant and aversive conditioning, have been viewed as appropriate to altering covert processes. In fact, Homme (1965) has offered the concept of "coverants" (covert operants) to describe covert behavior within a learning framework.

Many of us now identified with CBM originally subscribed to the conditioning conceptualization of behavior-therapy techniques and to the analyses of cognition offered by conditioning theory (although others associated with CBM were originally trained in more traditional fields of psychotherapy rather than in behavior therapy). However, we gradually became uneasy about the adequacy of conditioning models and at the same time began to believe that cognitive processes were central to the process of therapeutic change. Many factors influenced the shift. Breger and McGaugh (1965) published an influential critique in which they challenged the appropriateness of accounting for the efficacy of behavior therapy in terms of conditioning theory. In 1969, Bandura published his classic *Principles of Behavior Modification,* in which he challenged unmediated conditioning models on empirical grounds. The criticism of unmediated (i.e., noncognitive) conditioning models has accelerated in recent years (see Bandura, 1974; Brewer, 1974; Mahoney, 1974; Meichenbaum, 1977). The swell of criticism now has reached the point where even studies of eyeblink conditioning apparently have fallen to the cognitive ax (Jennings, Crosland, Loveless, Murray, & George, 1978; Maltzman, 1977). In order to underscore this point, we offer the following quotes from the Maltzman article, which appeared in the June 1977 issue of the *Journal of Experimental Psychology: General:*

It now seems apparent that classical conditioning in normal adults, as ordinarily studied in the laboratory, is a consequence of thinking rather than vice versa. . . . The GSR-OR (orienting reflex) is generated by the participants' covert problem-solving activities. It is not a response elicited by the CS signal as the result of the establishment of an association; it is a consequence of the discovered significance of the CS as a signal for the UCS. (Maltzman, 1977, pp. 112, 113)

Whether we should go so far as to conclude that there is *no convincing evidence for operant or classical conditioning* in adult humans, as Brewer (1974) does, we are not sure. But it is clear that fundamental questions are being raised about the appropriateness of conditioning models. We would emphasize in passing that, to the degree that all learning is cognitive (as opposed to nonmediated), the conceptual distinction between behavior therapy and CBM seems to be eroded.

While the assault on nonmediated conditioning theories was taking shape, clinical research was beginning to suggest that the efficacy of traditional behavior-therapy procedures could be enhanced by incorporating cognitive training with behavioral interventions (Meichenbaum, 1977) or by presenting the intervention as skill training (Goldfried, 1971). Self-instructional training and stress-inoculation training (see Meichenbaum, 1977, for a detailed review), as well as training in coping skills (see reviews by Goldfried, 1977, 1979), were thus initiated.

At present, then, we find ourselves in the position of having a number of CBM techniques that focus on altering behavior and cognition. These techniques do not easily lend themselves to conceptualization in terms of conditioning theory. (Of all the approaches that are apt to be associated with CBM, covert conditioning appears to be most amenable to conceptualization in conditioning terms. However, a critical review by Kazdin, 1977, casts doubt upon the adequacy of a conditioning conceptualization for even this approach.) In any case, conditioning theory is seen by many as moribund. A major current challenge involves developing a comprehensive theory of learning and the change process into which CBM techniques may be integrated.

As Wilson (1979) has noted, there appears to be considerable affinity between CBM and social learning theory as developed by Bandura (1969, 1974, 1977). Bandura's theory takes into account the role of environmental stimuli in eliciting and maintaining behavior. However, the individual is not viewed as a passive respondent to environmental events. The role of cognitive processes in selectively attending to and interpreting the environment is emphasized. Cognitions are also given a central role in the form of self-regulating processes that influence behavior. Bandura's model, then, is compatible with CBM techniques in that, like most CBM approaches, it takes into account environmental stimuli and consequences, overt behavior, and cognitive processes. The theoretical model also includes a concept of "reciprocal determinism": A continuous interplay between behavioral, cognitive, and environmental variables is envisioned. This model has much in common with Meichenbaum's (Meichenbaum, 1977; Meichenbaum & Butler, 1980; Meichenbaum, Butler, & Gruson, 1981) conceptualization of psychological functioning as involving interactions among cognitive structures, cognitive processes, overt behaviors, and their environmental consequences. In our judgement, a major challenge at present involves working out a model of psychological functioning that is comprehensive, integrative, and consistent with available data. Our own theoretical efforts have been directed toward the related, but more modest, objective of attempting to formulate a comprehensive cognitive–behavioral model of the change process, as discussed below.

In closing this section on the nature and origins of CBM, we would like to emphasize that we do *not* see the development of CBM as a revolution or paradigm shift. Instead, we see the field of behavior change as beginning to focus once more on concerns that have always been central to psychology. Victor Raimy (1975), in his book *Misunderstandings of the Self,* has traced the roots of cognitive–semantic therapy. The tradition includes Immanuel Kant, who proposed that mental illness occurs when a person fails to correct his "private sense" with "common sense." More than a century later, Alfred Adler viewed this "private sense" as "mistaken opinions" that underlie neurotic behavior, while H. S. Sullivan highlighted the role of "parataxic distortions" and "consensual validity" in the adaptive process. Raimy traces the recurrent past of the cognitive theme through the notions of the hypnotists in the 19th century who emphasized the role of "morbid ideas," to Paul Dubois's notion (1909) of "incorrect" ideas and Pierre Janet's notion (1907) of "fixed ideas" as contributing to maladaptive behavior. Modern-day versions of this tradition are found in the writings of Snygg and Combs (1949), who emphasized the role of "inadequate differentiations" as contributing to psychological disturbance, while Rotter (1954) spoke of the role of "erroneous expectations"; Kelly (1954) of "disordered constructs"; Frank (1961/1974) of "erroneous assumptions and faulty assumptive worlds"; and Ellis (1962) of "irrational ideas." Many other names (ranging from Epictetus to Korzybski and Horney) could be added to this list of semantic therapists who have suggested or implied the role of cognitive factors as a contributor to maladaptive behavior.

The present CBM treatment approach combines the clinical concerns of such cognitive–semantic philosophers and therapists with the technology of behavior therapy. We feel that such a combination will result in more effective treatment interventions, the critics notwithstanding. It is for future research to determine whether our optimism is well founded. We will now consider what we see as current, central conceptual issues in the field.

COGNITIVE-BEHAVIOR MODIFICATION WITH CHILDREN

Our discussion of CBM focuses first on issues pertaining to CBM interventions with children, and then on issues related to CBM with adults. We believe that at present the field requires (1) clarification of the conditions under which CBM treatments are likely to be effective; (2) understanding of ways in which CBM procedures can be integrated with nonpsychological interventions (e.g., medication) in clinical settings; (3) strategies for promoting maintenance and generalization of therapeutic gains; and (4) analysis of processes whereby CBM procedures exert their influence. Our discussion of CBM interventions is organized around these issues.

The impetus for the work on CBM interventions with children has several origins. One primary source was mounting evidence that available treatment programs, especially behavior-management procedures, were *not* fostering changes that were generalizable and durable. Problems with generalization and maintenance have plagued attempts by those who have used operant procedures to reduce children's disruptive behavior or to increase appropriate, task-relevant behavior. (See Coates & Thoresen, 1980; Conway & Bucher, 1976; Emery & Margolin, 1977; Keeley, Shemberg, & Carbonell, 1976; and Wahler, Berland, & Coe, 1979, for review and discussion.) The hope was that by supplementing behavioral procedures with cognitive interventions, such as self-instructional training or social problem solving, the efficacy, generalization, and maintenance of our interventions could be enhanced. This hope was predicated on the assumption that if a therapist "changed the child" by training self-regulatory cognitive skills, the intervention would have greater impact than would a procedure that influenced the child only indirectly by controlling environmental contingencies. The goal was to train the child to regulate his or her behavior so that he or she would act more effectively in the environment across situations. We return to the issues of generalization and maintenance later in this section.

The studies that were initially conducted focused primarily on impulsive, hyperactive, and aggressive children, generally in a laboratory setting. Results of these studies have been encouraging. (See recent reviews by Craighead, Craighead-Wilcoxon, & Meyers, 1978; Karoly, 1977; Kendall & Finch, 1979; Mash & Dalby, 1978; Meichenbaum & Asarnow, 1979; Rosenthal, 1980.) Although these early findings have been promising, results do not give rise to a sense of complacency. It is becoming apparent that we are beginning to be more sophisticated in our understanding of CBM procedures in that we are starting to develop an appreciation of the limitations of our procedures. It is to be hoped that increased understanding of conditions under which CBM procedures fail will lead us to take steps to ensure that requisite conditions for success are met before and during treatment interventions.

At present, there is not enough data to establish definitively the potential and limitations of CBM procedures. However, some broad themes do seem to be emerging. Recent reports (Higa, 1975; Robin, Armel, & O'Leary, 1975; Wein & Nelson, 1975) have suggested that self-instructional training may be most appropriate for children who have elemental performance skills in their repertoires, but who fail to regulate their own behavior appropriately. It is quite likely that training in self-regulatory skills will not promote improved performance unless the subskills requisite for successful execution of the target behaviors are in a child's repertoire. Meichenbaum (1977) has emphasized the importance of conducting a detailed analysis of task-related subskills before embarking on self-regulatory treatment, and has provided suggestions for conducting such subskill assessments. Both Kendall (1977) and Lloyd (1981) have also commented on the importance of ensuring that performance-related subskills are in a child's repertoire before initiating self-regulatory training.

Friedling and O'Leary (1979) have reported recently that they were unable to replicate Bornstein and Quevillon's finding (1976) of improved classroom behavior following self-instructional training with impulsive children. While Friedling and O'Leary point out a number of potentially important methodological differences between the two studies that might account for the difference in outcome, we would like to highlight just a few of their suggestions that are pertinent to the present discussion. They note that it might be important to identify and alter existing maladaptive or idiosyncratic self-statements rather than merely to train new and presumably adaptive private speech. As Friedling and O'Leary indicate, Thorpe, Amatu, Blakey, and Burns (1976) demonstrated that practice in identifying maladaptive self-statements effectively reduced speech anxiety among high-school students. Indeed, Thorpe *et al.* concluded from their study that "insight" into unproductive thinking may be a more important ingredient of self-instructional training than overt rehearsal of positive self-statements might be. Further research is required to clarify the value of explicitly identifying and altering negative private speech prior to undertaking training of positive self-statements. At present, it seems possible that identification of existing negative self-statements might enhance the efficacy of CBM procedures.

Friedling and O'Leary go on to suggest that "teaching children why and when to use self-instruction, and ensuring that they do, may be as important as teaching them how to self-instruct" (1979, p. 218). It is quite possible that CBM with children would be more successful if training included explicit coaching and practice in the appropriate use of the skills being trained. Intuitively, it seems reasonable to believe that this might be so.

While negative findings of the sort just described may be helpful for clarifying the conditions that must be met for CBM to be effective, logical analysis, clinical experience, and common sense also suggest some guidelines. Kendall (1977) has outlined some considerations that should be taken into account prior to initiating CBM interventions. Kendall emphasizes the importance of tailoring CBM interventions to the cognitive capacity of the child (pretraining requisite skills if necessary). He also points out that the therapist is more likely to be successful if he or she arranges intervention in a way that maintains the child's interest and attention and fosters a positive relationship with the therapist. In this regard, Kendall observes that one investigator who found self-instructional training ineffective with impulsive children (Weinreich, 1975) reported that treatment efficacy appeared to be vitiated by problems with incentives (scheduling problems and absence of contingent incentives). (It might be noted parenthetically that Meichenbaum (1977) has emphasized the importance of maintaining an animated and enthusiastic rather than a mechanical, "rote" attitude during training to hold interest and attention.) Kendall concludes his paper by considering training conditions that might be expected to enhance generalization: He advocates the use of training materials and settings that will maximize the likelihood of change in the target problem outside the treatment situation; he recommends using individualized rather than predetermined self-statements to ensure that the private speech trained is compatible with the style of the individual child; and he encourages the use of conceptual (i.e., general) rather than concrete (i.e., task-specific) labels to maximize generalization. We anticipate that training metacognitive skills (see below) will also enhance generalization.

The preceding discussion suggests that while some of the initial CBM interventions may have been somewhat naive, we are becoming more sophisticated as they acquire data and experience. The reader is directed to Kendall (1977) and to Meichenbaum (1977) for a more detailed discussion of ways in which CBM procedures with children may be implemented effectively. We anticipate that research over the next few years will enable us to clarify further the limitations of our procedures and to modify our interventions so as to minimize these limitations.

As the field develops and CBM moves from the laboratory to the clinic, we are starting to realize that we face the challenge of finding ways of integrating CBM procedures with other interventions. As Keogh and Glover (1980) indicate, different interventions such as those based on medication, behavioral, and cognitive regimens influence different aspects of performance and are only selectively effective. In clinical work, it is therefore quite common for a variety of interventions to be used in combination. Henker, Whalen, and Hinshaw (1981) have called attention to the fact that all forms of intervention—pharmacological, behavioral and cognitive—have message value, or, to use their terms, "cognitive sequelae and emanative effects." In a very thoughtful fashion, Henker *et al.* highlight the important role of the child's cognitive reactions (especially attributional processes) that follow from any intervention. As therapists introduce CBM techniques to clinical settings, they would do well to be concerned with (and to investigate systematically) these complex reactions.

As we noted at the beginning of this section, CBM procedures were developed largely in response to a concern with developing interventions that would have generalized and enduring results. The issues of generalization and maintenance of therapeutic improvement represent ongoing concerns. Indeed, after reviewing the state of the art of CBM with children, Meichenbaum and Asarnow arrived at the following conclusion:

In summary, as one surveys the cognitive-behavior modification literature, the evidence for treatment efficacy for children who have self-control problems is promising. Evidence for treatment generalization, however, especially across response modes and settings, is less convincing and often equivocal. *Perhaps more careful consideration must be directed at what we mean and expect when we seek generalization.* (Meichenbaum & Asarnow, 1979, p. 15; emphasis added)

As Baer, Wolf, and Risley (1968) and Stokes and Baer (1977) have indicated, generalization must be programmed rather than assumed. We anticipate that the next decade of CBM studies will investigate factors that enhance and inhibit generalization and maintenance of treatment effects.

Some interesting possibilities are beginning to emerge. Work on metacognitive training with retarded children (Borkowski & Cavanaugh, 1979; A. Brown & Campione, 1978) is of particular interest. J. Brown (1974) has outlined a series of steps that seems to be required for successful cognitive training with retardates. Since the outline appears to have application with populations other than retarded children, we review it (with some adaptation) in detail. Brown recommends that the therapist proceed as follows:

1. Analyze the desired target behavior into its component strategy and capacity requirements. The implication is that strategy training may have to be preceded by or accompanied by skill training, if deficits in requisite skills are discovered.
2. Test for spontaneous use of necessary strategies for performing the task. If they are absent or deficient, systematically train their effective use. We would add that if maladaptive strategies are observed, these might be identified and altered at this stage. Training tasks should approximate "real-world" demands as closely as possible. Graduated training that proceeds from simple to complex tasks might be useful.
3. Determine that acquired strategies are maintained over time before making a decision to terminate training.
4. Demonstrate that the child can transfer or adapt the strategy to a variety of tasks before discontinuing training.
5. Devise and train superordinate (or metacognitive) strategies that enable the child to monitor, regulate, and develop his or her own production of strategies, and to evaluate realistically the interaction between the task demands and his or her own capacities and repertoire of skills.
6. Take into account and address any motivational problems that emerge. Sternberg (in press) has suggested that once a repertoire of strategic skills is

acquired, motivation may increase "spontaneously." However, since there is no assurance that this will occur, it may be necessary to attempt to boost motivation directly. Adopting a playful attitude and presenting tasks as games, and ensuring that treatment does not occur during times that require students to miss favorite activities, represent just a couple of ways in which motivational issues might be addressed.

We would add the following guidelines for fostering generalization to Brown's prescriptions.

1. Insure that the purpose and rationale of the treatment is explained to the child as fully as possible.
2. Provide explicit feedback about the effectiveness with which the child implements the strategy.
3. Explicitly encourage the child to generalize the strategy to certain types of tasks or situations. This coaching might be supplemented by having the child enumerate situations where the strategy could be used and having him or her imaging using the strategy in a variety of situations.
4. Conduct training in multiple settings. This may involve training other agents (e.g., teachers, parents) to prompt or model self-regulating behaviors in "natural" settings.

Borkowski and Cavanaugh (1979) have summarized many of the objectives that we need to accomplish in order to develop effective interventions that will generalize:

First, we need to identify several strategies each of which is operative in different learning situations. Second, we need to train children on several strategies, making sure that they know when and how to apply them. Third, we need to train the instructional package so that common elements between training and generalization contexts are evident, and distractors minimal. Fourth, we need to develop child-generated search routines, probably through the use of self-instructional procedures, that encourage the child to analyze a task, scan his or her available strategic repertoire, and match the demands of the task with an appropriate strategy and retrieval plan. Fifth, we need to instruct children in such a way that we utilize whatever skills they possess, in order to bring each child to an awareness of the advantage of executive monitoring and decision-making in solving problems. Finally, we may need to reinforce, in a very explicit way, successful executive functioning in order for it to come under the control of natural environmental contingencies, such as the child's good feelings about solving a difficult problem. (p. 54)

As research into CBM enters its second decade, increased attention is being devoted to the issues of generalization and maintenance (e.g., see Kendall & Wilcox, 1978). The less than compelling evidence of generalized, enduring changes following CBM interventions with children may be due in large part to the excessively narrow approach to training that we have taken (Sternberg, 1981). It is noteworthy that concerns with generalization and maintenance of treatment effects also arise with CBM treatments directed toward adults. The cognitive–behavioral work on relapse prevention among adults being conducted by Marlatt and Gordon (1980) is particularly noteworthy. It is quite possible that the principles of relapse prevention being developed for adults may be adapted for use with children, complementing the guidelines we have reviewed here. As we attempt to develop a technology of behavior change, the issues of generalization and maintenance continue to be the biggest challenges that face this attempt.

The history of CBM has been primarily a history of "technological" developments, and our discussion up to this point has concentrated on technological issues. However, we should not lose sight of the interplay between technology and theory. Most of the technological innovations were originally inspired in part by theoretical research. For instance, the "self-instructional training" paradigm, and the "stress-inoculation" paradigm that evolved from it, were partly inspired by the work of Vygotsky (1962) and Luria (1961, 1969). As our field has developed, we have become preoccupied with applied issues. We stand to enrich our field if we remain mindful that theoretical developments in developmental, social, and clinical areas may provide new technological inspirations. Conversely, we should bear in mind that technological explorations have theoretical implications. In applied work, we circle around a number of fundamental theoretical issues. For instance, how are interpersonal instructions—modeled by a therapist, teacher, or parent—transformed into the child's own private speech and thought? How does private speech come to influence, the child's overt behavior on the one hand, and his or her cognitive structures (i.e., beliefs, attributions, and expectations) on the other hand? What is the process by which conscious regulation of behavior becomes "automatic"? Under what circumstances does "automatically" regulated behavior become consciously and intentionally regulated? Vygotsky (1962) observed in his book *Thought and Language* that the processes of "internalization" and "abbreviation" should not be viewed simply as faded speech; instead, he maintained that qualitative transformations occur as interpersonal speech becomes internalized as thought. As we continue to conduct CBM research, we have excellent opportunities to study the basic transformation processes (e.g., see Wertsch, 1979). If we can explicate the means by which interventions exert their influence, we will profit both technologically and and theoretically.

A recent theoretical development that promises to be quite valuable is the emerging concept of "metacognition." "Metacognition" refers to "thinking about thinking," or, to use A. Brown's phrase, "knowing about knowing.'' The concept of metacognition is still emerging, and its referents are still being elucidated (e.g., A. Brown, 1978; Flavell, 1979; Meichenbaum, Burland, Gruson, & Cameron, in press). An extended illustration first presented by Flavell (1976) nicely captures the essence of metacognitive activity:

Metacognition refers to one's knowledge concerning one's own cognitive processes and products or anything related to them, e.g., the learning-relevant properties of information or data. For example, I am engaging in metacognition (metamemory, metalearning, metaattention, metalanguage, or whatever) if I notice that I am having more trouble learning A than B; if it occurs to me that I had better scrutinize each and every alternative in any multiple-choice type task situation before deciding which is the best one; if I sense that I had better make a note of D because I may forget it . . . Metacognition refers, among other things, to the active monitoring and consequent regulation and orchestration of these processes in relation to the cognitive objects or data on which they bear, usually in the service of some concrete goal or objective. (p. 232)

The concept of metacognition may be construed as being related to processes that in other contexts have been referred to as "executive processes" (Belmont & Butterfield, 1977), "executive routines" (Neisser, 1967), "cognitive strategies" (Gagne & Briggs, 1974), "self-management behaviors" (Skinner, 1968), "plans" (G. Miller, Galanter, & Pribram, 1960), and "control processes" (Atkinson & Shiffrin, 1968).

Preliminary studies have examined metacognition in relation to attentional processes (P. Miller & Bigi, 1979), reading comprehension (Ryan, 1981), self-control (Mischel, Mischel, & Hood, 1978), communication (Markman, 1977), and other areas. (See Flavell, 1979, and Meichenbaum *et al.,* in press, for more extended reviews and references.) From a clinical perspective, what is exciting about this line of research is that a variety of clinical populations, including children with learning disabilities (Kauffman & Hallahan, 1979; Torgesen, 1977), mental retardation (Belmont & Butterfield, 1977; J. Brown, 1974; Campione & Brown, 1977), and hyperactivity (Douglas & Peters, 1981), have been identified as having metacognitive deficits.

Researchers with a bent toward CBM have been involved in assessing cognitions, and have reported findings suggesting that cognitive factors may contribute to clinical problems in children (e.g., Spivack & Shure, 1974) and adults (e.g., Schwartz & Gottman, 1976). However, until recently these assessments focused on task-specific self-regulating (or self-impeding) cognitions. With the advent of interest in metacognition, we will undoubtedly broaden our focus and study the superordinate metacognitive processes that regulate the regulating cognitions. We look forward to the development of a taxonomy of metacognitive processes and a model of the processes that result in the ontogenetic evolution of various metacognitive functions. As we develop a clearer understanding of the range of metacognitive strategies, we may be in a position to train metacognition. One objective we can envision is to structure therapy so that the focus of treatment is on training metacognitive strategies that will enable clients (children and adults) to be "self-correcting." Thus, by teaching children (1) to analyze the problems at hand; (2) to reflect upon what they know or do not know that may be necessary for a solution; (3) to devise a plan for attacking the problem; and (4) to check and monitor their progress, metacognitive skills can be enhanced. Progress in this direction may have a salutory effect on the problems of generalization and maintenance of treatment effects described above. While we obviously are enthusiastic about the potential of conducting metacognitive assessments (and eventually metacognitive interventions), we would also emphasize that progress in this area depends upon developing reliable and valid approaches to assessing cognition.

COGNITIVE-BEHAVIOR MODIFICATION WITH ADULTS

While we cannot review outcome studies in the present context, we would like to note in passing that CBM procedures have been applied to a wide range of populations in recent years. Populations treated include clients presenting with interpersonal anxiety (e.g., Goldfried, 1977; Heppner, 1978; Lange & Jakubowski, 1976; Thorpe, 1975); test anxiety (e.g., Denney, 1980; Wine, 1980); uncontrolled anger (Novaco, 1979); pain (Turk *et al.,* in press); depression (Beck *et al.,* 1979); addictions (Marlatt & Gordon, in press; Rychtarik & Wollersheim, 1978); sexual dysfunction (Rook & Hammen, 1977); and alcohol abuse (Chaney, O'Leary, & Marlatt, 1978; Intagliata, 1978). The proliferation of applications is exciting, although again we sometimes fear that enthusiasm is disproportionate to data. (See the annual *Cognitive-Behavior Modification Newsletter;* Meichenbaum, 1975–1979.)

As we survey the diverse procedures associated with CBM that are used to treat adults, it seems that a common process occurring across procedures is that therapy consists of training the client to think and behave like a scientist. We would like to elaborate on this theme. As we indicated at the outset, CBM views cognitions, behavior, and affect as interacting domains of experience. Although these domains are seen as interacting, the rationale underlying most or all CBM procedures is that an individual's affect and behavior are largely determined by the way in which he or she construes the world. CBM therapies are intended to help the client identify, reality-test, and correct maladaptive, distorted beliefs and perceptions. In a sense, the implicit model of the individual in CBM is "the individual as a scientist." It is important to emphasize that CBM therapists do *not* see human beings as armchair philosophers who do not empirically evaluate their ideas. They attempt to guide our clients both to think and to *act* like scientists. When they come for treatment, they usually have an undifferentiated interpretation of their problems. The therapists challenge them to generate a series of alternative hypotheses, and in some cases they suggest such. They evolve with the clients a formulation of their problems in a way that attributes difficulties to self-defeating ways of thinking and behaving. A client is challenged to test out the formulation empirically both by monitoring the experience to ensure that experience is consistent with the formulation, and by altering his or her ways of thinking and behaving to establish whether this results in an alteration in the problem. In other words, therapy may be seen as a process in which the client is prompted to generate alternative hypotheses and to evaluate them by conducting experiential experiments. We deal with the process of change at length in the next section. Our purpose in developing the metaphor of "client as scientist" has been simply to suggest the commitment to this image of the individual that seems to represent a central defining characteristic of CBM approaches. Whether therapists use "rational–emotive," "cognitive," or "self-instructional" procedures, or whether they are treating anxiety as anger, a common thread that influences their objectives and therapeutic strategies is their propensity to construe clients as "scientists" and to take an evidential approach to therapy. This is evident in the following CBM model of behavior change.

TOWARD A COGNITIVE–BEHAVIORAL THEORY OF THERAPEUTIC CHANGE

Students of psychotherapy and the process of behavior change are faced with a conundrum. Many therapists, embracing a wide variety of theories and techniques, claim to be therapeutically effective. In some cases, these claims are supported empirically. Moreover, it is widely believed that behavior change also occurs as a consequence of contacts with nonprofessional persons during the course of day-to-day life. The challenge that confronts us involves formulating a theory of change that specifies the necessary and sufficient conditions that bring about change. Ideally, the theory to which we aspire should be catholic in the sense that it takes into account empirical data, regardless of the theoretical system that originally inspired the collection and interpretation of the data in question. Developing such a theory is clearly a challenge of the first magnitude. In our view, however, efforts to outline a comprehensive theory of change are desirable both for integrating existing theoretical and empirical work and also for developing a basis for a strategic, programmatic approach to research. While other authors have also outlined ingredients that they regard as central to the change process (e.g., Bandura, 1977; Frank, 1961/1974), we focus in the present chapter on developing Meichenbaum's observations (1976, 1977).

Meichenbaum (1977) has suggested that effective therapy brings about client change in three domains. First, the *behavior* of the clients (and thus the environmental reactions to the clients) are altered. Second, the clients' *private speech* and *images* are modified: the clients learn to interpret their world, themselves, and their behavior in a way that has more heuristic value than did the previous manner of interpreting; the clients also learn to use their private speech and images to regulate effective coping behaviors. In other words, the clients change what they are saying to themselves before, during, and in response to their behavioral productions. And, third, the clients' *cognitive structures*—their basic implicit assumptions and their habitual styles of thinking—are changed. This framework suggests that a comprehensive theory of change will have to account for changes in each of these areas. The outline is presented tentatively, with a sense that undoubtedly it will require extension, elaboration, and revision.

If it is accepted that effective therapy induces change in behavior, self-regulatory cognition, and cognitive structures, the challenge is to specify the clinical operations that will promote such target changes effectively. Meichenbaum (1976, 1977) has suggested that therapy may be construed as progressing through three phases. While these phases are isolated for purposes of explication, it should perhaps be stated explicitly that in practice there is considerable overlap among the three phases.

Phase 1: Self-Observation

The first step in the process of change involves training clients to be better observers of their own behavior. Virtually all forms of therapy encourage client "self-exploration" or train the client to monitor behavior and cognitions formally. This period of data collection allows therapist and client alike to define the problem and to formulate therapeutic possibilities.

There are at least two distinct processes that seem to occur during this self-observational period. First, clients become aware of pertinent data that have been previously disregarded, and they develop a more differentiated understanding of the problem. For instance, a client may learn to specify the environmental conditions under which problematic behavior is manifest. As the client "reviews the data," he or she may redefine the presenting problem (e.g., "As we've talked, it's occurred to me that my real problem is not my headaches per se; it's becoming evident that they are a byproduct of my difficulty in being assertive").

The second important process that occurs during this phase is a process of translation. As a therapist selectively responds to a client's statements, asks questions, gives homework assignments, offers interpretations, or provides explanations, the therapist implicitly or explicitly encourages the client to reconstrue the problems discussed. It is our belief that the therapist begins to impart to the client his or her own theoretical constructs, so that the client gradually comes to interpret events and experiences in terms of the theoretical constructs used by the therapist. It is being suggested that this translation process is inherent in all therapies. The translation process serves a number of therapeutically important functions. First, it provides clients with an explanation for their problems that is likely to be considerably more benign than the clients' initial interpretation of the problems. Whereas clients may have interpreted debilitating anxiety as symptomatic of an impending "mental breakdown," they come to view it as the result of unwarranted transference, conditioning processes, or irrational beliefs, for example; the particular constructs used depend upon the theoretical bents of therapists. These more benign interpretations are likely to be quite reassuring. Second, the translation generally recasts the problems in a form that renders them amenable to solution: Therapists are committed to conceptualizing problems in terms that point the way to effective intervention. This provides a basis for clients to move from feeling helpless and hopeless to experiencing a sense of positive anticipation. A number of observers (e.g., Frank, 1961/1974; Seligman, 1975) have suggested that the fostering of hope is a central, vital ingredient in the therapeutic process. It is our belief that helping clients reconceptualize their problems in a form that suggests viable solutions is one of the best ways of fostering hope and one of the key challenges that faces therapists.

We should emphasize at this point that we do *not* assume that any therapeutic conceptualization will prove to be as good as any other conceptualization for bringing about change. At present, practitioners have the responsibility of interpreting a somewhat ambiguous literature in such a way as to arrive at their own conclusions regarding what sorts of conceptualizations and interventions are most appropriate for particular sorts of clinical problems. We feel that pertinent data are already available to guide clinicians, even though it is obvious that the discipline is a long way from providing complete, compelling data upon which to base clinical decisions. Given this ambiguity, clinicians should look for conceptualizations that have been found empirically to result in specific behavioral changes that may be transferred to real-life situations.

If our analysis has heuristic value, and the translation process is central to therapeutic endeavors, the practical challenge that faces the clinician is that of effectively orchestrating this translation process. Some therapists are very didactic and directive, and they seem to force upon clients a particular conceptualization by the power of their personalities, jargon, or positions. In some instances, this "hard-sell" approach may prove successful. Therapists must, however, be concerned not only with their clients' self-statements and attributions concerning their presenting problems, but also with those statements and attributions concerning the therapists and the therapeutic process (see Cameron, 1978; Meichenbaum & Gilmore, in press). If a client construes a therapist as dogmatic and intimidating, he or she presumably will be disinclined to express misunderstanding or reservations about a conceptualization and may "go through the motions" of therapy, or terminate prematurely, or both. An alternative way for therapists to proceed is to establish a *collaborative relationship* with their clients. Clients and therapists work together to identify and interpret pertinent data, and they cooperate in evolving a common conceptualization of the problem. An important advantage of proceeding in this way is that it increases the likelihood that therapists will develop a clearer sense of their clients' construct system.

Once clients have defined their problems in more differentiated and relatively benign terms that point the way to effective solutions, a sense of reassurance and hope develop, and the groundwork for more concrete change has been laid.

Phase 2: Developing New Thoughts and Behaviors

Habitual ways of thinking and behaving do not seem to change abruptly with clients. As clients begin to redefine their problem(s), their internal dialogues sometimes reflect the old ways of thinking and sometimes the new. The clients may have to learn to execute complex new behaviors (such as those called for in effective interpersonal communication) or to produce familiar behaviors in situations where such behaviors had been inhibited previously. It requires time and practice for clients to execute these new behaviors smoothly and with some consistency, and therapists must be concerned with the nature of the clients' internal dialogues in response to the failures and successes of implementing these new behaviors.

In the present model, the objectives of the second stage of therapy are (1) to continue the clients' reconceptualization of their problems; (2) to ensure that the clients can execute the behaviors requisite for dealing effectively with their problems; (3) to ensure that the clients learn to monitor their thoughts and behaviors during daily activities; and (4) to establish that the clients gradually implement their new ways of thinking and behavior with more consistency. In short, the essential goal of this phase of therapy is to induce clients to change both cognitions and behaviors as they engage in daily affairs.

The relationship between cognitive change and behavior change appears to be complex and interactive. Positive behavior change promotes positive cognitive change, and positive cognitive change gives rise to positive behavior change. Behavior change may induce a number of therapeutically important cognitive changes. If a client with a behavioral deficit acquires the capability to execute a behavior smoothly (delivering assertive statements convincingly, actively listening to and drawing out a spouse or other person when arguments arise, etc.) through modeling, role playing, or *in vivo* practice with coaching and feedback, the client is almost certain to think of himself or herself as more resourceful and better able to deal with problems. This self-perception of increased resourcefulness heightens a sense of control (Frank, 1961/1974; Seligman, 1975) and self-efficacy (Bandura, 1977); these cognitive changes, coupled with the client's newly established behavioral skills, increase the probability that the client will behave differently in problem situations. Moreover, Lazarus (1966) has theorized that the amount of stress individuals experience in response to a threatening stimulus is directly proportionate not only to the threatening qualities of the stimulus situation, but also to the extent to which the individuals see themselves as lacking resources to cope with the threat. Lazarus's analysis suggests that persons who have acquired relevant coping behaviors will interpret previously threatening stimuli as less threatening. In brief, if clients acquire new behavioral skills, they are likely to experience an increased sense of optimism and self-efficacy, which in turn increases the likelihood that they will deal with problem situations directly and effectively. The clients are also likely to experience less stress in previously threatening situations, since they now interpret these as less threatening on the strength of their newly acquired behavioral resources.

Once a client has acquired a new behavior, it is crucial for the therapist to arrange, as far as possible, for the client to try out the behavior under conditions that will enhance his or her self-statements pertaining to competence and self-efficacy. Bandura (1977) has suggested that a person's sense of self-efficacy requires not only confidence that he or she can produce the required behavior, but also a belief that the desired outcome will be elicited when the behavior is executed. Ideally, it would seem desirable for the therapist to arrange for the client to engage in the new behavior (1) *in vivo;* (2) where there is a high probability that the behavior will evoke the desired response; and (3) under conditions that lead the client to attribute his or her success to his or her own capability rather than to some external circumstance (see Bandura, 1977).

The preceding discussion is intended to make the general point that behavioral changes induced by the therapist may give rise to therapeutically desirable cognitive changes. Indeed, as noted previously, it has been suggested that the most effective way to modify cognitions may be to modify behavior (Mahoney, 1979).

It seems clear, however, that cognitive changes also give rise to behavioral changes. Due to space limitations, discussions of this point must be more brief than we might wish, and we focus here on just one way in which we think that cognition exerts a key influence on behavior. If clients are to modify their behavior, they must "catch themselves" when they are beginning old, well-rehearsed, maladaptive behavioral sequences and "remind themselves" that they now have alternative ways of behaving. In other words, the clients must monitor themselves and use their private speech and images to regulate behavior, at least until the new behavioral sequences become automatic. A key to successful therapeutic change appears to inhere in clients' learning to monitor themselves closely and to use the incipient low-intensity components of maladaptive behavior sequences as signals to initiate cognitions and behaviors incompatible with the old sequences. In order to achieve this, therapists may find it valuable to clarify with clients which aspects of the maladaptive behavioral sequences might effectively serve to "cue" production of the new, incompatible responses. It would seem desirable to find cues that are salient for clients and that occur early in the maladaptive response sequences (i.e., before affect has intensified and before other persons in the environment have begun their usual complementary reactions to the clients' maladaptive behavioral chain). It may also be helpful to develop with clients specific reorienting self-statements that switch them out of the old sequences and into the new.

Phase 3: Cognitions Concerning Change

According to our model, the first phase of therapy is concerned with defining clients' problems in terms of a framework that makes the problems amenable to solution. The second phase is concerned with actually promoting cognitive and behavioral change. The tasks of the third phase, to which we now turn, are to consolidate the changes, to promote generalization, and to lay a foundation for maintenance of the changes. Our assumption is that the way in which clients interpret the changes they have made will influence the degree to which changes are generalized and maintained.

In general, therapists would like to have clients regard themselves as having changed as persons as a result of therapy. This implies that (1) the clients recognize that a meaningful change has occurred, and (2) the clients attribute this change to an alteration in themselves instead of attributing it to external circumstances. Clients are more likely to see "real" changes if there are demonstrable changes not only in the relationship with their therapist (these changes can easily be attributed to the efforts of the therapists, the special relationship existing in therapy, etc.), but also in their daily functioning outside the therapy sessions. This is not intended as an attack on therapeutic approaches that focus on the relationship between therapist and client. However, it is doubtful that clients will perceive "significant" change occurring if they are not seeing changes in functioning in the course of daily activity as well. Even if changes are taking place outside therapy, it is not clear that the clients will spontaneously notice this. By having clients note and discuss changes occurring in the "real" world, therapists may encourage the clients to collect and remain mindful of "data" that can reasonably lead them to the conclusion that they are indeed changing. Behavior therapists have long emphasized that collection of such data is of value not only to clients, but also to therapists as they attempt to gauge progress in order to determine whether the therapeutic strategy is promoting change.

Given that the clients are aware of change occurring, it is important that the clients attribute change to themselves. Therapists may encourage such self-attribution in at least two ways. First, they may lay the groundwork for such attributions early in treatment by conceptualizing therapy as an educational, skill-training process. Second, whenever clients report positive alterations in their experience, it may be advantageous for therapists to encourage the clients to analyze in detail how they brought about the changes. The objective here is not only to have the clients make self-attributions, but also to ensure that they have a clear conceptual grasp of how they brought about the changes; presumably, they will be in a better position to engage in comparable performances in the future if they have developed coping strategies out of their own experience.

Enhanced treatment maintenance is likely to result if clients anticipate intermittent relapses. Anxiety, marital conflict, depression, poor eating habits, and most of the problems with which clients present are pervasive, commonly shared experiences in Western society. Even if clients are successfully treated, they are likely to reexperience their problems to some degree after therapy ends. Medical treatment, which aims ideally to provide permanent symptomatic relief by eradicating underlying pathology, represents the implicit model that most people probably have in mind when they seek "treatment" in this culture. If clients in psychological therapy expect to become and remain symptom-free, they are likely to react negatively to relapses that occur during and after treatment. It is easy for the clients to interpret such failures as evidence that "the treatment is not effective," or "the therapist is not competent," or "I am not capable of really changing, I'm just my same old self." It may be helpful to have clients anticipate relapses and to anticipate how they will cope with the problem behavior when these recur (Marlatt & Gordon, 1980). In our CBM skills-training interventions, we emphasize that recurrence of presenting problems is normal and should be expected. What therapy aims to change are clients' responses to problems as they arise; the goal is to have the clients acquire ways of thinking and behaving that help them cope productively with issues on an ongoing basis. When relapses occur, we want clients to interpret this as a signal for coping, as opposed to interpreting relapse as evidence of failure and an occasion for "catastrophizing." Factors that may influence client cognitions about the change process have been reviewed in more detail by Cameron (1978) and by Meichenbaum and Gilmore (in press).

In short, what is being suggested is an "evidential" theory of change, by which therapists help the clients generate, collect, and reconstrue data. The focus of therapy is on training cognitive and behavior skills that lead to alterations in the clients' behavior and private speech and ultimately to changes in the clients' cognitive structures. The clients are encouraged to review continually the evidence that they are changing, and to attribute the changes to alterations that they have made in their behavior and cognitions. Thus, therapists not only are concerned about the nature of clients' inferences, thinking styles, and conceptualization processes, but are concerned equally about the adequacy of the clients' behavioral and interpersonal repertoires and the resultant consequences. In this way, CBM reflects the marriage of the clinical concerns of cognitive–semantic therapists and the technology of behavior therapy—an integrative approach.

REFERENCES

Allport, G. W. *Becoming*. New Haven: Yale University Press, 1955.

Atkinson, R., & Shiffrin, R. Human memory: A proposed system and its control processes. In K. Spence & J. Spence (Eds.), *The psychology of learning and motivation* (Vol. 2). New York: Academic Press, 1968.

Baer, D., Wolf, M., & Risley, T. Some current dimensions of applied behavior analysis. *Journal of Applied Behavior Analysis*, 1968, *1*, 91–97.

Bandura, A. *Principles of behavior modification*. New York: Holt, Rinehart & Winston, 1969.

Bandura, A. Behavior theory and models of man. *American Psychologist*, 1974, *29*, 859–869.

Bandura, A. Self-efficacy: Toward a unifying theory of behavior change. *Psychological Review*, 1977, *89*, 191–215.

Bandura, A. The self-system in reciprocal determinism. *American Psychologist*, 1979, *33*, 344–358.

Bandura, A., Blanchard, E., & Ritter, B. The relative efficacy of desensitization and modeling treatment approaches for inducing affective, behavioral, and attitudinal changes. *Journal of Personality and Social Psychology*, 1969, *13*, 193–199.

Beck, A., & Mahoney, M. Schools of thought? *American Psychologist*, 1979, *34*, 93–98.

Beck, A., Rush, A. J., Shaw, B., & Emery, G. *Cognitive therapy of depression*. New York: Guilford, 1979.

Belmont, J., & Butterfield, E. The instructional approach to developmental cognitive research. In R. Kail & J. Hagen (Eds.), *Perspectives on the development of memory and cognition*. Hillsdale, N.J.: Erlbaum, 1977.

Borkowski, J. *Signs of intelligence: Strategy generalization and metacognition*. Paper presented at the University of Wisconsin Conference on Growth of Insight, Madison, 1979.

Borkowski, J., & Cavanaugh, J. Maintenance and generalization of skills and strategies by the retarded. In N. Ellis (Ed.), *Handbook of mental deficiency: Psychological theory and research* (2nd ed.). Hillsdale, N.J.: Erlbaum, 1979.

Bornstein, P., & Quevillon, R. The effects of self-instructional package on overactive boys. *Journal of Applied Behavior Analysis*, 1976, *9*, 179–188.

Bower, G. Contacts of cognitive psychology with social learning theory. *Cognitive Therapy and Research*, 1978, *2*, 123–146.

Breger, L., & McGaugh, J. Critique and reformulation of "learning theory": Approaches to psychotherapy and neurosis. *Psychological Bulletin,* 1965, *63,* 338–358.

Brewer, W. There is no convincing evidence for operant or classical conditioning in adult humans. In W. Weimer & D. Palermo (Eds.), *Cognition and the symbolic processes.* Hillsdale, N.J.: Erlbaum, 1974.

Brown, A. Knowing when, where, and how to remember: A problem of metacognition. In R. Glaser (Ed.), *Advances in instructional psychology.* Hillsdale, N.J.: Erlbaum, 1978.

Brown, A., & Campione, J. Permissible inference from the outcome of training studies on cognitive development research. *Quarterly Newsletter of the Institute for Comparative Human Development,* 1978, *2,* 46–53.

Brown, J. The role of strategic behavior in retardate memory. In N. Ellis (Ed.), *International review of research in mental retardation* (Vol. 7). New York: Academic Press, 1974.

Butler, L., & Meichenbaum, D. The assessment of interpersonal problem-solving skills. In P. Kendall & S. Hollon (Eds.), *Cognitive–behavioral interventions: Assessment methods.* New York: Academic Press, 1980.

Cameron, R. The clinical implementation of behavior change techniques: A cognitively oriented conceptualization of therapeutic "compliance" and "resistance." In J. Foreyt & D. Rathjen (Eds.), *Cognitive behavior therapy: Research and applications.* New York: Plenum, 1979.

Campione, J., & Brown, A. Memory and metamemory development in educatable retarded children. In R. Kail & J. Hagen (Eds.), *Perspectives on the development of memory and cognition.* Hillsdale, N.J.: Erlbaum, 1977.

Chaney, E., O'Leary, M., & Marlatt, G. A. Skill training with alcoholics. *Journal of Consulting and Clinical Psychology,* 1978, *46,* 1092–1104.

Coates, T., & Thoresen, C. Self-control and educational practice, or do we really need self-control? In D. Berliner (Ed.), *Review of research in education.* New York: Praeger, 1980.

Conway, J., & Bucher, B. Transfer and maintenance of behavior change in children: A review and suggestions. In E. J. Mash & L. C. Handy (Eds.), *Behavior modification and families.* New York: Brunner/Mazel, 1976.

Craighead, E., Craighead-Wilcoxon, L., & Meyers, A. New directions in behavior modification with children. In M. Hersen, R. Eisler, & P. Miller (Eds.), *Progress in behavior modification* (Vol. 6). New York: Academic Press, 1978.

Dember, W. Motivation and the cognitive revolution. *American Psychologist,* 1974, *29,* 161–168.

Denney, D. Self-control approaches to the treatment of test anxiety. In I. G. Sarason (Ed.), *Test anxiety: Theory, research, and applications.* Hillsdale, N.J.: Erlbaum, 1980.

Dollard, J., & Miller, N. *Personality and psychotherapy.* New York: McGraw-Hill, 1950.

Douglas, V., & Peters, K. Toward a clearer definition of the attentional deficit of hyperactive children. In G. Hale & M. Lewis (Eds.), *Attention and the development of cognitive skills.* New York: Plenum, 1981.

Dubois, P. *The psychic treatment of nervous disorders.* New York: Funk & Wagnalls, 1909.

Ellis, A. *Reason and emotion in psychotherapy.* New York: Lyle Stuart, 1962.

Emery, R., & Margolin, D. An applied behavior analysis of delinquency: The irrelevancy of relevant behavior. *American Psychologist,* 1977, *32,* 860–873.

Eysenck, H. Behaviour therapy and the philosophers. *Behaviour Research and Therapy,* 1979, *17,* 511–514.

Flavell, J. Metacognitive aspects of problem solving. In C. Resnick (Ed.), *The nature of intelligence.* Hillsdale, N.J.: Erlbaum, 1976.

Flavell, J. Metacognition and cognitive monitoring: A new area of cognitive–developmental inquiry. *American Psychologist,* 1979, *34,* 906–911.

Foreyt, J., & Rathjen, D. (Eds.). *Cognitive behavior therapy: Research and applications.* New York: Plenum, 1979.

Frank, J. *Persuasion and healing: A comparative study of psychotherapy* (Rev. ed.). Baltimore: Johns Hopkins University Press, 1974. (Originally published, 1961.)

Franks, C. M., & Wilson, G. T. (Eds.). *Annual review of behavior therapy.* New York: Brunner/Mazel, 1977.

Friedling, C., & O'Leary, S. G. Effects of self-instructional training on second- and third-grade hyperactive children: A failure to replicate. *Journal of Applied Behavior Analysis,* 1979, *12,* 211–219.

Gagne, R., & Briggs, L. *Principles of instructional design.* New York: Holt, Rinehart & Winston, 1974.

Goldfried, M. Systematic desensitization as training in self-control. *Journal of Consulting and Clinical Psychology,* 1971, *37,* 228–234.

Goldfried, M. The use of relaxation and cognitive relabeling as coping skills. In R. Stuart (Ed.), *Behavioral self-management.* New York: Brunner/Mazel, 1977.

Goldfried, M. Anxiety reduction through cognitive–behavioral intervention. In P. Kendall & S. Hollon (Eds.), *Cognitive–behavioral interventions: Theory, research, and procedures.* New York: Academic Press, 1979.

Greenspoon, J., & Lamal, P. Cognitive behavior modification: Who needs it? *Psychological Record,* 1978, *28,* 343–357.

Henker, B., Whalen, C., & Hinshaw, S. The attributional contexts of cognitive intervention strategies. *Exceptional Education,* 1981.

Heppner, P. A review of problem-solving literature and its relationship to the counseling process. *Journal of Counseling Psychology,* 1978, *25,* 366–375.

Higa, W. *Self-instructional versus direct training in modifying children's impulsive behavior.* Unpublished doctoral dissertation, University of Hawaii, 1975.

Homme, L. Perspectives in psychology: Control of coverants, the operants of the mind. *Psychological Record,* 1965, *15,* 501–511.

Intagliata, J. Increasing the interpersonal problem-solving skills of an alcoholic population. *Journal of Consulting and Clinical Psychology,* 1978, *46,* 489–498.

Janet, P. *The major symptoms of hysteria.* London: Macmillan, 1907.

Jennings, L., Crosland, R., Loveless, S., Murray, J., & George, S. Cognitive control of extinction of classically conditioned pupillary response. *Psychological Record,* 1978, *28,* 193–205.

Karoly, P. Behavioral self-management in children: Concepts, methods, issues and directions. In M. Hersen, R. Eisler, & P. Miller (Eds.), *Progress in behavior modification* (Vol. 5). New York: Academic Press, 1977.

Kauffman, J., & Hallahan, D. Learning disability and hyperactivity (with comments on minimal brain dysfunction). In B. Lahey & A. Kazdin (Eds.), *Advances in clinical child psychology* (Vol. 2). New York: Plenum, 1979.

Kazdin, A. Research issues in covert conditioning. *Cognitive Therapy and Research,* 1977, *1,* 45–58.

Keeley, S., Shemberg, K., & Carbonell, J. Operant clinical intervention: Behavior management or beyond? Where are the data? *Behavior Therapy,* 1976, *7,* 292–305.

Kelly, G. *The psychology of personal constructs* (Vols. 1 & 2). New York: Norton, 1954.

Kendall, P. On the efficacious use of verbal self-instructional procedures with children. *Cognitive Therapy and Research,* 1977, *1,* 311–341.

Kendall, P., & Finch, A. Developing non-impulsive behavior in children: Cognitive–behavioral strategies for self-control. In P. Kendall & S. Hollon (Eds.), *Cognitive–behavioral interventions: Theory, research, and procedures.* New York: Academic Press, 1979.

Kendall, P., & Hollon, S. (Eds.), *Cognitive–behavioral interventions: Theory, research, and procedures.* New York: Academic Press, 1979.

Kendall, P., & Wilcox, L. *A cognitive–behavioral treatment with impulsivity: Concrete versus conceptual labeling with nonself-controlled problem children.* Unpublished manuscript, University of Minnesota, 1978.

Keogh, B., & Glover, A. The generalizability and durability of intervention effects. *Exceptional Education,* 1981.

Kieslar, D. Some myths of psychotherapy research and the search for a paradigm. *Psychological Bulletin,* 1966, *65,* 110–136.

Lange, A., & Jakubowski, P. *Responsible assertive behavior: Cognitive–behavioral procedures for trainees.* Champaign, Ill.: Research Press, 1976.

Lazarus, R. *Psychological stress and the coping process.* New York: McGraw-Hill, 1966.

Ledwidge, B. Cognitive-behavior modification: A step in the wrong direction? *Psychological Bulletin,* 1978, *85,* 353–375.

Ledwidge, B. Cognitive-behavior modification, or new ways to change minds: Reply to Mahoney and Kazdin. *Psychological Bulletin,* 1979, *85,* 1050–1053.

Locke, E. Behavior modification is not cognitive—and other myths: A reply to Ledwidge. *Cognitive Therapy and Research,* 1979, *3,* 141–146.

Lloyd, J. Academic instruction and cognitive techniques: The need for attack strategy training. *Exceptional Education,* 1981.

Luria, A. *The role of speech in the regulation of normal and abnormal behaviors.* New York: Liveright, 1961.

Luria, A. Speech and formation of mental processes. In M. Cole & I. Maltzman (Eds.), *A handbook of contemporary Soviet psychology.* New York: Basic Books, 1969.

Mahoney, M. *Cognition and behavior modification.* Cambridge, Mass.: Ballinger, 1974.

Mahoney, M. Psychotherapy and the structure of personal revolutions. In M. Mahoney (Ed.), *Cognition and clinical science.* New York: Plenum, 1979.

Mahoney, M., & Arnkoff, D. Cognitive and self-control therapies. In S. Garfield & A. Bergin (Eds.), *Handbook of psychotherapy and behavior change* (2nd ed.). New York: Wiley, 1978.

Mahoney, M., & Kazdin, A. Cognitive behavior modification: Misconceptions and premature evacuation. *Psychological Bulletin,* 1979, *86,* 1044–1049.

Maltzman, I. Orienting in classical conditioning and generalization of the galvanic skin response towards: An overview. *Journal of Experimental Psychology: General,* 1977, *106,* 111–119.

Markman, E. Realizing that you don't understand: A preliminary investigation. *Child Development,* 1977, *48,* 986–992.

Marlatt, G. A., & Gordon, J. Determinants of relapse: Implications for the maintenance of behavior change. In P. Davidson (Ed.), *Behavioral medicine: Changing health life styles.* New York: Brunner/Mazel, 1980.

Mash, E. J., & Dalby, J. Behavioral interventions for hyperactivity. In R. Trites (Ed.), *Hyperactivity in children: Etiology, measurement and treatment implications.* Baltimore: University Park Press, 1978.

Meichenbaum, D. Toward a cognitive theory of self-control. In G. Schwartz & D. Shapiro (Eds.), *Consciousness and self-regulation: Advances in research.* New York: Plenum, 1976.

Meichenbaum, D. *Cognitive-behavior modification: An integrative approach.* New York: Plenum, 1977.

Meichenbaum, D. *Cognitive-behavior modification newsletter.* Unpublished manuscripts, University of Waterloo, 1975–1979.

Meichenbaum, D. Cognitive-behavior modification: The need for a fairer assessment. *Cognitive*

Therapy and Research, 1979, *3,* 133–140.

Meichenbaum, D., & Asarnow, J. Cognitive-behavior modification and metacognitive development: Implications for the classroom. In P. Kendall & S. Hollon (Eds.), *Cognitive-behavioral interventions: Theory, research, and procedures.* New York: Academic Press, 1979.

Meichenbaum, D., Burland, S., Gruson, L., & Cameron, R. Metacognitive assessment. In S. Yussen (Ed.), *Growth of insight.* New York: Academic Press, in press.

Meichenbaum, D., & Butler, L. Toward a conceptual model for the treatment of test anxiety: Implications for research and treatment. In I. G. Sarason (Ed.), *Test anxiety: Theory, research, and applications.* Hillsdale, N.J.: Erlbaum, 1980.

Meichenbaum, D., & Butler, L. Cognitive ethology: Assessing the streams of cognition and emotion. In K. Blankstein, P. Pliner, & J. Polivy (Eds.), *Advances in the study of communication and affect: Assessment and modification of emotional behavior* (Vol. 6). New York: Plenum, 1981.

Meichenbaum, D., Butler, L., & Gruson, L. Toward a conceptual model of sound competence. In J. D. Wine & M. D. Smye (Eds.), *Social competence.* New York: Guilford, 1981.

Meichenbaum, D., & Gilmore, J. B. Resistance: From a cognitive–behavioral perspective. In P. Wachtel (Ed.), *Resistance: A behavioral and psychodynamic analysis.* New York: Plenum, in press.

Miller, G., Galanter, E., & Pribram, K. *Plans and structure of behavior.* New York: Holt, Rinehart & Winston, 1960.

Miller, P., & Bigi, L. The development of children's understanding of attention. *Merrill-Palmer Quarterly,* 1979, *25,* 235–250.

Mischel, W., Mischel, H., & Hood, S. *The development of knowledge of effective collection to delay gratification.* Unpublished manuscript, Stanford University, 1978.

Neisser, U. *Cognitive psychology.* Englewood Cliffs, N.J.: Prentice-Hall, 1967.

Novaco, R. The cognitive regulation of anger and stress. In P. Kendall & S. Hollon (Eds.), *Cognitive–behavioral interventions: Theory, research, and procedures.* New York: Academic Press, 1979.

"Observer." The recycling of cognition in psychology. *Psychological Record,* 1978, *28,* 157–160.

Raimy, V. *Misunderstandings of the self.* San Francisco: Jossey-Bass, 1975.

Robin, A., Armel, S., & O'Leary, D. The effects of self-instruction on writing deficiency. *Behavior Therapy,* 1975, *6,* 178–187.

Rook, K., & Hammen, C. A cognitive perspective on the experience of sexual arousal. *Journal of Social Issues,* 1977, *33,* 7–29.

Rosenthal, T. Applying a cognitive behavioral view to clinical and social problems. In G. Whitehurst & B. Zimmerman (Eds.), *The functions of language and cognition.* New York: Academic Press, 1980.

Rotter, J. *Social learning and clinical psychology.* Englewood Cliffs, N.J.: Prentice-Hall, 1954.

Ryan, E. Identifying and remediating failures in reading comprehension: Toward an instructional approach for poor comprehenders. In T. Waller & J. MacKinnon (Eds.), *Advances in reading research* (Vol. 2). New York: Academic Press, 1981.

Rychtarik, R., & Wollersheim, J. The role of cognitive mediators in alcohol addiction with some implications for treatment. *JSAS Catalog of Selected Documents in Psychology,* 1978. (Ms. No. 1763)

Schwartz, R., & Gottman, J. Toward a task analysis of assertive behavior. *Journal of Consulting and Clinical Psychology,* 1976, *44,* 910–920.

Seligman, M. E. P. *Helplessness.* San Francisco: W. H. Freeman, 1975.

Skinner, B. F. *Science and human behavior.* New York: Macmillan, 1953.

Skinner, B. F. *The technology of teaching.* New York: Appleton-Century-Crofts, 1968.

Snygg, D., & Combs, A. *Individual behavior.* New York: Harper, 1949.

Spivack, G., & Shure, M. *Social adjustment of young children: A cognitive approach to solving real-life problems.* San Francisco: Jossey-Bass, 1974.

Sternberg, R. Cognitive–behavioral approaches to the training of intelligence in the retarded. *Journal of Special Education,* 1981, *15,* 165–183.

Stokes, T., & Baer, D. An implicit technology of generalization. *Journal of Applied Behavior Analysis,* 1977, *10,* 349–367.

Thorpe, G. Desensitization, behavioral rehearsal, self-instructional training and placebo effects on assertive-refusal behavior. *European Journal of Behavioral Analysis and Modification,* 1975, *1,* 30–44.

Thorpe, G., Amatu, H., Blakey, R., & Burns, L. Contributions of overt instructional rehearsal and "specific insight" to the effectiveness of self-instructional training: A preliminary study. *Behavior Therapy,* 1976, *7,* 504–511.

Torgesen, J. The role of nonspecific factors in the task performance of learning disabled children: A theoretical assessment. *Journal of Learning Disabilities,* 1977, *10,* 27–34.

Turk, D. C., Meichenbaum, D., & Genest, M. *Pain and behavioral medicine.* New York: Guilford, in press.

Vygotsky, L. *Thought and language.* Cambridge, Mass.: MIT Press, 1962.

Wahler, R., Berland, R., & Coe, T. Generalization processes in child behavior change. In B. Lahey & A. Kazdin (Eds.), *Advances in clinical child psychology* (Vol. 2). New York: Plenum, 1979.

Wein, K., & Nelson, R. *The effect of self-instructional training in arithmetic problem solving skills.* Unpublished manuscript, University of North Carolina at Greensboro, 1975.

Weinreich, R. *Inducing reflective thinking in impulsive, emotionally disturbed children.* Unpublished master's thesis, Virginia Commonwealth University, 1975.

Wertsch, J. From social interaction to higher psychological processes: A clarification and application of Vygotsky's theory. *Human Development,* 1979, *22,* 1–22.

Wilson, G. T. Cognitive behavior therapy: Paradigm shift or passing phase? In J. Foreyt & D. Rathjen (Eds.), *Cognitive behavior therapy: Research and applications.* New York: Plenum, 1979.

Wilson, G. T. Cognitive factors in life-style changes: A social learning perspective. In P. Davidson (Ed.), *Behavioral medicine: Changing health life styles.* New York: Brunner/Mazel, 1980.

Wine, J. Cognitive attentional theory of test anxiety. In I. G. Sarason (Ed.), *Test anxiety: Theory, research, and applications.* Hillsdale, N.J.: Erlbaum, 1980.

Wolpe, J. Behavior therapy and its malcontents: II. Multimodal electicism, cognitive exclusivism, and "exposure" empiricism. *Journal of Behavior Therapy and Experimental Psychiatry,* 1976, *7,* 109–116.

Wolpe, J. Cognition and causation in human behavior and its therapy. *American Psychologist,* 1978, *33,* 437–446.

8

SOCIAL LEARNING THEORY

TED L. ROSENTHAL

Department of Psychiatry
University of Tennessee College of Medicine and Mid-South Hospital

As a professional breed, psychologists tend to be quite concerned with self-definitions. Research data suggest that self-awareness is a mixed blessing. It can assist efficient conduct under some circumstances, but can impair harmonious performance under others (Carver, 1979). The utility of seeking to distinguish between "cognitive–behavioral" interventions and applications drawn from "social learning theory" would, on the face of it, seem questionable if controversy were not emerging—as evidenced by the request for this chapter. Otherwise, many researchers and clinicians would be quite content with some analogy, such as this: Their relationship is much like that between the study of animal husbandry in dogs and the study of the art of training retrievers to fetch. Both involve aspects of basic and applied science, but their relative weights differ. If the goal is to win prizes at field trials, they overlap a great deal. In other contexts, their divergence grows sharper. Yet neither emphasis holds any monopoly on cognition, behavior, or the hyphens mediating between them. With the hope of restoring these common-sense premises, the long-cut back to them is begun.

WHAT IS SOCIAL LEARNING THEORY?

In fact, a number of social learning approaches have been formulated over the years. N. E. Miller and Dollard (1941) proposed one; Rotter (1954) suggested another; and the impact of Sullivan's views (e.g., 1953) toward psychiatry, and Lewin's (1953) toward psychology, helped arouse interest in the interplay between cultural factors and individual adjustment. Many developmental psychologists, among others, use the term in a rather broadly descriptive manner, not identified with any particular intellectual lineage (Yussen, 1979). However, in the realm of behavioral views about etiology and treatment, the usual meaning of "social learning theory" (SLT) is confined to the orientation exemplified in the work of Albert Bandura. This use of the term is meant henceforth.

SLT has evolved into a rather general theoretical approach toward human thought and action. It draws on research contributed or influenced by Bandura and his associates, as well as on much work not fostered by the theory itself. In this wide-screen sense, it has come to offer an integrating framework for a broad swath of empirical data and to play a heuristic role in pointing out new and needed directions for study. At a macroconceptual level, it is one of perhaps three major general standpoints that presently address molar human behavior. In assumptions and emphases, it appears to fall somewhere between the two other main approaches. Those are "organismic" (e.g., Piagetian, structuralistic) and "conditioning" (e.g., operant, neo-Hullian) or frankly behavioristic positions. It is beyond the scope of the present discussion to compare the assets and liabilities of these competing stances (see Bandura, 1977a; Rachman & Wilson, 1980; Rosenthal & Bandura, 1978; Rosenthal & Zimmerman, 1978). None of them is a tightly unified theory of the sort proposed by Hull. Each contains or spans a number of more narrowly focused relatively specific smaller theories. For example, Piagetians have written on such topics as language, problem solving, and moral judgment, not always with precisely the same assumptions or conclusions. Eysenck (1979) has put forward a rather elegant analysis in defense of a conditioning explanation for neurosis. Bandura (1977b, 1978, in press) has advanced his self-efficacy theory to account for the role of self-referential processes in clinical behavior change. Note that each of these major thrusts must take account of and subsume the data generated by the others when there is overlap. If not, in essence, the one view yields ground to the other in that common arena. Thus, there is competition between social learning and conditioning views to explain problem solving and other symbolic behavior (Rachman & Wilson, 1980). But the competition rarely takes place at the macroconceptual level, as formulated across multiple spheres of interest; far more often, argument arises about more circumscribed matters in dispute. It is, perhaps, the result of many such bones of narrow contention that gives rise to more inclusuve lines of theoretical cleavage.

SOME MAIN TERRAIN OF SLT

It thus may be helpful to sketch some of the content domains to which SLT has contributed and in which it has, so to speak, vested interests. Among the long-standing concerns of SLT are the social and cultural variables that affect people's perceptions, judgments, reactions to interpersonal influence, and self-control. How societal forces and partners in face-to-face interactions mediate the evolution and change of individual behavior has been a consistent emphasis. For example, the parental priorities and child-rearing practices that encourage an adolescent to adopt aggressive styles of conduct were studied by Bandura and Walters (1959). They later (1963) drew on cross-cultural, field, and laboratory data to analyze the social influences that enter into personality development. They attempted to relate social stimuli, often neglected by prior learning theorists, to such topics as aggression, dependency, sexual behavior, morality, self-control, and psychological treatment. Rather than relying on response consequences in the form of social reactions and tangible reinforcements to dominate the organization and change of behavior, they proposed a number of mediating mechanisms that, at the time, were alien to most learning formulations. One illustration is that of the internalized *standards,* derived from social experience, that set the acceptable levels for a person's own performance or achievement. These standards serve as symbolic criteria that steer a person's aspirations and later judgments of whether his or her efforts deserve self-reward or self-censure. Much subsequent research on self-reinforcement processes (Bandura, 1971, 1976) has confirmed this line of reasoning and grown from it. Yet it is a kind of conceptualization, characteristic of SLT, that appears to confuse, frustrate, or outrage some proponents of peripheralistic S-R views.

Likewise, well before the current surge of interest in covert symbolic activities as determinants of therapeutic behavior change, Bandura (1969) put forth an information-processing conception. He took issue with traditional assumptions that much complex and even simple behavior should be attributed to rather direct connections between external cues and overt action. Instead, he said that the lion's share of human behavior was governed by executive processes which, in part, involve "strategic selection of the stimuli to which attention is directed, symbolic coding and organization of stimulus inputs, and acquisition, through informative feedback, of mediating hypotheses or rules which play an influential role in regulating response selection" (1969, p. 564). This framework assigned far more priority to central events in determining human action than did most other behavioral approaches, and it gave a structural diagram of the working components assumed to be the most critical. It committed SLT to a strategy of explanation derived from cognitive and not from conditioning theory, an alliance others have noted (Bower, 1978). Thus, such phenomena as verbal and classical conditioning, social influence, incentive effects, and self-referent mediation of inhibitory and antisocial conduct were addressed in cognitive terms. Other writers (e.g., Kanfer & Phillips, 1970) were moving from S-R toward information-processing conceptions of behavior therapy, but it seems fair to assert that Bandura's strides were longer, faster, and more explicitly tied to verifiable process mechanisms.

A main function of theory is to organize data in ways that spark and guide the work of others. Among Bandura's many colleagues and former students who have been influenced by the SLT perspective are the following: Blanchard (e.g., Blanchard, 1970; Eisler, Blanchard, Fitts, & Williams, 1978) has studied the effects of varying guidance information upon psychiatric and medical treatment outcomes. I. Brown (e.g., Brown, 1979; Brown & Inouye, 1978) has studied the role of referent clarity in language learning and perseverance as a function of self-perceived competence. Gelfand and Hartmann (e.g., Gelfand & Hartmann, 1975; Peterson, Hartmann, & Gelfand, 1977) have together studied treatment, moral judgments, and altruism in children. Harris (e.g., Harris, 1977; Harris & Siebel, 1976) has studied sex-role and ethnic variables in regard to language and personal influence. Jeffery (e.g., Jeffery, 1976; Jeffery & Wing, 1979) has studied rehearsal processes in motor learning and session pacing to aid weight loss. Mahoney (e.g., Mahoney, 1974; Mahoney & Arnkoff, 1978) has studied cognitive–behavioral techniques to improve self-control over many kinds of problems. Mischel (e.g., 1977) has addressed personality in social learning terms and, with his colleagues (e.g., Moore, Mischel, & Zeiss, 1976; Patterson & Mischel, 1976), has studied attentional and representational strategies to foster delay of gratification. Zimmerman (e.g., Zimmerman, 1979; Zimmerman & Blotner, 1979) has studied children's learning, transfer, and persistence on concept tasks. Many other names could be added, as could research on other topics by the workers cited. Contributions dealing with ethical issues in clinical science and scholarship might also be mentioned (e.g., Gagnon & Davison, 1976; Mahoney, 1976). The point of the foregoing list is to illustrate the breadth of impact that SLT has had on both basic and applied psychology. Its conceptual stance has detractors, including structuralistic critics who dispute aspects of its formulations (e.g., Smedslund, 1979). Yet its fruitful heuristic value appears beyond controversy.

VICTORIES VARIOUS VIA VISTAS VICARIOUS

To resist an entrenched stereotype, the word "modeling" has, by design, not been used till now. SLT is not confined to a clinical frame of reference, nor are vicarious processes its primary concerns. True, a very great fraction of the research it has sponsored does involve social modeling operations as independent variables. This in part has stemmed from intrinsic interest in how social example can guide human symbolic, adjustmental, and stylistic acts. Thus, an enormous range of both adroit and maladaptive behavior seems to derive from the social precedents and emphases to which people are exposed.

Grammar patterns and language labels; solutions and strategies for solving conceptual problems; categories for grouping or separating events; expressive and assertive styles of personal conduct; haste or deliberation before performance and the pace of response; criteria to steer such abstract judgments as ethical decisions; and approach to subjectively threatening events in the clinical realm—all have been amenable to teaching through demonstrations (Bandura, 1969, 1977a; Rosenthal & Bandura, 1978; Rosenthal & Zimmerman, 1978). Likewise, modeled example can dictate observers' own standards for personal achievement (Brown & Inouye, 1978), generosity (Peterson, Hartmann, & Gelfand, 1977), persistence (Borden & White, 1973; Zimmerman & Blotner, 1979), and tolerance of noxious pain (Craig, 1978). The populations studied have ranged downward in age from adults to toddlers (Leonard, 1975; Nelson, 1977) and to babies in their second year of life (Stewart & Hamilton, 1976). Thus, learning from teaching models is a potent form of guidance in a host of spheres.

However, there is another important reason accounting for the attention given to observational learning in research stimulated by SLT; this concerns the role it assigns to symbolic events and social forces in explaining human acquisition. The issues are historical and theoretical. When Bandura began his research program on modeling, two opposing conceptions were dominant. At the behavioristic pole, it was thought that "real" learning demanded overt practice (and, in some views, reward) for stimuli and responses to be joined. The emphasis was on tangible antecedent and consequent events, but the central regulation and organization of behavior was neglected or relegated to a few Hullian constructs that were made to subsume higher mental processes. Indeed, in some current views of covert conditioning, symbolic events seem to be treated as topographic variants or, in their nature, as close analogues of overt stimulus and response operations. At the opposite, structuralistic pole, it was thought that learning was dominated by cognitive maturation. Although experience was critical in taxing present mental organization, thus disrupting the status quo and provoking advance toward more refined levels, inner structure was largely set biologically and predestined to follow a fixed sequence of prototypic patterns; sociocultural events received scant attention as to the similarities and differences of their arrangements or effects. Both polar stances mainly ignored the precedents of others to convey skill and knowledge. Learning by observation was equated with copying, reproducing, or "mimicking" a model's responses. Little distinction was made among an infant's vocalization of sounds, a choreographer's demonstrations of movements for a ballerina, and a writer's stylistic emulation of subtle aspects of literary style: All were *imitation*. Further, imitation was supposed to be a weak teaching method. For example, in a pivotal study, Hillix and Marx

(1960) made adult observers the control group for a maze-learning task, because it was assumed that little if any progress would result. Instead, the observers learned better than did peers who overtly practiced on the maze. The results created a stir because they challenged the then-dominant conception that modeling was weak guidance.

In contrast, SLT has construed modeled examples as sources of information that can epitomize new behavioral configurations, guide inferential reasoning, and promote understanding. Modeling is treated as just one important channel, among many, to inform and modify conduct. These differences in the assumptions held by respective positions have made it important for SLT to seek to validate its conception of vicarious phenomena. Thus, empirical research on modeling has become a stadium in which SLT contests the macroconceptual premises of competing viewpoints. Well-organized social demonstrations will often compel more attention from learners and convey information more clearly than many other teaching methods will. Yet vicarious learning has not been assigned a unique or privileged status by SLT. People can grasp equivalent meanings from instruction of varied forms. All along, an effort has been made to integrate modeling tactics with other means of transmitting information in analyzing symbolic processes and overt action. Apart from language and conduct illustrated by others, people make use of many other cues. These include the experience and consequences of direct performance attempts, the rules and directions supplied orally or in writing by teachers, the opinions and feedback expressed by interaction partners, the solution strategies and self-regulatory plans that are received or constructed from diverse cultural sources, and so forth. Further, information from all sources must be subjectively weighted for importance and relevance, organized into working guidelines, harmonized for smooth execution, and judged for utility once implemented. Interpretive processes, including inferential reasoning about how best to combine, extrapolate from, and apply knowledge, are continually at work to integrate information, whatever its origins. Especially to introduce *new* information, in contexts where little prior familiarity exists, demonstrations have proven very useful, but so has giving neophytes plans and principles to guide their early efforts. Research suggests that, to create a basic grasp of new materials, symbolic exemplars and strategies are generally more efficient than learning by overt practice, which usually yields the needed information more slowly, with a weaker overview of interrelationships and with more errors made. This is because performance feedback is relatively discrete (i.e., linked to the quality and topography of one's specific efforts), and because the activities of selecting and executing responses can divert attention and thought away from grasping the cue messages and reworking them into enduring covert mediators.

THERAPEUTIC FUNCTIONS

Neither has modeling been assigned a privileged status in terms of clinical applications. It is one among a range of methods that can alter defective patterns of thought and conduct. Especially if clients' problems truly require new behavior for solution, demonstrating by social example—for example, demonstrating how to fend off others' illegitimate demands—can be very helpful. Such research thrusts are not the same as making demonstrations the keystones of a "school" of treatment. For clinical purposes, much evidence confirms that overt practice is more effective and reassuring in restoring known (i.e., familiar) but inhibited responses than are any kinds of simulated approach trials (Bandura, 1977b, 1978, 1981). It is hard to restrain wincing if one perceives a favorite racehorse confused with the art of racing. Attributing to SLT a primary *clinical* concern with modeling is to equate a topic of study with conceptual explanation. In the terms of Rachman and Wilson (1980), this is a confusion between process and procedures. Indeed, writers on SLT have warned against exclusive reliance on modeling techniques, symbolic or participant, to achieve optimal treatment progress. For example, the value of independent, self-directed client practice after the completion of approach trials with the therapist has been discussed (Bandura, Jeffery, & Gajdos, 1975). The need to combine modeling with other interventions—for example, self-instructions, group discussion, and feedback—that draw on a host of historical and conceptual forebears has been plainly stated: "Rarely will one procedure yield outcomes as good as [those achieved] with an array of tools" (Rosenthal & Bandura, 1978, p. 647). The equation of techniques with theory seems to reside in the eye of some beholders, perhaps because SLT has studied and hence exemplified modeling options. Yet demonstration is just one arrow in the SLT quiver, and it is not essential to the framework proposed to explain how behavior is acquired, regulated, and changed. That framework, it may be suspected, is uncongenial to some because it not only relies on a complex view of cognition, but also assumes that the subjective construction of events is a main contributor to observables. If this surmise is correct, there may be extralogical bases to dissociate modeling from the rest of SLT and treat the part as the whole; vicarious phenomena may be the relatively more palatable of SLT's "mentalistic heresies" for workers whose underlying assumptions remain associationistic or reinforcement-dependent. In turn, if a theory of treatment made the value judgment that people can and should minimize reliance on others and strive to live in splendid relative isolation from social influences, SLT would again become vexing. Its assumptions of factual and desirable reciprocity between a person's own standards and those of others would clash with an autarkic view of the human situation. In such cases, a gadfly reminder that exhortations favoring autonomy and communal disengagement are also forms of social influence would probably fall on unreceptive ears.

COMPONENT PROCESSES IN COGNITION

Among the many conceptualizations that have begotten basic research, SLT too has contributed to a scientific understanding of cognition. The picture etched by experimental data is far from complete. Yet for people to obtain, retain, and act upon information, whatever its mode of transmission, a number of mediating steps appear critical.

Attention processes register cues actively, emphasizing relevant, meaningful stimuli and muting access to extraneous signals. Cues are screened for identity and impact, often in microseconds. For example, a word cue may start a search through memory and culminate in the provisional selection of an entry item that then is tested for match against the stimulus. If the match is judged acceptable, the word cue has been recognized; if not, the process begins again and continues until a stored item is judged identical to the cue. Note that features of decision making are assumed to enter the scanning of sensory cues. Further, the semantic context affects the speed and priorities of search. After a stimulus such as "doctor," a related word (e.g., "nurse") will be discerned faster than a word (e.g., "cat") not semantically connected (Antos, 1979). Likewise, if an arrow pointing up is high in a spatial frame, perception is faster than if the direction and elevation (e.g., up–low) connote different meanings (Clark & Brownell, 1975). Once attention has detected the cue, that cue enters short-term memory and will be lost unless it is given a stable representation.

Retention processes involve the coding of information into durable symbols and frameworks. Much information is preserved in the form of verbal, visual, tactile, and motor images. The use of several imagery modes often enhances storage, whatever the sensory topography of the cue. In fact, most physical events undergo rather elaborate covert transformations or recodings before they are stabilized in memory. Active reworking of information, in diverse but subjectively graphic forms, far surpasses overt or mental repetition of the cues themselves without personal elaboration. There seems to exist great flexibility in how stimuli are coded, depending in part on the form and meaning of the cues and in part on subjective priorities in organizing data. At some point, however, the new or discrete information is synthesized with prior knowledge into categories, summaries, and other covertly meaningful networks, rubrics, and groupings. These maintain the key features of content, subordinate specific details to common themes, and offer structured "hooks" that can prevent a person from losing track of known information and hence becoming unable to retrieve it. Attentional and retentive processes are recursive in that similar or functionally equivalent information-working acts may recur many times and, in response to feedback, additional data, and the executive events of judgment and interpretation, a nominally later may revert to a nominally prior step of processing. These issues are dealt with in greater detail elsewhere (Bandura, 1977a; Rosenthal & Bandura, 1978; Rosenthal & Zimmerman, 1978).

Once knowledge is available in stable form, its utilization may depend on *motor reproduction* processes. Stored information, such as grasp of a satisfactory high jump or pirouette, does not ensure the motor skill needed to perform well, even if the properties and criteria of excellence are known. Finally, *motivation and incentive* processes determine whether or not acquired competence will be expressed as performance under given conditions. Thus, judgments such as "I can't get up before an audience and orate," or "My best efforts will be disparaged," may prevent persons with much knowledge and potential eloquence from ever speaking in public.

The foregoing thumbnail sketch exemplifies the SLT approach to the determinants of learning and performance. It bears a family relationship to other current viewpoints that assume that cognition weighs heavily in the occurrence and regulation of molar behavior (e.g., Bower, 1978; Gholson, 1980).

Central events of the sorts just capsuled will remain alive and well, whatever the labels bestowed upon them by behavioral scientists. However, a key difference between Bandura and writers who favor a "conditioning" stance, such as Eysenck (1979), reflects the degree to which SLT has sought to integrate contemporary research on information processing into its conceptualizations. To do so, it has made fairly intimate contact with research—mainly published in nonapplied journals—that seems to have had less impact on most other neobehavioral and cognitively oriented clinical standpoints, including some that appear to confuse an *emphasis on* with an *explanation of* central mediating events. From the fonts of basic research has sprung SLT's frame of reference as sketched above. It attempts more articulation of component mental processes than would seem defensible if the burgeoning experimental literature were not addressed. Those studies collectively argue for a conception of symbolic activity along the lines adopted by SLT. To illustrate such current data, Table 8-1 presents some main conclusions (with a sampling of supportive citations) suggested by many basic studies reported over the past several years. It is hoped that this listing will steer interested readers to some of the representative literature on which the SLT view is based.

TABLE 8-1. Some Representative Conclusions from Recent Experimental Research on Cognitive Processes

1. Subjective interpretations, familiarity, and provisional definitions open to validation enter into the perception of cues (Aaronson & Scarborough, 1976; Ambler & Proctor, 1976; Antos, 1979; Avant & Lyman, 1975; Bassili, 1976; Johnston & Heinz, 1979).

2. Attention is selective and depends on the meaning, relevance, and intelligibility of cues. Disattention is an *active* process (Banks, Clark, & Lucy, 1975; Bregman & Rudnicky, 1975; Clark & Brownell, 1975; Duncan, 1979; Farrell, 1979; Neill, 1977; Schvaneveldt, Meyer, & Becker, 1976; Yussen, 1974).

3. The processing of information occurs in recursive steps, dictated by executive processes, rather than in a fixed or linear S-R sequence (Bundesen & Larsen, 1975; Chow & Murdock, 1976; Cooper & Shepard, 1975; Finke & Schmidt, 1977; Malin, 1979).

4. Thus, encoding and representation are flexible and may shift repeatedly during information processing (Dykes, 1979; Hawkins, Reicher, Rogers, & Peterson, 1976; Kallman & Massaro, 1979; Smith, 1979; Spoehr & Smith, 1975).

5. Organizing frameworks may differ in pattern or dimensions among cue categories (Bell & Handel, 1976; Matsuda & Robbins, 1977; Robinson, 1977; Rosch, 1975; Rosch, Simpson, & Miller, 1976; Solso & Raynis, 1979).

6. Retaining information and enacting it for applied purposes often depends on how the information is symbolically coded (Bandura & Jeffery, 1973; Bandura, Jeffery, & Bachicha, 1974; Gerst, 1971; Kazdin, 1979; J. Miller, 1979).

7. Motor tasks—especially once they become familiar—are regulated at least as much or more by central as by peripheral events (Ells & Gotts, 1977; Jeffery, 1976; Kelso, 1977; Kelso, Southard, & Goodman, 1979; Rubin, 1978; Warren & Schmitt, 1978).

8. A host of cognitive aids, very different in form and specific features, can assist the processing and utilization of information (Andre & Womack, 1978; Bjorklund, Ornstein, & Haig, 1977; Cosgrove & Patterson, 1977; Dansereau, Collins, McDonald, Holley, Garland, Diekhoff, & Evans, 1979; Frase & Schwartz, 1979; Glynn & DiVesta, 1977; Greiner & Karoly, 1976; Raugh & Atkinson, 1975; Rigney & Lutz, 1976; Royer & Cable, 1976).

ONLY TRUE OR USEFUL TOO?

Whether making provision for data such as those tabled as building materials in the architecture of SLT will have viable *applied* payoff still remains an empirical question. Sexual enjoyment and expertise need not demand a profound understanding of anatomy. Likewise, the sequential intricacies by which cognition unfolds need not improve the ability of researchers and clinicians to intervene in the covert equilibrium states that symbolic processes eventually attain. Where thought gets to may often be more practically important than how it got there. For instance, Bandura's self-efficacy formulations fuse the prior complexities of self-referent thinking into fewer variables. Myriad antecedent events are condensed into their terminal, relatively stable forms as one of two main classes of expectation. This molar partition is conceptually more manageable for scientific grasp and leads more easily to treatment utilization by working clinicians. As to whether an organizing scheme for cognition of the sort espoused by SLT has applied value, there seem grounds for optimism. These include current analyses of sexual dysfunction in information-processing terms (Ruble & Brooks-Gunn, 1979) and research showing that guidance to adopt efficient recoding of covert modeling scenes can assist therapy outcomes (Kazdin, 1979). Further, a stance like SLT's can suggest new thrusts and explanations not readily produced by competing orientations. Some concrete steps for mass-media applications of vicarious guidance have been proposed (e.g., Bandura, 1977a; Rosenthal & Bandura, 1978; Rushton, 1979) that would be less promptly apparent if modeling were construed as imitation or as an instance of the matching-to-sample operant paradigm. An S-R view that gives highest priority to tangible, experimenter-defined operations may be strained to account for the similar outcomes achieved by procedural variants of systematic desensitization, or for the instances when such methods as desensitization, symbolic modeling, and covert modeling yield the same benefits (Bandura, 1977b). Functional equivalence has even been found when such nominally distinctive techniques as interpersonal skill training, the rewarding use of pleasant-activity schedules, and guidance in improving self-control were compared in the treatment of dysphoria (Zeiss, Lewinsohn, & Muñoz, 1979). Pains were taken to focus each method on different and specific target behaviors. Yet not only was progress similar for all treated client groups, but the respective methods had effects that were *not* confined to the specific changes each was expected to produce. The results were no different across a range of dependent measures presumably more tied to one or another therapy. Unlike "black box" or peripheralistic views, SLT can subsume such results handily in terms of equivalent subjective meanings: Because of commonalities in cognitive processes, patterns of self-referent thought, and social influence cues from therapists, it is expected that clients often will mediate externally distinctive operations in ways that lead to identical effects (Rosenthal, 1980; Rosenthal & Bandura, 1978).

Reasoning of this sort has another advantage for "trouble shooting" when applied guidance fails to bring about the benefits desired. Therapists are invited to scrutinize how their clients attend to, cognize, interpret, and judge the utility and "do-ability" of treatment information. Phenomenology and mishaps in distinguishable steps of information handling by the clients receive at least as much analytical concern as do the therapists' strategy and procedures. If, for example, a patient cannot concentrate on guidance that is hard to bridge to familiar knowledge or that violates personal value judgments, much time can be lost in fruitless efforts to rectify reinforcement contingencies or to review the elements of effective terminal response. Of course, a gifted therapist will consider covert interferences, but an intuitive hunt may take longer and proceed more haphazardly without some map of the key trouble spots that need to be checked. In contrast, most conditioning positions give highest priority to the manipulation of observables, as with Eysenck's ingenious suggestions (1979) about the parameter of cue duration in raising or lowering the threat value of phobic stimuli. Put simply, an S-R bias in the name of scientific "parsimony" (for which, in fact, no operational criteria or definitions seem to be available) can divert a therapist's attention from a relevant—albeit complex—covert obstacle that may determine the success or failure of treatment. Should these points seem overly self-evident, consider how long it has taken for patients' deviant personal standards of bodily pulchritude to be recognized as among the important determinants of anorexia nervosa. In a similar vein, writers influenced by SLT have raised related issues in discussing the causes that may underlie sexual deviations (Alford, Webster, & Sanders, 1980) and the maintenance of weight loss by formerly obese youngsters (Cohen, Gelfand, Dodd, Jense, & Turner, 1980).

Nonetheless, effective applications need not rest on so elaborated a view of cognitive mediating processes. Meichenbaum, for example, has been influenced by aspects of rational–emotive therapy and by Russian thinking about internal dialogue in the maintenance and change of maladaptive behavior. From these roots, he and his colleagues have evolved creative treatment interventions of major importance (e.g., Meichenbaum, 1977; Meichenbaum & Asarnow, 1979; Meichenbaum & Butler, 1980). Yet this work does not appear to rely on or derive from the current technical literature on information processing to any visibly great extent. Instead, a number of guidance strategies have been devised, tested, and refined to alter maladaptive self-referent and self-regulatory patterns, with most fruitful impact. For practical purposes, what actually works to enhance human happiness must take precedence over the comprehensiveness of its empirical origins or, for that matter, over the relative conceptual elegance of alternative explanatory frameworks. Whether operant, SLT, other cognitive–behavioral, or yet-to-be-conceived views are under the gun, researchers and clinicians must not succumb to the definition of tragedy attributed to Herbert Spencer—that is, to have a beautiful theory murdered by an ugly fact. As criteria for therapeutic decision making, the primacy of outcome should not be subordinated to the allure of process, even when the process captivates the scientific imagination. In this respect, it is risky to depart from the brass-instrument-bounded, T-maze-trodden legacy of behaviorism.

On the other hand, in the longer run, it is difficult to suppose that cognitive–behavioral clinicians of any allegiance will be able to afford indefinite lack of interest in the mental mechanisms uncovered by basic research on cognition. For instance, some of the deficits now alluded to by such terms as "minimal brain dysfunction" and "learning disabilities" may involve malfunction or maldevelopment of some but not other component cognitive processes that are not yet ordinarily separated for assessment or treatment. By the same token, the role of biological variables that contribute to psychological experience is undergoing active and productive study (see Akiskal & Webb, 1978). For example, by means of reasoning based on biochemical and genetic premises, it was possible to show similarities (e.g., in REM latency) between dysthymic but subpsychotic depressives and full-blown, unipolar depressed patients; but both these groups differed on a variety of measures from cases whose depression resulted from personality disorders that seem to be associated with "acting-out" character patterns (Akiskal, Rosenthal, Haykal, Rosenthal, & Scott-Strauss, 1980). Likewise, Davis, Buchsbaum, and Bunney (in press) present evidence suggesting that endorphins may play an important part in somatosensory attentional mechanisms, and perhaps also in visual and auditory attention. Advances of these kinds will need to be reckoned with and, in turn, will need to make meaningful contacts with new breakthroughs in the behavioral realm.

Despite the hope that continued investigation of such component processes as those just illustrated will, eventually, lead to rich applied yields, the returns are not yet in. If one tries to stand back from the enormous research literature on cognition and asks what it seems to be telling us as clinicians, its present message appears to be that molar tendencies and meanings dominate over molecular coordinates and details. Consistent with the recursive nature earlier ascribed to executive cognitive processes, clinicians (and clients) can get to the same place by many and varied routes. For example, consider the final assertion in Table 8-1 and its citations. What is implied is that any procedures that clarify, organize, and help integrate information meaningfully can improve client response in many problem areas. More concretely, here are some practical rules-of-thumb derived from experimental work to improve clients' grasp and retention of guidance messages: Use vivid illustrations and exemplars, clear analogies with known material, and familiar, concrete words to express the message. Give structure through preparatory orientations and rationales to make guidance meaningful and convincing. Provide strategies, plans, outlines and other mnemonic devices to maintain principles and facts in organized form. Introduce techniques that encourage active reworking of guidance content in personally compelling terms. Such options include inviting personal elaboration and periodic self-questioning; teaching clients to restate information in alternative ways, such as by paraphrase and visual imagery; and separating the critical ideas from supplementary or subordinate points and details.

If the foregoing is viewed as a sample of guidelines for intervention, it seems doubtful that any locus within the cognitive–behavioral spectrum would take issue with the thrust of the suggestions offered. Reciprocally, how could any particular standpoint claim that it—but not its brethren—held title to the tactics summarized? It would be no mean feat to disentangle the relative claims to ownership of what seems most accurately described as common property.

WHO GOT THERE FIRST?

As sex therapists will promptly recognize, the answer to this question will, to a substantial extent, depend on the subjective frames of reference of consenting participants. However, collective harmony is probably more critical than respective priority is. If one precedence must be assigned among North American psychologists for emphasizing the kinds of events (e.g., imagery, inferential reasoning, mental organization) that are essential elements of cognitive–behavioral therapies, credit likely belongs to William James (1890). The path of progress was hewn by so many workers—some now remembered, others forgotten—that decisions become more an exercise in differential attention than in rational drawing of conclusions. Every generation rewrites history in tune with its own perceptions and priorities. For example, in current thinking, both basic and applied, the role of attentional processes receives much weight. From a heuristic (if not an experimental) standpoint, James M. Baldwin (e.g., 1906) probably had as much of value to communicate as any other 20th-century writer. He drew notice to differential attention in selecting stimuli and helping organize them into networks or "mental categories," and he extended this thrust into an analysis of abstraction based on feedback and classification. Nevertheless, his direct impact was probably minor, as a result of historical forces. When the young Ayatollahs of behaviorism deposed the structuralistic Shahs, contributions like Baldwin's were relegated to the dusty archives of discredited discourse (see Rosenthal & Zimmerman, 1978). Since history is usually penned by chroniclers on the victorious side, it is only fairly recently that such writers as Baldwin have begun to earn posthumous rehabilitation.

Therefore, it seems more fitting for historians than for psychologists to award the laurels of priority in the realm of cognition. Should European—especially Greco–Roman—thinking be excluded from consideration? Here is a brief excerpt from Wheelwright's translation (1951) of the part of Aristotle's *Psychology* that deals with the process of cognition:

The thinking faculty thinks its ideas in terms of images. Not only do sensations determine for the mind its objects of pursuit and avoidance, but independently of sensations, when the mind is wholly preoccupied with its mental images, it may likewise be moved to action. We may, for example, perceive a lighted beacon, and then, observing by our "central sense" that it is in motion, take it to mean that the enemy is coming. But at other times we base our reasoning on the images and thoughts within the soul, building our deliberations about the future on those images now present. And when we declare an object of sense-experience to be pleasurable or painful, our subsequent thoughts about it eventuate in pursuit or avoidance, or, generally speaking, in action. (p. 150)

These ideas are hardly alien to Seligman's conception (e.g., 1978) of learned helplessness or to Bandura's views about the role of outcome expectations in the regulation of behavior. Likewise, when Wilson and Abrams (1977) showed that the *perception* of having ingested alcohol rather than tonic water was more important in restraining heart rate increases to a stressor than was the *fact* of which substance was actually consumed, the passage quoted seems rather modern. Their data seem at least as concordant with Aristotle's as with Skinner's views. Beyond this acknowledgment, attempting finer-grained judgments of relative merit would soon reach sharply diminishing intellectual returns or would run aground of imponderables (e.g., what was really meant by the word translated as "soul").

DIFFERENT AND SAME IN FACT OR IN NAME?

No doubt, there are real divergences in what procognitive therapists do and recommend to aid patients. Some fine intervention thrusts and programs have become identified with such individuals as Beck (1976), Mahoney (1974), and Meichenbaum (1977). Given that they are not Siamese triplets, whether their special emphases are opposing or conflicting is a moot point. Their methods surely are related in various concrete elements and, perhaps more saliently, in their conception of the treatment enterprise. Among workers who are self-defined adherents of these (or any other) procognitive views, variability will also exist. Since SLT has not advocated any "school" approach to therapy, the odds are that its proponents will also spread across that clinical bandwidth that loosely spans the cognitive–behavioral segment of the wider distribution of clinical positions. It would be difficult to cluster the cadres of SLT at some common point, distinct from others; they are dispersed throughout the procognitive range. Under such conditions, the statistical convention is to accept them as part of that same range or population. When the variance among persons is comparable to that among identified groups, no significant differences appear to exist, (i.e., between SLT in particular and cognitive–behavioral treatment approaches more generally). Even if some slight cleavage—demanding elaborate criteria or a very large n to detect—could be found in certain respects, at present the search would have dubious worth. The gain from rejecting the null hypothesis would not seem to justify the efforts required. Under such constraints, a struggle to find "differences" by making overly fine discriminations invites McNemar's retort that "Sometimes a 'what of it' is not an impertinence" (1955, p. 70). This conclusion drawn at the outset, however, rests on some assumptions about how common terms should be defined—that is, on a value judgment (see below).

Rather than trying to mark out arbitrary borders of a nonexistent social learning recipe for giving therapy, some stylistic motifs in thinking about therapy can be mentioned. These are like one band's rendition of a popular song—characteristic, but not unique. Such themes may best be illustrated by contrasting two studies recently completed by my colleagues and myself in Memphis. The first concerned treating dysphoria. Instead of assuming that pleasant cues would help but dreary cues worsen blue mood, we wondered whether *any* events that could interfere with dwelling on sorrowful, self-referent thoughts might be useful. Thus, matched for severity, one client group was taught to engage in and another to imagine pleasant experiences contingent on a blue mood. A third group instead practiced and a fourth visualized annoying events to punish blue moods. All four variations made substantial but equal progress. Another group was guided to attend to impersonal content (e.g., the Equal Rights Amendment) at noncontingent, arbitrarily fixed times of day. These clients expected and judged their treatment to be significantly less helpful than all others found theirs, yet they improved just as much —and far more than untreated controls—on multiple dependent measures (Catanese, Rosenthal, & Kelley, 1979). Our goal was to question whether the reinforcement valence of competing or distracting behavior was critical, or whether disattention to grim ruminations was itself useful (Rosenthal, 1980). Nonetheless, it seems plausible that many procognitive workers not allied with SLT would have similar interests and might raise identical issues, perhaps with the same or with a better research design.

Such overlap appears less likely for the second study. An impression exists that similarity between a client and a treatment model is necessarily desirable, as found in the results that coping models surpass mastery models. Drawing on principles from theories of social judgment and adaptation level, we instead reasoned that if a client were made to feel relatively advantaged in comparison with most fellow sufferers, this might raise self-judged efficacy and hence spur more effort and willingness to strive. Unassertive adults were matched for severity and were read a case description of a "typical" client. In one group, the comparison script depicted a person vastly more submissive than most actual clients were. In a second group, the person was somewhat more assertive, and in a third no less assertive than most clients. Finally, a control group heard no script but was otherwise given all the procedures. On an immediate behavioral test, the results were mainly as predicted. Clients exposed to the severely submissive model were the most assertive. Those given a model whose handicap was similar in degree to their own were the least assertive. The control group and the group with the moderately more submissive model were intermediate in assertiveness (Hung, Rosenthal, & Kelley, 1980). These essential results, showing that severely submissive models promoted more client assertion than similar models, have since been replicated with scripts that were both read aloud and presented in a videotape of a peer in the role of the "typical" case (Hung, 1979).

For good or ill, it seems doubtful that clinicians with views remote from SLT would have been led to undertake research of this kind. We assumed that clients' comparing themselves to a far more handicapped model would lead to a favorable reappraisal of their own competence and hence to more striving in a prompt assertion test. Our reasoning was social-psychological in impetus, and it was related to other experimental work in that area (e.g., Brickman, 1975; Brickman, Coates, & Janoff-Bulmann, 1978). Indeed, many aspects of SLT rest on experimental social psychology and sponsor research that is published in social journals. Just as with experimental cognition, there seems to be more interchange between ongoing work in social psychology and SLT than is true for many other cognitive–behavioral positions. This is asserted as a descriptive statement of why SLT is more liable to explore some paths than it is others. No evaluative tone is intended. As with cognition research, clinical value must be judged by outcome data. Thus, when some applied thrust drawing on sociopsychological thought generates promising results, it ought to be tried—and very likely will be—by neobehavioral and procognitive clinicians who adhere to diverse special allegiances. One may be persuaded that it is desirable in principle to interpenetrate social psychology or cognition as experimental topics. One may even suspect it is shortsighted of one's conceptual cousins not to do likewise. Yet such biases do not seem germane criteria for the purpose of comparing the therapeutic facets of SLT with other procognitive views.

Moreover, psychotherapy in all its forms, viewed in terms of economics, is a salable product like any other. That sober realization needs special attention, because these are hard times for higher education in the academic marketplace and in competing for a share of society's resources. In such circumstances, there may be a temptation to proliferate brands and to overstate their unique assets in order to capture a larger share of the market. As a long-range strategy, this may be self-defeating. The lures of superficial product differentation and the robustness of brand recognition to serve as magnets to entice consumers have their just limits. When too many, and too trivial, features are made the bases of claims to superiority, consumers may decide that there are no meaningful differences among products anyway. Such causation may underlie the declining sector of the market now occupied by American auto producers, who seem progressively to have been losing ground to foreign competition for the kinds of reasons at issue. The glut in food processors, which are now being discounted at drug and variety stores despite extensive media hawking of the several machines, seems another case in point. Scholars should perhaps take heed from these analogies. If inflation of course grades has to some extent debased the meaning of college degrees, parallel hazards may lie in wait if scholastic producers drench their consumers with a myriad of "better" brands involving cosmetic distinctions among largely overlapping ideas and tactics. Perhaps the best way to forestall Senator Proxmire's Golden Fleece Awards is not to invite them.

"A" OR "THE": INSTANCE VERSUS PROTOTYPE

What, then, are the meaningful differences between "social learning" and "cognitive-behavioral" stances toward therapy? If the latter term is used descriptively, to mean views that assign covert processes weight commensurate with that given to overt behavior, then a social learning approach becomes one among several falling within the more general category of *a* cognitive-behavioral orientation. There is much to recommend this labeling strategy. Most important, it makes "cognitive" just an adjective pertaining to cognition—a term in such wide and frequent use that it seems rather risky to confine it at this late point to some more narrow sphere of reference. Further, as earlier noted, many progenitors (both basic and applied) have nourished our present understanding of mental processes and enriched present techniques for changing maladaptive covert patterns. Before the Greeks, very likely, scholars in Egypt, Babylonia, and elsewhere originated and recorded cogent observations that may have informed Hellenic thought, even if those roots are now lost or neglected. On the contemporary stage, SLT is only one among multiple actors. It has lent new insights in some contexts and has borrowed in others. That is, after all, the routine path of evolution in science.

However, if there are those who wish to restrict the term to *the* cognitive-behavioral therapy, and they are further convinced they know which denomination it should be, "the" becomes an article of faith. It is also an invitation to a Tower of Babel, because commonplace, descriptive phrases such as "cognitive-behavioral therapy" or "cognitive-behavior modification" will become equivocal: Does a writer mean a nonperipheralistic approach to applied behavior change, or instead his or her preferred brand? Likewise, it is rash to assume that consensus would leap forward as to which of several somewhat different but largely similar treatment blends should be granted a copyright over the contested sobriquet. In that case, labeling warfare might expand to wider realms of nomenclature and eventually to language at large. (Should this calamity transpire, here and now let me claim verbs for SLT.) More earnestly, at a recent panel discussion (Wilson, 1979) on these issues, speakers not identified with SLT or procognitive views made the point that they have become quite literally confused about the spread of reference and inconsistent usage that seems endemic when procognitive treatment labels are invoked. In the court of ultimate resort, the worth of a defined position toward therapy or "school" of therapy procedures—not its name—will determine its acceptance.

A relatively conventional solution exists to dispel the boding impasse. It is offered here as a modest proposal. Historically, it has not been rare to particularize a common term with a qualifying or identifying cue. Hull, for example, did not conspire to preempt the words "behavior theory." Instead, he and his colleagues spoke of "Hullian" behavior theory, and most audiences knew pretty clearly what was meant. In like vein, litigators for the cognitive mantle might just say who they are, as in "Smithian" or "Jonesian" Cognitive Therapy. Alternatively, some other cue word could be chosen to split one from a second or third variant brand. Take the label "cognitive-behavior modification," for instance, and suppose it has led to several differing emphases, each claiming a higher degree of wholeness, harmony, and radiance. Any one of them could further designate its territory with some such prefix as "idealistic" or "iatrogenic" cognitive-behavior modification. Few of us encountering a solution of this kind would be moved to quibble about proprietorial rights to those words, or even their acronym, ICBM. Failing some analogous resolution, we may face a futile spectacle of semantic disputes about authenticity, ownership of terms, and the like, distracting communal attention from constructive debate over substantive issues.

REFERENCES

Aaronson, A., & Scarborough, H. S. Performance theories for sentence coding: Some quantitative evidence. *Journal of Experimental Psychology: Human Perception and Performance,* 1976, *2,* 56–70.

Akiskal, H. S., Rosenthal, T. L., Haykal, R. F., Rosenthal, R. H., & Scott-Strauss, A. Characterological depressions: Clinical features separating "dysthymic" from "character spectrum" subtypes. *Archives of General Psychiatry,* 1980, *37,* 777–783.

Akiskal, H. S., & Webb, W. L. (Eds.). *Psychiatric diagnosis: Exploration of biological predictors.* New York: SP Medical & Scientific Books, 1978.

Alford, G. S., Webster, J. S., & Sanders, S. H. Covert aversion of two interrelated deviant sexual practices: Obscene phone calling and exhibitionism. A single case analysis. *Behavior Therapy,* 1980, *11,* 15–25.

Ambler, B. A., & Proctor, J. D. The familiarity effect for single-letter pairs. *Journal of Experimental Psychology: Human Perception and Performance,* 1976, *2,* 222–234.

Andre, T., & Womack, S. Verbatim and paraphrased adjunct questions and learning from prose. *Journal of Educational Psychology,* 1978, *70,* 796–802.

Antos, S. J. Processing facilitation in a lexical decision task. *Journal of Experimental Psychology: Human Perception and Performance,* 1979, *5,* 527–545.

Avant, L. L., & Lyman, P. J. Stimulus familiarity modifies perceived duration in prerecognition visual processing. *Journal of Experimental Psychology: Human Perception and Performance,* 1975, *1,* 205–213.

Baldwin, J. M. *Mental development in the child and the race* (3rd rev. ed.). New York: Macmillan, 1906.

Bandura, A. *Principles of behavior modification.* New York: Holt, Rinehart & Winston, 1969.

Bandura, A. Vicarious and self-reinforcement processes. In R. Glaser (Ed.), *The nature of reinforcement.* New York: Academic Press, 1971.

Bandura, A. Self-reinforcement: Theoretical and methodological considerations. *Behaviorism,* 1976, *4,* 135–155.

Bandura, A. *Social learning theory.* Englewood Cliffs, N.J.: Prentice-Hall, 1977. (a)

Bandura, A. Self-efficacy: Toward a unifying theory of behavioral change. *Psychological Review,* 1977, *84,* 191–215. (b)

Bandura, A. Reflections on self-efficacy. *Advances in Behaviour Research and Therapy,* 1978, *1,* 237–269.

Bandura, A. Self-referent thought: The development of self-efficacy. In J. H. Flavell & L. D. Ross (Eds.), *Development of social cognition.* New York: Cambridge Press, 1981.

Bandura, A., & Jeffery, R. W. Role of symbolic coding and rehearsal processes in observational learning. *Journal of Personality and Social Psychology,* 1973, *26,* 122–130.

Bandura, A., Jeffery, R. W., & Bachicha, D. L. Analysis of memory codes and cumulative rehearsal in observational learning. *Journal of Research in Personality,* 1974, *7,* 295–305.

Bandura, A., Jeffery, R. W., & Gajdos, E. Generalizing change through participant modeling with self-directed mastery. *Behaviour Research and Therapy,* 1975, *13,* 141–152.

Bandura, A., & Walters, R. H. *Adolescent aggression.* New York: Ronald Press, 1959.

Bandura, A., & Walters, R. H. *Social learning and personality development.* New York: Holt, Rinehart & Winston, 1963.

Banks, W. P., Clark, H. H., & Lucy, P. The locus of the semantic congruity effect in comparative judgments. *Journal of Experimental Psychology: Human Perception and Performance,* 1975, *1,* 35–47.

Bassili, J. N. Temporal and spatial contingencies in the perception of social events. *Journal of Personality and Social Psychology,* 1976, *33,* 680–685.

Beck, A. T. *Cognitive therapy and the emotional disorders.* New York: International Universities Press, 1976.

Bell, H. H., & Handel, S. The role of pattern goodness in the reproduction of backward masked patterns. *Journal of Experimental Psychology: Human Perception and Performance,* 1976, *2,* 139–150.

Bjorklund, D. F., Ornstein, P. A., & Haig, J. R. Developmental differences in organization and recall: Training in the use of organization techniques. *Developmental Psychology,* 1977, *13,* 175–183.

Blanchard, E. B. The relative contributions of modeling, information influences, and physical contacts in the extinction of phobic behavior. *Journal of Abnormal Psychology,* 1970, *76,* 55–61.

Borden, B. L., & White, G. M. Some effects of observing a model's reinforcement schedule and rate of responding on extinction and response rate. *Journal of Experimental Psychology,* 1973, *97,* 41–45.

Bower, G. H. Contacts of cognitive psychology with social learning theory. *Cognitive Therapy and Research,* 1978, *2,* 123–146.

Bregman, A. S., & Rudnicky, A. I. Auditory segregation: Stream or streams? *Journal of Experimental Psychology: Human Perception and Performance,* 1975, *1,* 263–267.

Brickman, P. Adaptation level determinants of satisfaction with equal and unequal outcome distributions in skill and chance situations. *Journal of Personality and Social Psycholo-*

gy, 1975, *32,* 191–198.

Brickman, P., Coates, D., & Janoff-Bulman, R. Lottery winners and accident victims: Is happiness relative? *Journal of Personality and Social Psychology,* 1978, *36,* 917–927.

Brown, I., Jr. Language acquisition: Linguistic structure and rule-governed behavior. In G. R. Whitehurst & B. J. Zimmerman (Eds.), *The functions of language and cognition.* New York: Academic Press, 1979.

Brown, I., Jr., & Inouye, D. K. Learned helplessness through modeling: The role of perceived similarity in competence. *Journal of Personality and Social Psychology,* 1978, *36,* 900–908.

Bundesen, C., & Larsen, A. Visual transformation of size. *Journal of Experimental Psychology: Human Perception and Performance,* 1975, *1,* 214–220.

Carver, C. S. A cybernetic model of self-attention processes. *Journal of Personality and Social Psychology,* 1979, *37,* 1251–1281.

Catanese, R. A., Rosenthal, T. L., & Kelley, J. E. Strange bedfellows: Reward, punishment, and impersonal distraction strategies in treating dysphoria. *Cognitive Therapy and Research,* 1979, *3,* 299–305.

Chow, S. L., & Murdock, B. B. Concurrent memory load and the rate of readout from iconic memory. *Journal of Experimental Psychology: Human Perception and Performance,* 1976, *2,* 179–190.

Clark, H. H., & Brownell, H. H. Judging up and down. *Journal of Experimental Psychology: Human Perception and Performance,* 1975, *1,* 339–352.

Cohen, E. A., Gelfand, D. M., Dodd, D. K., Jense, J., & Turner, C. Self-control practices associated with weight loss maintenance in children and adolescents. *Behavior Therapy,* 1980, *11,* 26–37.

Cooper, L. A., & Shepard, R. N. Mental transformations in the identification of left and right hands. *Journal of Experimental Psychology: Human Perception and Performance,* 1975, *1,* 48–56.

Cosgrove, G. M., & Patterson, C. J. Plans and the development of listener skills. *Developmental Psychology,* 1977, *13,* 557–564.

Craig, K. D. Social modeling influences on pain. In R. A. Sternbach (Ed.), *The psychology of pain.* New York: Raven Press, 1978.

Dansereau, D. F., Collins, K. W., McDonald, B. A., Holley, C. D., Garland, J., Diekhoff, G., & Evans, S. H. Development and evaluation of a learning strategy training program. *Journal of Educational Psychology,* 1979, *71,* 64–73.

Davis, G. C., Buchsbaum, M. S., & Bunney, W. E., Jr. Alterations of evoked potentials link research on attention dysfunction to peptide response symptoms of schizophrenia. In M. Trabucchi & E. Costa (Eds.), *Neurology, peptides and neuronal communication.* New York: Raven Press, in press.

Duncan, J. Divided attention: The whole is more than the sum of its parts. *Journal of Experimental Psychology: Human Perception and Performance,* 1979, *5,* 216–228.

Dykes, J. R., Jr. A demonstration of selection of analyzers for integral dimensions. *Journal of Experimental Psychology: Human Perception and Performance,* 1979, *5,* 734–745.

Eisler, R. M., Blanchard, E. B., Fitts, H., & Williams, J. G. Social skill training with and without modeling on schizophrenic and non-psychotic hospitalized psychiatric patients. *Behavior Modification,* 1978, *2,* 147–172.

Ells, J. G., & Gotts, G. H. Serial reaction time as a function of the nature of repeated events. *Journal of Experimental Psychology: Human Perception and Performance,* 1977, *3,* 234–242.

Eysenck, H. J. The conditioning model of neurosis. *The Behavioral and Brain Sciences,* 1979, *2,* 155–166.

Farrell, W. S., Jr. Coding left and right. *Journal of Experimental Psychology: Human Percep-*

tion and Performance, 1979, *5,* 42–51.

Finke, R. A., & Schmidt, M. J. Orientation-specific color aftereffects following imagination. *Journal of Experimental Psychology: Human Perception and Performance,* 1977, *3,* 599–606.

Frase, L. T., & Schwartz, B. J. Typographical cues that facilitate comprehension. *Journal of Educational Psychology,* 1979, *71,* 197–206.

Gagnon, J. H., & Davison, G. C. Asylums, the token economy, and the metrics of mental life. *Behavior Therapy,* 1976, *7,* 528–534.

Gelfand, D. M., & Hartmann, D. P. *Child behavior analysis and therapy.* New York: Pergamon, 1975.

Gerst, M. S. Symbolic coding processes in observational learning. *Journal of Personality and Social Psychology,* 1971, *19,* 7–17.

Gholson, B. *The cognitive–developmental basis of human learning: Studies in hypothesis testing.* New York: Academic Press, 1980.

Glynn, S. M., & DiVesta, F. J. Outline and hierarchical organization as aids for study and retrieval. *Journal of Educational Psychology,* 1977, *69,* 89–95.

Greiner, J. M., & Karoly, P. Effects of self-control training on study activity and academic performance: An analysis of self-monitoring, self-reward, and systematic planning components. *Journal of Counseling Psychology,* 1976, *23,* 495–502.

Harris, M. B. Sex role stereotpyes, models' race, and imitation. *Psychological Reports,* 1977, *41,* 875–885.

Harris, M. B., & Siebel, C. E. Effects of sex, occupation, and confidence of model and sex and grade of subject on imitation of language behavior. *Developmental Psychology,* 1976, *12,* 80–90.

Hawkins, H. L., Reicher, G. M., Rogers, M., & Peterson, L. Flexible coding in word recognition. *Journal of Experimental Psychology: Human Perception and Performance,* 1976, *2,* 380–385.

Hillix, W. A., & Marx, M. H. Response strengthening by information and effect in human learning. *Journal of Experimental Psychology,* 1960, *60,* 97–102.

Hung, J. H. F. *Harnessing of social comparison effects in assertion training.* Unpublished doctoral dissertation, Memphis State University, 1979.

Hung, J. H. F., Rosenthal, T. L., & Kelley, J. E. Social comparison models spur immediate assertion: "So you think you're submissive?" *Cognitive Therapy and Research,* 1980, *4,* 223–234.

James, W. *The principles of psychology.* New York: Holt, 1890.

Jeffery, R. W. The influence of symbolic and motor rehearsal in observational learning. *Journal of Research in Personality,* 1976, *10,* 116–127.

Jeffery, R. W., & Wing, R. R. Frequency of therapist contact in the treatment of obesity. *Behavior Therapy,* 1979, *10,* 186–192.

Johnston, W. A., & Heinz, S. P. Depth of nontarget processing in an attention task. *Journal of Experimental Psychology: Human Perception and Performance,* 1979, *5,* 168–175.

Kallman, H. J., & Massaro, D. W. Similarity effects in backward recognition masking. *Journal of Experimental Psychology: Human Perception and Performance,* 1979, *5,* 110–128.

Kanfer, F. H., & Phillips, J. S. *Learning foundations of behavior therapy.* New York: Wiley, 1970.

Kazdin, A. E. Effects of covert modeling and coding of modeled stimuli on assertive behavior. *Behavior Research and Therapy,* 1979, *17,* 53–61.

Kelso, J. A. S. Motor control mechanisms underlying human movement reproduction. *Journal of Experimental Psychology: Human Perception and Performance,* 1977, *3,* 529–543.

Kelso, J. A. S., Southard, D. L., & Goodman, D. On the coordination of two-handed movements. *Journal of Experimental Psychology: Human Perception and Performance,* 1979, *5,* 229–238.

Leonard, L. B. The role of nonlinguistic stimuli and semantic relations in children's acquisition of grammatical utterances. *Journal of Experimental Child Psychology,* 1975, *19,* 346–357.

Lewin, K. *A dynamic theory of personality.* New York: McGraw-Hill, 1935.

Mahoney, M. J. *Cognition and behavior modification.* Cambridge, Mass.: Ballinger, 1974.

Mahoney, M. J. *Scientist as subject: The psychological imperative.* Cambridge, Mass.: Ballinger, 1976.

Mahoney, M. J., & Arnkoff, D. Cognitive and self-control therapies. In S. L. Garfield & A. E. Bergin (Eds.), *Handbook of psychotherapy and behavior change* (2nd ed.). New York: Wiley, 1978.

Malin, J. T. Information-processing load in problem solving by network search. *Journal of Experimental Psychology: Human Perception and Performance,* 1979, *5,* 379–390.

Matsuda, N., & Robbins, D. Prototype abstraction and distinctive feature learning: An application to Chinese characters. *Journal of Educational Psychology,* 1977, *69,* 15–23.

McNemar, Q. *Psychological statistics* (2nd ed.). New York: Wiley, 1955.

Meichenbaum, D. *Cognitive-behavior modification.* New York: Plenum, 1977.

Meichenbaum, D., & Asarnow, J. Cognitive-behavior modification and metacognitive development: Implications for the classroom. In P. C. Kendall & S. D. Hollon (Eds.), *Cognitive-behavioral interventions: Theory, research, and procedures.* New York: Academic Press, 1979.

Meichenbaum, D. C., & Butler, L. Toward a conceptual model for the treatment of test anxiety: Implications for research and treatment. In I. G. Sarason (Ed.), *Test anxiety: Theory, research, and applications.* Hillsdale, N.J.: Erlbaum, 1980.

Miller, J. Cognitive influences on perceptual processing. *Journal of Experimental Psychology: Human Perception and Performance,* 1979, *5,* 546–562.

Miller, N. E., & Dollard, J. *Social learning and imitation.* New Haven: Yale University Press, 1941.

Mischel, W. On the future of personality measurement. *American Psychologist,* 1977, *32,* 246–254.

Moore, B., Mischel, W., & Zeiss, A. Comparative effects of the reward stimulus and its cognitive representation in voluntary delay. *Journal of Personality and Social Psychology,* 1976, *34,* 419–424.

Neill, W. T. Inhibitory and facilitatory processes in selective attention. *Journal of Experimental Psychology: Human Perception and Performance,* 1977, *3,* 444–450.

Nelson, K. E. Facilitating children's syntax acquisition. *Developmental Psychology,* 1977, *13,* 101–107.

Patterson, C. J., & Mischel, W. Effects of temptation-inhibiting and task-facilitating plans on self-control. *Journal of Personality and Social Psychology,* 1976, *33,* 209–217.

Peterson, L., Hartmann, D. P., & Gelfand, D. M. Developmental changes in the effects of dependency and reciprocity cues on children's moral judgments and donation rates. *Child Development,* 1977, *48,* 1331–1339.

Rachman, S. J., & Wilson, G. T. *Effects of psychological therapies.* New York: Pergamon, 1980.

Raugh, M. R., & Atkinson, R. C. A mnemonic method for learning a second-language vocabulary. *Journal of Educational Psychology,* 1975, *67,* 1–16.

Rigney, J. W., & Lutz, K. A. Effect of graphic analogies in chemistry on learning and attitude. *Journal of Educational Psychology,* 1976, *68,* 305–311.

Robinson, G. M. Rhythmic organization in speech processing. *Journal of Experimental Psychology: Human Perception and Performance,* 1977, *3,* 83–91.

Rosch, E. The nature of mental codes for color categories. *Journal of Experimental Psychology: Human Perception and Performance,* 1975, *1,* 303–322.

Rosch, E., Simpson, C., & Miller, R. S. Structural bases of typicality effects. *Journal of Experimental Psychology: Human Perception and Performance,* 1976, *2,* 491–502.

Rosenthal, T. L. Social cueing processes. In M. Hersen, R. M. Eisler, & P. M. Miller (Eds.), *Progress in behavior modification* (Vol. 10). New York: Academic Press, 1980.

Rosenthal, T. L., & Bandura, A. Psychological modeling: Theory and practice. In S. L. Garfield & A. E. Bergin (Eds.), *Handbook of psychotherapy and behavior change* (2nd ed.). New York: Wiley, 1978.

Rosenthal, T. L., & Zimmerman, B. J. *Social learning and cognition.* New York: Academic Press, 1978.

Rotter, J. B. *Social learning and clinical psychology.* Englewood Cliffs, N.J.: Prentice-Hall, 1954.

Royer, J. M., & Cable, C. W. Illustrations, analogies, and facilitative transfer in prose learning. *Journal of Educational Psychology,* 1976, *68,* 205–209.

Rubin, W. M. Application of signal detection theory to error detection in ballistic motor skills. *Journal of Experimental Psychology: Human Perception and Performance,* 1978, *4,* 311–320.

Ruble, D. N., & Brooks-Gunn, J. Menstrual symptoms: A social cognition analysis. *Journal of Behavioral Medicine,* 1979, *2,* 171–194.

Rushton, J. P. Effects of prosocial television and film material on the behavior of viewers. In L. Berkowitz (Ed.), *Advances in experimental social psychology* (Vol. 12). New York: Academic Press, 1979.

Schvaneveldt, R. W., Meyer, D. E., & Becker, C. A. Lexical ambiguity, semantic context, and visual word recognition. *Journal of Experimental Psychology: Human Perception and Performance,* 1976, *2,* 243–256.

Seligman, M. E. P. Comment and integration. *Journal of Abnormal Psychology,* 1978, *84,* 165–179.

Smedslund, J. Between the analytic and the arbitrary: A case study of psychological research. *Scandinavian Journal of Psychology,* 1979, *20,* 129–140.

Smith, M. C. Contextual facilitation in a letter search task depends on how the prime is processed. *Journal of Experimental Psychology: Human Perception and Performance,* 1979, *5,* 239–251.

Solso, R. L., & Raynis, A. Prototype formation from imaged, kinesthetically, and visually presented geometric figures. *Journal of Experimental Psychology: Human Perception and Performance,* 1979, *5,* 701–712.

Spoehr, K. T., & Smith, E. E. The role of orthographic and phonotaxic rules in perceiving letter patterns. *Journal of Experimental Psychology: Human Perception and Performance,* 1975, *1,* 21–34.

Stewart, D. M., & Hamilton, M. L. Imitation as a learning strategy in the acquisition of vocabulary. *Journal of Experimental Child Psychology,* 1976, *21,* 380–392.

Sullivan, H. S. *Conceptions of modern psychiatry.* New York: Norton, 1953.

Warren, D. H., & Schmitt, T. L. On the plasticity of visual–proprioceptive bias effects. *Journal of Experimental Psychology: Human Perception and Performance,* 1978, *4,* 302–310.

Wheelwright, P. (trans.). [*Aristotle.*] New York: Odyssey, 1951.

Wilson, G. T. (Chair). *Cognition and behavior therapy.* Featured panel discussion presented at the Association for Advancement of Behavior Therapy convention, San Francisco, December 1979.

Wilson, G. T., & Abrams, D. Effects of alcohol on social anxiety and physiological arousal: Cognitive versus pharmacological processes. *Cognitive Therapy and Research,* 1977, *1,* 195–210.

Yussen, S. R. Determinants of visual attention and recall in observational learning by preschoolers and second graders. *Developmental Psychology,* 1974, *10,* 93–100.

Yussen, S. R. Observational learning. *Science,* 1979, *204,* 400.

Zeiss, A. M. Lewinsohn, P. M., & Muñoz, R. F. Nonspecific improvement effects in depression using interpersonal skill training, Pleasant Activity Schedules, or cognitive training. *Journal of Consulting and Clinical Psychology,* 1979, *47,* 427–439.

Zimmerman, B. J. Concepts and classification. In G. R. Whitehurst & B. J. Zimmerman (Eds.), *The functions of language and cognition.* New York: Academic Press, 1979.

Zimmerman, B. J., & Blotner, R. Effects of model persistence and success on children's problem solving. *Journal of Educational Psychology,* 1979, *71,* 508–513.

IV

ASSESSMENT
AND METHODOLOGY

9

BEHAVIORAL ASSESSMENT

FREDERICK H. KANFER
Department of Psychology
University of Illinois

W. ROBERT NAY
Department of Psychology
University of Illinois

This chapter presents a brief review of the development of strategies for behavioral assessment within the process of clinical assessment. Two critical assessment issues are repeatedly addressed: (1) those relating to the clinician's judicious selection of information to formulate task-relevant hypotheses; and (2) those relating to the selection and evaluation of methods to test these hypotheses in a manner that furthers the process of making clinical decisions and case recommendations. The common idealized sequence in behavioral assessment is presented in these steps: (1) definition of the assessment task to determine what information would be most useful for a decision that a referring agent or the clinician must make; (2) selection of the most promising combinations of persons, situations, and behavior patterns for detailed analysis; (3) selection of a method or test instrument to assess the chosen behaviors, by persons and in situations; (4) consideration of the effects of the assessment procedure on the client(s); and (5) evaluation of the utility and cost–benefit ratios of various possible assessment procedures, including the assessment task itself.

INTRODUCTION

Until the middle of the 1960s, a major task of clinical psychologists was the diagnosis of behavioral disorders. Based on various psychodynamic models of personality and roughly parallel to the operation of medical doctors in the treatment of infectious and bacterial diseases, it was a widely held assumption that psychological deviations and disturbances represented common disease processes. In a theoretical framework that presumed that neuroses and psychoses had common etiological factors, either in the biological or genetic constitution of the person or in some deviant developmental processes, it was logical to expect that a proper categorization of a syndrome would yield information about the etiological factors, the nature of the psychological disease process, and the probable future course of this process. Proper diagnosis, therefore, together with a body of knowledge about effective means for arresting or reversing the disease process, was expected to yield a prognostic statement and indications for a particular treatment. In this framework, the assessor's task was the assignment of persons to diagnostic categories. Numerous attacks on this model (Schmidt & Fonda, 1956; Zigler & Phillips, 1961) have well documented the limitations of this assumption. Not only is there serious question that the majority of psychological disturbances represent unitary psychological syndromes; it is also doubtful that most psychological complaints can be dealt with by sole focus on the patient, to the exclusion of a maintaining environment. Current trends in assessment point to the increasing use of a systems approach (e.g., Kanfer & Grimm, 1975; Nay, 1979; Sundberg, 1977; Zifferblatt, 1973), in which both levels and interaction of levels are selected for assessment, and the information is integrated to suit the questions formulated by the assessor (e.g., Sundberg, Tyler, & Taplin, 1973).

Experience has also shown that diagnosis based on a description of personal characteristics, developmental histories, and particular behavior patterns may not yield useful information for formulating specific intervention procedures or for predicting clients' responses to treatment. The rejection of diagnosis is illustrated at its extreme by the admonitions of the pioneers of behavior therapy to focus only on the patients' symptoms—the current observable behavioral deviations—and to abandon attempts at a diagnostic classification system altogether. For example, Eysenck (1959) advised clinicians to get rid of the symptom, thereby eliminating the neurosis.

Early behavioral alternatives to diagnosis stressed the need for a functional analysis of a client's behavior, the controlling environment, and the relationships between these, as a basis for treatment formulation (Baer, Wolf, & Risley, 1968; Bijou & Peterson, 1971; Ferster, 1965; Kanfer & Saslow, 1965). Given the assumption that abnormal behavior is the result of specific untoward person–environment interactions, a major focus of assessment was the determination of variables that control deviant behaviors. The change process consisted of the unlearning of habitual behavior patterns, the alteration of inappropriate or undesirable environmental controlling factors, or the development of new skills to enable the person to better handle everyday environmental demands.

Application of functional behavior analysis to a variety of populations yielded two clear trends. First, an emphasis on observable behaviors resulted in a shift toward the use of systematic applications of learning programs to specific target behaviors. Increased effectiveness, albeit often in the achievement of well-defined but narrow goals, becomes possible at a reduced cost and time (e.g., in reduction of phobias, bedwetting, aggressive child behaviors, and others). Second, despite the inherent idiosyncratic nature of a functional analysis, it became clear that many groups showed similar patterns of disturbance. Although it is not clear whether such common features are a product of similar cultural expectations, similar social environments, or similar biological predispositions, this possibility suggests that generic change programs may be more feasible and certainly more economical than idiosyncratic treatments.

While behavioral analysis thus began as a general directive for the collection of information, analysis of behavioral determinants, and selection of targets, it did not provide guidelines to assist the clinician in selecting among many symptoms as the critical targets along some dimension of priorities. Nor did it help to develop treatment objectives in the sequence for greatest efficacy. A survey of behavioral clinicians (Kanfer, 1972) suggested that traditional personality tests, and particularly the interview, were widely used in the contest of discovery (Reichenbach, 1951)—that is, in the development of hypotheses about appropriate target selection, rather than in their verification. In essence, the behavioral analysis is used as a broad guide for scanning the range of behaviors and determinants relevant to the clinical problem. Application of a systematic analysis yields further suggestions for the class of events to be considered for closer scrutiny, following the general S-O-R-K-C model (Kanfer & Phillips, 1970).

The relevance of an observed functional relationship to a presented problem has often been judged less in terms of content than in terms of quantifiable relationships among the elements of the analysis. For example, early analyses of depressive behavior were couched in terms of a reduction of obtainable reinforcers (Ferster, 1973; Lewinsohn, 1974). Similarly, phobias were understood in terms of emotional reactions to items on a graded hierarchy (Wolpe, 1969). While this approach has been criticized as excessively "peripheral," a more proper question may be raised about its limitations for providing the necessary analysis of the sociocultural context in which the individual lives and in which such "responses" are expected. For example, before treatment decisions can be made, excessive fears or deficits in assertive skills must be understood in relation to the demands made on persons by prevailing social norms and to the consequences of the behavior in specific situations.

We now bring these points into focus in the context of two major components of the process of clinical assessment and decision making: (1) the wise selection of information to formulate hypotheses that facilitate successful interventions; and (2) the verification (or refutation) of these hypotheses by use of assessment methods that meet commonly accepted criteria of objectivity, reliability, and validity. A consideration of the first component involves epistemological issues inherent in the diagnostic process—the means by which information is selected and organized from among person-by-situation possibilities, and the relative importance attributed to various categories of this information in explaining life problems. The second component includes methodological issues of measurement—selection of appropriate, valid, and economical methods for translating hypotheses into testable operations. The two components parallel the contexts of scientific work described by Reichenbach (1951) as the context of discovery and the context of verification. A clear separation of the components is, of course, illusory. As hypotheses are put to the test, assessment operations suggest refinements of old hypotheses or formulations of new ones, which must be evaluated. The discovery component relies heavily on the clinician's experience, skill, familiarity with psychological principles, prevailing sociocultural norms, and awareness of nonpsychological variables (e.g., biological, sociological, economic). The verification component deals with problems for which measurement theory, psychometric procedures, and scientific rules of procedure provide more definitive guidelines. An overview of issues important to each component would seem to provide a useful context for the substantive material that follows.

SELECTION OF INFORMATION

Apart from the presented complaint and collateral information, an almost endless number of facts about the person or the life situation could be assessed as potential sources for understanding current patterns of behavior. Whether obtained from life histories, behavior observations, or self-reports, the relevance of the data usually depends upon the clinician's particular conceptualization about human behavior and its determinants. It is obvious that the way in which the clinical task is defined and the clinician's biases about what is a desirable state for the client (the way things *ought to be*) also affect the selection of information about the current state (the way things *are*), as well as the means by which the transformation is planned.

In an analysis of the clinical process, Kaminski (1970) has proposed that at least five stores of knowledge can be tapped for hypothesis formulation and the selection and organization of client data. They are as follows:

1. Scientific theories or comprehensive models of human behavior and social systems. For some phenomena, there may be "miniature theories" or principles that are restricted in scope but thoroughly substantiated. This domain of resources is generally well established and contains knowledge that has withstood close scrutiny and experimental tests.
2. Empirically established and tested relationships, yielding statements of some generalizable scope.
3. Clinical lore about specific aspects of human behavior based on the ac-

cumulation of shared clinical experiences with many clients in different places and at different times. However, stringent experimental tests of these assertions are either lacking or have yielded uncertain conclusions.

4. Professional experience in dealing with clinical problems. This knowledge is gained from training, clinical reports and literature, and information exchange with and observation of colleagues, as well as personal experience. The generalizations derived from these experiences are based on limited evidence and are often speculative.

5. Personal experiences in everyday life, nonprofessional reports, and general information about people and settings. This store of information, shared by professional and lay persons, simply constitutes observations and common wisdoms about human nature that an adult gathers over a lifetime.

When we speak of a science of clinical psychology, we hope that the first two stores of knowledge are predominant sources of the clinician's hypotheses. Theoretical principles serve mainly as a guide in our search for variables that may be critical and may help us focus on possible outcomes (Cronbach, 1977). Thus, even well-established principles of behavior cannot be assumed to operate or to be useful unless their implications are tested in a particular clinical case. But as we bring to bear on a case information from the stores of knowledge already reviewed, we add power and increase the likelihood that we will be more skilled in posing relevant questions than the average lay person will be. The differences between professionals and lay persons should become even more significant as procedures are applied to test the appropriateness and utility of the formulation.

Much of the literature on clinical diagnosis has addressed itself to the testing of hypotheses derived from theories of personality and behavior. Some attention has also been given to the clinician's behavior in diagnosis, particularly as it concerns the process of person perception and the influence of sociocultural variables on the kinds of information employed for making inferences about the person in a situation. Unfortunately, little has been offered to guide clinicians in their task of seeking and ordering information about clients for the purpose of defining objectives and planning behavior change.

VERIFYING THE FORMULATION

A second consequence of an emphasis on the clinician's role as an agent of behavior change is that the development of behavior-assessment techniques has been neglected. It is interesting to note that behaviorally oriented clinicians have attended to the objectivity, replicability, and validity of various change procedures, but have given little attention to applying these criteria in the service of evaluating the information on which change procedures are based. This relative lack of attention to the validity of assessment methods has led

Sundberg (1977) to comment that "the same general psychometric concepts and principles apply to behavioral measures as to any other; the APA standards for tests (1974) need to be studied by behaviorists, too" (p. 168).

Psychology has long been concerned with the measurement of persons and situations, and the study of psychometric issues in test development has a long-standing and respected history. British behavioral psychologists, under the influence of Eysenck (1953, 1960), Shapiro (1951, 1966), and others, tended to continue to use and develop methods for assessing psychopathology and individual behavior patterns as a basis for intervention. In contrast, American behavior therapists generally proceeded directly to modification of target behaviors. Only recently did they recognize the importance of integrating test and theory into the diagnostic clinical process. Goldfried and D'Zurilla (1969) were among the first to describe procedural rules for developing standardized behavioral tests. During the last several years, this concern has come to the forefront and is reflected in the publication of books on assessment tools, in increased research, and in the establishment of new journals concerned with measurement within the clinical process. This shift is also noticed in the widespread use of the term "behavioral assessment" as a substitute for "clinical diagnosis."

The increased attention to the methodological component of assessment does not lessen the importance of integrating both epistemological and methodological issues in providing the clinician with improved rules for carrying out the behavioral assessment.

In the remainder of this chapter, we discuss issues that are relevant to the usual sequence of steps in designing, implementing, and evaluating a behavioral-assessment procedure.

DEFINING THE ASSESSMENT TASK

In actual practice, it is rare that the assessor is called upon to apply an assessment instrument to answer a well-articulated question. Most frequently, the clinical assessment is initiated by a referral statement that might be constructed either by one or more persons who are themselves experiencing some degree of discomfort or inefficiency in life (e.g., an individual, a couple, a family); by an interested party (e.g., a physician or friend); or by a social agent (e.g., a teacher, a social worker, or a court). The statement is couched in a language that makes sense to the referring person and reflects the vantage point from which that individual perceives the client's behavior (e.g., self, significant other, or distant other). But the aspects of the client's behavior that are detected and reported by the referring person, even if accurately observed, may represent only a small part of the total configuration of the client's behavior in a situation. For example, when a child is referred by a teacher because of a "lack of attentiveness" in class and "inadequate class preparation," the assessor may decide not only to assess the child's abilities, interests, or classroom behavior; he or she may also wish to examine the child's home situation and other potential sources of influence, such as the length of time spent in nonacademic pursuits or availability of peer models.

Thus the referral statement is merely a place to begin. From it a series of questions are developed, and these questions must be linked to the decisions the assessor will have to make at the end of the assessment process. Before proceeding to a review of the kinds of assessment tasks that the assessor might entertain, as a prelude to discussing important issues associated with each step in clinical assessment, it is worth noting that the articulateness and specificity of these initial questions limit in advance what can possibly be detected. The nature of these questions also defines the limits of generalizability of any information obtained. In addition, it should be obvious that once specific assessment questions are posed, new questions may be generated or questions may be altered as new information is collected. Thus, the important interrelationship between the posing of questions and the gathering of information is a dynamic process that cannot be fully predicted in advance. An important implication of this analysis is that a thoroughgoing, methodologically sophisticated assessment with respect to an initial question may be totally inadequate for answering questions that emerge as the assessment process unfolds. Therefore, the selection of methods must continually mesh with modification of the questions. And these questions implicitly express the assessor's purpose.

This chapter strongly emphasizes the linkage between the purposes, the assessment methodology, and the ultimate generalizations that can be made about information obtained by the methods described here. We feel that the interactive and heuristic nature of the assessment process needs to be underscored in view of recent publications on behavioral assessment, which have tended to overemphasize specific methodologies as exhibiting this or that psychometric property, or as useful across quite diverse situations and settings without regard to the limits of their generalizability. We stress that any evaluation of a behavioral-assessment procedure must be clearly and carefully linked to the purposes to which it is applied. It exhibits no properties outside of those purposes.

COMMON ASSESSMENT TASKS

Assessors are often asked to compare an individual or group to a defined population with respect to some characteristic or behavior, or to characterize the functioning of an individual or an interpersonal unit (e.g., a couple or family) across diverse conditions and situations. The first assessment category might be termed "interindividual" assessment, while the second is an "intraindividual" task (whether "individual" is defined to include a single client or a group of clients). As has already been mentioned, the initial task of the assessor is to recast the referral question in such a way that a series of steps can be developed to amass evidence for or against a decision implied by the referral. The process begins with a preliminary definition of the assessment task, to which methods must then be applied. In some cases the assessor may be asked only to report the presence or magnitude of some variables contributing to a problem. In others, the assessor may have full responsibility not only for describing critical aspects that influence a problem in living, but also for initiating a remedial program to transform or eliminate certain areas of complaint. In attempting a brief description of the most common tasks that an assessor faces, it should be made clear that several of them may be called for in a specific case. The ultimate sequence and priority of those tasks, of course, will depend upon the purpose of the assessment and the role or responsibility of the assessor in managing the case.

The following are the most frequent tasks that the assessor faces in clinical practice. These are reviewed to underscore the various ways in which behavioral assessment can be utilized in a total clinical process. The categorization of tasks clearly suggests that what is demanded of an assessor determines the selection of tests or methods, the needed degree of confidence in a conclusion, the structure of the procedure as represented to the client, and the minimal time and effort needed. While a test battery or a set of standardized procedures can satisfy some screening questions, they may be of limited utility, or may even be detrimental, when specific intervention questions are asked or when advice on a decision or disposition is needed.

It is our experience in working with beginning therapists in various clinical settings that costly and time-consuming assessments are frequently carried out in the context of a poorly defined purpose and ambiguously explicated task definition, perhaps in the hope that some important clues will develop out of a large set of data. Readers may have found themselves at times processing many "bits" of assessment information that did not seem to make sense or were difficult to integrate, merely because the assessment was not carefully planned and orchestrated according to a clear statement of purpose.

Assignment to a Diagnostic Category

The diagnostic assignment task usually requires that a person be located within a common psychiatric classification scheme, such as the DSM-III or any other taxonomic system. Interpretations derived from personality tests, interview data, or scores on well-established inventories may be used as a basis for classification. Assignment of a client to a category implies both the applicability of the constructs upon which the category rests to the individual's particular life situation (a question of generalizability), and a decision based on the clinician's personal and theoretical experiences with respect to behaviors expected of persons in the selected category.

While such an assessment request may be useful for administrative, research, or screening purposes, it must be acknowledged that the relationship between a diagnostic label and expected behavior under specified circumstances is relatively tenuous. Thus a diagnostic label should not be used as the sole basis for prediction of future behaviors of an individual across a range of situations that are not yet specified.

Evaluation of Specific Aptitudes, Abilities, Skills, or Situation-Specific Behaviors

The evaluation category includes referrals for information about the client's particular behavioral potentials. The referring person usually has some alternative plan for action in mind, but is uncertain whether the client's personal qualifications are appropriate for successful implementation. The assessor is frequently not asked to comment on the contemplated alternatives for action, as it is most often presumed that the referring person can handle the remainder of the assessment task. Requests for assessments of intellectual ability in school placements, or for evaluations of vocational choices, interpersonal skills, or the expectations of partners in premarital counseling, illustrate this type of request. The request may specify a broad area of functioning, such as perceptual–motor coordination or emotional stability, and the assessor then needs to select appropriate tools. Assessment tasks for screening purposes (e.g., need for hospitalization, suitability for a specific job) also belong in this category. The clinician may be able to safeguard against abuse of this information by indicating the need for interpreting the test results in the light of the broader assessment question. There are innumerable situations in which well-routinized procedures or specific referral by competent professionals permit assessors to play a significant role within this limited domain. In reality, however, such assessment tasks are components of a larger task, which remains the responsibility of the referring person.

Both the selection of tests or assessment techniques and the interpretation of the results require judgment by the clinician. First, the assessor's own experience will influence the selection of instruments that are seen to be most relevant to the task. Second, the client's performances are assessed in terms of sociocultural norms. As the individual is compared on a test or in a behavioral sample to other individuals who have undergone similar procedures, deviations from the norm are presumed to have important implications for the client's potentials. The assessor is therefore called upon to interpret scores, or observed excesses or deficits in perceptual, cognitive, motoric, or emotional channels, in the context of established norms. Often clinical judgments of how "the average" person with similar demographic characteristics would perform under the circumstances must be made in the absence of formal norms. Although the assessor may not have responsibility for further integration of this information into the total picture, he or she is expected to report any significant deviations from the norm in the context of the client's current situation and life goals. The conditions under which the test scores or behavioral samples are obtained must also be considered.

In the behavioral-assessment literature, the role of norms in the process of clinical decision making has been underemphasized (Evans & Nelson, 1977). In clinical studies, criterion-referenced tests (Carver, 1974) are frequently used because of their direct relevance to a treatment goal. But the norm-referenced approach has been too narrowly interpreted. Too often, norms are considered as applicable only as standard scores or stanines reported for an aptitude or intelligence test. But norms as criteria against which an individual's performance is compared are utilized by assessors in all assessment situations, be they standard tests, interviews, behavioral observations, questionnaires, or reports by other persons. When insufficient normative data are available for a procedure, the clinician often compares the person to a reference group with which he or she has had previous experience. Judgments about the position of a person in comparison with a larger population on some dimension may also be made when a clinician evaluates the probability that an adolescent will continue to be delinquent; considers the advisability of therapeutic intervention; or assesses the degree to which a person's interpersonal, sexual, cognitive, or emotional functioning may be sufficiently deviant from sociocultural norms to require change. This issue has been repeatedly stated in the literature on person perception and is at the heart of the controversy of actuarial versus clinical judgment. The assessor's knowledge of base rates for various behaviors in a demographically similar population becomes the unspecified "norm" against which the clinical comparison is often made. It is obvious that the clinician who is unfamiliar with common practices in the subculture in which the client lives can badly misinterpret the significance of test or behavior-sample findings. Among our own experiences illustrating these problems are the serious consequences of erroneous interpretations of aggressive, sexual, competitive, or intellectual behaviors for persons from geographic locations, ethnic minorities, socioeconomic classes, or religious orientations about whose practices the clinician has insufficient prior knowledge.

In contrast to the common practice of providing a clear statement of criteria for admission to research projects, the norms against which an assessor judges a person prior to selecting a treatment strategy or making a decision to terminate are often not clearly stated, even in well-documented published case reports. These omissions may be partly due to a lack of systematically developed norms for a given population in a situation. Or, given the current lack of such reporting in the literature, norms may be based on subjective criteria and therefore may vary in adequacy as a function of the assessor's competence and experience.

We believe that the development of interindividual norms to complement the intraindividual, criterion-referenced approach (e.g., the percentage of change for a given individual across time; see Hartmann, Roper, & Bradford, 1979) is badly needed for many of the decisions that assessors must make.

Transformation of Vague Complaints into Specific Assessment Questions

By far the most common task facing an assessor is the selection and identification of a problem that can be translated into a well-articulated series of assessment questions. In fact, the establishment of the assessor's task represents the initial step. The assessor needs to ask, "What can I contribute (1) to clarify the situation by pinpointing a problem, and thereby (2) to help toward planning a resolution of the problem?" In this group of assessment procedures, an attempt is made to evaluate the discrepancies between a client's behavior and self-generated or environmental demands. A resolution of such discrepancies may be brought about by assessing the relative contributions of situational, psychological, and biological factors that limit the client's behavioral choices, make inordinate demands upon him or her, or cause subjective discomfort. It is important to evaluate personal discomfort, whether or not behavioral dysfunctions are noted by others or interfere with effective daily functioning.

As previously discussed, the comparison of the client's behavior with norms derived from the assessor's experience or from publicly available information about the behavior of others in similar life situations will lead the assessor toward defining some events as solvable problems. Two types of situations should be differentiated: (1) events, states, or deficits for which no resolution can be expected (e.g., advancing age, incapacity due to physical illness, or irretrievable loss of a situation, property, or person); and (2) events or states that can be transformed by altering some aspect of the environment or the behavior of the client. In the former case, the assessment task may focus on means by which the client can learn to adjust to the irreversible situation or to minimize its detrimental impact. In the latter, the assessor must further analyze the problem in terms of component contributions of the various life factors uncovered in order to arrive at an intervention plan.

Assessment for Intervention

Assessment tasks related specifically to possible therapeutic intervention may be manyfold. The assessment problem may be to evaluate the suitability of various intervention methods to achieve a stated therapeutic objective. For this purpose, the assessor would have to be familiar with the treatment under consideration and have some knowledge of the required client skills, resources, and motivations in order to carry out the component procedures.

Another common task is the preparation of the client for subsequent intervention. Or the assessment may have the dual purpose of obtaining further information but also of serving as an intervention technique per se. Thus the reactivity of the assessment procedures may be purposely enhanced, as is the case with many categories of self-observation methods (e.g., Kanfer, 1970; Kazdin, 1974; Nay, 1979). Other intervention-related tasks may focus on the assessment of intraindividual change as a means of evaluating the effectiveness of ongoing therapy. When initial assessment has been thorough and clear therapeutic objectives have been defined, pretherapy versus posttherapy comparisons are relatively easily made, because the assessor has anticipated the behavioral domains in which change is expected and has provided base rates for the events. In the absence of adequate pretreatment assessment, evaluation of behavioral change during treatment remains tenuous and is often subjective. Recourse to descriptions of critical incidents in case records, evaluations of the client by others, or quantified performance evaluations (e.g., grades, job performance, etc.) may provide indirect evidence about therapeutic effectiveness when these items of information are relevant to the therapeutic objective.

Prediction of Future Behavior under Given Conditions

Essentially, the set of predicting tasks differs from evaluating tasks in that the assessor is given more information about the particular setting in which the client will function and then is asked to estimate the probable future occurrence of various behaviors under those conditions. For example, while an intellectual evaluation may be requested for a child who is having difficulties in school, another task might be to assess the probability that this child will function adequately in a school setting where expectations, peers, and discipline methods are known. The assessor may rephrase the task as one of ascertaining the strength of particular behaviors and evaluating their probable occurrences in the projected situation. One of the problems in completing this task is that most actions taken on the basis of assessment rest on the assumption that there is continuity and generality of behavior. But in real life the accuracy of behavioral predictions is frequently distorted by changes in a person's status and by the intervention of unforeseen or unforeseeable future events.

Assessment of Availability of Personal and Environmental Resources

After a problem has been identified and a plan of action has been developed, detailed inquiry may be required to assess the potentials of environmental resources, as well as the client's motivation and repertoire for participating in the proposed course of action. Most frequently, this task addresses the client's motivation for achieving changes that are necessary to assure the success of an intervention program. This task is often formulated in the early stages of treatment or in situations where environmental resources or client cooperation is questionable (Kanfer & Grimm, 1980).

While this list of categories does not cover the innumerable tasks presented to assessors, it illustrates the importance of shifting from a broad initial question to a specific task definition *prior to* undertaking the assessment procedure. In many cases an assessor is asked to contribute relevant psychological information in order to facilitate an administrative decision, or to assist a client in selecting among courses of action with reference to problems that do not lie fully in the psychological domain. For example, in rehabilitation programs, in vocational advising, in medical evaluations, or in legal procedures, the clinical assessment contributes only a small part to the total evaluation process. The contribution of the assessor to this effort often requires an understanding of the full scope of the problem in order to be able to define an assessment task that can make a meaningful contribution.

A final critical issue in defining the task concerns the role of the assessor. The assessment will be affected by the assessor's self-perception as one who gives or collects information, makes decisions, assists the client in making decisions, integrates information to recommend action, or considers the client for therapy. In any case, the assessor must continually reevaluate the appropriateness of the task definition. Once an initial task definition has been accomplished, the assessor turns to the gathering of information. This process first involves segmenting the stream of the client's behavior to limit the domain of inquiry.

SEGMENTING THE STREAM OF BEHAVIOR

Once the task has been defined, the next step is to draw together information gathered from the client or from significant others in order to formulate a list of preliminary assessment questions. These questions refine the purpose of the assessment beyond the global task definition already described in the previous section. The skillful phrasing of these questions is the essential ingredient of a successful assessment enterprise. It must be kept in mind, however, that clients' self-reports alone are often confused or distorted representations of actual events and situations in the clients' lives. Therefore, they are insufficient as the exclusive source of information. Indeed, the report of the clients and of others in their environment may be at odds. Nevertheless, useful information can be obtained with respect to how the clients are presenting themselves and how the clients view the world around them. Often it is the incongruity between a client's view and the perceptions of others that is a central part of the client's problem. This disparity can create difficulties for the client in his or her interactions with others. Therefore information from those other persons may be essential.

Information for posing provisional questions may also be derived from observations of clients during interviews. While behavioral assessors have generally prided themselves on the technological sophistication of observation protocols and self-report inventories, it is surely not coincidence that interviews have long remained a favorite technique for assessment. Their flexibility and the potential they provide for continued observation of clients make them rich sources for both formulation and verification of hypotheses (cf. Nay, 1979). In addition to interviews, a rough assessment of the particular milieu in which the client functions, as well as of the sociocultural norms from which the client and others evaluate a client's behavior and from which some complaint typically emerges, provides additional information for the formulation of questions.

The assessor's theoretical bias determines the relative importance assigned to a client's cognitive structures, attitudes, values, or self-statements; to overtly accessible client behaviors; or to the analysis of the client's interpersonal relationships and the social–ecological milieu within which the client functions. To counter the effects of this bias, it is imperative for the assessor to survey the full range of possible areas of inquiry and to ask, "What components of the person's situation and behavior do I need to look at in order to understand the full context of the apparent problem?" Furthering the earlier recommendations of Kanfer and Saslow (1965), we believe that a premature focus upon a "target" and a technology for change frequently results in the neglect of other important life domains for which the assessor may not have a ready-made intervention strategy at hand. A series of levels and questions should be considered by the assessor at the *planning stage* of the assessment process. This insures that a comprehensive consideration of a problem occurs in the context of the ecological milieu within which the client functions. It guards against excessive attention to targets that are most conspicuous but may not be central to resolution of the client's problems.

The four major levels that define the possible foci for assessment are shown in the columns of Figure 9-1. They range from assessment of an identified client to analysis of the subculture in which the problem occurs. Along the rows of this matrix, six major categories of questions are shown. They subsume information necessary for a comprehensive understanding of a client's life problems. While the general titles are borrowed from journalism for easy recall, the specific information collected in each of these major categories can vary considerably, depending upon the assessor's theoretical orientation. It may be worthwhile to review briefly each column and row heading. Their selective combination provides a multitude of assessment options, and it is expected that for any case only a few cells will be selected for intensive inquiry.

FIGURE 9-1. Matrix of levels and categories of questions for assessment.

	Individual	Significant others	Proximal others	Subculture/ society
What				
Where				
Who				
When				
When . . . then				
Why				

The "individual" level focuses exclusively upon a person or persons (a couple or family) who are initially defined as experiencing some problem in living. Particular individuals are often singled out as experiencing a sufficient amount of discomfort or inefficiency (or provoking a sufficient amount of discomfort among life partners) to warrant intervention of some kind. But frequently such target selection is premature—for example, when an entire family unit may represent a better target for intervention. An early focus on the individual level may lead to developing a program for behavior change that is not crucially related to the client's life difficulties, or to a piecemeal attack upon a limited sphere of dysfunction within the life context. As noted by Goldfried and Davison (1976), Morganstern (1976), and others, the best of programs directed at problematic but trivial aspects of the client's life may fail to produce meaningful improvement. And there is the strong possibility that undetected but important life problems may actually interfere with even the most limited behavioral objectives. Missed appointments, failures to carry out "homework" assignments, and other roadblocks should not be easily discounted as "resistance" on the part of an unmotivated client. Often it is an inaccurate or prematurely formulated assessment that has failed by focusing on a trivial target. As a result, the client may be motivated, but not toward the therapist's objectives. A lack of skill to carry out an assigned task or subservience to the expert's judgments may also prevent the client from correcting the erroneous assessment.

Thus, the remaining levels focus upon aspects of the interpersonal domain that may hold implications for understanding the client's current functioning. These levels include that of "significant others"—those family members, friends, or vocational colleagues who interact with the client on a sufficiently frequent and meaningful basis to be affected by or to have a role in the client's life concerns. Exploration of this level is useful because these persons may also be in a position to assist in an intervention plan. Next, the level of "proximal others" includes those members of the client's immediate community who interact with the client in a less meaningful fashion. The nature of the association, however, may still influence the client's life choices. Examples of proximal others include neighbors, colleagues on the job, fellow students, community leaders, teachers, physicians, and others who have contact with the client. In many cases the characteristics, attitudes, values, and beliefs of proximal others may be summarized in a manner that helps the assessor understand the client's personal orientation and view of the world. Thus, phenomena ranging from norms within a housing subdivision in which the client lives (e.g., norms related to home maintenance, child care, or involvement in community activities), through informal traditions or work norms expressed by coworkers or superiors in a job situation, to the religious values proposed by organized or informal groups with which the client worships all may have an important impact upon the client's life. The final level, and a much more global one, is that of "subculture/society." Community psychologists have focused upon the implications of various facets of the subculture in which an individual resides, as well as of the overarching society within which that subculture is placed, as important predictors and limitors of options for the person in question (e.g., see Rappaport, 1977). At this level, knowledge of client membership in a particular ethnic, socioeconomic, or even political group may assist the assessor in understanding certain life problems; or such memberships may essentially represent the problems themselves.

It is easier to appreciate the importance of the "individual" and "significant others" levels in assessing such targets as a parent's inability to control temper toward a child or inadequate communications between two marital partners than it is to appreciate that of the "proximal others" or "subculture/society" levels. In these two examples, however, it is worth noting that the community (the "subculture/society" level) may greatly influence the client's attitudes, values, and behavior with respect to punishment and violence. Similarly, popular media stereotypes of the "ideal" marital relationship may set up expectations for a couple that are unrealistic or unfortunate. For these reasons, we feel that an appreciation and a brief scan of the impact of these levels upon the client's life are essential.

In summary, we have presented four major levels within which the client might be assessed. It is obvious that the assessor may be unequipped to perform a detailed analysis at all levels for each client, and none may be needed in a given case. Nevertheless, a rough estimate of the significance of each of these levels in the client's current life adjustment is feasible and can be obtained with minimal cost as part of the usual interview or observation strategy.

Following this rough scan, the assessor should be able to *exclude* a given level or levels from further assessment consideration. When justified by a preliminary sketch of the client's life, it may be useful to make inquiries in the community in which the client lives. This may involve collaborating with other professionals, studying archival records of demographics and other characteristics of the client's particular subculture, and interviewing persons other than the client's immediate family. When an assessor cannot intervene at the levels of "significant others" or "proximal others" and their cooperation is critical, a comprehensive intervention plan should ideally be developed with the assistance of other professionals who are capable of such intervention. For example, such collaboration might be required when relocations, adoptions, or job changes represent the optimal alternative.

With respect to the rows of the matrix in Figure 9-1, the questions listed for general assessment will be formulated in terms of the theoretical orientation of the assessor. In the "what" category, an analysis of "what the problem is'' may require scanning major domains of the client's overt behaviors, cognitive and metacognitive events, feelings, and psychophysiological and biochemical phenomenona. Or the "what" may be expressed in terms of an analysis of the characteristic communications between the client and other significant persons (e.g., Haley, 1976; Watzlawick, Beavin, & Jackson, 1967). Elements of the functioning system may have to be assessed (cf. Gurman & Kniskern, 1978).

The "where" row deals with the specific settings in the client's environment where life problems seem to occur. Their selection is critical, because further assessments must focus on them and intervention ultimately must take place within them. Also, ecological characteristics of the settings may have predictive significance for the client's behavior (Barker, 1963; Barker & Wright, 1955; Wright, 1967). For example, investigators have found that the frequency and even the presence of certain "problems" among children are significantly predicted by the setting within which a child is assessed (e.g., Lichstein & Wahler, 1976; Raush, 1958). Thus, whether an individual is viewed as deviant may depend primarily upon the setting in which the assessment occurs.

The next category, "who," details the characters who are imporant for assessment within a given level. Such persons might vary from family members and friends to a probation officer or school principal, depending upon the nature of the relationship (which thus reflects a particular level).

The category of "when" defines the conditions under which relevant persons behave—the interaction of person and setting within an occasion such as a family conference, a classroom session, or a court learning. Thus, "when" describes activities that inextricably bind together individuals during specified times in given settings. "Where" and "when" overlap considerably, as locations often define times and content (e.g., recess in schoolyard, church attendance, etc.). "When" can also come to mean the past and present frequency and/or duration of behavior on the part of individuals or societal entities.

The next category, "when . . . then," specifies the consequences to the client or other persons of any event that is the focus of the assessor's interest. "When . . . then" might include such sequences as the attention an individual receives from making an "inappropriate" statement, the reaction of a child following a parental argument, or the potential human and financial costs of a legislative or court decision.

Finally, the category "why" offers the most direct expression of the assessor's theoretical bias in explaining how the selected phenomenon has developed. "Why" may be expressed in terms of antecedents and consequences, self-statements or irrational beliefs, or pushes and/pulls or balances of a family system.

The use of the proposed matrix *requires* a scanning of broad categories of life events and stimulates an awareness of the context of the client's problem. It provides a "map" that can aid the assessor in organizing a comprehensive assessment plan—one that stresses the larger picture at the outset and reduces both excessive analyses at nonrelevant levels and long-run costs and inefficiency resulting from overly narrow assessment.

SELECTION OF METHOD

Before an assessment technique is employed, the clinician or researcher should specify the decisions that will be made on the basis of the assessment information or the domains of populations, settings, times, or situations to which the information will be generalizable. We have already noted that methods do not exhibit fixed or specific reliability or validity coefficients and do not hold constant properties of generalizability. The characteristics depend upon the purpose of the assessor and the desired *inferences*. For instance, observational data collected in the home under a fixed set of conditions (e.g., employing a given set of time-sampling parameters, limiting family members to certain locations during home observations, or observing only during evening periods when certain family members are present; cf. Patterson, Cobb, & Ray, 1973) may not be generalizable and therefore may not be of use in answering questions about those same family members interacting at different times, at places other than the home, and with other persons. Indeed, we must even be cautious in drawing inferences about family interactions when observers are not present. If we are interested in examining those persons in the family who typically seek each other out or avoid contact, we must clearly make this question a part of our assessment purpose and insure that the assessment technique provides the best representation of that behavior.

There are a variety of methodological options available to an assessor. The choice among them depends on the clinician's preference as well as on the nature of the events to be assessed. Some clinicians and researchers place high credence in overt behavior that can be independently assessed by several observers. Others value self-reports. But it is impossible to make value statements about the worth of any particular technique apart from the specific purpose to which it is applied. For a single case, the mere recounting of data from other studies with respect to psychometric properties of the technique (as is often done in published reports) is not meaningful if the purpose of the assessment is not identical.

A similar point can be made in regard to efforts to evaluate the psychometric properties of a method. One of the hallmarks of a behavioral-assessment approach is a consideration of what is best called the "dependability of measures" (e.g., Cattell, 1964). It is most frequently expressed as the calculation of the percentage of the time that two observers or an observer and some criterion (e.g., scores on a videotape or a previously scored protocol) agree, either with respect to intervals during which some targeted behavior is observed or with respect to overall session totals (see Hartmann, 1977). Much concern has been expressed in recent years about the characteristics of one or another ideal measure of agreement, and attention has been given to reducing the probability of chance agreement and to better representing the population characteristics of the data (e.g., Cohen, 1960; Hartmann, 1977; Nay, 1979). It is unfortunate, however, that little discussion has addressed the issue of what *specific psychometric properties* a given instrument should *ideally* possess.

Occasionally, the constructors of behavioral-assessment methods have performed more traditional evaluations of the stability as well as of the internal consistency of their instruments (e.g., see Jones, Reid, & Patterson, 1975), while others have noted the potential applicability of generalizability theory (e.g., Cronbach, Gleser, Nanda, & Rajaratnam, 1972) to the observation arena (e.g., Cone, 1977). Generalizability theory is, in fact, atheoretical. It does not inform the user of precisely what domains of generalizability are relevant to assess and report. Also, generalizability theory makes no distinction between reliability and validity. Thus, the behavioral assessor is forced to specify in advance those specific domains (e.g., generalizability across observers, settings, or time) that are relevant to the assessment purpose. We feel that this approach is a good model for any clinical assessment in requiring that the assessor *plan* in advance and specify the desired generalizations about the assessment data, even if a formal generalizability study is not performed.

The current state of affairs may be due to the lines of demarcation frequently drawn between "traditional" and "behavioral" assessment (e.g., Goldfried & Kent, 1972). It is our belief that, unlike the theoretical differences that frequently emerge when researchers and practitioners of human behavior discuss the etiology of some "target" or "disorder," the necessary psychometric operations for evaluating an instrument depend *exclusively* upon the specific goals of the assessment enterprise and not upon the domain of the method that is employed (e.g., a personality measure versus a naturalistic observation). Our point moves us fully into the "home court" of construct validity (e.g., Cronbach & Meehl, 1955). While the construct of validity conceptualization was originally developed to permit an evaluation of certain theoretical ideas about individual personality characteristics, we believe that the behavioral assessor in certain important respects operates as a theorist, whether the assessment task involves preintervention assessment, assessment for purposes of clinical decision making, assessment of outcome, or assessment to describe or understand some phenomenon (e.g., Wiggins, 1973).

To illustrate the relationship between issues of construct validity, the selection of a specific behavioral-assessment methodology, and the resultant implications for the best approach to evaluation of that methodology, the reader is referred to Table 9-1. This table shows a variety of criteria that can be employed to characterize almost any behavioral-assessment instrument. We use the example of an observational approach to assessment to illustrate the points already raised. Within each of the categories listed at the top of the columns of Table 9-1, the reader will note a series of method facets, not meant to be exhaustive, that frequently characterize behavioral-assessment instruments employed in the literature. Thus, a "self-observation" approach might employ the client as a supplier of information, perhaps recording each occurrence (event) of some target in the client's natural life situation on a continuous basis. Indeed, almost any variant of observation methods can be represented merely by combining elements across the columns of Table 9-1. For example, participant observation in the home employs an independent observer or significant other ("information supplier"), to produce a written record ("operation") in the home (natural "setting") on a continuous basis ("sampling"). Novel observation methods might be suggested by unique combinations of the column elements, and such a matrix can be constructed for any kind of behavioral-assessment methodology.

Thus, the selection of a multivariate coding system to be employed by independent observers during specified periods (e.g., evenings for 1 week) tells us something about the information that the assessor considers important to an understanding of the client. In selecting a previously established coding

TABLE 9-1. Multiple Criteria for Defining Observation Methods

OPERATION	INFORMATION SUPPLIER	SETTING	SAMPLING
Mechanical (e.g., wrist counter, movement transducer, audio/video recording)	Client Significant other	Natural Clinical natural	Continuous record (e.g., specimen recording)
Product (e.g., trace, erosion, archive, task product)	Independent (e.g., behavior change agent, trained observer)	Contrived clinical	Time sampling
Written (e.g., checklist, symbol system)	Instrumentation (e.g., camera)		Event sampling

Note. From Nay (1979).

system, it is obvious that the assessor implicitly assumes that the present family does not differ from the population for which the observation categories were originally developed. Embedded in this selection of an observation system is the assessor's working definition of each of the behaviors to be assessed. Since a behavior will be detected and encoded *only* when it meets the definitional requirements of the selected observation system, the assessor's selection places important limitations on what can be learned about this family and what targets are likely to be treated. For example, when a particular coding system defines "aggressive behavior" in terms of physical body contact between two parties, this tells us that certain aspects of paralinguistic and kinesic (e.g., facial) communications, as well as characteristics of the setting and situational context within which the behavior occurs, are not seen by the assessor as relevant aspects of aggressive interactions between family members. Assessors could argue exhaustively about the difference between aggressive behavior as a "sign" of a trait or merely a "sample" of the client's behavior. Regardless, this particular assessor's construction of aggressiveness is expressed as soon as the assessor makes predictions about family members that go beyond the specific occasion of assessment (e.g., how the family might behave when the assessor is not present). In summary, when a limited behavioral observation is used to describe a client as "aggressive," this implies that the assessor is satisfied that the person has shown a sufficient subset of behaviors that fit the *assessor's* construction of aggressiveness.

The nature of the assessor's constructs also relates to selection of an evaluation strategy for the methods employed. For example, it is clear that the reporting of internal consistency for the multivariate coding system just discussed would imply that the investigator has selected items that in some way represent some core construct, and that behavioral scores on those items should converge in a meaningful way. There are, however, many behavioral-assessment instruments for which the report of an internal consistency coefficient would be irrelevant. Checklists of diverse categories of cognitive self-statements or of behavioral problems in children are examples of methods that would not usually be expected to show high internal agreement among items (perhaps among certain clusters of items related to a given problem area, but not overall). In this case, the purpose of the instrument is not to tap one central construct or domain of behavior (e.g., Ghiselli, 1964), but to survey many unrelated domains. Similarly, the reporting of a test–retest or stability coefficient for an instrument would be meaningless if the assessor in fact holds the view that the situation within which an individual functions is a major determinant of behavior expressed (e.g., Willems & Raush, 1969), unless the assessor has reason to believe that the situations to which the individual is exposed remain relatively constant across time. There are even cases in which high levels of agreement between observers, the sine qua non of behavioral assessment, may be irrelevant. Thus, a series of participant observers who function within the same setting but who assume divergent roles (e.g., Fry, 1973) might not be expected to agree on their perceptions of attitudes, their perceptions of values, or even their interpretations of overt behavior, because of the divergent perspectives from which the information is obtained.

IS THE ASSESSMENT DOING MORE THAN ASSESSING?

We have presented a variety of issues that should be considered in defining the tasks and goals of assessment and in selecting a method that will reasonably fulfill the assessor's purpose. The yield of assessment methods is further affected by the assessor's manner of presentation. Such diverse factors as the assessor's appearance or demeanor; instructions, prompts, and feedback during information collection; and the importance of the assessment itself for the client's life influence the assessment products. The reader may be familiar with the issue of reactivity of observational assessment (e.g., Hagen, Craighead, & Paul, 1975; Weick, 1968; White, 1972). Investigators have presumed that the salience of the assessment as an elicitor of behavior (rather than as an instrument for change) is a function of the level of activity associated with the assessment procedures; of the client's history with respect to the assessment methodology (e.g., over time a client might adapt to the assessment procedures); and of any deliberate effort to *promote* behavior change by means of the assessment methods (e.g., as in self-monitoring or goal-attainment scaling). A number of writers have noted that very little is known about those factors that promote reactivity (Kent & Foster, 1977), and this issue has been raised most often in the context of observational assessment. Rarely has reactivity been studied in the "behavioral" interview or as a function of the administration of a self-report instrument. In contrast, writers in other disciplines have described a variety of phenomena that must be taken into account to minimize the impact of the interview itself upon the data collected (e.g., Cannell & Kahn, 1968). Reactivity effects within the observational arena are no doubt a complex function of the characteristics of the assessor and the assessment methodology in interaction with the characteristics of the client and the presenting problem. To expand the traditional discussion of reactivity as applied to observational methodology, it is worthwhile to discuss additional ways in which the nature of the interactions between assessor and client in the interview may affect the data and the ultimate success of intervention. The client's initial expectations of roles, of the purpose of assessment, and of the therapeutic process will influence participation and the extent and accuracy of self-disclosure, and will establish a model for involvement in any subsequent therapeutic endeavor. In other words, the nature of these early transactions sets the stage for the manner in which the client comes to understand what is expected of him or her, what can be expected of the assessor, and what the structure and purpose of the relationship is. Thus, the interview is not a vehicle for "objective" data collection in which the client is a passive respondent. It is an intimate interaction between two persons who develop certain basic rules for communicating with each other.

At a practical level, Wallen (1956), in an excellent early analysis of the initial stages in the interview, noted that the client enters the relationship with certain expectations. These may involve viewing the clinician as a powerful expert—a "sage" capable of providing critical insights into the client's life or of magically provoking life changes. The client is motivated to maintain this role distance as a means of continuing his or her dependency upon the clinician without having to take the responsibility for behavior changes. Other client expectations might involve viewing the clinician as capable of interceding in some critical way in the client's life (e.g., in court referrals or involvements with family members). Many clients come to a behavioral clinician with firm ideas that past events (e.g., early life traumas) are the causes of adult maladjustment. Such clients are easily prompted to relate early childhood experiences to their current life predicaments. It is impossible to catalogue the array of expectations that a client can bring to the therapy situation. Many of them are shaped by the media, by popular psychological literature, or by traditional ways in which the client's family views help seeking (particularly in the "mental health" domain). Obviously, a client looking for a powerful change agent to provide a quick solution to his or her problems will not comprehend the need for time-consuming and elaborate assessment. If this issue is not addressed openly by both client and assessor, the conflict of expectations may result in the client's failure to cooperate in the assessment procedures or in termination of the relationship (Kanfer & Grimm, 1980). The situation just outlined illustrates how an unfortunate outcome may result from a poor relationship in an otherwise excellent assessment strategy.

Another problem resulting from role structure can develop when interviews are conducted in an impersonal style (e.g., the assessor plays the role of an active questioner). Once the clinician's role as advisor or provider of information is established and the client is "shaped" to be a passive respondent, it may be very difficult to induce the client later to take increasing responsibility as needed for therapy or for a critical decision.

We therefore recommend strongly that the assessor consider the potential impact of metacommunications in presenting the assessment procedures. What often seem straightforward instructions or innocuous comments to the clinician should be evaluated in terms of the client's expectations and their potential impact on defining the structure of the relationship (cf. Kanfer & Grimm, 1980). The client's expectations should be carefully explored, inappropriate ones should be corrected, and a rationale for the assessment should be given. The assessor should provide a mechanism allowing the client and the assessor to comment about the assessment process itself; he or she should also be aware of aspects of the client's paralanguage, kinesic communications, and other signs of behavior that suggest whether or not the client's view of the assessment is congruent with the clinician's purpose and objectives. Various phases of assessment (e.g., early information collection versus preparation for intervention) should be initiated with transitional statements that prepare the client for what is to follow. The client should have a rationale for what is to be learned from a given assessment procedure and the way in which the assessor intends to employ the information. The structure of a collaborative atmosphere also prepares a smooth transition from assessment to later intervention.

THE UTILITY OF THE ASSESSMENT: ISSUES IN CLINICAL DECISION MAKING

Clinical assessment is designed to provide information for making decisions that affect the client. In some cases, a diagnostic label or a characterization of the client in terms of certain behaviors may have important implications for the client's life. Decisions may lead to various forms of intervention and may even result in such sweeping changes for the client as institutionalization, adoption, or school dismissal. Depending upon the purpose of the assessment and the setting in which it occurs, the decisions can also have serious effects on the social group in which the person functions. From this perspective, many writers have emphasized that it is important to examine the cost of clinical decisions. In a comparison of the relative effectiveness of various assessment approaches for a case, costs of the administration of each must also be considered and balanced against the costs associated with carrying out the respective recommendations. In addition, the cost (and risk) of erroneous decisions must also be taken into account.

Broadly, there are three categories of costs that should be considered in selecting a methodology for making particular decisions. First, there are the personal costs to the client. An inexpensive and quickly administered procedure that leads to inaccurate decisions can gate the client into ineffective but time-consuming and costly interventions and can reduce the opportunities for efficient help. On the other hand, an expensive and time-consuming procedure that enhances the assessor's ability to make accurate decisions can result in quick and inexpensive help. Thus, for each cost factor in assessment, there is the potential benefit to the client against which the cost must be weighed.

Another category, societal costs, has to do with negative outcomes for society at large if poor decisions are made. Many decisions involve institutional admissions. The high cost to society of a wrong decision may include the possibility of harm coming to its citizens (e.g., when a potential for repeated violence is overlooked) or to the client (e.g., when discharge is unduly delayed). Other less dramatic examples of societal costs include the financial losses when persons are removed from the work community. A more subtle cost to society is produced by such diverse effects as the misuse of diagnostic labels, therapy-induced dependency, support of asocial behaviors, or other "iatrogenic" problems that affect both the client and his or her role in society.

Finally, the third category might be termed administration costs. It should be noted that any assessment, whether it is an interview or a battery of observational methods, involves personnel costs for administration as well as copyright fees or costs for replacement items. These costs must also be considered in relation to the costs of subsequent services that are required to implement good or poor decisions.

In attempting systematically to review the costs of a given strategy for assessment and decision making, the assessor must decide on some metric that can be used across the three cost categories. While many of the costs and benefits already reviewed might be expressed in dollars, it is clear that human costs are difficult to quantify. Nonetheless, to enter such potential costs and benefits into a rational "equation" for decision making, they must ultimately be reduced to a numerical format, as explained below.

It is important to attempt to relate costs and benefits to possible outcomes of the process of assessment and decision making. An excellent conceptualization that has been relatively ignored in the behavioral-assessment literature is the application of "decision theory" as presented by Meehl and Rosen (1955) and Wiggins (1973). There is a long history of the application of decision theory to the development and use of standardized tests. The following discussion is a brief review of several points that are particularly relevant to assessors. The material is not applicable when assessors seek only to gather information and believes that their clinical acumen and experience allow them to weigh questions of utility on the basis of clinical judgment without confirming computations. But the concepts can assist the practicing clinician as a reminder of some critical considerations that can improve clinical judgment.

To illustrate the range of possible outcomes, imagine that after a thorough assessment, using interviews with teachers and parents as well as observations, an assessor decides to label a little girl as "deficient in social skills" and to admit her to a program in social skills training. With respect to this decision (e.g., "socially deficient; can benefit from program"), there are two possible outcomes. After the child is admitted to the program, staff observations as well as her response to the program may indicate that the decision was valid—in other words, that the child was actually deficient in a manner that permitted her to benefit from the program. In this case, the strategy of assessment and decision making might be viewed as a success. However, the assessor might find that the reverse is true—that the child assessed as appropriate for the program has proved not to be socially deficient and thus has not benefitted. In both cases, the assessment labels the child as a "positive" (i.e., "socially deficient"). However, children who are labeled "socially deficient" may be accurately labeled positives ("valid positives," or VPs) or falsely labeled positives (FPs). To obtain the greatest benefit from the procedure of assessment and decision making , we want to maximize the probability of VPs. But we must also consider the personal and societal costs of FP outcomes when we offer an expensive program to persons who are misclassified and cannot really benefit from that intervention. In most cases, acceptance of an FP means that someone else (who could have benefited from the program) will be excluded.

On the other side, it is clear that any time we make decisions to classify individuals or to admit them to a program, we also decide to exclude those persons who were labeled "negatives" ("not socially deficient") on the basis of the assessment data. In the present example, if the little girl were assessed as *not* displaying deficient social skills appropriate to the intervention program's goals, this predicted "negative" outcome could prove to be either accurate (a "valid negative," or VN)or inaccurate (a "false negative," FN).[1] Clearly, there are costs and benefits associated with each of these two outcomes. We obviously want to maximize VPs and minimize FNs. Since persons falsely labeled as "negatives" and turned away from an intervention that would have been beneficial are rarely followed up, the personal and other costs of the FNs are almost never assessed directly. In contrast, a VN assessment outcome ("no social deficits, program inappropriate") has saved the individual and society the cost of intervention.

Thus, from a framework of decision theory, there are four possible outcomes. Each has different costs that must be taken into account in evaluating whether a given assessment methodology achieves its purpose. The costs and benefits can therefore be calculated and a course of action planned after considering what risks and costs are acceptable in order to reach the proposed objective. While it is beyond the scope of this chapter to review decision theory in detail, there are certain concepts and practical procedures that can help the individual assessor and the institutional administrator to determine in advance which criteria (and associated methods) will yield the best decision.

First is the issue of "base rate" (BR) for a given classification. By "base

---

1. It should be noted that the designation "positive" or "negative" may not always be clear-cut, as some children may benefit partially from a program. Thus, once again, the clinician's judgment must enter into the equation.

rate," we mean here the probability that an individual, randomly selected from a given population, will display the behavior of interest (e.g., in the previous example, deficient social skills appropriate to the treatment program). Obviously, the BR for a given behavior will vary considerably, depending upon the population that is assessed. For example, the BR of unskilled social behavior in a psychiatric ward would be much greater than the BR for such behaviors would be in the population at large, when age and other demographic characteristics are controlled for. But an assessment instrument is expected to do better than decisions made on the basis of BR information alone would. This implies that the utility of an instrument for making decisions is not fixed. It depends on the particular population (and its BR) to which it is applied.

An example illustrates the importance of considering the BR as a context for evaluating an assessment methodology. If the BR for some target behavior (actual positives) is 95% in an institutional population, it is clear that a good assessment procedure must yield better than 95% accuracy to improve over predictions made from the BR alone (e.g., if an assessor predicts the behavior to occur for all cases, this will be accurate in 95% of the cases). The relationship between BR and predictions from a given assessment methodology becomes less obvious as the BR drops. Thus, as the BR drops from 100% and the costs of making wrong decisions increase, the use of a good assessment technique should permit assessors to make decisions that are better than BR judgments.

Another important concept in decision theory is that of the "selection ratio" (SR); that is, the number of persons, on the average, labeled as "positive" through the use of an assessment method. The SR depends on the "cutoff" employed, and this decision is quite arbitrary. For personality assessment devices, the cutoff is usually some preset score on a personality scale. In behavioral assessment (even though assessors may not be aware of it at times), scores, frequencies, or proportions of certain behaviors serve as "cutoffs" for treatment decisions. The cutoff employed may depend upon implicit "norms," as noted in a previous section of this chapter. Sometimes practical considerations determine the SR. For example, assume that only 10% of the residents in a given setting can be admitted to a treatment program. A behavioral or scale-related cutoff for the assessment method must be adjusted so that 90% of the assessed residents are excluded. Given that we know both the BR and the SR, we have the essential information to evaluate the likelihood of making correct decisions from our knowledge of the BR alone. This computation is the proportion of VPs that can be predicted from merely knowing the BR.

$$BR \times SR = p(VP)$$

In deciding whether to employ a formal assessment method, we should be able to compare its ability to provide correct decisions with that of the BR alone. In addition, the costs of the possible outcomes as well as of administering the method must serve as a context for this evaluation. Combining outcomes and costs to compare the *utility* of method possibilities is aided by a series of easily performed computations offered by Cronbach *et al.* (1972). To provide an illustration of how procedures from decision theory might be employed, the Appendix (see pp. 395–399) extends our social skills example to a computation of expected utility. The interested reader may pursue these computational illustrations, which we think show the practical benefits that the conceptualization from decision theory offers to the behavioral assessor.

The procedures that have been presented may seem removed from the everyday world of the applied behavior analyst or the clinician in private or public practice. However, we present this information in the hope that it will prompt the reader to give some attention to the role of desired outcomes and associated costs with reference to the BR and SR. Even if a formal computation of expected utility is not undertaken, a consideration of these issues should encourage the assessor to be more aware of the factors that affect the utility of a given approach to assessment, as well as of the alternatives that should be considered to meet the assessor's objectives.

SUMMARY

In this chapter, we have attempted to sketch some of the issues to which behaviorally oriented assessors have given less than the deserved attention. As the area of behavioral assessment grows toward the status of a well-established subspecialty, it becomes important to make explicit the context and judgments as well as the methodological issues that characterize the assessment process. The eventual development of conceptual guides and rules that a clinician can apply under the constraints of practical settings requires a full evaluation (as well as supportive research) of the theoretical, logical, and methodological underpinnings of assessment and their relevance to the clinician's daily tasks. Continued examination of actual goals and practices can assist in this accomplishment when used as criteria for selection of appropriate principles and methods.

APPENDIX

To extend the social skills example of pp. 392–395, imagine that staff members in a juvenile residential facility are interested in screening 50 randomly selected children for possible placement within a social skills training program. They wish to employ the base rate (BR) alone as a means of selecting students. Suppose that previous program research has shown that about 10% of children placed in this institution are sufficiently unskilled to benefit from this program (BR = .10). In addition, assume that a selection ratio (SR) of 20% is chosen, since the program can accept only 10 children. Remember, $BR \times SR = p(VP)$. The following computation can be quickly made.

$$BR = .10$$
$$SR = .20$$
$$(.10) \times (.20) = .02, \text{ or } 2\%$$

Given this information, a decision matrix that includes cells representing each possible outcome can now be completed (see Figure 9-2).

Looking along the columns of this matrix, the staff members can see that, for the SR we have chosen (SR = .20), a total of 40 of the 50 children are predicted as negatives (FN + VN), while 10 of the 50 children are predicted as positives (VP + FP). Along the rows of the matrix, it can be seen that 10% of the children, or five of them, will actually display social skills deficits appropriate to the program, given that BR = .10 (FN + VP). Correspondingly, 90%, or 45 students, are actual negatives (VN + FP). In the present case, since it is known that 2% of the 50 students would be predicted to be VPs on the basis of chance alone, this prediction amounts to one child out of the 50, and this is included in the VP cell. By simple subtractions, the predicted number of students that fall into the remaining three cells of the matrix can be ob-

FIGURE 9-2. Decision matrix employing BR and SR as exclusive predictors.

Actual (+)	(BR = .10) = 5	FN 4 (.08)	VP 1 (.02)
Actual (−)	(1 − BR = .90) = 45	VN 36 (.72)	FP 9 (.18)
		= 40 (1 − SR = .80) Predicted (−)	= 10 (SR = .20) Predicted (+)

$$n = 50$$
$$BR = .10$$
$$SR = .20$$

tained. Looking at Figure 9-2, it can be seen that from knowledge of the BR alone, the staff members are likely to correctly classify 37 children—VP(1) + VN(36) = correct decisions (37)—in the absence of a formal assessment. Is this decision strategy really successful? As is true for any example of clinical assessment, success depends upon the purpose and goals for which the method is applied. While 37 out of 50, or 74%, are likely to be correctly classified in this case, it is also obvious that among the 10 children admitted to the program (the Ps, or positives: VP + FP), 9, or 90%, of entering children are likely to be misclassified (the FPs). Thus a huge proportion of children who do not need the program are being treated, while a number of youngsters who could benefit are being excluded. If the goal is to enhance the number of VPs among those students who are predicted positives (and thus admitted to the program), it is obvious that using the BR alone has severe limitations.

To justify the use of any more formal clinical assessment procedure, the staff members must be sure that it produces an *increase* in the VP rate beyond that achieved by using the BR alone. To give an example, imagine that the staff members have decided to administer a hypothetical Social Skills Inventory or SSI (a paper-and-pencil, 40-item checklist completed by staff members after brief observation of the children). Imagine also that each checklist requires about 1 hour of a single staff member's time for administration and scoring. Again, the staff cannot admit more than 10 children out of the 50 into the program, so an SR of .20, or 20%, is employed (SR = .20); the BR remains the same (BR = .10). Assume that at the end of a 6-month period (after classification with the SSI), of the 10 children admitted, 4 are viewed by staff as skills-deficient (correctly classified = VP). Since the VP rate for this procedure of assessment and decision making is now known, only the BR and SR are needed to complete a decision matrix, again subtracting to determine the remaining three cells (FP, FN, and VN). Figure 9-3 is laid out in a fashion similar to Figure 9-2. However, in this case, the VP rate has been increased (4 out of 10 predicted Ps are VPs). It can easily be seen that the "hits" (VPs and VNs) have been increased over the "hit" rate obtained using the BR alone (see Figure 9-2).

Of the 50 children, the staff members are likely to classify correctly 43 children: VP(4) + VN(39) = correct decisions (43). This compares favorably to the 37 correct decisions out of 50 that result from use of the BR alone. Also, and most importantly, 40% of the admitted children (4 out of 10 predicted Ps) are appropriate for the program. While there is still a rather high proportion of FPs to total Ps, the way in which the staff members evaluate the utility of the SSI now depends upon the staff's objectives.

The potential personal, societal, and administrational costs of each potential outcome should be taken into account as a part of the assessor's planning. In our previous examples, increasing the positive prediction rate

		FN	VP
Actual (+)	(BR = .10) = 5	1 (.02)	4 (.08)
Actual (−)	(1 − BR = .90) = 45	VN 39 (.78)	FP 6 (.12)
		= 40 (1 − SR = .80) Predicted (−)	= 10 (SR = .20) Predicted (+)

$$n = 50$$
$$BR = .10$$
$$SR = .20$$

FIGURE 9-3. Decision matrix employing hypothetical Social Skills Inventory as predictor.

from 10% to 40% (Figure 9-2 vs. Figure 9-3) might not cause us to select the SSI for future use (even though it predicts better), if this inventory were instead an observational battery costing $400 in staff time to administer on each occasion. A gain in making more accurate decisions may not outweigh the high costs involved in employing such an instrument.

The computation of expected utility now permits a more formal relation of outcomes and costs. In employing this computational procedure, the assessor must first decide on a cost–benefit ratio that pertains to each of the four possible outcomes (VP, FN, VN, FP). It has already been mentioned that assigning such costs is a difficult enterprise at best, and attempting to quantify certain human costs might seem to be a bit mechanical. Typically, costs are placed on a scale that might range from + 1 (benefit) to − 1 (cost), and a scaled cost is computed for each potential outcome. The numbers on the scale are typically related to dollars, as this is a metric that most categories of cost and benefit can be related to. The procedure also takes into account the cost of administration of the assessment procedure. Now that the probability of each possible outcome has been figured and a cost–benefit ratio has been calculated for each, a sample computation of expected utility can be provided.

Assume that the following costs are assigned to outcomes: $VP = + 1.00$; $FP = − .75$; $VN = + .20$; $FN = − 1.00$. Also, assume that on this same scale (and in relationship to dollars), the costs of administration are equal to − .10. Thus, the assignment of costs suggests that the attainment of VPs and the minimizing of FNs (+ 1.00 vs. − 1.00) are of maximum importance, whereas other outcomes are less critical. It is clear then that the values and goals, and in a broader sense, the purpose of the assessment, are expressed by the costs assigned to each of the possible outcomes.

Imagine that the goal of assessment is to evaluate the expected utility of the SSI. From Figure 9-3, the assessor can go back and compute the probability of each of the four possible outcomes merely by dividing the number of cases that fall within each cell by the n ($n = 50$). The following probabilities are obtained: $p(\text{VP}) = .08$; $p(\text{FP}) = .12$; $p(\text{VN}) = .78$; $p(\text{FN}) = .02$. Entering probabilities of each outcome along with the costs into the following formula enables us to compute the expected utility.

$$\text{Expected utility} = [p(\text{VP}) \times \text{cost (VP)}] + [p(\text{FP}) \times \text{cost (FP)}] + [p(\text{VN}) \times \text{cost (VN)}] + [p(\text{FN}) \times \text{cost (FN)}]$$
$$- \text{cost of assessment administration}$$

Using the data that have been collected, this works out as follows (numbers are rounded off):

$$\text{Expected utility} = [(.08)(+1.00)] + [(.12)(-.75)] + [(.78)(+.20)]$$
$$+ [(.02)(-1.00)] - (.10)$$
$$= .08 - .09 + .15 - .02 - .10$$
$$= +.02$$

Using this formula, the information can now be translated into a numerical statement about the expected utility of the SSI. This expected utility can be compared to that of making a decision on the basis of some other assessment strategy or of the BR alone. For example, to find the expected utility of a BR prediction the same calculations are performed, substituting the probability of each outcome from Figure 9-2 into our formula for expected utility.[2]

The advantage of this procedure is that it enables assessors to express values and objectives in a numerical format. Such a procedure permits assessors over time to maximize certain kinds of outcomes and minimize other, more unfortunate outcomes in a way that can reduce human as well as financial costs.

REFERENCES

American Psychological Association. *Standards for educational and psychological tests.* Washington, D.C.: Author, 1974.

Baer, D. M., Wolf, M. M., & Risley, T. R. Some current dimensions of applied behavior analysis. *Journal of Applied Behavior Analysis,* 1968, *1,* 91–97.

2. The expected utility of BR prediction (from Figure 9-2) works out to be $-.06$. Thus the SSI, taking into account outcomes and costs, is the method of choice.

Barker, R. *The stream of behavior.* New York: Appleton-Century-Crofts, 1963.

Barker, R., & Wright, H. *Midwest and its children: The psychological ecology of an American town.* New York: Row & Peterson, 1955.

Bijou, S. W., & Peterson, R. F. The psychological assessment of children: A functional analysis. In P. McReynolds (Ed.), *Advances in psychological assessment* (Vol. 2). Palo Alto, Calif.: Science & Behavior Books, 1971.

Cannell, C. F., & Kahn, R. L. Interviewing. In G. Lindzey & E. Aronson (Eds.), *The handbook of social psychology* (2nd ed.). Reading, Mass.: Addison-Wesley, 1968.

Carver, R. P. Two dimensions of tests: Psychometric and edumetric. *American Psychologist,* 1974, *29,* 512–518.

Cattell, R. B. Beyond validity and reliability: Some further concepts and coefficients for evaluating tests. *Journal of Educational Psychology,* 1964, *55(1),* 1–22.

Cohen, J. A. A coefficient of agreement for nominal scales. *Educational and Psychological Measurement,* 1960, *20,* 37–46.

Cone, J. D. The relevance of reliability and validity for behavioral assessment. *Behavior Therapy,* 1977, *8,* 411–426.

Cronbach, L. J. Beyond the two disciplines of scientific psychology. *American Psychologist,* 1975, *30,* 116–127.

Cronbach, L. J., Gleser, G. C., Nanda, H., & Rajaratnam, N. *The dependability of behavioral measurements: Theory of generalizability for scores and profiles.* New York: Wiley, 1972.

Cronbach, L. J., & Meehl, P. E. Construct validity in psychological tests. *Psychological Bulletin,* 1955, *52,* 281–302.

Evans, J. M., & Nelson, R. O. Assessment of child behavior problems. In A. R. Ciminero, K. S. Calhoun, & H. E. Adams (Eds.), *Handbook of behavioral assessment.* New York: Wiley, 1977.

Eysenck, H. J. *The structure of human personality.* London: Methuen, 1953.

Eysenck, H. J. Learning theory and behaviour therapy. *Journal of Mental Science,* 1959, *105,* 61–75.

Eysenck, H. J. (Ed.). *Handbook of abnormal psychology.* London: Pitman, 1960.

Ferster, C. B. Classification of behavior pathology. In L. Krasner & L. P. Ullmann (Eds.), *Research in behavior modification: New developments and implications.* New York: Holt, Rinehart & Winston, 1965.

Ferster, C. B. A functional analysis of depression. *American Psychologist,* 1973, *28,* 857–870.

Fry, P. S. Effects of desensitization treatment of core-condition training. *Journal of Counseling Psychology,* 1973, *20,* 214–219.

Ghiselli, E. E. *Theory of psychological measurement.* New York: McGraw-Hill, 1964.

Goldfried, M. R., & Davison, G. C. *Clinical behavior therapy.* New York: Holt, Rinehart & Winston, 1976.

Goldfried, M. R., & D'Zurilla, T. J. A behavioral-analytic model for assessing competence. In C. D. Spielberger (Ed.), *Current topics in clinical and community psychology* (Vol. 1). New York: Academic Press, 1969.

Goldfried, M. R., & Kent, R. N. Traditional versus behavioral personality assessment: A comparison of methodological and theoretical assumptions. *Psychological Bulletin,* 1972, *77,* 409–420.

Gurman, A. S., & Kniskern, D. P. Research on marital and family therapy: Progress, perspective and prospect. In S. L. Garfield & A. E. Bergin (Eds.), *Handbook of psychotherapy and behavior change* (2nd ed.). New York: Wiley, 1978.

Hagen, R. L., Craighead, W. E., & Paul, G. L. Staff reactivity to evaluative behavioral observations. *Behavior Therapy,* 1975, *6,* 201–205.

Haley, J. *Problem-solving therapy.* San Francisco: Jossey-Bass, 1976.

Hartmann, D. P. Considerations in the choice of interobserver reliability estimates. *Journal of Applied Behavior Analysis,* 1977, *10,* 103–116.

Hartmann, D. P., Roper, B. L., & Bradford, D. C. Some relationships between behavioral and traditional assessment. *Journal of Behavioral Assessment,* 1979, *1,* 3–21.

Jones, R. R., Reid, J. B., & Patterson, G. R. Naturalistic observation in clinical assessment. In P. McReynolds (Ed.), *Advances in psychological assessment* (Vol. 3). San Francisco: Jossey-Bass, 1975.

Kaminski, G. *Verhaltenstheorie und Verhaltensmodifikation.* Stuttgart: Drnst Klett Verlag, 1970.

Kanfer, F. H. Self-monitoring: Methodological limitations and clinical applications. *Journal of Consulting and Clinical Psychology,* 1970, *35,* 148–152.

Kanfer, F. H. Assessment for behavior modification. *Journal of Personality Assessment,* 1972, *36,* 418–423.

Kanfer, F. H., & Grimm, L. G. Managing clinical change: A process model of therapy. *Behavior modification: Ten related areas in need of exploration.* In W. E. Craighead, A. E. Kazdin, & M. J. Mahoney (Eds.), *Behavior modification: Principles, issues and applications.* Boston: Houghton Mifflin, 1975.

Kanfer, F. H., & Grimm, L. G. Managing clinical change: A process model of therapy. *Behavior Modification,* 1980, *4,* 419–444.

Kanfer, F. H., & Phillips, J. S. *Learning foundations of behavior therapy.* New York: Wiley, 1970.

Kanfer, F. H., & Saslow, G. Behavioral analysis: An alternative to diagnostic classification. *Archives of General Psychiatry,* 1965, *12,* 529–538.

Kazdin, A. E. Self-monitoring and behavior change. In M. J. Mahoney & C. E. Thoresen (Eds.), *Self-control: Power to the person.* Monterey, Calif.: Brooks-Cole, 1974.

Kent, R. N., & Foster, S. L. Direct observational procedures: Methodological issues in naturalistic settings. In A. R. Ciminero, K. S. Calhoun, & H. E. Adams (Eds.), *Handbook of behavioral assessment.* New York: Wiley, 1977.

Lewinsohn, P. M. Clinical and theoretical aspects of depression. M. K. Calhoun, H. Adams, & K. Mitchell (Eds.), *Innovative treatment methods in psychopathology.* New York: Wiley, 1974.

Lichstein, K. L., & Wahler, R. G. The ecological assessment of an autistic child. *Journal of Abnormal Child Psychology,* 1976, *4,* 31–54.

Meehl, P., & Rosen, A. Antecedental probability and the efficiency of psychometric signs, patterns, and cutting scores. *Psychological Bulletin,* 1955, *52,* 194–216.

Morganstern, K. P. Behavioral interviewing: The initial stages of assessment. In M. Hersen & A. Bellack (Eds.), *Behavioral assessment: A practical handbook.* New York: Pergamon, 1976.

Nay, W. R. *Multimethod clinical assessment.* New York: Gardner Press, 1979.

Patterson, G. R., Cobb, J. A., & Ray, R. S. A social engineering technology for retraining the families of aggressive boys. In H. E. Adams & I. P. Unikel (Eds.), *Issues and trends in behavior therapy.* Springfield, Ill.: Charles C Thomas, 1973.

Rappaport, J. *Community psychology: Values, research and action.* New York: Holt, Rinehart & Winston, 1977.

Raush, H. L. On the locus of behavior: Observations in multiple settings within residential treatment. In *Observation research with emotionally disturbed children* (Symposium, Session I), 1958.

Reichenbach, H. *The rise of scientific philosophy.* Berkeley: University of California Press, 1951.

Schmidt, H. O., & Fonda, C. P. The reliability of psychiatric diagnosis: A new look. *Journal of*

Abnormal and Social Psychology, 1956, *52,* 262–267.

Shapiro, M. B. An experimental approach to diagnostic psychological testing. *Journal of Mental Science,* 1951, *97,* 748–764.

Shapiro, M. B. The single case in clinical-psychological research. *Journal of General Psychology,* 1966, *74,* 3–23.

Sundberg, N. D. *Assessment of persons.* Englewood Cliffs, N.J.: Prentice-Hall, 1977.

Sundberg, N. D., Tyler, L. E., & Taplin, J. R. *Clinical psychology: Expanding horizons* (2nd ed.). Englewood Cliffs, N.J.: Prentice-Hall, 1973.

Wallen, R. W. *Clinical psychology: The study of persons.* New York: McGraw-Hill, 1956.

Watzlawick, P., Beavin, J. H., & Jackson, D. D. *Pragmatics of human communication: A study of interactional patterns, pathologies, and paradoxes.* New York: Norton, 1967.

Weick, K. E. Systematic observational methods. In G. Lindzey & E. Aronsen (Eds.), *The handbook of social psychology* (2nd ed.). Reading, Mass.: Addison-Wesley, 1968.

White, G. *The effects of observer presence on mother and child behavior.* Unpublished doctoral dissertation, University of Oregon, 1972.

Wiggins, J. S. *Personality and prediction: Principles of personality assessment.* Reading, Mass.: Addison-Wesley, 1973.

Willems, E. P., & Raush, H. L. *Naturalistic viewpoints in psychological research.* New York: Holt, Rinehart & Winston, 1969.

Wolpe, J. *The practice of behavior therapy.* New York: Pergamon, 1969.

Wright, H. *Recording and analyzing child behavior.* New York: Harper & Row, 1967.

Zifferblatt, S. Behavior systems. In C. E. Thoresen (Ed.), *Behavior modification in education* (72nd yearbook of the National Society for the Study of Education). Chicago: University of Chicago Press, 1973.

Zigler, E., & Phillips, L. Psychiatric diagnosis: A critique. *Journal of Abnormal and Social Psychology,* 1961, *63,* 607–618.

10

METHODOLOGICAL STRATEGIES IN BEHAVIOR-THERAPY RESEARCH

ALAN E. KAZDIN

Department of Psychiatry
University of Pittsburgh School of Medicine

The emergence of behavior therapy has been associated with a variety of advances in treatment and treatment evaluation. The advances can be attributed to several factors, including careful specification of treatment in terms that facilitate research; reliance upon theoretical and laboratory paradigms that foster specific hypotheses, which can be extrapolated to treatment; assessment of overt performance; and other factors as well. Many of the advances can be attributed to specific methodological approaches within behavior therapy. Whether the approaches owe their origin to behavior therapy can be readily argued. However, the important point is that behavioral research has developed and exploited various methodological approaches in research.

The purpose of the present chapter is to consider selected methodological advances in behavior-therapy research. The topics included in the chapter are single-case experimental research; treatment-evaluation strategies in outcome research; analogue research; and social validation to evaluate the clinical importance of treatment effects. The special importance of each of these approaches for treatment evaluation is discussed, along with sources of controversy and limitations. It is important to acknowledge at the outset that other topics might have been chosen to illustrate innovative methodological approaches in behavioral research. Hence, the topics selected might be viewed as illustrative areas within the field where distinct contributions have been made to treatment evaluation.

SINGLE-CASE EXPERIMENTAL DESIGN

Single-case experimental designs have been employed extensively with a variety of clinical populations and in a wide range of inpatient and outpatient settings (see Hersen & Barlow, 1976; Kazdin, 1978a). Although the designs can evaluate interventions for groups of individuals, their unique methodological contribution to experimentation is examination of the individual case. From the standpoint of clinical psychology, an experimental methodology to study the individual case is highly significant. Single-case research offers an alternative to the uncontrolled case study, which has been heavily relied upon to make conclusions about the individual case.

Use of single-case experimentation has been largely restricted to behavior-modification interventions. Although this can be explained historically (Kazdin, 1978c), it is unfortunate to view the approach as uniquely applicable to one conceptual approach over another. Single-case methodology provides a variety of options for combining clinical treatment and empirical evaluation. The methodology can be extended beyond a particular set of techniques, problems, and clients to provide a broad basis for validating clinical techniques.

UNDERLYING RATIONALE

In all experimental research, the underlying rationale for drawing inferences is based upon comparing performance under different conditions. In single-case research, the different conditions are compared within a subject or among several subjects. The comparison usually is achieved by presenting alternative conditions to the subject(s) at different points in time. Single-case designs depend upon continuous assessment of behavior to provide the basis for comparing different conditions. "Continuous assessment" refers to observations that are obtained often (e.g., daily) for extended periods (e.g., several weeks). Behavior is assessed for extended periods so that inferences can be made about treatment based upon patterns of the data across different treatment conditions.

Single-case designs usually begin with assessment of client behavior for several days prior to treatment. This period of observation, referred to as the "baseline" phase, is required to describe the extent of a client's problem and to predict the level of performance in the immediate future if treatment is not provided. The logic of the designs depends heavily upon the predictive function, because single-case research is fundamentally based upon testing predictions about performance.

The baseline data predict what behavior will be like in the future if treatment is not implemented. A projection of baseline performance into the future is the implicit criterion against which treatment is eventually evaluated. After the baseline data are stable and performance can be extrapolated into the future with some degree of confidence, treatment is implemented. Assessment of behavior continues during treatment to determine whether the level of performance during this phase departs from the level previously predicted by the baseline data. If treament is effective, the actual level of behavior should deviate considerably from the projected level of behavior projected from the baseline data. If the data during the treatment phase suggest that changes are occurring that would not be predicted by the original baseline, the changes may well have resulted from the intervention. Yet it is premature to make this claim with confidence.

The data from the treatment phase are not only compared with the level of behavior projected from the baseline data, but also are used to predict how the client will perform in the future. Treatment data are used to project future performance in the same way that baseline data are used. Perhaps performance during the treatment phase is not really the result of treatment, but the result of some extraneous event that will continue to account for the level of performance after treatment is withdrawn. To test this, treatment is withdrawn, and the new level of behavior during this (third) phase is compared with the projected level from the treatment phase. In addition, by withdrawing treatment, the investigator reinstates the conditions of the original baseline. By withdrawing treatment, a direct test is made to determine whether the prediction of the original baseline was accurate.

The method of making predictions and testing them within a subject illustrates the general rationale for single-case research. The precise manner in which the predictions are made and tested depart slightly from the description as a function of the specific experimental design. Brief descriptions of several basic designs can convey the logic and utility of the single-case approach for clinical research.

AN OVERVIEW OF SPECIFIC DESIGNS

Several single-case designs are available, and each of these includes multiple variations (see Hersen & Barlow, 1976; Kazdin, 1978d, 1982; Kratochwill, 1978; Leitenberg, 1973). Four basic designs are considered below to illustrate the methodology and the ways in which it is applied.

ABAB Design

The ABAB design is the basic design of single-case research, because it follows and illustrates the logic of the approach in the clearest fashion. Indeed, the above discussion of the rationale underlying single-case designs illustrates the ABAB design, in which the effects of treatment are evaluated by alternately presenting and withdrawing treatment at different points in time. The design usually begins with a baseline (or A) phase, in which behavior is observed without treatment. After a stable rate of behavior is evident, the treatment (or B) phase is implemented. When behavior during the treatment phase departs from the level of performance projected during the baseline and stabilizes, treatment is withdrawn. The baseline phase usually is then reinstated. This phase, often referred to as a "reversal" phase, is designed to return behavior to or near its original baseline level. Several procedures can achieve this goal, but usually treatment is simply withdrawn (Kazdin, 1980a). After behavior reverts to baseline levels, treatment is again reinstated so that the final phase of the ABAB design is implemented. If behavior approaches the level achieved in the previous treatment phase and departs from that achieved in the reversal phase, the effect of the intervention is quite clear.

The ABAB design and its variations depend upon the manifestation of improvements in performance with the implementation of treatment and of decrements upon withdrawal or alteration of the treatment. This latter characteristic, of course, raises serious problems when considering the design for clinical work. Withdrawing treatment to demonstrate a relationship between the intervention and behavior raises obvious ethical issues. Once behavior has improved, it is difficult to justify withdrawing treatment to make performance worse. And indeed, for many situations where clinically important behaviors are treated, it may be impractical and undesirable to suspend the intervention temporarily if the possibility exists that performance will become worse. Even if ethical and clinical concerns did not preclude withdrawing treatment temporarily to demonstrate a relationship between the intervention and performance, other problems may arise as well. In many instances, withdrawal of treatment does not result in reversions of behavior toward baseline levels. In such cases, the intervention may have caused therapeutic change. However, without a reversal of performance, it is not clear that the intervention is responsible for change.

In general, the ABAB design and its variations provide a compelling experimental demonstration of the effects of treatment on performance. Unfortunately, the problems raised by the use of a reversal phase often make the designs inapplicable to the clinical situation. Several other single-case designs are available that do not require temporary suspensions of treatment.

Multiple-Baseline Design

In a multiple-baseline design, an experimental effect is demonstrated by showing that behavior change occurs whenever treatment is introduced at different points in time. Once the intervention is presented, it need not be withdrawn or altered, so that the clinically objectionable feature of the ABAB design does not apply to the multiple-baseline design. In a multiple-baseline design, treatment is examined through the concurrent collection of data on two or more baselines. The variations of the design are distinguished on the basis of the specific baselines that are observed. The baselines can consist of *different responses* for a particular individual, the same response across *different persons,* or the same response for a given individual across *different situations.* For example, in multiple baselines across behaviors, several behaviors for an individual (or group) are observed each day. Each of the behaviors is one that will eventually be subjected to treatment. After baseline data stabilize for each behavior, treatment is applied to one of the responses. Baseline conditions remain in effect for the other responses, although data continue to be collected for all of the responses. The initial behavior to which treatment was applied is expected to change, while the other responses are expected to remain at baseline levels. When the treated behavior stabilizes, the intervention is applied to the next behavior, and observations continue to be taken. Eventually, each response is exposed to treatment, but at different points in time. A causal relationship is evident if each response changes when and only when the intervention is introduced, and not before.

The multiple-baseline design can demonstrate the effect of the intervention without a return to baseline conditions and the risk of a temporary loss in the gains that have been achieved with treatment. The clarity of the relationship is a function of the magnitude of treatment effects and the number of baselines across which this effect is demonstrated. In most applications, three or more baselines are used. Thus, if one of the baselines changes even before treatment is implemented, unambiguous inferences can be derived from the pattern of data for all of the other baselines.

One of the problems that may arise in the design is that alteration of one of the baselines may be associated with changes in the other baselines as well. Thus, multiple baselines across behaviors, persons, or situations may show changes in behaviors, persons, or situations, respectively, that have yet to receive treatment (Kazdin, 1982). If generalized treatment effects occur across baselines, the results would not show that behavior changed when and only when the intervention was applied.

Changing-Criterion Design

With the changing-criterion design, the effect of the intervention is demonstrated by showing that behavior changes in increments to match a performance criterion. A functional relationship is demonstrated if behavior matches a constantly changing criterion over the course of treatment (Hartmann & Hall, 1976). After initial baseline observations, the intervention phase is introduced. The intervention includes specification of a criterion for performance that the client is to meet. The criterion indicates the number of responses that need to be performed to achieve a particular response consequence. For example, a certain number of cigarettes smoked, calories consumed, minutes of exercise engaged in, or social activities participated in might be set up as a performance criterion, after negotiation with the client. Consequences such as monetary incentives or prizes are provided on a daily basis only if performance meets the criterion. Essentially, the client receives reinforcement for performing up to (or better than) the criterion level. After performance stabilizes at or above the criterion level, the criterion is altered so that a slightly more stringent demand is made to earn the reinforcer. The criterion is repeatedly changed throughout the intervention phase until the terminal goal of the program is achieved. The effect of the intervention is demonstrated if behavior matches the criterion as that criterion is changed. If behavior matches each criterion, it is likely that the intervention and criterion change, rather than extraneous influences, have accounted for the behavior change.

The design relies upon repeated alterations in the performance criterion and evaluations of whether behavior matches the new standard. The gradual approach toward a terminal goal is especially well suited to many clinical problems in which the skills that are needed on the part of the client are practiced and achieved gradually. If performance is likely to change abruptly and completely, the small incremental steps required by the design may not be evident.

A possible ambiguity of the changing-criterion design is that it usually looks for unidirectional changes (i.e., increases or decreases in performance, depending on the criterion in question, during the intervention phase). If performance does not closely follow changes in the criterion, it may be difficult to discern a clear effect of treatment, as opposed to a general trend toward an increase (or decrease) in performance. If there is ambiguity about whether a general improvement in performance can be attributed to criterion changes during the intervention phase, the design can be strengthened by making bidirectional changes in the criterion. Instead of making the criterion increasingly stringent, the investigator can make the criterion more stringent at some points and less stringent at others. The less stringent criterion shifts amount to "minireversal" phases and can indicate whether the performance follows the criteria set by the investigator.

Simultaneous-Treatment Design

The previous designs are well suited to evaluating the effects of a particular intervention. However, the designs are difficult to use for comparing alternative interventions. If two or more interventions are applied to an individual client, one intervention will be administered before the other, and the relative effectiveness of the interventions may be influenced by the sequence or order in which they are presented.

The simultaneous-treatment design permits comparison of different treatments within single-case experiments (Barlow & Hayes, 1979; Kazdin & Hartmann, 1978). The unique characteristic of the design is the concurrent administration of different treatments in the intervention phase. Because of the manner in which the alternative interventions are administered, the relative effectiveness of the interventions can be assessed.

The design begins with baseline observations of performance for a given client. The behavior must be observed under different circumstances or at different times during the day, so that there are at least two observation periods. If this requirement cannot be met for practical reasons, a single observation can be divided in half so that "separate" periods can be discerned. After baseline observations, two or more interventions are implemented to alter behavior. The interventions are implemented concurrently (i.e., on the same day), but during the different observation periods. The interventions are varied daily so that they are *balanced* across the separate observation periods and so that their effects can be separated from these periods. The intervention phase is continued until the response stabilizes under each of the separate interventions. If one of the interventions emerges as superior to the other(s), it can be implemented across each period in the final phase.

The simultaneous-treatment design is useful for identifying the more (or most) effective intervention among likely alternatives for a particular client. If the different interventions have different effects on behavior, the pattern of results is not likely to be explained by extraneous events that coincide with the onset of treatment. Also, because the interventions are balanced across different observation periods, it is unlikely that unique events during these periods would favor one intervention over another.

The design depends upon balancing the interventions across time periods. If more than two interventions are compared, the task of balancing the interventions may become formidable, because a very large number of occasions may be needed. Also, in some variations of the design, the interventions are balanced across time periods and staff members who administer treatment. In such cases, the number of occasions required for balancing alternative treatments becomes prohibitive if more than two interventions are compared. In most applications, however, alternating treatments across time periods is not difficult to achieve and allows use of the design.

The design also depends upon having interventions with few or no carryover effects from one intervention to another. For example, drug treatment usually would be inappropriate as one of the treatments, as it is possible that drug effects may continue throughout the day and influence performance during a period in which the other intervention is to be administered. If the separate effects of the interventions are of interest — and they usually are — the types of interventions employed should have no carryover effects.

One type of carryover effect may be difficult to predict or detect. It is possible that administering two (or more) interventions concurrently will dictate the effects that each of the interventions exerts on performance. The effect of a given treatment may be determined, in part, by the other treatment with which it is juxtaposed. This influence may lead to conclusions about the alternative treatments that would not be reached had the treatments been evaluated separately in another design.

ASSESSMENT AND DESIGN REQUIREMENTS

The designs highlighted above illustrate several options of the single-case approach. However, other facets than design need to be considered as well. The designs place several requirements on the clinical investigator that often are relevant in deciding whether the methodology can be readily applied.

Trends in the Data

Evaluation of intervention effects is greatly facilitated when baseline data show little or no trend. Trend in the data is a problem when behavior during baseline is changing in the same direction that the intervention is likely to produce. During baseline, behavior may be improving, even though the rate of improvement may not be sufficient for therapeutic purposes. If a trend is present in a therapeutic direction, it may be especially difficult to evaluate intervention effects in single-case designs. Essentially, the investigator needs to evaluate whether the existing trend is improved upon by adding the intervention. Judgments of this sort tend to be more difficult to make than those based upon stable data without initial trends.

Several recommendations have been provided regarding the presence of trends in the data. The usual recommendation, of course, is to wait until baseline stabilizes so that no trend is present before intervening (Baer, Wolf, & Risley, 1968). For obvious practical reasons, this often cannot be achieved in clinical situations, where interventions may need to be implemented quickly. Another recommendation is to select designs in which trends in the data create minimal ambiguity in the interpretation of the results. For example, multiple-baseline designs are likely to create minimal ambiguity when trends exist in baseline, because several baselines are used. If one or two baselines show initial trends, several other baselines may not. The effects of the intervention can be inferred from the data pattern across all baselines. Similarly, in a simultaneous-treatment design, trends in the data need not interfere with conclusions about treatment. Different treatments are implemented, and their relative impact on performance is evaluated. Differences in performance among the treatments, where they exist, presumably can be detected even if superimposed upon an overall trend pervading the baseline and treatment phases.

A final recommendation for the handling of trends is the application of statistical techniques. Time-series analysis, in particular, provides a statistical tool for identifying whether change occurs at the point in time that the intervention is implemented and whether a change in trend occurs between phases (Glass, Willson, & Gottman, 1975; Jones, Vaught, & Weinrott, 1977; Kazdin, 1976). The analysis can determine whether the changes in the data surpass those that might have occurred as a function of preexisting trends.

Variability

A trend in the data in the direction of therapeutic change is only one of the obstacles that can compete with drawing unambiguous inferences about intervention effects. Excessive variability in the data is likely to be a more common problem obscuring the effects of treatment. "Variability" here refers to the fluctuation of the client's performance over time within a particular phase. As a general rule, the greater the variability in the data is, the more difficult it is to infer a treatment effect. If the client's performance fluctuates between the most extreme points on the continuum of the measure (e.g., 0% to 100%), demonstrating clear changes in performance across phases may be difficult. A highly variable baseline does not provide a clear basis for predicting a particular level of performance against which intervention effects are evaluated.

Evaluation of interventions sometimes is facilitated by averaging data points across consecutive days or weeks; this reduces the appearance of variability. For example, fluctuations in daily performance will be reduced in graphical presentation of the information, if the average performance for 2- or 3-day blocks of time is plotted. As more data points are combined, the variability in graphical presentation is likely to decrease. More stable data points (based upon several days) provide a clearer basis for subsequent predictions. If large fluctuations exist in the data, however, merely altering the graphical appearance of the data may not resolve the difficulties for altering behavior and evaluating the results. In such cases, it may be useful to try to standardize conditions in the situation further so that a more consistent pattern of data emerges, or to develop the program in such a way that reductions in variability, if desirable, are trained directly.

UTILITY OF SINGLE-CASE RESEARCH FOR
CLINICAL PSYCHOLOGY

Single-case research represents a methodological approach that has been utilized for both basic and applied research in a number of disciplines. The approach has special utility for applied research in areas such as clinical psychology, which has a special commitment to the study of the individual (e.g., Korchin, 1976; Watson, 1951). Much of clinical work is directed to the diagnosis, assessment, and treatment of the individual, as seen in inpatient and outpatient work. Traditionally, investigation of the single individual has been restricted to case studies in which a person is studied in depth. Although the case study often provides fascinating analyses, the material usually is based upon anecdotal reports. The absence of experimental control removes the case study from the realm of scientific knowledge. Case studies provide extremely important hypotheses for subsequent research, but the information itself usually is insufficient to provide empirically based knowledge. Single-case research provides an opportunity for combining the richness of clinical application with the requirements of scientific methodology.

Scientific Study of Rare Phenomena

For many problems that are seen in treatment, the number of cases presented at the same time or location is insufficient to permit large-scale investigation. Hence, the only basis for information is the intensive study of the individual case. With rare clinical problems, even the traditional case study is very useful, for lack of alternative resources. For example, much of what is known about multiple personality as a clinical problem derives from intensive elaboration of clinical material (Thigpen & Cleckley, 1957).

Single-case experimental designs provide a unique opportunity to investigate rare phenomena and to provide scientifically based information for subsequent applications. An excellent instance of single-case investigation of a relatively rare phenomena was provided by Barlow, Reynolds, and Agras (1973), who reported the treatment of a 17-year-old male who desired to be a female. The patient's behaviors and attitudes reflected his transsexual interest, as evident in attraction to other males; a history of cross-dressing; interest in traditionally feminine role behaviors, such as knitting, crocheting, and embroidering; sexual fantasies in which he imagined himself as a woman; effeminate mannerisms in sitting, standing, and walking; and so on. Extensive treatment based upon modeling, rehearsal, and feedback was used to alter a variety of effeminate mannerisms, speaking patterns, social skills, sexual fantasies, and sexual arousal. The effects of training were demonstrated in a combination of ABAB and multiple-baseline designs showing specifically that the intervention accounted for change. The report is unique in demonstrating the successful psychotherapeutic treatment of transsexuality. It is unlikely that this treatment could have been evaluated without the use of single-case experimentation, if for no other reason than the difficulty in recruiting such clients in sufficient numbers who would be interested in treatment other than direct physical change through surgery. Yet the information provided is extremely valuable in demonstrating an effective treatment that may be of use with similar patients who might be interested in psychotherapy as a possible alternative to surgical intervention.

Precursor to Large-Scale Application

Several advantages of single-case experimentation pertain to the manner in which treatment can be implemented and evaluated. For many problems that are seen in treatment, multiple procedures may need to be applied to produce the desired changes in clients. Single-case designs allow initial tests of whether treatment is likely to achieve the desired changes before it is applied widely or over a protracted period. There are several ways in which this gradual approach to therapeutic change can be valuable.

For clients with several problems or problems that encompass several situations, treatment can be implemented in a gradual fashion. At the beginning of treatment, the procedures can be applied to one behavior or to behavior in one situation. The modest initial focus provides information about the effectiveness of the intervention before it is applied widely. Baseline information may be obtained to encompass several areas of client functioning. However, treatment is first applied only to one area. If the intervention is successful, it can be extended to other problem areas. If it is not successful or produces less than dramatic effects, changes can be made in an exploratory fashion until the desired changes are produced. Once an effective treatment has been identified, it can be applied more widely across the range of problem areas in need of treatment. This gradual approach is consistent with the clinical demands of treatment and also is based upon the rationale underlying the multiple-baseline designs, highlighted earlier.

In institutional settings, a multiple-baseline design has other advantages in the implementation of treatment. Typically, staff members implement treatment to alter the behavior of individual patients or groups of patients. The multiple-baseline design permits the staff to focus on one behavior initially and to extend the treatment to other behaviors as initial successes are achieved. This approach has an obvious practical advantage of allowing gradual proceeding in situations where staff members are not likely to have the resources to implement larger-scale multifaceted treatments all at once.

For the individual client, other single-case designs are well suited to the demands of treatment. The alleviation of many problems seen in treatment calls for new learning on the part of clients, and this learning can be developed gradually. For example, developing social skills in withdrawn and reticent adults can proceed gradually by having them practice and rehearse specific skills and engage over time in more of the behaviors that approach the terminal goal. The approach of a changing-criterion design is suitable for many clinical problems because the final behaviors of interest are approached gradually as a function of the client's ability to meet the performance criteria. Hence, treatment can proceed gradually and can take the individual client's rate of improvement into complete consideration.

Another practical feature of single-case designs is their usefulness in exploring new treatments. Hypotheses about effective treatments can be tested with individuals first before large-scale evaluation is undertaken in group research. Even if large numbers of clients are available for investigation, single-case research permits the investigator to develop treatment and to receive feedback about its success. When treatment is well developed in the individual case, larger treatment questions can be proposed and addressed in group investigations.

PROBLEMS AND LIMITATIONS

Single-case experimental designs offer a number of advantages for treatment outcome research. Perhaps the most obvious advantage is that the methodology allows investigation of the individual client and experimental evaluation of treatment for that client. The fact that only one individual is involved does not necessarily preclude careful evaluation of treatment, but it nevertheless imposes a number of limitations on research.

Range of Outcome Questions

Single-case experimental designs focus primarily on demonstrating that a particular treatment or treatment package produces therapeutic change. This focus is obviously important. However, the full spectrum of treatment evaluation and clinical change involves a wide range of questions, many of which are detailed later in this chapter. For present purposes, it is sufficient to note that after an effective treatment is developed, several questions arise about the components of the treatment that account for change, the variations of treatment that may be more effective, and the effectiveness of treatment relative to alternative procedures.

For the most part, single-case designs are not well suited to address many questions of outcome research. Part of the problem is that the designs usually evaluate treatments within a subject and that treatments are presented in sequence. For example, if two treatments are evaluated in an ABAB or multiple-baseline design for a particular person, one treatment will be followed by the other. The obvious problem that arises pertains to the order in which the alternative treatment are presented. It is possible that the treatment presented first (or second) may be more (or less) effective than the other. However, the effects of a given treatment or treatment variation, as well as the relative effectiveness of the alternatives under investigation, may be determined by the specific techniques and/or the order in which they appeared. Thus, treatment is confounded with order. The issue is not academic, as evident in some studies where treatments and order effects can be evaluated. The order in which a treatment is presented often contributes to its effectiveness, with first treatments usually showing a greater or greatest change (e.g., Everaerd, Rijken, & Emmelkamp, 1973; Hackmann & McLean, 1975). In single-case designs, the effects of the sequence in which treatment is presented usually cannot be identified, because alternative orders are not presented across subjects (i.e., in a between-group strategy).

Some designs, such as the simultaneous-treatment design, are represented as options for comparing alternative treatments or treatment variations. However, comparing two treatments within a given subject, whether in separate phases (ABAB design) or within a single phase (simultaneous-treatment design), allows for the possibility that the effects of one treatment will depend upon the other treatment that the client also receives.

Aside from comparing alternative treatments or treatment variations, single-case research is not especially well suited to examine whether a treatment is more or less effective as a function of particular client characteristics. The usual way that research approaches this question is through factorial designs in which subjects and treatment types are compared. The analyses examine whether the effectiveness of treatment interacts with the type of client; clients are grouped according to such variables as age, diagnosis, socioeconomic status, severity of behavior, and so on. If only a few subjects are studied and respond differently, the investigator cannot determine whether treatment was more or less effective as a function of particular characteristics of the subject. Actually, the client characteristics that may interact with treatment raise questions about the generality of results among clients. Generality is an important topic for evaluating single-case methodology, and hence is treated separately below.

Generality of the Findings

Perhaps the major objection that arises in evaluating single-case research is that the results may not be generalizable to persons other than the client or clients in question. This objection raises several important issues. To begin with, single-case experimental research has grown out of an experimental philosophy that attempts to discover laws of individual performance (Kazdin, 1978c). There is a methodological heritage of examining variables that affect performance of individuals. Of course, interest in studying the individual reflects a larger concern with identifying generalizable findings that are not idiosyncratic. Hence, the ultimate goal, even of single-case research, is to discover generalizable relationships.

The generality of findings from single-case research often is discussed in relation to between-group research. Because between-group research utilizes large numbers of subjects, the findings are often assumed to be more generalizable. As proponents of the single-case approach have noted, the use of large numbers of subjects in research does not by itself ensure generalizable findings (Sidman, 1960). In the vast majority of between-group investigations, results are evaluated on the basis of average group performance. The analyses do not shed light on the generality of treatment effects among individuals. Thus, if a group of 20 patients who received treatment show greater change than do 20 patients who did not receive treatment, little information is available about the generality of the results. It is not clear from this group analysis alone how many persons in the treatment group were affected, or how many were affected in any important way. Ambiguity about the generality of findings from between-group research is not inherent in this research approach; however, investigators rarely look at the individual subject data as well as the group data to make inferences about the generality of effects among subjects within a given treatment condition. Certainly, if individual data were examined in between-group research, a great deal might be said about the generality of the findings.

The generality of results from single-case research is not necessarily weak merely because one or only a few clients are examined at any one time. Actually, inherent features of the single-case approach and the ways in which it is used may increase rather than decrease the generality of the findings. Investigators who use single-case designs have emphasized the need to seek interventions that produce dramatic changes in performance. Thus, visual inspection rather than statistical significance is advocated. Interventions that produce dramatic effects are likely to be more generalizable across individuals than are effects that meet the relatively weaker criterion of statistical significance. Indeed, in any particular between-group investigation, the possibility remains that a statistically significant difference was obtained on the basis of "chance." The results may not generalize to other attempts to replicate the study, much less to other subjects. In single-case research, extended assessment across treatment and no-treatment phases, coupled with dramatic effects, reduces or may even rule out the possibility that the changes in performance could be attributed to chance.

Proponents of single-case research sometimes have suggested that the results may even be more generalizable than those obtained in between-group research because of the methodology and goals of these alternative approaches. The relative generality of findings from one approach over another may not be resolvable. However, it is important to note that generality is not necessarily a problem for single-case research. Findings obtained in single-case demonstrations appear to be highly generalizable because of the types of interventions that are commonly investigated. For example, various techniques based upon reinforcement have been effective across a large range of populations, settings, and target problems (e.g., Kazdin, 1978a).

The problem of single-case research is not that the results lack generality among subjects. Rather, the problem is that there are difficulties largely inherent in the methodology for assessing the dimensions that may dictate generality of the results. Within single-case research designs, there are no provisions for identifying client–treatment interactions. Focusing on one subject does not allow for the systematic comparison of different treatments among multiple subjects who differ in various characteristics, at least within a single experiment. Examining subject variables is more readily accomplished in between-group research.

General Comments

Although limitations of single-case research can be identified, it is important to place the designs in perspective. The development and elaboration of single-case methodology have had marked impact on treatment evaluation (see Hersen & Barlow, 1976). The designs have helped introduce empirical evaluation into clinical situations where group experimental evaluation would not be possible. The methodology provides several designs, many of which can be suited to specific clinical demands. Perhaps part of the problem in clinical psychology is that the designs have been used almost exclusively for evaluating behavioral techniques. The designs are not necessarily restricted to a particular sort of treatment, although some of the demands for assessment may dictate the sorts of measures that are used to evaluate change. An extremely important contribution of behavior modification has been to increase the utilization of single-case research in clinical work.

TREATMENT-EVALUATION STRATEGIES

Research in behavior therapy has generated an overwhelming amount of evidence on treatment outcome. A wide range of outcome questions has been addressed. The questions can be elaborated by examining the different treatment-evaluation strategies that have been exploited (Kazdin, 1980b).

TREATMENT-PACKAGE STRATEGY

Treatment-package strategy refers to the evaluation of the effects of a particular treatment as that treatment ordinarily is used. The notion of a "package" emphasizes that the treatment is examined *in toto*. Many techniques are multifaceted and include several components, each of which may exert influences in its own right. For example, self-instruction training is a cognitively based technique that includes the use of self-statements, modeling, external reinforcement, self-reinforcement, and practice (Meichenbaum, 1977). The components can be readily distinguished conceptually and can even be separated to some extent in practice. The treatment-package approach does not address the influence of the separate components, but rather asks whether the technique works for a particular problem. The strategy represents the simplest experimental paradigm, including treatment and no-treatment control groups. The treatment-package strategy has obvious priority because it asks the most basic question about treatment: Does it work? No matter how treatment has been devised, either from practice, theory, or some combination, the first research question addresses its efficacy.

The treatment-package approach in clinical work is fundamental. The approach emphasizes the priority of ameliorating a specific clinical problem (Azrin, 1977). Once the technique has been shown to be effective for a particular problem, a variety of other research questions can be raised to understand how the technique works, how it can be improved, and how its relative effectiveness can be assessed in comparison with various alternatives.

DISMANTLING-TREATMENT STRATEGY

Dismantling strategy consists of analyzing the components of a given treatment package (Lang, 1969). After a particular package has been shown to produce therapeutic change, research that begins to analyze the basis for change assumes importance. To dismantle treatment, individual components are eliminated or isolated from the treatment. In a dismantling investigation, some subjects may receive the entire package, and others may receive the package minus one or more components. The purpose of such research is to determine the necessary and sufficient components for therapeutic change.

Dismantling research serves multiple purposes. First, the approach points to the specific ingredients or combinations of ingredients that are responsible for change. Hence, clinical practice can be improved by emphasizing the aspects that are more important than others to outcome. Second, the approach often has important theoretical implications. When crucial ingredients are identified, the investigator may be in a position to comment upon the reasons *why* treatment produces change. The theoretical uses of dismantling-treatment research are important because they may suggest changes for a technique or new techniques that may prove to be more effective.

The dismantling strategy has been used extensively in the evaluation of systematic desensitization. When desensitization was first proposed, several specific components were delineated as crucial for therapeutic change

(Wolpe, 1958). These included (1) training the client in a response that could compete with anxiety (e.g., relaxation); (2) developing a hierarchy of items related to the source of anxiety; and (3) pairing the competing responses with the individual hierarchy items in a graduated fashion. Such a well-delineated technique lends itself extremely well to dismantling research, and several studies examining the specific components have been completed (e.g., Davison, 1968; Krapfl & Nawas, 1970). The above ingredients, originally thought to be crucial, are not essential for therapeutic change (Wilkins, 1971). The only component that appears to be important is the imagined or overt rehearsal of the response that is to be developed. These findings have important implications about the mechanism of behavior change. The original theoretical interpretation of the technique is much less tenable now since the emergence of research that has dismantled the overall package. The dismantling strategy requires that the treatment package consist of a delimited and reasonably well-specified set of treatment components. Dismantling research cannot be done if the ingredients cannot be carefully specified as part of the treatment. Not all components need to be separable from one another. Dismantling research is greatly facilitated by having a tentative theoretical basis for explaining the technique. The theory helps specify the crucial interpretation of the mechanism of treatment and directs the investigator to a particular set of components that warrant investigation. And the results of the investigation ultimately may reflect upon the specific theoretical proposition from which the research was derived.

CONSTRUCTIVE-TREATMENT STRATEGY

Constructive-treatment strategy refers to the development of a treatment package by the addition of components that may enhance outcome. In this sense, the constructive approach is the opposite of the dismantling strategy. Constructive-treatment research begins with a particular treatment, which may consist of one or a few ingredients or a larger package, and adds various ingredients to determine whether the effects can be enhanced. The strategy asks the question, "What can be added to treatment to make it more effective?" As constructive research continues, a given technique may theoretically grow to encompass more and more procedures. Actually, in constructive research, some ingredients are likely to enhance treatment and others are not. Those that improve outcome are retained and added, and those that do not are not retained.

An example of constructive-treatment research in behavior modification is evident in the work of Greenberg, Scott, Pisa, and Friesen (1975), who used a token economy to treat hospitalized psychiatric patients. Token reinforcement has been shown to be effective in altering behavior of psychiatric patients within the hospital and after discharge as well (Kazdin, 1977b; Paul & Lentz, 1977). Greenberg *et al.* (1975) used a constructive approach to see whether a token economy could be enhanced by combining it with milieu therapy, an entirely different treatment. One group of patients received a token economy, while another group received the token economy plus the milieu approach, which included participation in group activities (e.g., group decision making in regard to discharge). The results indicated that patients in the combined procedure spent more days out of the hospital than did patients without the milieu condition. The above study shows that adding one procedure to an already effective treatment enhanced performance.

Constructive-treatment research need not always combine two distinct procedures, such as token economy and milieu therapy. Smaller additions can be made to a treatment. For example, desensitization alone might be compared to desensitization plus home practice (engaging in anxiety-provoking responses at home). The basic treatment is not changed, but a new ingredient is added to assess whether performance improves as a result.

A constructive-treatment approach helps to develop a treatment package. Constructive research can begin with one or a few components, but it systematically builds a treatment that is more effective than the original variation. The advantage is that progress along the way toward the most effective treatment is empirically based.

As with the dismantling strategy, the constructive approach may have implications for the theoretical basis of therapy and perhaps even for the nature of the clinical problem. The investigator may select components for treatment on the basis of theory. For example, on the basis of self-efficacy theory (Bandura, 1977), investigators may wish to add an overt behavioral-rehearsal component to a treatment that consists of imagining various events. Self-efficacy theory has suggested that greater therapeutic change will be achieved if the client overtly rehearses the desired responses than will be achieved if rehearsal is omitted.

Of course, the construction of treatments need not rely on theory alone. Clinical practice or research may provide guidelines for variables that may lead to improved treatment, even though the theoretical basis is unclear. Subsequent research may show that such additions to treatment enhance change and perhaps serve as an impetus for developing good theory.

PARAMETRIC-TREATMENT STRATEGY

Parametric-treatment strategy refers to the alteration of specific aspects of a treatment in order to determine how to maximize therapeutic change. The dimensions or parameters of the treatment are altered to find the optimal manner of administering the procedure. The approach resembles the dismantling and constructive strategies because variations of a particular treatment are evaluated. However, components of treatment are not withdrawn (as in the dismantling approach) or added (as in the constructive approach). Rather, variables within the existing treatment are altered to find the optimal variation. Essentially, the parametric research focuses on refining a particular technique. In parametric research, variations often are made along quantitative dimensions by presenting more or less of a given portion of treatment. Different groups may receive the same general treatment but may differ in quantitative dimensions of a particular variable associated with that treatment.

The parametric approach can be illustrated by a study that examined the effects of flooding as a technique to treat agoraphobic patients (Stern & Marks, 1973). "Flooding" consists of confronting the client with the stimuli that cause distress until the adverse reaction is eliminated. Two parameters of flooding were evaluated, namely, the duration of continuous exposure to the feared stimuli (one long period of exposure vs. several short exposures), and the mode of flooding (in imagery or in actual situations). The most effective variation of treatment was the longer exposure period conducted in the actual situations. These results indicate that the two dimensions that can be manipulated within flooding can enhance treatment effects.

Most techniques include several dimensions that are unspecified in practice or research, such as the content of various discussions; the length of time for which certain topics are addressed; and the timing of various activities in treatment, such as presentation of imaginal or role-practiced stimuli, relaxation training, and so on. Furthermore, a particular treatment can be conducted in many different ways and still qualify as that same treatment. For example, modeling generally consists of observing others engage in responses that are to be developed in the client. However, the general procedure leaves unspecified many important variables, such as who the model is, how the model performs, how many models are presented, and so on (Rosenthal & Bandura, 1978). These variables all influence the effectiveness of the procedure as investigated in parametric research.

Parametric-treatment research is extremely important because it attempts to develop a particular technique. Relatively little parametric work exists. This is unfortunate, because techniques often are proposed as effective or discarded as relatively ineffective before basic research has been conducted to explore parametric variations that maximize therapeutic change.

Parametric research can have important implications for the theoretical basis of treatment, in addition to developing more effective variations. The parametric variations that influence outcome may suggest the mechanism responsible for therapeutic change. Also, and as noted with other strategies, understanding the mechanisms of change may lead to eventual improvements in treatment.

COMPARATIVE-TREATMENT STRATEGY

Comparative-treatment strategy consists of comparing two or more different treatments. The question addressed by this strategy is that of which treatment is better (or best) among various alternatives for a particular problem. This strategy is extremely familiar to researchers because of the very wide interest that comparative studies often hold. The interest derives from the specific treatments that are compared. Often the treatments are based on opposing conceptual approaches. Hence, investigations of alternative techniques are often viewed as critical and even as definitive tests of the constituent techniques.

Comparative-treatment studies involving behavior therapy and traditional outpatient and inpatient care have been conducted (e.g., Paul, 1966; Paul & Lentz, 1977; Rush, Beck, Kovacs, & Hollon, 1977; Sloane, Staples, Cristol, Yorkston, & Whipple, 1975). These studies attract wide attention because they place into the empirical arena the many conflicting and hyperbolic claims made for their superiority of one technique over another. Indeed, the comparative question often attracts such wide interest that it serves as the basis for larger evaluations of the literature (e.g., Kazrin, Durac, & Agteros, 1979; Luborsky, Singer, & Luborsky, 1975; Smith & Glass, 1977), in which conclusions are drawn about the relative efficacy of alternative techniques.

Comparative research often evaluates alternative techniques within a broad conceptual approach (e.g., Bandura, Blanchard, & Ritter, 1969; Linehan, Goldfried, & Goldfried, 1979). However, these comparisons often attract less attention than do investigations that contrast techniques with less conceptual compatibility.

The comparative-treatment strategy has obvious value. In the long run, comparisons are essential to determine which technique should be applied to a given problem. And the goal of all treatment is to determine the best available method, which makes comparative work crucial. The importance of comparative research and the wide interest it attracts may lead to premature comparisons, however. Techniques often are compared long before they are well investigated or well understood. Hence, the versions that are compared may not provide the optimal treatment, and conclusions that are drawn are not very meaningful.

Comparative research also introduces a number of special research problems that make it one of the more complex treatment-evaluation strategies (Kazdin, 1980b). When opposing techniques are compared, special difficulties often arise in keeping the techniques distinct; in holding constant variables considered to be irrelevant or incidental to treatment (e.g., amount of treatment, spacing of treatment); in utilizing therapists who can conduct both (or all) of the treatments; and in ensuring the integrity of the individual treatments. In many comparative studies, questions can be raised about whether one treatment, usually the one to which the investigator may be less committed, has received a fair representation.

CLIENT-AND-THERAPIST-VARIATION STRATEGY

Previous evaluation strategies emphasize the technique as the major source of treatment outcome. However, the effectiveness of many treatments is likely to vary as a function of characteristics of the clients and therapists. The strategy of client and therapist variation examines whether attributes of the client or therapist contribute to outcome.

The usual way in which the strategy is implemented is to select clients (or therapists) according to a particular variable. Variables for clients include age, gender, socioeconomic standing, marital status, education, severity of the disorder, level of anxiety or introversion, and so on. Therapist variables include such characteristics as therapist training, years of experience, age, interests, empathy, warmth, and so on (e.g., Meltzoff & Kornreich, 1970).

When clients and therapists are classified according to a particular variable, the main question addressed is that of whether treatment is more or less effective with certain kinds of participants. The question is directed to the generality of treatment effects through consideration of the types of clients to whom treatment can be extended. Examination of the generality of treatment effects in this fashion greatly increases information about treatment and addresses sophisticated questions about outcome. The question of which treatment or treatment variation produces greater effects is a very global one. It might well be that the techniques are differentially effective as a function of other variables related to the clients and therapists.

Occasionally, the investigation of therapist variables introduces direct manipulation of therapist behavior rather than classification of therapists according to a particular characteristic. For example, the effects of having therapists vary their behavior during treatment to convey greater warmth, empathy, or reinforcement can influence therapy. In such cases, the therapist variable is directly manipulated, rather than simply examined.

The strategy of client and therapist variation has received little attention in behavior-therapy research. In a few cases, the approach has been examined by looking at factors pertaining to the therapist or to the client–therapist relationship and relating to outcome (Alexander, Barton, Schiavo, & Parsons, 1976; Ford, 1978). However, few predictions have been generated in regard to client and therapist characteristics that may mediate treatment. Indeed, the behavioral approach has emphasized the search for techniques that work largely independently of the persons who administer or receive them.

GENERAL COMMENTS

The above strategies reflect questions that are frequently raised about treatment outcomes. The specific question posed by each strategy reflects a range of issues required to understand fully how a technique operates and can be applied for optimal effects. The questions reflect a general progression. The treatment-package strategy is an initial approach, and it may be followed by the various analytic strategies based upon dismantling, constructive, and parametric research. The comparative strategy probably warrants attention after prior work has been conducted that not only indicates the efficacy of the individual techniques but also shows how the techniques should be administered to increase their efficacy. Obviously, comparative research can be conducted before very much is known about the constituent techniques. However, the yield from such research may be quite limited if it is completed prematurely.

As noted earlier, behavior therapy has not devised the therapy questions or research strategies outlined above. Historical precedents for each strategy in individual studies and programs of research can readily be identified. Behavior-therapy research has simply highlighted the importance of the many different strategies and has made them researchable. A characteristic of behavior therapy is the specification of treatment procedures so that they can be studied empirically.

A high degree of operationalization is needed to investigate dismantling, constructive, and parametric questions. In each case, specific components or ingredients of therapy have to be sufficiently well specified to be added, withdrawn, or varied in an overall treatment package. Behavior therapy has been well suited to such operationalization.

Although behavior therapy has explored many of the strategies highlighted above, the research has not pursued each of the areas encompassed by the strategies. Behavior therapy has virtually neglected the strategy of client and therapist variation, with very few exceptions. The conceptualization of most behavioral techniques has not taken into account factors associated with client characteristics or developmental history that might make clients more or less responsive to treatment in general or to specific techniques in particular. The neglect of client and therapist variables might be easily justified if the sparse literature that already exists in behavior therapy on the issue had yielded little. However, several investigations have suggested the role of factors other than the techniques themselves (e.g., Alexander *et al.,* 1976; Devine & Fernald, 1973; Ford, 1978; Gordon, 1976; Morris & Zuckerman, 1974).

The process of therapeutic change is another area to which behavior therapy has devoted little attention. Process research, traditionally, has referred to questions about transactions between the therapist and client—about the type of interactions and their interim effects on client and therapist behavior. For example, process research may examine the perceptions of clients and therapists over the course of treatment (e.g., Orlinsky & Howard, 1975). Although such process factors may eventually be related to outcome, they have been studied independently of treatment efficacy.

Within behavior therapy, interest in process over the course of treatment as an end in itself has not been systematically pursued. Interim assessment of treatment effects is commonly used, as, for example, in single-case research or biofeedback research, where ongoing assessment is essential to evaluation of treatment effects. In these areas, continual assessment during the course of treatment usually consists of the same measures used at outcome. Processes of the treatment that may operate independently of the usual outcome measures are not included.

Behavior therapy might profit from empirical excursions into these therapy processes. For example, cognitive-behavior therapy might look at the effects of various techniques and therapist variables that influence changes in cognitive processes over the course of treatment. Cognitive processes may be important because they reflect, lead to, or covary with overt behavioral changes, or because they may ultimately lead to a client's redefinition of aspects of the environment that have been regarded as problematic. Even if interim processes of therapy are not of direct interest, they may be useful as a way of understanding behavior. Interim examination of client reactions during treatment may be useful in opening up areas of research that *are* of interest in behavior therapy. The correspondence, or rather lack of correspondence, among several modalities of assessment and among measures within these modalities may be better understood by looking at the course of changes from the beginning of therapy through outcome as well as at follow-up. Also, interim treatment processes may have implications for relapse, since they are early signs of the kinds of effects that take place. In general, what happens during treatment, in addition to the obvious outcome questions, may provide additional leads for research.

ANALOGUE RESEARCH

The treatment-evaluation strategies addressed above illustrate the specific outcome questions usually addressed in behavior-therapy research. Outcome research in behavior therapy has proliferated, in part because of the specification of the treatment techniques in terms that can be translated into specific operations. For research purposes, a high degree of specification is essential, so that highly refined and analytic questions about treatment can be studied.

Specification of treatment is an important component, but insufficient in its own right to foster a great deal of outcome research. Conducting outcome research raises a host of problems that can impede careful experimentation. To begin with, it may be difficult with many problems to obtain a sufficient number of clients with the same or similar problems. Similarity among the clients is important, too, so that the same sorts of measures can be used. Even if enough clients with similar problems can be found, there often are restraints on assigning clients to conditions. Random assignment, dictated by sound methodology, often cannot be permitted because of clients' preferences for treatment and administrative demands for assigning persons to groups (e.g., inpatient treatment).

Difficulties also arise in obtaining therapists who are willing to participate in an outcome study and who can administer alternative treatments or treatment variations. Certainly, the usual incentives (e.g., fame and fortune) are not offered to therapists for their services in outcome research. Also, therapists usually have skills in one particular technique, and ensuring equal degrees of skill in alternative techniques may present problems.

Even if practical problems could be resolved, certainly ethical issues can impede clinical research. Many of the important questions of therapy require control groups that withhold specific aspects of treatment. Assigning clients to control conditions that have a low probability of producing change would be an obvious violation of the professional commitment to treatment. Also, the possible ineffectiveness or relative ineffectiveness of various treatment or control conditions can lead to high levels of attrition, which can greatly interfere with research.

The sample of research problems highlighted here suggests that clinical settings may not be the place to address all or perhaps even most of the questions entailed by therapy. To overcome many of the obstacles, research has been conducted in situations *analogous* to those present in the clinical situation. Research that evaluates treatment under conditions that only resemble or approximate the clinical situation has been referred to as "analogue research."

Different types of analogue research have been employed to evaluate aspects of behavior change and therapeutic processes. Analogue research can vary widely in the degree of resemblance to the clinical situation to which the investigator may wish to generalize. At one extreme, animal (infrahuman) analogues have been used to study phenomena that appear to be relevant for therapy (Adams & Hughes, 1976). Animal research often bears close conceptual and occasionally even procedural ties to clinical research. For example, procedures to overcome anxiety and avoidance reactions in infrahumans resemble procedures used with clinical patients (e.g., Baum, 1970; Masserman, 1943; Wolpe, 1958). Another type of analogue research utilizes human subjects to isolate specific processes that occur in therapy (Heller, 1971). The complexity of client–therapist interaction militates against investigating isolated processes such as the impact of therapist verbalizations on the client. Analogue research in which an interviewer and subject respond to highly structured tasks (e.g., sentence construction) has been used to assess the influence of specific categories of statements that may reflect the sorts of processes evident in treatment.

Another type of analogue research resembles the therapy situation more closely than it does the laboratory situation mentioned above. In this research, the procedures are investigated in the context of treatment but are not conducted in a clinical setting. Certainly a historical landmark for behavior therapy was the research program of Lang and Lazovik, who evaluated the effectiveness of systematic desensitization in well-controlled laboratory-based research (e.g., Lang & Lazovik, 1963; Lang, Lazovik, & Reynolds, 1965; Lazovik & Lang, 1960). Several features of the research facilitated evaluation of treatment, including the use of volunteer undergraduate college students with relatively circumscribed fears; the standardization of treatment; the assessment of overt performance in the presence of a feared stimulus (approach toward a nonpoisonous snake); and the expressed focus of evaluating a new and, by implication, experimental method of treatment. This research was significant not only for the results that were produced, (i.e., in support of the efficacy of desensitization), but for providing a methodology to address many outcome questions encompassed by the treatment-evaluation strategies mentioned earlier (see Borkovec & Rachman, 1979; Kazdin, 1978b).

ADVANTAGES OF THERAPY ANALOGUES

In behavior therapy, a considerable amount of laboratory-based research has been conducted. In most of these studies, college students with relatively mild or highly circumscribed problems are seen in treatment. The manner in which the subjects are recruited, the types of problems they evince, the training of the therapists who see them, and the manner in which treatment is applied all differ from the usual clinic situation.

Analogue studies allow the investigator to control the conditions of experimentation to a much greater extent than do clinical investigations. The subjects who receive treatment can be selected because of their similarities in types of problems and the severity of the problems. Aspects of treatment can be carefully controlled that otherwise would vary tremendously in actual treatment. The entire treatment process can be relatively standardized. For example, therapists can be selected because of their similarities in age, experience, and training. The number of sessions, duration of treatment, and tasks assigned to the clients in the sessions can be controlled. Standardization of the treatment conditions serves to minimize variability among subjects and therapists and, of course, increases the power of the experimental test.

Aside from standardization, analogue studies permit use of control groups to a degree that otherwise might be impossible. Perhaps the most obvious problem to arise is that of withholding treatment, as in no-treatment and waiting-list control groups. In research with analogue treatments, clients usually are solicited instead of seeking out treatment, and the urgency of intervention is considerably less than in the clinical situation. The freedom of providing or withholding treatment in laboratory-based research greatly expands the range of questions that can be asked about therapy.

Another advantage of analogue research derives from the careful specification of treatment. Because many aspects of treatment are well specified, replications of treatment are possible. Relatively explicit guidelines, such as therapist manuals and schedules for administering treatment, are available for subsequent investigators who wish to replicate the original research.

In general, the superiority of control that laboratory research affords in comparison with clinical research is a function of the priorities of these different research methods. In laboratory research with volunteer subjects, rather than with patients who seek treatment, higher priority is given to the demands of experimentation. Sacrifices of treatment can be and often are made to meet the requirements of the design. For example, treatment can be standardized to ensure homogeneity of conditions, instead of having to take into account individual differences for each client's problem. In contrast, when clients seek treatment, as in clinical settings, the rigors of laboratory research often have to be sacrificed for the priority of providing service. For example, the individual treatment program and duration of treatment are likely to vary widely as a function of a client's needs.

DIMENSIONS THAT DISTINGUISH ANALOGUE RESEARCH

Several dimensions that distinguish analogue research from clinical treatment can be identified. Analogue-therapy investigations may vary from the clinical situation on one or more of these dimensions and in varying degrees. Thus, it is not especially meaningful simply to speak of analogue research as distinct from clinical research. There are varying degrees of resemblance of research to the clinical situation.

Target Problems

Analogue research often has been distinguished from clinical treatment on the basis of its target problems. In analogue research in behavior therapy, treatment has focused upon such problems as fear of small animals, test anxiety, anxiety in social situations, and so on. These problems in fact do appear in clinical treatment. However, in behavior-therapy research, the criteria for defining persons who have a particular problem are generally lenient (e.g., performance on a specific test or two). Performance on the screening criteria does not necessarily reflect a clinically debilitating problem (Bernstein & Paul, 1971). Hence, with few exceptions, the severity of the problem studied in analogue research is much less than that normally brought to clinical treatment.

The specific problems also seen in treatment in analogue research may differ from the ones usually brought to clinical treatment. For example, fears of small animals may respond to treatment quite differently from other sorts of fears (e.g., fears of social situations) (Borkovec & O'Brien, 1976). The results of research on a particular category of problems in analogue research may have little generality to problems seen in the clinic. It is likely that problems focused upon in analogue research differ greatly from those seen in the clinic. Even when problems closely resemble each other, clinical versions are likely to be more intertwined with other problems involving the client's functioning (Woolfolk & Lazarus, 1979). Hence, at first glance, it is quite possible or perhaps even likely that results with superficial problems in analogue studies might not extend to other problems seen in the clinic.

Population

The subjects who serve in analogue research usually are quite different on a number of characteristics, other than the target problem, from persons who are seen in clinical treatment. Typically, analogue studies focus on college students whose age, social class, education, and occupation differ from those of persons who usually seek treatment. This is not to say that college students never seek treatment. However, students serve almost exclusively as subjects in analogue research and yet only comprise a small portion of persons who are seen in clinical treatment. Conclusions reached about treatments using students may differ somewhat from those reached with patients seen in treatment.

Manner of Recruitment

In outpatient therapy, clients usually solicit treatment on their own or through their families. In contrast, subjects who serve in laboratory-based research usually are sought out by those who provide treatment. Often, undergraduate university students are solicited as volunteers and receive credit toward coursework for their participation. On other occasions, volunteers from the community are sought. Presumably, the incentives for the subjects who volunteer for laboratory-based research vary considerably from those of patients who seek treatment.

Therapists

In the clinical situation, experienced professional therapists provide treatment. In most analogue outcome research, graduate students usually administer treatment. Student therapists and professional clinicians are likely to vary on a wide number of dimensions and to behave differently toward their respective clienteles. The range of variables that could vary between types of therapists is extensive, including the types of expectancies held about treatment, the degree of credibility established, and so on.

Selection, Set, and Setting of Treatment

In clinical treatment, clients have a major role in determining the treatment they receive. Clients usually choose their therapists and treatments, a feature that itself may contribute to therapeutic change (Devine & Fernald, 1973; Gordon, 1976). Also, clients are in need of treatment and bring to therapy strong expectations and hopes about what will be accomplished. Perhaps because of their distressed state, clients may be especially receptive to the procedures and techniques administered by their therapists. The hope for relief may be bolstered by seeing a *therapist* at a *clinic* that is designated as a bona fide treatment facility.

The selection, set, and setting of treatment in analogue research may depart significantly from the situation characterizing clinical treatment. Students in laboratory-based research do not select treatments and therapists in the way that clients can. Also, they are less likely to come to treatment in a distressed state. As noted, students often are sought for laboratory-based treatment studies instead of seeking them out, so their initial motivation differs from that of clinical patients. The expectations of students may be attenuated by the fact that they are participating in an *experiment* or are seen in a laboratory or psychology building rather than in a treatment setting. In short, the selection, set, and setting of treatment differ in clinical and laboratory-based research.

INTERPRETATION OF ANALOGUE RESEARCH

The dimensions outlined above do not exhaust the range of characteristics that can distinguish laboratory-based analogue research from clinical treatment (see Kazdin, 1978b). However, the fact that laboratory-based and clinical treatment can be distinguished on so many dimensions raises an obvious question, namely, can the findings obtained in the laboratory-based research be extended to the clinical settings?

A major controversy has emerged within behavior therapy about the external validity of analogue research (e.g., Bandura, 1978; Bernstein & Paul, 1971; Cooper, Furst, & Bridger, 1969; Levis, 1970; Woolfolk & Lazarus, 1979). The controversy has been manifest in the treatment literature on anxiety because of the plethora of studies utilizing students who fear small animals such as harmless snakes or rats. Comments about the generality of laboratory-based research results from studies using students have varied among authors. Some authors have suggested that the generality of treatment may be especially weak if subjects are screened so leniently that only mildly fearful students are included (Bernstein & Paul, 1971). Others have suggested that college students with some fears rather than others (e.g., socially based fears rather than fears of small animals) may bear a closer resemblance to clients presenting with clinical problems (Borkovec & O'Brien, 1976). In still another view, it has been suggested that investigation of subjects who fear harmless snakes may provide an even better or more stringent test of treatment than investigation of clinical problems may, because treatment effects are unlikely to be obscured by extratreatment influences (Bandura, 1978).

In fact, it is difficult to evaluate the generality of analogue research. The influence of variations along each of the dimensions mentioned above on generality of the results is unknown. It is not necessarily the case that focusing on students, using student therapists, or conducting treatment in a university rather than a clinical setting, for example, alter the conclusions reached about treatment. Actually, variations of treatments explored in laboratory-based research often exclude many of the features that would enhance treatment outcome, such as individualized treatment plans, protracted treatment sessions, and patients who are highly motivated for and receptive to treatment. This is not to say that analogue research provides a more stringent test of treatment, but it suggests that the generality of results from analogue research is not necessarily weak. Whether the results from laboratory-based research can be extended to clinical treatment is a function of the particular dimensions along which laboratory research and clinical treatment differ, as well as of the dimension's actual relation to generality of the findings (Kazdin, 1978b). At present, the requisite research to draw conclusions about the generality or lack of generality of analogue research has not been completed.

Although the generality of analogue research is unclear, the fact remains that direct tests of the clinical efficacy of behavior-therapy techniques in clinical settings are needed. Many promising areas of treatment have not been extended to the target populations of direct interest. For example, treatments derived from behavior therapy and cognitive therapy have been developed for depression. However, the bulk of the research has examined depression in college students, and the effectiveness of treatments for clinical depression has been studied in relatively few instances (Rehm & Kornblith, 1979). So additional research is needed to investigate techniques with the clinical populations of direct concern.

The importance of analogue research does not rest simply on the generality of findings to the clinical situation, although the generality issue has occupied the majority of the discussions on the topic. Laboratory-based research is the best and perhaps the only place to address a large number of questions about therapy. Research that is interested in evaluating the analytic questions about treatment reflected in dismantling, constructive, and parametric strategies, for example, will invariably require extremely careful control over treatment and control conditions provided by the laboratory. Research that is interested in understanding the theoretical mechanisms of treatment or the processes of change require highly controlled situations only available in so-called analogue situations (Bandura, 1978; Borkovec & Rachman, 1979). Behavior therapy has made important breakthroughs in developing various treatments because of its heavy but certainly not exclusive reliance upon laboratory-based research.

SOCIAL VALIDATION OF TREATMENT EFFECTS

Therapy outcome usually is evaluated on the basis of changes in performance from pretreatment to posttreatment assessment. In most research on the various treatment-evaluation strategies, conclusions are based upon statistically significant differences among groups. In single-case experimental research, visual inspection rather than statistical criteria usually serves as the basis for evaluating treatment effects. Statistical and visual methods of data evaluation still leave unanswered questions about the clinical significance or importance of changes. Of course, concerns over the clinical significance of therapeutic changes are by no means restricted to any single approach to treatment, but apply to outcome research in general (Garfield, 1978). However, research in behavior therapy has begun to assess the clinical importance of treatment effects, and this represents an extremely important methodological development.

In some areas of treatment, the clinical importance or lack of importance of treatment effects is relatively obvious. For example, treatment may successfully reduce the head banging of an autistic child from 100 to 50 instances per hour. Such a change, over a period of several days, will probably produce a highly statistically significant effect. On the other hand, without a virtual or complete elimination of self-injurious behavior, the clinical value of the treatment can be challenged. To achieve a clinically important change or one that is clearly significant, the behavior needs to be eliminated completely. Of course, with most of the problems brought to treatment, the clinical importance of change cannot be evaluated by a simple observation as to whether the behavior is present or absent. The importance of the change may depend upon the extent to which behaviors are performed and the situations in which they occur. Hence, systematic criteria are needed to evaluate whether the magnitude of change is clinically significant.

Recently, Wolf (1978) has introduced the notion of "social validation," which encompasses methods of evaluating whether interventions produce change of clinical importance. Even though the methodology has been developed within behavior therapy, the evaluation techniques can be readily extended to outcome research in general. Social validation refers generally to consideration of social criteria for evaluating the *focus of treatment,* the *procedures* that are used, and the *effects* that these procedures have. For present purposes, the features related to evaluating the effects of treatment are especially relevant. Two methods for evaluating the clinical importance of treatment effects are referred to as social comparison and subject evaluation (Kazdin, 1977a).

SOCIAL COMPARISON

"Social comparison" refers to comparing the behavior of a client before and after treatment with the behavior of peers who are considered to be nondeviant and to be functioning adequately in their everyday environment. The question addressed by this procedure is that of whether the client's behavior after treatment is distinguishable from the behavior of his or her peers. To answer this question, persons who resemble the client in subject and demographic variables need to be identified. These persons are not a clinical population, but rather are identified because they are functioning normally. For many but certainly not all clinical problems, treatment can be evaluated by the extent to which it produces a change that brings clients to the performance levels of their nondeviant peers.

As an example, Kazdin (1980c) evaluated different imagery-based and rehearsal procedures to develop assertiveness among persons who volunteered for outpatient treatment at an assertion-training clinic. To evaluate the extent to which changes achieved in therapy were clinically significant, several persons were solicited as volunteers who regarded themselves as assertive and especially competent in social situations. These persons served as a group for social comparison to assist in the evaluation of treatment effects.

Prior to treatment, persons who participated in the program were well below the mean (approximately 1.5 standard deviations) of the normative or comparison sample. However, after treatment and at a 6-month follow-up, clients in different treatment groups were above the mean of their nondeviant peers. The improvements achieved in treatment brought clients to the level of peers who considered themselves to be functioning well in their everyday life and who had not sought treatment.

In an institutional setting, O'Brien and Azrin (1972) developed appropriate eating behaviors in mentally retarded residents who seldom used utensils, constantly spilled food on themselves, stole food from others, and ate food previously spilled on the floor. Using prompts, verbal praise and food reinforcement, these inappropriate behaviors were reduced dramatically. To address whether the changes were clinically important, the investigators compared the eating behaviors of the retarded residents who received training with those of "normals." The normal sample consisted of customers in a local restaurant, who were unobtrusively watched by observers recording their eating behaviors. The level of inappropriate mealtime behaviors among the retarded prior to training was much higher than was the level of the normal sample. Interestingly, after training, inappropriate behaviors of the retarded fell slightly below the level of the normative sample. These results suggest that the magnitude of changes achieved with training brought the residents to acceptable performance levels of people functioning in everyday life.

Several investigators have utilized social comparison to evaluate the clinical importance of change. For example, research has shown that children with conduct problems differ from their nonproblematic peers prior to treatment on a variety of disruptive and unruly behaviors, including aggressiveness, teasing, whining, and yelling. However, after treatment, the disruptive behavior of these children has been brought into the range that appears to be acceptable for the same-age peer group. Similarly, social behaviors of withdrawn, highly aggressive, and predelinquent children have been brought to the normative level of their peers. Behavioral treatments applied to a variety of adult and child populations have been evaluated through the use of social comparison (see Kazdin, 1977a).

SUBJECTIVE EVALUATION

Another method of evaluating the importance of behavior change is that of "subjective evaluation." The term refers to determining the importance of a treatment change by assessing the opinions of persons who are likely to have contact with a client. The question addressed by this method of evaluation is that of whether behavior changes are perceived as important among other persons with whom the client interacts. People who are in a special position to do so, through expertise or relation to the client, are asked to judge whether the changes in performance are important. Global evaluations are used to address the importance of the changes.

As an example, research with delinquents occasionally has used subjective evaluations to examine treatment effects. In one report, delinquent girls who resided in a home-style treatment facility were trained to engage in conversational skills, such as answering questions and attending to others who were talking (Maloney, Harper, Braukmann, Fixsen, Phillips, & Wolf, 1976). To evaluate the impact of training on overall conversation, persons with whom the delinquent girls might interact (e.g., a probation officer, a teacher, a counselor, a social worker) rated tapes of their conversations. These judges rated posttreatment conversation as superior to pretraining conversation. These results suggest that concrete behaviors altered during treatment had implications for more general evaluations of overall conversation.

Subjective evaluation has been used to assess treatment effects for a variety of target behaviors and populations. For example, interventions that have trained delinquent boys to interact differently in their conversations with police have been reflected in improvements on ratings of suspiciousness, cooperativeness, and politeness; improvements in specific public-speaking behaviors have been reflected in audience ratings of enthusiasm, sincerity, knowledge, and overall speaker performance; and improvements in specific writing behaviors among children have led to improvements in ratings of creativity of the compositions (see Kazdin, 1977a). In these and other cases, changes in specific behaviors had important implications for more general characteristics of behavior.

CONSIDERATIONS IN VALIDATING BEHAVIOR CHANGE

The use of normative data and global evaluations of client behavior represents an important step toward quantifying the extent to which changes produced in treatment are important. However, the methods of evaluating change raise problems that will need to be addressed in future research. For social comparison, problems arise in identifying a normative group. To whom should chronic psychiatric patients, the mentally retarded, prisoners, and other populations be compared in evaluating treatment and rehabilitative programs? Developing normative levels of performance in clinical populations may be an unrealistic ideal in many cases. Also, it is not clear how to match clients in treatment to a normative sample. Perhaps the sample should be the same on subject and demographic variables, such as age, gender, social class, education, and so on. Yet the level of normative performance may depend upon the variables used to match normal and clinical populations.

The importance of the comparison group for social validation of treatment effects is illustrated by a study designed to improve the social behavior of psychiatric patients (Stahl, Thomson, Leitenberg, & Hasazi, 1974). For one of the patients, verbalizations improved after treatment and closely approximated the level of verbal behavior of other patients of similar education who were not verbally deficient. Yet the increase in verbalizations was quite discrepant from the level of intelligent, normally functioning persons who were not patients. Thus, the clinical impact of treatment would be evaluated quite differently, depending upon the comparison group.

Even if a normative group can be identified, the range of behaviors that would be defined as "acceptable" is difficult to specify. It is relatively simple to identify deviant behavior when that behavior departs markedly from normative levels. As behavior becomes slightly less deviant, it is difficult to identify the point at which behavior is within the normative range. The difficulty of defining the normative range arises in identifying treatment-worthy problems to begin with and in deciding that the level of change produced is clinically important.

For many problems, social comparison may not seem relevant. For example, clients who are depressed or overly self-critical may not evince specific overt behaviors that depart from their less distressed peers. Functioning in everyday life in terms of social, work-related, and recreational performance may match that of nondistressed peers. The overt behavior may not be discrepant from normative standards, but the clients' evaluations of themselves and of their lives may be distinctly negative. In such cases, therapy may focus on a client's assumptions and self-dialogue. Data from social comparison may still be relevant if it examines the client's assumptions, evaluations, and affect, which might depart from normative levels to begin with and approach these levels after treatment. Admittedly, for many problems, client satisfaction may not depend upon a normative standard, and social comparison may be of unclear relevance in evaluating treatment.

Problems exist when applying subjective evaluation as well. Reliance upon the global opinions of others to evaluate treatment effects raises familiar problems. Subjective evaluations have been accorded a significant role in traditional treatment evaluation, in which therapists and clients judge the benefits of treatment; subjective evaluations of behavior, however, are subject to a variety of biases on the part of the raters. The ambiguity of criteria for the basis of making the ratings distracts from the ultimate meaning of the data. Thus, data based upon subjective evaluations must be treated very cautiously. Subjective evaluations may reflect change when overt behaviors do not (Kazdin, 1973; Patterson, Cobb, & Ray, 1973; Schnelle, 1974). Also, the fact that persons who interact with the client claim that there is a difference in behavior as a function of treatment does not necessarily mean that the amount of change in the client is clinically significant. A small change in behavior, or even no change in behavior, may be reflected in the global ratings while the client's behavior departs considerably from the normative level.

GENERAL COMMENTS

Evaluation of the clinical significance of treatment through social comparison and subjective evaluation raises several problems. Several ambiguities arise in the assessment and interpretation of normative and global rating data. However, the potential advantages of using social validation methods are manifold. First, social validation methods provide criteria to evaluate the impact of treatment in relation to practical considerations about the client's functioning in everyday life. The methods provide a way of relating outcome criteria used for research purposes with clinically relevant client objectives.

Second, social comparison directs attention to persons who are functioning adequately in everyday life. In obtaining normative data, it may be useful to look further into how people who are not identified for or seen in treatment behave. An area of research worthy of attention in its own right is the behavior of persons considered to be functioning well. Perhaps this is even a research area logically prior to treatment outcome, because normative information to some extent provides the goals toward which much of treatment is directed. For example, research might lead to clues as to how social skills are acquired by children and adults who function well in their everyday lives; why very active boys and girls do not become or are not seen as hyperactive; or why many children from high-risk family situations (e.g., broken homes, poverty, high-crime areas) develop normally. Examination of normative samples has relevance for prevention and diagnosis, as well as for treatment.

Finally, examination of normative data and subjective evaluations is part of a larger interest within behavioral research. Increasingly, proponents of behavior therapy are interested in the *social context* in which therapy is provided (see Kazdin, 1980a). Social context refers here to the opinions and values of persons in everyday life that are relevant for deciding on the problems that warrant intervention, the specific techniques that are appropriate, and the extent to which treatment outcomes are important. The social importance of the views of persons in everyday life in evaluating aspects of treatment has been widely recognized in research on therapy outcome in general (Kazdin & Wilson, 1978; Strupp & Hadley, 1977).

CONCLUSION

Behavioral research has made increased demands on the sorts of questions asked of treatment. Hence, several methodological approaches and evaluation techniques are commonly used. Although the behavioral literature can be readily characterized by the amount of research generated, perhaps of greater interest is the range of questions that is encompassed by this research. The present chapter has addressed some of the major approaches to illustrate the methodology of behavioral research.

It is not entirely accurate to imply that the topics addressed in the present chapter are unique to or developed by behavior-modification research. For example, although behavior-modification research is giving increased attention to the clinical significance of behavior change, the topic has been of perennial concern in treatment evaluation. Similarly, elaboration of the treatment-evaluation strategies only details questions of recognized importance in outcome research, independent of behavior modification.

Perhaps the most significant characteristic of the field is that the underlying theories, techniques, and approaches have fostered methodological developments and innovations. Indeed, the topics examined in the present chapter represent only some of the areas that might have been discussed. Progress in methodology has been made in a number of other areas, including the assessment of multiple response channels, evaluation of so-called nonspecific treatment factors, examination of costs and cost-effectiveness, and so on. Methodological approaches in the field often have played a role secondary to that of the innovative treatment approaches that have emerged. However, as the definitions of behavior therapy have evolved over the years, methodological characteristics have been given increased attention. The present chapter has attempted to detail those portions of the methodology that have epitomized behavioral research.

ACKNOWLEDGMENT

Completion of this chapter was facilitated by a Research Scientist Development Award (K02 MH00353) from the National Institute of Mental Health.

REFERENCES

Adams, H. E., & Hughes, H. H. Animal analogues of behavioral treatment procedures: A critical evaluation. In M. Herson, R. M. Eisler, & P. M. Miller (Eds.), *Progress in behavior modification* (Vol. 3). New York: Academic Press, 1976.

Alexander, J. F., Barton, C., Schiavo, R. S., & Parsons, B. V. Systems–behavioral intervention with families of delinquents: Therapist characteristics, family behavior, and outcome. *Journal of Consulting and Clinical Psychology,* 1976, *44,* 656–664.

Azrin, N. H. A strategy for applied research: Learning based but outcome oriented. *American Psychologist,* 1977, *32,* 140–149.

Baer, D. M., Wolf, M. M., & Risley, T. R. Some current dimensions of applied behavior analysis. *Journal of Applied Behavior Analysis,* 1968, *1,* 91–97.

Bandura, A. Self-efficacy: Toward a unifying theory of behavioral change. *Psychological Review,* 1977, *84,* 191–215.

Bandura, A. On paradigms and recycled ideologies. *Cognitive Therapy and Research,* 1978, *2,* 79–103.

Bandura, A., Blanchard, E. B., & Ritter, B. Relative efficacy of desensitization and modeling approaches for inducing behavioral, affective, and attitudinal changes. *Journal of Personality and Social Psychology,* 1969, *13,* 173–199.

Barlow, D. H., & Hayes, S. C. Alternating treatments design: One strategy for comparing the effects of two treatments in a single subject. *Journal of Applied Behavior Analysis,* 1979, *12,* 199–210.

Barlow, D. H., Reynolds, J., & Agras, W. S. Gender identity change in a transsexual. *Archives of General Psychiatry,* 1973, *29,* 569–576.

Baum, M. Extinction of avoidance responding through response prevention (flooding). *Psychological Bulletin,* 1970, *74,* 276–284.

Bernstein, D. A., & Paul, G. L. Some comments on therapy analogue research with small animal "phobias." *Journal of Behavior Therapy and Experimental Psychiatry,* 1971, *2,* 225–237.

Borkovec, T. D., & O'Brien, G. T. Methodological and target behavior issues in analogue therapy outcome research. In M. Herson, R. M. Eisler, & P. M. Miller (Eds.), *Progress in behavior modification* (Vol. 3). New York: Academic Press, 1976.

Borkovec, T., & Rachman, S. The utility of analogue research. *Behaviour Research and Therapy,* 1979, *17,* 253–261.

Cooper, A., Furst, J. B., & Bridger, W. A brief commentary on the usefulness of studying fears of snakes. *Journal of Abnormal Psychology,* 1969, *74,* 413–414.

Davison, G. C. Systematic desensitization as a counterconditioning process. *Journal of Abnormal Psychology,* 1968, *73,* 91–99.

Devine, D. A., & Fernald, P. S. Outcome effects on receiving a preferred, randomly assigned, or nonpreferred therapy. *Journal of Consulting and Clinical Psychology,* 1973, *41,* 104–107.

Everaerd, W. T. A. M., Rijken, H. M., & Emmelkamp, P. M. G. A comparison of "flooding" and "successive approximation" in the treatment of agoraphobia. *Behaviour Research and Therapy,* 1973, *11,* 105–117.

Ford, J. D. Therapeutic relationship in behavior therapy: An empirical analysis. *Journal of Consulting and Clinical Psychology,* 1978, *46,* 1302–1314.

Garfield, S. L. Research problems in clinical diagnosis. *Journal of Consulting and Clinical Psychology,* 1978, *46,* 596–607.

Glass, G. V., Willson, V. L., & Gottman, J. M. *Design and analysis of time-series experiments.* Boulder: Colorado Associated University Press, 1975.

Gordon, R. M. Effects of volunteering and responsibility on the perceived value and effectiveness of a clinical treatment. *Journal of Consulting and Clinical Psychology,* 1976, *44,* 799–801.

Greenberg, D. J., Scott, S. B., Pisa, A., & Friesen, D. D. Beyond the token economy: A comparison of two contingency programs. *Journal of Consulting and Clinical Psychology,* 1975, *43,* 498–503.

Hackmann, A., & McLean, C. A comparison of flooding and thought stopping in the treatment of obsessional neurosis. *Behaviour Research and Therapy,* 1975, *13,* 263–269.

Hartmann, D. P., & Hall, R. V. The changing criterion design. *Journal of Applied Behavior Analysis,* 1976, *9,* 527–532.

Heller, K. Laboratory interview research as an analogue to treatment. In A. E. Bergin & S. L. Garfield (Eds.), *Handbook of psychotherapy and behavior change: An empirical analysis.* New York: Wiley, 1971.

Hersen, M., & Barlow, D. H. *Single-case experimental designs: Strategies for studying behavior change.* New York: Pergamon, 1976.

Jones, R. R., Vaught, R. S., & Weinrott, M. Time-series analysis in operant research. *Journal of Applied Behavior Analysis,* 1977, *10,* 151–166.

Kazdin, A. E. Role of instructions and reinforcement in behavior changes in token reinforcement programs. *Journal of Educational Psychology,* 1973, *64,* 63–71.

Kazdin, A. E. Statistical analyses for single-case experimental designs. In M. Hersen & D. H. Barlow, *Single-case experimental designs: Strategies for studying behavior change.* New York: Pergamon, 1976.

Kazdin, A. E. Assessing the clinical or applied significance of behavior change through social validation. *Behavior Modification,* 1977, *1,* 427–452. (a)

Kazdin, A. E. *The token economy: A review and evaluation.* New York: Plenum, 1977. (b)

Kazdin, A. E. The application of operant techniques in treatment, rehabilitation, and education. In S. L. Garfield & A. E. Bergin (Eds.), *Handbook of psychotherapy and behavior change* (2nd ed.). New York: Wiley, 1978. (a)

Kazdin, A. E. Evaluating the generality of findings in analogue therapy research. *Journal of Consulting and Clinical Psychology,* 1978, *46,* 673–686. (b)

Kazdin, A. E. *History of behavior modification: Experimental foundations of contemporary research.* Baltimore: University Park Press, 1978. (c)

Kazdin, A. E. Methodological and interpretive problems of single-case experimental designs. *Journal of Consulting and Clinical Psychology,* 1978, *46,* 629–642. (d)

Kazdin, A. E. *Behavior modification in applied settings* (2nd ed.). Homewood, Ill.: Dorsey, 1980. (a)

Kazdin, A. E. *Research design in clinical psychology.* New York: Harper & Row, 1980. (b)

Kazdin, A. E. *Single-case research designs: Methods for clinical and applied settings.* New York: Oxford University Press, 1982.

Kazdin, A. E., & Hartmann, D. P. The simultaneous-treatment design. *Behavior Therapy,* 1978, *9,* 912–922.

Kazdin, A. E., & Wilson, G. T. Criteria for evaluating psychotherapy. *Archives of General Psychiatry,* 1978, *35,* 407–416.

Kazrin, A., Durac, J., & Agteros, T. Meta-meta analysis: A new method for evaluating therapy outcome. *Behaviour Research and Therapy,* 1979, *17,* 397–399.

Korchin, S. J. *Modern clinical psychology.* New York: Basic Books, 1976.

Krapfl, J. E., & Nawas, M. M. Differential ordering of stimulus presentation in systematic desensitization. *Journal of Abnormal Psychology,* 1970, *75,* 333–337.

Kratochwill, T. R. (Ed.). *Single-subject research: Strategies for evaluating change.* New York: Academic Press, 1978.

Lang, P. J. The mechanics of desensitization and the laboratory study of fear. In C. M. Franks

(Ed.), *Behavior therapy: Appraisal and status.* New York: McGraw-Hill, 1969.

Lang, P. J., & Lazovik, A. D. Experimental desensitization of a phobia. *Journal of Abnormal and Social Psychology,* 1963, *66,* 519–525.

Lang, P. J., Lazovik, A. D., & Reynolds, D. J. Desensitization, suggestibility, and pseudotherapy. *Journal of Abnormal Psychology,* 1965, *70,* 395–402.

Lazovik, A. D., & Lang, P. J. A laboratory demonstration of systematic desensitization psychotherapy. *Journal of Psychological Studies,* 1960, *4,* 238–247.

Leitenberg, H. The use of single-case methodology in psychotherapy research. *Journal of Abnormal Psychology,* 1973, *82,* 87–101.

Levis, D. J. The case for performing research on nonpatient populations with fears of small animals: A reply to Cooper, Furst, and Bridger. *Journal of Abnormal Psychology,* 1970, *76,* 36–38.

Linehan, M. M., Goldfried, M. R., & Goldfried, A. P. Assertion therapy: Skill training or cognitive restructuring. *Behavior Therapy,* 1970, *10,* 372–388.

Luborsky, L., Singer, B., & Luborsky, L. Comparative studies of psychotherapies: Is it true that "everyone has won and all must have prizes"? *Archives of General Psychiatry,* 1975, *32,* 995–1008.

Maloney, D. M., Harper, T. M., Braukmann, C. J., Fixsen, D. L., Phillips, E. L., & Wolf, M. M. Teaching conversation-related skills to predelinquent girls. *Journal of Applied Behavior Analysis,* 1976, *9,* 371.

Masserman, J. H. *Behavior and neurosis.* Chicago: University of Chicago Press, 1943.

Meichenbaum, D. H. *Cognitive-behavior modification.* New York: Plenum, 1977.

Meltzoff, J., & Kornreich, M. *Research in psychotherapy.* New York: Atherton, 1970.

Morris, R. J., & Zuckerman, K. R. Therapist warmth as a factor in automated desensitization. *Journal of Consulting and Clinical Psychology,* 1974, *42,* 244–250.

O'Brien, F., & Azrin, N. H. Developing proper mealtime behaviors of the institutionalized retarded. *Journal of Applied Behavior Analysis,* 1972, *5,* 389–399.

Orlinsky, D. O., & Howard, K. I. *Varieties of psychotherapeutic experience.* New York: Teachers College Press, 1975.

Patterson, G. R., Cobb, J. A., & Ray, R. S. A social engineering technology for retraining families of aggressive boys. In H. E. Adams & I. P. Unikel (Eds.), *Issues and trends in behavior therapy.* Springfield, Ill.: Charles C Thomas, 1973.

Paul, G. L. *Insight versus desensitization in psychotherapy: An experiment in anxiety reduction.* Stanford, Calif.: Stanford University Press, 1966.

Paul, G. L., & Lentz, R. J. *Psychosocial treatment of chronic mental patients: Milieu versus social learning programs.* Cambridge, Mass.: Harvard University Press, 1977.

Rehm, L. P., & Kornblith, S. J. Behavior therapy for depression: A review of recent developments. In M. Hersen, R. M. Eisler, & P. M. Miller (Eds.), *Progress in behavior modification* (Vol. 7). New York: Academic Press, 1979.

Rosenthal, T. L., & Bandura, A. Psychological modeling: Theory and practice. In S. L. Garfield & A. E. Bergin (Eds.), *Handbook of psychotherapy and behavior change* (2nd ed.). New York: Wiley, 1978.

Rush, A. J., Beck, A. T., Kovacs, M., & Hollon, S. Comparative efficacy of cognitive therapy and pharmacotherapy in the treatment of depressed outpatients. *Cognitive Therapy and Research,* 1977, *1,* 17–38.

Schnelle, J. F. A brief report on invalidity of parent evaluations of behavior change. *Journal of Applied Behavior Analysis,* 1974, *7,* 341–343.

Sidman, M. *Tactics of scientific research.* New York: Basic Books, 1960.

Sloane, R. B., Staples, F. R., Cristol, A. H., Yorkston, N. J., & Whipple, K. *Psychotherapy versus behavior therapy.* Cambridge, Mass.: Harvard University Press, 1975.

442   ASSESSMENT AND METHODOLOGY

Smith, M. L., & Glass, G. V. Meta-analysis of psychotherapy outcome studies. *American Psychologist,* 1977, *32,* 752–760.

Stahl, J. R., Thomson, L. E., Leitenberg, H., & Hasazi, J. E. Establishment of praise as a conditioned reinforcer in social unresponsive psychiatric patients. *Journal of Abnormal Psychology,* 1974, *83,* 488–496.

Stern, R., & Marks, I. M. Brief and prolonged flooding. *Archives of General Psychiatry,* 1973, *28,* 270–276.

Strupp, H. H., & Hadley, S. W. A tripartite model of mental health and therapeutic outcomes. *American Psychologist,* 1977, *32,* 187–196.

Thigpen, C. H., & Cleckley, H. M. *Three faces of Eve.* New York: McGraw-Hill, 1957.

Watson, R. I. *The clinical method in psychology.* New York: Harper, 1951.

Wilkins, W. Desensitization: Social and cognitive factors underlying the effectiveness of Wolpe's procedure. *Psychological Bulletin,* 1971, *76,* 311–317.

Wolf, M. M. Social validity: The case for subjective measurement, or how applied behavior analysis is finding its heart. *Journal of Applied Behavior Analysis,* 1978, *11,* 203–214.

Wolpe, J. *Psychotherapy by reciprocal inhibition.* Stanford, Calif.: Stanford University Press, 1958.

Woolfolk, R. L., & Lazarus, A. A. Between laboratory and clinic: Paving the two-way street. *Cognitive Therapy and Research,* 1979, *3,* 239–244.

V

OUTCOME AND EVALUATION

11

CHILDHOOD DISORDERS

K. DANIEL O'LEARY
Department of Psychology
State University of New York at Stony Brook

EDWARD G. CARR
Department of Psychology   ,
State University of New York at Stony Brook

INTRODUCTION

In 1967, when the first author taught an abnormal child psychology course emphasizing behavioral treatment, there were no texts on the topic, and selected readings in the area were sparse. In approximately 15 years, however, the field of child behavior therapy has clearly become a prominent treatment force. There are now a number of texts and books of readings bearing the title *Child Behavior Therapy* or some variation thereof (e.g., Erickson, 1978; Gelfand & Hartmann, 1975; Graziano, 1975; A. O. Ross, 1980), and there are frequent job advertisements for child behavior therapists.

The writings of Ullmann and Krasner (1965) and Bijou (1965) were instrumental in helping child psychologists to conceptualize abnormalities of children in behavioral terms and in prompting a Zeitgeist that was characterized by tremendous optimism and zeal. An investigator could readily get the impression in the late 1960s from reading treatises on behavior modification that autism, retardation, delinquency, aggression, hyperactivity, and social isolation could be readily cured or markedly ameliorated. In addition, the impact of the conceptual paradigm was so strong that behavioral treatment was seen by some as a treatment that would surpass any other.

The optimistic Zeitgeist of the late 1960s and early 1970s encouraged clinicians and researchers to try to change myriad acute and chronic behavior problems. The New Frontier and Great Society eras of Presidents Kennedy and Johnson were similarly optimistic, and they may actually have been influential in promoting the enthusiasm of psychologists. In fact, the vast amount of money earmarked for mental retardation programs and Head

445

Start–Follow Through efforts was a concrete sign that legislators also felt these problems could be ameliorated by psychological and educational means. The Head Start–Follow Through program was one of the largest social–educational experiments ever conducted by the United States government. Optimism regarding behavioral treatment fortunately continues today, but in a tempered sense. As we make clear in this chapter, certain critical problems of children—autism, aggression, delinquency, hyperactivity, and social isolation—have all been altered quite markedly, and maintenance effects have been observed. It is important to note, though, that few of these problems have been seen as "cured"; chronic conditions like autism, delinquency, and severe hyperactivity may never be "cured" in the usual sense of this term. However, as we note, the conditions can be changed in a fashion so that children with such problems can exist in an environment generally free of psychotropic medication, in conditions that are minimally restrictive, and in situations that prompt children to feel that they have an important impact on significant others.

The seminal influences of Ullmann and Krasner and of Bijou on the field of clinical child psychology were especially instrumental in changing conceptualizations of the causes of abnormalities from intrapsychic events to observable events (e.g., reinforcers). At present, mediational or cognitive events as well as observable events are viewed as important by behavioral psychologists (Mahoney, 1977). Nonetheless, cognitive–behavioral interventions with children have been largely promissory notes, as indicated by several recent reviews on self-control and self-instructional strategies with children (Hobbs, Moquin, Tyroler, & Lahey, 1980; Meichenbaum, 1980; S. G. O'Leary, 1980; S. G. O'Leary & Dubey, 1979; Rosenbaum & Drabman, 1979).

Despite the failures to document the success of cognitive interventions, the interest in such interventions continues. Such interest is probably well-founded, because the cognitive interventions are now seen by some not as singular interventions, but as part of a treatment approach involving operant, cognitive, and modeling strategies (cf. Douglas, 1980). The clinical efficacy of self-control strategies as the sole intervention is not clear, but teaching self-control strategies seems useful in a *multifaceted* treatment program for two reasons. First, self-control strategies are likely to facilitate generalization and maintenance of change. Second, self-control strategies are likely to lead to an increased sense of self-esteem or self-efficacy.

There has been a clear tendency in child behavior therapy to rely on principles of operant learning. The field of applied behavior analysis is philosophically consistent with Skinner's operant, behavioristic position (1953), and the *Journal of Applied Behavior Analysis* has been a major publication source for research with excellent single-subject methodology focusing on the change of significant overt behaviors. The emphasis in these articles has been largely atheoretical, and the research has been designed to develop a technology of behavior change (Dietz, 1978; Hayes, Rincover, & Solnick, 1980). We believe that the atheoretical focus should and will change in the next few years. At a minimum, new concepts and methods are needed to deal with family and social systems, and it seems unlikely that operant concepts can be relied upon to explain most phenomena in these systems.

We sense that seasoned operant researchers are becoming tired of demonstrating that reinforcement principles can be used to change countless behaviors. Further, sole reliance on current operant concepts, principles, and technology seems myopic and likely to lead to intellectual stagnation. Fortunately, there is a trend by child behavior therapists well known for their operantly oriented interventions toward introducing new concepts or using concepts from other orientations that have not been discussed in the operant literature. Such concepts include insularity (Wahler, 1980), cognitive operations (Becker & Carnine, 1980), assessment of feelings (K. D. O'Leary & Turkewitz, 1978a), pragmatics of language (Hart, 1980; Hart & Risley, 1978), resistance (Patterson, Chamberlain, & Reid, 1980), and subjective measurement (Wolf, 1978). The heuristic value of some of these concepts is illustrated in this chapter.

Of course, investigators can use operant terminology to describe what happens in other predictive and explanatory systems, and Skinner has repeatedly used operant terminology to discuss economic, sociological, educational, and mental health phenomena. If such translations have heuristic value, the translation is certainly useful. Unfortunately, the area of child behavior therapy has not recently had an infusion of concepts translated from other theoretical positions into operant terms that seem heuristically salient. A major value of the operant orientation has been the ease with which many phenomena can be conceptualized—especially treatment concepts that can readily be used for treatment planning. In order to prevent fragmentation that can result from studying sets of principles and procedures in an isolated fashion, it seems wise to place such principles and procedures in an overall theoretical framework (Wilson & O'Leary, 1980) or an atheoretical rubric (Skinner, 1953). In such an exercise, the limits and advantages of the model become apparent, as illustrated by Birchler and Spinks (1980) in their integration of behavioral and systems approaches to marital therapy.

This chapter is organized according to childhood problem areas. Developmental disabilities (autism, retardation, and childhood schizophrenia), fears, conduct disorders (aggression and hyperactivity), delinquency, enuresis, and behavioral pediatrics (asthma and obesity) are covered, and summaries are provided for each of these topical areas. Finally, a section on future directions represents our opinions regarding needed research and clinical directions. We attempt to relate the suggested directions to the previous sections, but we also relish the privilege to raise issues for consideration that have received little or no attention by behavior therapists.

DEVELOPMENTAL DISABILITIES

Developmentally disabled children have traditionally received labels such as "autistic," "retarded," or "schizophrenic." These labels denote certain distinctive behavioral patterns. For example, autistic children show extreme social isolation. They display an inability to comprehend sounds and develop language, problems that manifest themselves in mutism and echolalia (i.e., parroting the speech of others). Much of their time is spent in self-stimulatory and ritualistic behaviors that have been described as "attempts to preserve sameness." Schizophrenic children are typically more social and verbal; however, their speech often has a disorganized and nonsensical quality. Finally, retarded children show a pervasive delay in motor, intellectual, and social development. These diagnostic distinctions may ultimately prove beneficial in understanding etiology and planning preventive measures. At present, however, differential diagnosis does not lead to effective differential treatment for the vast majority of developmentally disabled children. In fact, traditional psychodynamic therapy, in which diagnostic categories are held to be important in determining treatment strategies, produces poor results (Rutter, 1966). These findings have helped to promote a significant trend away from treatment focused on a diagnostic categories toward treatment focused on specific *behavior problems*. Thus, developmental disability is now conceptualized as a deficit in adaptive behavior and not as a sign of underlying emotional disturbance. To put it another way, there has been a shift from a medical model to an educational model.

COMPONENTS OF BEHAVIORAL TREATMENT PROGRAMS

Since broad-spectrum behavioral approaches to these problems generally involve a combination of procedures aimed at remediating specific excesses and deficits, it is useful to review briefly some of the more important components of such programs before discussing outcome.

Many developmentally disabled children display self-injurious behavior, such as head banging and self-biting. Severe episodes of aggression and tantrums are also common. Since a child who displays these problems is very difficult to educate, considerable effort is devoted to controlling these problems at the outset of treatment. The basic strategy is to reinforce alternative behaviors that are incompatible with the problem behaviors (Carr, Newsom, & Binkoff, 1980; Lovaas, Freitag, Gold, & Kassorla, 1965). Sometimes this procedure is ineffective when used alone. In such cases, punishment (of the problem behavior) is added to the treatment package (Carr & Lovaas, in press). Punishment has also been used to control self-stimulatory behaviors (Foxx & Azrin, 1973).

Once behavior problems are brought under control, speech and language training begins. This activity constitutes the core component of most behavioral programs for developmentally disabled children. The emphasis on speech and language is justified in view of data suggesting that competence in this area of functioning is correlated with a more favorable prognosis (Lotter, 1978). For mute children, the intervention is based on the training of skills in verbal imitation (Lovaas, Berberich, Perloff, & Schaeffer, 1966). Once the child has mastered these skills, more complex semantic and syntactic behaviors are built, using the child's newly acquired imitative repertoire (Lovaas, 1977) Some children fail to make progress in speech training. For them, sign language may be used as an alternative communication system (Carr, 1979). Finally, in the case of more verbal children whose problem is excessive echolalia, a useful treatment strategy has been to teach a variety of more appropriate verbal responses to those stimuli that are discriminative for echolalic behavior. When this is done, echolalia is eliminated or greatly reduced (Carr, Schreibman, & Lovaas, 1975; Schreibman & Carr, 1978).

Since widespread deficits in social behavior are a common problem, these children are also taught simple social behaviors such as greeting and showing affection (Lovaas, Freitas, Nelson, & Whalen, 1967), as well as play (Koegel, Firestone, Kramme, & Dunlap, 1974). In addition, a variety of self-help skills has been taught, including self-feeding (Barton, Guess, Garcia, & Baer, 1970), toilet training (Azrin & Foxx, 1971), and dressing (L. S. Watson, 1973). Such skills presumably function to make the child more independent and better adjusted to community living.

COMPREHENSIVE HOME AND SCHOOL TREATMENT

There have been a number of attempts to combine several of the above treatment components in a comprehensive manner in both home and school settings. One of the earliest and most influential studies involved a young autistic child named Dickey (Wolf, Risley, & Mees, 1964). When first seen, he was self-destructive, nonsocial, echolalic, and lacking in self-help skills. Following behavioral treatment, he acquired normal speech and appropriate social and self-help skills; further, he was no longer self-destructive. His treatment was extended both at school and at home over a number of years.

Interestingly, he continued to improve to the extent that he was eventually transferred to a regular public-school classroom, where he was accepted by his peers and regarded as socially appropriate by his teacher (Nedelman & Sulzbacher, 1972). This successful outcome set a model for future studies. Most important was the emphasis on parent and teacher training, early intervention, and systematic follow-up to ensure maintenance of treatment gains as well as continued acquisition of new behaviors.

Later investigators have adopted the naturalistic, early-intervention approach initially developed by Wolf *et al.* (1964). Thus, Nordquist and Wahler (1973) treated a 4-year-old autistic boy by training his parents to use standard operant procedures in the home environment on a daily basis. An important feature of their program was the use of reinforcers, such as TV and drawing, that were indigenous to the home setting and thereby provided a potent, readily accessible motivational source for the various teaching programs. The child showed a decrease in crying and rituals and an increase in compliance and imitative abilities. Further, these gains were maintained and enhanced over the 2-year period of the study. The report is particularly noteworthy, since the parents had been repeatedly advised by other professionals to institutionalize their child. The fact that the child continued to improve at home and to show growth in important areas of development may be construed as evidence of a successful treatment outcome.

The above studies, though suggestive, leave open the question of generality, since each study involved only one child. Fortunately, there are two major studies that deal with larger samples of autistic children. Working with a group of 20 children, Lovaas, Koegel, Simmons, and Long (1973) employed a variety of measures to assess the outcome of their behavioral intervention which, for some of the children, was home-based and involved extensive parent training. Follow-up measures taken 1 to 4 years after treatment termination showed that the children displayed substantial decreases in psychotic behaviors such as self-stimulation and, to some extent, echolalia. Also, there were major gains in play behavior and, to a lesser degree, in compliance. Appropriate speech increased as well, although the gains were not as dramatic in this area. Interestingly, children who were initially echolalic eventually reached a higher overall level of functioning than those who were initially mute, suggesting the existence of subgroups with differing prognoses. An additional important finding was that there was marked behavioral deterioration at follow-up for those children who had been institutionalized at the end of treatment. In contrast, children who were discharged to trained parents maintained their gains and continued to improve in many areas. There is a noteworthy implication for public policy in these data—namely, that funds allocated for the treatment of developmentally disabled children are better spent in the training of parents in the community, than in perpetuating the institutional system. Yet, in spite of these data, substantial numbers of children are placed in institutions every year (Lotter, 1978).

Although Lovaas *et al.* (1973) were able to demonstrate significant gains in their children, there was still some questions regarding whether or not these gains would have been produced in any case without extensive behavioral intervention. A study of Hemsley, Howlin, Berger, Hersov, Holbrook, Rutter, and Yule (1978) sought to answer this question through the use of control groups. The experimental group, consisting of 16 children, received an intensive behavioral intervention. Parents of these children were trained to use a variety of behavioral techniques and worked with their children for a 30-minute period each day at home. In addition to the experimental group, there were two control groups. One control group consisted of 14 children who were not in treatment. A second control group consisted of 16 children who were seen only occasionally on an outpatient basis. This group received a much less intensive behavioral program than that received by the experimental group and are referred to here as the minimal-treatment group. These three groups were matched on several variables, such as IQ and language impairment, known to be related to outcome. Following 6 months of treatment, the experimental group showed much greater improvement in the conversational use of spoken language than did the no-treatment group. Also, they showed substantially less ritualistic behavior. Further, mothers of children in the experimental group showed an increase in behaviors relevant to teaching (e.g., corrections, directions, praise), whereas mothers in the no-treatment group did not. An 18-month follow-up showed that the experimental group maintained their gains and continued to improve. Further, compared with the minimal-treatment group, they showed less deviant behavior and were more socially responsive. Overall, this study suggests that intensive behavioral treatment appears more therapeutic than does minimal treatment or no treatment at all. The positive outcome of the Hemsley *et al.* study must be tempered, however, by the fact that the children in this study had relatively high IQs (i.e., nonverbal IQ of 60 or more). By way of comparison, Lovaas *et al.* (1973), who worked with children having substantially lower IQs, reported much smaller gains. This might suggest that there are subgroups of autistic children, distinguishable on the basis of level of intellectual functioning, who have differing prognoses even following behavioral intervention.

In spite of the emergence of a number of programs for parent training, it may still not be possible to treat some children in their own homes. Home treatment becomes extremely difficult in the aftermath of divorce, when many mothers may have to leave the home in order to go to work. Sometimes, parents cannot be trained because they have serious personal crises to deal with. Finally, a child may exhibit behavior problems that are too severe or dangerous to be dealt with at home. In these cases, treatment may have to be carried out in a group-home setting. That is, it may be possible to treat the children through surrogate parents who have been trained to use behavioral intervention techniques (Lovaas, 1978). Research using this model is just beginning.

The classroom is the other major intervention setting for developmentally disabled children. Early work showed that the amount of schooling received by psychotic children correlated positively with their level of social adjustment at adolescence (Rutter, Greenfeld, & Lockyer, 1967). This finding might suggest that outcome would be most favorable following intensive behavioral intervention in the classroom. A systematic analysis of this possibility has been carried out in England (Bartak, 1978). Three different classroom programs ("units") were compared. Unit A employed psychodynamic techniques with minimal attention to skill development. Unit B combined a permissive classroom environment in the context of psychodynamic techniques and a special-education curriculum. Unit C was a structured, organized program that emphasized the development of perceptual, motor, and cognitive skills. This program, in fact, included many features found in standard behavioral approaches. Follow-up measures were taken 3½ to 4 years after the program had begun. Children in Unit C (the behavioral prototype) displayed the lowest frequency of stereotyped behavior and spent the most time engaged in planned activities. In Unit C, most of the children (approximately 80%) were using phrase speech communicatively, whereas only half the children in the other Units were doing so. Further, the children in Unit C did best in terms of formal scholastic achievement (i.e., reading accuracy, comprehension, and arithmetic scores). It is important to note, however, that the very positive outcomes reported here were for children who functioned primarily in the mildly retarded range. Whether the outcomes would be as positive for children with lower IQs is at the moment an unanswered question. The studies discussed next, however, provide a partial answer to this question.

There have been a number of classroom studies done with moderately and severely retarded children. The major strategy has been to combine token reinforcement for various aspects of good classroom work, with time out for misbehavior. In a controlled study, Baker, Stanish, and Fraser (1972) found that children in a behavioral-treatment group displayed significantly less negative behavior than children in the control group. Birnbrauer, Wolf, Kidder, and Tague (1965) found that a token system was valuable for a majority of their retarded children in that it increased classroom productivity and/or helped control behavior problems. In general, then, behavioral intervention has proved beneficial in increasing academic productivity and in controlling behavior problems. However, when this mode of intervention is evaluated using standardized measures of academic achievement, the results are much less dramatic (Birnbrauer, 1976). This latter observation is congruent with that made by Rutter (1978) concerning the impact of treatment on autistic children. Rutter noted that educational intervention seemed to make little difference on a child's overall level of cognitive development. In short, then, behavior modification does not appear to "cure" the basic intellectual deficits that characterize developmental disabilities; however, it does enhance a variety of adaptive skills involving social and communicative behavior. Further, it helps in the control of serious problem behaviors. Perhaps, in the long run, the gains made in these areas will be sufficient to keep a child from being institutionalized. If so, the achievement is noteworthy, even if it does not constitute a "cure."

GENERALIZATION AND MAINTENANCE

A major concern in evaluating the above research is the lack of systematic data pertaining to generalization and maintenance of treatment (Carr, 1980b). This problem was highlighted in the data presented by Lovaas *et al.* (1973), who demonstrated how readily treatment gains are reversed in the absence of carefully planned follow-through. The major implication of that study is that continued improvement is to a great extent a function of the posttreatment environment. Researchers must be guided by this fact; that is, a researcher needs to plan for a child's future needs *now* by structuring the educational curriculum so that it will facilitate the child's adjustment to his or her future school and home situation. By teaching a child behaviors that are functional in subsequent placement, the researcher is adhering to the dictum that the "criterion of ultimate funcitoning" (L. Brown, Nietupski, & Hamre-Nietupski, 1976) must be paramount in determining what is to be taught now. Detailed research in this area is just beginning. For example, it is known that children who are to be eventually placed in regular classrooms (i.e., integrated or mainstreamed) must have skills such as independent work habits; also, they must be able to profit from group instruction (i.e., not just one-on-one treatment). It is encouraging to note, therefore, that both of these critical skills can be taught to children (Rincover & Koegel, 1978). Thus, by carefully structuring the educational curriculum so that it emphasizes the teaching of those behaviors that are requisite for successful, more normalized placement, an investigator can positively influence classroom outcome. In contrast to the school situation just described, almost nothing is known as yet concerning the skills a child must have in order to succeed in the home setting. This area should be a research priority, since a child who can be helped to adjust successfully to living at home is far less likely to be institutionalized.

To some extent, the problems of generalization and maintenance have been exacerbated by the piecemeal approach that has characterized intervention from the earliest behavioral studies. In the early studies, investigators tended to concentrate on only a few problems in a few restricted settings, using artificial (e.g., appetitive) reinforcers—a strategy that made discrimination of treatment and nontreatment environments easy, and durability of gains therefore improbable. This fragmented approach to intervention, though initially necessary in order to identify effective treatments, must now give way to more programmatic efforts. That is, young children must receive treatment from both trained parents and trained teachers. Such treatment must continue for as long as the children exhibit serious deficits in adaptive behaviors. Treatment in restrictive, artificial environments must be replaced with naturalistic treatment in which children are presented with many opportunities to associate with and be integrated into the community of normal peers. The data reviewed above suggest that this more holistic approach is likely to yield dividends with respect to promoting generalization and maintenance.

THE QUESTION OF SUCCESSFUL OUTCOMES

Since very few developmentally disabled children are "cured" by the treatment interventions discussed above, an important question is this: What will be their fate as they reach adulthood? From the standpoint of living arrangements, the group-home model is likely to be the final placement for many developmentally disabled individuals, in lieu of institutionalization. However, since schooling for these individuals usually ends at age 21, it is uncertain how they will occupy themselves as adults. Follow-up data (Lotter, 1978) show that the number of autistic persons employed ranges from 0% to 13% on the average, a very dim prospect. Notwithstanding this poor outcome, there is almost no systematic research on the vocational habilitation of the autistic. The picture for retarded persons is only a little brighter. It is worth noting, however, that Gold (1973) has shown the feasibility of using behavioral principles to facilitate the work activity of retardates. In view of the possibility that many developmentally disabled individuals, even those who are lower-functioning, could potentially spend much of their adult lives gainfully employed in a sheltered environment, more attention needs to be paid to a vocational component in the educational curriculum. In particular, there is a need for detailed task analyses and for the training of skills that are readily usable in a wide variety of work environments, thereby maximizing vocational opportunities (Bellamy, Wilson, Adler, & Clarke, 1980). At the present time, behavior therapists have provided very little systematic data on the procedures necesary for bringing about such gains. Nor have they provided data on the long-term effi cacy of vocational habilitation in helping developmentally disabled individuals to escape institutionalization.

In evaluating the outcome of behavioral intervention for developmental disabilities, it becomes clear that the diagnostic label, whether it be "autism," "mental retardation," or "childhood schizophrenia," is much too broad to be meaningful. Instead, it appears that there are subgroups of children that can be readily identified as being more or less benefited by treatment intervention. Thus, with respect to autism, echolalic children have a better outcome than mute children do (Lovaas *et al.*, 1973). Children with high IQs generally do better than do children with low IQs (Lotter, 1978). Further, a number of studies have suggested that intensive behavioral intervention with *young* mildly retarded children can produce substantial academic and intellectual gains (Bereiter & Engelmann, 1966). Likewise, studies with autistic children suggest that younger individuals might be particularly amenable to treatment (Nordquist & Wahler, 1973; Wolf, Risley, & Mees, 1964). Finally, a major study in progress suggests that early intervention with young autistic children (i.e., those under 30 months of age) may produce a *cure* rate of 50% (Lovaas, 1980): Given that the cure rate is normally only 5% to 17% (Lotter, 1978), these figures are most impressive; if substantiated by systematic data, they would represent the most significant breakthrough in the treatment of autism to date. The implication is that intervention with very young children will produce a substantially better outcome than that with older children will. This does not mean, of course, that older children should be abandoned. Rather, what it suggests is that we must redouble our efforts at early identification and intervention, while at the same time continuing to provide services for older, less tractable individuals. The above data, taken as a whole, would suggest (1) that behavior modifiers should pay more attention to individual differences among children; and (2) that the outcome of behavioral intervention may be highly dependent on subgroup characteristics, irrespective of diagnostic label.

Finally, the question of what ultimately constitues a successful outcome may be raised. To answer this question, we must consider the fact that about 50% of autistic children are institutionalized and that the percentage goes higher as the child grows older (Lotter, 1978). Further, about 25% of moderately and severely retarded children are in institutions, and 35% to 40% of the profoundly retarded are institutionalized (Conley, 1973). A minimum criterion of success could be that of whether or not behavioral interventions can improve upon these rates. Currently, these comparative data do not exist.

Given that a child has escaped institutionalization (i.e., is living at home), different levels of successful outcome can be defined in terms of the type of school placement in which the child is being educated. These levels, hierarchically arranged in order of increasing value, are as follows: The child is (1) attending a special school; (2) attending a special class in a regular school; (3) attending a partially integrated class in a regular school; (4) attending a regular class and receiving some additional remedial tutoring; (5) attending a regular class and functioning at grade level. In this last case, if the child is also judged as behaviorally indistinguishable from his or her peers, the outcome would probably be labeled a "cure." At present, data are sorely needed in order to evaluate what level of success (according to the criteria just outlined) behavioral interventions can produce.

In spite of all the progress described in this section, there is a compelling need to recognize that there are significant lacunae in behavioral intervention programs. For example, as noted above, while we are able to improve children's behavior and academic productivity, we are still in the dark about how to enhance overall cognitive and intellectual functioning. Such problems may best be approached by carefully considering the *content* of educational curricula; important gains have been produced in these areas of functioning by making detailed task analyses that take into account a child's current level of development (cf. D. M. Ross & S. A. Ross, 1974). Another unresolved problem is that we have yet to normalize the child's social behavior. Many developmentally disabled children, especially those labeled "autistic," respond poorly to social reinforcement, display inappropriate affect, and typically do not appear "attached" to significant others such as parents and siblings. This autistic "barrier" remains in effect even when a child shows gains in other areas. An analysis of social–affective behavior and the variables that enter into its remediation is long overdue. Finally, a great deal more attention must be paid to the social validity of behavioral intervention (Wolf, 1978). That is, will significant individuals such as parents, teachers, and neighbors judge a child as less deviant following intervention? If not, the child is likely to continue to be rejected and stigmatized, even though objective behavior recordings demonstrate substantial gains. Only recently has research in this neglected but critical area been undertaken (Dunlap, Egel, Killion, Koegel, & Schreibman, 1978).

SUMMARY

In sum, behavioral interventions for developmental disabilities seldom produce a cure, but they do produce marked improvements in a number of adaptive behaviors. Further, these improvements are greater than those achieved with more traditional interventions or with no intervention at all. The outcome of behavioral treatment is highly dependent on such subgroup characteristics as level of language development, level of intellectual functioning, and age of a child. There is a need for a more holistic and programmatic approach to treatment that involves parent and teacher training and continued intervention over time. Only then will the problems of generalization and maintenance be overcome. There is a need to investigate areas relating to cognitive and social behavior as well as to social validity. Such research is likely to enhance therapeutic effectiveness and to provide a more realistic assessment of the normalizing value of behavioral intervention. Finally, researchers and clinicians must evaluate the success of their interventions with respect to a standard set of outcome criteria, such as the hierarchy described above. By comparing their results against set criteria, they will be in a better position to judge the ultimate efficacy of their efforts.

FEARS

ACQUISITION

At birth, a child displays fearful responses to two stimuli only—loud noises and falling. The child's response to noises and falling, called the "Moro reflex," is a fanning of the arms in a clutching fashion and a simultaneous arching of the back. The presence and form of the Moro reflex are important in the neurological development of the child. Children rapidly develop various fearful responses to many stimuli, and the form of their responses changes from the reflexive nature of the Moro response to cautious avoidance and trembling. Jersild and Holmes (1935) described the development of children's fears in a classic monograph. Most important, they showed how children's fears changed from fears of specific objects to fears of imaginary objects and creatures when the children were between 4 and 6 years old.

Fear acquisition is a very complex phenomenon. Some discussion about the acquisition of fears is very important, because the development and treatment of children's fears was purported to be accounted for by a conditioning model, and thus was a milestone in the development of behavior therapy. In young children, fears of loud noises, falling, pain, depth, and strangers are thought to be innate. They do not occur invariably, but they are so common across highly different cultures that innate mechanisms seem to be the most likely causes of the fears in infants (Hetherington & Parke, 1979). Fears in children from the ages of 3 to 8 vary with social class, race, and intensity of parents' fears (Kennedy, 1971). Lower-class children are most fearful of robbers, scolding, and animals, while upper-class children are most fearful of being hurt, being alone, darkness, and physical danger. Girls generally have more fears in social situations than boys do. As the number and intensity of parents' fears increase, so do the fears of their children. Finally, according to Kennedy (1971), faulty communication between parents and children is one of the greatest causes of childhood fears. More specifically, parents often convey generalized fear reactions when clear communication about specific concerns would be much more beneficial for the child.

A more simplistic view of acquiring fears was promulgated in 1920 by John B. Watson, the famous radical behaviorist. Watson and Rayner (1920) published the first conditioning experiment of fearful behavior. A healthy 9-month-old male, Albert, was initially not frightened by a white rat, a white rabbit, masks with and without hair, a dog, or a newspaper. However, when a hammer struck a steel bar, the child started, cried, and trembled. After determining the child's usual responses to these various stimuli, the investigators created the loud noise by hitting the steel bar with a hammer as Albert reached out to touch the white rat. In short, "conditioning" trials were in operation to ascertain whether Albert would learn to fear the rat and similar objects. After several pairings of the noise and the touching of the rat, Albert reportedly showed a fearful response to the presence of the rat as well as to similar objects (e.g., the white rabbit and a Santa Claus mask). A month later, Albert continued to exhibit some fearful responses to the white laboratory rat and similar objects. Watson and Rayner concluded that they had established conditioned fear that generalized across time and objects.

Mary Cover Jones (1924) published a now-famous sequel to the Albert case. Jones worked with a 34-month-old boy, Peter, who feared rabbits, rats, and wool. Peter presented a natural opportunity to assess whether fears could be unlearned or deconditioned. The methods of treating the fear included the following:

1. Peter was placed in a playroom with other children who had been selected because they did not fear any of the aforementioned objects.
2. Peter was placed in a high chair and was given food he liked while the rabbit was gradually brought closer to Peter.

The study proved successful in that eventually Peter was able to touch the objects without evidence of fear. In brief, it now appeared that fears could be conditioned and deconditioned.

Several unsuccessful attempts were made to replicate the Watson and Rayner (1920) work (Bregman, 1934; English, 1929). However, Watson and Rayner's study of little Albert is one of the most widely cited studies in undergraduate psychology textbooks. Further, major graduate texts on psychopathology have used this study as a model of fear acquisition (Harris, 1979). In several recent detailed reanalyses of the Watson and Rayner study (Harris, 1979; Samuelson, 1980), critics have noted several distortions of the procedure, results, and interpretations of the study. In fact, this case is used to illustrate how lack of critical scrutiny and replications can lead a discipline to be misled for decades. These historical perspectives on the social science scene are humorous and enlightening, but at the same time sobering. The analyses should alert investigators to the way in which "classic" studies may be misrepresented, misinterpreted, and molded into a history of a discipline. The failure to replicate conditioning of fears in children leads to the conclusion that the conditioning accounts of fear acquisition in children are unproven. The variations of classic treatment procedures for children's fears by Jones (1924) have been used by many investigators, although conditioning accounts of treatment seem highly oversimplified.

DIFFERENTIATION OF FEARS AND PHOBIAS

A "fear" is defined as an emotion of violent agitation or fright in the presence (actual or anticipated) of danger or pain (English & English, 1958). Fears are characterized by physiological reactions such as avoidance and withdrawal. A "phobia" is "a special form of fear which (1) is out of proportion to the demands of the situation, (2) cannot be explained or reasoned away, (3) is beyond voluntary control, and (4) leads to avoidance of the feared situation" (Marks, 1969, p. 3). With the exception of school phobias, there are few phobias for which children are referred to mental health clinics. In an evaluation of types of DSM-II diagnoses used for 330 children attending a child clinic, phobias (phobic neuroses) were only diagnosed .6% of the time, and anxiety neuroses were diagnosed .3% of the time (Cerreto & Tuma, 1977). Further, on the basis of several related studies, it appears that clinicians see school phobias infrequently (approximately 1% of clinic cases), whereas clinicians see many more children (10% to 25% of clinic cases) with anxious and generally fearful symptoms (Johnson & Melamed, 1979). Finally, even in those cases where clinicians use the diagnosis "phobia," it is often for school phobias, and the extent to which a "school phobia" of older children is best conceptualized as a phobia is unclear (K. D. O'Leary & Wilson, 1975). Because of the infrequent treatment of specific phobias in children, treatment evaluations are here restricted to fears, school phobia, and social withdrawal.

TREATMENT OF SPECIFIC FEARS

Melamed and her colleagues have conducted a series of excellent studies of children with fear of surgical and dental situations. For children undergoing elective surgery, Melamed and Siegel (1975) used a film entitled *Ethan Has an Operation*, which depicted the experiences of a 7-year-old boy undergoing a hernia operation. In the film Ethan describes his apprehension, his fear, and his coping methods; he is depicted in the admission room, the ward orientation room, the operating room, the recovery room, and the hospital discharge area. To assess the impact of this film, 30 children about to undergo surgery for hernias, tonsillectomies, or urinary problems were shown either this experimental film or a control film about a boy's trip in the country. All children received the usual preoperative hospital preparation; this included demonstrations and explanations of surgery and the recovery process, as well as a visit from the surgeon, who again explained the surgery to the child and his or her parents. An excellent feature of the Melamed and Siegel study (1975) was their collection of data from three major response modalities: children's self-reports of anxiety, staff observations of anxiety, and the Palmar Sweat Index. Children who saw the experimental film showed greater reduction of anxiety in all three response modalities than did the children who saw the control film. It is important to note that the film was effective enough for changes to be detected, even though all children had received the regular detailed hospital preoperative procedures. Similar work by Vernon (1973, 1974) and Vernon and Bailey (1974) indicates the efficacy of film models in reducing fear or anxiety regarding general anesthesia or injections.

Melamed and her colleagues have begun to define more precisely the situations in which a film model will work (Melamed, Robbins, Smith, & Graves, 1980). It appears that children who have been hospitalized previously show less responsivity to the modeling film, and that the *pattern* of responding across modalities during film viewing is very important. That is, children with *high* prefilm levels of sweat gland activity showed the greatest retention of information about the film. Cardiac deceleration and self-reports of low anxiety are correlated with retention of information.

Fear of dentists has also been reduced by means of film-modeling procedures. Melamed and her colleagues have shown that all three response modalities (self-report, direct observation, and physiological indicators) showed reduction of anxiety when children about to have a dental examination were shown the film. In the dental situation, as in the surgical environment, cardiac deceleration during film viewing was associated with retention of information (Melamed *et al.,* 1980). The approach of using filmed peer models seems especially useful in a general preventive framework. However, from discussions with dentists who have used related films (Adelson, Liebert, Poulos, & Herskovitz, 1972), it appears that intensive and varied procedures are necessary to help some children overcome fears of dentists.

Bandura and his associates (Bandura, Grusec, & Menlove, 1967; Bandura & Menlove, 1968) conducted a series of studies in the late 1960s demonstrating that children who saw filmed peer models gradually approaching dogs showed significant approach responses to dogs. Of clinical interest was the finding that children who also had fears of various interpersonal situations showed less improvement than did children with a singular fear of dogs. This finding is similar to that of Lang, Lazovik, and Reynolds (1965), who found that adult phobic patients who had multiple fears improved less than patients with an isolated phobia.

In summary, the viewing of film peer models who successfully cope with the feared situation is associated with reductions of children's fears regarding surgery, dentists, and dogs. The film procedure seems most effective when used in a preventive sense—that is, before the fear has been well established. It should be noted that none of the subjects in the above studies were referred for treatment of fears. Instead, they viewed the film in the course of their dental or surgical treatment or during their regular nursery school day.

SCHOOL PHOBIA

As noted earlier, the term "school phobia" is one that represents a clear oversimplification. Generally, "school phobia" refers to a child's refusal to attend school where it is assumed that the child is irrationally afraid of something related to the school. The decision regarding whether the refusal is due largely to fear or something else is not always clear. Factors ordinarily associated with school phobia are maternal overprotection, eating problems, abdominal pain and nausea, sleeping problems, and clinical indications of anxiety. School truancy, on the other hand, is characterized by inconsistent home discipline, juvenile court appearance, persistent lying, wandering from home, and stealing (Hersov, 1960). In brief, the school phobic is generally characterized by fear and anxiety, whereas the school truant is characterized by delinquent behavior.

Several investigators of varying theoretical persuasions have found that forced school attendance is effective in treating school-phobic children if the failure to attend school is not a chronic problem (Kennedy, 1965; Rodriguez, Rodriguez, & Eisenberg, 1959). Ignoring a child's complaints and rewarding school attendance may be especially effective when the child's refusal to attend school has been inadvertently reinforced by parents' attention. Primary concentration on the operant components of school phobia has been exemplified by several investigators who have reported successful treatment (Ayllon, Smith, & Rogers, 1970; R. Brown, Copeland, & Hall, 1974). No assessment instruments have been devised that offer empirical support in the choice of treatment emphasis, (i.e., operant or respondent). Until more assessment research and well-controlled outcome studies are conducted, it seems reasonable to address both operant and fear components of the school phobia. With adolescents, very careful and sensitive probing is necessary to ascertain what an individual really fears.

SOCIAL WITHDRAWAL

Social isolation, shyness, withdrawal from peers, and overanxious reactions are characteristic of 10% to 25% of child clinic cases. Modeling and reinforcement have been the primary behavioral interventions to prompt and maintain social approach responses of children. Modeling was used as early as 1934 (Jack, 1934), and many studies have demonstrated the efficacy of modeling in modifying social withdrawal of children. O'Connor (1969) selected nursery-school children who were seen as socially withdrawn by their teachers and who exhibited low rates of social interactions, as indicated by classroom observations. Half the socially withdrawn children viewed a 23-minute modeling film that portrayed scenes of children interacting with other children, and the remaining children viewed a control film about dolphins. The peer-modeling film was highly effective. The withdrawn children showed great increases in social interactions in their classroom and were indistinguishable from classmates immediately following the film. In a subsequent study, O'Connor (1972) found that the modeling film was again effective in both prompting and maintaining approach responses and was more effective than a procedure involving direct reinforcement from teachers was. However, the particular method of reinforcing children and the schedule of reinforcement may have favored the modeling condition in this comparison. Nonetheless, these studies have been replicated with some variations, and both acquisition and short-term maintenance effects have been found (Evers & Schwarz, 1973; Keller & Carlson, 1974). Some attempts to increase social approach behavior in children by means of filmed peer models have failed (see Gelfand, 1978, for review). Sources of failure appear to be (1) inappropriate match of models for age of viewers; (2) lack of coping narration; and (3) modeling of other shy children if the isolated children view the films in a group of other shy children (Gelfand, 1978).

Reinforcement of social approach behavior has been used to treat social withdrawal since the hallmark studies of Bijou and his associates at the University of Washington in the early 1960s. Physical prompting and reinforcement have been especially useful in increasing social responding in retarded children (e.g., Whitman, Mercurio, & Caponigri, 1970). While it has been clear that social approach behavior can be modified with teacher attention, it is not clear that a reinforcement procedure is clinically effective in helping maintain durable changes, with or without a modeling film (Walker & Hops, 1973).

SUMMARY

Children's fears and anxieties have been successfully treated using behavioral interventions in well-controlled studies. Studies of modeling effects exemplify the best experimental work in the area of children's fears, and the research can provide a good prototype for others who wish to use behavioral procedures in a community-preventive sense. On the other hand, modeling research has not indicated under what conditions such interventions are effective, and the clinical efficacy of modeling films with children who have chronic fears has begun to be seriously questioned. Reinforcement procedures have proven effective in altering social withdrawal, but the reinforcement procedures have to be tailored to a child's age, and the fading of reinforcers must be carefully programmed.

Controlled research on school phobias is difficult to conduct, and the natural course of the problem is unclear. Treating acute school phobias in young children by forced school attendance seems highly advisable, and this approach has been used successfully by therapists of varying theoretical persuasions. No controlled-group studies with adolescent school phobias have been conducted, but focus on operant components in these children has proven fruitful, as judged from single-case research. Clinical experience leads us to conclude that emphasis on both operant and respondent factors is very important in adolescents and that sensitive probing assessments are crucial throughout assessment and treatment.

The absence of work with families is surprising, because, as mentioned in the introduction to this section, children often have fears that are similar to those of their parents, and the communication a child has with his or her mother may be especially important. We expect that successful clinical treatment of children with general fearful reactions will have to include work with the parents to address the modeling of their fearful reactions, the inadvertent reinforcement of their child's fears, and the modeling of social approach behavior.

CONDUCT DISORDERS:
AGGRESSION AND HYPERACTIVITY

There has been considerable debate regarding whether an independent syndrome of hyperactivity exists. More specifically, the concern is whether hyperactivity exists as a syndrome independent from aggression. We discuss this issue before evaluating treatment programs for aggressive and hyperactive children, because researchers and clinicans may ask whether the problems are really different, and concomitantly, whether the treatments for such children should be different.

DIFFERENCES IN AGGRESSION AND HYPERACTIVITY?

Hyperactivity has become prominent in part because a pharmacological treatment, namely psychostimulant medication, has been seen both by researchers and clinicians as an effective treatment. Children who receive psychostimulants such as Ritalin definitely show increased attention span, enhanced psychomotor skills, and more cooperative behavior in the classroom (Conners & Werry, 1979). Further, the effects of the medication are evident within 30 minutes after ingestion, and the medication is not physically addictive for children. At present, approximately 2% of all American elementary-school children receive such psychostimulant medication, and the Department of Health, Education, and Welfare (1971) reported that 5% of all American elementary-school children can be deemed "hyperactive." Recently, however, concern has been raised by journalists (Schrag & Divoky, 1975) and professionals (K. D. O'Leary, 1980) about the use of medication with children. The concern stems in large part from the evidence (1) that hyperactive children treated with psychostimulant medication do not fare better academically than hyperactive children who do not receive such medication, and (2) that hyperactive children treated with psychostimulant medication for several years do not show social and academic gains at follow-up greater than those of children who did not receive such medication.

To return to the issue of diagnosis, there is a concern that hyperactivity does not exist as an entity separate from aggression and conduct problems in general. For example, the title of an article in *Clinical Pediatrics* evaluating treatment efficacy was titled, "Pharmacological Management of Children with Hyperactive/Aggressive/Inattentive Behavior Disorders" (Winsberg, Yepes, & Bialer, 1976). Correlations of approximately +.70 have generally been found between factors of hyperactivity and aggression on a standardized teacher rating scale, and until 1978, evidence did not exist for a syndrome of hyperactivity that was relatively distinct from aggression.

Loney, Langhorne, and Paternite (1978) made a hypothetical distinction between "primary" or "core" syndromes (e.g., hyperactivity and inattention) and "secondary" or "resultant" symptoms (e.g., low self-esteem and delinquent behavior) that were thought to arise from the hyperkinetic child's "flawed interactions with his/her environment" (p. 432). More specifically, low self-esteem and delinquent behavior were thought to result from the central problems of inattention, hyperactivity, and their sequalae. Using judges' ratings from case records of primary and secondary syndromes of children treated primarily for hyperactivity, Loney *et al.* found two relatively independent major factors: aggression and hyperactivity. These factors had intercorrelations of only .27. Using the same variables that Loney *et al.* rated from case folders, S. G. O'Leary and Steen (in press) factor-analyzed teacher rating data from two widely used teacher rating scales (Conners, 1969; Quay & Peterson, 1979). More specifically, O'Leary and Steen categorized the items in the two teacher rating scales in order to conform to the conceptual framework of Loney *et al.*, and they also found two relatively independent factors in both an original and a cross-validation sample. The correlations between aggression and hyperactivity were .12 in the original sample and .21 in the cross-validation sample.

It can be concluded from the Loney *et al.* (1978) work and the S. G. O'Leary and Steen (in press) results that hyperactivity *can* be relatively independent of aggression. However, both Loney *et al.* and O'Leary and Steen started with populations that were high on indices of hyperactivity. Thus, it can be concluded that children who are hyperactive need not be aggressive. Further, the Loney *et al.* 1978 result has been replicated almost exactly by S. G. O'Leary and Steen (in press) with two different cross-validation populations totaling approximately 100 children. These results do not necessarily allow a clinician to take a sample of children with a mixed group of behavioral problems and reliably assign them to hyperactive or aggressive groups. Nonetheless, this research represents the first practical utilization of Loney *et al.*'s theoretical work. More specifically, a straightforward mathematical analysis of two standardized rating scales led to two separate dimensions: hyperactivity and aggression (S. G. O'Leary & Steen, in press).

Because aggression has been a target of intervention by behavior therapists for a longer period of time than hyperactivity has, we first evaluate the effects of treatment efforts with aggression.

AGGRESSION

Patterson and his colleagues (e.g., Patterson, Reid, Jones, & Conger, 1975) have conducted some of the most programmatic research with aggressive children and adolescents. His research has focused primarily on helping families with aggressive boys. The research began in the mid-1960s with a series of individual case studies involving careful collection of data during baseline and intervention. This research was summarized by Patterson (1974), who treated 47 children for behavior problems in the home and school. Interventions included training in behavioral procedures for all parents and consultation with school personnel for 14 of the children who had significant problems at school. Total treatment time per case averaged 31.5 hours in the home and 28.6 hours in the classroom. In addition, an average of 1.9 hours of consultation was provided during the 12-month follow-up period.

After treatment, the rate of problem behaviors at home was reduced to a level that was deemed "within the normal range," and this reduction was maintained at 12-month follow-up. Patterson's work is exemplary of clinical innovation and careful documentation of repeated interventions. However, the absence of an untreated control group makes it difficult to conclude unequivocally that the changes attributed to treatment did, in fact, result from the treatment. While we believe that the treatment certainly had some salutary effects, it is not possible to ascertain how much of the treated groups' changes were due to the treatment rather than maturation.

A brief treatment program involving contingency management and skills in communication and conflict resolution was more effective than was no treatment for a group of children with a variety of problems; some of the children were aggressive, while others had problems of withdrawal and fear (Martin, 1977). On the other hand, Camp, Blom, Herbert, and Van Doorninck (1977) had mixed results when they implemented a program of cognitive-behavior modification with aggressive boys. More specifically, they found greater changes in the treated than in a nontreated group on laboratory measures designed to measure aggression, but not on classroom ratings of aggression.

Kent and O'Leary (1976) established a treatment program for aggressive boys who were selected on the basis of a standardized teacher checklist and classroom observations. The treatment program involved weekly consultations with each boy, his parents, and/or his teachers across 3–4 months. The treatment was conducted by experienced clinical psychologists. The procedures that were most important in the treatment of school problems were (1) teacher and parental praise, encouragement, and other forms of positive attention (e.g., a pat on the back or a wink); (2) decreased use of teacher threats and reprimands, with substitution of occasional reprimands audible only to the treated child; and (3) special privileges, such as extra television or special desserts when the child evidenced improvement on the daily report completed by the teacher. Factors that received emphasis in treating problems at home were praising appropriate behavior; ignoring inappropriate behavior whenever possible; and restricting privileges, contact with peers, and television viewing for brief periods when punishment was necessary. In addition, the therapist discussed the undesirable effects of physical punishment and angry scoldings. It should be noted that the program at home was provided in large part as a means of assisting children with their homework and tutorial materials. That is, parents were expected to aid their children for 20–30 minutes each school day in either math or reading.

A total of 16 treated children were compared with 16 nontreated control children at baseline, at the end of treatment, and at a 9-month follow-up. (The study involved one treated or control child per class; thus 32 classes were involved during baseline and treatment, and 3 additional classes were included at follow-up.) Both observational recordings and teacher ratings of social and academic behavior indicated that treated children improved more than did nontreated children. However, at the 9-month follow-up, the control group had improved sufficiently that the differences in social behavior were no longer significant. On the other hand, actual academic changes (as opposed to teacher ratings) were not greater for treated children at termination, but they were at follow-up, as reflected by both grades and achievement test scores. Ratings of therapists by teachers and parents were uniformly positive, and there were no dropouts during the 3–4 months of treatment.

As Kent and O'Leary indicated, 20 hours of consultation is sufficient to serve some families of highly aggressive elementary-school children, but others may need at least double that number of produce lasting improvement in school. Further, the investigators noted that marital and family problems would require attention in an ongoing clinical treatment. Of greatest interest methodologically was the finding that the untreated control children improved significantly on standardized teacher ratings and classroom observations of aggression. Had the control group not been included, the authors would have concluded that the behavior-therapy program was responsible for the clear behavioral improvement that was maintained with slight deterioration 9 months after termination of therapy.

Kent and O'Leary (1977) extended the aforementioned program with a BA-PhD consultation team and compared their effectiveness with treatments implemented by PhD clinical psychologists only. Aggressive boys again served as the treated subjects ($n = 16$), and they were compared to untreated aggressive controls boys ($n = 8$). The treatment program was basically the same as the one described earlier (Kent & O'Leary, 1976), and a replication of effects was found in that treated children improved more than did untreated children, as assessed by classroom observations and teacher ratings at termination of therapy. The treatments of the BA-PhD team were as effective as the treatments implemented by the PhD clinical psychologists alone were. Unfortunately, no effects on academic behavior were attributable to treatment, and no differences between treated and untreated children were evident at follow-up. The absence of academic effects resulting from treatment may have been due to the absence of parental tutoring support during the school year and summer.

Measurements of aggression pose a difficult problem when an investigator is conducting lengthy treatment research that includes a significant follow-up period, since the topography of aggression changes significantly with age. For example, it is likely that an 8-year-old child may very frequently display aggressive behavior such as biting, pushing, and name calling. When the child is 11 years old, he or she may become much more selective in the way aggression is displayed, yet may not be clinically improved. More specifically, the 11-year-old may occasionally take another youngster's books in the hall between classes, and may beat the tar out of a peer in a locker room during gym on several occasions during the school year. Because of this developmental phenomenon, it seems wise to utilize some clinical judgment measures until investigators can acquire a reasonable understanding of what decreases in aggression mean across age. The issue is especially important, since very aggressive boys who are not treated do show less frequent aggression as they get older (Kent & O'Leary, 1976, 1977), but the clinical status of the children is not clear.

HYPERACTIVITY

Behavioral treatments for hyperactive children have also been associated with clear changes in social behavior in the classroom. The approaches that have been successful have emphasized reinforcement of behavior in the classroom, teacher consultation, and home-based reinforcement. Salutary changes have been obtained on standardized teaching ratings as well as on independent observations of children's classroom behavior (K. D. O'Leary, 1980). Specific academic targets such as amount of work completed have also been changed, but changes have not been observed on standarized academic achievement tests. It is likely that such changes have not occurred simply because the interventions have generally been only several months in duration.

Interventions employing cognitive-behavior therapy with hyperactive children have been shown to be useful in changing behavior on laboratory tasks and some achievement tests. On the other hand, there is almost no evidence that cognitive interventions lead to changes in classroom behavior. Drawing upon the work of Palkes, Stewart, and Freedman (1972), Douglas and her colleagues (Douglas, Parry, Marton, & Garson, 1976) developed a program emphasizing self-instruction and modeling to improve attentional difficulties and impulsivity in hyperactive children. The self-control training (24 sessions over 3 months) was augmented with direct instruction and contingency-management consultation (18 sessions) to parents and teachers. The treated group of 18 hyperactive boys made significant gains on several nonacademic laboratory tasks, both at posttreatment and at a 3-month follow-up, as compared to 11 boys in an untreated but equivalent control group. Some effects were also noted on achievement tests. In contrast, no significant results of self-instructional training were observed in classroom behavior.

Failures in the cognitive-training approach, however, are widespread, and the effectiveness of the cognitive element of certain behavior-therapy approaches is unclear. Several detailed reviews of the self-control and self-instructional research have appeared (S. G. O'Leary & Dubey, 1979; Rosenbaum & Drabman, 1979). These reviews all question the utility of the self-instructional approach with hyperactive children specifically. On the other hand, few if any investigators argue against teaching self-control or self-instructional strategies. Rather, the general sentiment appears to be that the self-control approach has merit when combined with other, more direct interventions.

Douglas (1980) has an excellent yet cautious interpretation of the cognitive-training approach for hyperactive children as she is developing it in a clinical fashion. The approach now has three levels of intervention: (1) helping children understand the nature of the disabilities that are creating problems for them; (2) increasing the youngsters' awareness of their own role as problem solvers and motivating them to assume this role more actively and successfully; and (3) teaching specific problem-solving strategies. This recommendation seems very reasonable, and Douglas enumerates the ways in which the strategy is designed to facilitate generalization to the classroom. Further, Douglas fully recognizes the need for combining cognitive training with drug treatment or contingency management.

SUMMARY

Behavioral treatments for both aggression and hyperactivity have been successfully implemented. More large-scale behavior-therapy interventions have been implemented with aggressive than with hyperactive children, in terms of numbers of children treated, length of the intervention, length of follow-up, and scope of intervention (e.g., inclusion of both home and school). There is sufficient evidence, both in terms of subjective and objective reports, to conclude that families of aggressive children can be helped by behavioral interventions. However, it is unclear that treatments lead to long-term gains. This ambiguity results from the improvement of untreated control children that is frequently documented empirically. In future research, more stress might be placed on significant others' perceptions of clinical changes and their maintenance. This focus might prove fruitful because overt rates of aggression might well decrease in children as they get older, but the intensity or seriousness of singular aggressive incidents may also become more significant. Methodological problems in measuring change abound in this area (K. D. O'Leary & Turkewitz, 1978b), but they are not elaborated here. However, it seems worthwhile to begin to attend more to correlates or moderators of treatment effectiveness, because several investigators have noted that their treatment effects may be mitigated by marital discord and overt parental hostility.

There is a need for interventions for hyperactive children to focus on the particular problems of such children, instead of simply using omnibus behavioral interventions for children with some constellation of conduct problems. More specifically, impulse control, short attention spans, problems with fine motor coordination, and inability to delay gratification are key problems of most hyperactive children. However, there are as yet no specific interventions for hyperactive children that show that the above problems can be changed. One exception here is the work of Douglas, who has developed a multipronged program for hyperactive children. Yet Douglas's program has limitations, one being that because of the variety of intervention strategies used, it is impossible to ascertain what particular procedures are effective. More importantly, the meager laboratory evidence that exists on Douglas's interventions does not readily translate into interventions that involve skill training in the natural environment.

One great challenge in the future will be whether behavioral interventions with hyperactive children can provide changes that are similar to those of psychostimulant medication. Psychostimulant medication is repeatedly and dramatically associated with increases in attention and cooperativeness in classrooms (Conners & Werry, 1979). These changes associated with medication use may be deceptive, and researchers and clinicians should be wary of the problems associated with widespread use of psychostimulants. More specifically, when children on these drugs are compared to untreated children, the psychostimulants do not appear to have long-term salutary effects of either an academic or social nature. Further, even though increases in attention are almost always associated with psychostimulant use in children, academic changes have not been detected even on short-term bases on standardized achievement tests. In this vein, K. D. O'Leary (1980) has recommended a large-scale multiclinic outcome study comparing the effects of psychostimulants, behavior therapy, and their combination. Satterfield, Cantwell, and Satterfield (1979) have provided data that suggest that a combined psychological, pharmacological, and educational intervention may be particularly useful on both a short-term and a long-term basis.

DELINQUENCY

Juvenile delinquency is increasing, in spite of massive funding from federal and state government agencies for intervention programs and in spite of a plethora of suggestions from social scientists on how best to control the problem. Between 1940 and 1968, the number of adolescents convicted of serious crimes doubled (Stratton & Terry, 1968). The Federal Bureau of Investigation *Uniform Crime Reports* for 1973 indicated that 34% of all crimes were committed by individuals under 18 years of age. The failure of traditional counseling and institutional programs has provided some of the impetus for developing new interventions based on behavioral principles. It is worth noting, at the outset, that "delinquency" is strictly a legal term, not a psychological one. It refers to youths who have committed a legal offense and have come into contact with the court system.

INSTITUTIONAL MODELS

Traditionally, the institution was the only program alternative available for delinquents who did not respond to parole and counseling services. It was in such institutions that important early behavioral work was conducted. Two programs are particularly noteworthy as institutional models of treatment: the CASE II project (Contingencies Applied to Special Education—Phase II) executed at the National Training School (NTS) in Washington, D. C. (Cohen & Filipczak, 1971), and the Youth Center Research Project implemented at two sites within the California Youth Authority (Jesness, DeRisi, McCormick, & Qedge, 1972). The youths in these programs had been convicted of a variety of crimes including assault, breaking and entering, and robbery.

The main objective of the CASE II project was to strengthen academic behaviors so that students could reenter the public school system. It was hoped that by getting the students back into the mainstream of society and teaching them the academic skills necessary for success, future acts of delinquency could be prevented. The basis of the program was a token economy in which youths earned points for reaching criteria in a number of individualized education programs and for displaying exemplary social behavior. Points could subsequently be exchanged for recreational activities and other special privileges. The average duration of treatment was 8 months. In terms of academic gains, the program was successful in that each youth improved an average of one or two grade levels during treatment. Most importantly, the rate of recidivism (i.e., the percentage of individuals who were imprisoned again) for the first year following discharge from the program was 27% for the CASE II youths, compared to an overall rate of 76% for released youths from the general NTS sample (i.e., youths who did not participate in the CASE II program). By the third year, however, the recidivism rate for CASE II youths was near the norm for other NTS students. Thus, the main effect of CASE II was to delay the delinquent's return to the institution. Apparently, the behavioral intervention conducted in the institution was by itself not sufficient to produce long-term maintenance of gains in the community setting.

The Youth Center Research Project is noteworthy in that it was one of very few studies attempting to compare a behavior-modification program with a nonbehavioral program—in this case, one based on a transactional-analysis model. The transactional model stressed counseling sessions in order to produce improvements in self-concept. It also provided for contracts between the youth and the counselor that set personal academic and social goals, although there were no explicit reinforcement contingencies associated with adherence to the contract. In contrast, the behavioral program made use of contracts with explicit contingencies. Further, a token economy was employed to develop social and academic skills. Surprisingly, both programs reduced behavior problems equally well during treatment; that is, the number of youths sent to detention dropped more than 60% in both programs. Most importantly, each program reported an almost identical recidivism rate of about 31%, 1 year after treatment, compared to an average rate of 46% for untreated youths from similar institutions in the California Youth Authority. Since the follow-up period was only 1 year, however, it is not known whether these gains would have persisted for longer periods of time. Nonetheless, the study remains of some interest because of the unexpectedly strong performance of the transactional group. Since the transactional model emphasizes, among other things, a positive interpersonal relationship between client and therapist, the study implies that behaviorists might do well to attend more to relationship variables. This point is considered again below.

COMMUNITY-BASED PROGRAMS

Traditionally, institutional programs, even those with a behavioral orientation, have not systematically assessed whether the behaviors targeted for treatment do indeed have survival value in the communities to which the youths are returning. Perhaps the lack of functional skills training in many of these programs is one reason why long-term maintenance has seldom been produced. The treatment of youths in facilities that are located far from the communities to which the youths must return is not conducive to developing programs that are sensitive to helping a youth adjust to his or her particular community. There are many home and school problems that can only be dealt with if the treatment intervention takes place in an integrated fashion within the community setting itself. In support of this notion, the current Zeitgeist in delinquency treatment involves a shift away from providing services in the institution toward providing services in the community where the individual lives.

One of the best examples of a community-based residential program is Achievement Place. This is a model in which delinquent youths who would normally be sent to institutions are instead retained in their local communities to live in a homelike setting with specially trained surrogate parents, referred to as "teaching parents" (Phillips, Phillips, Fixsen, & Wolf, 1974). The surrogate parent functions to teach each youth a variety of social, academic, and vocational skills thought to be essential for successful reintegration into the community. This model offers several advantages over traditional institutional treatment. The most important advantage is that since the youth continues to live in the community during treatment, liaisons can be formed between the teaching parents and a youth's actual teachers and parents, enabling close monitoring of youths during weekend visits with their parents as well as daily monitoring of progress at school. Thus, problems can be dealt with as soon as they arise. Further, parent and teacher training provided by the surrogate parents can help to ensure a smoother transition back into the community once the youth is ready to leave Achievement Place.

The Achievement Place model (or, as it is sometimes called, the Teaching Family program) has several different phases, depending on the progress that a youth is making. At the start, the youth is placed on a token economy in which points are earned and lost for appropriate and inappropriate behaviors respectively, and subsequently are traded in for a variety of privileges. Over time, as the youth improves, he or she is put on a merit system in which points are no longer required for privileges; that is, as long as the youth is behaving appropriately, all privileges are free. Finally, youths are advanced to the Homeward Bound phase, in which they spend more and more time at home with their parents. At the same time, the teaching parents instruct the youths and their families as to how to negotiate behavioral contracts—that is, how to specify which behaviors parents desire from the youths and what privileges the youths can earn for fulfilling parental expectations. In short, while at Achievement Place, youths gradually move from an artificial motivational system (i.e., points) to a naturalistic system (i.e., negotiation and contracting).

Many of the components making up the program, such as the motivational system and the interface with the school system, have been evaluated and found to be effective in modifying youths' behavior (e.g., Bailey, Wolf, & Phillips, 1970; Phillips, Phillips, Fixsen, & Wolf, 1971). For present purposes, however, the critical question concerns the long-term outcome of such procedures. There have been several such evaluations conducted. An early evaluation by Trotter (1973) compared 16 boys from Achievement Place with 15 boys from a state institution. The Achievement Place group had a much lower recidivism rate 2 years following treatment (19%) than did the institutional group (53%). This finding was replicated in a later study (Kirigin, Braukmann, Fixsen, Phillips, & Wolf, 1975) that also demonstrated a lower recidivism rate 2 years following treatment for the Achievement Place group (22%) as compared to an institutional group (47%). An independent, large-scale evaluation was recently reported by R. R. Jones (1979), who compared

27 programs using the Achievement Place model with 25 other home-based programs not using the model. The results of this investigation complicate any interpretation of the efficacy of Achievement Place as far as outcome is concerned. If offense rates from preprogram to postprogram (i.e., 2 years following entry into a program) are compared, the postprogram reductions are approximately 65%. However, there was *no difference* between Teaching Family and other programs in the degree of reduction in offense rates from pretreatment to posttreatment. The Teaching Family model was superior in some respects, however. For example, school performance for Teaching Family youths was superior to that of youths in other programs. Also, the cost of Teaching Family programs was less than that for the other programs. Finally, the Teaching Family programs received significantly more favorable community reaction. In spite of these advantages in favor of the Teaching Family model, one central question remains—namely, what could account for the similarities between the two types of programs in terms of offense rate outcomes? Jones has provided a partial answer. Apparently, there is considerable variability among programs that use the Teaching Family model. Some programs spend substantially more time than others on therapy as opposed to nontherapy activities (e.g., on counseling and tutoring as opposed to cooking meals and washing clothes). A critical finding is that the amount of therapy effort in the Teaching Family models during treatment correlates .45 with differences in posttreatment outcome with respect to offense rates. In short, the heterogeneity that exists across various Teaching Family programs may be an important variable helping to explain why there is no difference between the Teaching Family model and the other models. Specifically, by pooling together the data from all Teaching Family programs, both intensive and less intensive, investigators may actually be underestimating the potential impact on outcome of a highly structured, therapeutically intensive model.

A number of other problems have beset the Achievement Place model, not the least of which concerns the issue of maintenance. Many youths began to experience problems again once they returned to their communities to live permanently with their parents. Problems with community agencies (including but not limited to the police and the courts) gave rise to the notion of an "aftercare advocate"—that is, a person who could help carry on the efforts of the teaching parents during the first 1 or 2 years following release from the program (Willner, Braukmann, Kirigin, & Wolf, 1978). Interestingly, this "youth advocacy" model has been systematically tested at the University of Illinois (Seidman, Rappaport, & Davidson, 1976). Youths who had been charged with a criminal offense were immediately referred to the advocacy program. Here, they were assigned a college student who functioned as an advocate. The student worked with each youth to teach that individual community survival skills, especially ways in which to attain personal goals by making use of negotiation and contracting with parents, teachers, and other authority figures. Thus, the thrust of the program was to help youths to resolve the kinds of conflicts and problems encountered daily in the community. The program produced a substantial decrease in the number of delinquency-related problems during the course of treatment. Most impressive, however, were the outcome data. Compared to control youths who were not in the program, youths dealt with through the advocacy model had substantially lower recidivism rates. More specifically, youths in the program had fewer contacts with the police during the second year of follow-up (fewer than .5 contacts on the average, compared to more than 1 contact for controls), and the offenses that they engaged in were much less serious than those for the control youths. Apparently, an advocacy model can be an important asset in enhancing maintenance in community-based behavioral treatments for delinquency.

FAMILY INTERVENTIONS

Because community interventions, such as Achievement Place and the "youth advocacy" model just described, emphasize family involvement in the treatment process, there has been a growing interest among behavioral practitioners in the question of whether some types of family intervention are more effective than others. In an important study, J. F. Alexander and Parsons (1973) provided data on the relative efficacy of several types of family therapy. One intervention was behaviorally based and involved an extension of the systems approach developed by Patterson and his colleagues (Patterson & Reid, 1970). The focus of this intervention was on changing the *process* of family interaction, rather than on intervening only on problem behaviors per se. Previous data showed that deviant families, as compared to normal families, are more silent, talk less equally, and exhibit fewer positive interactions. The behavioral intervention aimed at changing family processes so that the patterns of interaction shown by the delinquent families would more closely resemble those displayed by normal families. To accomplish this goal, therapists trained the families to communicate both feelings and information in a clear manner, to establish a system of rules and privileges by means of contingency contracting, and to negotiate solutions to problems of mutual concern. Several comparison groups were also examined. One of these was a client-centered group in which the focus was on exploring attitudes and feelings concerning family relationships and adolescent problems. A second comparison group, psychodynamic in orientation, placed emphasis on insight as a means for producing therapeutic change. Finally, there was no-treatment control group that was assessed but not placed into any of the above programs. The youths in all of these groups had been at Juvenile Court for a variety of offenses, including truancy, shoplifting, and drug possession. The dependent variables included rate of recidivism and the measures of family processes described above. The outcome data were collected 6 to 18 months following termination from treatment. The no-treatment controls had a recidivism rate of 50%. The client-centered group was comparable to the no-treatment group, with a recidivism rate of 47%, while the psychodynamic group, paradoxically, did worse than the no-treatment group and had a rate of recidivism of 73%. The behavioral-intervention group fared substantially better than all the others did, with a recidivism rate of only 26%. Interestingly, recidivism rates were inversely correlated with improvements in family process measures. Apparently, a behavioral intervention that focuses on changing patterns of family interaction can be effective in facilitating stable reductions in delinquent behavior.

Some families benefited more than others did from behavioral intervention. This finding led J. F. Alexander, Barton, Schiavo, and Parsons (1976) to ask what aspects of intervention might be most highly correlated with good outcome. At the outset, these investigators noted that while a therapist can present the principles of behavior modification to parents of delinquent youths, there is no guarantee that the parents will use or be influenced by the suggestions of the therapist. Thus, the issue of client motivation arises. Typically, in traditional counseling work, much effort is spent in establishing rapport with the client as a prelude to motivating the client to accept and implement treatment suggestions. Behaviorists have paid little systematic attention to this variable. J. F. Alexander *et al.* (1976) sought to determine whether such relationship variables might be important predictors of outcome. They used the model of behavioral intervention developed in their earlier work as described above, but, focused in addition, on correlating therapist characteristics with outcome. The important finding was that a variety of characteristics such as warmth and humor were positively correlated with favorable outcome. Those therapists who received high ratings on these qualities were most effective in altering patterns of family interaction. Further, their clients had lower recidivism rates 12–15 months following treatment termination than did clients of therapists who were rated low on relationship variables. Nonrelationship skills—that is, those having to do with implementing behavior-modification procedures—accounted for only 15% of the outcome variance. It is important to note that all of these data pertain to the effects of *behavioral* treatment. Relationship variables alone are not sufficient for producing positive outcomes. This was demonstrated in the earlier study by J. F. Alexander and Parsons (1973), which, as noted, showed that client-centered therapy (based primarily on relationship factors) did not reduce recidivism below the rate reported for no-treatment controls. It appears, then, that it is the *combination* of positive relationship factors and structured behavioral intervention that is most likely to produce a good outcome.

Not all families profit from the behavioral interventions described above. There are suggestions in the literature that outcome is adversely affected by several variables pertaining to family structure. First, youths who lack strong social support systems (e.g., who have minimal levels of home involvement) often do poorly even when participating in an otherwise successful program such as the "youth advocacy" project described earlier (Seidman, Rappaport, & Davidson, 1977). Second, mothers who are socially insulated from friendly community contacts are less able than noninsular mothers are to maintain treatment programs for delinquent sons (Wahler, 1980). Not surprisingly, this failure to maintain the programs results in higher incidences of behavior problems. Third, treatment is difficult with families characterized by a high degree of disorganization (Reid & Hendriks, 1973). These three variables—lack of social support systems, mother insularity, and family disorganization— may all contribute to poor outcome *despite* the use of behavioral intervention. Therefore, if such interventions are to have maximum impact, it becomes critical to assess the effect of such variables systematically and to investigate ways of reversing the negative consequences of each. Perhaps the heterogeneity of outcomes typically reported in behavioral delinquency research is the result of a failure to address adequately the problems produced by these family variables.

IMPORTANCE OF "TYPES" OF DELINQUENCY

Just as variables pertaining to family structure have not been adequately addressed by behavior therapists, so too, not enough attention has been paid to the question of whether all *types* of delinquent acts can be remediated with a single behavioral strategy. This latter issue is particularly important in light of data reported by Reid and Hendriks (1973). These investigators found that a social learning intervention for boys who were aggressive but did not steal was twice as effective as that for boys who engaged in stealing as well as aggression. Following treatment, only 6 of the 14 stealers had a successful outcome, compared to 9 of 11 nonstealers. A 2–9 year follow-up showed that 77% of the stealers subsequently had court contacts, compared to only 13% of those who had been treated initially for aggression only (Moore, Chamberlain, & Mukai, 1979). It thus appears that treatment outcome may be highly dependent on the kind of problem initially presented. Therefore, the common practice of reporting outcome data for "delinquents," irrespective of the kinds of behavior problems represented, probably obscures some important differences that are a function of the type of behavior problem being treated. Future research should therefore distinguish delinquents both at intake and follow-up according to the type of behavior problem.

ROLE OF COGNITIVE VARIABLES

Finally, the role that cognitive factors play in treatment outcome may be considered. For a better understanding of the reasons for focusing on this particular issue, it is important to note that delinquents often have a long history of failure. They fail at school. They fail with their families. They fail in the larger world of their community in endeavors such as gaining meaningful employment and social respectability. With this background, it is not hard to see why such individuals might seek out unorthodox, perhaps illegal, ways of adapting to society. It is also not hard to see why such individuals might come to believe that they are incompetent and are unable to control events to their own advantage. In this context, it may be that one important element in producing long-term therapeutic change would be to alter the way that such individuals *think* about the world, rather than attempting merely to reduce socially offensive behaviors. A great many of the interventions that we have discussed may be effective precisely because they induce youths to perceive themselves as capable of producing beneficial changes in others by performing a variety of prosocial acts. Such a notion is akin to the proposition put forth by Bandura (1977) that psychological interventions are successful only insofar as they change an individual's perception of self-efficacy. Efficacy expectations are most powerfully influenced by an individual's performance accomplishments—that is, by the success or failure of given patterns of behavior. In this light, many of the behavioral interventions for delinquency may be interpreted in terms of their ability to influence a youth to believe that he or she is effective in producing changes in the behavior of others through prosocial means. This contrasts sharply with the traditional philosophy of intervention, in which an external agent intervenes and the youth is the passive recipient of treatment benefits. Even in a program that purportedly stresses external control, such as Achievement Place, there is a tremendous emphasis on strategies such as self-government. Youths are taught how to participate in setting rules, presenting arguments to adults, and being responsible for the behavior of their peers. Similarly, in "youth advocacy" approaches (e.g., Seidman *et al.,* 1976) there is great stress on training youths how to deal effectively with adults by using procedures such as contracting (cf. Stuart, 1971), and negotiation skills (cf. Kifer, Lewis, Green, & Phillips, 1974). These procedures presumably help enhance youths' perceptions that they *can* affect important aspects of their social environment. Recently, there has been a growing interest in explicitly teaching youths those behaviors that are likely to recruit positive reinforcers from others (e.g., Seymour & Stokes, 1976). In fact, in one large-scale study of institutionalized youths (R. R. Ross & McKay, 1979), the youths were allowed, within broadly defined limits, to run their own peer behavior-modification program. These youths had actually become worse when a behavioral program had earlier been externally imposed (i.e., run exclusively by the staff). In contrast, under the new regimen, offenses involving assault, property damage, and abscondance decreased to negligible levels. Unfortunately, much of this research was uncontrolled. However, it remains of considerable interest, given the notion that long-term maintenance of behavior gains (i.e., positive outcome) may be enhanced when individuals see *themselves* as the agent of behavior change (cf. Bandura, 1977). Such self-attribution and the accompanying change in expectations of self-efficacy may be an important element in producing positive outcome in delinquency intervention. To date, it has only been hinted at in the literature. Perhaps the time has come to address the problem explicitly by systematically programming procedures to enhance youths' perceptions that *they* are responsible for positive behavior change, and that, by behaving prosocially, *they* can influence the behavior of others in desirable directions (Carr, 1980a).

SUMMARY

In sum, behavioral interventions for delinquents in institutions, while often producing positive short-term effects on offense rates, are not well maintained over time. In contrast, community-based models emphasizing social survival skills are considerably more effective in producing long-term maintenance, particularly when posttreatment efforts are built into the program on an "as needed" basis. Finally, the behavioral treatment of delinquency no longer concentrates solely on modifying specific problem behaviors. Instead, the current trend is toward facilitating positive outcomes by paying greater attention to altering patterns of family interaction; providing systematic aftercare; building upon client–therapist relationship factors during the course of intervention; taking cognizance of differences in family structures and subtypes of delinquency; and, finally, attempting to strengthen youths' perception of behavior change as one depending upon self-control rather than upon external control.

ENURESIS

CLASSICAL-CONDITIONING MODEL

The treatment of nocturnal enuresis has been dramatically successful. Mowrer and Mowrer (1938) developed the first practical conditioning device, a urine-sensitive pad that is connected to an alarm which sounds when the child urinates. Mowrer and Mowrer found that all 30 enuretic children treated with the bell-and-pad device became continent within 2 months after beginning treatment. Many investigators have replicated the Mowrer work, and initial cure rates vary from 53% to 100% 6 months following treatment. Although relapse rates are often as high as 35%, with booster treatments the overall cure rate can be as high as 100% 6 months after treatment (Yates, 1970).

Various theories have been used to explain why the bell-and-pad procedure and the associated accoutrements (e.g., daily progress charts, changing sheets) are so often effective and why the treatment gains are so well maintained. Mowrer and Mowrer (1938) based their intervention on a Pavlovian-conditioning model, which they conceptualized as follows:

If the child is repeatedly awakened at a time when the bladder is partially filled, but not so distended as to produce reflex emptying, the attendant bladder stimulation will eventually become specifically associated with the response of *awakening* [italics ours], before the point has been reached at which voiding tends to occur automatically. . . . If some arrangement could be provided so that the sleeping child would be awakened *just after the onset of urination,* and only at this time, the resulting association of bladder distension and the response of awakening and inhibiting further urination should provide precisely the form of training which would seem to be most specifically appropriate. (p. 445)

It has become evident, however, that the classical-conditioning model is much too simple to account for the enuresis cures. The model was not able to account for the cures associated with sleeping through the night without awakening to go to the bathroom. Further, it is unclear how the conditioning would move backward so that the child would awaken before urinating.

OPERANT-CONDITIONING MODEL

Azrin, Sneed, and Foxx (1973) applied a model of enuresis training with profoundly retarded adults (mean IQ = 12) that incorporated specific operant components. The bell-and-pad device was supplemented with specific operant interventions, such as positive reinforcement for having a dry bed, positive reinforcement for nighttime urination in the toilet, practice and reinforcement for arising to urinate, and punishment for accidents (i.e., being reprimaded and having to clean and remake the bed). Fully 95% of the retarded adults learned to toilet themselves at night in an average time period of 3 days.

The methods used with retarded adults were then modified for use with normal children in a program called Dry-Bed Training (Azrin, Sneed, & Foxx, 1974). The intervention was especially novel in that it involved a full night of *intensive* training, followed by use of the bell and pad for 1 week. Major aspects of the training included giving rationales to the children and parents for each part of the intervention; having the children drink large amounts of fluid to increase the desire to urinate; use of minimal cues from trainers to arouse the children hourly to go to the toilet; use of the bell and pad, with the bell ringing in both the children's and parents' rooms; reprimands for wetting the bed; having the children change the sheets after each wetting incident; and 20 practice trials in which the children had to lie in bed and then get up to make trips to the bathroom to attempt to urinate.

After *one* all-night training session, the 24 treated children had an average of only two bedwetting accidents before achieving 2 weeks of consecutive dry nights. An initial relapse occurred in 29% of the children, but following the booster sessions with the bell and pad, no further relapses occurred during the remainder of the 6-month follow-up period. In brief, the all-night training program produced rapid treatment effects that maintained well across 6 months, and the treatment was more efficient than was the standard bell-and-pad treatment.

In Australia, Bollard and Woodworth (1977) utilized the Dry-Bed procedure just described with an important variation—namely, the parents rather than a professional trainer administered the intensive all-night training program. All 14 children treated by their parents stopped bedwetting, but the median time to the last night of wetting was 12 days. There were two children who had initial relapses, but after booster sessions with the bell and pad, no further wetting occurred.

The role of the bell-and-pad device has been assessed in the use of the Dry Bed procedure by several investigators at two different sites. Bollard and Woodworth (1977), who had parents administer the Dry-Bed procedure, found that the bell-and-pad alarm device was very beneficial in achieving continence. On the other hand, Azrin and his colleagues (Azrin & Thienes, 1978; Azrin, Thienes-Hontos, & Besabel-Azrin, 1979) have not found it necessary to use the bell and pad with intensive Dry-Bed training in the late afternoon and evening by professionals. Further, they did not find it necessary to use the bell-and-pad device following a 1.5-hour office visit to teach the parents to conduct the toilet training. In brief, the bell-and-pad device may be a useful adjunct to the Dry-Bed procedure, but it does not always appear to be a necessity.

BLADDER SIZE AND TREATMENT EFFECTIVENESS

Several studies have demonstrated that enuretics have a smaller functional bladder capacity than nonenuretics do, and this fact has been confirmed by cystometric studies (i.e., studies involving internal measurement of bladder size). It is also known that enuretics void more often during the day than do children who are not enuretic (Starfield, 1972).

Allen and Hasazi (1978) assessed children who were successfully treated with the bell and pad in order to ascertain whether pretreatment bladder capacity was a predictor of amont of change in bladder capacity at the end of treatment. They found that children with a bladder capacity of less than 200 cc increased their capacity by an average of 47%, whereas those with bladder capacities of greater than 200 cc increased their bladder capacities by only 10% on the average. In a related vein, however, they found that all children with bladder capacities of less than 200 cc arose "every night or nearly every night" in order to remain continent. Children with bladder capacities greater than 200 cc sometimes awakened to urinate and sometimes learned to sleep through the night without urinating. The correlation between bladder capacity and awakening for all children was − .69. In brief, bladder capacity is an excellent predictor of whether the child will need to awaken to urinate during the night in order to remain dry.

Explanations of treatment success have not generally included analyses of whether a child learns to awaken and urinate or to sleep through the night without urinating. Such a dichotomy seems very useful; given the data just presented, it appears critical. If a child has a small bladder capacity even after repeated attempts at bell-and-pad treatment, training to increase bladder capacity or to help the child awaken with increasingly minimal cues might be critical. While a number of reviews of sleep patterns of enuretics have indicated little evidence for deeper sleeping of enuretics than of nonenuretics (e.g., Johnson, 1980), it seems very likely that ease of arousing a child with a small bladder capacity would be predictive of treatment success.

SUMMARY

The behavioral treatment of enuresis is an outstanding success story. Cure rates average approximately 80% with the standard bell-and-pad conditioning device. More recently, intensive training sessions conducted by parents and including a variey of treatment procedures have been effective with almost all children.

The existing evidence leads us to conclude that no simple extant model of enuresis treatment is adequate to account for the facts. Instead, an explanation of successful enuresis treatment appears to require a broad-based social learning model that also takes into account biological constraints on behavior, such as arousability, bladder capacity, and detrusor muscle control. Further, studies of maintenance should be conducted in which family stress and reinforcement of continence are used as predictors of success in treatment. In this vein, it is interesting to note that family deviance, separation of mother and child, and punitive parental practices are all correlated with enuresis.

BEHAVIORAL PEDIATRICS

Physicians have long recognized that organic conditions can be influenced by an individual's behavior patterns and by certain social–environmental factors. With the growth of behavior therapy, techniques have been developed that can alter such behavioral and environmental variables in ways that ameliorate physical conditions. Two points need to be made at the outset, however. First, no claim can be made that behavior therapy per se can cure an organically based condition, except in some rare cases. Rather, it is the *combination* of behavioral and medical knowledge that will most likely prove fruitful. Secondly, the behavioral-medicine approach to children's physical problems is a relatively new enterprise. Therefore, it would be misleading to characterize this area of inquiry as a breakthrough. It is, however, clearly a promising area. The problems that have been most researched are those of asthma and obesity, and we therefore highlight these two conditions in what follows.

ASTHMA

This condition is one of the most common psychophysiological disorders of childhood. It consists of temporary but extensive narrowing of the airways, with the result that breathing, particularly expiration, becomes very difficult—hence, the characteristic "wheezing" sounds of this condition. Asthma, like many medical conditions, is multiply determined. It is influenced by respiratory infections, allergies to specific airborne substances, and psychological factors. In approximately 37% of the cases, psychological factors, including anxiety, anger, depression, and pleasurable excitement, are suggested as dominant determinants of asthmatic attacks (Rees, 1964). Such findings have led some investigators to consider using psychologically based treatments to ameliorate asthma.

In an early study, Purcell, Brady, Chai, Muser, Molk, Gordon, and Means (1969) sought to identify those asthmatic children who might improve following interventions that had a psychological basis. They did this by asking parents to rate the degree to which their children's asthma was elicited by intense emotional states. Based on prior data, Purcell *et al.* predicted that children for whom emotional factors were rated as frequent precipitants for attacks would show improvement following separation from their families. This group was labeled as "predictive positives." The other group, for whom emotions were not rated as important precipitants, were labeled "predicted negatives." Several measures were taken, including peak expiratory flow rate (a measure of how rapidly a child can expel air), degree of wheezing, quantity and potency of medication required, and daily frequency of asthmatic attacks. These measures were taken at several points during the study. One measure was taken just before the parents were separated from their children (i.e., during the baseline period); another while the separation was in effect; and another following the children's reunion with their families. For the predicted positive group, there was an improvement from baseline to separation, and a deterioration from separation to reunion. For the predicted negative group, there were no systematic changes. In interpreting these data, two points are especially worth noting. First, the improvement in respiratory functioning (peak expiratory flow rate) was only 11%, a change that is statistically significant but not clinically significant, particularly in the case of a client who is suffering an attack. Secondly, the outcome data are not favorable, since respiratory functioning rapidly deteriorated during the reunion period. Despite these criticisms, this study is of theoretical interest because of the gains observed during the separation period—gains that were a result of temporarily changing the home environment. Purcell *et al.* have suggested that the data support the notion that there are subgroups of asthmatics, some of whom are influenced strongly by psychological factors. Two explanations have been offered for the findings. One explanation is that asthma has an *operant* component. That is, the family typically reinforces asthmatic attacks through solicitous attention. During the separation period, of course, the family is not around to give such reinforcement, and that is why the asthma may improve. A second explanation is that asthma has a *respondent* component. That is, the family typically presents certain psychological stressors that elicit attacks. Again, during separation, the asthma improves, only this time perhaps because the family is not around to present stressors.

There have been several studies following up on the notion that asthma may have respondent components. One study (A. B. Alexander, Miklich, & Hershkoff, 1972) tested the effects of relaxation training on respiratory functioning in asthmatic children. If emotional stressors are important as elicitors of asthmatic attacks, then some form of relaxation training might be expected to improve respiration. Accordingly, Alexander *et al.* trained one group of asthmatic children in progressive relaxation techniques, while another (i.e., a control) group was simply instructed to sit quietly. All children in this study had chronic respiratory problems, even in the absence of asthmatic attacks per se. The results were that the peak expiratory flow rate improved by 11% for the relaxation group, but remained essentially unchanged for the control group. However, it is important to emphasize again that an 11% improvement, while statistically significant, is not clinically significant. Further, there was no test to see whether this improvement generalized outside the laboratory situation or maintained over time. More alarming still is the lack of replicability of these initial findings. Specifically, A. B. Alexander, Cropp, and Chai (1979) ran an extended version of the above study, in which multiple measures of respiratory functioning were taken to assess the effects of relaxation training. While such training seemed to prevent the subjects from getting worse, there was no systematic evidence that it made them better. Bronchodilating drugs, on the other hand, produced an immediate, clinically significant improvement. Thus, outcome studies that have emphasized the conceptualization and treatment of asthma in terms of respondent characteristics have been notably unsuccessful. These findings are perhaps more understandable when it is considered that laboratory studies designed to test the classical-conditioning interpretation of asthmatic responding have also failed to find evidence to support such an interpretation (Dekker, Pelse, & Groen, 1957). Perhaps, for many clients, anxiety and other states of emotional distress are the result rather than the cause of chronic asthma.

The second set of behavioral interventions for asthma conceptualizes some of the respiratory distress as reflecting the operant or instrumental nature of the problem. There is evidence that many forms of childhood psychopathology function as escape or avoidance responses (e.g., Carr, Newsom, & Binkoff, 1980). It appears that asthma may also function in this manner. Some asthmatic children learn that by exaggerating symptoms, they may be able to escape an aversive school stituation (Creer, Weinberg, & Molk, 1974) and be placed in a hospital environment rich in social and entertainment possibilities (Creer, 1970; Creer et al., 1974). In these cases, the problem has been treated by making the hospital environment less reinforcing (e.g., not allowing the child to socialize with other children while in the hospital), a variant of time out. In addition, the child may be given remedial school work so that he or she can catch up in academics, thereby making the school experience a successful and presumably a less aversive one. Under this regimen, a decrease in the number and rate of hospitalizations is obtained (Creer et al., 1974). Anecdotal reports suggest that these gains last up to a year. Other data are also relevant to the notion that some aspects of respiratory distress may be operant in nature. Specifically, Neisworth and Moore (1972) presented results suggesting that, in some instances, asthmatic responding may be an attention-getting behavior. They taught the parents of an asthmatic child to ignore the nighttime coughing and wheezing (once it had been determined that there was no danger in doing so) and to provide tangible reinforcers contingent on a gradually lowered frequency of coughing. The results showed a dramatic decrease in the duration of bedtime asthmatic responding. This decrease was maintained during an 11-month follow-up. Although the above studies suggest that asthma may have operant (i.e., attention-getting, or escape) components, there are several important qualifications that need to be made. First, in none of the studies were direct measures of respiratory functioning taken. Thus, it is possible that even those children who profit from the above interventions in showing a decrease in the rate of hospitalization may nonetheless continue to show the same degree of respiratory impairment as existed before the intervention. It seems that the above studies can best be understood as reflecting the remediation of corollary behaviors that are secondary to chronic asthmatic distress. A further qualification is that these studies involved only one or two subjects. This fact underlies the necessity for running broader-scale studies to determine the extent to which operant factors enter into the control of asthmatic episodes. Finally, it is important to note that none of the above studies demonstrates that asthma is an operant resulting from differential reinforcement of symptomatology by parents. Rather, taken as a whole, the data suggest that the most likely explanation can be found in a diathesis–stress model. In this model, the diathesis consists of a genetically determined impairment of the respiratory tract—a plausible point, given the observation that 86% of asthmatics have been reported to have had respiratory infections before their asthma developed (Rees, 1964). In addition, children with chronic asthma may over time evoke a great deal of parental attention (the stress component of the model) contingent upon displaying asthmatic symptoms. At that point, the operant component of the condition may be said to have developed. On the basis of the model just outlined, it is clear that behavioral intervention may ameliorate asthmatic responding, but it will not cure it. The best approach would appear to be a combination of medical and psychological intervention—drugs to alleviate the respiratory impairment, and behavioral treatment to decrease adult reinforcement of symptom exaggeration and to increase reinforcement of "well" behaviors.

OBESITY

Estimates of childhood obesity range from 5% to 26% of the juveniles in the United States (Stimbert & Coffey, 1972). Approximately 80% of obese children become obese adults (Abraham, Collins, & Nordsieck, 1971). The widespread prevalence of this problem is all the more serious when one considers that adults who suffer from juvenile-onset obesity have a problem that is "more severe, more resistant to treatment, and more likely to be associated with emotional disturbances" than that of individuals who suffer from adult-onset obesity (Stunkard & Mahoney, 1976, p. 51). Thus, outcome studies of childhood obesity have a special significance from the standpoint of prevention of more serious problems in adulthood.

Because mothers are in a strong position to control the amount and type of food their children receive, most programs have involved parents as the primary treatment agents. The program outlined by Stuart and Davis (1972) forms the core of most behavioral interventions for childhood obesity. This program emphasizes the learning of better eating habits and does not focus on weight loss per se. Thus, children may be taught stimulus control such as limiting their eating to one setting or not watching TV while eating. The goal of this strategy is to limit the number of cues that set off eating. Further, children may be taught how to eat more slowly and how to establish contracts with their parents in which reinforcers are earned for adhering to the weight loss program.

In a prototypical study, Kingsley and Shapiro (1977) compared the efficacy of standard behavioral treatment (as described above) with that of a no-treatment control. The children involved were 10 to 11 years old. Following an 8-week program, treated children lost an average of 3.5 pounds, as opposed to a gain of 2 pounds for children in the control group. However, at a 20-week follow-up, treated children had gained back the weight they had lost. Similar results were obtained in a study by Aragona, Cassady, and Drabman (1975). These investigators worked with 5- to 10-year-old obese girls. A standard behavioral treatment package implemented over a 12-week period resulted in weight loss. In contrast, girls in a no-treatment control group gained weight during the same time period. However, as was the case with the Kingsley and Shapiro study, follow-up data collected 31 weeks after treatment termination showed that the girls in the treatment groups had gained back the weight they had lost. Aragona *et al.* have suggested the use of periodic booster sessions (in which treatment is briefly reinstated) as a way to produce maintenance. Nonetheless, the above two studies demonstrate that the transiency of treatment effects so often reported in the literature on adult obesity also characterizes the outcome for interventions with childhood obesity.

Not all efforts to control childhood obesity have produced transient treatment effects. In an important study reported by Weiss (1977), several different treatment approaches were compared. Some children were put on simple diets; others were treated by means of stimulus-control procedures; and still others received a combination of the two. In addition, there was a no-treatment control group. Subjects were 9.5 to 13 years old. By the end of the 12-week treatment program, all groups were superior to the no-treatment controls, with the two groups receiving the stimulus-control intervention being the most effective. Importantly, from the standpoint of outcome, the stimulus-control groups *continued* to show weight loss at the end of a 1-year follow-up. In evaluating the significance of this outcome (or, for that matter, any outcome study in the area of childhood obesity), it is important to realize that children, unlike adults, are expected to *gain* weight over time as part of the normal process of physical growth. Since a child's height will typically change during the course of a lengthy follow-up, the appropriate index of weight loss is not how many pounds a child loses, but rather the degree to which he or she is overweight for the height (and sex) norms at a given age. By this standard, obese children who maintain a constant weight but grow taller will show a decrease in the degree to which they are overweight. Given these considerations, Weiss reported data in terms of the percentage of overweight (as well as pounds lost). At the 1-year follow-up, children in the stimulus control groups showed a net drop of 9% to 10.5% in the amount that they were overweight. What could account for the favorable results of this study? One possibility is that, whereas the other studies described above placed emphasis on external control (i.e., parents dispensed reinforcers contingent on weight-loss behaviors), Weiss emphasized self-control procedures. That is, Weiss taught the children to reinforce themselves for behaviors leading to weight loss; parents were asked not to interfere with the program. It may be that this procedure heightens a child's perception of control over the problem—a factor that several theoreticians suggest may be important for producing long-term maintenance (cf. Bandura, 1977).

In the above studies, some children profited from a given behavioral intervention much more than others did. It is possible that there are different subgroups of obese children and that outcome could be enhanced by attending to these differences. Wheeler and Hess (1976) systematically explored this possibility by designing individualized treatments for a group of children 2 to 11 years of age. They identified several different problematic patterns. For example, for some children, the main problem was that they ate too many sweets; for others, the problem was that they ate extra large portions at meals; and for still others, the problem centered on a lack of exercise. By designing interventions aimed at remediating problems on an individual basis, these investigators slowly altered a given child's eating and/or exercise pattern over a period of many months. Following 7 months of this individualized approach to treatment, children in the intervention group showed a decrease of 4.1% in the amount that they were overweight, compared to a gain in weight of 6.3% for untreated controls. Thus, individualized programming may be another factor that contributes to maintenance of weight loss.

With so much literature available on adult obesity and so little available on childhood obesity, it would be a mistake for child researchers to ignore the lessons learned from research with adults. For example, a recent study by Brownell, Heckerman, Westlake, Hayes, and Monti (1978) demonstrated that by training the spouses of obese adults to practice good eating habits and monitor their obese mates, substantial weight losses could be achieved and maintained, with even further losses, at the 6-month follow-up. The equivalent procedure with obese children would be to train peers or siblings to act as monitors, models, and sources of social support for the overweight children. Such an intervention has yet to be systematically tested. Secondly, certain biological facts relevant to weight loss should not be ignored (cf. Wooley, Wooley, & Dyrenforth, 1979). For example, caloric restriction generally causes a slowing of body metabolism, which decreases the rate of weight loss over time. Thus, children who show smaller and smaller weight losses over time may not be cheating on their diets, but may simply be the victims of a natural biological process. Some form of exercise may therefore need to be added as the rate of weight loss becomes asymptotic. Finally, Stuart and Guire (1978) point out several interesting correlates of successful maintenance of weight loss in the case of adults. These factors may be relevant for children and adolescents as well. One variable lies in the fact that adults who successfully lose weight generally institute a greater number of changes in life style to support their weight-control efforts than do adults who are unsuccessful at losing weight. Although this finding is only a correlation, it is possible that such a factor might act causally to help improve outcome in the case of childhood obesity as well.

In sum, the maintenance problems that have plagued research in adult obesity also plague research with overweight children. Making use of booster sessions, enhancing perception of self-control, and attending to individual differences in eating behavior may all act to produce better maintenance and are worthy of systematic research efforts. In addition, the literature on adult obesity suggests that social support systems, biological factors, and changes in life style may also affect outcome. Thus, these variables too might profitably be researched with child clients.

OTHER PEDIATRIC PROBLEMS

There are a number of other areas of behavioral pediatrics that are promising, although they are less well developed than the areas we have been discussing. For instance, chronic ruminative vomiting of nonorganic origin is a serious problem seen in some infants and young children. This behavior produces marked weight loss and occasionally death. Contingent use of aversives, such as shock or forced ingestion of lemon juice, has proven effective in eliminating or drastically reducing rumination and producing weight gain. These effects have been maintained during follow-up periods of 3 months to 1 year after treatment termination (Kohlenberg, 1970; Lang & Melamed, 1969; Luckey, Watson, & Musick, 1968).

Anorexia or food refusal is another problem that has been researched. This problem is most typically seen in adolescent girls. Initial research suggested that the problem could be controlled by making pleasurable activities such as TV and walking contingent on food intake (Leitenberg, Agras, & Thomson, 1968). Weight gains were maintained at 4- to 9-month follow-ups. More recent research has suggested that feedback concerning weight gain or loss and caloric intake is the effective component of behavioral intervention (Agras, Barlow, Chapin, Abel, & Leitenberg, 1974).

A final area is that of seizure control. Punishment of stereotyped pre-seizure behavior can eliminate or greatly reduce the rate of seizures in selected children. This effect may be maintained several months later at follow-up (Zlutnick, Mayville, & Moffat, 1975).

The above areas—ruminative vomiting, anorexia, and seizures—are promising avenues for future research. Two points must be borne in mind, however, when evaluating treatment outcomes in these areas. First, all the studies cited involved only a few subjects, and thus the generality of the interventions has not been established. Second, outcome may be influenced by the subgroup characteristics, each subgroup requiring a different treatment. Thus, some seizures appear to be respondent in nature and can be ameliorated using modified classical extinction procedures (Forster, 1966). Other seizures may respond best to punishment, as described above. Anorexia, too, may have multiple causes and therefore may require individualized treatments that take cognizance of subgroup characteristics (Bemis, 1978).

SUMMARY

In summarizing the area of behavioral pediatrics, it is worthwhile to emphasize that this is a relatively new field of inquiry. Yet, in spite of its youth, this research area has generated suggestive data demonstrating benefits to asthmatic and obese children as well as to ruminators, anorexics, and seizure-prone individuals. It appears that many of these conditions can be broken down into subgroups, each with a different etiology and each requiring a carefully individualized treatment. Behavioral interventions rarely, if ever, "cure" the conditions discussed above. Rather, they can be useful in helping to ameliorate a given medical problem. Full resolution of the problem, however, requires active collaboration with physicians. The medical model is in fact appropriate in this area of psychological inquiry. Some of the traditional antagonism between behavioral and medical models has yielded to collaborative efforts that produce benefits for the child client.

FUTURE DIRECTIONS

FAMILY INTERVENTION AND LONGER TREATMENT

There appears to be considerable agreement among behavioral researchers who conduct clinical outcome research that treatments for most chronic social problems of children are likely to take more time than many behavior therapists had envisioned. This conclusion seems especially clear in work with conduct problems, hyperactivity, autism, and delinquency. More specifically, Kent, O'Leary, Patterson, Reid, and Lovaas all appear to advocate treatments that may last a year or more. Further, the treatments are not solely directed at changing children's behavior. Instead, family correlates of the above problems of children are becoming increasingly recognized—for example, marital discord (Porter & O'Leary, 1980), family disorganization (Reid & Hendriks, 1973), mother insularity (Wahler, 1980), and mother's negative perception of self (Patterson, 1976).

The recognition of the need to address familial variables in treatment will likely serve to provide greater integration of behavioral conceptualizations with psychodynamic and family-systems conceptualizations. This rapprochment has already occurred in the treatment of marital problems (Paolino & McCrady, 1978). While there are clear differences in conceptualization and treatment of cases among behavioral, systems, and psychodynamic therapists, there are also important similarities. Differing conceptual approaches to the same problem may provide useful integrations and may prompt new conceptualizations. The phenomena described as "displacement," "resistance," and "transference" are problems worthy of attention from therapists of all theoretical backgrounds.

PROBLEM-SOLVING AND SELF-CONTROL STRATEGIES

Cognitive-behavior modification has enjoyed increased attention in the past decade, but cognitive or self-control interventions with children have not enjoyed much success when evaluated by clinical standards. In fact, recent reviews of cognitive programs with children have been generally quite ambivalent about the success of the cognitive interventions (Hobbs, Moquin, Tyroler, & Lahey, 1980; S. G. O'Leary & Dubey, 1979; Rosenbaum & Drabman, 1979). Several reasons for the tempered optimism are as follows: (1) the failure to find that self-control strategies (e.g., self-instruction, self-recording, self-evaluation, and self-reinforcement) have consistent effects that surpass externally controlled reinforcement (e.g., reinforcement by teacher, parent, or ward attendant); (2) the difficulty in getting children to use self-control strategies reliably and to monitor them experimentally; and (3) the absence of a significant body of research demonstrating unequivocally that maintenance effects are enhanced when self-control or problem-solving strategies are used.

Despite the above concerns, many behavior therapists advocate using self-control strategies whenever possible, and we concur with the recommendation. We believe the evidence indicates that self-control strategies with intermittent monitoring are often *as good as* externally controlled programs (e.g., Drabman, Spitalnik, & O'Leary, 1973). We also see a consistent theme in successful programs with adolescents and delinquents, in that the programs are designed to help the individuals believe that they can have influence over their environment (e.g., the self-government system of Achievement

Place, "youth advocacy" programs, and the teaching of problem-solving and negotiation skills with parent–adolescent dyads). In research with token-reinforcement programs with elementary-school children, there is clear evidence that the reversal effects so commonly seen in token-reinforcement programs of the late 1960s do not occur if self-control strategies are taught to the children and external token and backup reinforcers are gradually removed (Wilson & O'Leary, 1980).

It seems that children and adolescents who learn to perform desired behaviors and ultimately do so with self-control strategies will gradually develop an important sense of self-esteem. The documentation of such effects has not occurred and will not be easy, because such effects would probably require lengthy treatment programs and sensitive instruments to measure self-esteem. However, the Head Start–Follow Through evaluations showed that the greater the children's academic progress was, the greater their self-esteem was also. Furthermore, children in the Direct Instruction behavioral programs improved more in their basic academic skills and in their self-esteem than did those in nonbehavioral programs (Becker & Carnine, 1980). Of course, it is possible that the skill building per se in these economically disadvantaged children leads to the increased self-esteem, and indeed we believe that skill building may be the most important determinant of self-esteem. However, the emphasis in these programs is on learning on one's own and on positive reinforcement ("Let me shake a smart hand! You are a terrific speller!"). Programs that teach good skill building along with problem solving and self-mastery are most likely to have long-range benefits.

A caution about self-control and self-learning should be sounded. As Becker and Carnine (1980) emphasized, self-directed learning, at least with economically disadvantaged children, is *not* best. Direct instruction methods with fading or prompts, and the shifting of teachers from a source of information to a guide to the use of new information, appear to be key elements in producing this overwhelming success story of a behavioral program for economically disadvantaged children. Self-esteem, a sense of self-efficacy, and self-mastery are variables that appear to have a useful function in the production and maintenance of behavior (Bandura, 1977); therapeutic and instructional programs should be designed to facilitate a sense of self-efficacy and self-esteem.

PREVENTION AND COMMUNITY INTERVENTION

Behavioral approaches to community problems have received increased emphasis, as exemplified by the research on energy conservation, use of mass-transit systems, teaching of self-help skills to community residents, and arrangement of day-care facilities to provide effective supervision of children (see the review by Fawcett, Mathews, & Fletcher, 1980). Unfortunately, we could not find any research that has focused on prevention of problem behaviors in children. For example, it is not known whether after-school activities such as sports and music programs appeal sufficiently to children with social and family problems to encourage their participation and possibly to prevent truancy, vandalism, and loitering. We simply underscore the need for research on prevention of child clinical problems by noting the research that relates to prevention of child clinical probelms. As becomes evident, the research comes from diverse areas and is only indicative of the types of intervention that could be used in a preventative manner.

The Head Start–Follow Through programs started in the Kennedy–Johnson administrations; as mentioned in the introduction to this chapter, this research was one of the largest social experiments of the 1970s. Many programs were both educational and community endeavors, since the parents were very actively involved in the programs for the children and since a parent organization served effectively as a school board for the programs. A behavioral model (the Direct Instruction of Engelmann and Becker) was the most effective model in producing academic change *and in maintaining academic gains* (Becker & Carnine, 1980). The Head Start–Follow Through programs were designed as broad-spectrum efforts to aid in children's total development. While the focus was on educational change, there were efforts to provide adequate meals, dental and medical checkups, and child management courses for parents. While we do not know of assessments of the effects of these programs on children's clinical status, it could certainly be expected that children who improve academically—as these children did—would have fewer social and legal problems than would children who have persistent school failure.

Cowen and his associates (Cowen, Lorion, Dorr, Clarfield, & Wilson, 1975) have utilized a preventive program in elementary schools for shy and aggressive children. This prevention program was designed to take children at risk for mental health problems and to give them help from paraprofessionals in their schools. The program has not been unequivocally successful with aggressive children, but it has demonstrable effectiveness with shy children. The program was not behaviorally oriented, but it is mentioned here because it represents the kind of prevention research that could be executed by behavioral researchers.

Treatment programs that are more focal, yet seem especially useful in a preventive sense, are exemplified by the following: teaching children to resist enticements by strangers (Poche & Brouwer, in press); teaching children to complete homework assignments (Anesko & O'Leary, in press); and teaching parents how to cope with behavioral problems in supermarkets (Greene,

Clark, & Risley, 1977). Research efforts like these should be strongly encouraged, because they may be associated with prevention of varied conduct and personality problems. The area of prevention and early intervention is generally neglected by behavioral researchers. We have chosen examples of research on frequent problems of normal children that could be expanded to ascertain whether changing such behaviors leads to prevention of other behaviors. The need for research at a community level on preventing aggression in children was recently underscored by Eron (1980), who argued for a need to socialize boys in such a manner that they will develop behaviors like those traditionally fostered in girls (sensitivity to feelings, nurturance, cooperation, and aesthetic appreciation). His thesis is of special interest, because he notes that the stability of aggression is about the same as that of intelligence and that many attempts to change childhood aggression may be doomed to failure if the prevention of the problem does not begin before the age of 6 years.

INVESTIGATIONS OF PREJUDICE

Much of the thrust of child clinical work centers on changing the child's behavior so as to make it more acceptable to society at large. But this question can be raised: Why not educate the public so that they are more tolerant of children's problems? To put it another way, current definitions of social abnormality may be excessively narrow and may act to exacerbate problems that are not particularly debilitating to the individual or harmful to society. Traditionally, in the United States, it has not required much in the way of "deviant behavior" to justify taking children from the mainstream of society and placing them in restricted settings. Children who display bizarre mannerisms, chronic impulsivity, or repeated conduct problems may be labeled as "emotionally disturbed," "learning-disabled," or "delinquent," respectively; they may then be sent away to special schools, or worse, to state institutions.

Recently, American society has begun to shift away from these intolerant, exclusionary practices and to recognize that "behaving differently from others" is not sufficient reason for a child to be removed from the mainstream of society. In enacting Public Law 94-142, the Education for All Handicapped Children Act of 1975, Congress explicitly reaffirmed that handicapped children too are entitled to due process and equal protection as specified by the Constitution. Now that the moral and legal arguments have been articulated and codified, the time has come to examine some of these issues empirically. Specifically, the issue that most needs to be researched concerns *prejudice*. Many handicapped children *do* behave differently from other children, and this difference causes the majority of adults to reject them as unsuitable candidates for public education and community living. Several questions can be raised, the most important of which is this: How can clinicians help break down these prejudices against the handicapped? We suggest that the processes that underlie prejudice against the handicapped are likely to be similar to the processes that produce sex and race prejudice. Perhaps, then, it would be wise for clinicians to use the social-psychological research on race and sex prejudice (e.g., Allport, 1954; Williams, 1977) as a starting point for understanding and alleviating prejudice against the handicapped.

HEURISTIC SUBCATEGORIES

One important principle that emerges from the research discussed above is that progress in child clinical psychology may be facilitated through the identification and elaboration of *heuristic subcategories.* The evidence reviewed suggests that the wholesale adoption of traditional clinical categories, such as "autism," "delinquency," and "hyperactivity" sometimes acts to impede the acquisition of new knowledge concerning these problems. Consider, for example, two investigators, each of whom is using the same social learning approach in the treatment of delinquency. One investigator is working primarily with children who are "stealers," while the other is working primarily with children who are aggressive toward their parents and peers but do not steal. The data reviewed above suggest that these two groups will respond quite differently to the same treatment; the aggressive children will probably improve, whereas the stealers probably will not. Further, in terms of prognosis, the stealers will have a much poorer outcome than will the children whose main problem is aggression. Given this situation, it can be seen that our hypothetical investigators are in fact comparing apples and oranges, even though, on the face of it, they are both treating "delinquents." The problem just described is not restricted to investigations of delinquency. The same difficulties arise in treating mute autistic children as opposed to those who are echolalic, or in treating children whose hyperactivity is associated with high rates of aggression as opposed to hyperactive children with problems primarily of attention and motor activity. In light of the above, it appears that an important step to be taken centers on the careful analysis and delineation of subcategories within a given child clinical population. By taking this step, investigators help to ensure that they are comparing similar populations in their research. Further, this approach should help in the development of *functional* treatments—that is, treatments that are designed to take cognizance of the different variables controlling behavior problems within each clinical subcategory.

REFERENCES

Abraham, S., Collins, G., & Nordsieck, M. Relationship of childhood weight status to morbidity in adults. *HSMA Health Reports*, 1971, *86*, 273–284.

Adelson, R., Liebert, R. M., Poulos, R. W., & Herskovitz, A. A modeling film to reduce children's fear of dental treatment. *International Association for Dental Research Abstracts*, March 1972, p. 114.

Agras, W. S., Barlow, D. H., Chapin, H. N., Abel, C. G., & Leitenberg, H. Behavior modification of anorexia nervosa. *Archives of General Psychiatry*, 1974, *30*, 279–286.

Alexander, A. B., Cropp, G. J. A., & Chai, H. Effects of relaxation training on pulmonary mechanics in children with asthma. *Journal of Applied Behavior Analysis*, 1979, *12*, 27–35.

Alexander, A. B., Miklich, D. R., & Hershkoff, H. The immediate effects of systematic relaxation training on peak expiratory flow rates in asthmatic children. *Psychosomatic Medicine*, 1972, *34*, 388–394.

Alexander, J. F., Barton, C., Schiavo, R. S., & Parsons, B. V. Systems–behavioral intervention with families of delinquents: Therapist characteristics, family behavior, and outcome. *Journal of Consulting and Clinical Psychology*, 1976, *44*, 656–664.

Alexander, J. F., & Parsons, B. V. Short-term behavioral intervention with delinquent families: Impact on family process and recidivism. *Journal of Abnormal Psychology*, 1973, *81*, 219–226.

Allen, R. B., & Hasazi, J. *Bladder capacity and awakening behavior as outcome variables in the conditioning treatment of enuresis.* Unpublished manuscript, University of Vermont, 1978.

Allport, G. W. *The nature of prejudice.* New York: Addison-Wesley, 1954.

Anesko, K. M., & O'Leary, S. G. The effectiveness of brief parent training for the management of children's homework problems. *Child Behavior Therapy,* in press.

Aragona, J., Cassady, J., & Drabman, R. S. Treating overweight children through parental training and contingency contracting. *Journal of Applied Behavior Analysis,* 1975, *8*, 269–278.

Ayllon, T., Smith, D., & Rogers, M. Behavioral management of school phobia. *Journal of Behavior Therapy and Experimental Psychiatry,* 1970, *1*, 125–128.

Azrin, N. H., & Foxx, R. M. A rapid method of toilet training the institutionalized retarded. *Journal of Applied Behavior Analysis,* 1971, *4*, 89–99.

Azrin, N. H., Sneed, T. J., & Foxx, R. M. Dry-bed: A rapid method of eliminating bedwetting of the retarded. *Behaviour Research and Therapy,* 1973, *11*, 427–434.

Azrin, N. H., Sneed, T. J., & Foxx, R. M. Dry-bed training: Rapid elimination of childhood enuresis. *Behaviour Research and Therapy,* 1974, *12*, 147–156.

Azrin, N. H., & Thienes, P. M. Rapid elimination of enuresis by intensive learning without a conditioning apparatus. *Behavior Therapy,* 1978, *9*, 342–354.

Azrin, N. H., Thienes-Hontos, P., & Besabel-Azrin, V. Elimination of enuresis without a conditioning apparatus: An extension by office instruction of the child and parents. *Behavior Therapy,* 1979, *10*, 14–19.

Bailey, J. S., Wolf, M. M., & Phillips, E. L. Home-based reinforcement and modification of pre-delinquent's classroom behavior. *Journal of Applied Behavior Analysis,* 1970, *3*, 223–233.

Baker, J. G., Stanish, B., & Fraser, B. Comparative effects of a token economy in nursery school. *Mental Retardation,* 1972, *10*, 16–19.

Bandura, A. Self-efficacy: Toward a unifying theory of behavioral change. *Psychological Review,* 1977, *84*, 191–215.

Bandura, A., Grusec, J. E., & Menlove, F. L. Vicarious extinction of avoidance behavior. *Journal of Personality and Social Psychology*, 1967, *5*, 16–23.

Bandura, A., & Menlove, F. L. Factors determining vicarious extinction of avoidance behavior through symbolic modeling. *Journal of Personality and Social Psychology*, 1968, *8*, 99–108.

Bartak, L. Educational approaches. In M. Rutter & E. Schopler (Eds.), *Autism: A reappraisal of concepts and treatment*. New York: Plenum, 1978.

Barton, E. S., Guess, D., Garcia, E., & Baer, D. M. Improvement of retardates' mealtime behaviors by time-out procedures using multiple-baseline techniques. *Journal of Applied Behavior Analysis*, 1970, *3*, 77–84.

Becker, W. C., & Carnine, D. W. Direct instruction. In B. B. Lahey & A. E. Kazdin (Eds.), *Advances in clinical child psychology* (Vol. 3). New York: Plenum, 1980.

Bellamy, G. T., Wilson, D. J., Adler, E., & Clarke, J. Y. A strategy for programming vocational skills for severely handicapped youth. *Exceptional Educational Quarterly*, 1980, *1*, 85–97.

Bemis, K. M. Current approaches to the etiology and treatment of anorexia nervosa. *Psychological Bulletin*, 1978, *85*, 593–617.

Bereiter, C., & Englemann, S. *Teaching disadvantaged children in the preschool*. Englewood Cliffs, N.J.: Prentice-Hall, 1966.

Bijou, S. W. Experimental studies of child behavior, normal and deviant. In L. Krasner & L. P. Ullmann (Eds.), *Research in behavior modification*. New York: Holt, Rinehart & Winston, 1965.

Birchler, G. R., & Spinks, S. H. Behavioral–systems marital and family therapy: Integration and clinical application. *The American Journal of Family Therapy*, 1980, *8*, 6–28.

Birnbrauer, J. S. Mental retardation. In H. Leitenberg (Ed.), *Handbook of behavior modification and behavior therapy*. Englewood Cliffs, N.J.: Prentice-Hall, 1976.

Birnbrauer, J. S., Wolf, M. M., Kidder, J. D., & Tague, C. Classroom behavior of retarded pupils with token reinforcement. *Journal of Experimental Child Psychology*, 1965, *2*, 219–235.

Bollard, R. J., & Woodworth, P. The effect of parent-administered dry-bed training on nocturnal enuresis in children. *Behaviour Research and Therapy*, 1977, *15*, 159–165.

Bregman, E. O. An attempt to modify the emotional attitudes of infants by the conditioned response technique. *Journal of Genetic Psychology*, 1934, *45*, 169–196.

Brown, L., Nietupski, J., & Hamre-Nietupski, S. The criterion of ultimate functioning and public school services for severely handicapped students. In A. Thomas (Ed.), *Hey, don't forget about me: Education's investment in the severely, profoundly, and multiply handicapped*. Reston, Va.: Council for Exceptional Children, 1976.

Brown, R., Copeland, R., & Hall, R. V. School phobia: Effects of behavior modification treatment by an elementary school principal. *Child Study Journal*, 1974, *4*, 125–133.

Brownell, K. D., Heckerman, C. L., Westlake, R. J., Hayes, S. C., & Monti, P. M. The effect of couples training and partner cooperativeness in the behavioral treatment of obesity. *Behaviour Research and Therapy*, 1978, *16*, 323–333.

Camp, B. W., Blom, G. E., Herbert, F., & Van Doorninck, W. J. "Think Aloud": A program for developing self-control in young aggressive boys. *Journal of Abnormal Child Psychology*, 1977, *5*, 157–169.

Carr, E. G. Teaching autistic children to use sign language: Some research issues. *Journal of Autism and Developmental Disorders*, 1979, *9*, 345–359.

Carr, E. G. Delinquents as behavior modifiers (review of *Self-mutilation* by R. R. Ross & H. B. McKay). *Contemporary Psychology*, 1980, *25*, 330–331. (a)

Carr, E. G. Generalization of treatment effects following educational intervention with autistic children and youth. In B. Wilcox & A. Thompson (Eds.), *Critical issues in educating au-*

tistic children and youth. Washington, D.C.: U.S. Department of Education, Office of Special Education, 1980. (b)

Carr, E. G., & Lovaas, O. I. Contingent electric shock as a treatment for severe behavior problems. In S. Axelrod & J. Apsche (Eds.), *Punishment: Its effects on human behavior.* New York: Academic Press, in press.

Carr, E. G., Newsom, C. D., & Binkoff, J. A. Escape as a factor in the aggressive behavior of two retarded children. *Journal of Applied Behavior Analysis,* 1980, *13,* 113–129.

Carr, E. G., Schreibman, L., & Lovaas, O. I. Control of echolalic speech in psychotic children. *Journal of Abnormal Child Psychology,* 1975, *3,* 331–351.

Cerreto, M. C., & Tuma, J. M. Distribution of DSM-II diagnoses in a child psychiatric setting. *Journal of Abnormal Child Psychology,* 1977, *5,* 147–155.

Cohen, H. L., & Filipczak, J. *A new learning environment.* San Francisco: Jossey-Bass, 1971.

Conley, R. W. *The economics of mental retardation.* Baltimore: Johns Hopkins University Press, 1973.

Conners, C. K. A teacher rating scale for use in drug studies with children. *American Journal of Psychiatry,* 1969, *126,* 152–156.

Conners, C. K., & Werry, J. S. Pharmacotherapy. In H. C. Quay & J. S. Werry (Eds.), *Psychopathological disorders of childhood.* New York: Wiley, 1979.

Cowen, E. L., Lorion, R. P., Dorr, D., Clarfield, S. P., & Wilson, A. B. Evaluation of a preventively oriented school-based mental health program. *Psychology in the Schools,* 1975, *12,* 161–166.

Creer, T. L. The use of a time-out from positive reinforcement procedure with asthmatic children. *Journal of Psychosomatic Research,* 1970, *14,* 117–120.

Creer, T. L., Weinberg, E., & Molk, L. Managing a hospital behavior problem: Malingering. *Journal of Behavior Therapy and Experimental Psychiatry,* 1974, *5,* 259–262.

Dekker, E., Pelse, H. E., & Groen, J. Conditioning as a cause of asthmatic attacks. *Journal of Psychosomatic Research,* 1957, *2,* 97–108.

Department of Health, Education, and Welfare, Office of Child Development. *Report of the conference on use of stimulant drugs in the treatment of behaviorally disturbed young school children.* Washington, D.C.: U.S. Government Printing Office, 1971.

Dietz, S. M. Current status of applied behavior analysis: Science versus technology. *American Psychologist,* 1978, *33,* 805–814.

Douglas, V. I. Treatment and training approaches to hyperactivity: Establishing internal or external control. In C. K. Whalen & B. Henker, (Eds.), *Hyperactive children: The social ecology of identification and treatment.* New York: Academic Press, 1980.

Douglas, V. I., Parry, P., Marton, P., & Garson, C. Assessment of a cognitive training program for hyperactive children. *Journal of Abnormal Child Psychology,* 1976, *4,* 389–410.

Drabman, R., Spitalnik, R., & O'Leary, K. D. Teaching self-control to disruptive children. *Journal of Abnormal Psychology,* 1973, *82,* 10–16.

Dunlap, G., Egel, A., Killion, J., Koegel, R., & Schreibman, L. *Parent training versus clinic treatment: Impact on family and child.* Paper presented at the meeting of the Association for Advancement of Behavior Therapy, Chicago, November 1978.

English, H. B. Three cases of the conditioned fear response. *Journal of Abnormal Social Psychology,* 1929, *24,* 221–225.

English, H. B., & English, A. V. *Psychological and psychoanalytic terms.* New York: Longmans, Green, 1958.

Erickson, M. T. *Child psychopathology.* Englewood Cliffs, N. J.: Prentice-Hall, 1978.

Eron, L. D. Prescription for reduction of aggression. *American Psychologist,* 1980, *35,* 244–252.

Evers, W. L., & Schwarz, J. C. Modifying social withdrawal in preschoolers: The effect of filmed modeling and teacher praise. *Journal of Abnormal Child Psychology,* 1973, *1,* 248–256.

Fawcett, S. B., Mathews, R. M., & Fletcher, R. K. Some promising dimensions for behavioral community technology. *Journal of Applied Behavior Analysis,* 1980, *13,* 505–518.

Forster, F. M. Conditioning in sensory evoked seizures. *Conditional Reflex,* 1966, *1,* 224–234.

Foxx, R. M., & Azrin, N. H. The elimination of autistic self-stimulatory behavior by overcorrection. *Journal of Applied Behavior Analysis,* 1973, *6,* 1–14.

Gelfand, D. M. Social withdrawal and negative emotional states: Behavior therapy. In B. B. Wolman, J. Egan, & A. O. Ross (Eds.), *Handbook of treatment of mental disorders in childhood and adolescence.* Englewood Cliffs, N.J.: Prentice-Hall, 1978.

Gelfand, D. M., & Hartmann, D. P. *Child behavior analysis and therapy.* New York: Pergamon, 1975.

Gold, M. W. Research on the vocational habilitation of the retarded: The present, the future. In N. R. Ellis (Ed.), *International review of research in mental retardation* (Vol. 6). New York: McGraw-Hill, 1973.

Graziano, A. M. *Behavior therapy with children.* Chicago: Aldine, 1975.

Greene, B. F., Clark, H. B., & Risley, T. R. *Shopping with children: Advice for parents.* San Rafael, Calif.: Academic Therapy Publications, 1977.

Harris, B. Whatever happened to little Albert? *American Psychologist,* 1979, *34,* 151–160.

Hart, B. Pragmatics and language development. In B. B. Lahey & A. E. Kazdin (Eds.), *Advances in clinical child psychology* (Vol. 3). New York: Plenum, 1980.

Hart, B., & Risley, T. Promoting productive language through incidental teaching. *Education and Urban Society,* 1978, *10,* 407–429.

Hayes, S. C., Rincover, A., & Solnick, J. V. The technical drift of applied behavior analysis. *Journal of Applied Behavior Analysis,* 1980, *13,* 275–286.

Hemsley, R., Howlin, P., Berger, M., Hersov, L., Holbrook, D., Rutter, M., & Yule, W. Treating autistic children in a family context. In M. Rutter & E. Schopler (Eds.), *Autism: A reappraisal of concepts and treatment.* New York: Plenum, 1978.

Hersov, L. A. Persistent non-attendance at school. *Journal of Child Psychology and Psychiatry,* 1960, *1,* 130–136.

Hetherington, E. M., & Parke, R. D. *Child psychology.* New York: McGraw-Hill, 1979.

Hobbs, S. A., Moquin, L. A., Tyroler, M., & Lahey, B. B. cognitive behavior therapy with children: Has clinical utility been demonstrated? *Psychological Bulletin,* 1980, *87,* 147–165.

Jack, L. M. An experimental study of ascendant behavior in preschool children. *University of Iowa Studies in Child Welfare,* 1934, *9,* 3–65.

Jersild, A. T., & Holmes, F. B. Children's fears. *Teachers College Child Development Monographs,* No. 20, 1935.

Jesness, C. F., DeRisi, W. J., McCormick, P. M., & Qedge, R. F. *The Youth Center Research Project.* Sacramento, Calif.: American Justice Institute, 1972.

Johnson, S. B. Enuresis. In R. Daitzman (Ed.), *Clinical behavior therapy and behavior modification.* New York: Garland, 1980.

Johnson, S. B., & Melamed, B. G. The assessment and treatment of children's fears. In B. B. Lahey & A. E. Kazdin (Eds.), *Advances in clinical child psychology* (Vol. 2). New York: Plenum, 1979.

Jones, M. C. The elimination of children's fears. *Journal of Experimental Psychology,* 1924, *7,* 382–390.

Jones, R. R. *Therapeutic effects of the Teaching Family group home model.* Paper presented at the meeting of the American Psychological Association, New York, September 1979.

Keller, M. F., & Carlson, O. M. The use of symbolic modeling to promote social skills in preschool children with low levels of social responsiveness. *Child Development,* 1974, *45,* 912–919.

Kennedy, W. A. School phobia: Rapid treatment of fifty cases. *Journal of Abnormal Psychology,* 1965, *70,* 285–289.

Kennedy, W. A. *Child psychology.* Englewood Cliffs, N.J.: Prentice-Hall, 1971.

Kent, R. N., & O'Leary, K. D. A controlled evaluation of behavior modification with conduct problem children. *Journal of Consulting and Clinical Psychology,* 1976, *44,* 586–596.

Kent, R. N., & O'Leary, K. D. Treatment of conduct problem children: B.A. and/or Ph.D. therapists. *Behavior Therapy,* 1977, *8,* 653–658.

Kifer, R. E., Lewis, M. A., Green, D. R., & Phillips, E. L. Training predelinquent youths and their parents to negotiate conflict situations. *Journal of Applied Behavior Analysis,* 1974, *7,* 357–364.

Kingsley, R. G., & Shapiro, J. A comparison of three behavioral programs for the control of obesity in children. *Behavior Therapy,* 1977, *8,* 30–36.

Kirigin, K. A., Braukmann, C. J., Fixsen, D. L., Phillips, E. L., & Wolf, M. M. *Are community-based corrections effective: An evaluation of Achievement Place.* Paper presented at the meeting of the American Psychological Association, Chicago, 1975.

Koegel, R. L., Firestone, P. B., Kramme, K. W., & Dunlap, G. Increasing spontaneous play by suppressing self-stimulation in autistic children. *Journal of Applied Behavior Analysis,* 1974, *7,* 521–528.

Kohlenberg, R. J. The punishment of persistent vomiting: A case study. *Journal of Applied Behavior Analysis,* 1970, *3,* 241–245.

Lang, P. J., Lazovik, A. D., & Reynolds, D. J. Desensitization, suggestibility, and pseudotherapy. *Journal of Abnormal Psychology,* 1965, *70,* 395–402.

Lang, P. J., & Melamed, B. G. Avoidance conditioning therapy of an infant with chronic ruminative vomiting: Case report. *Journal of Abnormal Psychology,* 1969, *74,* 1–8.

Leitenberg, H., Agras, W. S., & Thomson, L. E. A sequential analysis of the effect of selective positive reinforcement in modifying anorexia nervosa. *Behaviour Research and Therapy,* 1968, *6,* 211–218.

Loney, J., Langhorne, J. E., & Paternite, C. S. An empirical basis for subgrouping the hyperkinetic/minimal brain dysfunction syndrome. *Journal of Abnormal Psychology,* 1978, *87,* 431–441.

Lotter, V. Follow-up studies. In M. Rutter & E. Schopler (Eds.), *Autism: A reappraisal of concepts and treatment.* New York: Plenum, 1978.

Lovaas, O. I. *The autistic child.* New York: Irvington, 1977.

Lovaas, O. I. Parents as therapists. In M. Rutter & E. Schopler (Eds.), *Autism: A reappraisal of concepts and treatment.* New York: Plenum, 1978.

Lovaas, O. I. Personal communication, August 2, 1980.

Lovaas, O. I., Berberich, J., Perloff, B., & Schaeffer, B. Acquisition of imitative speech by schizophrenic children. *Science,* 1966, *151,* 705–707.

Lovaas, O. I., Freitag, G., Gold, V. J., & Kassorla, I. C. Experimental studies in childhood schizophrenia: Analysis of self-destructive behavior. *Journal of Experimental Child Psychology,* 1965, *2,* 67–84.

Lovaas, O. I., Freitas, L., Nelson, K., & Whalen, C. The establishment of imitation and its use for the development of complex behavior in schizophrenic children. *Behaviour Research and Therapy,* 1967, *5,* 171–181.

Lovaas, O. I., Koegel, R. L., Simmons, J. Q., & Long, J. S. Some generalization and follow-up measures of autistic children in behavior therapy. *Journal of Applied Behavior Analysis,* 1973, *6,* 131–165.

Luckey, R. E., Watson, C. M., & Musick, J. K. Aversive conditioning as a means of inhibiting vomiting and rumination. *American Journal of Mental Deficiency,* 1968, *73,* 139–142.

Mahoney, M. J. *Cognitive and non-cognitive views in behavior modification.* Paper presented at the meeting of the American Psychological Association, San Francisco, 1977.

Marks, I. M. *Fears and phobias.* New York: Academic Press, 1969.

Martin, B. Brief family intervention: The effectiveness and importance of including the father. *Journal of Consulting and Clinical Psychology,* 1977, *45,* 1002–1010.

Meichenbaum, D. Cognitive behavior modification with exceptional children: A promise yet unfulfilled. *Exceptional Education Quarterly,* 1980, *1,* 83–88.

Melamed, B., Robbins, R., Smith, S., & Graves, S. *Coping strategies in children undergoing surgery.* Paper presented at the meeting of the American Psychological Association, Montreal, September 1980.

Melamed, B., & Siegel, L. Reduction of anxiety in children facing hospitalization and surgery by use of filmed modeling. *Journal of Consulting and Clinical Psychology,* 1975, *43,* 511–521.

Moore, D. M., Chamberlain, P., & Mukai, L. H. Children at risk for delinquency: A follow-up comparison of aggressive children and children who steal. *Journal of Abnormal Child Psychology,* 1979, *7,* 345–355.

Mowrer, O. H., & Mowrer, W. M. Enuresis: A method for its study and treatment. *The American Journal of Orthopsychiatry,* 1938, *8,* 436–459.

Nedelman, D., & Sulzbacher, S. I. Dickey at thirteen years of age: A long-term success following early application of operant conditioning procedures. In G. Semb (Ed.), *Behavior analysis and education.* Lawrence, Kan.: Follow-Through Project, 1972.

Neisworth, J. T., & Moore, F. Operant treatment of asthmatic responding with the parent as therapist. *Behavior Therapy,* 1972, *3,* 95–99.

Nordquist, V. M., & Wahler, R. G. Naturalistic treatment of an autistic child. *Journal of Applied Behavior Analysis,* 1973, *6,* 79–87.

O'Connor, R. D. Modification of social withdrawal through symbolic modeling. *Journal of Applied Behavior Analysis,* 1969, *2,* 15–22.

O'Connor, R. D. Relative efficacy of modeling, shaping, and the combined procedures for modification of social withdrawal. *Journal of Abnormal Psychology,* 1972, *79,* 327–334.

O'Leary, K. D. Pills or skills for hyperactive children. *Journal of Applied Behavior Analysis,* 1980, *13,* 191–204.

O'Leary, K. D., & Turkewitz, H. Marital therapy from a behavioral perspective. In T. J. Paolino & B. S. McCrady (Eds.), *Marriage and marital therapy: Psychoanalytic, behavioral and systems theory perspectives.* New York: Brunner/Mazel, 1978. (a)

O'Leary, K. D., & Turkewitz, H. Methodological errors in marital and child treatment research. *Journal of Consulting and Clinical Psychology,* 1978, *46,* 747–758. (b)

O'Leary, K. D., & Wilson, G. T. *Behavior therapy: Application and outcome.* Englewood Cliffs, N.J.: Prentice-Hall, 1975.

O'Leary, S. G. A response to cognitive training. *Exceptional Education Quarterly,* 1980, *1,* 89–94.

O'Leary, S. G., & Dubey, D. R. Applications of self-control procedures by children: A review. *Journal of Applied Behavior Analysis,* 1979, *12,* 449–465.

O'Leary, S. G., & Steen, P. Subcategorizing hyperactivity: The Stony Brook Scale. *Journal of Consulting and Clinical Psychology,* in press.

Palkes, H., Stewart, M., & Freedman, J. Improvement in maze performance of hyperactive boys as a function of verbal-training procedures. *Journal of Special Education,* 1972, *5,* 337–342.

Paolino, T. J., & McCrady, B. S. (Eds.). *Marriage and marital therapy: Psychoanalytic, behavioral and systems theory perspectives.* New York: Brunner/Mazel, 1978.

Patterson, G. R. Interventions for boys with conduct problems: Multiple settings, treatment, and criteria. *Journal of Consulting and Clinical Psychology,* 1974, *42,* 471–481.

Patterson, G. R. *Mothers: The unacknowledged victims.* Paper presented at regional Social Research–Child Development meeting, Oakland, April 1976.

Patterson, G. R., Chamberlain, P., & Reid, J. *A treatment comparison for families with antisocial children.* Unpublished manuscript, University of Oregon, Eugene, 1980.

Patterson, G. R., & Fleischman, M. J. Maintenance of treatment effects: Some considerations concerning family systems and follow-up data. *Behavior Therapy,* 1979, *10,* 168–185.

Patterson, G. R., & Reid, J. B. Reciprocity and coercion: Two facets of social systems. In C. Neuringer & J. Michael (Eds.), *Behavior modification in clinical psychology.* New York: Appleton-Century-Crofts, 1970.

Patterson, G. R., Reid, J. B., Jones, R. R., & Conger, R. E. *A social learning approach to family intervention: I. Families with aggressive children.* Eugene, Ore.: Castalia Press, 1975.

Phillips, E. L., Phillips, E. A., Fixsen, D. L., & Wolf, M. M. Achievement Place: The modification of the behaviors of pre-delinquent boys within a token economy. *Journal of Applied Behavior Analysis,* 1971, *4,* 45–59.

Phillips, E. L., Phillips, E. A., Fixsen, D. L., & Wolf, M. M. *The teaching family handbook.* Lawrence: University of Kansas Printing Service, 1974.

Poche, C., & Brouwer, R. Teaching self-protection to young children. *Journal of Applied Behavior Analysis,* in press.

Porter, B., & O'Leary, K. D. Marital discord and childhood behavior problems. *Journal of Abnormal Child Psychology,* 1980, *8,* 287–295.

Purcell, K., Brady, K., Chai, H., Muser, J., Molk, L., Gordon, N., & Means, J. The effect on asthma in children of experimental separation from the family. *Psychosomatic Medicine,* 1969, *31,* 144–164.

Quay, H. C., & Peterson, D. R. *Manual for the Behavior Problem Checklist.* Unpublished manuscript, 1979. (Available from the second author at 39 North Fifth Avenue, Highland Park, N. J. 08904.)

Rees, L. The significance of parental attitudes in childhood asthma. *Journal of Psychosomatic Research,* 1964, *7,* 253–262.

Reid, J. B., & Hendriks, A. F. C. J. Preliminary analysis of the effectiveness of direct home intervention for the treatment of predelinquent boys who steal. In L. Hamerlynck, L. Handy, & E. Mash (Eds.), *Behavioral change: Methodology, concepts, and practice.* Champaign, Ill.: Research Press, 1973.

Rincover, A., & Koegel, R. Research on the education of autistic children: Recent advances and future directions. In B. B. Lahey & A. E. Kazdin (Eds.), *Advances in clinical child psychology* (Vol. 1). New York: Plenum, 1978.

Rodriguez, A., Rodriguez, M., & Eisenberg, L. The outcome of school phobia: A follow-up study based on 41 cases. *American Journal of Psychiatry,* 1959, *116,* 540–544.

Rosenbaum, M. S., & Drabman, R. S. Self-control training in the classroom: A review and critique. *Journal of Applied Behavior Analysis,* 1979, *12,* 467–485.

Ross, A. O. *Child behavior therapy.* New York: Wiley, 1980.

Ross, D. M., & Ross, S. A. *Pacemaker primary curriculum.* Belmont, Calif.: Fearon, 1974.

Ross, R. R., & McKay, H. B. *Self-mutilation.* Lexington, Mass.: D. C. Heath, 1979.

Rutter, M. Prognosis: Psychotic children in adolescence and early adult life. In J. K. Wing (Ed.), *Early childhood autism: Clinical, educational, and social aspects.* London: Pergamon, 1966.

Rutter, M. Language disorder and infantile autism. In M. Rutter & E. Schopler (Eds.), *Autism: A reappraisal of concepts and treatment.* New York: Plenum, 1978.

Rutter, M., Greenfeld, D., & Lockyer, L. A five-to-fifteen year follow-up study of infantile psychosis. II. Social and behavioural outcome. *British Journal of Psychiatry*, 1967, *113*, 1183-1199.

Samuelson, F. J. B. Watson's little Albert, Cyril Burt's twins, and the need for a critical science. *American Psychologist*, 1980, *35*, 619-625.

Satterfield, J. H., Cantwell, D. P., & Satterfield, B. Y. Multimodality treatment. *Archives of General Psychiatry*, 1979, *36*, 965-974.

Schrag, P., & Divoky, D. *The myth of the hyperactive child*. New York: Pantheon, 1975.

Schreibman, L., & Carr, E. G. Elimination of echolalic responding to questions through the training of a generalized verbal response. *Journal of Applied Behavior Analysis*, 1978, *11*, 453-463.

Seidman, E., Rappaport, J., & Davidson, W. S. *Adolescents in legal jeopardy: Initial success and replication of an alternative to the criminal justice system.* Paper presented at the meeting of the American Psychological Association, Washington, D. C., August 1976.

Seidman, E., Rappaport, J., & Davidson, W. S. Adolescents in legal jeopardy: Initial success and replication of an alternative to the criminal justice system. In National Institute of Law Enforcement Assistance Administration (Ed.), *The adolescent diversion project: A university's approach to delinquency prevention.* Washington, D.C.: U.S. Government Printing Office, 1977.

Seymour, F. W., & Stokes, T. F. Self-recording in training girls to increase work and evoke staff praise in an institution for offenders. *Journal of Applied Behavior Analysis*, 1976, *9*, 41-54.

Skinner, B. F. *Science and human behavior*. New York: Macmillan, 1953.

Starfield, B. Enuresis: Its pathogenesis and management. *Clinical Pediatrics*, 1972, *11*, 343-350.

Stimbert, V. E., & Coffey, K. R. *Obese children and adolescents: A review*. ERIC Document Reproduction Service, 1972.

Stratton, J. R., & Terry, R. M. *Prevention of delinquency: Problems and programs*. New York: Macmillan, 1968.

Stuart, R. B. Behavioral contracting within families of delinquents. *Journal of Behavior Therapy and Experimental Psychiatry*, 1971, *2*, 1-11.

Stuart, R. B., & Davis, B. *Slim chance in a fat world*. Champaign, Ill.: Research Press, 1972.

Stuart, R. B., & Guire, K. Some correlates of the maintenance of weight loss through behavior modification. *International Journal of Obesity*, 1978, *2*, 225-235.

Stunkard, A. J., & Mahoney, M. J. Behavioral treatment of the eating disorders. In H. Leitenberg (Ed.), *Handbook of behavior modification and behavior therapy.* Englewood Cliffs, N.J.: Prentice-Hall, 1976.

Trotter, R. J. Behavior modification: Here, there, and everywhere. *Science News*, 1973, *103*, 16, 260-263.

Ullmann, L. P., & Krasner, L. *Case studies in behavior modification.* New York: Holt, Rinehart & Winston, 1965.

Uniform Crime Reports for the United States, 1973. Washington, D.C.: U.S. Government Printing Office, 1974.

Vernon, D. T. Use of modeling to modify children's responses to a natural, potentially stressful situation. *Journal of Applied Psychology*, 1973, *58*, 351-356.

Vernon, D. T. Modeling and birth order in responses to painful stimuli. *Journal of Personality and Social Psychology*, 1974, *29*, 794-799.

Vernon, D. T., & Bailey, W. C. The use of motion pictures in the psychological preparation of children for induction of anesthesia. *Anesthesiology*, 1974, *40*, 68-72.

Wahler, R. G. The insular mother: Her problems in parent–child treatment. *Journal of Applied Behavior Analysis*, 1980, *13*, 207-219.

Walker, H. M., & Hops, H. Group and individual reinforcement contingencies in the modification of social withdrawal. In L. A. Hamerlynck, L. C. Handy, & E. J. Mash (Eds.), *Behavior change: Methodology, concepts, and practice*. Champaign, Ill.: Research Press, 1973.

Watson, J. B., & Rayner, R. Conditioned emotional reactions. *Journal of Experimental Psychology, 1920, 3,* 1-12.

Watson, L. S. *Child behavior modification*. New York: Pergamon, 1973.

Weiss, A. R. A behavioral approach to the treatment of adolescent obesity. *Behavior Therapy, 1977, 8,* 720-726.

Wheeler, M. E., & Hess, K. W. Treatment of juvenile obesity by successive approximation control of eating. *Journal of Behavior Therapy and Experimental Psychiatry, 1976, 7,* 235-241.

Whitman, T. L., Mercurio, J. R., & Caponigri, Y. Development of social responses in two severely retarded children. *Journal of Applied Behavior Analysis, 1970, 3,* 133-138.

Williams, J. H. *Psychology of women*. New York: Norton, 1977.

Willner, A. G., Braukmann, C. J., Kirigin, K. A., & Wolf, M. M. Achievement Place: A community treatment model for youths in trouble. In D. Marholin (Ed.), *Child behavior therapy*. New York: Gardner Press, 1978.

Wilson, G. T., & O'Leary, K. D. *Principles of behavior therapy*. Englewood Cliffs, N. J.: Prentice-Hall, 1980.

Winsberg, B. G., Yepes, L. E., & Bialer, I. Pharmacological management of children with hyperactive/aggressive/inattentive behavior disorders. *Clinical Pediatrics, 1976, 15,* 471-477.

Wolf, M. M. Social validity: The case for subjective measurement, or how applied behavior analysis is finding its heart. *Journal of Applied Behavior Analysis, 1978, 11,* 203-214.

Wolf, M. M., Risley, T. R., & Mees, H. Application of operant conditioning procedures to the behaviour problems of an autistic child. *Behaviour Research and Therapy, 1964, 1,* 305-312.

Wooley, S. C., Wooley, O. W., & Dyrenforth, S. R. Theoretical, practical, and social issues in behavioral treatments of obesity. *Journal of Applied Behavior Analysis, 1979, 12,* 3-25.

Yates, A. J. *Behavior therapy*. New York: Wiley, 1970.

Zlutnick, S., Mayville, W. J., & Moffat, S. Modification of seizure disorders: The interruption of behavioral chains. *Journal of Applied Behavior Analysis, 1975, 8,* 1-12.

12

ADULT DISORDERS

G. TERENCE WILSON
Department of Clinical Psychology
Rutgers University

INTRODUCTION

Beginning with Wolpe's bold assertion (1958) that 90% of the 210 adult neurotic patients he had treated were either "cured" or "much improved," behavior therapists have generally claimed that their methods are demonstrably effective and, at least in some cases, significantly superior to other psychological treatment approaches. Predictably, these claims have often generated heated controversy. Given the high personal and professional stakes that are involved in evaluations of the efficacy of competing therapeutic methods for the psychological disorders, the frequently subjective and emotional nature of the controversy is not difficult to understand. Moreover, the empirical evidence, even where it exists, is not always as unequivocal as investigators would wish. The same data can stimulate genuine disagreement even among those men and women of goodwill and methodological sophistication who are disposed to evaluate the evidence with dispassionate objectivity. Behavior therapists themselves are far from unified on the many thorny issues of treatment evaluation and outcome (Franks & Wilson, 1973–1980). Disagreement with nonbehavioral colleagues can therefore come as little surprise.

Yet whatever the controversy about the overall or ultimate efficacy of behavior therapy, it seems to me that there are three issues about which there can be no serious dispute. The first is that the current evaluation of behavior therapy is focused not on the question of whether it *can* be effective, but rather on the specific questions of *how* effective it is with particular problems. As the 1980s begin, the value of behavior therapy is, by and large, clearly recognized in the fields of clinical psychology, psychiatry, and education. In the remarkably brief time span of 20-odd years since Wolpe (1958) published his landmark text, behavior therapy has developed from the heavily

criticized and often vehemently denounced approach of a handful of therapists to a widely accepted and routinely used form of treatment (e.g., American Psychiatric Association Task Force, 1973; Bergin & Lambert, 1978; Risley, 1977). The once total rejection of the therapeutic value of behavioral
techniques is a thing of the past. Second, I submit that the quantity and, more
importantly, the quality of research on treatment outcome in behavior therapy, with all its imperfections, far exceeds that available in traditional psychotherapy. Much of this behavioral research has been facilitated by the development of innovative and powerful research strategies for evaluating therapy
outcome, strategies that are discussed by Kazdin in Chapter 10 of this volume. These methodological innovations provide the means for conducting
the detailed empirical analyses of the specific outcome questions that need to
be asked. There is no need to rehash here the numerous conceptual and methodological inadequacies of what Rachman and Wilson (1980) have identified
as conventional outcome research in psychotherapy. The reader is referred to
detailed analyses by Kazdin and Wilson (1978) and Rachman and Wilson
(1980) of conventional outcome research that compared "behavior therapy"
to "psychotherapy." Suffice it to state here that there is now consensus that
questions such as "Is behavior therapy more effective than psychotherapy?"
defy answer and only mislead the process of evaluation. The appropriate
question that must guide outcome research is "What method, administered
by whom, is effective on what measures for what problem in which populations and at what cost?"

The third issue about which there can be no debate is that behavior therapy is demonstrably more applicable to a broader range of psychiatric, medical, and educational problems than is traditional psychotherapy. The view
that behavior therapy is appropriate mainly for the treatment of simple phobias or habit disorders, or that it is really a useful adjunct to psychotherapy,
can be decisively dismissed (Kazdin & Wilson, 1978; O'Leary & Wilson, in
press).

Adopting a position that appears to have had some influence, Marks
(1976) has declared that behavior therapy "can help perhaps 10% of all adult
psychiatric patients when used as the chief instrument of change. This means
that 90% of all adult cases require other approaches as the main form of
treatment" (p. 254). More recently, Marks (1981b) has gone on to assert:

The commonest neuroses presenting for treatment are those dominated by mild depression and/or anxiety, and these are unfortunately the least amenable so far to behavioral treatment . . . those problems where good research evidence suggests that behavioral psychotherapy is currently the approach of choice . . . include phobic and
obsessive–compulsive disorders, social skills problems, sexual dysfunction, and enuresis. Together these make up about 25% of neurotic patients who present to psychiatric
outpatient clinics. In running an efficient behavioral service it is obviously critical to

select patients who have problems suitable for behavioral psychotherapy or one otherwise wastes not only one's own time but also that of the patient, unless of course one is trying out new research methods. (p. 138)

Quantitative estimates of this sort are most arbitrary and will vary across settings as a function of several variables. Furthermore, the view that "the commonest neuroses," namely, "those dominated by mild depression and/or anxiety," are unsuitable for behavior therapy, as claimed by Marks in the passage just quoted, can be seriously questioned. Consider the treatment of unipolar depression.[1] That behavior therapy has been applied to mild and even severe cases of depression is amply documented in the behavioral-treatment literature (e.g., Beck, Rush, Shaw, & Emery, 1979; Craighead, 1980; Rehm, 1980). Moreover, evidence from controlled outcome studies suggests that self-control and cognitive–behavioral interventions are effective in treating depressives. This evidence can be illustrated by reference to three of the more important studies.

Beck's "cognitive therapy" (actually an explicit amalgam of cognitive and behavioral methods) has emerged as a major form of psychological treatment of depression (Beck *et al.,* 1979). Rush, Beck, Kovacs, and Hollon (1977) compared this form of cognitive restructuring to pharmacotherapy in the treatment of depression. On average, the clients had been continually or intermittently depressed for about 9 years, and 75% reported suicidal ideas. The majority had had previous psychotherapy without success, and 22% had been hospitalized on account of their depression. Treatment for both groups averaged 11 weeks.

Depression was substantially reduced by both treatments; however, cognitive therapy produced significantly greater improvement on self-ratings and clinical ratings of depression. A total of 79% of the clients in the cognitive-therapy condition underwent marked improvement or complete remission, as compared to 23% of the clients in the pharmacotherapy condition. These treatment differences were maintained at 3- and 6-month follow-ups. Aside from being more effective, cognitive therapy was associated with a significantly lower dropout rate over the course of the study. This is an important finding, since there is good evidence that clients who drop out of treatment are almost inevitably treatment failures. If statistical analysis of outcome results is based only on those clients who complete treatment, a biased picture may emerge. In this study by Rush *et al.* (1977), cognitive therapy was superior to pharmacotherapy irrespective of whether the dropouts were included in the analysis.

---

1. By "neuroses . . . dominated by . . . anxiety," barring phobic and obsessive–compulsive disorders, Marks refers primarily to anxiety states. The treatment of these disorders is discussed in a later section.

The apparent superiority of Beck's cognitive–behavioral method warrants serious attention, since pharmacotherapy represents the most powerful comparative treatment method that could have been chosen. Tricyclic antidepressant drugs have been shown to be more effective than other treatments, including traditional psychotherapy, and are widely viewed as the recommended therapy for depression. Moreover, the results obtained with pharmacotherapy in this study were said to be comparable to previous findings with antidepressant drugs. It should be noted, however, that the adequacy of the pharmachotherapy treatment in the Rush *et al.* (1977) investigation has been queried. Thus, Becker and Schuckit (1978) argued that the pharmacotherapy condition was not an optimal test of drug treatment for depression. Specifically, Becker and Schuckit contended that imipramine may be less effective with the sort of chronically depressed population that Rush *et al.* treated. They suggested that lithium carbonate is more appropriate for recurrent depressions. They also argued, and with success, that the drug dosages might have been inadequate. Most critical of all, the drugs were not administered for a satisfactory period. Rush *et al.* replied that their results were comparable to other findings obtained with drug treatments, but this is open to dispute. The possibility that comparative pharmacotherapy treatment might not have been properly tested, together with the fact that the evaluations of treatment outcome were conducted by assessors who were not blind to the respective treatments, necessitates caution in interpreting Rush *et al.*'s findings. Nonetheless, the results obtained with cognitive–behavioral treatment are most promising.

A 1-year follow-up showed good maintenance of treatment effects. As Kovacs, Rush, Beck, and Hollon (1981) put it, "Self-rated depressive symptomatology was significantly lower for those who, one year earlier, had completed cognitive therapy than for those who had been in the clinical trial's pharmacotherapy cell. While there were several other interesting trends in favor of the cognitive-therapy patients, none of the between-group differences were significant" (p. 33).

In a study by McLean and Hakstian (1979), 196 depressed patients were randomly assigned to either behavioral therapy, psychotherapy, pharmacotherapy, or an attention placebo (relaxation training). The patients were drawn from a typical outpatient clinical population and met the following requirements: They were between 20 and 60 years old; they had been depressed for at least the last 2 months; they were functionally impaired as a result of their depression; they were not involved in any other form of therapy; they were diagnosed as presenting with primary depression on the basis of a clinical interview; they met the diagnostic criteria for psychiatric research in clinical depression as suggested by Feighner, Robins, Guze, Woodruff, Winokur, and Muñoz (1972); and they scored within or beyond the moderate range of well-established tests of depression such as the Beck Depression Inventory (BDI) and the MMPI D scale (D scale scores average 25 for men and 29.5 for women). In all, 72% of the sample were women, with an average age of 39 years, over half of whom were married and employed. On average, they had been depressed for close to 11 years; 25% reported at least one serious suicide attempt, and 54% reported frequent suicidal thinking.

In the behavior-therapy treatment, *in vivo* practice and modeling were used to develop adequate coping skills in seven areas of functioning: communication, behavioral productivity, social interaction, assertiveness, decision making, problem solving, and cognitive self-control. Structured homework assignments were employed, and patients were equipped with well-rehearsed plans for coping with the experience of future depressive episodes. Psychotherapy was based upon a psychodynamic model, and patients in the pharmacotherapy treatment were given a biochemical rationale for their depression and received amitriptyline for a total of 11 weeks. The relaxation-training or attention-placebo treatment involved patients learning to relax in the therapist's office and practicing this skill at home. The relationship between depression and muscle tension was emphasized, and the occurrence of depressive symptoms was attributed to the presence of tension.

Assessment of treatment outcome was based on multiple measures of functioning, including the BDI and measures of cognitive activity, coping, personal activity, social functioning, somatic indicators, mood, and overall satisfaction. An analysis of patients who terminated treatment prematurely shows that the dropout rate for behavior therapy (5%) was significantly lower than that for either the psychotherapy group (30%) or the pharmacotherapy group (36%). The dropout rate in the relaxation-training group was 26%. Dropouts were not included in the data analyses and were replaced by additional patients in order to reduce the effects of a differential attrition rate.

The results at posttreatment showed that behavior therapy was significantly superior to psychotherapy on 6 of the 10 main outcome measures (scores on the BDI, subjective complaints, rating of goal attainment, social functioning, general satisfaction, and mood) and significantly superior to all other treatments on three measures (complaints, goal attainment, and mood). Patients were also divided into three categories at the end of treatment in terms of their BDI scores: A score of less than 7 represented the normal range; a score of less than 23 but more than 7 represented the mildly depressed range; and a score of greater than 23 represented the moderate to severe range of depression. Of the behavior-therapy patients, 50% were in the normal range, as compared to 25% of the patients in both the psychotherapy and pharmacotherapy groups. There was no effect for therapist experience. A 3-month follow-up indicated fewer statistically significant differences. Behavior therapy was more effective than all other treatments were in terms of social functioning, and it was superior to psychotherapy on the mood measure. Similarly, pharmacotherapy produced greater improvement on the mood measure. Overall, behavior therapy registered the greatest improvement on 7 of the 10 measures, while psychotherapy produced the weakest effects on 7 of the 10 outcome variables.

The results are consistent with the Rush *et al.* (1977) findings summarized above that show the superiority of cognitive–behavior therapy over imipramine. Similarly, the fact that behavior therapy resulted in a significantly lower attrition rate than did pharmacotherapy is consistent with the Rush *et al.* findings. Nevertheless, consistent with Kovacs *et al.*'s 1-year follow-up (1981), McLean and Hakstian's follow-up data indicate only one significant difference between behavior therapy and pharmacotherapy.

Finally, Blackburn, Bishop, Glen, Whalley, and Christie (in press) compared Beck's cognitive–behavioral approach to pharmacotherapy and a combined therapeutic approach in the treatment of depressed patients in general clinical practice and a hospital outpatient department respectively. The results were generally consistent with those of the preceding two studies. Patients treated with pharmacotherapy responded less well in both hospital and general practice, and the combination of treatments was superior to drug treatment in both hospital and general practice. In general practice, cognitive therapy was superior to drug treatment. The presence of endogenous features did not affect response to treatment.

The findings of the studies referred to above not only demonstrate the applicability of cognitive–behavioral treatments to mild to severe types of unipolar depression, but they also indicate that these treatments may offer specific therapeutic advantages. Whether or not they will be shown to be the preferred form of psychological therapy must be determined by future outcome research.

To conclude this brief discussion of the applicability of behavior therapy, it is appropriate to cite an appraisal that is more in keeping with current practice than are Marks's estimates. It comes from another psychiatrist, Chesser (1976). He points out that "if one considers behavior therapy as a broad approach which informs and influences the total management of the patient not only in hospital, then the range of applicability can be extended to crisis intervention in families . . . social work . . . group therapy . . . marital problems . . . family therapy . . . interpersonal problems, chronic neurotic depression, weight disorders, alcohol and drug abuse, some organic disorders, and the rehabilitation of patients with organic deficits or chronic schizophrenia" (p. 302). The general applicability of behavior therapy is all the more significant when it is remembered that traditional psychodynamic psychotherapy has always been restricted to carefully selected neurotic and personality disorders (see Candy, Balfour, Cawley, Hildebrand, Malan, Marks, & Wilson, 1972; Kernberg, 1973; Luborsky, Singer, & Luborsky, 1975; Sloane, Staples, Cristol, Yorkston, & Whipple, 1975).

THE SCOPE OF THE PRESENT CHAPTER

Given the broad applicability of behavior therapy to diverse problems in clinical psychology and psychiatry, education, and, increasingly, medicine too, it is impossible to survey the available outcome evidence in one chapter, even in summary form. General reviews of the data bearing on the efficacy of behavior therapy with adults can be found elsewhere (e.g., O'Leary & Wilson, in press; Rachman & Wilson, 1980). Rather than attempting a general overview of the evidence on therapeutic efficacy, the present chapter focuses specifically on two major areas of application—anxiety disorders and sexual disorders. There are a few reasons for this choice.

First, anxiety and sexual disorders are two of the areas in which behavior therapy has been most extensively applied and evaluated. A substantial body of research exists, illustrating both the strengths and weaknesses of the approach in these areas and attempts to evaluate it scientifically. Second, although several excellent reviews of this literature have been published in the past (e.g., Emmelkamp, 1980; Leitenberg, 1976; Marks, 1978; Rachman & Hodgson, 1980), the rapidly moving events in these areas require that these reviews be updated and new issues critically examined. Third, not only is there a concentration of research on the effects of behavior therapy in the treatment of anxiety disorders, but this research has also been directed at investigating some of the basic theoretical underpinnings of behavior therapy as a formal therapeutic system (see Chapters 2, 5, and 8 in this volume, for example). The present chapter does not address theoretical issues; however, a clear understanding of the relative efficacy of different techniques that derive directly from competing theoretical positions is vital to the clarification and ultimate resolution of theoretical conflicts (Bandura, 1969; Rachman & Wilson, 1980). Finally, a searching evaluation of the efficacy of behavioral sex therapy seems most timely in view of recent, well-publicized claims that sex therapy has been uncritically and prematurely accepted and that it is without the empirical foundations that have been allegedly claimed for it.

The material is organized according to the diagnostic categories of the most recent version of the American Psychiatric Association's *Diagnostic and Statistical Manual of Mental Disorders* (DSM-III) (1980). I have adopted this framework because it is convenient to readers who are familiar with this diagnostic grouping; such an adoption is not necessarily an endorsement of the utility of this particular system. No attempt is made at theoretical analysis or at an evaluation of the adequacy of current conceptual models. However, as I note in what follows, outcome studies should be designed to shed light on significant theoretical questions (see Rachman & Wilson, 1980).

Another characteristic of behavior therapy in its third decade is its complexity and diversity. Behavior therapy can no longer be defined neatly as the application of modern learning theory to clinical disorders. Taking a broad view of the field, it is clear that behavior therapy encompasses a wide range of heterogeneous procedures with frequently different theoretical rationales. Contemporary behavior therapy can be best conceptualized as including the following different approaches: applied behavior analysis (e.g., Baer, Wolf, & Risley, 1968; Brigham & Catania, 1979); a neobehavioristic mediational model (e.g., Eysenck, 1976; Wolpe, 1976); social learning theory (e.g., Bandura, 1969; Wilson & O'Leary, 1980), and cognitive-behavior modification (e.g., Mahoney & Arnkoff, 1978; Meichenbaum, 1977). As the reader will observe, this analysis of the conceptual mainstreams of modern-day behavior therapy has provided the framework for Section III of the present volume. This broad view of behavior therapy is adopted for the purpose of evaluating relevant treatment outcome evidence in the remainder of this chapter.

ANXIETY DISORDERS

The subject of Wolpe's pioneering applications of behavioral treatment methods (1958), anxiety disorders (anxiety neuroses) have always been a major focus of behavioral research and therapy. Among the anxiety disorders, phobic reactions have been the most commonly reported targets of behavioral treatment.

PHOBIC DISORDERS

There is a huge literature on the behavioral treatment of phobic disorders, with several comprehensive reviews of treatment outcome (e.g., Emmelkamp, 1980; Marks, 1978; Mavissakalian & Barlow, 1981; Rachman & Wilson, 1980). Here I provide an update of outcome studies, review briefly the status and comparative efficacy of different behavior therapy methods, and relate controlled research to clinical practice.

Simple Phobias

Specific phobias of small animals, snakes, heights, and so on have been the major testing ground of a number of well-known behavior-therapy techniques. A wealth of clinical and experimental evidence has been amassed that must convince even the most begrudging of the critics of behavior therapy that behavioral methods are the treatment of choice for simple phobias. Expositional convenience dictates that these quick and effective treatment techniques be discussed individually.

Systematic Desensitization. One of the earliest and most widely used of all behavior-therapy techniques (see Wolpe, 1958), systematic desensitization has also remained one of the most intensively investigated treatment methods in all of the psychological therapies. In a classic review of the evidence of the efficacy of systematic desensitization, Paul (1969) was able to conclude that "the findings were overwhelmingly positive, and for the first time in the history of psychological treatments, a specific treatment package reliably produced measurable benefits for clients across a broad range of distressing problems in which anxiety was of fundamental importance. 'Relapse' and 'symptom substitution' were notably lacking, although the majority of authors were attuned to these problems" (p. 159). In a still more detailed review 2 years later, Rachman (1971) summarized the experimental evidence on systematic desensitization as follows:

Desensitization therapy effectively reduces phobic behavior. It is unnecessary to ascertain the origin of the phobia in order to eliminate it and neither is it necessary to change the subject's basic attitudes or to modify his [or her] personality. The elimination of a phobia is rarely followed by symptom substitution. The response to treatment is not related to the trait of suggestibility. Relaxation alone, or accompanied by pseudo-therapeutic interviews, does not reduce phobias. The establishment of a therapeutic relationship with the patient does not of itself reduce the phobia. Interpretive therapy combined with relaxation does not reduce phobic behavior. The induction of a state of subjective relaxation facilitates desensitization but is not a prerequisite. The technique can be used effectively even when the subject is not in a state of muscular relaxation. (p. 124)

In 1976, Leitenberg stated that "it seems safe to conclude that systematic desensitization is demonstrably more effective than both no treatment and every psychotherapy variant with which it has so far been compared" (p. 131).

Despite the massive clinical and experimental support that systematic desensitization enjoys, the evidence has not gone unchallenged. Objections to the internal validity of studies of systematic desensitization can be illustrated by reference to Kazdin and Wilcoxon's expert methodological evaluation (1976) of systematic desensitization and nonspecific treatment effects. Simply stated, Kazdin and Wilcoxon's challenging thesis is that there is insufficient evidence that meets demanding methodological criteria to gainsay the hypothesis that the favorable results obtained with systematic desensitization are attributable to so-called nonspecific treatment effects, such as placebo influences and expectations of therapeutic improvement.

In order to exclude alternative explanations of treatment effects in terms of nonspecific therapeutic influences and thus to establish the specific therapeutic power of systematic desensitization in controlled outcome studies, Kazdin and Wilcoxon required that the placebo conditions in these studies had to have been empirically demonstrated to generate expectations of therapeutic improvement that were comparable to those elicited by systematic desensitization. They found that only 5 of the 92 studies they reviewed met these demanding methodological requirements—the studies of D'Zurilla, Wilson, and Nelson (1973); Gelder, Bancroft, Gath, Johnston, Mathews, and Shaw (1973); McReynolds, Barnes, Brooks, and Rehagen (1973); Steinmark and Borkovec (1974); and Wilson (1973). Kazdin and Wilcoxon's evaluation of these five controlled studies is that they "do not support the proposition that desensitization includes a specific therapy ingredient beyond expectancies for improvement" (p. 745).

Of these five studies, the one that is clearly the most important and directly concerned with clinical phobias is the Gelder *et al.* (1973) study. This is also the only study that Kazdin and Wilcoxon view as an exception to the rule that systematic desensitization is no more effective than an equally credible placebo treatment is. Gelder *et al.* compared systematic desensitization and flooding to an attention-placebo condition in the treatment of 18 agoraphobics, 9 social phobics, and 9 simple phobics. In the placebo condition, the therapist presented phobic images to initiate each client's free association, but made no attempt to control the content of subsequent imagery or verbal responses. The clients were told that this exploration of their feelings would enhance self-understanding and decrease their anxiety. All treatments were carried out by experienced therapists explicitly trained in the administration of the different methods. An attempt was made to induce a high expectancy of success in half of the subjects by describing the treatment and therapist chosen in half of the subjects by describing the treatment and therapist chosen in very favorable terms and showing them a videotape of a client who had benefited from the treatment they were to receive. Treatment effects were evaluated in terms of measures of behavioral avoidance, blind psychiatric ratings, client self-ratings, physiological responsiveness, and standardized psychological tests. The adequacy of the control group in eliciting expectancies of treatment success, in comparison with those evoked by the two behavioral methods, was assessed directly; the effects were shown to be comparable across all three treatments.

As noted, half of the clients were agoraphobics, while the other half was a mixed group of simple and social phobias. Clients were assigned to treatments and therapists in a factorial design that permitted an analysis of the possible interactions among treatment effects, therapist differences, type of phobia, and levels of expectancy. Treatments were administered in 15 weekly sessions. In all, the Gelder *et al.* (1973) study was sufficiently well designed and well executed to answer the question, "What treatment method has what specific effect on what problem in whom?" It provided one methodological model according to which specific treatment methods could be compared with each other and with an interpretable placebo control condition.

Both behavioral treatments produced greater improvement than the control condition on the behavioral avoidance tests, physiological arousal measures, psychiatric ratings of the main phobia, and patients' self-ratings of improvement. Simply put, both systematic desensitization and flooding were twice as effective as the convincing pseudotherapy control treatment was. This difference was particularly marked with the agoraphobic patients, indicating that the failure of some studies to demonstrate clear-cut superiority of systematic desensitization over stringent control treatments might have been due to the use of insufficiently phobic subjects. The more disturbed the patients were, the greater the difference between specific behavioral methods and suitable pseudotherapy control was (Mathews, 1978).

Of the remaining four studies identified by Kazdin and Wilcoxon, careful inspection, as Rachman and Wilson (1980) point out, reveals that the Steinmark and Borkovec (1974) and Wilson (1973) investigations actually provide support for the specific therapeutic efficacy of systematic desensitization as opposed to nonspecific therapeutic influences. Moreover, other evidence not considered by Kazdin and Wilcoxon points in the same direction. For example, consider the well-known Paul study (1966, 1967) of speech-anxious college students, in which desensitization was shown to be significantly more effective than were an abbreviated form of psychotherapy, an attention-placebo control, and a no-treatment control at posttreatment and at a 2-year follow-up. This well-controlled study was not counted as evidence for the efficacy of desensitization per se by Kazdin and Wilcoxon, because Paul did not report an assessment of how credible his attention-placebo control treatment was in developing positive expectations of therapeutic outcome. Both Borkovec and Nau (1972) and McReynolds *et al.* (1973) have reported findings that suggest that the rationale provided for Paul's attention-placebo group was less convincing and credible than that provided for desensitization proper. However, it must not be forgotten that Paul demonstrated conclusively that systematic desensitization was greatly superior to the form of short-term psychotherapy he evaluated. Although it is clear that this result cannot be used to argue that psychotherapy is ineffective or that systematic desensitization would be more effective than alternative forms of psychotherapy, to dismiss Paul's psychotherapy treatment as less credible to the subjects in that study than systematic desensitization was would seem to be highly implausible. The psychotherapy treatment was administered by well-qualified, practicing psychotherapists who were using their preferred method of therapy; these psychotherapists reported that they were confident that the psychotherapy they conducted would be effective; and the subjects rated the therapists in the psychotherapy condition as no less competent nor less likeable than those in the systematic-desensitization treatment were rated. The psychotherapy condition in Paul's study is viewed best as a stringent and persuasive placebo treatment that was significantly less effective than systematic desensitization.

The same argument can be made for other studies that were included in the Kazdin and Wilcoxon review but deemed deficient with respect to ensuring equal credibility between desensitization and placebo controls. An example is the Gillan and Rachman (1974) study of 32 multiphobic patients, 11 of whom were agoraphobic, in which desensitization was shown to be significantly superior both to a pseudotherapy control *and* to a psychotherapy condition administered by psychiatrists with training in psychotherapy. Independent assessments of therapeutic expectations generated by these different treatments were not reported, but, whatever the fate of the pseudotherapy condition, it is highly unlikely from everything that is known that the psychotherapy treatment was not perceived by the subjects in this investigation as comparable to desensitization in plausibility as a form of treatment.

To summarize the discussion up to this point, it is argued that the available evidence does provide support for the view that the well-established efficacy of systematic desensitization is attributable to the specific components of this technique itself, rather than to more general expectations of therapeutic improvement that are created by highly credible and persuasive treatment rationales.

Flooding. "Flooding" involves therapist-directed, prolonged exposure to high-intensity anxiety-eliciting stimulation. It is important to distinguish between flooding and "implosion therapy," a treatment that relies solely upon exposure to threatening material in imagination (Stampfl & Levis, 1967). In implosion therapy, the aversive nature of the phobic situations is deliberately exaggerated, with an emphasis on horrifying scenes that include adverse consequences to the client. Another characteristic of implosion therapy is that much of the material the client is instructed to imagine is based on psychoanalytic concepts, such as Oedipal themes, repressed sexuality, and so on. By contrast, flooding is increasingly conducted *in vivo,* although several studies have examined the effects of flooding in imagination. No attention is paid to psychoanalytically inspired stimulus material; exposure is to the actual cues that the client fears.

There is no evidence that the inclusion of psychoanalytically based cues in flooding has any therapeutic effect. Marshall, Gauthier, Christie, Currie, and Gordon (1977) showed that the inclusion of implosion-type material in the flooding procedure impaired treatment outcome. Immediate *in vivo* exposure to the feared object proved to be most effective in reducing avoidance behavior. These findings contradict the claims of proponents of implosion therapy, who emphasize the necessity of including psychoanalytic cues. Similarly, Foa, Blau, Prout, and Latimer (1977) found that adding "horror" imagery to the flooding procedure had little effect on treatment outcome. At this point, it can be concluded that the unrealistic and physically damaging imagery that is induced in implosion therapy is unnecessary for successful treatment.

Several detailed reviews of flooding (Leitenberg, 1976; Marks, 1978; Mathews, 1978) and implosion (Levis & Hare, 1977) have been published. In evaluating the efficacy of flooding as a treatment technique, it appears that it is particularly important to take account of the subject populations and problems with which it has been used (Mathews, 1978). In an early review of flooding and implosion therapy, Morganstern (1973) concluded that these methods, at best, were no more effective than systematic desensitization was; that they were often less effective than desensitization was; that they entailed such disadvantages as high relapse rates or increased variability in outcome at follow-up; and that they frequently produced negative side effects, such as nightmares and resistance to continued treatment (e.g., Barrett, 1969). However, the vast majority of the early studies on flooding consisted of studies of college students, the intensity of whose fears was not very severe and whose motivation for therapy was probably questionable. Mathews (1978) points out that the only study of clinically phobic patients in the Morganstern review was that by Marks, Boulougouris, and Marset (1971). In this study, flooding was more effective than systematic desensitization; a favorably low subject attrition rate was obtained; and adverse consequences, such as patient resistance to treatment sessions, were found to be generally nonexistent. This discrepancy might well be accounted for by the fact that participants in the laboratory-based studies of college students were less motivated and committed to treatment than were the phobic patients treated by Marks *et al.* (1971).

Marks *et al.* compared flooding to systematic desensitization in a study of seven simple phobics and nine agoraphobics, using a crossover design in which the patients received six sessions of the one treatment followed shortly thereafter by six sessions of the other. The results showed that, although both treatments produced improvements on the combined ratings of the therapist and independent assessor in the main and total phobias, flooding produced significantly greater improvement. A 1-year follow-up indicated that gains made during therapy were maintained.

In the study by Gelder *et al.* (1973) referred to above, flooding was significantly more effective than was a stringent placebo control, showing that flooding produces successful treatment of simple phobias and agoraphobia independent of placebo influences. However, this same study revealed no differences between flooding and systematic desensitization, nor were there any differences in the response of different types of phobias to flooding. Using subjects with phobias of snakes or spiders, Marshall *et al.* (1977) found that a combination of flooding in imagination and *in vivo* was more effective in reducing fear and avoidance behavior than was either systematic desensitization or an attention placebo. To summarize, flooding is an effective treatment for simple phobias and may even be superior to systematic desensitization in this respect.

Modeling. Several types of modeling procedures have been shown to reliably eliminate simple phobias (Rachman, 1976; Rosenthal & Bandura, 1978). A series of studies by Bandura and his colleagues, using snake-phobic subjects, has not only documented the efficacy of modeling as a means of reducing fear and phobic behavior, but has also contributed to a theoretical analysis of fear-reduction mechanisms in all behavioral-treatment methods that are discussed in this chapter (Bandura, 1977). In an illustrative study from this impressive program of research, Bandura, Blanchard, and Ritter (1969) compared systematic desensitization with symbolic modeling, participant modeling, and a no-treatment control. "Participant modeling" is a multicomponent approach in which the person's feared activities are repeatedly modeled without the model's experiencing any adverse consequences. The client is then encouraged and physically assisted by the therapist in performing carefully graduated subtasks of previously threatening activites, in increasing order of difficulty. The basic principle involves arranging the environment and supporting the client in such a way that the likelihood of the feared consequences is reduced; a sufficient reduction allows the client to engage in previously avoided behavior and to experience success in practicing his or her newly developed sense of emotional freedom and lack of behavioral restraint across a variety of everyday living situations. As the treatment progresses, the therapist gradually withdraws supportive aids until the client can fearlessly engage in the behaviors without assistance.

Following comprehensive pretreatment assessment of the cognitive, affective, and behavioral components of their phobia about snakes, one group of subjects received orthodox desensitization treatment, in which imaginal representation of increasingly aversive scenes involving snakes was paired with relaxation. A second group receiving self-administered symbolic modeling relaxed themselves while observing a graduated film showing children and adults engaging in progressively more threatening interactions with a snake. The rate of presentation of the modeled stimuli was regulated by the subjects by means of a remote-controlled projector, so that any anxiety-provoking scene was repeatedly viewed until completely neutralized before they moved on to the next scene in the hierarchial sequence. The third group received participant modeling.

Desensitization and symbolic modeling resulted in considerable improvement at posttesting, while participant modeling produced the greatest gains, eliminating phobic behavior in 92% of subjects. Nontreated control subjects showed no change in any response measure. The control subjects subsequently received symbolic modeling without relaxation training. The results indicated no difference between symbolic modeling administered with or without relaxation. Several other findings from this well-designed study are noteworthy. First, not only did the treatment techniques effect substantial behavioral changes, but they also produced favorable changes in subjects' affective and attitudinal responses toward snakes with participant modeling proving to be the most powerful form of treatment. Second, an analysis of a comprehensive fear inventory that was administered to the subjects before and after therapy revealed decrements in other types of reported anxiety than the snake phobia specifically treated. Desensitization reduced the intensity of fears about animals in general, but only the modeling groups, particularly those receiving modeling with guided participation, produced an overall decrease in the number of fears about animals and a reduction in anxieties related to other areas of functioning, including both interpersonal and nonsocial situations. Nontreated controls showed no changes in either the intensity or number of fears. Finally, Bandura *et al.* (1969) administered the participant modeling procedure to all subjects who had shown only partial improvement at posttesting, with the result that their phobic behavior was completely eliminated in all cases. This demonstration indicates that specific technique variables, rather than any characteristic of the subjects, were responsible for the therapeutic improvement. All therapeutic gains were maintained at a 1-month follow-up.

"Covert modeling" is a procedure in which the patient does not observe a live or filmed model, but imagines a model engaging in phobic behavior. In a series of well-controlled studies using snake phobics, Kazdin (see Kazdin & Smith, 1979) has demonstrated the efficacy of this method and identified some of its important procedural parameters. The following factors enhance treatment outcome: imagination of multiple models; reinforcement of models for overcoming their problem; and imagination of a coping model who gradually overcomes initial fear, as opposed to a "mastery" model who performs fearlessly from the outset.

Conclusion. The evidence clearly shows that performance-based methods such as participant modeling are more efficient and effective than either symbolic modeling or imagery-based techniques such as covert modeling and systematic desensitization are (Bandura, 1977; Wilson & O'Leary, 1980).

There appears to be little differential effectiveness among symbolic and covert modeling and systematic desensitization (Rosenthal & Bandura, 1978). Participant modeling has also been shown to be significantly more effective than is a cognitive restructuring treatment derived from Ellis's (1970) rational–emotive therapy (RET) and Goldfried's (1979) rational restructuring technique (see Biran & Wilson, 1981). In this study, 22 phobics with fears of heights, elevators, or darkness were treated with either participant modeling or cognitive restructuring. Participant modeling produced significantly greater improvement across behavioral, subjective, and physiological measures of fear than cognitive restructuring did. Over 80% of subjects treated with participant modeling obtained complete relief from their phobias after only five therapy sessions. Moreover, these treatment-produced gains were fully maintained at a 6-month follow-up. Cognitive restructuring resulted in relatively minimal improvement, calling into question the value of this approach in treating simple phobias.

Behavior therapy is the obvious treatment of choice for simple phobias. No other approach, psychological or pharmacological, can rival behavior therapy in terms of efficiency or efficacy in eliminating these problems.

The Issue of Analogue versus Clinical Research. A frequent criticism of many of the studies of snake-phobic subjects described above is that the findings of this analogue research are not applicable to clinical populations (e.g., Marks, 1978). The relevance of analogue studies in outcome research is discussed by Kazdin in Chapter 10 of this volume. The reader is also referred to detailed discussions of this issue in Borkovec and Rachman (1979), Kazdin and Wilson (1978), and Rachman and Wilson (1980). Suffice it to point out that the applicability of analogue studies to clinical practice will depend upon the intensity and type of problem studied rather than upon the status of the subject sample (namely, subjects recruited for a study as opposed to patients seen in a clinic). As Rachman and Wilson (1980) note, "if the fears of analogue subjects are intense and similar in type to those of the clinical subjects, then generalizing from one group to the next is likely to be successful in most instances. The main objection to analogue research falls away. . . . The wholesale dismissal of analogue research cannot be justified on empirical or on theoretical grounds. Calling a study an 'analogue' is a description, not a criticism" (p. 263).

Consider, for example, the snake-phobic subjects in Bandura's research on fear-reduction methods. Unlike so many laboratory-based investigations using only mildly fearful college students whose motivation change was questionable, at best, and hence of little relevance to an evaluation of therapy outcome, the snake-phobic subjects in these studies exhibited intense phobic reactions that they were strongly motivated to overcome. As a result of their phobias, these subjects were unable to participate in highly desired activities. Examples of this functional impairment of their daily life styles included the inability to walk in the garden, go on camping trips, live in wooded areas, and so on. Aside from this behavioral hindrance, the vast majority of subjects reported recurrent nightmares and a variety of distressing thoughts and ruminations about snakes. There is no reason for considering these problems different from the sort of simple phobias therapists encounter in routine clinical practice.

Social Phobias

Several of the studies described in the previous section included subjects who were social phobics, for example, 9 in the Gelder *et al.* (1973) study and 5 in the Gillan and Rachman (1974) investigation. The findings from these and other studies indicate that social phobias can be treated as effectively as simple phobias can by either systematic desensitization or flooding. Additional support for this conclusion comes from a 4-year follow-up of different phobic patients who had originally been treated either with systematic desensitization or psychotherapy (Marks, 1971). Over 20% of these 65 patients suffered from social phobias. No differences were observed between these patients and their counterparts with simple phobias or agoraphobia, either at posttreatment or the long-term follow-up.

A comparative outcome study by Shaw (1979) examined the relative efficacy of systematic desensitization, flooding, and social skills training in the treatment of 30 seriously incapacitated social phobics. Systematic desensitization and flooding were carried out entirely in imagination, whereas the social skills training was performance-based. Treatment outcome was assessed using multiple measures of subjects' fear and avoidance behavior. The results showed that all three methods produced substantial therapeutic improvement that was maintained at a 6-month follow-up. No differences were found between treatments. It is impossible to rule out an explanation of these findings in terms of a "nonspecific" therapeutic factor such as therapist contact, as Shaw observes.

It is usually the case in behavioral research on phobic disorders that patients with the same diagnosis (e.g., social phobia or agoraphobia) are grouped together than then randomly assigned to different treatment methods. Ost, Jerremalm, and Johansson (1981) went beyond this customary design in taking account of individual differences in patterns of fear response. Following participation in a structured social interaction test, 40 social phobics were classified as either "behavioral" or "physiological" responders. The former were rated as high on behavioral indices of social anxiety and showed low physiological arousal. The latter displayed the opposite pattern. Subjects within each of these experimentally structured groups then received either relaxation training or social skills training (a similar procedure to that used by Shaw, 1979). In sum, Ost *et al.* compared a treatment that corresponded to the subjects' response pattern with treatment that did not.

Treatment consisted of 10 individual sessions. The within-group comparisons showed that both treatments yielded significant improvements on most measures. The between-group comparisons showed that for the behavioral reactors, social skills training was significantly better than applied relaxation was on most of the measures; for the physiological reactors, relaxation was significantly better than social skills training on some of the measures. Ost *et al.* concluded that these data indicate that superior treatment effects are obtained when the method meshes with the patient's response pattern.

Excessive fear and avoidance of public speaking are often diagnosed as social phobia. Paul's standard-setting study (1966), referred to in the discussion of simple phobias, unequivocally demonstrated the efficacy of systematic desensitization with such individuals. It should be noted, however, that the subjects in Paul's investigation were drawn from a normal college undergraduate population and cannot be said to have been neurotic in the light of their performance on standardized tests of anxiety and neuroticism. Treating a comparable population of speech-anxious subjects, Meichenbaum, Gilmore, and Fedoravicius (1971) replicated the superiority of systematic desensitization over placebo and no-treatment controls and also showed that the technique of self-instructional training was as efficacious as systematic desensitization was. Self-instructional training in particular, and cognitive-behavior therapy in general, have been broadly used to treat a range of social anxieties that are not unrelated to specific social phobias, including interpersonal anxiety, lack of assertiveness, heterosexual anxiety, and test anxiety. Some significant successes have been achieved in these areas (Rachman & Wilson, 1980), and representative findings are summarized below in a dicussion of social anxiety.

Despite the reported success of cognitive restructuring methods in the treatment of social anxiety, Biran, Augusto, and Wilson (1981) were unable to obtain comparable findings in the treatment of three specific social phobics. Each patient suffered from a debilitating fear and avoidance of writing or signing her name in public, particularly if the situation involved the possibility of being scrutinized by strangers. Cognitive restructuring, based on Goldfried's (1979) method of rational restructuring, failed to reduce the patients' fear or phobic avoidance. Nevertheless, a therapist-assisted *in vivo* exposure procedure produced prompt and lasting eradication of phobic avoidance, although some subjective anxiety persisted at a 9-month follow-up. The efficacy of cognitive restructuring for specific social phobias thus remains to be demonstrated. At present, the treatment of choice, as in the case of simple phobias, would appear to be systematic exposure, preferably *in vivo,* to the fear-producing situations.

Agoraphobia

Agoraphobia is generally regarded as the most complex and most difficult to treat of all the phobic disorders. Yet the Gelder *et al.* (1973), Gillan and Rachman (1974), and Marks *et al.* (1971) studies referred to above have all provided convincing evidence of the efficacy of behavioral treatment methods for this disorder. Clinical experience and experimental research have shown that the most effective procedures are those that rely upon systematic *in vivo* exposure to the feared situations (Marks, 1978; Mathews, 1978). Imaginal systematic desensitization or flooding, without explicit *in vivo* practice, cannot be recommended.

Different forms of *in vivo* exposure treatment have been used to treat agoraphobic patients: flooding *in vivo,* which is designed to elicit maximum anxiety by confronting the patient with his or her most intense anxiety-eliciting cues as soon as possible; graduated *in vivo* exposure, which is conducted on a graduated or hierarchical basis so as to confront the patient with his or her feared situations but without evoking intense anxiety; and participant modeling, a procedure that is similar to graduated *in vivo* exposure but that also explicitly incorporates a number of "response-induction aids"—prior modeling by the therapist, verbal support and reassurance, and so on—deliberately designed to enable reluctant patients to confront their feared situations or activities. Controlled clinical research, much of it carried out in England and Holland, has established a number of factors that critically influence the therapeutic effects of these *in vivo* exposure methods. These factors can be summarized as follows:

1. Flooding *in vivo* is more effective than flooding in imagination is (e.g., Emmelkamp & Wessels, 1975). It is noteworthy that in such impressive demonstrations of the efficacy of flooding in the treatment of agoraphobic patients as the Gelder *et al.* (1973) and Marks *et al.* (1971) studies, imaginal exposure was followed in each session by *in vivo* exposure to the feared situation. The superior efficacy of flooding *in vivo* is consistent with other evidence showing that all fear-reduction techniques, including desensitization and modeling procedures, appear to be more successful when conducted *in vivo* rather than on a symbolic level (Bandura, 1977).

An informative study in this regard was conducted by Mathews, Johnston, Lancashire, Munby, Shaw, and Gelder (1976). Three treatments were compared: (1) 8 sessions of imaginal flooding followed by 8 sessions of flooding *in vivo*; (2) 16 sessions of combined imaginal and *in vivo* treatment; and (3) 16 sessions of *in vivo* exposure alone. The dependent measures were similar to those used by Gelder *et al.* (1973), as described above. The results showed no significant difference among treatments at 8 weeks, at 16 weeks, or at a 6-month follow-up.

The failure to find differences among the three treatments could be due to the fact that they were all equally effective. Alternatively, this outcome could merely reflect the operation of nonspecific treatment factors common to all methods. However, the Mathews group rejected the latter explanation on the grounds that the improvement observed in these agoraphobic patients was comparable to that obtained by Gelder *et al.* (1973) and significantly better than the minimal improvement achieved by the highly credible placebo control in the Gelder *et al.* study. A more plausible interpretation of the results bears on the nature of the patients' activities between rather than during treatment sessions. Considerable emphasis was placed on the patients' self-directed practice attempts at *in vivo* exposure in their home settings. This is all the more likely, since treatment spanned a relatively long time—16 weeks —whereas previous studies demonstrating the superiority of *in vivo* over imaginal methods were much briefer in duration. This longer period provided more time to practice. Johnston, Lancashire, Mathews, Munby, Shaw, and Gelder (1976) conducted an analysis of the weekly measures of change in the study just described and related these within treatment measures to outcome at follow-up. Aside from confirming the presence of a therapist effect, Johnston *et al.*'s analyses show that the immediate effects of the treatment were different. Thus, *in vivo* exposure had immediate positive effects, whereas imaginal flooding had no obvious short-term effect. The authors suggested that both methods facilitated self-directed practice between sessions and that this was the effective agent of therapeutic change.

2. The longer the exposure to the feared situation is, the more effective flooding is likely to be. For instance, Stern and Marks (1973) found that 2 hours of continuous exposure *in vivo* was significantly more effective than 4 separate half hours in one afternoon in the treatment of agoraphobics. Too short a duration of exposure may, in certain circumstances, actually result in a temporary increase in phobic arousal (McCutcheon & Adams, 1975; Stone & Borkovec, 1975).

3. It is unnecessary to elicit intense expression of anxiety during *in vivo* exposure, a finding that discredits the original learning rationale behind flooding and implosion therapy (Levis & Hare, 1977). The evidence is consistent in showing that patients' anxiety level during flooding does not correlate with subsequent outcome (Hafner & Marks, 1976; Johnston *et al.*, 1976; Mathews, 1978; Mathews & Rezin, 1977; Stern & Marks, 1973).

4. Consistent with the previous point, there is evidence that gradual *in vivo* exposure to the phobic situation is as effective as instant exposure to the maximally fear-producing situation (as in flooding).

5. Flooding and graduated *in vivo* exposure conducted within a group setting are as effective as individual treatments (e.g., Bandura, Adams, Hardy, & Howells, 1980; Hand, Lamontagne, & Marks, 1974).

6. *In vivo* exposure treatment in which the exposure is client-controlled may be as effective as therapist-controlled exposure is, and it is more cost-effective (e.g., Emmelkamp, 1980).

7. Home-based treatment, making use of a treatment manual, and active spouse involvement, produces improvement comparable to that achieved with more intensive therapist-administered treatment in the clinic (Jannoun, Munby, Catalan, & Gelder, 1980; Mathews, Teasdale, Munby, Johnston, & Shaw, 1977). Home-based, spouse-assisted treatment is not only cost-effective but might also result in superior maintenance of treatment-produced change (Munby & Johnston, 1980).

8. *In vivo* exposure treatment conducted by nursing personnel under the supervision of a professional behavior therapist appears to be comparable to treatment carried out by clinical psychologists or psychiatrists. This increases the cost–benefit ratio for efficient delivery of treatment services (e.g., Marks, Hallam, Connolly, & Philpott, 1977). Yet it would be well to note that a therapist effect was evident in two major studies, despite the highly standardized treatment format (Jannoun *et al.,* 1980; Mathews, Johnston, Lancashire, Munby, Shaw, & Gelder, 1976).

9. Supplementing *in vivo* exposure with self-instructional training does not increase therapeutic efficacy (Emmelkamp & Mersch, in press; Williams & Rappoport, 1980). *In vivo* exposure has been significantly more effective than cognitive restructuring methods alone have been (Emmelkamp, Kuipers, & Eggeraat, 1978). However, *in vivo* exposure methods have not always been strictly behavioral interventions. Rather, they also involve an explicit focus on the patient's thoughts and feelings that would qualify them as "cognitive–behavioral" methods, according to some classifications of treatment methods (Wilson, in press).

10. Although consistently effective in the majority of cases, programmed *in vivo* exposure is not essential for the successful treatment of agoraphobia. Aside from the effects of pharmacotherapy in some instances (see below), a problem-solving treatment aimed at lowering a patient's level of arousal by identifying relevant life stresses and finding ways of reducing or resolving them, with the active cooperation and involvement of the patient's spouse, has shown therapeutic promise (Jannoun *et al.,* 1980). (See DeSilva & Rachman, 1981, for an extended discussion of this theoretically important point.)

Long-Term Efficacy of Treatment. Systematic evaluations of the long-term efficacy of treatment are relatively rare in research on the psychological therapies, including behavior therapy. Encouragingly, lengthy follow-ups of the behavioral treatment of agoraphobia have been reported. In Oxford, England, Munby and Johnston (1980) conducted a long-term follow-up of the agoraphobic patients of the Gelder *et al.* (1973), Mathews, Johnston, Lancashire, Munby, Shaw, and Gelder (1976), and Mathews *et al.* (1977) studies. Of the 66 patients who had been treated in these three studies, 95% were interviewed by a psychiatric research worker 5 to 9 years later. Follow-up measures, repeating those used in the original studies, were compared with those obtained prior to treatment and 6 months after treatment ended. On most measures of agoraphobia, the patients were much better at follow-up than they had been before treatment. The assessor's ratings suggested that there had been little change in the patients' agoraphobia since 6 months after treatment. Some of the patients' self-ratings showed evidence of a slight improvement over this period. No evidence of any symptom substitution was found. The patients who showed the greatest reductions in agoraphobia were, at follow-up, among the least anxious and depressed. However, interpretation of these findings must be tempered by the report that a sizeable number of these former patients had received additional treatment over the follow-up period. Excluding these subjects from the analysis of the data did little to change the outcome, however. Another result that suggests caution in evaluating these data is that at the end of follow-up, 8 of the 12 patients treated with behavior therapy in the Gelder *et al.* (1973) study, 25 of the 34 patients treated by Mathews, Johnston, Lancashire, Munby, Shaw, and Gelder (1976), and 4 of the 11 patients in the Mathews *et al.* (1977) study were receiving psychotropic drugs.

Three other long-term follow-ups provide further support for the durable effects of *in vivo* exposure treatments of agoraphobic patients. In Holland, Emmelkamp and Kuipers (1979) followed up 70 outpatient agoraphobics, derived from a sample of 81 patients who had received exposure treatments 4 years previously. All information was obtained from questionnaires that were mailed to patients. Improvements in phobic fear and avoidance obtained during treatment were maintained, and on some of the measures further improvement occurred; there was also a reduction in depression in the follow-up period, and no new neurotic disturbances developed. In Scotland, McPherson, Brougham, and McLaren (1980), using a postal follow-up of 56 agoraphobics who had shown improvement when treated with *in vivo* exposure, similarly found that treatment gains were maintained 4 years later. Finally, Marks (1971) reported satisfactory maintenance of treatment-produced change in phobic patients at a 4-year follow-up.

Comparative Efficacy of Behavior Therapy and Alternative Treatments. Few comparative outcome studies have been completed, and those that are available have their methodological limitations (see Kazdin & Wilson, 1978, for a detailed analysis of this literature). Gillan and Rachman (1974) found that systematic desensitization was significantly superior to psychotherapy in their study, while Gelder, Marks, and Wolff (1967) showed that systematic desensitization was more efficient than individual or group psychotherapy. In this study, desensitization was significantly superior to individual and group psychotherapy. At the end of treatment, the difference in favor of desensitization was not statistically significant. However, this assessment was made at the end of the treatment of longest duration, group psychotherapy, after 18 months. Systematic desensitization had been terminated after 9 months. Thus, what was posttreatment assessment for group psychotherapy represented a 9-month follow-up for the behavioral treatment. Moreover, the number of clients whose phobias were rated as "much improved" by two or three raters at the final evaluation were as follows: systematic desensitization, 9 of 16 (56%); individual psychotherapy, 3 of 10 (33%); and group psychotherapy, 2 of 16 (12.5%). In terms of this criterion, systematic desensitization was clearly more effective. These meager data do not permit a definitive conclusion that behavioral methods are superior to alternative psychological treatments. However, the dearth of any independent evidence indicating that psychotherapy is effective in treating agoraphobia clearly leaves behavior therapy as the psychological treatment of choice at present.

A handful of studies have compared behavioral methods with antidepressant drugs. Lipsedge, Hajioff, Huggins, Napier, Pearce, Pike, and Rich (1973) found no differences among combined drug (an MAO inhibitor) and systematic desensitization, systematic desensitization plus a placebo, and the drug alone, although all three treatments were more effective than the placebo alone. Similarly, Solyom, Heseltine, McClure, Solyom, Ledwidge, and Steinberg (1973) obtained no differences between pharmacotherapy (an MAO inhibitor) and behavioral treatment (systematic desensitization and flooding), although both methods seemed to be more effective than a combination of a placebo and supportive psychotherapy. Neither study tested performance-based behavioral methods, which are clearly the most effective of the behavior-therapy techniques, and both relied upon inadequate clinical ratings as dependent measures.

The first of two studies by Zitrin and her associates (Zitrin, Klein, & Woerner, 1978) compared imipramine plus systematic desensitization, imipramine plus supportive psychotherapy, and systematic desensitization plus a placebo in the treatment of chronic agoraphobics, mixed phobics, and simple phobics. Both drug treatments were superior to desensitization plus placebo treatment for the agoraphobics, but not for the simple phobics. Systematic desensitization was not significantly different from supportive psychotherapy with any of the groups of phobics. However, among the simple phobics, 60% treated with systematic desensitization were rated by the independent assessor as "markedly improved," compared to 29% of the patients treated with supportive psychotherapy. This difference appears more impressive when it is realized that 42% of the patients treated with supportive psychotherapy plus imipramine dropped out of therapy. The comparable figures for behavior therapy plus imipramine and placebo, respectively, were 29% and 10%. This differential attrition rate can be seen as artefactually inflating the success of the supportive psychotherapy. Two other findings are important. The attrition rate was higher for patients treated with imipramine than for those treated with the placebo. Similarly, during a 1-year follow-up, the relapse rate was greater (but statistically nonsignificant) among patients treated with imipramine than it was among patients who received the placebo.

Several shortcomings with this study complicate interpretation. All results are based on global clinical ratings, the limitations of which are well established (see below). Furthermore, debatable differences between the behavior-therapy and supportive-psychotherapy treatments (Kazdin & Wilson, 1978) and the absence of a direct comparison between imipramine and behavioral treatments (Hollon & Beck, 1978) tend to obscure the findings.

In a second study, Zitrin, Klein, and Woerner (1980) treated 75 agoraphobic women in groups using *in vivo* exposure. Half of the patients received imipramine; the other half received a placebo. Following an initial 4 weeks of drug treatment, *in vivo* exposure sessions were begun that lasted for an additional 10 weeks. Thereafter, imipramine treatment was continued for another 3 months. The same limited, global clinical ratings once again indicated the greater efficacy of imipramine as compared to placebo. The attrition rate was a high 29% in both conditions.

Zitrin (1981) observes that in both of these studies, "the vast majority of patients were moderately to markedly improved both globally and in relation to the primary phobia at the completion of the treatment" (p. 166). Zitrin also notes that over 60% of these patients had previously been treated unsuccessfully with traditional psychoanalytic psychotherapy. However, the inadequacy of the dependent measure calls for caution in interpreting these results. Finally, consistent with other behavioral outcome studies, Zitrin found no evidence of either symptom substitution or therapy-induced negative effects. "On the contrary," she comments, "we found a significant improvement in the quality of their lives; better functioning at home and at work, increased social life, expanded interests and activities, and improved interpersonal relationships. In general, there was a greater richness in the fabric of their lives. With stresses and traumas, there often was a recurrence of the old phobic behavior, rather than the emergence of new symptoms" (p. 169).

Lastly, research has failed to show any therapeutic advantages of combining behavioral methods of fear reduction with diazepam or intravenous administration of Brevital (e.g., Chambless, Foa, Groves, & Goldstein, 1979; Marks, 1978).

Caveats and Conclusions. The preceding summary of controlled research on the behavioral treatment of agoraphobics has been based on reports of statistically significant differences between treatments and control conditions. These criteria leave unanswered the question of clinical significance—namely, precisely what is meant by "treatment success"? What is the likelihood that an individual agoraphobic seeking therapy will be helped, and, specifically, what can that person expect if therapy is successful? Regrettably, the answers to these pressing clinical concerns are difficult to come by.

Summarizing the effects of behavior therapy for agoraphobia, Barlow, Mavissakalian, and Hay (1981) have the following to say:

Although summary statements are difficult, due to differing methods of assessment and lack of follow-up in some studies, it appears that the dropout rate from exposure *in vivo* treatments ranges between 8[%] and 40%, with a median of about 22%. Similarly, the improvement rate among those who complete treatment seems to average between 60[%] and 75%, and this is without specifying the degree of improvement (Mavissakalian & Barlow, 1981). Thus, the number of patients who are unimproved or perhaps worse off as the result of this procedure is as high as 40% of those who complete treatment. Interpersonal factors must play a role in this high failure rate. (p. 246)

Estimates of this sort are naturally somewhat arbitrary, and a host of moderating factors, some of which are discussed below, could affect the treatment outcome across different settings. Nonetheless, even if it is assumed that this estimate has reasonable validity, it still remains to specify the nature of the therapeutic changes that these methods effect. To rely upon "at least some clinically relevant effect" is unacceptably vague. Yet careful reading of the research reports makes it difficult to construct an adequate picture of clinical change.

Ideally, multiple objective and subjective measures of outcome, using the triple-response system to analyze changes in fear and avoidance, and including measures of generalized change (e.g., interpersonal functioning, marital satisfaction, work productivity, etc.) can be called for (Rachman & Wilson, 1980). Available outcome evidence is simply inadequate on many of these counts. The primary dependent measure in a majority of studies has been independent clinical ratings of treatment outcome (e.g., Marks, 1978). The limitations of these clinical ratings have been detailed elsewhere (e.g., Kazdin & Wilson, 1978; Rachman & Hodgson, 1980). Changes of 1 or 2 points on a 5- or 9-point rating scale that assesses phobic anxiety and avoidance in different situations (e.g., a supermarket, public transportation, a busy street, etc.) provide a very limited view of therapeutic progress, irrespective of the high reliability among assessors using these scales (Emmelkamp & Kuipers, 1979; Marks, 1971). Moreover, the validity of these scales has yet to be firmly established. Williams and Rappoport (1980) found that the 9-point fear questionnaire used in many of these studies was only modestly correlated with objective behavioral assessment of agoraphobics' functioning. The rating tended to strongly overestimate subjects' degree of improvement compared to the behavioral test, and the authors concluded that "such measures may at times overestimate the value of weak treatments while obscuring real differences in effectiveness existing between treatment methods."

Commendably, some studies have included behavioral assessment of treatment outcome, such as the Williams and Rappoport (1980) investigation just mentioned. Yet there are problems with this type of measurement as well. Typically, behavioral assessments focus narrowly on one particular aspect of agoraphobics' functioning. Thus Williams and Rappoport only assessed their subjects' actual driving behavior. The degree to which changes were produced across other areas of functioning is unclear. In their research program, Emmelkamp and his colleagues employed the following measure of behavioral change. The patient had to walk along a certain route from the hospital toward the center of town. He was instructed to stay outside until he began to feel uncomfortable or tense, then he had to come directly back. The duration of time spent outside by the patient was measured by the therapist. The maximum time was set at 100 minutes in connection with the calculations to be made. While yielding statistically significant differences, therapists might question the clinical significance of an overall difference between two treatment groups of roughly 30 minutes' time spent walking outside the hospital. Indeed, it might be concluded that this represents progress but hardly the stuff of which "cures" are made. In these, as in other studies, readers are left to form an overall impression of therapeutic change from the clinical ratings.

Zitrin and her associates attempted to obtain behavioral measures of their patients' performance, but gave up, claiming that such a measure "proved to be highly unreliable because the patients, in order to please the examiner, put pressure on themselves to do things that they had not done for long periods of time. For example, a patient who had not been in an elevator for years, when taken by the evaluator before treatment to an elevator and asked to go in, could comply" (1981, pp. 149–150). Far from dismissing such a finding as evidence of "unreliability," the contemporary behavioral researcher, guided by the triple-response system, would attach considerable significance to this result. It raises questions about the nature of patients' phobic distress and leaves readers to guess at the pattern of results that might have emerged were behavioral measures to have been consistently gathered.

The most adequate assessment of behavioral change has been reported by the Oxford group (Gelder *et al.,* 1973; Mathews, Johnston, Lancashire, Munby, Shaw, & Gelder, 1976). For each subject, a 10-item hierarchy was constructed of testable situations, covering the range from a situation that the patient found totally unfearful to the most frightening situation the patient could imagine. Typical hierarchy situations were going up two floors in an elevator alone (item 3), driving along an elevated motorway (item 6), and walking across a suspension bridge (item 9). The Oxford group also had patients record in diaries the time spent away from their houses each week (Mathews *et al.,* 1977). The findings from this study indicated that the average time spent out of the house prior to treatment was 15.8 hours, with figures of 23.3 hours and 27 hours reported at the 6-month and 5-year follow-ups respectively. However, Munby and Johnston (1980) caution that over the long-term follow-up, the diaries provided "rather unsatisfactory measures for comparison . . . since large changes in life style seriously threaten the validity of time out of the home as a measure of agoraphobia; for example, two patients had babies during the follow-up period and this had reduced the time they spent out of the house without affecting the severity of agoraphobia assessed in other ways" (p. 423).

The clinical picture of agoraphobics after behavioral treatment shows that they do not develop other neurotic symptoms, that depression frequently decreases, and that no evidence of symptom substitution can be found (Emmelkamp, 1980; Marks, 1971; Munby & Johnston, 1980; Zitrin, 1981). However, patients do continue to be troubled by their primary agoraphobic problems (Marks, 1971; McPherson *et al.,* 1980). Of 57 patients treated by the Oxford group in their series of studies 21 reported, at the 5- to 9-year follow-up, having experienced "a period of severe relapse, lasting at least a month" (Munby & Johnston, 1980). It must also be remembered that a large number of the same patients treated by the Oxford group received subsequent care following therapy, and that many had been placed on psychotropic drugs (drugs and reasons unspecified)—factors that cloud the interpretation of these otherwise heartening results. Finally, despite ill-considered reports by Hafner (1976, 1977), there is no evidence showing that successful treatment of agoraphobics' fear and avoidance through the use of *in vivo* exposure methods tends to lead to increases in marital conflict. Marks (1981a) reanalyzed the data on which this view was based and reached a different conclusion: "The evidence is clearly that greatest improvement in phobias was associated with greatest improvement to other areas of function, including marital satisfaction. This result is the opposite of that to be expected from the symptom substitution model or from general systems theory. Patients with poor marriages to start with improved least in all areas" (p. 238). Even if marital conflict were to increase, interpretation of this correlated event is not always straightforward. For example, an agoraphobic woman who, as a result of successful behavioral treatment, is no longer crippled by her phobic anxiety, and who then expresses dissatisfaction with an unhappy and unfulfilling marriage that she had been too fearful to challenge in the past, can be said to be displaying additional evidence of the efficacy of the therapy. Unresolved marital issues may then become the focus of further treatment—an option that simply was not available to her prior to successful treatment of her agoraphobia.

Cobb, McDonald, Marks, and Stern (1980) assigned phobic obsessional patients and their spouses to one of two treatment groups: *in vivo* exposure directed at reducing the phobias and rituals, and marital therapy designed to improve the relationship. In the *in vivo* exposure, no attention was focused on marital issues, although the spouses were asked to help the patients comply with their exposure homework assignments. Spouses acted as cotherapists in both conditions, however, to control for simple participation in treatment. All couples had experienced chronic marital dissatisfaction. After a 12-week follow-up, all couples received the alternative therapy in a crossover design. The exposure treatment produced not only the expected reduction in phobic and obsessional complaints, but also an improvement in the couples' marital relationships. Marital therapy improved couples' marital relationships, but had little effect on phobias and obsessions.

In the study by Barlow *et al.* (1981), six agoraphobic women and their husbands took part in a group-therapy program consisting of *in vivo* exposure, covert rehearsal of coping, and cognitive restructuring. The husbands acted as cotherapists, and both spouses independently completed ratings of marital satisfaction and severity of the phobic complaints throughout the course of treatment and follow-up. The results were grouped into two distinctive patterns. In four of the couples, a parallel relationship was observed between improvement in the phobic disorders and increases in marital satisfaction. In the other two couples, improvements in the agoraphobic condition were accompanied by decreases in marital satisfaction. In both these latter cases, the husbands reported decreases in marital satisfaction that were correlated with improvements in their wives' phobic conditions. Significantly, and in contrast to results reported by Milton and Hafner (1979), 12-month follow-ups revealed that these two wives continued to improve, despite the decreases in marital satisfaction. These observations refute the clinically popular but empirically unsubstantiated notion that agoraphobia cannot be treated successfully if the interpersonal context is poor.

Finally, it is important to bear in mind that the studies reviewed above evaluated the effects of a specific therapeutic technique—namely, some form of exposure. The requirements of controlled research militated against individual assessment of each patient's problems, as would be standard clinical practice. Such individual assessment, a cardinal feature of clinical behavior therapy, would in all likelihood have led to multifaceted interventions in many cases. *In vivo* exposure would have been supplemented with such diverse strategies as assertion training, behavior rehearsal, marital therapy, and self-regulatory procedures where appropriate. In short, it can be argued that the therapeutic results obtained in the controlled research described above represent a conservative index of the outcome that could be achieved with clinical practice, which is not inevitably constrained by the demands of experimental rigor.

ANXIETY STATES

Surprisingly, little controlled research has been carried out with anxiety disorders. Nevertheless, an indication of the value of behavior therapy can be gleaned from the Sloane *et al.* study (1975), in which 57 of the 94 patients were diagnosed as anxiety reactions using the DSM-II classification. The findings of this study showed that in terms of the target symptoms, 48% of the control group and 80% of the behavior-therapy and psychotherapy groups were considered improved or recovered. Behavior therapy produced significant improvement in both work and social adjustment, whereas psychotherapy resulted in only marginal improvement in work. Moreover, behavior therapy was significantly superior to the other groups on the global rating of improvement. At the 1-year follow-up, there was no overall difference among the three groups on any of the dependent measures.

It would be unwise to make too much of this slight superiority of behavior therapy, in view of the conceptual and methodological problems with this study in particular and with this kind of conventional comparative outcome research in general (see Kazdin & Wilson, 1978). Aside from inadequacies in the measures used, the "behavior-therapy" treatment was insufficiently specified and included a range of methods such as imaginal desensitization, assertion training, direct advice, relaxation training, and so on. Furthermore, the waiting-list control group did not control for nonspecific placebo influences.

Woodward and Jones (1980) compared the following four conditions in the treatment of 27 outpatients diagnosed as suffering from anxiety states: (1) cognitive restructuring, consisting of elements of both rational–emotive therapy and Meichenbaum's (1977) self-instructional training; (2) modified systematic desensitization, emphasizing coping rather than mastery imagery; (3) a combination of (1) and (2); and (4) a waiting-list control. The combined treatment proved to be significantly superior to all others in reducing anxiety. Cognitive restructuring alone had little therapeutic effect. This finding is consistent with the poor results obtained with cognitive restructuring in the treatment of other anxiety disorders, as indicated above (e.g., Biran & Wilson, 1981; Emmelkamp *et al.,* 1978). Commenting on the poor showing of cognitive restructuring, Woodward and Jones suggested that it "may reflect many factors, but the choice of subject group seems particularly important. General anxiety patients are 'different customers,' not often used as subjects in studies of treatment efficacy. They display a high level of physiological arousal, together with rather nebulous symptomatology. Perhaps this experiment has in fact demonstrated that a multidimensional approach to treatment, for example cognitive behavior modification, is more likely to succeed with this type of patient than treatments comprising one element only, as does cognitive restructuring" (p. 407).

OTHER ANXIETY PROBLEMS

Behavioral methods have been extensively used to treat other anxiety problems that do not fall readily under the previous categories of anxiety disorders. Thus interpersonal anxiety has been rapidly and effectively treated with different cognitive–behavioral methods. DiLoreto (1971), for example, found that systematic desensitization was significantly more effective than either client-centered therapy or a placebo control was, while Kanter and Goldfried (1979) showed that rational restructuring and modified desensitization were more effective than a waiting-list control. The subjects in the latter study experienced "anxiety, tension, or shyness in social situations." Cognitive–behavioral methods have similarly been shown to be highly successful in reducing test anxiety. (See Goldfried, 1979, and Rachman & Wilson, 1980, for comprehensive reviews of cognitive-behavior therapy and the treatment of interpersonal and test anxiety.)

Finally, mention should be made of some conventional comparative outcome studies that have pitted "behavior therapy" against some form of "psychotherapy" in the treatment of what have been imprecisely referred to as "neurotic disorders." The Luborsky, Singer, and Luborsky (1975) review of comparative outcome research summarizes much of this literature. It will be recalled that Luborsky et al. concluded that there were no differences between behavior therapy and psychotherapy. The reader is referred to detailed analyses of the inaccuracies and inadequacies of Luborsky et al.'s review and reasoning (Kazdin & Wilson, 1978; Rachman & Wilson, 1980). Suffice it to note here that the evidence on the treatment of neurotic disorders that Luborsky et al. restricted themselves to is so badly flawed, conceptually as well as methodologically, that it is essentially uninterpretable. Contrary to the self-defeating policy of assessing the comparative effects of ill-defined therapies with heterogeneous clumps of disorders on inadequate, global measures (as exemplified by Luborsky et al. and an equally errant review by Smith & Glass, 1977), evaluation of therapy outcome requires testing of well-specified treatment methods applied to particular problems with multiple measures of outcome, as discussed above.

OBSESSIVE–COMPULSIVE DISORDERS

Obsessive–compulsive disorders are among the most severe and disabling psychiatric problems there are. They have remained notoriously resistant to successful treatment of any kind, and they provide a searching and decisive testing ground for potentially effective therapies. As in other areas, the behavioral-treatment literature shows a definite progression toward the development of increasingly refined and effective therapeutic techniques. After methods such as imaginal systematic desensitization proved to be largely ineffective, more effective methods were developed—namely, *in vivo* exposure and response prevention (Rachman & Hodgson, 1980).

Most of the evidence on the efficacy of these behavioral methods comes from uncontrolled clinical series and a few controlled studies. More rigorous evaluations remain to be completed, especially since the controlled research to date has lacked the methodological sophistication that has characterized behavioral research on phobic disorders. Nonetheless, the consistency of findings by investigators using *in vivo* exposure and response prevention in different countries and between controlled and uncontrolled reports is an encouraging development.

Illustrative of the controlled research on the treatment of obsessive-compulsive disorders are two studies by Rachman, Marks, and their colleagues at the Institute of Psychiatry in London. In the first study (Marks, Hodgson, & Rachman, 1975), three methods were compared: flooding *in vivo;* modeling *in vivo* (essentially participant modeling); and a combination of flooding and *in vivo* modeling. Patients were selected whose disorders were sufficiently severe to merit admission to an inpatient unit. All of them had previously received other forms of treatment. After an initial week's evaluation, all subjects received 15 1-hour sessions of relaxation training over the next 3 weeks. This extended period of relaxation therapy was designed to serve as an attention-placebo control. Thereafter, the subjects were randomly assigned to the three treatment conditions for an additional 15 sessions of therapy during the final 3 weeks. Subjects were assessed before treatment, after the 3 weeks of relaxation therapy, at the end of flooding or modeling, and at a 6-month follow-up. The measurements taken included self-ratings, psychiatric rating scales, attitudinal responses, behavioral avoidance tests that were tailored to individuals' specific problems, and direct measures of compulsive acts.

Both flooding and modeling were significantly more effective than the relaxation control was on all measures, but they did not differ from each other. The combined treatment did not increase the success of either method alone. A subsequent 2-year follow-up (Marks, Hodgson, & Rachman, 1975) revealed that of the 20 clients who had been treated, 14 were judged to be much improved, 1 improved, and 5 unchanged. Subjects who had improved at the 6-month follow-up maintained their progress. Improvements in obsessional–compulsive problems were accompanied by improvement in other aspects of the patients' functioning.

The limitations of this important study should be noted. Relaxation is not necessarily a stringent control condition against which to compare the effects of flooding and participant modeling. Furthermore, the latter techniques were administered after the relaxation training was, confounding order effects with the effects of different treatments. Finally, the efficacy of the specific behavioral methods at the 2-year follow-up is difficult to determine, because many subjects received additional treatment during this period. Eleven subjects had to be treated in their home settings after being discharged from the hospital.

In the second study (Rachman, Cobb, Grey, McDonald, Mawson, Sartory, & Stern, 1979), the effects of behavioral treatment (*in vivo* exposure with modeling and self-imposed response prevention), alone and in combination with an antidepressant drug (clomipramine), were investigated with 40 chronic obsessive–compulsive patients. Consistent with previous findings, the behavioral method produced significantly greater reductions in compulsive rituals than did a relaxation-training control. The flooding treatment did not, however, result in an improvement in the patients' depressed mood. The use of the clomipramine did produce a general improvement in patients' mood states, as well as some change in compulsive behavior. The specificity of the treatment effects argues against alternative interpretations in terms of placebo factors or the therapeutic relationship. The therapeutic effects of the *in vivo* exposure treatment were maintained at 1- and 2-year follow-ups (Marks, Stern, Mawson, Cobb, & McDonald, 1980). Indeed, improvement had generalized to social adjustment during follow-up. Discontinuing clomipramine after 40 weeks of treatment resulted in frequent relapses, although the patients improved again after readministration of the drug. As in the previous study (Marks *et al.*, 1975), several patients required additional therapy following the end of the formal treatment period (4 weeks of pharmacotherapy as outpatients, followed by 6 weeks of behavioral treatment as inpatients). Marks *et al.* (1980) describe this in the following manner: "Domiciliary sessions were carried out when necessary (mean of 2.5 sessions per patient for the whole group), and in cases where the patient lives a long way from [the] hospital a local therapist was enlisted to provide treatment cover after discharge. During follow-up only essential psychological treatment was given, and 12 patients brought their families to a six-weekly therapeutic group for a mean of 4 sessions" (p. 4). Furthermore, Marks *et al.* report that during the 2-year follow-up, 8 patients had to be readmitted to the hospital (4 each from the drug and placebo conditions) and that "extra counseling and support was given to 5 clomipramine and 5 placebo patients, to a mean of 5 sessions" (p. 17).

In both of the foregoing studies, patients were simply instructed to desist from engaging in their rituals during and between treatment sessions, and compliance seemed to affect outcome. Response prevention can be ensured by continuous nursing supervision during inpatient treatment, and those studies that have followed such a procedure have obtained particularly positive outcomes (Foa & Goldstein, 1978; Meyer, Levy, & Schnurer, 1974; Mills, Agras, Barlow, & Mills, 1973). For example, using *in vivo* exposure and strict response prevention, Foa and Goldstein demonstrated significant improvements in their sample of 21 obsessive–compulsive patients after only 2 weeks of treatment. In the majority of cases, these gains were maintained and even increased during follow-ups ranging from 3 months to 3 years. The therapeutic improvements spread beyond the target symptoms to include improvements in occupational adjustment, social life, sexual adjustment, and family relations. The most striking feature of their results is that two-thirds of the patients became asymptomatic after treatment. It is of course true that no control group was employed in this series, but the results are nevertheless very promising. The therapeutic changes were large, stable, and generalized. Moreover, the major changes took place within the remarkably short time of 2 weeks of intensive treatment. The possible contribution of nonspecific factors cannot be excluded, but the fact that no changes were observed in the pretreatment period, with or without therapist contact, rules out at least some of the commonly encountered nonspecific therapeutic factors. The magnitude of the success rate—two-thirds of the patients becoming asymptomatic within 2 weeks of intensive treatment—conclusively rules out the possibility that the results can be attributed to spontaneous remission.

The Mills *et al.* study (1973), employing rigorous single-case experimental methodology, demonstrated that response prevention per se, independent of any placebo factors, produces substantial improvements in compulsive rituals. Strictly supervised response prevention conducted with inpatients has yet to be compared to self-imposed response prevention. It may be that the additional resources and practical problems entailed by the former are a relatively small price to be paid if, in the ultimate analysis, it proves to be more efficient and possibly more effective than the latter.

Other findings on the behavioral treatment of obsessive–compulsive disorders can be summarized as follows:

1. As in the case of agoraphobia, self-controlled *in vivo* exposure appears to be as effective as therapist-controlled exposure (Emmelkamp & Kraanen, 1977).

2. Combining self-directed *in vivo* exposure with cognitive restructuring

has not been found to increase therapeutic efficacy (Emmelkamp, van der Helm, van Zanten, & Plochg, 1980).

3. Trainee nurse–therapists working under the direction of psychologists and psychiatrists achieve success with severely incapacitated patients that is comparable to the outcome obtained by highly trained professional therapists (Marks, *et al.,* 1977).

4. Preliminary data indicate that including patients' spouses in self-directed *in vivo* exposure treatment may produce results that are superior to those obtained by treating the patients alone (Emmelkamp, in press).

5. Although *in vivo* exposure and response prevention seem to be essential elements in eliminating compulsive rituals, effective treatment must often include supplementary behavioral strategies. Recall the additional treatment (visits to patients' home and involvement of family members in the treatment process) given patients in the Marks *et al.* (1975) and Marks *et al.* (1980) outcome studies. Spouses or family members are not always easily co-opted into the treatment program, and formal marital or family therapy may be necessary to produce treatment effects in the first place, let alone to facilitate the maintenance of therapeutic improvement. Similarly, Emmelkamp (in press), noting that a complete behavioral assessment of individual cases occasionally reveals patients who are hampered by social anxiety and lack of assertiveness, has reported clinical findings showing that assertion training may be a necessary component of effective treatment. It is necessary to reiterate the point made in connection with the treatment of complex agoraphobia. In the clinical practice of behavior therapy, the therapist must assess the particular needs of the individual patient and use whatever techniques are necessary in order to help that person. A large number of strategies are available to the therapist, in addition to *in vivo* exposure and response prevention, and treatment may often take the form of multifaceted intervention.

6. Aside from supplementing *in vivo* exposure and response prevention with other behavioral methods, therapists may also find drugs to be necessary components in the total clinical management of many obsessive–compulsive patients. This is especially the case where the obsessive–compulsive disorder is associated with depression (Marks *et al.,* 1980).

7. Less progress has been made in the treatment of obsessional thoughts than in the treatment of compulsive rituals such as hand washing and checking. Prolonged exposure in imagination (Emmelkamp & Kwee, 1977) or satiation treatment (Rachman, 1978) appear to be the most promising methods to date, but acceptable empirical evidence of therapeutic efficacy is still conspicuously lacking.

8. The evidence from uncontrolled clinical trials and the better-controlled outcome studies reveals a consistent failure rate ranging from 10% to 30% (Rachman & Hodgson, 1980). The reasons for these failures are unclear.

The presence of depression and patients who hold overvalued ideas (i.e., they do not believe their obsessional fears to be irrational or groundless) may be indicators of a poor prognosis (Foa & Tilmanns, 1979).

PSYCHOSEXUAL DYSFUNCTIONS

The treatment of sexual dysfunctions has been a prominent part of behavior therapy from its earliest days (e.g., Wolpe, 1958; Wolpe & Lazarus, 1966). The use of the Semans "stop-start" technique in the treatment of premature ejaculation; graded sexual contact and stimulation to ensure the dominance of positive sexual arousal over neurotic anxiety; a deemphasis on sexual intercourse as the only means of sexual satisfaction; nondemand procedures; and imaginal and *in vivo* desensitization—all were part and parcel of the initial clinical practice of behavior therapy. For the most part, however, it was the publication in 1970 of Masters and Johnson's influential book *Human Sexual Inadequacy* that led to the enthusiastic public and professional acceptance of what has come to be called "sex therapy." Masters and Johnson do not identify their methods as "behavior therapy," but their treatment program can be accurately characterized as such (O'Leary & Wilson, 1975). It is with the Masters and Johnson treatment approach that the evaluation of the efficacy of behavioral sex therapy can begin.

UNCONTROLLED CLINICAL TRIALS

At the outset, it must be remembered that Masters and Johnson's results were the product of an uncontrolled clinical trial, lacking any control group. It is within this context that their findings must be evaluated. In short, of the 790 patients they treated, only 142 (18.9%) were treatment failures at the end of the 2 weeks of therapy. Follow-up data were obtained through regularly scheduled phone calls that included both members of each couple as well as both cotherapists. In addition, personal interviews in or near the couples' home environments were conducted with 226 clients from 4½ to 5½ years after the rapid-treatment phase of the program. The overall failure rate 5 years after the end of therapy, including both initial treatment failures and subsequent reversals, was only slightly higher (25.5%) than that immediately following treatment. The 5-year follow-up figures are based on 313 of the original 790 patients treated. Reversals of therapeutic successes tended to occur within the first year following treatment. Couples who returned to the program for additional treatment that proved to be successful, as well as many individuals who voluntarily reported achieving fully effective sexual functioning in periods ranging from 72 hours to 6 months after leaving the program without intervening therapy of any description, were all listed as therapeutic failures—a commendably conservative tack to take. There were no overall differences between failure rates with men and women when all types of sexual dysfunction were considered, despite a lower success rate in treating impotence.

The rapidity and apparent efficacy of the Masters and Johnson program combined to make a dramatic impact. However, while enthusiastically greeting the apparently unprecedented efficiency of the Masters and Johnson program, behavioral investigators were quick to point out their scientific shortcomings (O'Leary & Wilson, 1975). As Masters and Johnson themselves pointed out, theirs was a highly select and selected sample of patients uncharacteristic of the general population. The majority were members of the upper middle class, including a disproportionate number of doctors and behavioral scientists, who were very highly motivated. (Nonetheless, it should be noted that over 50% of the sample had received previous psychotherapy without success.) This is important to bear in mind, because many investigators believe that the type of patients who seek sex therapy today may differ from the type of patients treated by Masters and Johnson. For example, LoPiccolo (1978) has observed that "some years ago, most couples seeking therapy were basically very naive about sex; an education and training approach was usually quite successful. Recently, fewer and fewer such cases appear. The current greater cultural acceptance of sexuality and the widespread availability of good information about sexual physiology and technique have apparently resulted in a lower incidence of sexual dysfunction caused by naivete and ignorance. Current cases more commonly involve deep-seated negative attitudes about sexuality and relationship problems" (p. 516). Moreover, without a long-term follow-up of all the clients who were treated, the overall outcome data, while suggestive, are still not conclusive.

More recently, Masters and Johnson (1979) reported the results of the treatment of sexual dysfunction in 84 male and female homosexual couples, using virtually identical treatment principles and procedures. Sexual adequacy in homosexuals was assessed in terms of how successfully the persons responded to three sources of sexual stimulation: masturbation, partner manipulation, and fellatio or cunnilingus. Given this yardstick of sexual adequacy, then, a "primarily impotent" homosexual male was defined as someone who had never been able to achieve and maintain an erection in response to any of the three sources of sexual stimulation. A "secondarily impotent" homosexual was one who had once been able to develop an erection to these sources of stimulation but had since lost this ability. A "situationally impotent" man was defined as one who had attained and maintained a full erection in response to one or two of the three sources of sexual stimulation, but never in response to all three. With respect to sexual dysfunctions in lesbians, a "primarily anorgasmic" woman was defined as one who had never been orgasmic in response to any of the three sources of stimulation. The definition of "situational anorgasmia" was based on the same criteria as those for situational impotence in the male, while the "randomly anorgasmic" woman was defined as one who had been orgasmic at least once in response to each of the three sources of sexual stimulation, but for whom orgasm was a rare occurrence, irrespective of the mode of stimulation.

The results of treatment of these male and female homosexuals show an overall failure rate of only 7% at posttreatment and 10.7% at the end of the 5-year follow-up. Of the 84 couples, 80 were included in the 5-year follow-up. These results are superior to those obtained earlier with heterosexual couples, a finding that Masters and Johnson attribute to two reasons: the absence of successful sexual intercourse as a criterion of sexual adequacy in the homosexual couples, and the greater experience and sophistication of the therapists.

Masters and Johnson's claims about treatment outcome have not gone unchallenged. In a sharp attack on these findings, Zilbergeld and Evans (1980) have made the following charge: "Our conclusion in brief: Masters and Johnson's sex-therapy research is so flawed by methodological errors and slipshod reporting that it fails to meet customary standards—and their own— for evaluation. This raises serious questions about the effectiveness of the 10-year-old discipline they created" (p. 31). Is this an accurate assessment?

Zilbergeld and Evans correctly point out many methodological inadequacies in Masters and Johnson's 1970 and 1979 reports. Aside from the methodological limitations already noted, the imprecision with which treatment outcome is defined is a problem. Masters and Johnson reported only failure rates, arguing that it is easier for therapist and patient to agree on what constitutes failure than on what constitutes success. The reader is therefore left without any operational definition of "therapeutic success"—or of "therapeutic failure," for that matter. Masters and Johnson define "failure" as indication that the 2-week rapid-treatment phase has failed to initiate reversal of the basic symptomatology of sexual dysfunction. Yet as Zilbergeld and Evans point out, "initiating reversal" is subject to different interpretations.

An anorgasmic woman, for example, might feel less guilty about sex, become less performance-oriented during sex, enjoy sex more, have an orgasm with masturbation, or have an orgasm in intercourse. . . . The need for specificity is illustrated in this example. Treatment for anorgasmic women often teaches patients to have orgasms with masturbation. This method is highly successful as long as success is defined as ability to have orgasms with self-stimulation. However, if the standard of success is the ability to have an orgasm via the partner's manual or oral stimulation, the success rate drops significantly. It takes an even greater plunge if the criterion is orgasm in intercourse. The results of therapy may differ tremendously depending upon which standards of success or failure are used. (1980, p. 33)

In addition, readers have to take Masters and Johnson's own word for the results; this leaves room for unwitting bias in evaluating success, especially in view of the global, imprecise criteria for therapeutic outcome. Systematic evaluation of treatment effects by the patients themselves, a necessary component of adequate assessment of therapy outcome, was not reported. Moreover, an independent, neutral assessor who was "blind" to the type of therapy used did not evaluate treatment outcome, as would typically be the case in scientific research.

Adequate evaluation of treatment outcome must include multiple subjective and objective measures, as pointed out in the discussion of anxiety disorders (Rachman & Wilson, 1980). The importance of gathering multiple measures of sexual responsiveness is illustrated by Wincze, Hoon, and Hoon's study (1978) of women who participated in a comprehensive sex-therapy program for low levels of sexual arousal. Outcome measures included vaginal photoplethysmographic recordings, a clinical interview, subjective ratings of sexual arousal and anxiety, and self-monitoring records of sexual behavior. At posttreatment, all five women in this study expressed "positive attitudes toward the therapists, increased capacity for sexual arousal, increased knowledge and understanding of sex, and general improvement in their sexual relationships. Glowing reports of continued improvement and satisfaction with the therapists and therapy persisted two years later in telephone follow-up interviews, and one patient who was inorgasmic at posttherapy now claimed that she was orgasmic" (p. 48).

Kazdin and Wilson (1978) have noted that one criterion for determining whether changes made in treatment are clinically important is whether the clients engage in normative levels of the behavior after treatment. Brender, Libman, Burstein, and Takefman (1980) compared measures of sexual and nonsexual dimensions of marital functioning for couples who sought sex therapy with those for a demographically similar group of well-adjusted couples. There was a marked similarity between the well-adjusted and the dysfunctional subjects, both before and after therapy, on ratings of nonsexual dimensions of marital functioning. In contrast, on most sexual items, the well-adjusted group's ratings were superior to those of the dysfunctional couples prior to treatment, and they remained so at posttreatment and at an 8-month follow-up. Despite substantial improvement in their levels of sexual functioning, the treated couples did not reach the level of sexual adjustment reported by the couples in the normative sample.

Lastly, Zilbergeld and Evans (1980) draw attention to a little-noticed feature of the Masters and Johnson program—namely, the degree to which they included a "maintenance phase" of sorts. According to Masters and Johnson, former patients were "instructed to call the Foundation if they encountered sexual distress." This was in addition to "regularly scheduled calls that include both members of the marital unit and both cotherapists. These calls continue on a specific schedule with lengthening intervals between conferences, unless sexual dysfunction redevelops" (p. 38). Within a social learning framework, this schedule of contacts would be viewed as an explicit maintenance strategy; it is one that may have been crucial in facilitating generalization of treatment-produced effects from Masters and Johnson's institute to the couples' home environments, as well as in maintenance of the effects over time. Results of the Zeiss (1978) study, discussed below, confirm the potential therapeutic relevance of telephone contacts of this sort.

Zilbergeld and Evans make a number of valid points about the inadequacy of Masters and Johnson's results, but their conclusion that sex therapy as a whole has no acceptable empirical support is unfounded. Masters and Johnson stated that in the last resort their therapeutic claims would have to be validated on the basis of independent replication of their results. Reports of uncontrolled clinical trials have claimed results that are comparable to those obtained by Masters and Johnson (Hartman & Fithian, 1972; Kaplan, 1974). However, the total absence of any systematic outcome data in these reports precludes any serious consideration. Wolpe and Lazarus (1966) reported comparable success rates using similar procedures with the same range of problems, while Laughren and Kass (1975), in a review of uncontrolled clinical findings on the use of *in vivo* desensitization, were led to remark that "considering some important differences in population and treatment methods, it is remarkable that the overall improvement rates tend to cluster around 80%" (p. 283). A report by Yulis (1976) indicates that 33 of 37 (89%) of premature ejaculators treated with Masters and Johnson's methods reported a "very satisfactory sexual relationship" at a 6-month follow-up, self-reports that were confirmed by their partners. "Very satisfactory sexual adjustment" was defined as between 80% and 100% "ejaculation-controlled sexual encounters" (p. 356). Other evidence of the efficacy of sex therapy is summarized by LoPiccolo and LoPiccolo (1978) in their comprehensive handbook on the subject of sexual dysfunction. In one of the chapters in that volume, Hogan (1978) concluded that "when uncontrolled studies repeatedly indicate a correlation between a particular therapeutic technique and a positive outcome, it can be assumed that this technique, rather than the numerous uncontrolled variables present in the various studies, was responsible for the improvement" (p. 58). Of greater importance, however, is the fact that controlled research has provided encouraging evidence that behavioral sex therapy is indeed effective.

CONTROLLED STUDIES

Most of the controlled studies have evaluated the relative efficacy of specific behavioral treatment methods against control conditions. Following a brief discussion of these investigations, those few comparative outcome studies pitting behavioral methods against alternative, nonbehavioral approaches are summarized.

Two studies in England evaluated the efficacy of a modified Masters and Johnson program suitable for the National Health Service there. The first study, by Mathews, Bancroft, Whitehead, Hackmann, Julier, Bancroft, Gath, and Shaw (1976), compared three methods—systematic desensitization plus counseling; directed practice (i.e., a modified version of the Masters and Johnson *in vivo* program, plus counseling); and directed practice with minimal therapist contact—in the treatment of male and female sexual dysfunction. The counseling consisted of discussing sexual attitudes, reviewing treatment progress, and encouraging free communication of sexual feelings between partners. In the minimal-contact condition, therapeutic instructions were mailed to patients, with only two actual treatment sessions (at midtreatment and at the end of therapy). The counseling component was absent from these sessions. All therapy consisted of 12 weekly sessions. Of the 36 couples, 18 presented with primarily male problems, such as erectile failure or premature ejaculation. The most common complaint among the female patients was that of low interest in and arousal by sexual encounters; 13 reported failure in achieving orgasm. Both members of each couple were seen together, but half the couples in each therapy condition were treated by a single therapist and half by a two-partner sex-therapy team. Outcome measures included ratings of patients' sexual adjustment by an independent psychiatrist before and after therapy and at a 4-month follow-up; patient self-ratings and estimates of sexual activities; and therapist ratings of patients' sexual adjustment.

The modified Masters and Johnson treatment was approximately twice as effective as the other two treatments were. Also, there was a marginally significant suggestion that the two-partner sex-therapy team was more effective than a single therapist was in the administration of directed practice plus counseling. Given the earlier discussion of the importance of specifying therapy outcome criteria, the following observation by Mathews and his colleagues is noteworthy: "The nature of the change occurring in couples whose treatment was rated relatively successful was often surprisingly unclear. This seems particularly true of 'female complainant' couples, where changes in orgasmic function were disappointingly few, even when there was general agreement that the sexual relationship had improved. One possibility is that some parts of treatment, particularly the mutual exchange and communication aspects of directed practice, succeeded in increasing sexual enjoyment, despite failure to attain orgasm'' (1976, p. 452). Marked variability in the outcome of patients receiving the directed practice with minimum therapist contact led the Mathews group to suggest that some patients will respond to straightforward behavioral techniques, whereas others, distinguished mainly by interpersonal and communication difficulties, will not respond to this treatment and may even become worse.

The second study, by Crowe, Gillan, and Golombok (1981), compared a modified Masters and Johnson program with male and female cotherapists to the same program conducted by a single therapist and to a third treatment comprising marital therapy and relaxation training. The subjects were 48 couples with a variety of problems, including primary and secondary impotence, primary and situational orgasmic dysfunction, and low sex drive. The outcome measures consisted of a number of questionnaires and rating scales that were completed by the subjects themselves and, in some instances, by an independent assessor. According to the authors, the results at posttreatment and at a 1-year follow-up showed improvement on ''variables associated with sexual and relationship satisfaction,'' with no differences among the three groups.

Several problems with this poorly designed study complicate interpretation of the findings. The inadequacy of global clinical ratings of therapy outcome such as those in this study need not be rehashed here (see Kazdin & Wilson, 1978). Aside from questionable validity, the ratings were not even reliable. The interrater reliability between subjects and assessor ranged from +.44 to +.68, unacceptably low coefficients. The authors also refer cryptically to ''problems with missing data'' at follow-up. Furthermore, both the modified Masters and Johnson groups are said to have received marital counseling and relaxation training, thereby obscuring the procedural differences between treatments. The integrity of the independent variable is further compromised when it is noted that all of this therapy could have been conducted in only 5 to 10 treatment sessions, each lasting for 30–40 minutes.

In a study by Everaerd (1977), 48 couples in whom the woman suffered from sexual dysfunction were assigned to the following four conditions: a modified form of Masters and Johnson's treatment; systematic desensitization followed by *in vivo* training at home; a combination of the modified Masters and Johnson method and systematic desensitization; and a waiting-list control. An independent assessor rated improvement in sexual and relationship satisfaction after 10 weeks of treatment and at a 6-month follow-up. Although the modified Masters and Johnson treatment showed significant within-group improvement, no between-group differences among the four treatments were obtained at either evaluation. Given the unknown reliability and validity of the measures, these results are not very informative. A second study, comparing the same modified Masters and Johnson treatment and systematic-desensitization method in the treatment of male sexual dysfunction similarly failed to show between-group differences. In commenting upon these studies, Everaerd observes that resistance or lack of cooperation, particularly in the men with sexual dysfunction, is a major obstacle to therapeutic progress. He also concludes that "therapy for sexual inadequacies can be done by therapists with minimum training" (i.e., approximately 16–23 hours of training). It is tempting to hypothesize that it is precisely with the inescapably real and difficult problem of patient resistance to treatment that well-trained, experienced therapists might demonstrate their mettle.

Impotence and premature ejaculation were the target problems in two outcome studies by Auerbach and Kilmann (1977) and Zeiss (1978). In the Auerbach and Kilmann study, 24 men with secondary impotence were matched in terms of age, severity of disorder, cooperativeness of partner, and marital status in being assigned either to group desensitization or to an attention-placebo control. The latter consisted of relaxation training (unrelated to specifically sexual functioning) and of developing rapport. Treatment lasted for 15 sessions and was assessed in terms of a success–experience ratio that comprises the number of successful sexual experiences (i.e., achievement and maintenance of full intromission) divided by total number of attempts at intercourse. Group desensitization proved to be significantly more successful in improving erectile functioning. Subjects' self-reports of successful attempts at intercourse were corroborated by their partners. Specifically, the desensitization group showed an improvement of over 40%, compared to less than 30% for the control group. This improvement was maintained over a 3-month follow-up period, and control subjects who were subsequently treated showed considerable change.

In the second study, by Zeiss, 20 couples who reported difficulties with premature ejaculation received one of three types of treatment. The first treatment consisted of a totally self-administered program based on a written manual. Couples in this condition were provided copies of a self-help book written by Zeiss and Zeiss (1978), a treatment manual describing a 12-week program based on the techniques of Masters and Johnson (1970) and requiring approximately 3 hours of sexual and talking assignments each week. In the second treatment condition, couples received copies of the same manual; in addition, however, they had minimal contact with a therapist, consisting of weekly, prearranged telephone calls. On average, each couple received about 6 minutes of phone contact per week. This phone contact was designed to be supportive in nature and "to check on couples' progress, to congratulate them on their successes, to provide encouragement when couples felt discouraged, and to help them resolve minor problems when they arose" (Zeiss, 1978, p. 1237). The third treatment condition consisted of more conventional therapist-administered treatment. Couples in this group received weekly individual therapy sessions in which the therapist followed the same procedures that were described in the self-help manual.

The results indicated that the therapist-administered and the minimal-contact treatments were significantly superior to the completely self-administered treatment, but did not differ from each other. All six of the couples in the therapist-administered group and five out of the six couples in the minimal-contact group were classified as treatment successes in terms of the following criteria: Latency to ejaculation in intercourse was more than 5 minutes and had improved by at least 3 minutes from pretreatment levels; and both partners expressed satisfaction about improvement in the male's ejaculatory control. In contrast to these highly favorable findings, the totally self-administered treatment failed to produce improvement. None of the six couples in this condition was classified as a treatment success. Five of the couples dropped out of treatment in the early stages, claiming that they were too busy with other activities to devote the necessary time to the treatment program. In the only couple to complete the totally self-administered treatment program, the female partner did not report greater satisfaction with the male's ejaculatory control as a result of treatment. It should also be noted that a follow-up of 8 of the 11 couples who were treatment successes, at 3 to 9 months after therapy, indicated that four couples had suffered some deterioration in ejaculatory performance.

Behavioral sex therapy for women has similarly registered some well-documented successes. The treatment of primary orgasmic dysfunction, particularly the use of directed-masturbation programs within the context of a Masters and Johnson approach, has shown impressive success in uncontrolled clinical reports, and it is reassuring to see these promising results confirmed in a controlled outcome study by Riley and Riley (1978). A directed-masturbation program was compared to a control treatment consiting of the sensate focus component of the Masters and Johnson program plus supportive psychotherapy. Patients were married, 26 years old on the average, and were known to have no organic problem. All patients were seen weekly, together with their husbands, for 6 weeks and then every fortnight for another 6 weeks. Assessment of progress was based on both partners' report of sexual functioning.

Of the 20 women in the directed-masturbation treatment, 90% were orgasmic at posttreatment. The comparable figure for the comparison treatment was 53%. Eighty-five percent of the women in the directed-masturbation group, as opposed to 43% of the comparison-treatment group, were orgasmic during intercourse at least 75% of the time. These results were maintained at a 1-year follow-up. Of eight failures in the comparison group who were subsequently offered directed masturbation treatment, seven became orgasmic, adding to the confidence that can be placed in these findings.

Symbolic modeling not only is effective in reducing phobic anxiety (as described in an earlier section of this chapter), but also is successful in improving inhibited sexual functioning. Nemetz, Craig, and Reith (1978) compared individual symbolic-modeling procedures, conducted on either an individual or a group basis, with a waiting-list control. The subjects were 22 inorgasmic women, 15 of whom suffered from secondary orgasmic dysfunction and 7 of whom reported primary orgasmic dysfunction. Treatment consisted of relaxation training followed by the viewing of 45 videotaped vignettes depicting graduated sexual behavior, with instructions to practice the modeled activities at home. Multiple outcome measures were used, including the frequency of specific sexual behavior as assessed by both the subject and her partner; global and specific measures of sexual attitudes; and subjective measures of anxiety about sexual behavior.

Treated subjects improved on all three categories of outcome measures. Women who did not receive treatment showed no improvement and even some evidence of deterioration. Successful treatment effects were maintained at a 1-year follow-up. McMullen and Rosen (1979) also demonstrated that a cost-effective symbolic-modeling procedure was substantially more effective than no treatment was in developing orgasmic responsiveness in women with primary orgasmic dysfunction.

A multifaceted behavioral-treatment program, consisting of systematic desensitization, assertion training, modeling, cognitive restructuring, direct education, and masturbation training with dilators and vibrators, was compared to a waiting-list control by Munjack, Cristol, Goldstein, Phillips, Goldberg, Whipple, Staples, and Kanno (1976) in the treatment of married women with either primary or secondary orgasmic dysfunction. Treatment was significantly more effective than was no treatment on several measures: (1) the percentage of patients experiencing orgasm during at least 50% of sexual relations; (2) the percentage of women reporting satisfactory sexual relations at least 50% of the time; (3) patients' ratings of positive reactions to various sexual activities; and (4) assessors' global clinical ratings of the women's sexual adjustment, as well as their feeling about sex. Only about one-third of the women were orgasmic in at least 50% of their sexual encounters at the end of the 20 sessions of treatment. At posttreatment, 22% of the women with primary dysfunction and 40% of the women with secondary dysfunction were orgasmic in at least 50% of their sexual relations, whereas none had been orgasmic before treatment. At follow-up, however, none of the patients with primary dysfunction was orgasmic more than 50% of the time, whereas the percentage of patients with secondary orgasmic dysfunction who were now orgasmic had increased to 60%. In terms of global ratings at follow-up, the women with secondary dysfunction were judged to be significantly more improved than were those with primary dysfunction.

Few controlled studies comparing behavioral methods to alternative treatments have been conducted, and those that have suffer from a number of methodological limitations. Obler (1973) compared behavioral treatment to traditional group therapy and to no treatment. The behavioral treatment consisted of 15 weekly sessions of systematic desensitization, supplemented by the use of sexual slides and films of sexual encounters, assertion training, and role playing of situations related to sexual problems. Group psychotherapy, 1½ hours weekly over a 10-week period, was conducted by two trained therapists employing the typical procedures they used in their daily treatment of neurotic clients. The therapists described themselves as neo-Freudian in orientation. The therapy focused on reducing misconceptions, promoting greater insight, and interpreting underlying dynamics and repressions associated with sexual dysfunction. Subjects were shown the same slides and films that were used in the behavioral treatment. The subjects in this investigation were intelligent, highly motivated individuals; they had been referred by professional clinicians from community-based psychotherapeutic clinics and university counseling services in New York City. Multiple measures of outcome were assessed, including galvanic skin responses (GSRs) and heart rate responses to filmed material depicting sexual dysfunction; a variety of questionnaire measures; and records of all successful and unsuccessful sexual experiences as defined by a success–experience form provided to each subject.

Based on the subjects' success–experience ratios from pretreatment to posttreatment, the behavioral treatment produced significantly greater improvement than did either group psychotherapy or no treatment. A total of 42% of the female subjects' and 61% of the male subjects' sexual encounters were successful, as compared to only 3% of sexual attempts in the other two groups. Behaviorally treated subjects also showed greater reductions in physiological arousal to scenes of sexual failure and greater improvement on questionnaire indices of sexual stress. Of the behaviorally treated subjects, 80% (18 of 22) became "sexually functional," and Obler stated that these gains were maintained at an 18-month follow-up, although the actual data were not reported.

Unfortunately, no information on treatment outcome for specific sexual problems is reported. It is unclear what the patients' problems were, and outcome criteria such as "sexually functional" or "successful sexual experiences" are not defined, leaving questions about the nature of therapeutic improvement.

Everaerd (1977) has published a brief report of a comparison of a modified Masters and Johnson method (which included systematic desensitization "in the case of high anxiety problems") with a form of communication therapy emphasizing "active and passive listening, verbalization and reflection of feelings, fair fighting and assertive behavior" (p. 154) in the treatment of 48 couples in whom the woman presented with sexual dysfunction. Evaluation of treatment outcome by an independent assessor who rated sexual and relationship satisfaction at posttreatment and at a 6-month follow-up indicated that only the modified Masters and Johnson method produced significant within-group improvement in sexual functioning. The between-group analysis showed that the superiority of the modified Masters and Johnson method over the communication therapy was only marginally significant ($p < .07$). Lacking details of the patients' specfic problems, data on the validity of the measures, and the reliability of the assessor's ratings, interpretation of these findings is beset with difficulty.

A comparative outcome study on marital therapy by Crowe (1978) provides relevant data on the relative efficacy of behavioral sex therapy and alternative psychological approaches. Crowe compared three treatments: behavioral marital therapy modeled after Stuart's methods (1969); an interpretative therapy; and a supportive control procedure. Couples who received the behavioral marital therapy and who exhibited sexual dysfunction were treated with a modified Masters and Johnson approach. The interpretative therapy is described by Crowe as follows: "The therapist made interpretations to the couple centering on conflict, defences, manipulation, avoidance of responsibility, and underlying emotional states such as depression or anger. Ventilation of feelings such as those of resentment and sadness was encouraged, and the therapist often intentionally took sides, but few transference interpretations were used. Advice of any sort was expressly excluded" (p. 624). Therapy lasted from 5–10 sessions, and outcome was evaluated using questionnaires and ratings of marital, sexual, and general adjustment. Commendably, Crowe established through independent ratings of taped therapy sessions that the three treatments were procedurally discriminable.

At posttreatment and at 3- and 18-month follow-ups, the behavioral treatment was significantly more effective than was either the interpretative therapy or the supportive control procedure in terms of sexual adjustment. The behavioral and interpretative treatments yielded roughly comparable success on ratings of marital and general adjustment, although only the behavioral treatment was significantly superior to the supportive control treatment at the 18-month follow-up. However, enthusiasm for this apparent superiority of behavioral sex therapy over more traditional interpretative therapy must be tempered by a number of considerations.

First, the measures of treatment outcome in Crowe's study (essentially those used by Crowe *et al.,* 1981, as described above) leave something to be desired. Aside from the inherent limitations of questionnaires and clinical rating scales, the reliability between patient and assessor ratings of target problems ranged from an unacceptably low .43 to a more reassuring .90. Interrater reliability on estimates of general adjustment was more acceptable and considerably higher than it was in the Crowe *et al.* (1981) study. Second,

fully 37 of the 42 couples in this investigation were treated by the same therapist, producing a therapist × treatment confound. Since the therapist himself predicted a slight superiority for the behavioral treatment, it is impossible
to exclude potential differential therapist influence as an explanation of these
results, as Crowe is quick to point out. These shortcomings notwithstanding,
the study is not without its informative features.

A modified form of the Masters and Johnson program was compared to
pharmacotherapy (oxazepam) and a placebo control by Ansari (1976) in the
treatment of erectile difficulties. Patients were classified as "recovered"
("patient completely satisfied with sexual functioning"); "improved" ("still
occasional failures, less satisfied than recovered group"); or "no change."
Posttreatment results indicated that 15 of 21 (67%) of the Masters and Johnson group, 10 of 16 (63%) of the chemotherapy group, and 13 of 18 (72%) of
the control group were considered to be either recovered or improved. An
8-month follow-up suggested that members of the two treatment groups had
deteriorated further than the members of the control group had. Unfortunately, these results are hard to interpret. Ansari failed to specify the treatment
procedures, the criteria for patient selection, or the assessment procedures.
The assumption that global labels such as "directive sex therapy" or a "Masters and Johnson-type program" subsume homogeneous treatment components is probably untenable. Different treatment methods in different programs that are labeled in the same way might explain differential success
rates. Furthermore, evaluating treatment outcome in terms of the qualitative, global categories described above tends to obscure potential treatment
differences.

Finally, Kockott, Dittman, and Nusselt (1975) compared systematic desensitization to "routine therapy" and a waiting-list control in the treatment
of impotence. "Routine therapy" was defined as the combination of advice
and medication given by general practitioners and psychiatrists in Munich,
West Germany. Patients in the desensitization condition received 14 treatment sessions, whereas those in the routine-therapy group were seen by psychiatrists for a total of four occasions at intervals of 3–5 weeks. A taped,
semistructured interview, subsequently scored by the interviewer and two independent psychiatrists, served as a pretreatment–posttreatment measure of
therapeutic efficacy. No reliability figures were reported. In addition, penile
plethysmographic measures were obtained from 10 of the patients while they
were asked to imagine two separate scenes involving sexual intercourse. All
subjects provided subjective ratings of these two imagery scenes.

Although patients who received systematic desensitization reported less
subjective aversion or anxiety to the thought of sexual intercourse at the end
of treatment, behavioral improvements, as determined from the semistructured interviews, were minimal in both treatment groups. Only two patients

in each group were judged to have been "cured"; a "cure" was defined as "erection maintained for at least 1 minute after intromission with intravaginal ejaculation before loss of erection" (p. 498). An increase in duration of erection of up to 20% was observed in only four patients (at least one in each group) at posttreatment. However, there was no association between this increase in tumescence and the clinical ratings.

Kockett *et al.* attributed the ineffectiveness of systematic desensitization to the fact that it is a technique for "dealing with anxiety-related problems alone," whereas "during the behavior analysis of the patients it became clear that there was a great number of other factors in addition to anxiety which seemed to maintain the behavioral disturbance" (p. 499). Unimproved patients were subsequently treated with a modified Masters and Johnson program that addressed some of these factors, such as unrealistic standards and negative attitudes about sex. Of the 12 patients treated in this manner, 8 were rated as "cured," 3 had shown no improvement, and 1 had relapsed shortly after therapy.

CONCLUDING COMMENTS

In summing up the current status of behavioral sex therapy, a number of conclusions—some more tentative than others, owing to the uneven nature of the available evidence—can be drawn.

1. Behavioral procedures have been shown to be quick and effective treatment for specific forms of sexual dysfunction, such as orgasmic difficulties in women, premature ejaculation, and some erectile problems. Behavior therapy reliably reduces sexual anxiety and can increase sexual responsiveness. Whatever its current limitations, and these cannot be overlooked, behavioral sex therapy is clearly the preferred form of treatment for psychogenic sexual dysfunction in men and women.

2. The brevity of these sexual treatment methods bears underscoring. Aside from the much-publicized 2-week rapid-treatment program of Masters and Johnson, most of the controlled outcome studies reviewed above ranged from approximately 5 to 20 sessions.

3. More compelling evidence of the long-term efficacy of these methods is needed. Only five of the controlled studies included follow-ups of 1 year or more (Crowe, 1978; Crowe *et al.,* 1981; Nemetz *et al.,* 1978; Obler, 1973; Riley & Riley, 1978). As in the other areas of behavior change, explicit maintenance strategies require development and evaluation (O'Leary & Wilson, in press).

4. The cost-effectiveness of behavioral sex therapy is evident from several other sources.

a. It appears that Masters and Johnson's insistence on highly trained two-partner sex-therapy teams in all instances is unfounded. Single therapists appear to achieve comparable success, and it may be that for selected problems these therapists can be effective with relatively limited training in sex therapy. Additional evidence on this point is needed.
b. Treatment manuals, at least for a relatively straightforward problem such as premature ejaculation, can be helpful, provided that there is some critical but nonetheless minimal level of therapist contact and direction (Zeiss, 1978).
c. Group treatment of couples has proved feasible and effective in certain cases (e.g., Leiblum, Rosen, & Pierce, 1976).
d. Preliminary data suggest that therapy for primary orgasmic dysfunction is as effective if the women alone are treated as a group as it is if the women are treated together with their male partners (Ersner-Hershfield & Kopel, 1979).

5. Behavioral sex therapy does not appear to result in any symptom substitution or other noticeable negative side effects. Contrary to some now infrequently voiced concerns, therapy-induced deterioration in the patients' functioning has not been reported (Wilson, 1978).

6. For optimal efficacy, behavioral sex therapy needs to be used flexibly, following a thorough assessment of each individual patient's (couple's) problems. As in the research on the anxiety disorders, this emphasis on tailoring the treatment to the individual couple's particular problem—a cardinal feature of the clinical practice of behavior therapy—has been rarely adopted in controlled outcome studies. Consistent with this emphasis on therapeutic flexibility and versatility, multifaceted treatment programs, including both sexual and nonsexual methods, will often be required. For example, effective treatment might necessarily include marital therapy or other explicit attention to alleviate the interpersonal ramifications of the problem; systematic desensitization to reduce focal anxieties; cognitive restructuring to alter distorted thinking; and so on. The behavior-therapy literature contains many telling illustrations of the need for broad-spectrum interventions of this kind (e.g., Brady, 1976; Leiblum & Pervin, 1980).

7. Clinical experience and much of the experimental evidence show that relationship problems tend to complicate sex therapy and to militate against its success (e.g., Brady, 1976; Mathews, Bancroft, Whitehead, Hackmann, Julier, Bancroft, Gath, & Shaw, 1976; Munjack *et al.,* 1976). This finding assumes added significance if, as is widely believed among sex therapists, the population seeking sex therapy today is somewhat different from and more likely to have fundamental relationship problems than the patients treated in the early 1970s (e.g., LoPiccolo, 1978). Of course, generalizations of this

nature are arbitrary. Libman, Takefman, and Brender (in press) have recently reported that couples seeking sex therapy were found "to be distinguishable from those seeking marital counseling in that the former group had a higher level of marital adjustment. In terms of satisfaction with communication and couple social activities, sex problem couples did not differ from contented couples. This result supports the view of sex therapists that numerous couples requesting sexual counseling can be treated by an intervention focused on their sexual interaction, with minimal if any attention to other marriage issues" (p. 225).

8. The precise relationship between the general level of psychological disturbance of the patient or couple and the efficacy of behavioral sex therapy remains to be delineated. Kaplan (1979), for example, has argued that whereas short-term behavioral sex therapy is reliably effective for a number of sexual dysfunctions, a subset of sexual problems characterized by greater psychopathology and intrapsychic conflict necessitates treatment along the lines of psychoanalytically oriented therapy. Kaplan calls her own amalgam of behavioral methods and psychodynamic principles "psychosexual therapy," and she claims that it works where behavior therapy fails. Whether or not this is the case is an empirical question. What can be said at this juncture is that the total failure of psychoanalytically oriented psychotherapy to have produced successful treatment results with sexual problems in decades past does not augur well for its presumptive efficacy in the subset of patients referred to by Kaplan (Rachman & Wilson, 1980).

9. Behavioral sex therapy is applicable to sexual dysfunction that is psychogenic in nature. Kaplan (1979) has stressed the difficulty in treating patients suffering from what she has termed "disorders of desire" with behavioral sex therapy. These are the patients for whom she recommends her psychosexual approach. However, Carney, Bancroft, and Mathews (1978) have shown that female sexual unresponsiveness (similar to Kaplan's "disorders of desire"?) might be beneficially treated with a combination of behavioral sex therapy and hormonal therapy. The potentially fruitful combination of hormonal and behavioral treatments remains to be explored further.

10. Attempts to evaluate the efficacy of the Masters and Johnson approach have focused on specific techniques (e.g., the squeeze technique) or individual components (e.g., sensate focus) of the overall program (e.g., Zeiss, 1978), or on methods usually described as "modified" Masters and Johnson programs (e.g., Mathews, Bancroft, Whitehead, Hackmann, Julier, Bancroft, Gath, & Shaw, 1976). Precise replication of Masters and Johnson's original program has not been attempted. One of the dimensions on which subsequent evaluations of behavioral sex therapy have differed from the original Masters and Johnson program is that of the format and intensity of therapy. The advantages of the Masters and Johnson treatment

format in terms of maximizing adherence to therapèutic directives and coping constructively with inevitable "crisis points" in the therapy are discussed elsewhere (Wilson, 1981). In the uncontrolled clinical trials and controlled studies summarized above, patients were usually scheduled for weekly sessions. It is possible that this format using spaced sessions may undermine adherence to homework assignments and allow minicrises to escalate into major threats to therapeutic progress. Ersner-Hershfield and Kopel (1979) found that weekly sessions were no less effective than were sessions held twice a week, but this does not approximate a satisfactory test of the "massed" versus "spaced" sessions.

REFERENCES

American Psychiatric Association Task Force on Behavior Therapy. *Behavior therapy in psychiatry* (Report No. 5). Washington, D.C.: American Psychiatric Association, 1973.

American Psychiatric Association. *Diagnostic and statistical manual of mental disorders* (3rd ed.). Washington, D.C.: Author, 1980.

Ansari, J. Impotence: A controlled study. *British Journal of Psychiatry,* 1976, *128,* 194–198.

Auerbach, R., & Kilmann, P. R. The effects of group systematic desensitization on secondary erectile failure. *Behavior Therapy,* 1977, *8,* 330–339.

Baer, D. M., Wolf, M. M., & Risley, T. R. Some current dimensions of applied behavior analysis. *Journal of Applied Behavior Analysis,* 1968, *1,* 91–97.

Bandura, A. *Principles of behavior modification.* New York: Holt, Rinehart & Winston, 1969.

Bandura, A. *Social learning theory.* Englewood Cliffs, N.J.: Prentice-Hall, 1977.

Bandura, A., Adams, N., Hardy, A., & Howells, G. Tests of the generality of self-efficacy theory. *Cognitive Therapy and Research,* 1980, *4,* 39–66.

Bandura, A., Blanchard, E. B., & Ritter, B. The relative efficacy of desensitization and modeling approaches for inducing behavioral, affective, and cognitive changes. *Journal of Personality and Social Psychology,* 1969, *13,* 173–199.

Barlow, D. H., Mavissakalian, M., & Hay, L. Couples treatment of agoraphobia: Changes in marital satisfaction. *Behaviour Research and Therapy,* 1981, *19,* 245–256.

Barlow, D. H., & Wolfe, B. Behavioral approaches to anxiety disorders: A report on the NIMH-SUNY, Albany, research conference. *Journal of Consulting and Clinical Psychology,* 1981, *49,* 448–454.

Barrett, C. L. Systematic desensitization versus implosive therapy. *Journal of Abnormal Psychology,* 1969, *74,* 587–592.

Beck, A. T., Rush, A. J., Shaw, B. F., & Emery, G. *Cognitive therapy of depression.* New York: Guilford, 1979.

Becker, J., & Schuckit, M. A. The comparative efficacy of cognitive therapy and pharmacotherapy in the treatment of depressions. *Cognitive Therapy and Research,* 1978, *2,* 193–198.

Bergin, A. E., & Lambert, M. J. The evaluation of therapeutic outcomes. In S. L. Garfield & A. E. Bergin (Eds.), *Handbook of psychotherapy and behavior change* (2nd ed.). New York: Wiley, 1978.

Biran, M., Augusto, F., & Wilson, G. T. A comparative analysis of cognitive and behavioral methods in the treatment of scriptophobia. *Behaviour Research and Therapy,* 1981, *19,* 525–532.

Biran, M., & Wilson, G. T. Cognitive versus behavioral methods in the treatment of phobic disorders: A self-efficacy analysis. *Journal of Consulting and Clinical Psychology,* 1981, *49,* 886–899.

Blackburn, I., Bishop, S., Glen, A., Whalley, L., & Christie, J. The efficacy of cognitive therapy in depression: A treatment trial using cognitive therapy and pharmacotherapy, each alone and in combination. *British Journal of Psychiatry,* in press.

Borkovec, T., & Nau, S. Credibility of analogue therapy rationales. *Journal of Behavior Therapy and Experimental Psychiatry,* 1972, *3,* 257–260.

Borkovec, T., & Rachman, S. The utility of analogue research. *Behaviour Research and Therapy,* 1979, *17,* 253–262.

Brady, J. P. Behavior therapy and sex therapy. *American Journal of Psychiatry,* 1976, *133,* 896–899.

Brender, W., Libman, E., Burstein, R., & Takefman, J. *Effectiveness of behavioral sex therapy in a clinical setting.* Paper presented at the meeting of the American Psychological Association, Montreal, September 1980.

Brigham, T., & Catania, A. C. *Handbook of applied behavior research: Social and instructional processes.* New York: Wiley, 1979.

Candy, J., Balfour, F. G. H., Cawley, R. H., Hildebrand, H. P., Malan, D. H., Marks, I., & Wilson, J. A feasibility study for a controlled trial of formal psychotherapy. *Psychological Medicine,* 1972, *2,* 345–362.

Carney, A., Bancroft, J., & Mathews, A. Combination of hormonal and psychological treatment for female sexual unresponsiveness: A comparative study. *British Journal of Psychiatry,* 1978, *133,* 339–346.

Chambless, D., Foa, E., Groves, G. A., & Goldstein, A. Flooding with Brevital in the treatment of agoraphobia: Countereffective? *Behaviour Research and Therapy,* 1979, *17,* 243–252.

Chesser, E. S. Behaviour therapy: Recent trends and current practice. *British Journal of Psychiatry,* 1976, *129,* 289–307.

Cobb, J., McDonald, R., Marks, I. M., & Stern, R. Marital versus exposure therapy: Psychological treatments of co-existing marital and phobic–obsessive problems. *European Journal of Behavioural Analysis and Modification,* 1980, *4,* 3–17.

Craighead, E. Away from a unitary model of depression. *Behavior Therapy,* 1980, *11,* 122–128.

Crowe, M. J. Conjoint marital therapy: A controlled outcome study. *Psychological Medicine,* 1978, *8,* 623–636.

Crowe, M. J., Gillan, P., & Golombok, S. Form and content in the conjoint treatment of sexual dysfunction: A controlled study. *Behaviour Research and Therapy,* 1981, *19,* 47–54.

DeSilva, P., & Rachman, S. Is exposure a necessary condition for fear-reduction? *Behaviour Research and Therapy,* 1981, *19,* 227–232.

DiLoreto, A. *Comparative psychotherapy.* New York: Aldine-Atherton, 1971.

D'Zurilla, T., Wilson, G. T., & Nelson, R. A preliminary study of the effectiveness of graduated prolonged exposure in the treatment of irrational fear. *Behavior Therapy,* 1973, *4,* 672–685.

Ellis, A. *The essence of rational psychotherapy: A comprehensive approach to treatment.* New York: Institute for Rational Living, 1970.

Emmelkamp, P. M. G. The behavioral study of clinical phobias. In M. Hersen, R. Eisler, & P. Miller (Eds.), *Progress in behavior modification* (Vol. 8). New York: Academic Press, 1980.

Emmelkamp, P. M. G. Recent developments in the behavioural treatment of obsessive–compulsive disorders. In J. C. Boulougouris (Ed.), *Applications of learning theories in psychiatry.* London: Wiley, in press.

Emmelkamp, P. M. G., & Kraanen, J. Therapist-controlled exposure *in vivo* versus self-controlled exposure *in vivo:* A comparison with obsessive–compulsive patients. *Behaviour*

Research and Therapy, 1977, *15,* 491–495.

Emmelkamp, P. M. G., & Kuipers, A. C. M. Agoraphobia: A follow-up study four years after treatment. *British Journal of Psychiatry,* 1979, *134,* 352–355.

Emmelkamp, P. M. G., Kuipers, A. C. M., & Eggeraat, J. B. Cognitive modification versus prolonged exposure *in vivo:* A comparison with agoraphobics as subjects. *Behaviour Research and Therapy,* 1978, *16,* 33–42.

Emmelkamp, P. M. G., & Kwee, K. Obsessional ruminations: A comparison between thought-stopping and prolonged exposure in imagination. *Behaviour Research and Therapy,* 1977, *15,* 441–444.

Emmelkamp, P. M. G., & Mersch, P. P. Cognition and exposure *in vivo* in the treatment of agoraphobia: Short term and delayed effects. *Cognitive Therapy and Research,* in press.

Emmelkamp, P. M. G., van der Helm, M., van Zanten, B. L., & Plochg, I. Treatment of obsessive–compulsive patients: The contribution of self-instructional training to the effectiveness of exposure. *Behaviour Research and Therapy,* 1980, *18,* 61–66.

Emmelkamp, P. M. G., & Wessels, H. Flooding in imagination versus flooding *in vivo:* A comparison with agoraphobics. *Behaviour Research and Therapy,* 1975, *13,* 7–15.

Ersner-Hershfield, R., & Kopel, S. Group treatment of preorgasmic women: Evaluation of partner involvement and spacing of sessions. *Journal of Consulting and Clinical Psychology,* 1979, *47,* 750–759.

Everaerd, W. Comparative studies of short-term treatment methods for sexual inadequacies. In R. Gemme & C. Wheeler (Eds.), *Progress in sexology.* New York: Plenum, 1977.

Eysenck, H. J. The learning theory model of neurosis: A new approach. *Behaviour Research and Therapy,* 1976, *14,* 251–268.

Feighner, J. P., Robins, E., Guze, S. B., Woodruff, R. A., Winokur, G., & Muñoz, R. Diagnostic criteria for use in psychiatric research. *Archives of General Psychiatry,* 1972, *26,* 57–63.

Foa, E. B. Failure in treating obsessive–compulsives. *Behaviour Research and Therapy,* 1979, *17,* 169–176.

Foa, E. B., Blau, J., Prout, M., & Latimer, P. Is horror a necessary component of flooding (implosion)? *Behaviour Research and Therapy,* 1977, *15,* 397–402.

Foa, E. B., & Goldstein, A. Continuous exposure and complete response prevention in the treatment of obsessive–compulsive neurosis. *Behavior Therapy,* 1978, *9,* 821–829.

Foa, E., & Tillmanns, A. The treatment of obsessive–compulsive neurosis. In A. Goldstein & E. Foa (Eds.), *Handbook of behavioral interventions.* New York: Wiley, 1979.

Franks, C. M., & Wilson, G. T. (Eds.). *Annual review of behavior therapy: Theory and practice* (Vols. 1–7). New York: Brunner/Mazel, 1973–1980.

Gelder, M. G., Bancroft, J. H. J., Gath, D., Johnston, D. W., Mathews, A. M., & Shaw, P. M. Specific and non-specific factors in behavior therapy. *British Journal of Psychiatry,* 1973, *123,* 445–462.

Gelder, M. G., Marks, I. M., & Wolff, H. H. Desensitization and psychotherapy in the treatment of phobic states: A controlled clinical inquiry. *British Journal of Psychiatry,* 1967, *113,* 53–73.

Gillan, P., & Rachman, S. An experimental investigation of desensitization in public patients. *British Journal of Psychiatry,* 1974, *124,* 392–401.

Goldfried, M. R. Anxiety reduction through cognitive–behavioral intervention. In P. Kendall & S. D. Hollon (Eds.), *Cognitive-behavioral interventions: Theory, research and procedures.* New York: Academic Press, 1979.

Hafner, R. J. Fresh symptom emergence after intensive behaviour therapy. *British Journal of Psychiatry,* 1976, *129,* 378–383.

Hafner, R. J. The husbands of agoraphobic women and their influence on treatment outcome. *British Journal of Psychiatry,* 1977, *131,* 289–294.

Hafner, J., & Marks, I. M. Exposure *in vivo* with agoraphobics: The contributions of diazepam, group exposure and anxiety evocation. *Psychological Medicine,* 1976, *6,* 71–88.

Hand, I., Lamontagne, Y., & Marks, I. M. Group exposure (flooding) *in vivo* for agoraphobics. *British Journal of Psychiatry,* 1974, *124,* 588–602.

Hartman, W., & Fithian, M. A. *Treatment of sexual dysfunction.* Long Beach, Calif.: Center for Marital and Sexual Studies, 1972.

Hogan, D. R. The effectiveness of sex therapy: A review of the literature. In J. LoPiccolo & L. LoPiccolo (Eds.), *Handbook of sex therapy.* New York: Plenum, 1978.

Hollon, S., & Beck, A. T. Psychotherapy and drug therapy: Comparisons and combinations. In S. L. Garfield & A. E. Bergin (Eds.), *Handbook of psychotherapy and behavior change.* New York: Wiley, 1978.

Jannoun, L., Munby, M., Catalan, J., & Gelder, M. A home-based treatment program for agoraphobia: Replication and controlled evaluation. *Behavior Therapy,* 1980, *11,* 294–305.

Johnston, D. W., Lancashire, M., Mathews, A. M., Munby, M., Shaw, P. M., & Gelder, M. G. Imaginal flooding and exposure to real phobic situations: Change during treatment. *British Journal of Psychiatry,* 1976, *129,* 372–377.

Kanter, N. J., & Goldfried, M. R. Relative effectiveness of rational restructuring and self-control desensitization in the reduction of interpersonal anxiety. *Behavior Therapy,* 1979, *10,* 472–490.

Kaplan, H. *The new sex therapy.* New York: Brunner/Mazel, 1974.

Kaplan, H. *Disorders of sexual desire.* New York: Brunner/Mazel, 1979.

Kazdin, A. E., & Smith, G. A. Covert conditioning: A review and evaluation. *Advances in Behaviour Research and Therapy,* 1979, *2,* 57–98.

Kazdin, A. E., & Wilcoxon, L. A. Systematic desensitization and nonspecific treatment effects: A methodological evaluation. *Psychological Bulletin,* 1976, *83,* 729–758.

Kazdin, A. E., & Wilson, G. T. *Evaluation of behavior therapy: Issues, evidence and research strategies.* Cambridge, Mass.: Ballinger, 1978.

Kernberg, O. F. Summary and conclusions of "Psychotherapy and psychoanalysis: Final report of the Menninger Foundation's psychotherapy research project." *International Journal of Psychiatry,* 1973, *11,* 62–77.

Kockott, G., Dittman, F., & Nusselt, L. Systematic desensitization of erectile impotence: A controlled study. *Archives of Sexual Behavior,* 1975, *4,* 493–500.

Kovacs, M., Rush, A. J., Beck, A., & Hollon, S. Depressed outpatients treated with cognitive therapy or pharmacotherapy. *Archives of General Psychiatry,* 1981, *38,* 33–39.

Laughren, T. P., & Kass, D. L. Desensitization of sexual dysfunction. In A. S. Gurman & D. G. Rice (Eds.), *Couples in conflict.* New York: Jason Aronson, 1975.

Leiblum, S. R., & Pervin, L. A. (Eds.). *Principles and practice of sex therapy.* New York: Guilford, 1980.

Leiblum, S. R., Rosen, R. C., & Pierce, D. Group treatment format: Mixed sexual dysfunctions. *Archives of Sexual Behavior,* 1976, *5,* 313–322.

Leitenberg, H. Behavioral approaches to treatment of neuroses. In H. Leitenberg (Ed.), *Handbook of behavior modification and behavior therapy.* Englewood Cliffs, N.J.: Prentice-Hall, 1976.

Levis, D., & Hare, N. A review of the theoretical rationale and empirical support for the extinction approach of implosive (flooding) therapy. In M. Hersen, R. Eisler, & P. Miller (Eds.), *Progress in behavior modification* (Vol. 4). New York: Academic Press, 1977.

Libman, E., Takefman, J., & Brender, W. A comparison of sexually dysfunctional, maritally disturbed and well-adjusted couples. *Personality and Individual Differences,* in press.

Lipsedge, M. S., Hajioff, J., Huggins, P., Napier, L., Pearce, J., Pike, D., & Rich, M. The management of severe agoraphobia: A comparison of iproniazid and systematic desensitization. *Psychopharmacologia,* 1973, *32,* 67–80.

LoPiccolo, J. The professionalization of sex therapy: Issues and problems. In J. LoPiccolo & L. LoPiccolo (Eds.), *Handbook of sex therapy.* New York: Plenum, 1978.

LoPiccolo, J., & LoPiccolo, L. (Eds.). *Handbook of sex therapy.* New York: Plenum, 1978.

Luborsky, L., Singer, B., & Luborsky, L. Comparative studies of psychotherapies: Is it true that everyone has won and all must have prizes? *Archives of General Psychiatry,* 1975, *32,* 995–1008.

Mahoney, M. J., & Arnkoff, D. Cognitive and self-control therapies. In S. L. Garfield & A. E. Bergin (Eds.), *Handbook of psychotherapy and behavior change* (2nd ed.). New York: Wiley, 1978.

Marks, I. M. Phobic disorders four years after treatment: A prospective follow-up. *British Journal of Psychiatry,* 1971, *118,* 683–688.

Marks, I. M. The current status of behavioral psychotherapy: Theory and practice. *American Journal of Psychiatry,* 1976, *133,* 253–261.

Marks, I. M. Behavioral psychotherapy of adult neurosis. In S. L. Garfield and A. E. Bergin (Eds.), *Handbook of psychotherapy and behavior change* (2nd ed.). New York: Wiley, 1978.

Marks, I. M. *Cure and care of neuroses.* New York: Wiley, 1981. (a)

Marks, I. M. Behavioural concepts and treatments of neuroses. *Behavioural Psychotherapy,* 1981, *9,* 137–154. (b)

Marks, I. M., Boulougouris, J. C., & Marset, P. Flooding versus desensitization in the treatment of phobic patients: A crossover study. *British Journal of Psychiatry,* 1971, *119,* 353–375.

Marks, I. M., Hallam, R. S., Connolly, J., & Philpott, R. *Nursing in behavioural therapy.* London: The Royal College of Nursing of the United Kingdom, 1977.

Marks, I., Hodgson, R., & Rachman, S. Treatment of chronic obsessive–compulsive neurosis by *in vivo* exposure. *British Journal of Psychiatry,* 1975, *127,* 349–364.

Marks, I. M., Stern, R. S., Mawson, D., Cobb, J., & McDonald, R. Clomipramine and exposure for obsessive–compulsive rituals: I. *British Journal of Psychiatry,* 1980, *136,* 1–25.

Marshall, W. L., Gauthier, J., Christie, M. M., Currie, D. W., & Gordon, A. Flooding therapy: Effectiveness, stimulus characteristics, and the value of brief *in vivo* exposure. *Behaviour Research and Therapy,* 1977, *15,* 79–87.

Masters, W., & Johnson, V. *Human sexual inadequacy.* Boston: Little, Brown, 1970.

Masters, W., & Johnson, V. *Homosexuality in perspective.* Boston: Little, Brown, 1979.

Mathews, A. Fear-reduction research and clinical phobias. *Psychological Bulletin,* 1978, *85,* 390–404.

Mathews, A. M., Bancroft, J., Whitehead, A., Hackmann, A., Julier, D., Bancroft, J., Gath, D., & Shaw, P. The behavioural treatment of sexual inadequacy: A comparative study. *Behaviour Research and Therapy,* 1976, *14,* 427–436.

Mathews, A. M., Johnston, D. W., Lancashire, M., Munby, M., Shaw, P. M., & Gelder, M. G. Imaginal flooding and exposure to real phobic situations: Treatment outcome with agoraphobic patients. *British Journal of Psychiatry,* 1976, *129,* 362–371.

Mathews, A., & Rezin, V. Treatment of dental fears by imaginal flooding and reasearsal of coping behaviour. *Behaviour Research and Therapy,* 1977, *15,* 321–328.

Mathews, A., Teasdale, J., Munby, M., Johnston, D., & Shaw, P. A home-based treatment program for agoraphobia. *Behavior Therapy,* 1977, *8,* 915–924.

Mavissakalian, M., & Barlow, D. H. (Eds.). *Phobia: Psychological and pharmacological treatment.* New York: Guilford, 1981.

McCutcheon, B., & Adams, H. The physiological basis of implosive therapy. *Behaviour Research and Therapy,* 1975, *13,* 93–100.

McLean, P. D., & Hakstian, A. R. Clinical depression: Comparative efficacy of outpatient treatments. *Journal of Consulting and Clinical Psychology*, 1979, *47*, 818–836.

McMullen, S., & Rosen, R. C. Self-administered masturbation training in the treatment of primary orgasmic dysfunction. *Journal of Consulting and Clinical Psychology*, 1979, *47*, 912–918.

McPherson, F. M., Brougham, L., & McLaren, L. Maintenance of improvements in agoraphobic patients treated by behavioural methods in a four year follow-up. *Behaviour Research and Therapy*, 1980, *18*, 150–152.

McReynolds, W. T., Barnes, A. R., Brooks, S., & Rehagen, N. J. The role of attention-placebo influences in the efficacy of systematic desensitization. *Journal of Consulting and Clinical Psychology*, 1973, *41*, 86–92.

Meichenbaum, D. *Cognitive-behavior modification*. New York: Plenum, 1977.

Meichenbaum, D., Gilmore, J., & Fedoravicius, A. Group insight vs. group desensitization in treating speech anxiety. *Journal of Consulting and Clinical Psychology*, 1971, *36*, 410–421.

Meyer, V., Levy, R., & Schnurer, A. The behavioral treatment of obsessive–compulsive disorder. In H. R. Beech (Ed.), *Obsessional states*. London: Methuen, 1974.

Mills, H. L., Agras, W. S., Barlow, D. H., & Mills, J. R. Compulsive rituals treated by response prevention. *Archives of General Psychiatry*, 1973, *28*, 524–529.

Milton, F., & Hafner, J. The outcome of behavior therapy for agoraphobia in relation to marital adjustment. *Archives of General Psychiatry*, 1979, *36*, 807–811.

Morganstern, K. P. Implosive therapy and flooding procedures: A critical review. *Psychological Bulletin*, 1973, *79*, 318–334.

Munby, M., & Johnston, D. W. Agoraphobia: The long-term follow-up of behavioural treatment. *British Journal of Psychiatry*, 1980, *137*, 418–427.

Munjack, D., Cristol, A., Goldstein, A., Phillips, D., Goldberg, A., Whipple, K., Staples, F., & Kanno, P. Behavioural treatment of orgasmic dysfunction: A controlled study. *British Journal of Psychiatry*, 1976, *129*, 497–502.

Nemetz, G. H., Craig, K. D., & Reith, G. Treatment of female sexual dysfunction through symbolic modeling. *Journal of Consulting and Clinical Psychology*, 1978, *46*, 62–73.

Obler, M. Systematic desensitization in sexual disorders. *Journal of Behavior Therapy and Experimental Psychiatry*, 1973, *4*, 93–101.

O'Leary, K. D., & Wilson, G. T. *Behavior therapy: Application and outcome* (1st ed.). Englewood Cliffs, N.J.: Prentice-Hall, 1975.

O'Leary, K. D., & Wilson, G. T. *Behavior therapy: Application and outcome* (2nd ed.). Englewood Cliffs, N.J.: Prentice-Hall, in press.

Ost, L., Jerremalm, A., & Johansson, J. Individual response patterns and the effects of different behavioral methods in the treatment of social phobia. *Behaviour Research and Therapy*, 1981, *19*, 1–16.

Paul, G. L. *Insight versus desensitization in psychotherapy*. Stanford, Calif.: Stanford University Press, 1966.

Paul, G. L. Insight versus desensitization in psychotherapy two years after termination. *Journal of Consulting Psychology*, 1967, *31*, 333–348.

Paul, G. L. Behavior modification research: Design and tactics. In C. M. Franks (Ed.), *Behavior therapy: Appraisal and status*. New York: McGraw-Hill, 1969.

Rachman, S. *Effects of psychotherapy*. Oxford: Pergamon, 1971.

Rachman, S. Observational learning and therapeutic modeling. In M. P. Feldman & A. Broadhurst (Ed.), *Theoretical and experimental bases of the behaviour therapies*. New York: Wiley, 1976.

Rachman, S. An anatomy of obsessions. *Behavioural Analysis and Modification*, 1978, *2*, 253–278.

Rachman, S., Cobb, J., Grey, S., McDonald, B., Mawson, D., Sartory, G., & Stern, R. The behavioural treatment of obsessional–compulsive disorders, with and without clomipramine. *Behaviour Research and Therapy,* 1979, *17,* 467–478.

Rachman, S., & Hodgson, R. *Obsessions and compulsions.* Englewood Cliffs, N.J.: Prentice-Hall, 1980.

Rachman, S., & Wilson, G. T. *The effects of psychological therapy.* Oxford: Pergamon, 1980.

Rehm, L. (Ed.). *Behavior therapy for depression.* New York: Academic Press, 1980.

Riley, A., & Riley, E. A controlled study to evaluate directed masturbation in the management of primary orgasmic failure in women. *British Journal of Psychiatry,* 1978, *133,* 404–409.

Risley, T. *Winning.* New York: BMA Audio Cassette Publications, 1977.

Rosenthal, T., & Bandura, A. Psychological modeling: Theory and practice. In S. L. Garfield & A. E. Bergin (Eds.), *Handbook of psychotherapy and behavior change* (2nd ed.). New York: Wiley, 1978.

Rush, A. J., Beck, A. T., Kovacs, M., & Hollon, S. Comparative efficacy of cognitive therapy and pharmacotherapy in the treatment of depressed out-patients. *Cognitive Therapy and Research,* 1977, *1,* 17–37.

Shaw, P. A comparison of three behaviour therapies in the treatment of social phobia. *British Journal of Psychiatry,* 1979, *134,* 620–623.

Sloane, R. B., Staples, F. R., Cristol, A. H., Yorkston, N. J., & Whipple, K. *Psychotherapy versus behavior therapy.* Cambridge, Mass.: Harvard University Press, 1975.

Smith, M. L., & Glass, G. V. Meta-analysis of psychotherapy outcome studies. *American Psychologist,* 1977, *32,* 752–760.

Solyom, L., Heseltine, G., McClure, D., Solyom, C., Ledwidge, B., & Steinberg, G. Behavior therapy versus drug therapy in the treatment of phobic neurosis. *Canadian Psychiatric Association Journal,* 1973, *18,* 25–31.

Stampfl, T., & Levis, D. Essentials of implosive theory: A learning-based psychodynamic behavioral therapy. *Journal of Abnormal Psychology,* 1967, *72,* 496–503.

Steinmark, W., & Borkovec, T. D. Active and placebo treatment effects on moderate insomnia under counterdemand and positive demand instructions. *Journal of Abnormal Psychology,* 1974, *83,* 157–163.

Stern, R., & Marks, I. Brief and prolonged flooding. *Archives of General Psychiatry,* 1973, *28,* 270–276.

Stone, N., & Borkovec, T. D. The paradoxical effect of brief CS exposure in analogue phobic subjects. *Behaviour Research and Therapy,* 1975, *13,* 51–54.

Stuart, R. An operant interpersonal treatment for marital discord. *Journal of Consulting and Clinical Psychology,* 1969, *33,* 675–682.

Williams, S. L., & Rappoport, J. A. *Behavioral practice with and without thought modification for agoraphobics.* Unpublished manuscript, Stanford University, 1980.

Wilson, G. T. Effects of false feedback of avoidance behavior: "Cognitive" desensitization revisited. *Journal of Personality and Social Psychology,* 1973, *28,* 115–122.

Wilson, G. T. Ethical and professional issues in sex therapy: Comments on Bailey's "Psychotherapy or massage parlor technology?" *Journal of Consulting and Clinical Psychology,* 1978, *46,* 1510–1514.

Wilson, G. T. Behavior therapy as a short-term therapeutic approach. In S. H. Budman (Ed.), *Forms of brief therapy.* New York: Guilford, 1981.

Wilson, G. T. Psychotherapy process and procedure: The behavioral mandate. *Behavior Therapy,* in press.

Wilson, G. T., & O'Leary, K. D. *Principles of behavior therapy.* Englewood Cliffs, N.J.: Prentice-Hall, 1980.

Wincze, J. P., Hoon, E. F., & Hoon, P. W. Multiple measure analysis of women experiencing low sexual arousal. *Behaviour Research and Therapy,* 1978, *16,* 43–50.

Wolpe, J. *Psychotherapy by reciprocal inhibition.* Stanford, Calif.: Stanford University Press, 1958.

Wolpe, J. Behavior therapy and its malcontents: II. Multimodal eclecticism, cognitive exclusivism and "exposure" empiricism. *Journal of Behavior Therapy and Experimental Psychiatry,* 1976, *7,* 109–116.

Wolpe, J., & Lazarus, A. A. *Behavior therapy techniques.* New York: Pergamon, 1966.

Woodward, R., & Jones, R. B. Cognitive restructuring treatment: A controlled trial with anxious patients. *Behaviour Research and Therapy,* 1980, *18,* 401–407.

Yulis, S. Generalization of therapeutic gain in the treatment of premature ejaculation. *Behavior Therapy,* 1976, *7,* 355–358.

Zeiss, R. A. Self-directed treatment for premature ejaculation. *Journal of Consulting and Clinical Psychology,* 1978, *46,* 1234–1241.

Zeiss, R. A., & Zeiss, A. M. *Prolong your pleasure.* New York: Pocket Books, 1978.

Zilbergeld, B., & Evans, M. The inadequacy of Masters and Johnson. *Psychology Today,* 1980, pp. 28–43.

Zitrin, C. M. Combined pharmacological and psychological treatment of phobias. In M. Mavissakalian & D. H. Barlow (Eds.), *Phobia: Psychological and pharmacological treatment.* New York: Guilford, 1981.

Zitrin, C. M., Klein, D. F., & Woerner, M. G. Behavior therapy, supportive psychotherapy, imipramine and phobias. *Archives of General Psychiatry,* 1978, *35,* 307–316.

Zitrin, C. M., Klein, D., & Woerner, M. Treatment of agoraphobia with group exposure *in vivo* and imipramine. *Archives of General Psychiatry,* 1980, *37,* 63–72.

AUTHOR INDEX

SUBJECT INDEX

585